国外大学优秀教材——工业工程系列（影印版）

International Logistics
The Management of International Trade Operations
Fourth Edition

国际物流
——国际贸易中的运作管理
（第4版）

[美]Pierre A. David

清华大学出版社
北京

International Logistics: The Management of International Trade Operations, Fourth Edition
EISBN-13: 978-0-9894906-0-3

Copyright © 2014, Pierre A. David

All Rights Reserved.

Authorized English language reprint edition by Pierre A. David is published by Tsinghua University Press. This edition is authorized for sale in the People's Republic of China only, excluding Hong Kong, Macao SAR and Taiwan.

本书英文影印版由 Pierre A. David 授权清华大学出版社在中国境内（中国香港、澳门特别行政区及台湾地区除外）独家出版、发行。

北京市版权局著作权合同登记号　图字：01-2014-4213 号

版权所有，侵权必究。举报：010-62782989，beiqinquan@tup.tsinghua.edu.cn。

图书在版编目(CIP)数据

国际物流：国际贸易中的运作管理：第 4 版=International logistics-the management of international trade operations,4th ed.：英文/（美）戴维（David, P.A.）著. --影印本. --北京：清华大学出版社，2014（2021.12重印）
国外大学优秀教材·工业工程系列
ISBN 978-7-302-37127-4

Ⅰ. ①国… Ⅱ. ①戴… Ⅲ. 国际贸易－物流－高等学校－教材－英文 Ⅳ. ①F252

中国版本图书馆 CIP 数据核字（2014）第 145992 号

责任编辑：冯　昕
封面设计：常雪影
责任印制：沈　露

出　版　者：清华大学出版社
　　　　网　　址：http://www.tup.com.cn，http://www.wqbook.com
　　　　地　　址：北京清华大学学研大厦A座　　　邮　　编：100084
　　　　社 总 机：010-62770175　　　　　　　　　邮　　购：010-62786544
　　　　投稿与读者服务：010-62776969，c-service@tup.tsinghua.edu.cn
　　　　质量反馈：010-62772015，zhiliang@tup.tsinghua.edu.cn
印 装 者：北京嘉实印刷有限公司
发 行 者：全国新华书店
开　　本：203mm×260mm　　　　印　张：30.5
版　　次：2014年8月第1版　　　　印　次：2021年12月第10次印刷
定　　价：79.00 元

产品编号：058561-03

出版说明

为了满足国内广大读者了解、学习和借鉴国外先进技术和管理经验的需要，清华大学出版社与国外几家著名的出版公司合作，影印出版了一系列工业工程英文版教材。《国际物流——国际贸易中的运作管理（第2版）》自引进以来，受到了广大师生的认可，被多所学校选为教材。因此，我们又积极引入了该书第4版。由于原书篇幅过长，且其中的部分内容与我国的教学需要不符，我们请作者删除了第10章"International Insurance"，并对图书重新进行了排版和索引编写。在此对 Pierre A.David 教授的积极配合与大力支持表示衷心的感谢！

欢迎广大读者给我们提出宝贵的意见和建议！

清华大学出版社理工分社
2014.7

Forward

This textbook series is published at a very opportunity time when the discipline of industrial engineering is experiencing a phenomenal growth in China academia and with its increased interests in the utilization of the concepts, methods and tools of industrial engineering in the workplace. Effective utilization of these industrial engineering approaches in the workplace should result in increased productivity, quality of work, satisfaction and profitability to the cooperation.

The books in this series should be most suitable to junior and senior undergraduate students and first year graduate students, and to those in industry who need to solve problems on the design, operation and management of industrial systems.

Gavriel Salvendy

Department of Industrial Engineering, Tsinghua University
School of Industrial Engineering, Purdue University
April, 2002

序 言

本教材系列的出版正值中国学术界工业工程学科经历巨大发展、实际工作中对工业工程的概念、方法和工具的使用兴趣日渐浓厚之时。在实际工作中有效地应用工业工程的手段将无疑会提高生产率、工作质量、合作的满意度和效果。

该系列中的书籍对工业工程的本科生、研究生和工业界中需要解决工程系统设计、运作和管理诸方面问题的人士最为适用。

加弗瑞尔·沙尔文迪
清华大学工业工程系
普渡大学工业工程学院（美国）
2002 年 4 月

Contents

Preface — xi

1 International Trade — 1
1.1 International Trade Growth — 4
1.2 International Trade Milestones — 4
1.3 Largest Exporting and Importing Countries — 7
1.4 International Trade Drivers — 12
1.5 International Trade Theories — 15
1.6 The International Business Environment — 23

2 International Supply Chain Management — 27
2.1 Historical Development — 27
2.2 Logistics and Supply Chain Management — 36
2.3 Elements of International Logistics — 41
2.4 The Economic Importance of Logistics — 42
2.5 International Reverse Logistics — 44

3 International Infrastructure — 51
3.1 Definitions — 51
3.2 Transportation Infrastructure — 52
3.3 Communication Infrastructure — 77
3.4 Utilities Infrastructure — 80
3.5 Services Infrastructure — 83
3.6 Legal and Regulatory Infrastructure — 84

4 International Methods of Entry — 91
4.1 Entry Strategy Factors — 91
4.2 Indirect Exporting — 92
4.3 Active Exporting — 96
4.4 Production Abroad — 103
4.5 Parallel Imports — 111
4.6 Counterfeit Goods — 113
4.7 Other Issues in Methods of Entry — 113

5 International Contracts — 119
5.1 *Lex Mercatoria* — 120
5.2 International Sales Contracts and the CISG — 121
5.3 Agency versus Distributorship Legal Issues — 124
5.4 Elements of an Agency or Distributor Contract — 126
5.5 Termination — 134
5.6 Arbitration — 136
5.7 Mediation — 137

6 Terms of Trade or Incoterms® Rules — 141
6.1 International Commerce Terms — 142
6.2 Understanding Incoterms Rules — 142
6.3 Incoterms Rule Strategy — 143
6.4 Ex-Works (EXW) — 146
6.5 Free Carrier (FCA) — 148
6.6 Carriage Paid To (CPT) — 150
6.7 Carriage and Insurance Paid To (CIP) — 151
6.8 Delivered At Terminal (DAT) — 152
6.9 Delivered At Place (DAP) — 154
6.10 Delivered Duty Paid (DDP) — 155
6.11 Free Alongside Ship (FAS) — 156
6.12 Free on Board (FOB) — 158
6.13 Cost and Freight (CFR) — 161
6.14 Cost, Insurance, and Freight (CIF) — 162

6.15 Summary of Incoterms® Responsibilities 163
6.16 Common Errors in Incoterms® Rules Usage 165
6.17 Incoterms Rules as a Marketing Tool 167

7 Terms of Payment 171
7.1 International Payment Characteristics 172
7.2 Alternative Terms of Payment 174
7.3 Risks in International Trade . 175
7.4 Cash in Advance 178
7.5 Open Account 178
7.6 Letter of Credit 180
7.7 Additional Types of Letters of Credit 190
7.8 Documentary Collection . . 192
7.9 Forfaiting 196
7.10 Purchasing Cards 197
7.11 TradeCard 198
7.12 Bank Guarantees 199
7.13 Terms of Payment as a Marketing Tool 200

8 Managing Transaction Risks 205
8.1 Currency Used in the Sales Contract 206
8.2 The System of Currency Exchange Rates 210
8.3 Theories of Exchange Rate Determinations 220
8.4 Exchange Rate Forecasting . 224
8.5 Managing Transaction Exposure 227
8.6 International Banking Institutions 231
8.7 Currency of Payment as a Marketing Tool 233

9 International Commercial Documents 237
9.1 Documentation Requirements 237
9.2 Invoices 238
9.3 Export Documents 242
9.4 Import Documents 250
9.5 Transportation Documents 261
9.6 Electronic Data Interchange 270
9.7 Document Preparation as a Marketing Tool 272

11 International Ocean Transportation 277
11.1 Types of Service 278
11.2 Size of Vessels 278
11.3 Types of Vessels 284
11.4 Flag 298
11.5 Liability Conventions 301
11.6 Non-Vessel-Operating Common Carriers 303
11.7 Security Requirements . . . 305

12 International Air Transportation 309
12.1 Cargo Airlines, Airports, and Markets 310
12.2 Types of Service 312
12.3 Types of Aircraft 316
12.4 Airfreight Tariffs 327
12.5 International Regulations . 328
12.6 Environmental Issues and Sustainability 328
12.7 International Air Cargo Security 329

13 International Land and Multimodal Transportation 337
13.1 Truck Transportation 338
13.2 Rail Transportation 341
13.3 Intermodal Transportation . 347
13.4 Freight Forwarders 359
13.5 Project Cargo 359
13.6 Alternative Means of Transportation 360
13.7 Ground Transportation Security 362

14 Packaging for Export 367
14.1 Packaging Functions 368
14.2 Packaging Objectives 369
14.3 Ocean Cargo 370
14.4 Air Transport 385
14.5 Road and Rail Transport . . 387
14.6 Security 389
14.7 Hazardous Cargo 391
14.8 Refrigerated Goods 392
14.9 Domestic Retail Packaging Issues 393
14.10 Packaging as a Marketing Tool 395

15 International Logistics Security 399
   15.1 The Impact of a Significant Disruption in International Logistics 401
   15.2 International Organizations 402
   15.3 The United States' Approach 406
   15.4 The European Union's Programs 414
   15.5 Other Countries' Approach 415
   15.6 Corporate Efforts 415

16 Customs Clearance 421
   16.1 Duty 421
   16.2 Non-Tariff Barriers 435
   16.3 Customs Clearing Process . 440
   16.4 Foreign Trade Zones 446

17 Developing a Competitive Advantage 453
   17.1 Communication Challenges 454
   17.2 International English 455
   17.3 Special English 457
   17.4 Metric System 458
   17.5 Cultural Sensitivity 461
   17.6 Specific Advice 462

Preface

A User's Perspective

The content of this textbook is directed at the users of international logistics services. It covers all of the concepts that are important to managers who are actively exporting or importing goods, or are otherwise involved in international trade operations. All of the relevant issues are thoroughly explained, including documentation, terms of payment, terms of trade (Incoterms® rules), exchange rate exposure, international insurance, Customs clearance, agency and distributorship sales contracts, packaging, transportation, and security issues.

The book is accessible to the reader: the concepts are clearly and accurately portrayed and the vocabulary is precise and accurate, which makes it an easy read for all, including non-native speakers of English. The presentation of the material is logical and the reader can understand a concept without having to refer to material that is presented later in the book. Nevertheless, the interested reader should attempt to read the book "quickly" once, before delving into some of its finer details, in order to get an indication of the interdependencies of the decisions to be made.

Since the book introduces topics that tend to be technical or unfamiliar to many readers, there are more than a hundred and forty color illustrations, tables, and figures in the text to support the core content. All were chosen carefully to accurately depict the concepts presented in the text.

This textbook has been adopted by most of the logistics programs in the United States and many abroad. It is the official reference textbook for the international portion of the Certification in Transportation and Logistics offered by the American Society of Transportation and Logistics, and is recommended for the Certified Global Business Professional examination of the North American Small Business International Trade Educators.

Instructors' Supplements

There is a series of **Powerpoint presentations** linked to all of the chapters in this book, which can be freely edited to reflect a particular pedagogical style.

There is a **test bank** available as well, written in Word, so the questions can be edited to reflect the style and the level of the classroom.

There is a brief **instructor's manual** with sample syllabi and other suggestions, to suit a particular academic emphasis.

Finally, there are three **DVDs of videos and photographs** that complement the materials in this book. They are available to faculty members upon request, by contacting Pierre David at pdavid@bw.edu.

Acknowledgements

This book is the result of the work of many: Richard Stewart, of the University of Wisconsin-Superior, who was my co-author for the second and third edition, and whose influence is most felt in Chapter 11, Robert Materna, of Embry-Riddle Aeronautical University Worldwide, who was instrumental on a revision of Chapter 12 in the third edition, and of Earl Peck, professor *emeritus* at Baldwin Wallace University, who gave much material for Chapter 8.

I am also thankful for all of the suggestions I received from many: Helmut Kellerman (Tacoma Community College), William Borden (John Carroll University), Bud Cohan (Columbus State Community College), Jim Chester (Baylor Law School), Frank W. Davis (University of Tennessee-Knoxville), Charles Kerr (Long Beach City College), Jeanne Lawrence (East Carolina University), Edison Moura (Sul Ross State University-Rio Grande College Del Rio), MyongSop Pak (Sungkyunkwan University), Stephen Hays Russell (Weber State University), Yavuz Agan (Western Illinois University), Syed Tariq Anwar (West Texas A&M University), Angelica Cortes (University of Texas-Pan American), Stanley Flax (St. Thomas University), Mary Jo Geyer (Robert Morris University), Tom Grooms (Northwood University), Jon Helmick (United States Merchant Marine Academy), Thuong T. Le (University of Toledo), Larry LeBlanc (Vanderbilt University), Michael Munro (Florida International University), Steve Swartz (University of North Texas), Evelyn Thomchick (The Pennsylvania State University), and Peter Weaver (Ferris State University).

Many students also helped me make this book a reality: I would like to recognize Steven Baer (Weber State University), Mark Forquer, Jeffrey Halaparda, Jamie Serenko, Elise Wallis, Andrew Ghanem, and Patrick LaGuardia (all of Baldwin Wallace University).

I am also indebted to Steve Scoble, Kendra Leonard, and Matt Walker at Atomic Dog-Thomson Publishing, as well as Sarah Blasco and Greg Albert at Cengage for their help with prior editions.

Finally, I must thank my wife Beth and our children Natalie, Caroline, and Timothy for their help and support in getting this fourth edition together. I could not have done it without your patience and understanding.

Thank you.

Chapter 1

International Trade

 1.1 International Trade Growth 4
 1.2 International Trade Milestones 4
 1.3 Largest Exporting and Importing Countries 7
 1.4 International Trade Drivers 12
 1.5 International Trade Theories 15
 1.6 The International Business Environment 23

The years since World War II have seen an unprecedented increase in international trade and a parallel improvement in the economic development of most nations. Countries that were barely able to feed their population sixty years ago are now economic powerhouses where inhabitants enjoy a modern standard of living and where many companies trade internationally. In most developing countries, political concerns have shifted from famine and abject poverty to pollution and urban gridlock, which were once the concerns of developed countries only.

This increase in international trade was triggered by the realization that countries' economies benefit by trading with each other and that trade increases the overall well-being of the world's population. Figure 1.1 illustrates how much international trade has grown in constant dollars, and the respective shares of the twenty-seven European Union countries, the United States, Japan, China, and of the remainder of the world in international trade from 1952 until 2012.[1] Although the economic crisis of 2008-2009 had an impact on the overall volume of international trade, this decrease was temporary. As people's standards of living increase worldwide, so do their abilities to purchase a greater number of goods, and therefore so does international trade.

Professionals in international logistics have been the main facilitators of that trade growth. They have been the managers responsible for the safe and timely deliveries of these millions of dollars worth of goods. They are responsible for:

- arranging transportation of these goods over thousands of miles

- understanding the trade-offs between the different modes of transportation available and making the correct decision

- making sure that the goods are packaged properly for their journey

international trade
The sale of goods and services across international borders.

constant dollars
Dollars adjusted for inflation so that it is possible to compare dollar values from one period to another.

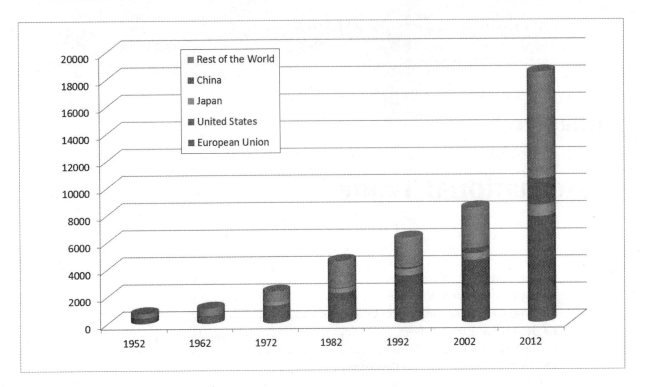

Figure 1.1: Growth in International Trade and Share of Selected Countries (in constant [2012] US$ billions)
World Trade Organization.

- understanding the risks the goods face while in transit, and insuring them appropriately

- minimizing the risks associated with international payments by selecting the right payment currency or the right hedging strategy

- making sure that the goods are accompanied by the proper documents so that they can clear Customs in the country of destination

- defining properly who, between them and their foreign counterparts, is responsible for which aspects of the voyage and which documents

- determining which method is most suitable for payment between the exporter and the importer

- following security measures designed to prevent damage to the goods while they are in transit, and following regulations imposed by the governments of importing countries and international organizations

- storing the goods in appropriate warehouses and distribution centers when they are not in transit.

While all of these responsibilities of an international logistics manager will be covered in the remainder of this textbook, this chapter gives an overview of the extent of international trade, of the economic theories of international trade and of some of the difficulties associated with conducting business in an international environment.

Figure 1.2: The maobi wood panels of the Alice Tully Theater in New York City
Photo ©Iwan Baan. Used with permission.

The Alice Tully Theater Project

The 2008 renovation of Lincoln Center's Alice Tully Theater (see Figure 1.2) in New York City included the complete renovation of its decorative and acoustic elements. The architectural firm in charge of the renovation collaborated with an acoustic-research firm to include walls which were shaped to give the theater better acoustic characteristics. The walls were covered by panels made with a very thin wood veneer, so thin that small lights placed behind the wood could shine through it and give the theater a warm, pleasant glow when the main lights were turned off. The theater can add a light show to some of its acoustic performances.
The wood veneer used in those panels came from a single moabi tree harvested in the forests of Gabon, a country in West Africa. The tree species is endangered, so a minimal amount was used; the hundreds of plywood sheets needed for the project were created from a single log that was about one meter in diameter (about forty inches). In order to achieve this enormous yield, the log was first shipped from Gabon to Ryugasaki City, Japan, where it was cut into slices that were two tenths of a millimeter thick (eight hundredths of an inch). The wood veneer was then shipped to Miami, Florida, where it was inspected before being shipped to Salt Lake City, Utah. There it was glued to a substrate and then formed to the shapes that the acoustic engineers had designed for the

theater. The resulting plywood sheets were then eventually shipped to New York City for final installation. Patrons of the Alice Tully Theater are undoubtedly enjoying these magnificent wood-veneered walls, but few of them can fathom that the wood that was used to build them had traveled more than 40,000 kilometers (25,000 miles), a distance equal to the circumference of the earth at the equator. The wood had traveled by road, rail and ocean before its final destination; all along the way, international logisticians made sure that it was transported economically, packaged properly, and that it cleared Customs and complied with international regulations without difficulty.[2,3]

1.1 International Trade Growth

current dollars
Dollars not adjusted for inflation. Their value is determined by the year they were actually received or paid.

In current U.S. dollars (that is, not corrected for inflation), international trade in merchandise has grown 30,600 percent between 1948 and 2012[4]—that is, international trade is 307 times larger—an average annual growth rate of 9.21 percent. In constant US dollars (corrected for inflation, and expressed in 2012 dollars), the growth was 3,180 percent for the same period—that is, international trade is 32.8 times larger—an average annual growth rate of 5.51 percent.

In constant US dollars (2012 dollars), international trade in merchandise and services has almost tripled since 1992, an average annual growth rate of 5.5 percent. Tables 1-1[5], 1-2[6], and 1-3[7] on the following two pages show the World Trade Organization's data for international trade for merchandise and services for the period for which it has kept that information. The differences between exports and imports reflect the different ways in which the values of exports and imports are calculated.

World Trade Organization
The international organization responsible for enforcing international trade agreements and for ensuring that countries deal fairly with one another.

The economic contraction of 2008-2009 had a substantial impact on world trade; the WTO reported that total exports decreased 22.3 percent between 2008 and 2009, from $16,140 billion to $12,542 billion. They increased 21.8 percent between 2009 and 2010 to reach $15,274 billion, but needed another year to recover completely. The total value of worldwide exports reached $18,255 billion in 2012.[8] The contraction was substantial for many countries, but it was a temporary setback in the overall growth of the worldwide economy.

The increase in international trade was triggered by a massive liberalization of international commerce following World War II and the creation of a number of international organizations designed to facilitate international commerce, as well as a significant decrease in transportation costs and transit times. During that period, a much greater consumer acceptance of things "foreign," from food to automobiles, allowed an increasing number of companies to expand their sales beyond their domestic borders.

1.2 International Trade Milestones

The development of international trade has been fostered over the years by several critical milestones, the ratification of several key international treaties, and the

1.2 International Trade Milestones

International Merchandise Trade Volume in US$ billions

Year	Current US dollars		2011 Constant US dollars	
	Exports	Imports	Exports	Imports
1957	114	121	931	989
1962	143	151	1,087	1,148
1967	218	228	1,499	1,567
1972	419	433	2,301	2,378
1977	1,128	1,171	4,274	4,437
1982	1,883	1,941	4,480	4,618
1987	2,516	2,582	5,085	5,219
1992	3,766	3,881	6,163	6,351
1997	5,591	5,737	7,998	8,207
2002	6,494	6,742	8,288	8,605
2007	14,017	14,325	15,525	15,866
2012	18,323	18,567	18,323	18,567

Table 1.1: International Merchandise Trade Volume in US$ billions
World Trade Organization.

International Service Trade Volume in US$ billions

Year	Current US dollars		2011 Constant US dollars	
	Exports	Imports	Exports	Imports
1982	368	404	876	961
1987	537	544	1,085	1,099
1992	932	949	1,525	1,553
1997	1,316	1,294	1,883	1,851
2002	1,597	1,561	2,038	1,992
2007	3,420	3,174	3,788	3,515
2012	4,347	4,106	4,347	4,106

Table 1.2: International Service Trade Volume in US$ billionsWorld Trade Organization.

establishment of international organizations designed to facilitate and support international trade activities.

Total International Trade Volume in US$ billions

	Current US dollars		2011 Constant US dollars	
Year	Exports	Imports	Exports	Imports
1982	2,251	2,345	5,356	5,579
1987	3,053	3,126	6,171	6,318
1992	4,698	4,830	7,688	7,904
1997	6,907	7,031	9,881	10,058
2002	8,091	8,303	10,326	10,597
2007	17,437	17,499	19,313	19,381
2012	22,670	22,673	22,670	22,673

Table 1.3: World's Total International Trade in Merchandise and Services in US$ billions

1.2.1 The Bretton-Woods Conference

Bretton-Woods
A 1944 conference at which many of the international institutions were created.

In the last year of World War II, world leaders of the Allied nations met in July 1944 in the resort town of Bretton-Woods in New Hampshire in the United States, a conference that led to the creation of several international institutions, two of which were specifically designed to facilitate world trade:

International Monetary Fund
The international organization created in 1945 to oversee exchange rates and develop an international system of payments.

- The International Monetary Fund (IMF), created on December 27, 1945, which established an international system of payment and introduced stable currency exchange rates.

- The General Agreement on Tariffs and Trade (GATT), which through multiple negotiation periods (in Geneva [1948], Annecy [1949], Torquay [1951], Geneva [1956], the Dillon Round [1960-61], the Kennedy Round [1964-67], the Tokyo Round [1973-79], and the Uruguay Round [1986-94]), led to a decrease of duty rate from an average of over 40 percent in 1947 to an average slightly above 4 percent in 2011.[9]

General Agreement on Tariffs and Trade
An agreement between countries to lower tariffs and trade barriers.

1.2.2 The World Trade Organization

tariff
A tax collected by an importing country on the value of imported goods.

The World Trade Organization (WTO) was officially created on January 1, 1995.[10] It replaced the GATT and is the organization in charge of enforcing free trade. From 2001 to 2008, the WTO worked on the Doha Developmental Round of multilateral negotiations, whose goal is to improve trade in agricultural commodities, which is impeded by a large number of non-tariff barriers, and replete with agricultural subsidies in developed countries. The round stalled in July 2008, and no progress has been made in the discussions since then. In April 2011, Pascal Lamy, the Director-General of the WTO, urged the reconsideration of the round, but recognized that there were major remaining obstacles.[11] The main points of dissention are the agricultural subsidies that the developed countries (specifically the United States and the European Union countries) continue to grant to their farmers. The United

1.3 Largest Exporting and Importing Countries

States and the EU want each other's subsidies to be eliminated, and the developing countries regard these subsidies as trade barriers, preventing their lower-priced commodities to compete in these developed countries' markets.

1.2.3 The Treaty of Rome

The Treaty of Rome in 1957 between Belgium, France, Germany, Italy, Luxembourg, and the Netherlands led to the eventual creation of the European Union and was emulated by countless other groups of countries that were more or less successful in designing their own common markets. The European Union expanded in 1973 (Denmark, Ireland, and the United Kingdom), in 1981 (Greece), in 1986 (Spain and Portugal), in 1995 (Austria, Finland, and Sweden), in 2004 (Cyprus, Czech Republic, Estonia, Hungary, Latvia, Lithuania, Malta, Poland, Slovakia, and Slovenia) and finally in 2007 (Bulgaria and Romania). It totals twenty-seven countries as of August 2012. The Treaty of Rome set the groundwork for the creation of the European Union, and it was extended by the Maastricht Treaty of 1992, which created the euro, and the Treaty of Lisbon in 2009, which modified the governmental processes of the European Union, specifically allowing a simple majority of states to rule, rather than the unanimity that was required originally.

Treaty of Rome
The treaty between six European countries that created the European Union.

The creation of the European Union triggered many other regional economic groups and other bilateral or multilateral agreements: most notable are the Association of South East Asian Nations (ASEAN), Mercosur, the Andean Community, and the North American Free Trade Agreement (NAFTA). A number of examples are given in Table 1.4 on page 9.

Maastricht Treaty
A 1992 Treaty between the European Union countries in which a number of standards were adopted, including a standard currency.

1.2.4 The Creation of the Euro

The euro is the European currency introduced in 1999 and put in circulation on January 1, 2002 in twelve of the fifteen countries of the European Union (Austria, Belgium, Finland, France, Germany, Greece, Italy, Ireland, Luxembourg, the Netherlands, Portugal, and Spain). The adoption of the euro was extended to the country of Slovenia in 2007, to the countries of Cyprus and Malta in 2008, to the country of Slovakia in 2009, and to Estonia in 2011.

euro
The common currency of 17 of the 27 countries of the European Union.

The euro is also the currency to which many of the remainder of the European currencies are tied; their exchange rate must remain within a certain percentage of the euro's value. Such is the case for Denmark, Latvia, and Lithuania. It has also become the currency of a number of smaller countries not part of the European Union (Andorra, Kosovo, Monaco, Montenegro, and San Marino), as well as the currency on which a number of other countries have pegged their currencies (Bosnia and Herzegovina, and the Communité Française Africaine, for example). It was the first multinational effort at replacing eleven strong legacy currencies, and it has become one of the most widely-traded currencies of the world.

1.3 Largest Exporting and Importing Countries

Figures 1.4 on page 10[12] and 1.5 on page 11[13] show the fifteen largest exporting and importing countries for 2012 according to the World Trade Organization's database.

Most of these countries have liberal trading policies and multiple free-trade agreements with many of their partners, confirming that liberal trade policies en-

Figure 1.3: The European Currency since 2001, the Euro
Photo ©MistikaS. Used with permission.

courage economic growth and development; more specific information about these countries' general trade policies can be found in the World Bank's "Doing Business" database.[14]

There are nevertheless substantial differences in the trade situation of the largest exporting countries. For example, three countries run a very large trade deficit; the United States, with a deficit of U.S.$ 788 billion, imports about 50 percent more than it exports. The United Kingdom imports U.S.$ 212 billion more than it exports—or 45 percent of its exports—and India imports 67 percent more than it exports, or U.S.$ 196 billion.

On the other end, China runs a trade surplus of U.S.$ 231 billion, importing only 89 percent of what it exports. Germany runs a trade surplus of U.S.$ 240 billion—it imports only 83 percent of what it exports. The Netherlands and Belgium also show a trade surplus with imports representing only 90 and 97 percent of their exports. Although China's surplus is due to its low manufacturing costs, Germany, the Netherlands and Belgium experience some of the highest labor costs in the world.[15]

Some countries are extremely dependent on world trade and export a very large percentage of their GDP. Belgium exports 87 percent of what it produces, the Netherlands exports 78 percent, and Germany 39 percent. In contrast, the United States export only 10 percent of its GDP and Japan exports only 14 percent. China exports 28 percent of its GDP.

trade deficit
A situation where the total exports of a country are worth less than its total imports.

trade surplus
A situation where the total exports of a country are worth more than its total imports.

1.3 Largest Exporting and Importing Countries

Economic Trade Blocs

Economic Group	Current Membership (2012)
(1958) European Union	Austria, Belgium, Bulgaria, Cyprus, Czech Republic, Denmark, Estonia, Finland, France, Germany, Greece, Hungary, Ireland, Italy, Latvia, Lithuania, Luxembourg, Malta, Netherlands, Poland, Portugal, Romania, Slovakia, Slovenia, Spain, Sweden, United Kingdom.
(1960) Central American Integration System	Belize, Costa Rica, El Salvador, Guatemala, Honduras, Nicaragua, Panama.
(1967) ASEAN (Association of South East Asian Nations)	Brunei, Cambodia, Indonesia, Laos, Malaysia, Myanmar, Philippines, Singapore, Thailand, Vietnam.
(1969) Andean Community	Bolivia, Colombia, Ecuador, Peru.
(1973) Caricom (Caribbean Community)	Antigua and Barbuda, Bahamas, Barbados, Belize, Dominica, Grenada, Guyana, Haiti, Jamaica, Montserrat, Saint Kitts and Nevis, Saint Lucia, Saint Vincent and the Grenadines, Suriname, Trinidad and Tobago.
(1975) ECOWAS (Economic Community of Western African States)	Benin, Burkina Faso, Cape Verde, Côte d'Ivoire, Gambia, Ghana, Guinea, Guinea-Bissau, Liberia, Mali, Niger, Nigeria, Senegal, Sierra Leone, Togo.
(1981) Gulf Cooperation Council	Bahrain, Kuwait, Oman, Qatar, Saudi Arabia, United Arab Emirates.
(1991) Mercosur (Southern Common Market)	Argentina, Brazil, Paraguay, Uruguay, Venezuela
(1994) NAFTA (North American Free Trade Area)	Canada, Mexico, United States.
(1994) ECOWAS (Economic Community of Central African States	Angola, Burundi, Cameroon, Central African Republic, Chad, Democratic Republic of the Congo, Republic of the Congo, Equatorial Guinea, Gabon, Rwanda, São Tomé and Príncipe.
(1996) Eurasian Economic Community	Belarus, Kazakhstan, Kyrgyzstan, Russia, Tajikistan, Uzbekistan.
(2001) East African Community	Burundi, Kenya, Rwanda, Tanzania, Uganda.
(2004) South African Customs Union	Botswana, Lesotho, Namibia, Swaziland, South Africa.

Table 1.4: Economic Trade Blocs

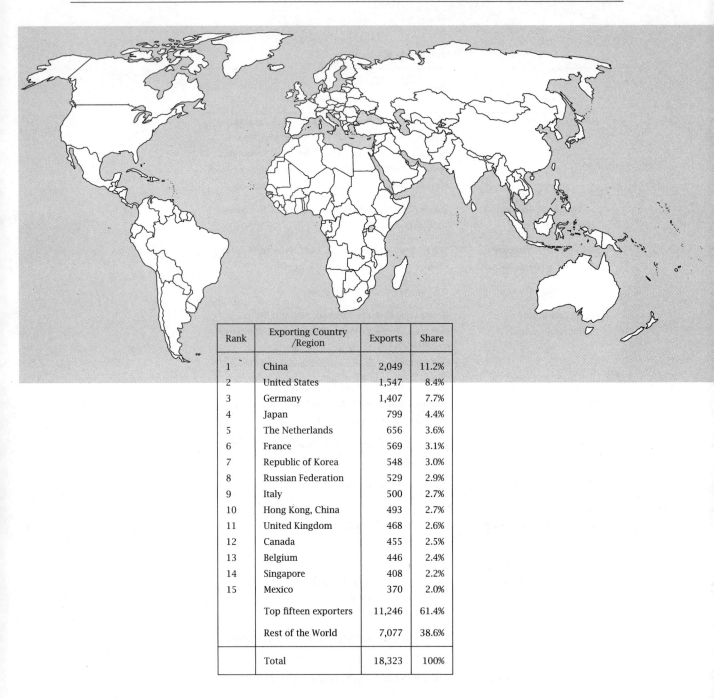

Figure 1.4: World's Largest Merchandise Exporting Countries/Regions (2012) in U.S.$ billions
World Trade Organization.

1.3 Largest Exporting and Importing Countries

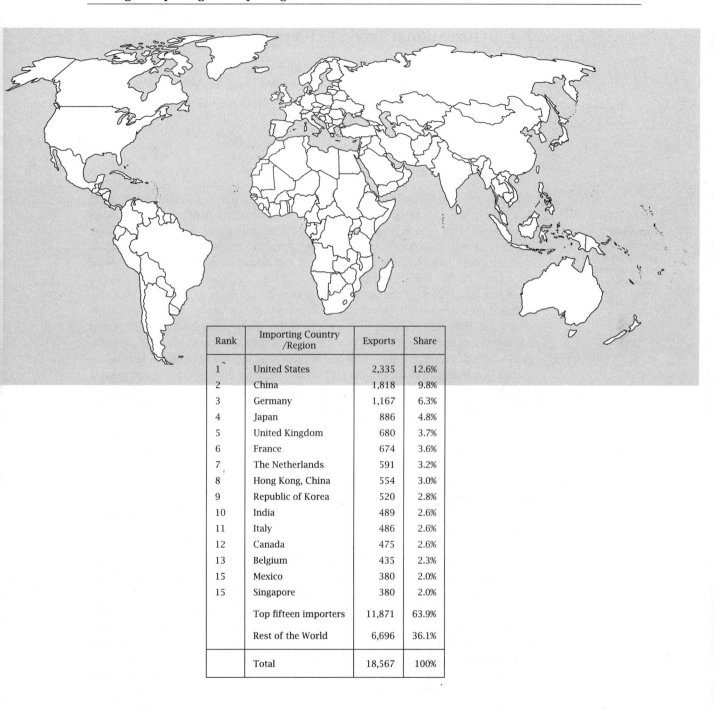

Rank	Importing Country/Region	Exports	Share
1	United States	2,335	12.6%
2	China	1,818	9.8%
3	Germany	1,167	6.3%
4	Japan	886	4.8%
5	United Kingdom	680	3.7%
6	France	674	3.6%
7	The Netherlands	591	3.2%
8	Hong Kong, China	554	3.0%
9	Republic of Korea	520	2.8%
10	India	489	2.6%
11	Italy	486	2.6%
12	Canada	475	2.6%
13	Belgium	435	2.3%
15	Mexico	380	2.0%
15	Singapore	380	2.0%
	Top fifteen importers	11,871	63.9%
	Rest of the World	6,696	36.1%
	Total	18,567	100%

Figure 1.5: World's Largest Merchandise Importing Countries/Regions (2012) in U.S.$ billions
World Trade Organization.

1.4 International Trade Drivers

There are many explanations for the enormous surge in international trade in the second half of the twentieth century. Companies found reasons to expand their sales in foreign countries, and others found reasons to purchase some of their raw materials and supplies from abroad. These international trade drivers can generally be divided into four main categories: cost, competition, market, and technology.

1.4.1 Cost Drivers

cost driver
One reason a firm may go international is to spread its costs over a large number of units.

For companies that require large capital investments in plants and machinery, there is a strong incentive to spread the costs of these fixed costs over a large number of units. For that reason, companies in the automobile industry have been among the first to seek customers outside of their domestic markets, and the companies that dominate that industry are present in just about every country: Ford Motor Company, Toyota Motors, and Volkswagen produce and sell automobiles in the most remote corners of the world. Those that do not have as strong of an international presence tend to be purchased by their competitors or enter partnerships with them. The consolidation of the automobile industry started in the 1970s and has evolved to include approximately eighteen multinational manufacturing groups, each of which produces more than one million vehicles: the newcomers are the automobile manufactures from India and China, and they have also purchased assets worldwide. For example, Tata Motors of India purchased Land Rover and Jaguar in 2008, and Geely Automobile of China purchased Volvo in 2010. The worldwide consolidation of automobile manufacturing is evident in Table 1.5 on the facing page, that shows the world's largest automobiles groups,[16] and in Table 1.6 on page 14, that shows the top fifteen car-manufacturing countries.[17]

Such cost drivers are not limited to plants and machinery. In industries where the developmental costs are very large and the costs of manufacturing are low, such as in the software industry, companies are keen to develop their international sales to dilute their developmental costs; such is the case for Microsoft, for example.

The other cost incentives to trade are found on the sourcing side; companies that assemble products from parts and subassemblies (called Original Equipment Manufacturers) seek suppliers that have the lowest possible prices. They will purchase their parts from companies located in countries that enjoy low labor costs or low energy costs. Such a purchasing pattern is called outsourcing. For example, Royal Appliance Manufacturing, a producer of vacuum cleaners under the brand Dirt Devil, used to manufacture all of its products in the United States. In 2006, it produced none in the United States, having outsourced all of its production.

outsourcing
A practice that consists of a business contracting with other businesses to have them perform some of the operations it used to handle in-house.

This outsourcing phenomenon is also called the "Wal-Mart effect" in the United States. Manufacturers are asked to provide products at certain prices, called "price points," and there is an unrelenting pressure to make these price points lower every year, in response to consumer preferences. Companies then seek the lowest-cost suppliers, invariably abroad.

The pursuit of lowest manufacturing costs has also caused a substantial shift in other industries as well, notably those that manufacture products that are sold to consumers at retail: textiles, toys, housewares, and so on. Many companies are faced with increased manufacturing costs abroad, particularly in China, as labor costs have increased and the Chinese currency, the yuan, has appreciated. The Boston

1.4 International Trade Drivers

Vehicle Manufacturers with automobile sales greater than 1,000,000 units (2011)

Automobile Group	Units sold worldwide	Brands
General Motors Corporation	9,146,000	Cadillac, GMC, Buick, Chevrolet, Opel, Vauxhall, Holden
Volkswagen Group AG	8,157,000	Volkswagen, Audi, Porsche, Łkoda, Scania, SEAT, MAN
Toyota Motors Corporation	8,050,000	Lexus, Scion, Daihatsu, Hino, Toyota
Renault-Nissan	7,457,000	Renault, Nissan, Dacia, Infiniti
Hyundai Motor Group	6,617,000	Hyundai, Kia
Ford Motor Company	4,873,000	Ford, Lincoln, Troller, Bedford
Peugeot-Citroën SA	3,582,000	Peugeot, Citroën
Honda Motors	2,909,000	Honda, Acura
Suzuki	2,726,000	Suzuki, Maruti
Fiat SpA	2,400,000	Fiat, Alfa-Romeo, Ferrari
Chrysler Group, LLC	2,005,000	Chrysler, Dodge, Jeep
BMW AG	1,738,000	BMW, Rolls-Royce
Daimler AG	1,528,000	Mercedes-Benz, Mitsubishi-Fuso, Setra, Smart, Freightliner
Mazda Motors	1,166,000	Mazda
Mitsubishi	1,140,000	Mitsubishi
DongFeng Motors(e)	1,100,000	
Tata Motors	1,061,000	Tata, Jaguar, Land-Rover
Geely(e)	1,000,000	
Rest of the world	12,144,000	
Total worldwide production	78,799,000	

Table 1.5: Vehicle manufacturers having produced more than 1,000,000 automobiles in 2011
International Organization of Motor Vehicle Manufacturers.

Consulting Group forecasts that China will have lost most of its cost advantages by 2015.[18] Consequently, a recent trend, called reshoring—or right shoring—has developed in the United States since 2010.[19] Some companies are bringing back the manufacturing of their products to the United States or to Mexico, because the savings that these companies had experienced by outsourcing to China or the Far East no longer cover the additional transportation costs. Other manufacturers are reshoring to be able to respond more quickly to their customers' requests.

reshoring
The practice of returning to the home country the manufacturing processes that had been outsourced abroad.

1.4.2 Competition Drivers

In some cases, competition incentives drive companies to expand overseas. For example, one of their domestic competitors may venture in a particular country and they feel compelled to follow suit, so as to not lose overall market share. Examples of such competitive behavior are more common in industrial goods than they are in consumer goods; however, this is the drive for the intense competition between the two largest retailers in the world. Carrefour of France and Wal-Mart of the United States compete in many different countries; as soon as one enters a foreign market,

Top Fifteen Countries in Vehicle Production (2011)	
Country	Automobiles Produced
China	18,419,000
United States	8,654,000
Japan	8,399,000
Germany	6,311,000
Republic of Korea	4,657,000
India	3,927,000
Brazil	3,406,000
Mexico	2,680,000
Spain	2,354,000
France	2,295,000
Canada	2,135,000
Russia	1,988,000
Iran	1,649,000
United Kingdom	1,464,000
Thailand	1,458,000
Rest of the World	10,312,000
Total	80,108,000

Table 1.6: Top Fifteen Countries in Total Vehicle Production (Automobiles and Trucks) for 2011
International Organization of Motor Vehicle Manufacturers.

competition driver
One reason a firm may go international is to compete more aggressively against its foreign competitors.

the other feels compelled to follow suit.

In other cases, companies expand their sales abroad in response to moves made by their competitors. When a new overseas competitor enters their home market, they retaliate by going overseas themselves and competing in that newcomer's home market. An example of such behavior would be The Gap entering the Italian market after Benetton started competing in the United States.

Competition drivers also exist on the sourcing side. If a competitor starts offering an entry-level product targeted at a segment of price-conscious consumers, a company may retaliate by offering a similar product in order to maintain its market share. Because the competitor's entry-level product tends to be manufactured in a low-cost country, the company has little choice but to source overseas as well.

1.4.3 Market Drivers

market driver
One reason a firm may go international is to follow its customers when they travel abroad.

As international tourism exploded, consumers have become increasingly global in their interests, and their tastes and preferences have become almost uniform worldwide. This phenomenon was originally observed for products that reflected this consumer mobility, such as camera film and hotel rooms. Should a consumer want film in any country, there were essentially only three choices everywhere (Kodak, Agfa, and Fuji), but they were easy to purchase with identical sizes, sensitivities, and processing technologies. For hotel rooms, the number of alternative brands is much greater, but the uniformity of choices is similar.

Firms faced with consumers who wanted to find their products everywhere had to expand overseas. In the 1970s, McDonald's restaurants in Germany, Great Britain, and France were mostly patronized by foreigners looking for an experience with which they were familiar. Although foreigners still represent a good portion of their sales today, McDonald's restaurants cater mostly to domestic consumers who have come to appreciate the convenience of fast food. This phenomenon of standardization of tastes is everywhere: television shows, clothing, books, music, food, sports, and so on.

Finally, as consumers become increasingly knowledgeable about the products they consume, they are more likely to purchase products with which they are unfamiliar. The wine industry is very typical in that aspect. French and Italian wines at one time dominated the higher segments of the market, but the way they were marketed demanded that the consumer learn a complex system of classification. When United States vintners simplified the industry by labeling the bottles with the name of the grape variety they used, it expanded the market by making it less intimidating to buy wine. Consumers were less likely to make mistakes and more likely to enjoy their wines. An unintended consequence of this simplification was a substantial increase in the sales of wines from countries that traditionally had sold exclusively domestically; Chile, South Africa, and New Zealand, for example.

1.4.4 Technology Drivers

Another reason people are more familiar with products is that the diffusion of information has become universal. Anyone with an Internet connection can quickly access Wikipedia or any other website that provides information. Consumers can conveniently purchase products everywhere, and it is just as convenient to purchase from overseas as it is to purchase next door. Companies that have a presence on the Internet are enticing consumers everywhere to purchase their products. Expanding on this concept of worldwide competition between companies, Thomas Friedman writes about how the world has become flat, and that individuals are now competing with each other on a worldwide scale for jobs: easy communications and transfer of information have made one's location irrelevant.[20]

technology driver
One reason a firm may go international is to respond to technologically savvy customers who buy products worldwide.

An easy example of the worldwide availability and sharing of information is the textbook that you are reading; in order to find good illustrations of certain concepts, the author searched for photographs on the Internet. There are a total of eighty-six different photographers, from twenty-four different countries, who provided the illustrations for this book. All were easily contacted to request their authorization to use their work. In a similar fashion, companies can easily find suppliers for just about any product on the Internet as well, using search engines such as the Hong Kong-based alibaba.com.[21]

1.5 International Trade Theories

On a formal level, economists have developed several theories to explain why countries trade, and all have empirical support. The following four theories are the ones most commonly used to explain bilateral trade between two countries.

1.5.1 Smith's Theory of Absolute Advantage

Adam Smith's Theory of Absolute Advantage was first defined in *The Wealth of Nations* in 1776: "If a foreign country can supply us with a commodity cheaper than we ourselves can make it, better buy it of them with some part of the produce of our own industry, employed in a way in which we have some advantage."[22]

absolute advantage
An economic theory that holds that when a nation can produce a certain type of product more efficiently than other countries, it will trade with countries that produce other goods more efficiently.

The principle of absolute advantage is very easy to understand. Suppose companies, located in France, can produce 20,000 liters of wine for each year of labor they employ, and, also using a year of labor, can produce two units of machinery. Suppose companies in Germany produce, with the same amount of labor, 15,000 liters of wine or three units of machinery. It is clear that the French enjoy an absolute advantage in making wine and that the Germans have an absolute advantage in making machinery, and therefore that it is in the best interest of both parties to have the French companies produce wine and the German companies make machinery.

Production before Trading	France	Germany	Combined Output
Wine	20,000 liters	15,000 liters	35,000 liters
Machinery	2 units	3 units	5 units

Production after Trading	France	Germany	Combined Output
Wine	40,000 liters	0 liters	40,000 liters
Machinery	0 units	6 units	6 units

Consumption after Trading	France	Germany	Combined Consumption
Wine	20,000 liters	20,000 liters	40,000 liters
Machinery	3 units	3 units	6 units

Table 1.7: A numerical example of the Theory of Absolute Advantage

Table 1.7 illustrates this point. Before trading, both countries use their respective resources to make wine and machinery. France produces 20,000 liters of wine and 2 units of machinery, while Germany produces 15,000 liters of wine and 3 units of machinery. If the two countries decide to trade and use their respective absolute advantages, France will take all of the resources it had been using to make machinery and divert them to make more wine, shifting production from 2 units of machinery to 20,000 additional liters of wine. Germany also shifts its emphasis; instead of making 15,000 liters of wine, it makes three additional units of machinery.

France then proceeds to buy 3 units of machinery from Germany. France would be willing to pay as much as 30,000 liters of wine (what it would have to give up in order to make those 3 units) for those units. Germany, reciprocally, proceeds to buy 20,000 liters of wine. Germany would be willing to pay 4 units of machinery (what Germany would have to give up to make those 20,000 liters). Overall production, consumption and satisfaction are higher in both countries.

The theory does not concentrate on labor alone, but on the sum of all of the re-

1.5 International Trade Theories

sources that are needed to make the product. A country (company) has an absolute advantage if it produces more goods than another, using the same amount of input; in other words, a company enjoys an absolute advantage if it is more efficient.

There are many examples of absolute advantage in international trade; countries specialize in specific crops or manufactures because they enjoy a worldwide absolute advantage over all other countries. For example, Kuwait produces crude oil more cheaply than any other country and imports most everything else its economy needs. Taiwan region produces most of the world's supply of Random Access Memory (RAM) chips, and uses these proceeds to import other products and goods it cannot produce as efficiently, such as soybeans from Brazil.

1.5.2 Ricardo's Theory of Comparative Advantage

Although most frequently attributed to David Ricardo, the Theory of Comparative Advantage was first outlined by Robert Torrens in his *Essay on the External Corn Trade* published in 1815.[23] It was Ricardo, though, who illustrated it with a numerical example in *On the Principles of Political Economy and Taxation* in 1817[24] and who is responsible for its great acceptance. The principle of comparative advantage is not as simple as that of absolute advantage.

To illustrate the comparative advantage theory, suppose that companies in Great Britain can manufacture, using one year of labor, five units of machinery or a hundred tons of wheat. Companies in Brazil can manufacture, using the same input of labor, three units of machinery and ninety tons of wheat. In this case, Britain enjoys an absolute advantage in both machinery and wheat, and therefore, at least according to the Theory of Absolute Advantage, the two countries would not trade.

comparative advantage
An economic theory that holds that nations will trade with one another as long as they can produce certain goods relatively more efficiently than one another.

Production before Trading

	Great Britain	Brazil	Combined Output
Wheat	100 tons	90 tons	190 tons
Machinery	5 units	3 units	8 units

Production after Trading

	Great Britain	Brazil	Combined Output
Wheat	80 tons	120 tons	200 tons
Machinery	6 units	2 units	8 units

Consumption after Trading

	Great Britain	Brazil	Combined Consumption
Wheat	105 tons	95 tons	200 tons
Machinery	5 units	3 units	8 units

Table 1.8: A numerical example of the Theory of Comparative Advantage

However, Britain enjoys a comparative advantage in the production of machinery and Brazil enjoys a comparative advantage in the production of wheat. For Britain to manufacture a hundred tons of wheat, it has to "give up" five units of machinery;

in other words, the cost of a piece of machinery is twenty tons of wheat. For Brazil, in order to produce ninety tons of wheat, it has to give up three units of machinery. The cost to Brazil of producing one unit of machinery is therefore thirty tons of wheat. Therefore, it makes sense for both countries to trade with one another; Britain can sell units of machinery in exchange for wheat from Brazil. Should the agreed-upon price be between the British value of twenty tons of wheat for each unit of machinery and the Brazilian value of thirty tons of wheat for each unit of machinery, both countries will find it beneficial to trade with each other. Assuming a market price of twenty-five tons of wheat for each piece of machinery, Britain is better off making machinery rather than growing wheat, and Brazil is better off growing wheat than making pieces of machinery.

Table 1.8 illustrates that example. Before trading, both countries use their respective resources to make wheat and machinery. Great Britain produces a hundred tons of wheat and five units of machinery, while Brazil produces ninety tons of wheat and three units of machinery. If the two countries decide to trade and use their respective comparative advantages, Great Britain may decide to take the resources it had been using to make wheat and divert them to make more units of machinery.

Britain decides to decrease its production of wheat by twenty tons and increase its production of machinery by one unit. Brazil also shifts its emphasis; it decreases its production of machinery by one unit, and increases its production of wheat by thirty tons. Using a market price of twenty-five tons of wheat for each unit of machinery, Britain then proceeds to buy twenty-five tons of wheat from Brazil in exchange for one unit of machinery. Brazil, reciprocally, proceeds to buy this unit of machinery by selling twenty-five tons of wheat. British companies now have a hundred-and-five tons of wheat available for consumption and Brazil has ninety-five tons. Overall, production, consumption and satisfaction are higher in both countries.

The Theory of Comparative Advantage is present in most of the exchanges that companies make internationally. Most firms specialize in making certain products efficiently and these specializations give them a comparative advantage. At one point in its history, the Ford Motor Company built the River Rouge plant where, at one end, iron ore and coal were delivered, and at the other, finished automobiles rolled off the assembly line. Today, Ford has gained a comparative advantage in designing and assembling automobiles and countless suppliers have made a business out of their own comparative advantage; Mittal Steel (India) in sheet metal, Alcan in aluminum products, TRW in airbags, and so on. Even though the Ford Motor Company is capable of producing these products, it chooses not to, and rather buys them from companies that can produce them relatively more efficiently than it can.

1.5.3 Heckscher-Ohlin Factor Endowment Theory

factor endowment
An economic theory that holds that a nation will have a comparative advantage over other countries if it is naturally endowed with a greater abundance of one of the factors of economic production.

The Factor Endowment Theory was developed by Eli Heckscher and Bertil Ohlin in 1933[25] and builds on Ricardo's comparative advantage concept. Ricardo's explanation of factor endowment was based on comparing the effectiveness of a country at using its labor to produce goods, and it assumed different levels of technology to account for the differences in the countries' ability to manufacture goods.

The Heckscher-Ohlin Theory extends that idea by assuming that, even when technology is identical, some countries enjoy a comparative advantage over others because they are endowed with a greater abundance of a particular factor of production. Since economists consider that there are four factors of production—land, labor, capital, and entrepreneurship—countries with a greater abundance of one of these factors enjoy an advantage over others.

A country may have a relative abundance of capital and relatively scarce labor resources; because capital is plentiful, it is inexpensive, and therefore the products made by industries that require a lot of capital tend to have a relatively low production cost when compared to products made by industries that require a lot of labor, since labor is relatively scarce and therefore expensive.[26]

For example, Japan has a relative abundance of capital, and therefore Japanese companies can manufacture products such as precision machinery, that are capital-intensive, at a relatively low cost. Japan has a heavily-subsidized agriculture, but still produces rice at a very high unit cost. There are two reasons for that high production cost; Japan has a relative scarcity of land (only about 12 percent of its land is arable) and of labor (it has a very low unemployment rate due to a decreasing labor force caused by a declining overall population and an aging workforce). Indonesia, on the other hand has an abundance of young labor and much agricultural land, and Indonesian farmers can produce rice at a very low cost. However, capital is relatively scarce in that country, and therefore manufacturing costs are high, and there are few companies producing precision machinery. Because they enjoy an abundance of capital, the output of Japanese precision-machinery companies is much greater than the output of their Indonesian counterparts. Similarly, because the Indonesian farmers have access to more labor and land, their production of rice is much greater than the output of Japanese farmers.

Total Country Output before Trading (1978)

	Japan	Indonesia	Combined Output
Automobiles	6 million cars	0.02 million cars	6.02 million cars
Rice	16 million tons	26 million tons	42 million tons

Production after Trading (2010)

	Japan	Indonesia	Combined Output
Automobiles	8.4 million cars	0.8 million cars	9.2 million cars
Rice	10.6 million tons	66.5 million tons	77.1 million tons

Table 1.9: A numerical example of the Heckscher-Ohlin Theory (based on actual data)

Table 1.9 illustrates that example more precisely and the figures are based on actual data.[27,28,29,30] In 1978, Japan produced 6 million cars and 16 million tons of rice a year. Its automobile industry used abundant capital, and therefore it enjoyed relatively low production costs. On the other hand, rice was produced using very-high priced labor and scarce land, and therefore it was a high-cost commodity. In Indonesia, the situation was reversed; the country produced fewer than 20,000 automobiles, because such production demanded a large amount of capital, which was scarce in Indonesia. However the country also produced 26 million tons of rice because of its abundant labor and agricultural land. There was relatively little trade between the two countries.

In 2010, Japan produced only 10.6 million tons of rice, a decrease of more than 30 percent, but Indonesia's production reached a record 66.5 million tons, more than twice what it had been in 1978. Japanese companies used their capital to expand their production to satisfy the needs of the Indonesian population in terms of automobiles, producing a total of 10 million vehicles at home. However, they also made capital investments in Indonesia; automobile production in Indonesia soared to about 838,000 vehicles in 2011, many of them made in plants owned by Japanese, European or U.S. manufacturers. Four distributors dominate the Indonesian market: P.T. Astra that sells Toyota, Daihatsu, Peugeot, BMW, and Lexus, P.T. Indomobil that sells Nissan, Volvo, Volkswagen, Audi, Renault, and Infiniti, P.T. Ford Motor, and P.T. GM Auto World Indonesia.[31]

The Factor Endowment Theory explains why certain countries specialize in the production of certain products. Argentina has abundant grazing land, and therefore enjoys a comparative advantage over other countries in beef production. India has abundant educated labor and therefore enjoys a comparative advantage in the staffing of call centers. The United States has an economic system in which entrepreneurship is handsomely rewarded, and it enjoys a comparative advantage in innovation and the development of intellectual property.

1.5.4 International Product Life Cycle

The International Product Life Cycle Theory was developed by Raymond Vernon in 1966.[32] This theory explains the development of international trade in three stages. Figure 1.6 illustrates the three stages devised by Vernon.

international product life cycle
An economic theory that holds that, over its life cycle, a product will be manufactured in different countries.

In the first stage, a company creates a new product to satisfy a market need. This generally takes place in a developed country, as the critical number of customers necessary for a new product launch is often only found in such countries. The product may also use proprietary technology that is only available in that country. The firm manufactures the product in the country of innovation because it needs to be able to monitor the manufacturing process carefully, since there are always unexpected problems in manufacturing a new product. As the product gains acceptance, the firm starts to export the product to other developed countries, where similar markets start to emerge.

In the second stage, sales in other developed countries start to grow and local competitors see that there are enough customers to justify production of products that imitate the original product. Alternative processes or patents are developed. Sales grow further and the product manufacturing process becomes much better controlled and somewhat standardized and many companies master the intricacies of making that product. At the same time, the higher-income segments of developing countries' markets import the product from developed countries, and a market in those countries starts to emerge.

In the third stage, the manufacturing process has become is almost routine. There are pressures to lower production costs. At the same time, the markets in developing countries start to reach such sizes that entrepreneurs in developing countries start to produce the products, frequently under contract from firms in the developed countries.

1.5 International Trade Theories

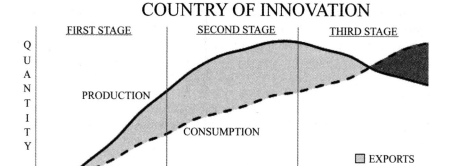

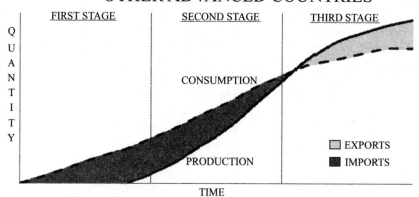

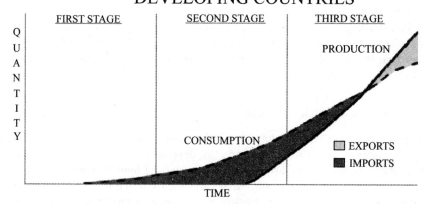

Figure 1.6: The International Product Life Cycle Theory
Adapted by Rémy d'Arras. Used with permission.

Because the manufacturing costs of a mature product tend to be mostly labor-related, these firms start to export massively toward developed countries, slowly replacing all of the manufacturing capacity in those markets.

There is much empirical evidence that supports the International Product Life Cycle Theory. The first televisions were first manufactured and sold in Great Britain. They eventually were manufactured in other developed countries in Europe, North America, Japan, and Australia-New Zealand. As their popularity increased, all of the manufacturing facilities in those developed countries were eventually replaced by manufacturing facilities in developing countries in Southeast Asia.[33] As of 2003, there were no longer any manufacturing facilities in the United States for televisions at all.

1.5.5 Porter's Cluster Theory

Michael Porter's Cluster Theory, developed in 1990,[34] is not a theory of international trade, but an explanation of the success of certain regions at developing a worldwide absolute (or comparative) advantage in a particular technology or product, despite having no particular advantage in any specific factor of production.

cluster
An observation that a firm can develop a substantial competitive advantage in manufacturing certain goods when a large number of its competitors and suppliers are located in close proximity.

The cluster theory argues that it is critical to have a cluster of companies in the same industry, as well as their suppliers, concentrated in one geographic area. The companies feed on each other's know-how, and their competitiveness pushes them to innovate faster. In addition, when such a cluster exists, the best and brightest employees are eager to move to that location, as they know that they will easily find employment. In addition, as these employees move from firm to firm, they also take with them the know-how they acquired with their previous employers and therefore innovation travels from firm to firm. In some cases, these employees develop technologies and ideas that their employers may not want to pursue further and they themselves then start a company to exploit these ideas. Innovation flourishes within the area.

There are several areas of the world where such clusters can be found. The most commonly mentioned location is Silicon Valley in California, where most of the innovation in computer technology took place in the latter part of the twentieth century. However, Porter studied the cluster of Sassuolo in Italy, which specializes in ceramic tiles and produces more than 30 percent of the world's ceramic tiles, and where more than 70 percent of the production is exported.[35] Another well-known cluster is the area around the Jura mountains in France and Switzerland, where, from the late eighteenth century until the mid-twentieth century, most of the mechanical watches produced worldwide were produced.[36]

1.5.6 Sheffi's Logistics Cluster Theory

Yossi Sheffi extended Michael Porter's Cluster Theory to the logistics industry in 2012.[37] He observed that some locations can develop into economic powerhouses because they combine in one area multiple providers of logistical services, a situation that attracts manufacturers since they can easily obtain their raw materials and ship their goods in the most cost-effective way possible. Some regions, such as Singapore, are poor in natural resources, yet develop into international hubs because of the concentration of logistical service providers.[38] Sheffi emphasizes that local governments and chambers of commerce can be instrumental in developing clusters, by facilitating the concentration of logistical services in one area. Sheffi was particularly impressed with the Zaragoza cluster, called PLAZA—*Platforma Logística de Zaragoza*—located in an area roughly equidistant from all of the manufacturing and population centers of Spain. PLAZA has attracted multiple logistical companies, and it has become the transportation hub of the country of Spain.[39]

1.6 The International Business Environment

On a more practical level, the international logistics professional should have some understanding of the particularities of the international business environment. While it is impossible to replace experience in dealing with people from different countries, it is often useful to know the relevant issues. These few paragraphs are no substitute for classes in international marketing, intercultural communication, international finance, and international economics, but neither are these classes substitutes for experience in world travel and frequent contact with people from different countries and the extensive study of a foreign language.

The international environment is often first described by differences in culture, a term that encompasses the entire heritage of the people living in a particular country or geographical area; their language, their customs, their traditions, their morals, their beliefs, and their relationships with one another. If there is one aspect of international business about which it is difficult to generalize, it is culture. Not only are there differences between countries, but there are often differences between regions of a country (in the United States, consider New York and Hawaii), between industries within a country (the bio-tech industry and the auto industry), and often between companies within an industry (IBM and Apple Computers). Therefore, stating that the normal business attire in the United States is a pin-striped suit, a white shirt, and a conservative tie is correct, but only in a certain industry, in a certain geographic location, and in a particular company. Making similar generalizations about other countries is just as incorrect.

The best strategy for a person interested in a career in international business would be to become familiar with the different techniques for intercultural communications. A number of excellent textbooks have been written in this field. For a person interested in conducting business with a firm in the United States, there are books dealing with the American business culture. For managers interested in a specific country, Brigham Young University publishes the Culturegrams, which are an excellent synopsis (a few pages) of a given country's culture.[40] Despite all of these tools, culture and cultural misunderstandings are probably the greatest sources of frustration for managers involved in international business. Several tools are presented in Chapter 18 to prevent some of these problems, but the best strategy is to be flexible and sensitive to other people's reactions.

The remainder of the international environment is simpler to understand; countries have different approaches to their legal system, to the way they run their governments, and to the way their economies function. Most information about a country can easily be found in the World FactBook published by the Central Intelligence Agency,[41] in the Country Commercial Guides published by the United States Department of Commerce,[42] in the Country Profiles and Country Reports published by The Economist's Intelligence Unit,[43] and in the Business Planet database of the World Bank.[44]

Further information on countries of a different nature can be found in other sources: the Culturegrams of Brigham Young University give excellent insights on the cultures of 190 countries in the world, in addition to the 50 U.S. states and 13 Canadian provinces. The United Nations' Human Development Report[45] gives a composite perspective on the quality of life in most countries.

Finally, and this is a "must see," data on multiple countries are vividly illustrated by Gapminder,[46] a website dedicated to illustrating data in graphic and dynamic form. This website is the result of a phenomenal effort undertaken by Hans Rosling of Sweden, his son Ola Rosling and his daughter-in-law Anna Rosling Rönnlund who created a software that makes data come alive. The software was purchased by Google in 2007.

Review and Discussion Questions

1. Given the total volume and importance of international trade and international exchanges, describe the implications to someone's career in business, and to your education in particular.

2. Consider two countries' situations: Country A can produce either six automobiles or twelve movies with the same amount of resources. Country B, using the same resources, can produce either five automobiles or eight movies. Using Ricardo's Theory of Comparative Advantage, determine which country would produce automobiles, which would produce movies, and the range of relative prices within which these products would trade.

3. Wal-Mart is famous for requesting ever lower price points from its suppliers: if a supplier offers a product for $45.00, Wal-Mart will ask the supplier to consider introducing a similar product for $39.00. According to the Heckscher-Ohlin Factor Theory, which consequences do such requests have?

4. In addition to the clusters of Silicon Valley and Sassuolo, Michael Porter identified a cluster for printing presses in Heidelberg, Germany, and others have written about clusters in Limoges, France, for porcelain and in Valenza Po, Italy, for gold jewelry. What characteristics do industrial clusters have that other cities do not have? Can you think of another industrial cluster in the United States or abroad?

Notes

[1] World Trade Organization Statistical Database, http://stat.wto.org/ StatisticalProgram/-WSDBViewData.aspx?Language=E, retrieved May 15, 2013.

[2] Scherer, Barrymore Laurence, "Alice Tully's Pleasing Makeover," *The Wall Street Journal*, April 14, 2009, p. D7.

[3] Crissey, Jeff, "On Center Stage," *Modern Woodworking*, March 2009, pp. 24-29.

[4] *World Trade Organization Statistical Database*, http://stat.wto.org/ StatisticalProgram/-WSDBViewData.aspx?Language=E, retrieved May 15, 2013.

[5] World Trade Organization Statistical Database, http://stat.wto.org/ StatisticalProgram/-WSDBViewData.aspx?Language=E, retrieved May 15, 2013.

[6] *Ibid.*

[7] *Ibid.*

NOTES

[8] *Ibid.*

[9] "WTO Tariff Analysis Online [TAO]," http://www.wto.org/english/ tratop_e/tariffs_e/tao_help_e.htm, retrieved August 18, 2012.

[10] "The WTO in Brief: History," http://www.wto.org/english/thewto_e/ whatis_e/inbrief_e/inbr00_e.htm, retrieved April 13, 2009.

[11] "Documents from the negotiating chairs, 21 April 2011," http://www. wto.org/english/tratop_e/dda_e/chair_texts11_e/chair_texts11_e.htm, retrieved August 18, 2012.

[12] World Trade Organization Statistical Database, http://stat.wto.org/ StatisticalProgram/WSDBViewData.aspx?Language=E, retrieved August 17, 2012.

[13] *Ibid.*

[14] Doing Business Database, The World Bank Group, 1818 H Street NW, Washington, DC 20433, http://www.doingbusiness.org/data, retrieved August 18, 2012.

[15] Bureau of Labor Statistics, United States Department of Labor, "International Comparison of Hourly Compensation Costs in Manufacturing—2011," http://www.bls.gov/fls/#compensation, retrieved May 30, 2013.

[16] "World Motor Vehicle Production," International Organization of Motor Vehicles Manufacturers—Organization Internationale des Constructeurs Automobiles, 4 rue de Berri, 75008 Paris, France, http://oica.net/wp-content/uploads/ranking-2010.pdf, retrieved August 18, 2012.

[17] Motor Vehicle Production Statistics (2011), International Organization of Motor Vehicles Manufacturers—Organization Internationale des Constructeurs Automobiles, 4 rue de Berri, 75008 Paris, France, http://oica.net/category/production-statistics, retrieved August 18, 2012.

[18] Sharma, Ruchir, "China Slows Down, and Grows Up," *The New York Times*, April 25, 2012.

[19] Kulish, Eric, "Right Shoring: Global Cost Structures have Manufacturers Reevaluating Outsourcing Phenomenon," *American Shipper*, June 2012, pp.8-17.

[20] Friedman, Thomas, *The World is flat: a brief history of the twenty-first century*, Farrar, Strauss and Giroux, New York, New York, 2005.

[21] www.alibaba.com

[22] Smith, Adam, *An inquiry into the nature and causes of the wealth of nations*, Bantam Classics, 2003.

[23] Torrens, Robert, The budget: On commercial and colonial policy, London, Smith, Elder, 1840.

[24] Ricardo, David, On the principles of political economy and taxation, Dover Publications, 2004.

[25] Ohlin, Bertil, *Interregional and international trade*, 1933, reproduced in Samuelson, Paul A., *Heckscher-Ohlin international trade theory*, MIT Press, 1991.

[26] Suranovic, Steven M., "The Heckscher-Ohlin Model Overview," *International Trade Theory and Policy*, http://www.internationalecon.com/ Trade/Tch60/T60-0.php, April 14, 2009.

[27] Paddy rice production, by country and geographical region, 1961-2007, Food and Agriculture Organization, http://beta.irri.org/solutions/ index.php?option=com_content&task=view&id=250, retrieved April 19, 2009.

[28] Paddy rice production, by country, 2010, Food and Agricultural Organization, http://faostat.fao.org/site/339/default.aspx, retrieved August 19, 2012.

[29] Fuss, Melvyn A. and Leonard Waverman, "Passenger car production 1961-1984," *Cost and*

Productivity in Japanese Production: The Challenge of Japanese Efficiency, Cambridge University Press, 1992.

[30] Motor Vehicle Production Statistics (2011), International Organization of Motor Vehicles Manufacturers—Organization Internationale des Constructeurs Automobiles, 4 rue de Berri, 75008 Paris, France, http:// oica.net/category/production-statistics, retrieved August 18, 2012.

[31] Overview of Automobile Industry in Indonesia, Indonesian Commercial Newsletter, April 2011, http://www.datacon.co.id/Automotive-2011Industry.html, retrieved August 19, 2012.

[32] Vernon, Raymond, "International Investment and International Trade in the Product Life Cycle," *Quarterly Journal of Economics*, May 1966, 80(2), pp. 190-207.

[33] Gao, Zhicun, and Clem Tisdell, "Television Production: Its Changing Global Location, the Product Cycle and China," *Economic Theory, Applications and Issues*, Working Paper No. 26, University of Queensland, http://ageconsearch.umn.edu/bitstream/90530/2/WP%2026.pdf, retrieved April 19, 2009.

[34] Porter, Michael E., *The competitive advantage of nations*, The Free Press, New York, New York, 1990.

[35] "Sassuolo cluster profile," United Nations Industrial Development Organization, http://www.unido.org/doc/4309, August 10, 2006.

[36] Glasmeier, Amy, "Why Switzerland?," *Manufacturing Time; Global Competition in the Watch Industry: 1790-2000*, Guilford Press, New York, New York, 2000.

[37] Sheffi, Yossi, *Logistics Clusters: Delivering Value and Driving Growth*, MIT Press, Cambridge, Massachusetts, 2012.

[38] Kulish, Eric, "Logistics Clusters," *American Shipper*, November 2012, pp.14-15.

[39] Bradley, Peter, "Logistics clusters as drivers of growth: Interview with Yossi Sheffi," *DC Velocity*, December 2012, pp. 38-40.

[40] Culturegrams, Pro-Quest and Brigham Young University, http://www.culturegrams.com.

[41] *The World Factbook*, Central Intelligence Agency, https://www.cia.gov/library/publications/the-world-factbook.

[42] Country commercial guides, United States Department of Commerce, http://www.state.gov/e/eb/rls/rpts/ccg.

[43] The Economist's Intelligence Unit, http://www.eiu.com/site_info.asp?info_name=about_eiu.

[44] Business Planet: Mapping the Business Environment, The World Bank Group, http://rru.worldbank.org.

[45] United Nations Development Programme, Human Development Reports, http://hdr.undp.org/en/statistics

[46] Rosling, Ola, Anna Rosling Rönnlund and Hans Rosling, Gapminder: Unveiling the beauty of statistics for a fact-based worldview, http://www.gapminder.org.

Chapter 2

International Supply Chain Management

> 2.1 Historical Development 27
> 2.2 Logistics and Supply Chain Management 36
> 2.3 Elements of International Logistics 41
> 2.4 The Economic Importance of Logistics 42
> 2.5 International Reverse Logistics 44

Before presenting the different aspects of international logistics, it is useful to understand how this function is currently included in the management of a firm engaged in international business. It is essential for the international logistician to understand the responsibilities of that profession and the interactions that this function has with the other operational functions of a firm, such as marketing, finance, and production.

Over the years, the responsibilities of an international logistics manager have evolved substantially. This chapter introduces a brief history of the development of the profession of international logistician, the evolution of the activities that have become his or her responsibility, and the current status of this managerial position. It should be made clear that the responsibilities of an international logistician are still changing; it is not known whether the profession will eventually include a greater number of activities or whether its responsibilities will be curtailed, especially in the light of the creation of the field of Supply Chain Management.

2.1 Historical Development

2.1.1 The Early, "Slow" Days

The globalization of markets is generally understood to be a recent phenomenon, triggered by the economic development explosion after World War II; however, while international trade has certainly increased dramatically in the second half of the last century, nations have engaged in international trade for eons. However, before the twentieth century and the advent of modern transportation, trade between nations had always relied on courageous traders who ventured in faraway places in the

international trade
The sale of goods and services across international borders.

hope of earning a living. The spice trade was well established in Roman times, and flourished during the Middle Ages,[1] bringing a vast array of different products to European consumers; a Florentine merchant listed 288 different spices that it could procure at the beginning of the fifteenth century. These goods moved either by sea or by caravans of pack animals, "with many transshipments, many tolls, and much danger of loss."[2]

The adventurers/logisticians of that period were responsible for determining what goods they should take along as payment for the goods they hoped to bring back, negotiating with foreigners with whom they did not share a language, and arranging for the transportation and safekeeping of the goods while in transit. They were exposed to the risks of international travel, of market preferences, and of political instability. They were willing to be pioneers.

Can these early traders be considered to have been the first involved in international logistics? Undoubtedly. The word "logistics" comes from the Greek *logistike*, which translates as "the art of calculating"[3] using concrete items, in contrast with *arithmetike*, which was the art of calculating using abstract concepts.* The latter eventually evolved into the modern concepts of arithmetic and algebra. The first gave birth to the modern term of "logistics," which has evolved into the art and science of determining eminently concrete aspects of business management, from transportation and packaging to warehousing and inventory management.

The first international traders were involved in logistics; they calculated how much their ships—or beasts—could carry, how much food to bring along, and how best to package the goods while in transit, decisions that parallel exactly what a modern logistics manager does when considering how many units to place in a modern container, how to balance the load evenly, and how to protect the goods for their international voyage. Early traders had to decide which payment method was most appropriate, just as a modern exporter must determine the best way of ensuring it will get paid. While many aspects of international logistics have changed, the main concerns of people involved in this field remain similar; they have to ensure that goods manufactured in one part of the world arrive safely to their destination.

Nevertheless, the modern interpretation of the term "logistics" has its origins in the military, where it was used to describe the activities related to the procurement of ammunitions and essential supplies to troops located at the front. It gave birth to the title of *Maréchal des Logis* in the French military, which is given to a sergeant in charge of a unit's supplies and housing. Interestingly enough, when the term applies to the branch of the military in charge of logistics on a large scale, the modern French military uses a different word altogether, "*le train.*"

Initially, logistics was understood as "physical distribution," and was based on the military concept encompassing mostly the physical movement of goods. The first author to expand the concept beyond this early interpretation was Shaw,[4] who incorporated it into the remainder of distribution activities, such as inventory and the selection of distribution intermediaries. Today, the term is much broader and includes not only all the activities related to the physical movement of goods, both upstream (procurement activities) and downstream (sales) activities, but also the management of the relationships with suppliers and customers.

Over the last thirty years, the focus of logistics has evolved substantially: early on, and probably until the mid-1980s, the main concern of logistics managers and

container
A large metallic box used in international trade that can be loaded directly onto a truck, a railroad car or an ocean-going vessel. The most common dimensions of a container are $8 \times 8.5 \times 20$ feet and $8 \times 8.5 \times 40$ feet.

---

*This interpretation may not be shared by all readers of Klein's work: the distinction is not very accessible.

2.1 Historical Development

specifically of international logistics managers, was to make sure that the goods arrived at their destination in good condition and at the lowest possible cost. Shorter transit times were considered, but generally only when the goods were perishable or because the goods were so urgently needed that the additional costs were justified; for most goods, however, long transit times were essentially considered normal. As time moved on, a transition was made to shorter transit times.

2.1.2 The Move Toward Speed

Containers—"boxes" in the logisticians' vernacular—changed the focus of international logistics. Even though they were introduced in 1956, containers had a limited impact on international trade until the early 1970s.

Before containers, the process of shipping internationally by ocean was cumbersome and very time consuming. The traditional method was to first pack the goods into a truck or a railroad car for their inland trip to the port. The goods were then unloaded in the port and loaded onto a ship using cranes and slings, as well as a large number of longshoremen who stowed them appropriately for their ocean voyage. The goods were then unloaded again in the port of arrival, loaded in a truck or railroad car for their inland trip, and finally unloaded at their destination. Packages had to be small and light enough to be handled by humans in the ship's holds, and very sturdy to withstand being handled numerous times. A transatlantic shipment took in excess of one month, with the majority of that time spent with the cargo delayed in the ports.

longshoreman
A person who performs manual labor in a port.

stevedore
A person who loads and unloads goods from a vessel in a port.

Stevedores

Before the advent of containers, stevedoring was back-breaking work. The goods to be shipped abroad would arrive to port in trucks or railroad cars in small packages or in pallets. They would then be unloaded in a warehouse located alongside the pier and counted. When the ship arrived, it would first have to be completely emptied of its current goods and that merchandise had to be removed from the pier before any loading could start. The merchandise to be loaded was then moved from the warehouse to the quay and counted once more. A loading plan was devised to determine what should be loaded first (the heavier, more resilient items), and what should be loaded last.

Longshoremen would then assemble the goods into "drafts," which were larger parcels that could be loaded onto the ship by cranes. They did this by hand, carrying, dragging, and rolling the merchandise to a point where the crane could pick them up; they eventually placed slings under each draft before they were loaded. The merchandise was then lifted onto the ship where another gang of longshoremen would unpack the drafts, count the goods once again, and position them into the holds of the ship (still using muscle power), making sure that every piece of cargo was tightly braced against the others so that it would not shift during the voyage.

Many of these goods were not packaged to be handled easily; some bags of grain weighed as much as 100kg (220 lbs.) and bags of sugar weighed 60kg (132 lbs.). A single longshoreman generally carried the bags of sugar, but two shared the work of moving a bag of

Figure 2.1: New York stevedores loading corn-syrup barrels, 1912
Photo ©Lewis Hine, National Archives of the United States. Used with permission.

grain. Bananas were regularly unloaded by walking down a gangplank on the side of the ship rather than by crane. Each weighed about 80kg (176 lbs.). With such working conditions, it is understandable that longshoremen accidents were common; every year, one in six was injured. Between 1947 and 1957, forty-seven longshoremen were killed in the port of Marseille.[5]

Unloading was not much different. The results of such labor-intensive work were millions of longshoremen employed worldwide, as many as 50,000 in each of the ports of New York, London, and Marseille. Most of these men were employed only part-time, working whenever there was a ship, idle when there were none, and competing for work when one was scheduled to arrive in port. They toiled in all sorts of weather, and had to learn to move anything; one day they would load and unload delicate goods, and the next, heavy, dirty, smelly bags.[6]

All this changed with the advent of containers, which allowed the mechanization of loading and unloading ships. The work of a stevedore became much less physical; although some dockworkers still have to be aboard the ship to position the twist locks that tie the containers to one another and lash down the two lower containers in a stack, many of them drive trucks to position containers alongside the ship or pick them up, or operate a gantry crane.[7,8,9]

With the advent of containers, shipments began to speed up. Instead of loading and unloading the goods several times, containers were loaded only once, in the shipper's plant, and unloaded only once, at the customer's facilities. Packaging did not have to be as sturdy. Ship loading and unloading operations were much faster. Ships no longer had to be completely empty to load new cargo; as soon as a stack of containers was empty, the crane that was unloading containers from the ship did not have to return to the ship empty; it could immediately pick up another container to be loaded onto the vessel. This single difference doubled the productivity of crane operators. Because of all of these improvements, the costs of ocean shipping came down: port labor costs were lower, ships were more productive because they spent less time idling in ports, and significant investments were made in container ships that became ever more efficient.

Figure 2.2: Thousands of Containers at Port Elizabeth, New Jersey
Photo ©Albert Theberge, National Oceanic and Atmospheric Administration. Used with permission.

Only a few years later, in the late 1970s and early 1980s, international logistics saw an explosion in the number of air shipments. Even though DHL had been founded in 1969 and Federal Express in 1973, neither of these services provided much coverage: DHL was strictly a San Francisco-Honolulu service until 1974, and Federal Express had only twenty-five domestic destinations until 1979. However, Federal Express sales rose quickly and by 1983, it had become a billion-dollar corporation strictly based on domestic shipments. It started international operations in 1984, and, by 2005, it had changed its name to FedEx, and become a $30 billion corporation. In the United States, the term "fedex" has become a verb. For its fiscal year 2012, the corporation reported global sales of $42 billion.[10]

The costs of air shipments also dropped considerably during this period. In the beginning, Federal Express operated with Dassault Falcon jets, which had limited cargo capacity. By the end of the 1970s, after a partial deregulation of the industry, it had acquired Boeing 727s and McDonnell-Douglas DC10s, which had much greater capacity. Further deregulation in the 1980s and open-sky agreements in the 1990s increased the number of aircrafts dedicated to freight, and air shipments became increasingly cost competitive with surface alternatives.

As customers' expectations of speedy delivery increased, it became clear that delivery speed had become one of the salient criteria in the selection of a supplier. David Hummels estimated that "each additional day spent in transport reduces the probability that [a company] will source from that country by 1 to 1.5 percent."[11]

Malcom McLean

Anyone observing one of the world's ports today would see a constellation of containers (see Figure 2.2 on the preceding page). Containers being hoisted off ships and onto trucks or trains, others being loaded onto ships, and still hundreds of others stacked and waiting their turn to be moved. Other than these boxes, there are no actual goods to be seen, and the observer would have no way of knowing what was coming and going. Inside the boxes could be televisions or shampoo, computers or potato chips. But the scene at these same ports just a few decades ago would have been very different.

The idea of one man, Malcom McLean, changed all that.

Before containerization, goods were delivered to the waterfront as separate pieces by truck or train. From there they were taken by hand to a storage shed to wait for longshoremen to load them onto a ship. The longshoremen would take each piece and place it by hand in the cargo hold. Loading thousands of goods onto a ship could take days and the process had to be reversed when the ship reached its destination.[12]

Those wishing to export their merchandise would typically have to arrive days or even weeks before the ship was to set sail in order to ensure their goods would be loaded. "Ships remained in port for days while longshoremen wrestled individual boxes, barrels and bales into and out of tight spaces below deck. Damage was frequent and expensive, as were losses from pilferage."[13] This process was terribly inefficient and slow, and was a major deterrent for many manufacturers who might consider transporting their goods overseas or even to other parts of the country.

This was the scene in 1937 when Malcom McLean drove a truck loaded with cotton intended for export to a port in New Jersey. He had to wait for days while he waited for longshoremen to load his cotton. He figured there had to be a better way. At the time McLean owned a small trucking company in North Carolina. After his experience in New Jersey he put his mind to building a better system of shipping which would grow his company into an efficient competitor in the shipping industry.

McLean went about hiring as many experts in containerization as he could find and learning everything he could about the field. He had the idea of driving truck trailers onto ships but found it was impractical. Eventually McLean and one of his engineers came up with a plan to use "containers thirty-three feet long, a length chosen because the available deck space aboard the T-2 tankers was divisible by thirty-three."[14] The boxes were much larger than anything seen before and would be loaded onto tankers by cranes. The tankers had specially designed frames that would hold the containers in place.

McLean put his idea to the test on April 26, 1956, when the converted tanker ship *Ideal X* set sail from Newark. McLean and his team watched a crane load fifty-eight containers onto the ship, one every seven minutes. What previously had taken days now took only hours. The ship left the Port of Newark destined for Houston, trailed the entire way by the Coast Guard to ensure its safety. Six days later the team watched the Ideal X come into port in Houston with all fifty-eight containers still safely aboard. This first test was a complete success.

When the transit costs of the journey were calculated McLean knew he had a real winner. Traditional shipping of loose cargo at the time cost about "$5.83 per ton" while shipping on the Ideal X container ship cost only "15.8 cents per ton."[15] These dramatically reduced costs drove the development of container shipping and an infrastructure was built to handle containers at ports around the world. McLean's company grew as did competitors and new technologies were developed to make containerization even more cost effective. Larger shippers were built that could handle more containers and the trend continues today as bigger ships are constantly in the works. Despite the protests of longshoremen, the old way of loading ships was quickly abandoned as containerization was embraced. This encouraged more businesses to ship their products further distances creating new markets. It also allowed new foods and other goods to be sent around the world to places they had never been seen before.

The idea of containerization is what fueled the spread of globalization around the globe.

2.1.3 The Emphasis on Customer Satisfaction

By the early 1990s, the increased speed of ocean shipments and the availability of affordable airfreight services had effectively changed the focus of logistics managers: they began to consider the shortest reasonable transit time in response to customers' request for speedy deliveries. Although it was still very important to make sure that the goods arrived in good condition and at the lowest possible cost, the managers' focus had shifted from these process-oriented concerns to the satisfaction of customers' requirements.

The major reason behind this change of objectives in the management of logistics was the increased focus by large manufacturers on the reduction of inventories during the 1980s. Starting in the mid-1970s, but culminating in the early 1980s, interest rates climbed to unprecedented heights, triggering a concern about all the money immobilized in inventories. In the 1980s, companies emphasized reductions in their "static" inventories, or the goods they kept in their warehouses or plants. By the early 1990s, they had shifted their attentions to their "mobile" inventories, or the goods that were in transit between two of their plants or between their suppliers and their plants. The tools they used were Materials Requirement Planning (MRP) and Manufacturing Resources Planning (MRP II), which allowed them to create Just-In-Time manufacturing processes. In turn, these processes triggered a need for

Materials Requirement Planning [MRP]
A management tool that allows a manufacturer to determine what to produce and in which quantity, in function of what it sells to its customers.

just-in-time
A management philosophy that consists of planning the manufacturing of goods in such a way that they are produced just before they are needed in the next step of the assembly process.

"time-defined" deliveries of assembly parts; plants demanded to have parts delivered just before they were used on the assembly line, and not later. The number of goods that were "in transit" had to be curtailed as well.

By the mid-1990s, all manufacturers had adopted such techniques and were requiring their suppliers to ship just-in-time. At the same time, large retailers and other distributors jumped on the same idea. They started to use techniques derived from MRP and MRP II, which they called Distribution Resources Planning (DRP) techniques, which used final consumer sales data to pull products through the distribution channel. Consumer sales data were collected through the point-of-sale (POS) scanners. If the products were selling briskly, then the DRP program reordered the goods from the manufacturer and had them delivered just-in-time to the appropriate warehouse or retail store. If a product did not sell well, none were ordered again. This strategy forced logistics managers to shift their attention to transit times and to become adaptable to frequent changes in their work. This came to be known as "agile logistics."

Distribution Resources Planning [MRP]
A management tool that allows a retail firm to determine what to order from its suppliers and in which quantity, in function of what it sells to its customers.

Materials Requirement Planning

In the late 1970s and early 1980s, Japanese manufacturers adopted a new manufacturing management philosophy that was based on reducing work-in-process inventory and delivering the goods to the assembly line just before they were needed. Such philosophy was called "Just-In-Time." Toyota's system for just-in-time (JIT) management was a technique using cards that it still uses today, called *kanban*. Other manufacturers also adopted the JIT philosophy, starting in the early 1980s, but implemented it using a technique called Materials Requirements Planning (MRP), especially in the United States.

MRP is a computer-based system that determines what needs to be manufactured on a given day, in which quantity, and whether that order should be expedited. It creates a Master Production Schedule based upon what is currently in inventory (on-hand), what is required to be produced (orders and forecasts of sales for the final product), and bill-of-materials files that spell out precisely what each product's components are. It is a "pull" system: nothing is manufactured unless there is an order for the final product (or a forecast of an order), and all parts and sub-assemblies are only manufactured to fulfill a particular order.

Although it was originally strictly a manufacturing program, MRP eventually expanded to include other functions related to production: purchasing, finance, and so on, and programs that included those functions came to be known as Manufacturing Resources Planning software, or MRP II. As of 2012, MRP II programs are present in almost all North American plants.

Another derivative of the MRP programs was the development of Distribution Requirements Planning (DRP) software. The idea behind a DRP is similar: whenever a consumer purchases a product in a retail store, that purchase is captured by point-of-sale scanners, and the DRP program orders another one to be shipped from

the distribution center, and one to be manufactured by the supplier. This also operates as a "pull" system: no product is manufactured or shipped by the supplier unless that product was sold by the retailer, and it minimizes the probability of unsold inventory in the supply chain.

Both MRP and DRP have strongly influenced the management of logistics; the traditional warehouse, which was once used to keep products in inventory until they were needed, has become a distribution center (DC), whose function is to take large shipments from manufacturers and separate them into smaller parcels to be delivered to retail stores. Such "cross-docking" operations, where trucks are being unloaded on one side and loaded on the other, are illustrative of the increased emphasis on just-in-time deliveries. Although there are some small differences, the concept is now called lean logistics.

Today, the requirements of most manufacturers and large retail chains are such that they penalize financially the suppliers that do not deliver on time (too early or too late) by withholding a portion of the invoice at the time of payment.

It is fair to say that customer satisfaction is now the primary concern of logisticians: not only does the shipment have to be accurate (the right parts, in the right quantity), complete (no back-ordered parts), and the packaging appropriate so that the goods arrive undamaged and ready to be sold, but it must also be delivered within a very specific time frame.

While international logisticians must make sure that the shipment is accurate, complete, and arrives on time, they also have many additional responsibilities. They must make certain that their shipment's paperwork is in perfect order so that it can clear Customs without delay. They must make sure that the packaging is sufficient to protect the goods during their long (and often eventful) international voyage. They must ensure that they meet a myriad of security requirements and must manage the intricacies of a transaction involving different currencies and different laws. They must choose the right mode of transportation and must make sure that the goods are properly insured. In short, they have many challenges with which to contend for each shipment.

2.1.4 The Transformation into a Strategic Advantage

The 1990s saw the integration of logistics into supply chain management, and the early 2000s saw the emergence of the management of the supply chain as a strategic tool; by the 2010s, it had clearly become a means by which corporations sought a competitive advantage, and it now commanded the attention of top managers, often with the creation of the position of Chief Supply Chain Management Officer.

The emphasis of logistics managers shifted to securing a differential advantage over competitors by providing better service to customers, by offering better delivery terms, by working with suppliers and customers to offer greater flexibility, by making the processes as seamless as possible. These tasks were made particularly challenging as the complexity of the global supply chain increased drastically during the same period: from 1995 to 2011, the number of companies involved in international trade (which the United Nations calls "transnational companies") increased from 38,000 to 103,000, and the number of foreign subsidiaries increased from 265,000 to 892,000.[16] The number of people employed by the foreign affiliates of these transnational companies represented 69,000,000 people.[17]

A study of Chief Supply Chain Officers conducted by IBM in 2008[18] identified the six greatest challenges faced by companies involved in international trade:

- Cost containment, in view of increased fuel costs, increased need for flexibility, and increased expectations of internal and external customers

- The "visibility" to the supply chain, which refers to the management of all of the information that is generated in the supply chain, and making sure it is collected, analyzed and distributed to the appropriate manager

- Risk management, in view of renewed problems in currency fluctuations, transportation risks, product recalls, tight shipping schedules and reduced inventory levels

- Increasing customer demands, in terms of delivery performance, cost containment, information availability, and levels of service

- The globalization of the economy, which has transformed itself into a source of additional revenues in addition to being just about cost savings

- Sustainability efforts, affecting product and packaging designs, transportation choices, and supplier selections. These efforts at reducing energy and water usage, as well as waste, reflect the changing preferences of consumers and the legislative efforts of many countries. Figure 2.3[19] shows the relative importance of sustainability practices in North America, Western Europe and the Asia-Pacific regions.

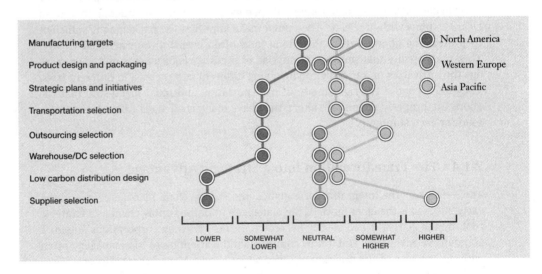

Figure 2.3: Relative implementation of "green" practices in different regions of the world
Diagram ©IBM Corporation. Used with permission.

2.2 Logistics and Supply Chain Management

As the fields of logistics and international logistics evolved, the managers working in those fields changed the definitions that they used to describe their profession.

2.2 Logistics and Supply Chain Management

Whereas "logistics" was the most commonly accepted term for all of the activities in which they engaged, the term was broadened, starting in the mid-1980s, to include additional activities; eventually, the profession was renamed "supply chain management" in the 1990s. Today, the term "logistics" is understood to encompass a number of activities that are a subset of the activities that constitute Supply Chain Management.

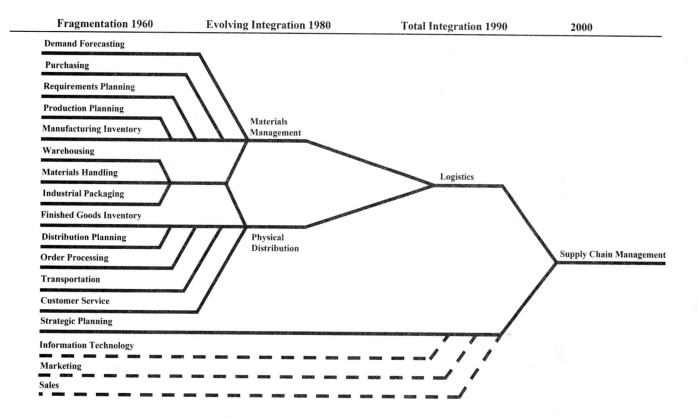

Figure 2.4: The Evolution of Logistics
Adapted from Alfred J. Battaglia. Reproduced by Natalie David.

2.2.1 Logistics

As it stands today, the term "logistics" is defined by the professionals in the field as:

> Logistics is that part of the supply chain process that plans, implements, and controls the efficient, effective forward and reverse flow and storage of goods, services, and related information between the point of origin and the point of consumption in order to meet customers' requirements.[20]

From this definition, it is clear that logistics managers see that the focus of their profession lies in those activities that are related to the physical aspects of the movement of goods from supplier to customer. Logisticians are mostly concerned about the transportation, packaging, warehousing, security, and handling of goods that their firm purchases or sells, and they interact daily with managers who hold other responsibilities closely related to the movement of these goods; manufacturing and production, purchasing and procurement, marketing, inventory management, finance, customer service, and so on.

Figure 2.4 summarizes a slightly different opinion of the evolution of logistics, as seen by Alfred Battaglia.[21] In his view, the logistical function of a company came to include the management of materials and manufacturing somewhat earlier than the 1990s. What is clear is that most logistics professionals referred to their profession as "supply chain management" by the early 2000s, and all did by 2010.

2.2.2 Supply Chain Management

In an international survey of logistics educators that was conducted in 2001, Larson and Halldorsson[22] found that there were four different viewpoints regarding the relationship between logistics and supply chain management, three of which are shown in Figure 2.5.

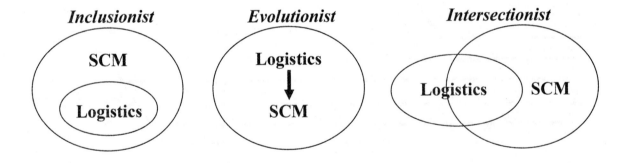

Figure 2.5: Three Different Perspectives on the Relationship between Logistics and SCM
Adapted from Larson and Halldorsson. Reproduced by Natalie David.

By 2004, the inclusionist viewpoint had prevailed, as the Council of Logistics Management changed its name to the Council of Supply Chain Management Professionals (CSCMP) to reflect what was perceived as the broader nature of the field, and produced the following definition:

> Supply Chain Management encompasses the planning and management of all activities involved in sourcing and procurement, conversion, and all Logistics Management activities. Importantly, it also includes coordination and collaboration with channel partners, which can be suppliers, intermediaries, third-party service providers, and customers. In

essence, Supply Chain Management integrates supply and demand management within and across companies.[23]

The most significant characteristic of this definition is that it reflects an extension of the concept of logistics to that of supply chain management. In the view of the CSCMP, the shift from logistics to supply chain management was a shift from an internal focus on the company's own processes to an external focus that includes all the firm's partners. The scope of Supply Chain Management is therefore much broader than the scope of logistics; not only does it include all of the tactical and managerial decisions on which logistics and operations managers tend to focus, but it also includes strategic issues that are more traditionally the domain of the managers in those top management positions that are now colloquially referred to as C-level positions (CEO, Chief Executive Officer, CFO, Chief Financial Officer, COO, Chief Operations Officer, and so on). Several companies have created positions of Chief Global Supply Chain Officers; IBM reported having interviewed 400 of them for its Supply Chain of the Future study in 2008.[24]

2.2.3 International Logistics

The role of international logistics in the global supply chain mirrors that of logistics in the domestic environment: international logistics professionals focus on the tactical aspects of the global supply chain, those activities that are inherent to the movement of goods and paperwork from one country to another, those activities that constitute the basis for export and import activities and operations.

The definition of logistics provided by the Council of Supply Chain Management Professionals can therefore be logically modified to define international logistics by including the elements of the international environment:

> International logistics is the process of planning, implementing, and controlling the flow and storage of goods, services, and related information from a point of origin to a point of consumption located in a different country.

The emphasis of international logistics is therefore on the creation of internal processes and strategies. These processes and activities are the focus of this textbook.

2.2.4 International Supply Chain Management

A characteristic of supply chain management is that it is inherently global in nature; just about every company outsources some percentage of its production abroad or sells to customers who are located abroad. If it does not, its suppliers or customers do. In 2006, Forbes Magazine reported that the percentage of the content of the quintessential American car (the Ford Mustang) that was made outside of the United States stood at 35 percent. In contrast, the Toyota Sienna, a Japanese minivan sold in the United States, was made of 90 percent American parts.[25]

It is not clear why the Council of Supply Chain Management Professionals did not include this global aspect of supply chain management in its definition. The Council's definition should more accurately read:

Supply Chain Management encompasses the planning and management of all activities involved in sourcing and procurement, conversion, and all Logistics Management activities. Importantly, it also includes coordination and collaboration with channel partners, which can be suppliers, intermediaries, third-party service providers, and customers, whether they are located in the United States or abroad. In essence, Supply Chain Management integrates supply and demand management within and across companies.

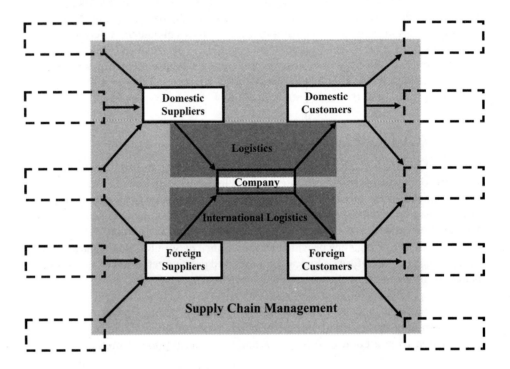

Figure 2.6: Logistics, International Logistics, and Supply Chain Management
Diagram by Pierre David. Reproduced by Natalie David.

Figure 2.6 outlines the current state of the relationships between logistics, international logistics, and supply chain management as of 2012. The activities included in the logistical function are those that include physical transportation of the goods from the supplier(s) to the company and from the company to its customer(s). Logistics also includes the warehousing and other inventory functions within the company that involve the products it purchases, manufactures, and sells.

International logistics works in a parallel form for foreign suppliers and customers. It includes additional activities, such as Customs clearance, documents handling, and international packaging, but the main function of international logistics is concentrated on the physical movement of goods from suppliers to the company and from the company to its customers. The fact that they are in an international arena makes fulfilling these activities much more complex. Supply chain management is a much broader term; it includes both the domestic logistics and the international logistics functions, but it is also the management of the relationships with suppliers and customers (domestic or foreign) and, to some degree, of their relationships with their suppliers and customers. It deals with the entire supply chain, attempting to manage a smooth flow of goods from the first supplier to the ultimate customer. A possible example of a supply chain management activity is the management of quality by the large U.S. Original Equipment Manufacturers (General Motors, Ford Motor Company, Chrysler, and General Electric), that implemented QS-9000, which includes a process by which they certify the quality function of their direct suppliers (called tier-one supplier), of these suppliers' suppliers (called tier-two), and of these firms' suppliers (called tier-three).

2.3 Elements of International Logistics

There are only a few activities that are exclusively specific to international logistics; however, the traditional logistical activities are managed differently in an international environment than they are in a domestic environment.

- The environment involved in international logistics is quite important. While there is obviously the issue of language and culture—neither of which should be underestimated, but are more appropriately covered in an intercultural management textbook—the physical environment of international logistics is quite distinct. The differences in the infrastructure of international logistics and the challenges they represent are covered in Chapter 3.

- The decisions regarding international transportation are eminently more complicated. Because of the distances involved, there are different modes of transportation, different carriers, different transportation documents, and much greater transit times. Chapters 11, 12, and 13 cover these transportation alternatives.

- The number of intermediaries involved is greater. Banks, insurance companies, freight forwarders, not to mention the governments of the exporting country and of the importing country, all have different paperwork requirements. Chapter 9 covers the multitude of documents that are utilized in international trade.

- The inherent risks and hazards of international transportation are much more significant. In order to protect the goods while they are in transit, the logistics manager must have a good understanding of the packaging options that are available. Chapter 14 covers the choices and decisions surrounding packing for international transport. Chapter 15 covers the management of security issues in international trade.

- International insurance is much more complex. The contracts are sometimes written using archaic language and terminology that varies in meaning depending on the country in which the insurance contract is drawn. Chapter 10 presents the different types of insurance coverage available in an international environment.

- International means of payment are more involved. The risks of nonpayment and currency fluctuations call for specific strategies that are never used in domestic transactions. Chapter 7 explains the different alternative means of payment and Chapter 8 presents the methods used by international traders to protect themselves against the risks presented by currency fluctuations.

- Terms of trade are much more complicated, as the greater number of nodes and links increases the number of possible alternatives for transfer of responsibility and ownership. The terms of trade used in international sales—the Incoterms© Rules of the International Chamber of Commerce—are presented thoroughly in Chapter 6.

- The crossing of borders represents specific challenges. Products sold abroad or purchased from abroad have to go through Customs, a complicated and paper-intensive process in most countries. The procedures involved in such a process are described in Chapter 16. In addition, when conducting business with foreign firms, issues arise in the contracts of sale, distribution agreements, and other legal documents. Chapters 4 and 5 present the options available to a firm engaged in international trade.

- Supply chain managers are becoming more conscious about sustainability issues, and are therefore making decisions that reduce the energy and the resources used in manufacturing, packaging and shipping goods across borders. Each chapter of this textbook, when appropriate, deals with the sustainability issues that are relevant to the chapter's topic.

2.4 The Economic Importance of Logistics

Logistical activities represent a substantial proportion of the economic activity of the world economy.

2.4.1 Logistics in the United States

In a yearly study of domestic logistics, Rosalyn Wilson calculates the percentage of the United States' Gross Domestic Product (GDP) that is spent on logistical activities (transportation, inventory, and other administrative costs linked to logistical activities). That percentage stood at 8.5 percent in 2003, but increased to 9.9 percent in 2007, due to rising energy costs, but continued on the downward trend started in 1960 to stand at 8.5 percent in 2011,[26] as shown in Figure 2.7 on the next page. This decrease is mostly due to corporations becoming more efficient in their use of inventory; the advent of Just-in-Time, Manufacturing Resources Planning, and their subsequent derivatives have decreased inventory levels from 24 percent of the United States' GDP in 1981 to a near-record low of 14.6 percent in 2011.[27]

Some of this decrease can also be attributed to more efficient means of transportation—for example, the increased use of containers—and to the deregulation of the U.S. transportation industry, especially during the 1980s and early 1990s. Collectively, American businesses spend almost U.S. $1.3 trillion on domestic logistical activities, including U.S. $806 million on transportation services in 2011.[28]

Since the late 1990s, the costs of transportation have been slowly rising, however; increased fuel costs, a shortage of truck drivers, additional security costs, and a transportation infrastructure stretched to its limits have considerably increased what businesses spend on transportation. Transportation costs rose almost 10 percent from 2009 to 2011, and represent 5.3 percent of the GDP of the United States.

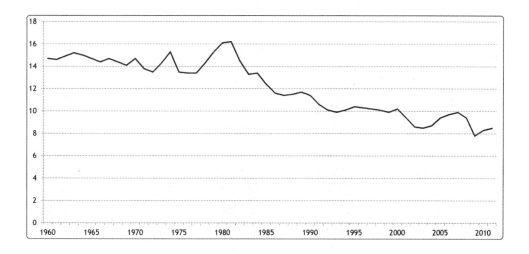

Figure 2.7: Logistics Costs (Percentage of U.S. Gross Domestic Product)
Annual State of Logistics Reports, 2000-2011.

2.4.2 Logistics in the World

The logistics functions of United States companies are much more efficient than many of its trade partners' companies. In 2000, the China Federation of Logistics and Purchasing estimated that logistics costs amounted to 20 percent of the Chinese GDP, and that they had only decreased to 18.3 percent in 2006.[29] This progress is due to improvements in infrastructure and the adoption of better inventory management techniques; nevertheless, it is still about twice the relative weight of the same function in the US.

Worldwide, it is estimated that logistical activities total U.S.$ 7.4 trillion. Figure 2.8 on the following page[30] shows the breakdown of these costs by region of the world. Since the total world output is estimated at U.S.$70 trillion,[31] logistical activities can be estimated to represent about 10.4 percent of the world's economy.

2.4.3 International Logistics

While there are no comprehensive data illustrating the total value of international logistics activities—logistical activities related to trade between nations—it can be conservatively estimated that the percentage spent on international logistics activities would be around 15 percent of the total volume of international trade. Because the total value of the world's merchandise trade is U.S. $18.2 trillion, the total expenditures on international logistics is approximately U.S. $2.7 trillion. This estimate takes into account the fact that international logistics activities are typically more costly due to more complex procedures, inefficient infrastructures, and longer distances.

There is one aspect of international logistics, though, that distinguishes it from domestic logistics regarding its impact on the world's economy; not only are the profits of corporations involved in logistics taxed by their respective governments, but international trade also generates a considerable amount of additional government revenues, as most imports are subject to tariffs. A conservative estimate of

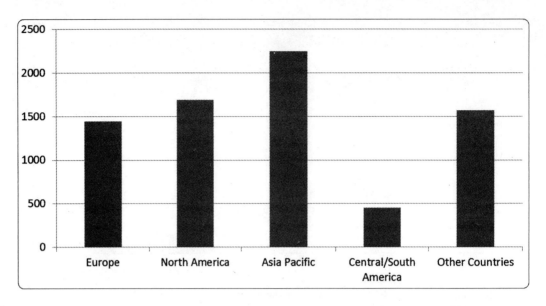

Figure 2.8: Logistics Costs by Region of the World *SupplyChainBrain*, March-April 2012.

the "value" of duty collection and other taxes directly linked to international trade would be about 5 percent[32] of the world's merchandise trade. International logistic activities therefore generate about U.S. $1 trillion in additional government revenues, or the equivalent of the entire GDP of Mexico or Republic of Korea.

2.5 International Reverse Logistics

A recent development in the field of logistics is the introduction of reverse logistics, or the management of products and packaging returned by customers. More broadly, the management of reverse logistics involves the handling of goods after they have been sold to the final consumer or customer. Reverse logistics is the "process of planning, implementing, and controlling the efficient, cost effective flow of raw materials, in-process inventory, finished goods and related information from the point of consumption to the point of origin for the purpose of recapturing value or proper disposal."[33] Essentially, the activities of reverse logistics are the same as the activities of traditional logistics, except in "reverse."

Goods are returned to the manufacturer for a number of reasons:

- The goods have completed their useful life for the consumer or customer and are returned because they can be remanufactured or refurbished by the manufacturer. There are multiple incentives for both the customer and the manufacturer to do so; either there are sustainability incentives to the consumer (laws to encourage the return of obsolete or depleted goods), or the costs of returning the goods are lower than the disposal costs for the customer, or the return and reuse costs for the manufacturer are lower than the costs of manufacturing new parts.

- The goods are returned because the consumer needs them to be repaired under warranty, or the goods do not meet the expectations of the customer.

2.5 International Reverse Logistics

- The goods are defective and the manufacturer issues a recall of the goods, so that they can be repaired or made conform to the requirements of the market.

- The packaging that was used to ship the goods from the manufacturer's plant to the customer's facilities can be reused for another shipment.

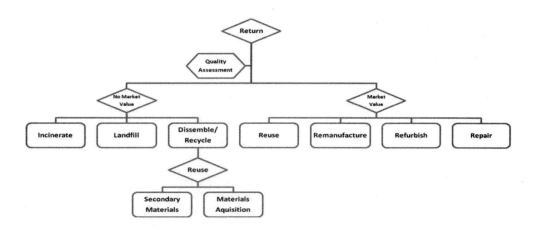

Figure 2.9: Typical Flow Diagram of a Reverse Logistics System
Lora Skarman. Used with permission.

Many companies are now realizing that a reverse logistics system combined with source-reduction processes can be used to gain competitive advantage through value creation.[34] Specific examples come from Kodak, Estée Lauder and Caterpillar. Kodak started a campaign in 1990 to take back, reuse, and recycle its single-use cameras, originally designed as disposables. In 1990 it collected 0.9 million cameras and by 1998 that figure had jumped to 61 million units. In 2008, Kodak had multiple recycling facilities where up to 86 percent of camera parts were reused in manufacturing new cameras.

Estée Lauder used to dump $60 million of its products into landfills annually. In the first year of its reverse logistics program, after an initial investment of $1.3 million, Estée Lauder was able to increase the number of returned products by twenty-four percent, reduce the number of destroyed products from 37 percent to 27 percent of returned products and save $0.5 million in labor costs. Estée Lauder has since created a $250 million product line from its return flows, the third most profitable product line in the company.

As for Caterpillar, it operates fourteen remanufacturing plants around the world. The plants are capable of disassembling and rebuilding diesel engines—cleaning, inspecting, and repairing as many as 20,000 parts along the way. The remanufacturing division of Caterpillar is its fastest growing division, at a rate of twenty percent per year, and annual revenues exceed $1 billion.[35]

In all cases, especially in an international environment, the process of getting the goods from the customer or consumer to the manufacturer involves the intermediaries that were present at the time of the original sale, making it somewhat cumbersome to import products that had originally been exported.[36] However, small-package shippers, such as United Parcel Service, have implemented processes to help exporters handle goods that are returned by their international customers.[37]

Many companies are starting to implement a "cradle to cradle" manufacturing system, in which the product is manufactured, used by consumers, recovered after use, and then reused, refurbished, resold or some combination of these activities, to put the product back into circulation. Figure 2.9 on the previous page shows the flows in a typical reverse logistics system from "cradle to cradle." [38]

Two Different Reverse Logistics Programs

In 1991, the German government passed a law that required all manufacturers of consumer packaged goods to take back all of the packaging that they used to ship their goods, including the final consumer containers. This law triggered the creation of a dual refuse collection system, ubiquitous in the country, called *Der Grüne Punkt*—The Green Dot—designed to collect and return all consumer packaging materials to the manufacturers.

Set up by the industry, this secondary garbage collection system is made up of yellow collection bins located near retail centers and of yellow plastic bags used by households on garbage collection days, and that are designed to collect used consumer packages. The materials collected are then sorted, recycled or re-used. The entire system is funded by the industry.

By 2009, German consumers recycled more than 88 percent of their packaging materials,[39] and German municipal household waste was 48 percent recycled and 18 percent composted, the highest percentage in the world.[40] The city of Curitiba, Brazil, has implemented its recycling program in a completely different way. It has placed recycling containers throughout the city, and has encouraged families to sort their household waste. It is an entirely voluntary program, but the city has managed to recycle more than two-thirds of its household refuse.[41]

The city hires homeless and very low income residents to collect recyclable items and exchanges what they collect for food and money. The city even has a "green exchange" program through which residents of the favelas that surround the city can take the household trash that they have collected and exchange it for food. This has the effect of keeping the slums cleaner, and improving the nutrition and income of its poorest residents.

2.5 International Reverse Logistics

Figure 2.10: The Colorful Recycling Bins of Curitiba, Brazil
Photo ©Gilberto de Oliveira Souza. Used with permission.

Manufacturers, especially in the United States, have not typically designed products for repair, reuse or recovery. There is a strong sentiment worldwide to change that business model with the introduction of extended producer responsibility laws. European environmental laws have been introduced with the concept of extended producer responsibility for everything from the products themselves to their packaging materials. Many firms are now realizing that designing products for not only the first use, but also subsequent use provides a cost advantage because these products can be sold in secondary markets with minimal work after recovery. The cost of raw materials, transportation, storage, and other supply chain components as well as regulations will drive international logistics professionals to get the most out of their product's life cycle.

Review and Discussion Questions

1. What are the elements that differentiate international logistics from domestic logistics?

2. What are the principal distinct components of international logistics?

3. What are the major costs of international logistics? Given what you read in Chapter 1 about the World Trade Organization, what trend do you expect these costs to follow?

4. MRP and DRP have allowed manufacturers and retailers to carry less and less inventory. What consequences would a major snowstorm or disruption of transportation have on such Just-In-Time management systems?

5. Describe the impact of international trade on your own life, using the products that you own or have purchased in the recent past.

Notes

[1] Turner, Jack, *Spice: The History of a Temptation*, Vintage Books, Random House, New York, New York, 2005.

[2] Gies, Frances and Joseph, *Cathedral, Forge and Waterwheel; Technology and Invention in the Middle Ages*, Harper-Collins Publishers, New York, New York, USA, 1995.

[3] Klein, Jacob, *Greek Mathematical Thought and the Origin of Algebra*, translated by Eva Brann, Dover Publications, Mineola, New York, USA, reprinted October 1992. Original publication by MIT Press, Cambridge, Massachusetts, USA, 1968.

[4] Shaw, Arch Wilkinson, *Some Problems in Market Distribution*, Harvard University Press, Cambridge, MA, 1915.

[5] Pacini, Alfred and Dominique Pons, *Docker à Marseille, Récits de vie*, Payot, T.S. Simey, ed„ Paris, 1996.

[6] Levinson, Marc, *The box; how the shipping container made the world smaller and the world economy bigger*, Princeton University Press, Princeton, New Jersey, 2006.

[7] Levinson, Marc, *The box; how the shipping container made the world smaller and the world economy bigger*, Princeton University Press, Princeton, New Jersey, 2006.

[8] Cudahy, Brian J., *Box boats: How containerships changed the world*, Fordham University Press, New York, New York, 2006.

[9] Donovan, Arthur, and Joseph Bonney, "The box that changed the world," *The Journal of Commerce*, Commonwealth Business Media, New York, New York, 2006.

[10] Fedex Annual Report, http://fedexannualreport2012.hwaxis.com/ Files/FedEx_Annual_Report_2012_Chairmans_Letter.pdf, November 1, 2012.

[11] Hummels, David, "Time as a Trade Barrier," Purdue University working paper, July 2001, http://www.unc.edu/depts/econ/seminars/ hummels.pdf, January 21, 2009.

[12] Levinson, Marc, *The box; how the shipping container made the world smaller and the world economy bigger*, Princeton University Press, Princeton, New Jersey, 2006.

[13] Donovan, Arthur, and Joseph Bonney, "The box that changed the world," *The Journal of Commerce*, Commonwealth Business Media, New York, New York, 2006.

NOTES

[14] Levinson, Marc, *The box; how the shipping container made the world smaller and the world economy bigger*, Princeton University Press, Princeton, New Jersey, 2006.

[15] Levinson, Marc, *The box; how the shipping container made the world smaller and the world economy bigger*, Princeton University Press, Princeton, New Jersey, 2006.

[16] *World Investment Report 1996: Investment, Trade, and International Policy Agreements*, United Nations, August 1996, and *World Investment Report 2012: Toward a new Generation of Investment Trade Policies*, United Nations, May 7, 2012, http://unctad.org/en/Pages/DIAE/World%20Investment%20Report/WIR2012_WebFlyer.aspx, November 1, 2012.

[17] *Ibid.*

[18] *The smarter Supply Chain of the Future; Global Chief Supply Chain Officer Study*, January 2009, IBM Global Services, Route 100, Somers, NY 10589, http://www-935.ibm.com/services/us/gbs/bus/html/ gbs-csco-study.html, May 13, 2009.

[19] *Ibid.*

[20] Council of Supply Chain Management Professionals, "Supply Chain Management / Logistics Management Definitions," http://cscmp.org/ aboutcscmp/definitions.asp, November 1, 2012.

[21] Delaney, Robert V. and Rosalyn Wilson, *Thirteenth Annual State of Logistics Report: Understanding Inventory—Stay Curious*, ProLogis and Cass Information Systems, Inc., June 10, 2002, http://www.cassinfo.com/ 2002 Press Conference Full.PDF, October 15, 2002.

[22] Larson, Paul D. and Arni Halldorsson, "Logistics vs. Supply Chain Management: An International Survey," *Journal of Supply Chain Management*, March 2004, pp. 17-31.

[23] Council of Supply Chain Management Professionals, "Supply Chain Management / Logistics Management Definitions," http://cscmp.org/ aboutcscmp/definitions.asp, November 1, 2012.

[24] *The smarter Supply Chain of the Future; Global Chief Supply Chain Officer Study*, January 2009, IBM Global Services, Route 100, Somers, NY 10589, http://www-935.ibm.com/services/us/gbs/bus/html/ gbs-csco-study.html, May 13, 2009.

[25] Fahey, Jonathan, "The parts paradox," *Forbes*, May 8, 2006.

[26] Wilson, Rosalyn, *Twenty-Third Annual State of Logistics Report: The Long and Winding Recovery*, Council of Logistics Management, June 13, 2012, http://cscmp.org/securedownloads/filedownload.aspx?fn=memberonly/23sol-report.pdf, November 1, 2012.

[27] *Ibid.*

[28] *Ibid.*

[29] "Several Issues in China's Logistics Industry," *Market Avenue*, January 28, 2008, http://www.marketavenue.cn/upload/articles/ARTICLES _1340.htm, May 14, 2009.

[30] Armstrong, Richard, "There Could be a great 3PL in your Future," *SupplyChainBrain*, March-April 2012, pp. 48-50

[31] World Development Indicators database, World Bank, 15 April 2013, databank.worldbank.org/databank/download/GDP.pdf, retrieved May 28, 2013.

[32] Tariffs and Import Fees, U.S. Department of Commerce International Trade Administration, http://export.gov/logistics/eg_main_018130.asp, November 1, 2012.

[33] Hawks, Karen, "What is Reverse Logistics?," *Reverse Logistics Magazine*, Winter-Spring 2006, pp.12-13.

[34] Jayaraman, Vaidyanathan, and Yadong Luo, "Creating Competitive Advantages Through New Value Creation: A Reverse Logistics Perspective," *Academy of Management Perspectives*, May 2007, pp. 56-73.

[35] *Ibid.*

[36] Stanton, Tom, "Avoiding the Pitfalls of International Returns," *Reverse Logistics Magazine*, June 2010, pp. 42-43 (part I), August 2010, pp. 39-42 (part II), and October 2010, pp.42-44 (part III).

[37] United Parcel Service, "International Returns Made Easy," advertorial, *DC Velocity*, April 2013, p.54.

[38] Stock, James R., *Development and Implementation of Reverse Logistics Processes*, Council of Logistics Management, 1998.

[39] "Trash Planet: Germany," *Earth911.com*, http://earth911.com/news/2009/07/13/trash-planet-germany, November 10, 2012.

[40] "German recycling system gets an overhaul," *The Local*, May 3, 2011, http://www.thelocal.de/society/20110503-34757.html, November 10, 2012.

[41] Alvarado, Paula, "Jaime Lerner and Sustainability in Curitiba and 'Urban Acupuncture'," November 12, 2007, http://www.treehugger.com/files/2007/11/jaime_lerner_interview_planeta_sustentavel.php, November 1, 2012.

Chapter 3

International Infrastructure

3.1 Definitions 51
3.2 Transportation Infrastructure 52
3.3 Communication Infrastructure 77
3.4 Utilities Infrastructure 80
3.5 Services Infrastructure 83
3.6 Legal and Regulatory Infrastructure 84

For the manager of international logistics, it is important to have a good understanding of the challenges presented by the different levels of infrastructure found abroad. It is always one of the first problems encountered by an international manager; things don't work abroad like they do at "home." There are different standards, there are different expectations of performance, there are things that work much better, and there are things that do not work as well—in some cases, not at all. Adapting to those differences, and anticipating problems before they arise, are part of the assets of an experienced international logistics manager.

infrastructure
A term that refers to all the public and private goods that facilitate transportation, communication, and business exchanges.

The issue with learning how to manage these differences in infrastructure is that they are difficult to generalize in one particular comment or statement. Most challenges tend to be concentrated in some small geographic areas, and in most cases are limited to a single location: a specific port is not equipped with sufficient cold-storage warehousing space, does not have an appropriately-sized crane, or is experiencing delays in getting the goods from the port to the remainder of the country; a road is particularly congested, a specific tunnel has recently been closed, or a railroad is experiencing shortages of appropriate cars. These challenges force the manager involved in international logistics to recognize the possibility of serious problems. The purpose of this chapter is to present enough information and examples to encourage him or her to ask questions at the onset of a transaction, so that there are no discrepancies between the expectations of the company and what can be achieved.

3.1 Definitions

Before going much further, it would be useful to determine what is meant by infrastructure in the context of international logistics. A few dictionary definitions would be a good start:

> The American Heritage Dictionary defines it in the broadest terms: "The basic facilities, services, and installations needed for the functioning of a community or society, such as transportation and communications systems, water and power lines, and public institutions including schools, post offices, and prisons."[1]
>
> The Oxford English Dictionary defines it more narrowly, using its military origins: "A collective term for the subordinate parts of an undertaking; substructure, foundation. The permanent installations forming a basis for military operations, as airfields, naval bases, training establishments, ... etc."[2]
>
> Merriam-Webster is the most succinct with "the system of public works of a country, state, or region,"[3] and ignores the privately-owned elements of infrastructure.

In the field of logistics, the definition must be very broad: infrastructure is a collective term that refers to all of the elements in place (publicly or privately owned goods) to facilitate transportation, communication, and business exchanges. It would therefore include not only transportation and communication elements, but also the existence and quality of public utilities, banking services, and retail distribution channels. To this list, it makes sense to add the existence and quality of the Court system, the defense of intellectual property rights, and the existence of standards. As these concepts are introduced in this chapter, their inclusion into the concept of infrastructure will become more acceptable.

The study of infrastructure is important because the movement of goods and of documents, as well as the movement of money and information, is dependent on these infrastructure components.

3.2 Transportation Infrastructure

The infrastructure that most obviously affects the movement of goods internationally is the transportation infrastructure. Without a good understanding of the transportation infrastructure that a shipment will face, a manager may package a product inappropriately, may face delays, or may even be faced with unexpectedly damaged merchandise.

3.2.1 Port Infrastructure

Panamax ship
A ship of the maximum size that can enter the locks of the Panama Canal.

post-Panamax ship
A ship whose size is too large to enter the locks of the Panama Canal.

Port infrastructure is made up of several items, most of which are interconnected, and obviously affect the type of ships that can call on a given port, as well as the type of merchandise that can transit through it.

With the advent of the much larger post-Panamax containerships, ports have been faced with many challenges. Specifically, the size of those ships is stretching the capabilities of the ports: they are much wider, longer, higher above the water, and have a much deeper draft. There were 175 containerships of a capacity greater than 10,000 TEUs—twenty-foot equivalent units, or twenty-foot containers—in operation as of May 2013, representing only 3.5 percent of the total containership fleet, but more than 13.5 percent of its capacity. There were another 111 to be built and delivered before 2016 (see Table 3.1 on the facing page), representing almost

3.2 Transportation Infrastructure

a quarter of all the ships ordered for that period,[4] and almost half of the capacity being built.[5] Most of these ships operate on the routes between Asia and Western Europe, although they will soon serve between Asia and North America.[6] Such large ships mean that as many as 6,000 forty-foot containers need to be unloaded and 6,000 loaded in a single port.

Containerships in Operations

TEU size range	Number of Ships	Percentage of Ships in Use	Capacity (in TEUs)	Percentage of Capacity
Ships smaller than Panamax				
0-1,999	2,252	45.5%	2,416,427	14.5%
2,000-2,999	671	13.5%	1,709,010	10.3%
3,000-3,999	279	5.6%	957,270	5.7%
Panamax				
4,000-5,099	751	15.2%	3,395,690	20.4%
Post-Panamax				
5,100-7,499	481	9.7%	2,957,465	17.7%
7,500-9,999	344	6.9%	2,985,039	17.9%
10,000-18,000	175	3.5%	2,242,377	13.5%
	4,953		16,663,278	

Containerships on Order

TEU size range	Number of Ships	Percentage of Ships on Order	Capacity (in TEUs)	Percentage of Capacity
Ships smaller than Panamax				
0-1,999	74	16.4%	103,853	3.2%
2,000-2,999	29	6.4%	72,570	2.2%
3,000-3,999	51	11.3%	187,261	5.7%
Panamax				
4,000-5,099	60	13.3%	282,501	8.6%
Post-Panamax				
5,100-7,499	28	5.8%	180,302	5.5%
7,500-9,999	97	21.6%	872,914	26.7%
10,000-18,000	111	24.7%	1,566,663	48.0%
	450		3,266,064	

Table 3.1: Containerships in Operations and on Order as of May 2013 (Alphaliner.)

Depth of Water

The first issue is undoubtedly the depth of the water of a port, which has to be sufficient to accommodate the draft of the ships that call at that port. In many ports, the depth of the channels and of the berths, which had been sufficient to accommodate Panamax ships, is not sufficient to accommodate the newer, larger ships. Therefore, in a great number of ports, the port authorities have had to engage in dredging activities in order to allow ships with drafts exceeding 13.5 meters [40 feet] to access the port. Only a few ports with naturally deep channels have been exempt from this activity.[7]

Despite the fact that the dredging of channels and ports can be exceedingly expensive, ports have little alternative but to undertake this improvement of their capabilities. One of the ports that has benefited from its natural assets is the Port of Prince Rupert in British Columbia, Canada, which started handling container freight in the fall of 2007. The port enjoys terminals with a natural draft of 20 meters [67 feet], as well as a Canadian National Railroad terminal in the port, giving it a direct link to the North American continent. Since it also is the North American port closest to the Asian rim ports, Prince Rupert is attempting to divert some of the traffic that traditionally called on West Coast ports in the United States; it can shorten transit times from China to Chicago by as many as 60 hours.[8] However, Prince Rupert has so far diverted only a small fraction of the cargo discharged on the West Coast of North America.

In a parallel fashion, longer ships require longer turning circles, and therefore a redesign—and dredging—of different access channels. As ships become yet longer, wider, and heavier, the challenge for the ports will be to keep up with these ships' requirements and adapt.

Bridge Clearance

Another factor of great importance is the clearance under the bridges over the waterways leading to the port; the ships that call that port have an air draft which dictates the minimum space that they need under a port's bridges. In many older ports, the bridges are too close to the water, leaving very little clearance for tall ships or ships carrying oversized cargo. In some cases, the ships have to be modified or designed so that they can clear the bridges: several of the ships that call the Port of New York-New Jersey were specifically designed to accommodate the Bayonne Bridge's low clearance: 45 meters [151 feet] above the water at high tide.[9]

All of these factors (depth of channels and berths, as well as bridge clearance) are likely to affect how ports are used in the future. There is a strong likelihood that some ports will not be able to make the necessary infrastructure adjustments to accommodate the largest ships and that there will be a need to create large port hubs, to and from which mega-containerships will travel. Smaller ports would then be served by smaller "feeder" ships that would not tax the ports' infrastructure beyond their capacity. Such ports were created in the 1990s in the Mediterranean Sea: Marsaxlokk in Malta and Cagliari in Sardinia (Italy) serve as trans-shipment ports, loading and unloading large containerships in a deep-water port and using feeder services to serve the local markets and shallower ports of France, Italy, and Spain.[10] There were once discussions of a large port fulfilling the same function on the Atlantic Coast of the United States, to alleviate the constraints presented by the current older ports of New York and Philadelphia,[11] but such plans were postponed

---

draft
The minimum depth of water that a ship needs in order to float.

berth
In a port, the location at which a ship can load and unload its cargo.

dredging
The removal of sediments or soil from the bottom of a water channel to increase its depth.

air draft
The minimum amount of space between the water and the lowest point on a bridge that a ship needs in order to enter a port.

3.2 Transportation Infrastructure

Figure 3.1: The port of Yangshan near Shanghai, China
Photo ©Bert van Dijk. Used with permission.

by the economic decline of 2009-2011.

China's most noticeable response to the increase in the number of mega-containerships is the deep-water Port of Yangshan, part of the Port of Shanghai, in China. As the Port of Shanghai became congested, and since it is relatively shallow and would require a lot of dredging, the government of China decided to build a deep-water port in the Hangzhou Bay, just South of Shanghai. It was built on a large landfill between two uninhabited islands and is linked to the mainland by the Donghai Bridge, a 32km-long (20-mile) bridge, most of which is above water.[12]

The combined ports of Shanghai and Yangshan constitute the largest port in the world, ahead of the two ports that had dominated the list for the past ten years: Singapore and Hong Kong SAR. In 2012, Shanghai handled 32.5 million TEUs, with Singapore and Hong Kong SAR at 31.6 and 23.1 million TEUs respectively.[13] As of 2013, the Port of Yangshan can handle 10 million TEUs with 16 berths. When it is completed in 2020, it will have 30 berths and will be able to handle 15 million TEUs.[14] For a sense of perspective, Table 3.2 on the next page[15] lists the twenty five largest container-handling ports in the world. The largest European port is Rotterdam with 11.9 millon TEUS, and the largest North American port is Los Angeles, with 8.1 million TEUs. Even with its sister port in Long Beach, their combined volume was only 14.1 million TEUs.

Cranes

Port terminals have found out that the width of post-Panamax ships can also be a challenge for their cranes. Traditional Panamax ships can be loaded with up to thirteen containers in the width of a ship (see Figure 3.2 on page 57). Some of the post-Panamax ships can be loaded with as many as eighteen containers side-by-side (see Figure 3.3 on page 58). This presents a problem for ports in which the cranes cannot reach the far side of the ship. Early on, ports managed their lack of crane capacity by loading ships from one side, turning the ships around, and then loading the remainder of the containers. The problem was one of balance, as the ships list

list
A ship that leans to one side is said to *list*.

Largest Container Ports of the World

Rank	Port	TEUs	Rank	Port	TEUs
1	Shanghai, CN	32,529,000	14	Hamburg, DE	8,863,896
2	Singapore, SG	31,649,400	15	Antwerp, BE	8,635,169
3	Hong Kong, HK SAR	23,097,000	16	Los Angeles, US	8,077,714
4	Shenzhen, CN	22,941,300	17	Dalian, CN	8,064,000
5	Pusan, KR	17,030,000	18	Tanjung Pelepas, MY	7,700,000
6	Ningbo, CN	16,830,000	19	Xiamen, CN	7,201,700
7	Guangzhou, CN	14,743,600	20	Tanjung Priok, ID	6,200,000
8	Qingdao, CN	14,500,000	21	Bremerhaven, DE	6,115,211
9	Dubai, UAE	13,280,000	22	Long Beach, US	6,045,562
10	Tianjin-Xingang, CN	12,300,000	23	Laem Chabang, TH	5,926,436
11	Rotterdam, NL	11,865,916	24	New York-New Jersey, US	5,500,000
12	Port Klang, MY	10,001,495	25	Lianyungang, CN	5,020,000
13	Kaohsiung, TW, CN	9,781,221			

Table 3.2: 2012 World's 25 Largest Container Ports (in TEU movements) Kaiji Press.

if they are heavier on one side. Today's ports have made considerable investments in new large-capacity cranes that can load these larger ships.

The existing cranes can be modified to reach higher and farther. These modifications can be quite costly for a port and new cranes capable of serving these ships can cost $50 million. [16] Another alternative, chosen by the Amsterdam Container Terminals at the Paragon Terminal, is to create an indented berth to allow the ship to be loaded from both sides. An advantage of this configuration is that it allows the ship to be loaded with up to twelve cranes rather than the maximum of six in a traditional port. This alternative speeds up the loading of the ship considerably, from a maximum of 160 containers per hour (the world record held by the Port of Singapore for a traditional berth) to up to 300 containers per hour, decreasing the time that a ship spends in port and therefore increasing its profitability.[17]

For shippers handling non-containerized cargo, the cranes' capacity is a major factor in deciding through which port to send a specific cargo. Cigna Insurance used to publish a directory called *Ports of the World* that listed the equipment of any port in the world, specifically the capacity of its cranes.[18] Unfortunately, ACE Limited, the company that purchased Cigna's international property-and-casualty insurance business, has not updated the booklet since the late 1990s, and the information has become obsolete. Fortunately, since 2005, the website *World Port Source*[19] has provided an excellent database about most ports in the world, based on the data contained in the World Port Index compiled by the National Geospatial Intelligence Agency. Table 3.3 shows an excerpt of the information included in the World Port Source database.

From a shipper's standpoint, it should be obvious that the crane at the port of destination should have at least the same capacity as the one that was used to load the cargo. Failure to pay attention to that fact is likely to lead to a dismantling of the cargo or to the use of an overloaded crane, both of which could place the cargo in jeopardy.

3.2 Transportation Infrastructure

Figure 3.2: A Panamax Containership Arriving in the Port of Savannah, Georgia, United States
Photo ©David Cannings-Bushell. Used with permission.

Port Operations

Another issue in ports is the way the port is managed, particularly its work rules, which are often dictated by strong unions. Some ports, such as the Port of Long Beach on the Pacific Coast of the United States, used to only operate eight hours a day[20] instead of the much more efficient twenty-four hours a day, seven days a week of most Asian Pacific Rim ports. Today, the port stevedores will load and unload a ship at any time, but the terminals' truck gates are only open from 7:00 am until 5:00 pm, and only on weekdays, ostensibly to accommodate the work hours of the businesses shipping goods to and from the port.[21] Nevertheless, since the immense majority of the goods transiting through the Ports of Long Beach and Los Angeles are destined for areas much beyond Southern California, the rule is very constraining.

Work rules can also be very complex and hamper the efficiency of ports to the point where they are less and less competitive: in the 1950s, unions dominating the ports of South America were refusing to unload containers, for example.[22] When there are attempts to modify these rules, strikes are common: some Japanese and European ports are plagued with recurring work stoppages. Finally, the issue of productivity is often linked to labor practices; while Japanese ports can handle routinely 45 container movements per hour per crane, most United States ports are stagnat-

Figure 3.3: A post-Panamax Containership in the Port of Amsterdam, The Netherlands

Photo ©Olivier Lantzendörffer. Used with permission.

ing at 25 movements per hour.[23] As productivity in the ports increases, the need for additional capital expenditures decreases; for many ports, physically constrained by the sea on one side and by a large city on the other, increases in productivity are the only possible avenues for handling the growth in cargo volume that they are experiencing.

Warehousing Space

Finally, it is critical to understand the amount of warehouse storage space that exists in the port. In most instances, it is necessary for merchandise to be placed in some storage area that is protected from the elements (specifically rain and sun). If these storage areas are not available or are overcrowded, then it's likely that cargo will be left exposed, leading to possible damages.

Similarly, the shipper should pay attention to the amount of space available in the port to store containers before and after their ocean voyage; the smaller the space, the greater the probability that the container will be moved multiple times, or that it will be stored in an inappropriate location. Even if the cargo can tolerate being left exposed to the elements, another concern is the possibility of flooding in the container—or cargo—staging area. It is not unusual, when bad weather strikes,

3.2 Transportation Infrastructure

Port of Gilbraltar

Latitude	36° 8'13" N	Longitude	5° 21'41" W

Water Depth

Channel	12.5-13.7 m	Anchorage	18.6-19.8 m
	(41-45 ft)		(61-65 ft)
Cargo Pier	7.1-9.1 m	Oil Terminal	6.4-7.6 m
	(26-30 ft)		(21-25 ft)
Tide	0.3 m (1 ft)		

Entrance Restrictions

Tide	no	Overhead Limit	no
Ice	no	Swell	no

Pilotage

Compulsory	no	Advisable	yes
Available	yes		

Cranes

100+ ton		Fixed cranes	yes
50-100 ton		Mobile cranes	yes
25-49 ton	yes	Floating cranes	
0-24 ton	yes		

Table 3.3: Excerpts from an Entry on World Port Source Website World Port Source.

to see a port's container yard flood, and the containers at the bottom of a stack partially immersed, even in a modern port. During the floods that devastated southern Brazil in 2008, hundreds of containers were affected by the water surge in the ports of Paranaguá, Itajaí and São Francisco do Sul.

For shippers involved with refrigerated cargo, those issues are compounded with the need for reliable power supply, as well as proper reefer storage areas, equipped with power outlets and personnel competent enough to monitor the temperature charts of the refrigerated containers.

Connections with Land-Based Transportation Services

Yet another issue in ports are their connections to the remainder of the country's transport infrastructure, such as rail and road access. In some cases, there is so much congestion in the access roads to port terminals that cargo can be delayed substantially. This is a major issue in just about every port in the world, but particularly in North and South America and in China.[24] Most ports are obviously located near the ocean, and the cities that developed around these ports are located between the port and the hinterlands, where the cargo eventually has to go. Therefore, every piece of cargo that is shipped through the port has to travel through the city, which creates a serious strain on road and railroad infrastructures to the port and engenders serious traffic jams and the resentment of the local population. Ports are actively looking at overcoming these bottlenecks.[25]

The Ports of Los Angeles and Long Beach inaugurated in 2002 the Alameda Corridor, a north-south, twenty-mile rail link between the ports and the transcontinental rail yards on the eastern edge of the city of Los Angeles (see Figure 3.4). The Corridor is a thirty-three-feet deep trench that cuts through the city's neighborhoods and is uninterrupted by road traffic.[26]

Figure 3.4: The Alameda Corridor between the Port of Los Angeles and East Los Angeles
Photo ©Alameda Corridor Transportation Authority. Used with permission.

Port Capacity

Yet another issue in ocean transportation is the strained capacity of ports, as many ports are operating at capacity or very near their capacity. Because ports tend to be physically located between an ocean and a city, there are limits in the ways that they can expand as their traffic increases. Many ports add capacity by gaining on the sea with landfills or by purchasing real estate that is then transformed into port terminals, both of which tend to be quite costly. For example, the port of Santos in Brazil is located on a river that stretches between an island and the main land. The older port is located on the island, and it cannot expand because it is constrained by the city of Santos on one side and the river on the other side, on which it cannot gain because the river cannot be made narrower. All of the port expansion has been on the other side of the river, but, there again, it is limited by the river and suburbs that are now growing along with the city.

In the United States, there is, for example, an increasing need for additional capacity in container terminals on the Pacific Coast, and this capacity cannot come from the expansion of the ports themselves; it has to come from increases in productivity, which are difficult to achieve, or from the addition of new ports. The creation of the Port of Prince Rupert (see Figure 3.5 on the next page), in a city of

3.2 Transportation Infrastructure

Figure 3.5: The Port of Prince Rupert, Canada
Photo ©Maher Terminals. Used with permission.

14,000 inhabitants unconstrained by urban sprawl, with a strong rail connection to the hinterland and a deep natural harbor, is a harbinger of what is to come.

The Panama Canal

On August 15, 1914 the *Ancon* became the first ship to officially pass through the Panama Canal. This unprecedented voyage ushered in a new era of shipping and international trade. This new route allowed ships to make the trans-pacific voyage from Asia to the Americas quickly and safely. With a construction cost of three hundred seventy-five million dollars (and twenty-five thousand lives), the Canal immediately put Panama at the center of global trade.[27]
Today, nearly one hundred years later, the canal is as important as ever, and as much as five percent of world trade's cargo transits through it. However, in the late 1990s, the canal was reaching its capacity, with some ships waiting several days for their turn [28] and the newly built giant containerships too large to fit through the canal's locks. The increasing number of these ships meant it had become a major issue, and the Panama Canal Authority was faced with the dilemma to either improve the canal or watch it become outdated. After years of planning, the Canal Authority has designed a new plan for the canal, one that will improve it and make it more viable for modern shipping needs.

Figure 3.6: Two Panamax containerships entering the Gatun Locks on the Atlantic Side of the Panama Canal

Photo ©Matthew Ragen. Used with permission.

The Panama Canal Authority decided to spend $5.25 billion to improve the canal, a project that will double the current canal's capacity and allow it to accept larger ships by 2015. This is a massive engineering project that will take advantage of the techniques learned in building the original canal and implement new methods to build the new canal faster as well as making it more efficient. The new canal will be able to accommodate 12,600 TEU ships that are 420 meters (1,400 feet) long, 54 meters (180 feet) wide, and draw 18 meters (60 feet) of water. allowing mega-ships previously labeled as "post-Panamax" to cross from the Atlantic to the Pacific in under ten hours.

The new canal will include two new sets of locks, one set on the Pacific side and one on the Atlantic. Two new navigational channels will also be built to connect to the existing canal. One major obstacle the engineers struggled with was getting access to enough water to supply the canal, which will require two billion gallons per day. They solved this by implementing a system that will reuse sixty percent of the water flushed out during each ship's passing. This means that although the new canal holds sixty-five percent more water than the old one it will actually use seven percent less water.[29]

The final obstacle the Canal Authority faced was how to pay for the project. The Panamanian government and citizens support the project but the small country can not afford to pay for the multi-billion dollar project. Executives eventually came up with a plan that will pay for the project through increased canal tolls, cash reserves, and international loans. Construction has started and authorities are hoping that a year after the one hundredth anniversary of the original canal, in 2015, the eyes of the world will once again turn to their country as the first mega-ship passes through the new Panama Canal.

3.2.2 Canals and Waterways Infrastructure

Maritime transportation is also quite dependent on the existence and proper maintenance of canals and other maritime channels. Their size, as well as the size of their locks, has a great influence on international trade. For example, ships sized to get through the Suez Canal are called Suez-Max ships, and those sized to get through the Panama Canal are called Panamax ships. From an international logistics standpoint, several waterways are fundamentally and strategically important. However, these waterways have lost their monopoly, as alternatives were developed to circumvent their shortcomings.

canal
A man-made waterway connecting two natural bodies of water.

- The Bosporus Strait in Turkey: joining the Black Sea to the Mediterranean Sea, it is the only water link between the Black Sea and the oceans. A large percentage of the merchandise trade between Russia and the rest of the world transits through it, creating severe congestion and raising safety concerns for the city of Istanbul, which is built on both sides of the Strait. Several efforts have been made to convert some of that traffic to a network of pipelines,[30] but none have yet been built. A rail tunnel, called Marmaray, is being built under the Bosporus to connect the European side and the Asian side of the country, and is set to open at the end of 2013.[31] A canal parallel to the Bosporus has been considered, but no specific plans have been drawn.[32]

- The Suez Canal: it cuts through the Sinai Desert (see Figure 3.7 on the following page) and allows ships to avoid traveling around the entire continent of Africa when they are going from the Persian Gulf to Europe. When it was closed after the Six-Day War in 1967, oil companies started to build much larger oil tankers, to make the voyage around the Cape (South Africa) more cost-effective. Since its reopening in 1975, the Canal has recaptured some of the traffic it had lost, through a widening and deepening effort. However, the Canal is still too shallow for many ships, and its tolls are prohibitive. The cost of a single trip through the Canal can exceed U.S.$500,000 (see Table 3.4 on page 65).[33]

- The Panama Canal: it allows ships to avoid traveling around South America. However, the Canal is remarkably "slow," because it is essentially running at its maximum capacity. Wait times to enter the Canal average twenty-two hours.[34] However, despite the emergence of land bridges in the United States, and the emergence of post-Panamax ships, the Canal still retains its commercial importance even though its tolls are expensive. For a 5,000-TEU Panamax containership, for example, a passage costs U.S.$ 360,000.[35]

land bridge
A term coined to describe the practice of shipping goods from Asia to Europe through the United States by using railroads.

- The Saint Lawrence Seaway: it links the Great Lakes to the St. Lawrence River and the Atlantic Ocean. Unfortunately, the Seaway is narrow and few ships

Figure 3.7: A Containership on the Suez Canal.
Photo ©Adrian Beesley. Used with permission.

can pass through its locks. It is also plagued by ice, and the Welland Canal—which links Lake Erie to Lake Ontario and bypasses the Niagara Falls—closes from January to March. This has forced companies to find alternative means of transportation, and the traffic through the Seaway is down 45 percent from what it was twenty years ago.[36]

- The Corinth Canal (see Figure 3.8 on page 66): it connects two parts of the Mediterranean Sea, the Ionian Sea and the Aegean Sea, by making a spectacular cut through the Isthmus of Corinth, between the Peloponnese peninsula and the remainder of the country of Greece. Designed by the Ancient Greeks and started by the Roman Emperor Nero, it was only completed at the end of the nineteenth century. It is mainly used by local traffic and tourist ships.

The absence of certain waterways is also detrimental to international trade and the efficient movement of goods. For example, there had been considerable talk about a canal through Nicaragua that would be "parallel" to the Panama Canal and be free of locks, an advantage that would speed up the transit time considerably.[37] In addition, the canal would be several hundred miles further North, which would also reduce transit times. A railroad "dry canal" was also once proposed for the same region, with two options. One suggested to transport ships from one ocean to the other, without unloading them, and by carrying the ships on a railroad cradle. The other was more conventional with simply a double-decker container service on railroad cars.[38] However, both of these projects have been abandoned, and the Panama

3.2 Transportation Infrastructure

Suez tariff for a laden containership — Northbound

Suez Canal Net Tonnage: 80,000 tons
Gross Registered Tons: 171,000 tons
Draft: 15.5m

First 5,000: 5,000 at SDR 7.88 per container	39,400.00
Next 5,000: 5,000 at SDR 5.41 per container	27,050.00
Next 10,000: 10,000 at SDR 4.20 per container	42,000.00
Next 20,000: 20,000 at SDR 2.94 per container	58,800.00
Next 30,000: 30,000 at SDR 2.73 per container	81,900.00
Next 50,000: 10,000 at SDR 2.15 per container	21,500.00
Rest: 0 at SDR 2.05 per container	0.00
Total Canal Tolls (SDR)	270,650.00
Tug: 1 tug at SDR 8,000 per tug	8,000.00
Mooring / Projector (SDR)	1,582.85
Pilotage (SDR)	427.00
Disbursements (SDR)	9,715.88
Total Disbursements (SDR)	19,725.73

Exchange Rate USD/SDR 1.48624662

Total Canal Tolls (USD)	431,569.95

Table 3.4: Toll Calculation for a Large-Size Laden Containership using the Suez Canal Northbound
Leth Agencies.

Canal is, for the foreseeable future, the only connection between the Atlantic and the Pacific. A canal through the Isthmus of Kra in Thailand—the Malay Peninsula—which would bypass the Strait of Malacca and the Port of Singapore would speed up the transit time between Europe and the Far East as well. This project has been in the planning stages on and off in the past decade within the Thai government and there is increased interest on the part of Malaysia, Indonesia, and particularly China.[39] No decision had been made by summer 2013.

The same lack of infrastructure is found in freshwater passages. After the War in the Balkans, there was a period during which there was no freshwater communication between the Black Sea and Northern Europe, as many bridges were demolished on the Danube River[40] and barges could not pass. There is still no large-capacity freshwater communication between the Mediterranean Sea and Northern Europe, as the expansion of an eighteenth-century canal between the Rhône River and the Rhine River is still being debated; however, the Europakanal, a canal between the Rhine and the Danube, was completed in 1992, and is heavily traveled.

Figure 3.8: The Spectacular Corinth Canal in Greece
Photo ©Danny de Bruyne. Used with permission.

3.2.3 Airport Infrastructure

Airports are also a fundamental part of the transportation infrastructure. There are fewer critical issues in the management of an international airport than there are in a port, but they can be just as constraining.

Runways

runway
The strip of concrete in an airport from which airplanes take off and land.

The runways of an airport determine the type of aircraft that it can serve. The lengths of the runways are particularly relevant, as they generally determine whether the airport can support direct flights to faraway places. Many airports in the world cannot accommodate the large jumbo jets that serve international destinations because the runways were designed mostly for smaller aircraft. As the cities around the airports grew, the airports became landlocked, unable to extend their runways.

Several cities have had to build airports far from their city centers in order to build facilities that can accommodate international flights. Whereas Charles de Gaulle Airport in Paris, France, and Heathrow Airport in London, UK, (both built in the 1970s) are about twenty-five kilometers (fifteen miles) from the cities they serve, the airports built in the 1990s are much further away: Denver International is thirty-seven kilometers (twenty-three miles) from the city and Malpensa in Milan, Italy, is forty-eight kilometers (thirty miles) away.

The Legendary Kai Tak

Kai Tak Airport in Hong Kong SAR was one of the most unusual airports in the world. As the airplanes landed, they flew a few hundred feet away from the high rises and the hills that surrounded the airport (see Figure 3.9). It was an uncomfortable experience for many passengers.

In 1998, its replacement, Chek Lap Kok Airport, opened. Dubbed the most expensive construction project in the world at U.S.$20 billion—the Chunnel under the English Channel cost U.S.$15 billion—it is an artificial island on the outskirts of the city, with its own dedicated tunnel, its own suspension bridge, its own commuter railroad, and the largest cargo facility in the world. It operates twenty-four hours a day, a boon for cargo shippers involved in the South-East Asian market, because Kai Tak closed at night.

Figure 3.9: The Approach at Kai Tak Airport in Hong Kong SAR
Photo ©Daryl Chapman. Courtesy of www.ailiners.net. Used with permission.

In addition to the challenges of building such a large infrastructure, the transfer from one airport to the other was completed in one night. As Kai Tak closed at midnight on July 5, 1998, all of its equipment was moved to Chek Lap Kok with 10,000 vehicle trips, seventy barge voyages, and thirty flights, and the new airport opened on July 6, at 6:30 A.M. Unfortunately, it did not happen as smoothly as expected, and the first couple of weeks were hectic, especially for cargo.

Nevertheless, the new airport has become the busiest international cargo airport in the world, handling more than 4.1 million tons in 2012, an increase of over 8 percent per year since its first full year of operation in 1999.[41]

A second concern is the number of runways, which determines the capacity of the airport. Most airports have more than one runway, but the busiest airport—in number of passengers—in the world has four runways (Hatfield Airport in Atlanta, Georgia, USA). Both Chicago O'Hare and Dallas-Fort Worth International have seven. An airport can be quite constrained by its lack of runways; for years, Narita Airport in Tokyo had only one runway to accommodate its traffic. It was stretched to capacity, and there was no way to build a second runway as a number of small farmers refused to sell their land to the airport.[42] Since, by law, the Japanese government cannot expropriate them, the airport cannot build the runway on their land, and travelers and cargo shippers are inconvenienced as the number of flights in and out of Narita is limited, increasing the landing fees. Narita finished a second runway that avoided the reluctant farmers' land, but it was too short to accommodate jumbo jets, which constitute 90 percent of the Narita traffic, so it is only used for local traffic. It was not until 2009 that Narita was able to extend its second runway to accommodate international flights.[43]

A single runway also increases the probability of delays as the slightest accident or malfunction will immobilize the entire airport.

Hours of Operation

Another concern of importance is the time frame during which airports are operating. Because most airports are geographically close to large cities, their hours of operations are generally limited by noise constraints and they operate only during day hours. Because cargo tends to fly at night, specialized cargo airports that are located outside of large cities and can operate twenty-four hours a day, seven days a week, have been built in smaller cities such as Prestwick in Scotland, Hahn in Germany, and Chateauroux in France.[44] To some extent, this development mirrors that of the Memphis airport, which has become the largest cargo airport in North America—and the second largest cargo airport in the world—with 4.0 million tons of freight in 2013[45] even though it is not located near a large metropolitan center.

Warehousing Space

Another concern of importance for cargo shippers is the existence of appropriate warehouse space at an airport; cargo should be protected while it is in transit, and not left to the elements. This is particularly important as air cargo tends to be—erroneously—not as well packaged as cargo destined for ocean shipping. The prob-

3.2 Transportation Infrastructure

lem is even more severe for refrigerated warehouse space, which can be in very short supply.

3.2.4 Rail Infrastructure

Another element of the transportation infrastructure of a country is its railroad network. In the eighteenth and early nineteenth centuries, railroads were the most important means of long-distance land transportation. In Europe, the United States, India, Africa, and Asia, a dense network of railroads was built, sometimes under the impetus of colonizing forces who wanted to be able to move troops quickly. This historical development led to some decisions that, a century and a half later, are causing significant problems. To prevent possible invaders from using their railroad infrastructures, Spain, Brazil, and Russia developed railroad gauges (the width between the rails) that were incompatible with the rest of Europe. While it did prevent military troops from using the network, this decision is still causing trouble for any type of rail transportation between these countries and their neighbors. For example, most trains stop at the French-Spanish border so that cargo can be shifted to railcars that are appropriate for the gauge used in the other country; others—including passenger trains—slow down to a crawl while specially designed axles expand or contract.[46] In Brazil, the cost of the rolling stock is substantially higher as every car and locomotive must be adapted to its unusual gauge size, whether they are purchased new or used, and trains have to travel slower because the cars are much wider than what the railroad was designed to handle and therefore are less stable.

Most countries updated their railroad infrastructure as their economies grew. However, in a few countries, the economy has grown much faster and the infrastructure has not been able to keep pace. Such is the case in China, where demand far outstrips supply in terms of rail transportation. The Chinese government has spent billions of yuans to develop its rail infrastructure, including a large network of high-speed rail lines, and to expand its road network. The Chinese government spends CN¥700 billion—U.S.$ 122 billion—per *year* to develop its railroad infrastructure in 2012-2020.[47] Such an investment is considerable. India is similarly making significant investments in its infrastructure, spending more than U.S.$ 12 billion per year,[48] though most of that money is not going to railroads, but roads.

The United States has a railroad infrastructure which is atypical; all railroads are privately owned, and that fact alone limits the amount of investment that can be spent on improving the overall rail infrastructure of the country. In addition, the geography of the United States presents several large obstacles; in particular, the Rocky Mountains present challenges because of their size and climate; the amount of snow that falls in the Rockies routinely exceeds 500 centimeters (200 inches). Because these challenges make it very expensive to build and maintain tracks, there are several miles of important East-West railroad connections in the United States that are still "single track," that is, traffic in both directions uses the same set of tracks. Since doubling the track often involves blasting rocks near the existing railroad, progress is time consuming and expensive. The trans-continental railway of the BNSF company is almost completely double-tracked, except for a small 30-mile section on the Red River. Double-tracking increases a rail segment's capacity by 500 to 600 percent.

In many countries, though, the railroads gradually lose their focus on shipping merchandise and shift their efforts to high-speed passenger transportation. Such is the case of Europe, where most merchandise is mostly shipped by means other than railroad, but where intercity rail passenger transportation is commonplace, convenient, fast, and competes with airlines over small distances. The best examples are the French (now European) Trains à Grande Vitesse (TGV), which connect Paris to London in two hours (dubbed the Eurostar) and Paris to Brussels in an hour and a half (the Thalys). There is only one TGV dedicated to merchandise transport, and it is used by the French Postal Service (La Poste) exclusively for mail transportation (see Figure 3.10). A similar switch from merchandise to high-speed passenger transport occurred in Japan; the Shinkansen train covers the 192 kilometers (120 miles) between Hiroshima and Kokura in less than forty-five minutes, for example. These high-speed trains run on dedicated tracks that are separate from the remainder of the slower rail infrastructure.

Figure 3.10: The Only Merchandise High-Speed Train, Used by the French Postal Service

Photo ©Mecdepaname. Courtesy of www.wikipedia.org. Used with permission.

Multi-Modal Emphasis

In the last two decades, three factors have contributed to the renewal of merchandise traffic on railroads: the congestion of roads has worsened, concerns about pollution and noise have increased, and the creation of the multi-modal container has eliminated the need to load and unload merchandise from traditional boxcars.

In the United States, railroads have invested heavily in the modernization of their rolling stocks; they have shifted from boxcars to piggy-back cars—allowing them to carry truck trailers—and container cars. At the same time, they have improved their infrastructure by increasing the height clearances in tunnels and other areas, allowing trains to transport containers "double-stacked" (*i.e.*, twice as many containers as a single-stack train would). Figures 13.8 on page 344 and 13.9 on page 345 illustrate these concepts. American trains tend to be exceedingly long, with at least 100 cars, allowing a crew of a few individuals to move in excess of 200 containers or truck trailers, making them particularly cost-effective. In addition, because passenger rail transport is almost nonexistent in the United States—with the exception of the northeastern part of the country—cargo trains have priority on the network and tend to be relatively fast.

Unfortunately, such improvements have not yet been made to the European infrastructure, which still consists mostly of aging boxcars. Moreover, the emphasis on passenger transportation gives priority to passenger trains, and relegates cargo trains to second-class status, making them slow and inefficient cargo movers. Multiple attempts to create high-speed cargo railroad links from ports in Northern Europe to ports in the Mediterranean have been made, but politics and administrative delays are unlikely to make this corridor a reality for some years.[49]

In the same fashion, the success of North American railroads has enticed several developments in Asia. There are plans to significantly modernize the trans-Siberian railroad, which would allow cargo to be shipped from Asia (Vladivostok) to Europe by rail. Some Japanese car manufacturers are already using the service to transport cargo to Eastern Europe.[50] There are also plans to create a Trans-Asian railroad, which would connect Singapore and Seoul to Europe via Turkey, using the tunnel being dug to connect the Asian side to the European side of Istanbul.[51].

Land Bridges

A consequence of the increased efficiency of the railroads in the United States has been the creation of land bridges. The concept of a land bridge is based on the idea that containerized ocean cargo sometimes needs to cross some landmass; for example, cargo from South-East Asia can be shipped through the Pacific Ocean, cross the North American continent, and then continue on its way to Europe by crossing the Atlantic Ocean. One alternative is to take the Panama Canal; however, it is a fairly long voyage south in the Pacific to reach Balboa, and a fairly long voyage north from Colón onto Europe in the Caribbean Sea and the North Atlantic. Another alternative is to take the cargo around India and through the Suez Canal, which is inconvenient and expensive. The latest consideration consists of shipping the goods *via* the Northwest Passage, through the Arctic Ocean, which is slowly becoming ice-free with climate change, bringing a host of issues, from pollution to government control over those waters.[52]

land bridge
A term coined to describe the practice of shipping goods from Asia to Europe through the United States by using railroads.

The alternative developed by the U.S. railroads is to cross North America on a land bridge; the cargo is unloaded from a large containership on the West Coast of the United States or Canada, and shipped by double-stack container train to the East Coast. The journey is faster and cheaper than by ocean and the Panama Canal. In addition, it allows shipping lines to use post-Panamax ships on their trans-Pacific and trans-Atlantic routes, which is also more efficient. A consequence of this trend is that cargo going from Taipei to Barcelona is going to transit through Chicago. Such variations from the traditional itinerary of Taipei-Panama-Barcelona are said to be "transparent" to the shipper, which means that the shipper is unaware of them. However, such a transparent voyage may expose the shipment to lower temperatures than those the shipper expected and a shipment may not be protected adequately enough for the extremes in temperature, from the tropical climate of Taipei to the sub-freezing temperatures of the mid-West of the United States.

3.2.5 Road Infrastructure

In addition to the infrastructure of ports, airports, and railroads, a great amount of shipping moves by road, especially on the last portion of the journey, from the port, airport, or rail terminal to its final destination. This part of the on-carriage is often called the "last mile."

The road infrastructure of a country is evaluated somewhat differently than the rest of its transportation infrastructure. In almost no country is there a shortage of roads, with only one exception, Russia, which still does not have a trans-Siberian road connection between the Western and Eastern parts of the country. Russians refer to a large percentage of their country's territory as *bezdorozhye*, or "place without roads."[53] However, this is the exception, and for all other countries, the issues are the quality and maintenance of the network, its congestion, as well as the existence of high-speed links between major metropolitan areas. The concern therefore is not one of density, but one of usability.

Quality

The road infrastructure of a country is generally described in documents such as the U.S. Department of Commerce's Country Commercial Guides[54] or the CIA's World Factbook[55] in terms of total miles of road, and of the percentage of these roads that are paved. For example, the country of Argentina is listed as having 231,474 kilometers (143,862 miles) of roads, of which 69,412 kilometers (43,140 miles)—30 percent—are paved.[56] In the United States, paved roads only represent 67 percent of the road infrastructure,[57] but they represent 100 percent of the network in Switzerland and Germany.

However, this is somewhat misleading, as most of the traffic obviously utilizes paved roads, and the unpaved roads serve remote rural areas. In addition, the condition of a paved road makes a substantial difference in its usefulness; an overcrowded, two-lane highway riddled with potholes is not very conducive to the safe transportation of cargo. Such is the case with the roads in the countries of Belarus, Albania, Romania, Lithuania, and Latvia. The government of Poland estimated once that 80 percent of its roads were in unsatisfactory or bad condition.[58] India[59] and China also suffer from a lack of quality road infrastructure, although both are spending considerable amounts of money to improve it.[60] Unfortunately, there is no statistical source that indicates the condition of the roads in a country, and because there are substantial variations from one region of a country to another, it is even more difficult to evaluate. The United States road infrastructure received a grade of "D" by the American Society of Civil Engineers[61] and by the U.S. Transportation Secretary, Ray Lahood.[62] Mostly, the U.S. infrastructure is not sufficiently well maintained for the traffic that it sustains, and delays cost U.S. businesses considerable amounts, not withstanding the dangers of poorly maintained roads and bridges.[63]

Congestion of the road infrastructure is also endemic to certain cities: there are too many cars, trucks, and other vehicles on the road, and deliveries are difficult to make (see Figure 3.11 on the next page). In Calcutta, India, the traffic is so congested that the average speed in the city is eight km/h (five mph); most people travel by rickshaw or by public transportation rather than by car.[64] In New Delhi,

Figure 3.11: Traffic Congestion in Lahore, Pakistan
Photo ©Voice of America. Used with permission.

the government has created a category of vehicles, called VVIP—Very Very Important Persons—that are allowed to zip through traffic with blaring sirens and flashing lights.[65] The traffic is Beijing is notorious for being at a standstill for a good percentage of the day. In order to resolve congestion, many developing countries' cities have instituted a system of alternating days for traffic; vehicles with odd-numbered license plates are only allowed to travel on odd-numbered days and vehicles with even-numbered license plates can only travel on even-numbered days. Such is the case in Lagos, Nigeria, for example. The problem is not resolved, as resourceful Nigerians obtain two license plates for every vehicle from corrupt civil authorities, and change the plates every morning.

Although congestion is a problem that is extreme in developing countries, it is certainly also present in large metropolitan areas in Europe, Japan, and the United States. As the number of automobiles increases, the situation will worsen further and make deliveries to customers more problematic and inefficient. Many delivery firms are now using motorcycles and mopeds, which are more maneuverable in large cities. London enacted a very effective tax system to prevent vehicles from entering the heart of the city; vehicles' license plates are monitored and recorded through a closed-circuit television system and commuters are charged £ 8.00 for each day they travel into the city. Residents receive a 90 percent discount of this daily rate. Fines for non-compliance are substantial. After it was enacted in February 2003, the program was judged so successful in the city (traffic decreased approximately 15 percent)[66] that it was expanded to a larger proportion of the city in February 2007, and that other cities have adopted a similar system or are considering adopting a similar system; Stockholm, Manchester, Singapore, Milan, San Francisco and New York.

Yet another issue in cities is the confusion that can be generated by the lack of signage and a different addressing system. While most Northern American cities are built on a grid of east-west and north-south streets, with a fairly logical numbering sequence of streets and buildings, European cities are plagued with a maze of different streets that change names at each—or so it seems—intersection. Mexico City has an extraordinarily confusing system of streets; there are nearly 800 streets named after Benito Juárez, 760 named for Miguel Hidalgo, and 300 streets renamed every year. To make things even more confusing, 80,000 city blocks have no signage at all.[67] Japan has the tradition of numbering buildings on a street in the order in which they were built, and not in a sequential order based on location. Most of Bombay's addresses are not based on street names, but defined by a succession of smaller and smaller areas: a person's address will include the name of the house, the name of the street, the name of the block, the name of the city, and the city code. In addition, there will be an east or a west, depending of which side of the railroad track the block is located, with parallel structures on either side. Such systems make it challenging to deliver goods to a new customer. The worst situation from this perspective is on the island of Saipan in the Northern Mariana Islands, with a population of 70,000, which still has no address system at all.[68]

To decrease the congestion in cities, countries have built a network of high-speed links that avoid smaller cities while connecting the larger ones. These limited access highways speed up considerably the transportation of goods between cities. Nevertheless, these highways are subject to a number of rules and regulations, some of which limit the size of the trucks that can travel on them and the speed at which they can travel. Because these rules vary from country to country, it can be a challenge to arrange international truck transportation of merchandise. In addition, in many countries, access to high-speed highways is limited to vehicles that pay a toll, making such roads an expensive alternative. In France, for example, the private company running the high-speed highway system charges approximately € 0.21 per kilometer (€ 0.35 per mile) for semi-trucks.

Civil Engineering Structures (Ouvrages d'Art)

If the country is mountainous, these high-speed thoroughfares are built with numerous bridges and tunnels designed to eliminate the constraints of the landscape. A perfect example of such a highway is the Italian Autostrade, which runs along the Appennine Chain and is seemingly an unending succession of tunnels and bridges. Such engineering structures are called collectively (in French) *ouvrages d'art*—art structures—and it is an apt moniker; unfortunately, there is no equivalent in English, so the French term will be used.

The dependence of international trade on such ouvrages d'art cannot be underestimated: most natural borders are either water (oceans or lakes) or mountains at the watershed separation. To cross these natural borders, bridges or tunnels have to be built. The Chunnel—the tunnel built under the English Channel, between France and Great Britain—is a case in point. Until its opening in 1994, shipping goods from one country to the other was delayed by a fairly lengthy ferry voyage, which sometimes could be delayed or cancelled due to bad weather. The Chunnel has substantially shortened shipping times between the two countries, although it is quite expensive; for private automobiles, the cost is £ 45, and it can reach £ 500

3.2 Transportation Infrastructure

for semi-trucks.

Another international route that has been radically changed by ouvrages d'art is the trade between Western Europe and the Middle East, with the opening of the two suspension bridges in Istanbul, one in 1973 (Bogaziçi Bridge), the other in 1988 (Fatih Sultan Mehmet Bridge). These are the only two bridges that allow road transportation between Europe and Asia, save for an itinerary north of the Black Sea, through Bulgaria, Romania, the Ukraine and Russia. To date, there is no rail link from Southern Europe to Asia—although one will open at the end of 2013 (see Section 3.2.2 on page 63), as the Orient Express ends on the European side of Istanbul, and the Baghdad Railway starts on the Asian side. No rail link is available between the two stations, and passengers and cargo cross the Bosporus by using ferries.

The so-called Øresund Fixed Link between Copenhagen, Denmark, and Malmö, Sweden, is another example of an ouvrage d'art that has significantly altered the transportation landscape of an international border: it actually is a succession of three bridges and a tunnel, with a switchover on an artificial island in the middle of Flinte Channel. It is the first terrestrial communication between the two countries, and it replaces a forty-five minute ferry ride with an eight-minute drive. More importantly, it is the first land link between Western Europe and the Scandinavian countries.

The Millau Bridge in southern France (see Figure 3.12) opened in 2004 and is another highway bridge that significantly reduces transportation times. It links two high plateaus that are separated by a deep river gorge, for which the only crossing was in the middle of the small town of Millau. Before the construction of the bridge, vehicles had to travel down approximately 300 meters (1,000 feet) through a series a

Figure 3.12: The Millau Bridge in Southern France
Photo ©Timothy David. Used with permission.

hairpin turns to the city, cross the river, and then climb up the same distance on the other plateau. The town was infamous for its traffic jam, and it was not unusual to spend two hours to go from one plateau to the other. With the bridge, it takes less than one minute. The bridge is 345 meters above the river (1,150 feet), about twenty meters higher than the Eiffel Tower, and was built in a little over three years.[69]

Some bridges are much less architecturally noticeable but no less important to the economies of the countries they link. For example, the United States and Canada, the two largest trade partners in the world, are only connected by a bridge and a tunnel between Detroit, Michigan and Windsor, Ontario, and two bridges near Buffalo, New York, for a significant portion of their common border. At least one of those bridges, the Ambassador Bridge between Detroit and Windsor, owned by a private company, has not been updated in 50 years; it is only a four-lane bridge and carries 3.3 million trucks every year. Similarly, the Peace Bridge between Buffalo and Fort Erie, Ontario, is used at its maximum capacity and has not been expanded since 1927. A new bridge between Detroit and Windsor has been proposed,[70] entirely financed by the Canadian government, but the owner of the Detroit-based owner Ambassador Bridge ran a campaign to prevent its construction. It was defeated.[71]

Another example of the critical nature of bridges and other structures can be seen in the tiny island nation of Palau, where a 1996 bridge collapse between the capital city of Koror and the main island of Babeldaob created an economic nightmare. People on the main island used to commute to the capital via the bridge, and the bridge collapse was a major setback to the Palau people and the country's economy; while the bridge was temporarily replaced by ferry services, it was a much less efficient alternative. The bridge was not rebuilt until 2002, with a Japanese grant.[72]

It is not just in developing countries that the failure of such infrastructures can be catastrophic: all ouvrages d'art are vulnerable. In March 1999, a deadly fire occurred in the Mont-Blanc tunnel between France and Italy, under the Alps; the tunnel was closed until April 2002. This forced trucks to use the Fréjus tunnel, the only other tunnel under the Alps between France and Italy, or to make a substantial detour along the Mediterranean coast, neither option being a good alternative. A fire in the Saint Gothard tunnel—the second longest road tunnel in the world, between Switzerland and Italy—forced its closure in October 2001; while the tunnel was reopened in December 2001, it was limited to half of its traffic capacity until April 2002, as traffic was only allowed in one direction at a time. There have been several truck fires in the Chunnel as well, which reduced the tunnel's capacity, while it was repaired.

The building of a bridge can also alter the character of a region; for example, Prince Edward Island is now connected to the rest of Canada by a recently built bridge, and its residents are divided on its impact on their life and economy. While the island has gained some additional tourism revenues and islanders have greater access to the amenities of the neighboring cities of Moncton and Halifax, it has also lost some of its quaint tranquility.

3.2.6 Warehousing Infrastructure

It is evident that transportation is dependent on an infrastructure that allows the movement of goods. However, it is equally important to realize that cargo is often stationary when it waits for the next transportation alternative to be available. Therefore, it is important for a shipper to obtain information about the warehousing infrastructure of the locations where a shipment will be in layover.

The issues revolving around the warehousing infrastructure concern the protection of the goods when they are waiting while in transit. Will they be protected from the rain? From the sun? From possible floods? From (unusual) cold? A savvy international logistics manager will attempt to determine the conditions under which the goods will be kept, and will then determine whether they are correctly packaged, or whether they need to be shipped through a different itinerary. With the disappearance of the The Cigna Insurance Company's *Ports of the World* booklet, there has not been a comprehensive source of the warehouse space available in each port; the World Port Source website (see Table 3.3 on page 59) has very limited information on the warehousing space available in a port.

In many cases as well, shippers will use public warehouses for storage purposes, in order to deliver goods to their customers without having to resort to an international shipment. This enables the company to provide much better customer service by delivering goods with a much shorter lead time.

Unfortunately, the warehousing infrastructure of a country is difficult to evaluate, as there are no general sources of information on the availability and quality of public warehouses. Therefore, in those cases where a company is considering using a public warehouse to serve its customers, it would be best to plan an actual visit to the location considered, as the standards used in public warehousing management may be quite different than the ones expected.

3.3 Communication Infrastructure

In addition to the transportation infrastructure, the communication infrastructure is also of substantial importance to international logistics. The ability to communicate with customers and suppliers, by mail, by phone, or through other electronic media, is very important to the smooth operation of an international transaction. Unfortunately, there are different expectations of service and performance in communication means from country to country.

3.3.1 Mail Services

The ability of the postal services to deliver mail on time and reliably should be a given in most developed countries. However, there is ample anecdotal evidence that it is not the case in all places. On many occasions, there are unacceptable delays and errors: while the European Union countries strive to deliver letters sent to a national address on the day after it is mailed—a so-called D+1 policy—and on the second day if it is international mail within the European community, this is a difficult standard to achieve. Italy, especially before its national postal service was privatized, was notoriously unreliable. France has periodic strikes of its mail service and of its national railway service, both of which can substantially delay the delivery of mail. In South Africa, the mail service has become so unreliable that businesses and individuals no longer trust it enough to send payments, forcing them to make payments in person or through banks.

Another issue is the safety of the mail: will a letter or package make it to its destination, or will it be lost, damaged, or stolen in transit? Because postal services tend to be very large employers, it is difficult to screen all employees effectively. There have been countless documented instances of postal employees stealing the contents of parcels, removing the contents of letters—especially cash and checks—before they reach their destination. Developing countries have an even greater problem, as public employees' wages tend to be modest. In some parts of the world, the mail services are so unreliable that emigrants sending a portion of their paychecks to their relatives use parallel services, such as the traditional *hawala* in the Middle East and North Africa, *fei-ch'ien* in China, *padala* in the Philippines, *hui kuan* in Hong Kong SAR, and *hundi* in India,[73] and similar parallel systems in Brazil.[74]

Many firms intent on ensuring that their postal communications are safely delivered have switched, especially for international documents' exchanges, to private services such as DHL or FedEx. While the costs of private services are much higher than the costs of the traditional postal services, these small-packet companies have gained significant market share, thanks to their reputation for greater reliability. In particular, the customers' ability to track packages and documents online has increased this perception. This tracking ability is now available for some of the postal servicesŠ products, but it is not available worldwide.

Another phenomenon is the exploitation (arbitrage) of the differences in prices and mail categories for international mail from one country to another. A direct marketer sending a substantial number of identical mail pieces internationally will determine in which country that particular mailing is going to cost the least amount; it will then ship the mailing materials in bulk to a company operating a re-mailing service in that country. The re-mailer will then place the individual items in the mail and so the overall mailing costs to the marketer will be lower. Commercial materials emanating from France have come to the author from Denmark, Great Britain, and the Netherlands; the lowest cost provider was probably determined by the fact that the weight of the materials being sent placed them in different price categories in different countries.

3.3.2 Telecommunications Services

Slightly different issues are facing telecommunication services; not only has the demand for voice telecommunication increased about 10 percent a year, but the demand for data telecommunication has essentially doubled every year for the past ten years, and it shows no sign of slowing down. Some countries have been able to build a sufficiently large domestic infrastructure to carry this increased load, often by using their already-existing infrastructure. For example, many gas and oil pipelines have been given the added responsibility of transmitting data through a fiber-optic line laid in their midst.[75] Many countries, though, have not been able to keep up with such growth, and telecommunications in those countries are slow and not very reliable.

This reliability is the primary concern in several countries where the economy has grown quickly; the domestic communication infrastructure did not follow. Phone service is notoriously unreliable, with phone conversations disconnected, phone calls regularly connected to wrong numbers, and dial tones all but absent. Table 3.5 on the next page shows the penetration rate of land-line phones for selected countries; it is calculated by dividing the total number of land-line phones by the population.[76] It does not refer to the percentage of the population with access to a land-line phone, because many of these phones are shared by a household.

leap frogging
The idea that some countries will "skip" a technology to adopt the most recent one available.

Fortunately, in some of those countries, a phenomenon known as leap frogging has taken place. Because the "old" land-based telephone infrastructure is not working properly, people have switched to cellular phones very quickly and bypassed the

3.3 Communication Infrastructure

Landlines per capita (2011)

Rank	Country/Region		Rank	Country/Region	
1	Taiwan	72.9%	11	Sweden	50.4%
2	Germany	63.8%	12	Australia	47.5%
3	France	60.5%	13	United States	46.1%
4	Hong Kong	60.5%	14	Israel	45.4%
5	Republic of Korea	60.2%	15	Denmark	45.3%
6	Switzerland	57.7%	16	Belgium	44.3%
7	Greece	53.3%	17	Slovenia	43.8%
8	Canada	52.7%	18	Belarus	43.7%
9	United Kingdom	52.4%	19	New Zealand	43.1%
10	Japan	50.8%	20	Ireland	42.9%

Table 3.5: Percentage of Population with a Landline, by Country/Region CIA's World Factbook.

land-based system. This switch is facilitated by the fact that many countries quickly adopted a single operating standard (Global System for Mobile Communications, or GSM), which makes for easy portability and for increased convenience. As of 2011, there were more than 70 countries in which the penetration rate for cellular phones was greater than 100 percent. Table 3.6 highlights the penetration rates for cellular telephones.[77] Since it is calculated as the number of cellular phones divided by the population size, the rate corresponds, roughly, to the number of cell phones that an average individual owns. Only one country/region (Hong Kong) is listed in both tables.

Cellular Telephones per capita (2011)

Rank	Country/Region		Rank	Country/Region	
1	United Arab Emirates	214.2%	14	Guatemala	144.1%
2	Hong Kong	212.9%	15	Uruguay	143.1%
3	Panama	189.2%	16	Lithuania	142.3%
4	Kuwait	183.1%	17	Kazakhstan	142.3%
5	Finland	169.8%	18	Sierra Leone	138.9%
6	Libya	166.6%	19	Vietnam	137.7%
7	Russia	166.1%	20	Gaza Strip	136.4%
8	Oman	164.9%			
9	Austria	158.4%	23	Germany	134.0%
10	Italy	156.2%	33	Taiwan	123.9%
11	Bulgaria	150.0%	84	United States	91.7%
12	Trinidad and Tobago	149.0%	86	France	90.7%
13	Estonia	147.1%			

Table 3.6: Percentage of the Population with a Cellular Telephone, by Country/Region CIA's World Factbook.

In China, there are almost more than three times the number of cellular phones (986 million) than there are land-based phones (285 million), and there is growth in the number of cellular phones and a decline in the number of traditional landline phones. Countries such as the United States, which have a strong land-based infrastructure, have been much slower at switching to cellular phone usage. As of 2011, the United States was not in the top seventy-five countries in the world when ranked by the percentage of the population that owned a cellular telephone. Although this ranking was due to the fact that the land-based infrastructure is very good (and people have much less of an incentive to switch), it was also due to the fact that there are four different operating technologies competing for cellular phone customers, and therefore that there are four times as many towers to be built (and paid), making cellular phone service particularly expensive.

On the international side, telecommunications are heavily dependent on a network of underwater cables that run across the Atlantic, the Pacific, the Mediterranean Sea, or other large bodies of water. As telecommunication traffic has increased, the capacity of these cables has also increased dramatically. Altogether, though, there are still very few cables (only seven cross the Northern Atlantic), and their vulnerability is extraordinary. Although they are buried on the portion of their route that is located in shallow water, they are for the most part simply laid on the floor of the oceans, at the risk of being snagged by fishermen's nets and boat anchors.[78] When these cables cross land, they are just as vulnerable and at the mercy of a careless backhoe operator or other accident. Whenever they are snagged or damaged, traffic on that cable ceases until it is repaired. In an outstanding article in Wired Magazine, Neal Stephenson followed the construction of the FLAG—Fiber-optic Link Around the Globe—and reported on the vulnerability of this network: for example, five of the major worldwide cables are routed through a single building in Alexandria, Egypt.[79]

Satellite telecommunications are no less dependent on a limited number of alternatives and therefore just as vulnerable; because satellites are increasingly heavily used for communications such as television programs, their capacity is entirely used, and the failure of a single satellite can wreak havoc on telecommunications. Other telecommunication infrastructures are vulnerable; the Internet, although touted as robust, is still very dependent on root-servers that keep the list of addresses on the Internet.

3.3.3 Internet Access

As the world economy relies further on the Internet for commerce and communication, it is interesting to note that only 8.6 percent of the world's population has broadband access to the Internet, with a digital subscriber line, cable modem, or other high-speed technology.[80] Table 3.7 on the next page lists the top 20 countries in their population's access to the Internet.

3.4 Utilities Infrastructure

Another area of concern for the manager involved in international logistics is the utilities infrastructure. While it is generally taken for granted that all utilities—electricity, water, sewage, gas—are available in most countries, experience shows that there is often a shortage of one or more of these commodities in many countries, including developed countries. And while utilities are not directly an issue in

Internet Access per capita (2011)

Rank	Country/Region		Rank	Country/Region	
1	Switzerland	40.0%	11	United Kingdom	32.7%
2	Netherlands	38.7%	12	Canada	31.8%
3	Denmark	37.6%	13	Sweden	31.8%
4	Republic of Korea	36.9%	14	Hong Kong	31.6%
5	France	36.0%	15	Malta	30.9%
6	Norway	35.4%	16	Andorra	29.9%
7	Iceland	33.9%	17	Finland	29.5%
8	Germany	33.1%	18	Japan	27.6%
9	Belgium	33.0%	19	United States	27.4%
10	Luxembourg	32.9%	20	New Zealand	25.8%

Table 3.7: Percentage of Population with Internet Access, by Country/Region
CIA's World Factbook.

transportation, they can become critically important when a company is considering operating a warehouse or establishing a corporate office.

3.4.1 Electricity

The most common problem with utilities is the availability and reliability of electrical power. It is common in countries where the rate of economic growth outpaces the rate of growth in electricity production to have blackouts for part of the day or frequent interruptions. Actually, the situation is endemic in sub-Saharan Africa, where there are scheduled blackouts because the production of electricity is much lower than the demand for it; households and businesses therefore plan their days around the availability of electricity. India and China are also affected by recurring blackouts, and so is Saudi Arabia. China has invested considerable amounts in electrical generation infrastructure, including the Three River Gorge Dam, which came on-line in 2008, and will eventually produce more than 10 percent of the electricity used by the country. However, there are still some disruptions in multiple areas of the country.

The availability of electricity is disrupted in many countries, as the problems tend to be regional as well as national. In the summer of 2001, there were substantial supply and demand imbalances and numerous shortages of electricity in California. However, recent evidence has shown that, even though there were infrastructural shortages at the root of the problem, the speculative behavior of the Enron Corporation was mostly responsible for the wild price fluctuations that Californians experienced. On the other hand, some countries have abundant electrical resources: Brazil and Paraguay share the Itaipu Dam which provides 82 percent of Paraguay's electrical needs and 26 percent of Brazil's. Nevertheless, for those areas of Brazil that are geographically far from Itaipu, there are still shortages and temporary blackouts.

In addition to problems of production, the utilities are sometimes the victims of theft; households and businesses bypass their meters or tap directly in the grid without the "inconvenience" of a meter, preventing utilities from collecting enough income to be able to invest in additional capacity. A World Bank loan to India to build additional power plants was actually made conditional on the utility getting paid for a greater percentage of its production.[81] In Russia, an endemic problem is the theft of the electrical wires for scrap, an activity that kills more than 500 thieves each year and forces the Russian government to replace miles of high-tension wires, without mention of the disruptions to businesses and individuals.

Figure 3.13: Tangled Utility Wires in New Delhi, India
Photo ©Joseph Routon. Used with permission.

In many countries, quick economic growth has prevented the orderly construction of the power grid, as is shown in Figure 3.13. Unfortunately, such jumble of wires is not uncommon, and it certainly affects the reliability of the power supply.

3.4.2 Water and Sewer

Water supply is also a concern in many countries in the world, leading to interruptions, rationing, and recurring water shortages. It is not uncommon for cities to ration water in the middle of a drought period, on some occasions reducing the availability of water to a few hours a day or a few days a week. As populations in cities increase, the infrastructure delivering water to the cities is often overtaxed, which can lead to potentially catastrophic problems, especially in cities with aging infrastructures. For example, New York City gets most of its water from reservoirs 125 miles away, and it is delivered by two tunnels that were built in 1917 and 1937. Neither of these tunnels has ever been shut down for repairs, as the city would not be able to function without the water they deliver. A new water tunnel is currently under construction and is scheduled to start operating in 2014.[82] Many cities have leaky pipes and lose a portion of their supply to those leaks; the city of Manila, in the Philippines, estimates it loses half of its water production through leaks and illegal siphoning of the water.[83]

The quality of the water is also a concern: in many cities, the water delivery infrastructure is not well protected, leaving a strong possibility of bacterial contamination, and forcing users to boil the water before they use it. This procedure is a common recommendation given by international travelers. The World Bank estimates that no more than 80 percent of the rural world population and that 95 percent of urban dwellers have "reasonable access" to clean water, defined as access to within one kilometer (0.62 miles) of the house.[84] For most people, that is a considerable distance.

On the other end, the infrastructure designed to remove used water is also critical. Many countries have inadequate or overburdened sewer treatment facilities, resulting in the pollution of water tables and adjacent bodies of water, or problems with sewer backups at times of heavy rains, even in developed countries.[85] While less critical than water availability to the proper operation of a warehouse or distribution center, sewer service is still important as it can be a nuisance to have employees deal with stench or frequent cleanups. The World Bank estimates that less than 60 percent of the world population has access to adequate sanitation.[86]

Similar observations can be made about refuse removal, a service generally provided by the municipalities, but which can be unreliable; strikes of municipal workers can take several days, during which no pickup is conducted, resulting in a problem in the operation of any type of business.

3.4.3 Energy Pipelines

The infrastructure of access to energy is also of importance. As most of the easily accessible oil and gas fields are near the end of their life expectancies, energy resources now come from remote areas that are difficult to operate and from where it is difficult to ship. Building energy pipelines from those areas is a challenge, and the obstacles include the weather, natural barriers, political issues, environmental challenges, and bickering between the oil companies and the governments of the countries in which they were building.

Nevertheless, the infrastructure of pipelines is growing and allows an ever-greater percentage of the energy needs of the world to no longer be transported by ships, trucks, and railroads.

3.5 Services Infrastructure

In addition to a transportation, communication, and utilities infrastructure, businesses need a commercial support services infrastructure to operate efficiently.

3.5.1 Banking Infrastructure

The banking infrastructure allows businesses to transfer funds, obtain foreign currency, move documents both domestically and internationally, and process consumer payments efficiently. This requires a network of bank branches and well-trained employees in multiple countries. In most parts of the world, the banking infrastructure is dominated by domestic banks, with no easy access to international banks. The only exceptions are in large metropolitan areas, such as New York, Tokyo, or Paris, and in large financial centers, such as Hong Kong SAR, London, or Singapore, where most multinational banks have offices.

Since the beginning of the twenty-first century, though, this traditional model has changed, mostly under the initial impetus of one bank, HSBC, that has tried to open branches in many smaller business centers, beyond the capital cities of most countries. The traditional model of international banks had been to be present in large cities only, and develop a network of correspondent banks to serve their international customers in smaller cities. Several other banks have now followed HSBC's lead, and it is not unusual to find multiple international banks in a medium-sized city. This is a very nice development for international logisticians, as they need this infrastructure to process foreign-currency payments and handle the documents linked to an international transaction.

3.5.2 Logistics Support Infrastructure

In addition to banking services, international logisticians need to have easy access to professionals in several fields: freight forwarders, couriers, carriers, delivery services, packing services, order fulfillment centers, and other third-party logistics service providers, are critical to the smooth operations of an international logistics department. The success of a logistics cluster is due primarily to the existence of a number of different services that can support a company involved in international trade, so that it can find those services quickly and at competitive prices.

Yossi Sheffi makes that point abundantly clear; the reason that many companies settled in the PLAZA—*Plataforma Logística de Zaragoza*—logistical cluster in Spain is because there was a conscious effort on the part of its owner, the Aragon Region government, to provide all sorts of logistical support services in one area. The park now covers 1,200 hectares (3,000 acres), and is expanding.[87]

3.6 Legal and Regulatory Infrastructure

3.6.1 Court Infrastructure

The court infrastructure of a country allows businesses to settle disputes quickly and fairly. This must include not only an efficient court system, but also a network of mediators and arbitrators, a number of competent lawyers, and the existence of clear jurisprudence. In many countries, if not most, the court infrastructure is slow, cumbersome and inefficient.

The World Bank publishes a *Doing Business* database, that list the number of days that it takes to resolve a contract dispute in the court system of all countries in the world, as well as the costs of resolving that dispute and the number of procedural steps that must be taken. The range is considerable. Whereas the average contract dispute takes 150 days to be resolved in the courts of Singapore, it takes an average of 510 days in OECD countries, and as many as 1,420 days in India. The costs also vary dramatically. The average cost of resolving a contractual dispute in the lowest-cost country, Iceland, is 8 percent of the disputed amount. For the OECD, the average is 20 percent. For the highest-cost country, the costs can exceed the amount of the dispute.[88]

When the court system is not operating efficiently, businesses turn to mediators and arbitrators to resolve their disputes. It is much more difficult to find aggregate information on the effectiveness of arbitration. However, most arbitrators and mediators are operating in multiple countries, unaffected by the local situation.

3.6.2 Intellectual Property Infrastructure

The intellectual-property infrastructure allows businesses to protect their intellectual property (copyrights, patents, and trademarks) with law enforcement services intent on enforcing intellectual property laws. In most developed countries, there is an effective way to deal with intellectual property, but in some newly industrialized countries, that is not the case. Most notorious are Nigeria and India, where intellectual property is frequently not respected, and where law enforcement officials and the court system do not enforce the rights of the intellectual-property owners.[89]

In many countries, there have been considerable efforts to attempt to protect international intellectual-property rights, but it is still a major issue. Partially, there is a priority aspect to this problem; countries in which there is widespread poverty or substantial economic inequalities, or crime, are not going to allocate resources to a problem that is perceived as not urgent. However, there is also a cultural aspect that hinders the resolution of these issues; it is politically difficult to favor a large foreign corporation over a local small-business owner who is struggling to make ends meet and whose customers want an affordable alternative to the foreign company's product.

It is likely that intellectual-property issues will be eventually resolved. The matter is always part of the negotiations when heads of state meet, and it has very high visibility. The current situation abroad is actually fairly similar to the situation in which high-income countries were in the 1980s and 1990s, with widespread copying of software, music, and movies. As intellectual-property companies became aggressive in the defense of these rights, the problem slowly abated.

3.6.3 Standards Infrastructure

The standard infrastructure allows businesses to determine the requirements that their products and operations must meet in order to be successful in a particular market. This includes safety, design, and performance standards. For a company involved in multiple countries, the preference is always for a unified national standard that is clear and widely available. It is much more difficult to sell a product when a country has multiple regional standards, or when the standards are not delineated clearly.

In terms of standards, the United States often stands at odds with the remainder of the world. Not only is the country still operating on a non-metric system, but it often has multiple standards that are state specific. This characteristic makes it one of the more challenging markets for a company trying to penetrate the U.S. market. However, it also makes it difficult for U.S. exporters, as they have to adapt to an unfamiliar environment.

Review and Discussion Questions

1. What are the main elements of the maritime transportation infrastructure? How would the quality and dependability of the maritime transportation infrastructure affect an international shipment?

2. What are the main elements of the air transportation infrastructure? How would the quality and dependability of the air transportation infrastructure affect an international shipment?

3. What are the main elements of the land transportation and warehousing infrastructure? How would the quality and dependability of these infrastructures affect an international shipment?

4. What are the main elements of the communication and utilities infrastructure? How would the quality and dependability of these infrastructures affect an international shipment?

Notes

[1] American Heritage Dictionary, Fifth Edition, 2012, Houghton-Mifflin Company, Boston, Massachusetts.

[2] Oxford English Dictionary, online edition, http://www.oed.com, March 4, 2013.

[3] Merriam-Webster Dictionary, http://www.merriam-webster.com/ dictionary/ infrastructure, March 4, 2013.

[4] "Cellular Fleet at 1st May 2013," Alphaliner, http://www.alphaliner.com/, retrieved June 1, 2013.

[5] "Cellular Fleet Forecast," Alphaliner, http://www.alphaliner.com/, retrieved June 1, 2013.

[6] Dupin, Chris, "Stretched: Ports, Terminals Prepare for Challenges from Bigger Ships, Expanding Alliances," *American Shipper*, May 2013, pp.42-46.

[7] Lipton, Eric, "Beneath the Harbor, it's Dig or Else," *The New York Times*, November 23, 2004.

[8] Whitman, Reg, "The Port of Prince Rupert—North America's Jewel of the Northwest," *Logistics Quarterly*, 14:5, 2008, pp. 48-49.

[9] Leach, Peter, "A bridge too low," *The Journal of Commerce*, June 5, 2006, pp. 30-31.

[10] Port of Marsaxlokk, Association of Ship Agents, /http://www.malta shipagents.org/port-of-marsaxlokk, retrieved May 31, 2013.

[11] Machalaba, Daniel, "Maersk is Ready to Start on Giant Port," *The Wall Street Journal*, June 5, 2000, p. A4.

[12] Ying, Wang, "Third Phase of Yangshan Port completed," *China Daily*, December 5, 2008.

[13] "Western Ports Disappear from top 10 Container Ports List," February 21, 2013, *Daily Cargo News*, http://www.daily-cargo.com/english/2013/0221/, retrieved July 7, 2013.

[14] Zhang, Lilian, "Further 20-billion yuan expansion of Yangshan port in pipeline," *South China Morning Post*, April 4, 2012.

[15] "Western Ports Disappear from top 10 Container Ports List," February 21, 2013, *Daily Cargo News*, http://www.daily-cargo.com/english/-

2013/0221/, retrieved July 7, 2013.

[16] Mongelluzzo, Bill, "With Cranes, Size is Everything," *The Journal of Commerce*, December 31, 1996, p. 1B.

[17] Bonney, Joseph, "Cranes to Work from Both Sides," *The Journal of Commerce*, August 25, 1999, p. 1.

[18] *Ports of the World*, Fifteenth Edition, Cigna Insurance Corporation, available from Publisher, Ports of the World, Cigna Insurance Companies, P.O. Box 7716, Philadelphia, Pennsylvania 19192, USA.

[19] http://www.worldportsource.com, March 10, 2013

[20] Mongelluzzo, Bill, "Extending Terminal Hours," *The Journal of Commerce*, March 5, 1997, p. 1B.

[21] "How successful is the effort to expand the hours of operations at Port shipping terminals?," FAQ page, The Port of Long Beach, http:// www.polb.com/contact/qc.asp/#474, May 18, 2009.

[22] Davies, John, "Slow Passage to Progress," *International Business*, December 1996-January 1997, pp. 14-17.

[23] Casper, Bill, "The 30-Container-per-Hour barrier," *Cargo Business News*, August 2008, pp. 24-25.

[24] Oster, Shai, "China's Boom Snarls Traffic in 60-mile Jam," *The Wall Street Journal*, August 25, 2010, p. A7.

[25] McCue, Dan, "Infrastructure can slow Emerging Markets," *World Trade*, April 2013, pp. 32-39.

[26] Fortner, Brian, "The Train Lane," *Civil Engineering*, 72(9), September 2002, pp.52-61.

[27] Beatty, Andrew, "Work stars on biggest-ever Panama canal overhaul," Reuters, September 4, 2007.

[28] Reagan, Brad, "The Panama Canal's Ultimate Upgrade," *Popular Mechanics*, February 2007, pp. 63-68.

[29] Bussey, John, "Ripples Likely from Wider Canal," *The Wall Street Journal*, November 11, 2011, p. B1.

[30] Moore, Molly, "Is the Bosporus Taking On More Than It Can Handle?," *The International Herald Tribune*, November 17, 2000, p. 2.

[31] O'Byrne, David, "Increased Trade adds to Strains on Creaking Infrastructure," *The Financial Times*, December 7, 2010, p. 4.

[32] Champion, Marc, "Turkey Plans Own 'Panama Canal'," *The Wall Street Journal*, April 28, 2011, p.A12.

[33] Suez Canal Toll Calculator, Leth Agencies, http://www.lethagencies.com/calculator.asp?Port=SUEZTREG, retrieved June 2, 2013.

[34] Prince, Theodore, "Panama Canal: Expansion: Game Changer or More of the Same?", *Supply Chain Quarterly*, Quarter 1, 2012, pp.32-44.

[35] Kulisch, Eric, "Panama Canal: Myths and Misconceptions," *American Shipper*, May 2012, pp.48-54.

[36] Urquhart, John, "U.S., Canada Try to Revive Once-Grand Waterway," *The Wall Street Journal*, March 12, 1998, p. A14.

[37] Tobar, Hector and Kris Kraul, "Rival to Panama Canal Planned," *Los Angeles Times*, September 30, 2006, p. C1.

[38] Rogers, Tim, "Is Russia eyeing Dry Canal?", *Nicaragua Dispatch*, February 6, 2012, http://www.nicaraguadispatch.com/news/2012/02/will-russia-get-the-trains-rolling-again/2084, retrieved June 4, 2013.

[39] Thapa, Rajesh B., M. Kusanagi, A. Kitazumi and Y. Murayama, "Sea Navigation, Challenges and Potentials in South East Asia: an Assessment of Suitable Sites for a Shipping Canal in the South Thai Isthmus." *GeoJournal*, 70, October 2007, pp. 161-172.

[40] Kim, Lucian, "Danube Trade Blocked by Bridges," *Christian Science Monitor*, October 6, 1999, p. 6.

[41] "Cargo Traffic for past 12 months," Airport Council International, January 2013, http://www.aci.aero/Data-Centre/Monthly-Traffic-Data/Freight-Summary/12-months, retrieved June 5, 2013.

[42] Bangsberg, P.T., "One-track mind," *Journal of Commerce*, May 31-June 6, 2004, pp. 46A-50A.

[43] "Runway extension at Narita finally opens," *Japan Times,*, October 23, 2009, http://www.japantimes.co.jp/news/2009/10/23/news/runway-extension-at-narita-finally-opens/#.Uc1_Ntjxn4s, retrieved June 28, 2013.

[44] Conway, Peter, "Taking the High Road," *Air Cargo World*, January 2000, pp. 62Ű67.

[45] "Airport Traffic Reports," Airports Council International-North America, http://www.aci-na.org/content/airport-traffic-reports, retrieved June 5, 2013.

[46] "Three Routes Lead to Iberia," *SBB Cargo*, http://www.sbbcargo.ch/en/index/sbbcargo_magazine/00_03/03_00_1.html, March 15, 2001.

[47] Fu, Bill, Brooks Bentz, and Mark McCalla, "Logistics in China: Thinking Ahead," *Logistics Management*, October 2011, pp. 36-40.

[48] Frentzel, David, "The Bright side of Logistics in India," *Inbound Logistics*, September 2011, pp.87-91.

[49] "The European Rail Network for Competitive Freight," European Commission, http://ec.europa.eu/transport/modes/rail/infrastructures/rail_freight_oriented_network_en.htm, retrieved June 5, 2013.

[50] Nakagawa, Hitoki and Tomoyoshi Isogawa, "Asia-Pacific cargo hitching rides on Trans-Siberian Railway," *The Asahi Shimbum*, August 20, 2012, http://ajw.asahi.com/article/economy/business/AJ2012082027, retrieved March 27, 2013.

[51] O'Byrne, David, "Increased Trade adds to Strains on Creaking Infrastructure," *The Financial Times*, December 7, 2010, p. 4.

[52] Schuetze, Christopher, "Deciding the Future of the Arctic," *The New York Times*, May 20, 2013.

[53] Blakely, Alexander, "The place without Roads; Russia paves the Trans-Siberian Gap," *Harper's*, December 2003, pp. 57-63.

[54] Country Commercial Guides, U.S. Department of Commerce, http://www.state.gov/e/eb/rls/rpts/ccg/, retrieved June 8, 2013.

[55] *World Factbook*, Central Intelligence Agency, https://www.cia.gov/library/publications/the-world-factbook/, retrieved June 8, 2013.

[56] Argentina, *World Factbook*, Central Intelligence Agency, https://www.cia.gov/library/publications/the-world-factbook/geos/ar.html, retrieved June 8, 2013.

[57] United States, *World Factbook*, https://www.cia.gov/library/publications/the-world-factbook/geos/us.html, retrieved June 8, 2013.

[58] Feller, Gordon, "For Truckers, Polish Roads are a Deep, Dark Pothole on Route Linking EU

NOTES

and Russia," *Traffic World*, September 8, 1998, p. 18.

[59] Bajaj, Vikas, "A High-Tech Titan Plagued by Potholes," *The New York Times*, August 26, 2010, p.B1.

[60] Fu, Bill, Brooks Bentz, and Mark McCalla, "Logistics in China: Thinking Ahead," *Logistics Management*, October 2011, pp. 36-40.

[61] Hessman, Travis, "Can the U.S. Revitalize its Infrastructure?", *Industry Week*, June 2012, pp.24-28.

[62] Schultz, John, "Man on the Move," *Logistics Management*, November 2011, pp.24-28.

[63] Millman, Joel, Zusha Elinson, and Jim Carlton, "One Link Proves a Bridge's Undoing," *The Wall Street Journal*, May 25-26, 2013, p. A3.

[64] Zubrzycki, John, "In City of Joy, Foot-Power Loses Pull with Rickshaw Ban," *The Christian Science Monitor*, December 11, 1996, p. 1.

[65] Marquand, Robert, "Driving in Delhi: Chaos of Cars, Carts and Cows," *The Journal of Commerce*, August 18, 1999, p. 1.

[66] Morris, Nigel, "The Big Question: Has the Congestion Charge been effective in reducing London's Traffic?," *The Independent*, February 13, 2008.

[67] Dillon, Sam, "Can't Find Juárez Street? There are Hundreds!", *The New York Times*, January 12, 2000.

[68] Faison, Seth, "Palm Trees and Sun (and Who Needs an Address)," *The New York Times*, February 23, 1999.

[69] Sciolino, Elaine, "A Soaring Bridge puts an Ancien Town on the Map," *The New York Times*, July 17, 2005.

[70] Davey, Monica, and Ian Austen, "Detroit-to-Canada Bridge to be Unveiled," *The New York Times*, June 14, 2012.

[71] "Michigan Vote Means new Canadian-Financed Detroit-Windsor Bridge one Step Closer," *National Post*, November 7, 2012.

[72] Anonymous, "The Koror-Babeldaob Bridge," *Wikipedia*, http://en.wikipedia.org/wiki/Koror-Babeldaob_Bridge, May 20, 2009.

[73] Al-Khalifa, Abdulrahman, "The Use of Hawala as a Remittance System," traccc.gmu.edu/pdfs/student_research/Hawala_AR.pdf, retrieved June 3, 2013.

[74] Cuevas-Mohr, Hugo, "An Introduction to Understanding The Gray Market Real Exchange in Brazil," International Money Transfer Conference, January 15, 2012.

[75] Ransdell, Eric, "Rolling Out the Future," *U.S. News & World Report*, August 12, 1996, pp. 47-48.

[76] *World Factbook*, Central Intelligence Agency, https://www.cia.gov/library/publications/the-world-factbook/, retrieved June 8, 2013.

[77] *World Factbook*, Central Intelligence Agency, https://www.cia.gov/library/publications/the-world-factbook/, retrieved June 8, 2013.

[78] Moore, Solomon, "Ships Sever Data Cables, Cutting East Africa Links," *The Wall Street Journal*, February 28, 2012, p. B3.

[79] Stephenson, Neal, "Mother Earth, Mother Board," *Wired*, December 1996, pp. 97-160.

[80] The World Bank, "Fixed broadband Internet subscribers," http://data.worldbank.org/indicator/IT.NET.BBND.P2/countries?display=default, retrieved June 9, 2013.

[81] Dugger, Celia W., "India Tries to Plug a Cash Drain: Its Power System," *The New York Times*, February 6, 2000.

[82] Fernandez, Manny, "For Water Tunnels, Age is Just a Number," *The New York Times*, January 14, 2011.

[83] Bangsberg, P.T., "Making a Splash," *The Journal of Commerce*, January 24, 1997, p.3A.

[84] The World Bank, "Improved water source, urban" and "Improved water source, rural," http://data.worldbank.org/indicator/SH.H2O.SAFE.UR.ZS/countries?display=default, retrieved June 9, 2013.

[85] Schwirtz, Michael, "Report Cites Large Release of Sewage From Hurricane Sandy," *The New York Times*, April 30, 2013.

[86] The World Bank, "Fixed Broadband Internet Subscribers," http://data.worldbank.org/indicator/SH.H2O.SAFE.UR.ZS/countries?display=default, retrieved June 9, 2013.

[87] Sheffi, Yossi, *Logistics Clusters: Delivering Value and Driving Growth*, MIT Press, Cambridge, Massachusetts, 2012.

[88] "Enforcing Contracts," The World Bank, http://www.doingbusiness.org/data/exploretopics/enforcing-contracts, retrieved June 9, 2013.

[89] Wong, Edward, and Didi Kirsten Tatlow, "China Seen in Push to Gain Technology Insights," *The New York Times*, June 5, 2013.

Chapter 4

International Methods of Entry

4.1	Entry Strategy Factors	91
4.2	Indirect Exporting	92
4.3	Active Exporting	96
4.4	Production Abroad	103
4.5	Parallel Imports	111
4.6	Counterfeit Goods	113
4.7	Other Issues in Methods of Entry	113

The first venture of most firms in the international arena is usually more the result of serendipity than of careful planning and thoughtful strategic thinking. The first few sales abroad emerge from a chance contact made at a trade show, an unexpected fax sent after a prospect viewed a domestic sales brochure, or a sales inquiry resulting from an ad in a trade magazine. After a few of these haphazard transactions, the firm then realizes that there may be a substantial market—at least large enough to warrant further consideration—for its products outside their original domestic market, and management starts considering selling on a more systematic basis abroad. The pitfalls usually start at this point. Firms need to assess correctly the market's characteristics, its potential, and, particularly, the advantages and disadvantages of a given method of entry, and must base their entry strategy on a basis other than a chance encounter at a trade show with a foreign agent or a distributor, or enter a joint venture with a partner met through casual business acquaintances. Countless headaches can be avoided if the correct strategy is determined early on, using as many pieces of information as possible.

4.1 Entry Strategy Factors

There are many factors that will influence a company's entry strategy into a foreign market. Some of these factors are related to the characteristics of the market that the firm is targeting, and others are related to the characteristics of the product and of the exporter.

Specifically, the exporter should analyze carefully the following determinant factors:

- **The size of the market.** While there is no easy rule, the method of entry is different for a market in which combined sales amount to € 10,000,000 (U.S. $13,000,000) per year and a market that exhibits sales in billions of euros.

- **The growth of the market.** A stable market, growing at a moderate rate, will call for a different entry strategy than one in which there is a substantial potential for growth.

- **The potential market share of the exporter.** A market in which the exporter can become a major player will call for a different strategy than one in which the exporter has no chance of being much more than a niche player.

- **The type of product.** Products with technology and a need for after-sale service and parts will require a different entry strategy than a disposable consumer good.

- **The market strategy of the firm.** Although self-evident, a firm whose strategy is to provide a top-of-the-line product will have a different entry strategy than a firm that has chosen to be the lowest cost provider.

- **The willingness of the firm to get involved.** Firms that actively want to develop foreign markets should have a different entry strategy than firms that believe that their domestic market is their primary concern and consider foreign sales as "bothersome."

- **The characteristics of the country considered.** The level of development, the infrastructure of the country, the business sophistication of potential trade partners, the overall climate under which business is conducted, the culture of the market, and the culture of customers should all be considered in the decision of an entry strategy.

- **The time horizon considered.** Products that have a short life cycle, or products that are likely to generate a lot of "me-too" competitors, demand a different entry strategy than products that are patent protected or are likely to have a long life cycle or engender a long line of complementary products.

Only after all of these factors are evaluated is it possible for a firm to decide appropriately which market entry strategy to pursue. Overall, great caution should be exercised in decisions regarding entry strategies: among all the decisions made by marketers regarding the marketing mix, the distribution decision is the one with the longest time horizon, and the least likely to be quickly adjusted. Not that product, promotion, and price can be easily adjusted, but a distribution change can be quite an undertaking, leading to ill feelings and trauma, and therefore the need for a correct initial decision is yet more critical.

The alternative entry strategies available to a casual exporter will be presented first, followed by those alternatives available to an active exporter, and then the strategies available to a company willing to manufacture abroad.

4.2 Indirect Exporting

Some firms are unwilling exporters in that they prefer to concentrate on their domestic markets and consider any foreign inquiry as a difficult sale. As such, they do not like to handle them. Under this banner of indirect exporting, several alternatives are possible, from the lowest level of involvement to some very moderate interest.

4.2.1 Export Trading Company (ETC)

In the case where a company is unwilling to undertake any of the activities of marketing abroad, the use of an export trading company is the simplest solution. An export trading company (ETC) is an intermediary that will purchase the goods in the exporting country and resell them to a customer in a foreign country.

export trading company A company that purchases goods in one country for the purpose of reselling them in another country at a profit.

The dominant ETCs are very large firms, with local offices in numerous countries. The trading companies operate in the following fashion: they take title to the goods in the exporting country, making this transaction a domestic transaction for the exporter, and transfer title to the importer in the importing country, making that transaction a domestic transaction as well. As far as either of the parties dealing with the trading company is concerned, the product is seemingly handled by a domestic company, its foreign origin is not a concern for the buyer, and its sale abroad is not an issue for the seller.

Trading companies were first created in the Netherlands, France, and Britain for trade with India and Indochina. As these trade routes disappeared, new trading companies were founded in Spain and Portugal for commerce with South America; eventually these trade routes also disappeared in the late nineteenth century. In the twentieth century, trading companies were resurrected in Japan to handle Japan's exporting efforts after World War II. These so-called *sogo shosha* have come to mightily dominate the export trading business: Mitsubishi, Mitsui, Itochu, Marubeni, and Sumitomo. All have sales in the trillions of yen, and trade in all sorts of goods. Mitsui claims to be involved from "noodles to missiles." Because of their presence in all countries of the world, these trading companies have acquired a wealth of information on potential sellers and buyers, and they leverage this knowledge into sales. They contact sellers when they are aware of a buyer in some foreign country, and contact buyers when they become aware of a particularly motivated seller. In addition, these trading companies have come to offer a complete package of international logistical services; they ship, insure, and finance international trade, and, in some cases, sophisticated traders rely on their services for complex transactions rather than handle them themselves: their expertise in handling international transactions is unmatched.

sogo sosha The Japanese term for a trading company.

Other ETCs are in existence, but they tend to specialize in one geographical area or one product line. However, they still offer the breadth of services that a *sogo shosha* can make available to an exporter; in particular, they take title to the goods in the exporting country. In the United States, since the passage of the Export Trading Companies Act in 1982, a number of firms have been created, all operating on this smaller scale. The United States has also created ETC cooperatives that allow trade associations to offer export services to competing companies. Most of these ETC cooperatives are involved in exports of agricultural goods.[1]

The use of an ETC makes great sense for the novice exporter or the company unwilling or unable to dabble in the complexities of an occasional international transaction. However, should the company decide to become more involved in the long run, choosing an ETC is a poor strategy, as the customers abroad are not the customers of the exporter but those of the ETC, and may not be known to the exporter. It is unlikely that the ETC will relinquish this information readily if it is no longer profiting from its efforts at developing the market for the exporter's products; it is equally unlikely that the exporter could benefit from the goodwill created by the ETC with its foreign customers as well.

4.2.2 Export Management Corporation (EMC)

export management corporation
A company that puts suppliers in touch with potential buyers, and earns a commission if a sale is completed.

Despite the similarity in name, an export management corporation (EMC) is an altogether different type of intermediary. An EMC is typically located in the exporting country and is operating as an export-oriented manufacturer's representative for the exporter. It does not take title to the goods but earns a commission on the sale.

Most EMCs are small firms, typically with fewer than fifteen employees. The firms rarely have an office abroad, although they do have contacts with a large number of potential importers, and regularly send employees—or, more likely, the owner of the agency—abroad to visit customers and actively attend trade shows and other promotional activities. EMCs tend to restrict their sales efforts to potential customers in one country and often specialize in selling one line of products in that country. Most of them represent more than one manufacturer abroad, usually in complementary lines.[2]

agent
The overseas representative of a manufacturer. The agent represents the manufacturer in sales negotiations.

Because an EMC acts as an agent, the exporter is slightly more involved in the foreign sale than with an ETC; for example, the exporter is responsible for shipping the goods, invoicing the importer, and collecting from it. The degree to which the EMC helps the exporter depends on the relationship they have established with each other and the level of sophistication of the exporter. In general, an EMC helps a lot rather than a little: it acts as the export department of the seller, handling every detail of the transaction, from freight forwarding to insurance and from invoicing to collection. The compensation of the EMC therefore varies in function of its involvement: it either earns a higher commission for handling all of the details of the sale or earns a commission on the sale and fixed fees for the remainder of its efforts. The range of alternative arrangements is such that it is difficult to generalize.

The use of an EMC makes great sense for the novice exporter; by working with an EMC, and by at least partially managing its foreign accounts, a firm gains substantial insights, which would become quite valuable should the company decide to become further involved in export sales. In practice, though, because the EMC is a small firm and has valuable contacts abroad, it is often absorbed—at least partially—and transformed into the export department of the exporter. This allows the firm to capitalize on the talent of the personnel of the EMC and the goodwill it generated abroad.

African Export Ventures

In a few areas in sub-Saharan Africa, local EMCs, such as Getrade and Fritete African Art Works in Ghana, are spurring the development of an export-led economy. They established contacts with importers in the United States and negotiated large purchases of local African artifacts for such companies as Pier 1 Imports, Cost Plus, and Body Shop International.

However, none of the local companies had the capacity to handle such large orders, so the EMCs coordinated the efforts of hundreds of small artisans and, after some initial difficulties, were able to procure most of the orders placed by the U.S. firms. As the artisans realized the profitability of such export sales, they started accepting orders for artifacts that were nontraditional in their colors or shapes, to accommodate the customers' requests, creating a perfect example of international marketing.[3]

In addition, as most small businesses in sub-Saharan Africa suffer from a lack of capitalization, the EMCs also brought in "micro-lenders," charitable organizations that will make very small loans (U.S. $500 to $3,000) to help entrepreneurs purchase machinery or obtain working capital. As these loans allow businesses to grow, it is expected that a business infrastructure will grow, allowing greater access to financing and triggering further business development. Such micro-lending efforts, pioneered by Muhammad Yunus when he created the Grameem Bank (literally translated as "rural bank" from his native Bengali), have lifted many local economies out of abject poverty. His efforts earned him the Nobel Prize in Economics in 2006.[4]

In addition, the United States African Growth and Opportunity Act (AGOA), passed in 2000 and renewed in 2004, allows duty-free access to the U.S. market for goods made in most sub-Saharan African countries, creating additional export growth opportunities for entrepreneurs in that part of the world.[5]

4.2.3 Piggy-Backing

A third alternative choice exists for a reluctant exporter: it is called piggy-backing and can refer to one of two possible situations:

1. A customer of a firm enters a foreign market by setting up a manufacturing facility. The customer tells its suppliers that they will need to supply parts for assembly and spare parts for customer service. The suppliers therefore end up selling their product abroad, piggy-backing on the strategy of an existing customer. In some cases, the suppliers develop their own independent sales in that market. This piggy-backing also happens with franchised businesses, which require that the equipment of the franchises they establish overseas be equipped with exactly the same machinery and utilize the same supplies worldwide.

2. A successful exporter involves one of its suppliers—or a company that makes a complementary product—in the markets that this exporter has developed. This form of piggy-backing is sometimes referred to as collaborative exporting; nevertheless, there is certainly an imbalance in the ability of the two partners, with one particularly competent and the other a novice.

piggy-backing
When a manufacturer goes overseas and asks its suppliers to continue doing business abroad with him, the suppliers are said to be *piggy backing* on that customer's efforts.

Piggy-backing can sometimes be seen as a passive arrangement (triggered by another firm), at which point it is difficult to call it a strategy. Nevertheless, should the opportunity present itself, it makes perfect sense for a company to seize it and acquire some knowledge about selling abroad (see Figure 4-1). If piggy-backing is initiated by a firm eager to develop its own sales in foreign markets, it is quite an appropriate strategy, as the experience gained from the experienced exporter can eventually develop into a solid export strategy with the use of agents, distributors, or even sales subsidiaries.

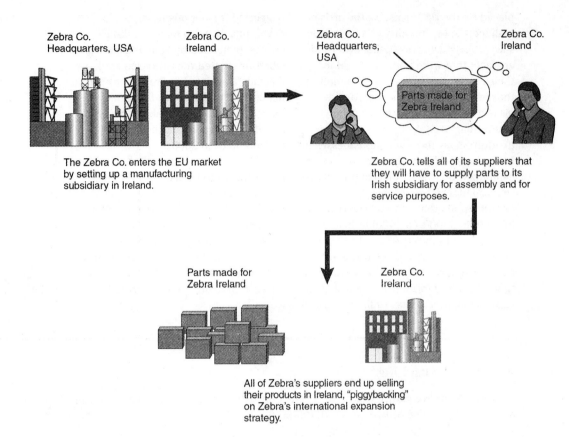

Figure 4.1: Piggy-backing

4.3 Active Exporting

Once a firm realizes that it wants to exploit the possibilities that sales abroad can bring and decides to become involved in export activities, a number of alternatives open up. Several alternatives are possible, differing not only in the level of involvement of the exporter, but also in the strategies pursued by the exporter.[6]

4.3.1 Agent

agent
The overseas representative of a manufacturer. The agent represents the manufacturer in sales negotiations.

principal
The manufacturer represented by an agent.

An agent is usually a small firm or an individual located in the importing country who acts as a manufacturer's representative for the exporter. The agent sells the manufacturer's products to customers in the importing country, using the terms of sale—price, delivery, discounts—determined by the exporter. An agent does do not buy product, but arranges sales directly from the principal to the customers. For this work, an agent is paid a commission, calculated as a percentage of the sale price of the product to the customer, and collected after the customer has paid the principal.

An agent often has several principals and generally sells a group of complementary products rather than products that compete directly with one another. The agent will handle all of the sales functions for the exporter, from the initial prospect-

4.3 Active Exporting

ing for customers to the close. The agent is usually given varying support by the exporter: some exporters provide only the bare minimum of a sales brochure and a price list, while the more experienced exporters provide training on the product's characteristics, analysis on the competitors' products, information on the sales and service philosophy of the company, sales support in the form of samples, catalogs (translated or adapted), trade advertising, and financial support to attend trade shows, technical visits by corporate engineers, participation in sales incentive programs, and so on.

Agents, as a whole, like to keep control over their schedule and over their sales approach, but the exporter's support of their efforts is critical to their success and to the extent to which they expend a lot of effort selling the exporter's product. In particular, requests for quotes and *pro forma* invoices should be handled quite promptly, and negotiations on price and delivery done diligently, so as to not delay the agent's sales efforts; time differences sometimes exacerbate the perception of a lack of responsiveness on the part of the exporter.

Sometimes, there is the suggestion that, given a set of guidelines, the agent could be trusted to reach decisions and negotiate with the customer on critical aspects of the sale: price, delivery, terms of trade (see Chapter 6), terms of sale (see Chapter 7), and collection. However, it is critical that all such negotiations be handled by the principal, with the agent acting as an intermediary between the exporter and the importer. If the agent is allowed to negotiate directly with the importer, then the agent is considered by a large number of countries' governments as a binding agent, and the exporter is considered to have a permanent establishment in the country of import. This determination has significant taxation implications; the profits realized on the sales made in that country are now considered taxable by the country of import. If there is no permanent establishment, the profits are not taxable in the country of import, although they are obviously taxable in the country of export.

binding agent An agent who is allowed to make decisions that are binding on the principal. The principal must abide by whatever statements the agent has made.

permanent establishment A fixed place of business abroad that subjects the exporter to tax liability in the importing country.

After the sale is concluded between the agent and the importer, all of the other aspects of the transaction, from the *pro forma* invoice to the actual collection of payment, from packaging to shipping the goods, are handled directly and solely by the exporter. Finally, the agent does not get paid until after the exporter has been paid by the importer.

The choice of an agent should obviously be made on a large number of criteria: its ability to represent the exporter and its product accurately, its ability to sell, its contacts, its knowledge of the industry that the exporter wants to target, the compatibility of its objectives with those of the exporter, and so on. Moreover, the choice of an agent is a long-term commitment; although the contract is often based on one-year increments, the duration of an effective relationship between an exporter and its agents is much longer.

There are several alternative routes to finding agents in foreign countries; among the most commonly used methods are contacts made at trade shows, participations in trade missions, inquiries with the commercial attachés of the exporter's country's consulates, and contacts with other successful exporters.

The use of an agent is generally driven by several factors, one or more of which can be enough to trigger this strategic decision:

1. When the firm estimates that its potential sales in that market are small (perhaps no more than 5 or 10 percent of its domestic sales), with moderate or no growth potential

2. When the product is not a stock item, but a product specifically designed and made for a particular customer

3. When the product is a very expensive item, such as operating machinery

4. When the company expects a short product life cycle

5. When the product does not require frequent after-sale service

6. When the exporter is unlikely to ever become one of the dominant players in the market and will remain a niche player

7. When the company is reasonably well equipped to handle export sales

8. When the company is not pursuing a top-of-the-line strategy and does not attempt to collect premium prices

9. When the company wants to keep a reasonable amount of control over its prices and delivery policies

4.3.2 Distributor

distributor
An overseas company that purchases a manufacturer's products with the goal of reselling them at a profit.

Another entry strategy is to use a firm located in the importing country—or, sometimes, in a neighboring country—that buys the goods from the exporter. Such an intermediary is called a distributor, that takes title to the goods, sells them, and earns a profit on the sales it makes. What characterizes a relationship with a distributor is that there are two sets of invoices: one set of international invoices between the exporter and the distributor, who is also the importer of record; and a set of domestic invoices between the distributor and its customers, who see these transactions as domestic sales of a foreign product. A distributor is therefore carrying inventory of the exporter's goods, and it also often carries inventory of spare parts and provides after-sale service. A distributor will carry complementary products but also may carry products that compete directly with those of the exporter.

A distributor is taking much more risk in its relationship with the exporter than does an agent, and experiences much higher costs. The distributor carries the traditional risks associated with inventory and invests a considerable sum of money in the inventory; should the goods not sell well, the distributor is saddled with the unsold or obsolete goods. In addition, it is traditional for a distributor to participate in the costs of advertising, trade show attendance, and so on. In exchange, the distributor has much more freedom in setting prices, negotiating terms with customers, and managing all matters not directly related to the exporter's trademarks or copyrights. However, there is a large number of exporting firms that attempt to limit these freedoms, specifically on price, in order to maintain a standard strategy from country to country and to eliminate or reduce "parallel imports" (see Section 4.5 on page 111).

A distributor should also be considered a long-term partner. Because it makes a substantial investment in inventory and in the training of its employees, the distributor considers itself involved for a long period of time, and great care should be taken in finding the right partner. The choice of a distributor should be made on a large number of criteria: its ability to represent the exporter and its product accurately, its ability to invest in the exporter's products, to sell them, and to provide after-sale service, as well as its employees, their contacts, its knowledge of the industry, the compatibility of its objectives with those of the exporter, and so on.

There are several alternative routes to identifying potential distributors in foreign countries; among the most commonly used methods are trade shows, trade missions, the commercial attachés of the exporter's country's consulates, and contacts with other successful exporters.

The use of a distributor is generally driven by several factors,[7] one or more of which can be enough to trigger this strategic decision:

1. When the firm estimates that the market is substantial (perhaps 20 or 25 percent of its domestic sales) or when it estimates that there is substantial growth potential

2. When the product is a stock item, and generally not tailored to the needs of a specific customer

3. When the product is a rather moderately priced item

4. When the company expects a fairly long product life cycle

5. When the product requires (frequent) after-sale service and/or maintenance parts

6. When the company estimates it will not become much more than a minor player in the market

7. When the company prefers to handle export sales with only one customer

8. When the company is not pursuing a prestige pricing strategy with premium prices and service

9. When the company is comfortable relinquishing control of its price and delivery terms.

4.3.3 Additional Issues in the Agent-Distributorship Decision

There are two other issues to consider when determining whether an agent or a distributor would be the most appropriate partner—both issues are legal in nature.

First, some countries will not allow agents at all, or will not allow agents to represent foreign manufacturers, or will mandate a physical after-sale service presence on the country's soil, all requirements that mandate the use of a distributor.

The second issue is more complicated: many governments make a substantive differentiation in the way agents and distributors are considered by their judicial systems. Most often, because agents tend to be individuals or very small firms, many countries have decided to place them under the protection of labor law, the code of laws that deals with the relationships between employers and employees (see Section 5.3.1 on page 125). In many countries, notably in Europe, labor law tends to be very restrictive in terms of what an employer can and cannot impose on an employee and, in those countries in which labor law applies to agents, what an exporter can and cannot require of an agent. For example, even though the principal-agent contract may call for a termination notice of thirty days and no compensation, labor law may call for a six-month notice and six-month loss-of-income compensation, overruling the terms of the contract. There are similar restrictions on the number of hours worked, the payment of taxes, the legal requirements of certifications, licenses, and so on.

labor law
A set of laws that govern relationships between employees and employers.

contract law
A set of laws that govern relationships established by contracts between two parties.

In contrast, distributors, because they tend to be larger and are assumed to be more sophisticated, are covered in almost all countries by contract law. Contract law is much less restrictive, and courts tend to render judgments based upon the terms of the contract; the only restrictions are limited to contracts that are obviously biased or coerced, a situation very unlikely to be observed if one of the International Chamber of Commerce model contracts or an equivalent is used.

There is another distinction that is often made between an agent and a distributor that presents some potential for misunderstandings; it is often said that a distributor has risks (it invests in inventory), whereas the agent does not. While it is a useful distinction, it is incomplete. It is correct to understand that the distributor has substantial financial risks, because it invests in inventory and is faced with the possibility of unsold inventory. However, the agent often has considerable risks as well. It invests time and effort in obtaining a sale for which it will not be compensated until after the product is delivered and paid. In some cases, especially if the product is custom-made for the importer, there may be a lag of several months between the sale and the receipt of the commission check.

4.3.4 Marketing Subsidiary

marketing subsidiary
An overseas firm owned by an exporter that is responsible for selling the exporter's products in a foreign market.

Finally, a firm may decide, rather than employ an agent or a distributor (over neither of which it has much control), to create its own sales or marketing subsidiary in a foreign country. A marketing subsidiary is a foreign office staffed by employees of the exporting firm who will sell its goods in the foreign market. A subsidiary is incorporated in the foreign market, so it is the importer of record as far as the foreign government is concerned, and the "export" takes place between two legal entities that are part of the same company, at a transfer price. Although transfer prices can sometimes create problems in the process of clearing Customs, the process is very smooth altogether, as the traditional concerns of payment, terms of sale, and terms of trade are eliminated. All sales made by the foreign subsidiary to its customers are domestic sales and therefore are simpler to manage. All profits earned in the importing country are taxable to the importing country's government.

The costs of a marketing subsidiary are higher, and a good portion of them are fixed: a building must be rented, an inventory built, and employees hired and trained before measurable sales can offset these expenses. This is in stark contrast with sales through an agent, which are variable-cost sales (the commission is paid only if the agent sells) or sales through a distributor, where that distributor is the one bearing the costs of establishing the business in the foreign market. These investments obviously also require a long-term commitment on the part of the exporting firm.

The choice of a sales or marketing subsidiary is made when the company wants to retain control over its sales in that country, usually when the company is faced with one or more of the following situations:

1. When the firm estimates that the market potential is considerable (more than 25 percent of its domestic sales) or when it estimates that there is very substantial growth potential or very substantial profits to be made

2. When the product is technology driven, with substantial intellectual property content

3. When the product is rather complicated to sell

4. When the company expects to be involved for the long run, with additional products to be introduced later on

5. When the product requires sophisticated after-sale service and/or maintenance parts

6. When the company expects to become one of the major players in the market

7. When the company is exacting premium prices from customers

8. When the company is uncomfortable relinquishing control of its products and prices.

4.3.5 Coordinating Direct Export Strategies

There are two types of factors included in the entry decision for an exporter: those factors that are market-driven and those that are company- or product-driven. Consequently, some firms elect to have a policy to always follow a strategy driven by their product line and always use a sales subsidiary or a distributor or an agent. However, some firms decide on a country-by-country basis which strategy is the most appropriate and juggle a combination of agents, distributors, and marketing subsidiaries. Each of these overall strategies has advantages and disadvantages.

When a company chooses to have the same entry strategy in all its export markets, it certainly simplifies the management of its exports and presents a unified front to its customers on all aspects of its marketing. In particular, if the firm uses agents or sales subsidiaries in all countries, its prices are bound to be well coordinated and its after-sale policies clearly controlled. If there are any discrepancies, they are known to the firm and can be clearly managed and understood. A firm choosing to use distributors in all of its markets can exercise the same level of control by using contracts that specify clearly which prices distributors are allowed to charge—a practice that is generally legal or, at least, tolerated—and which after-sale service they must provide. However, there are problems with this "fit-all" strategy, as inappropriate strategies may lead to a poor match with the market: a potentially very lucrative market may be given away to an agent, or a sales subsidiary may have to be established in a small market. Moreover, a firm may have to postpone entry into a lucrative market because of a lack of resources if it adheres to a strategy of building only subsidiaries.

When a firm chooses to have different entry strategies in different countries, or when it decides to sell through a series of independent distributors, the coordination of prices and after-sale service is more difficult to achieve, and the possibility of parallel imports (see Section 4.5 on page 111) looms. However, the most appropriate strategy is chosen for each country, and, generally, the greatest profits can be extracted from the foreign markets. For a firm, the decision to have a coordinated entry strategy is based on criteria that can be interpreted differently by different management teams.

However, there is one significant issue to consider once a choice has been made: the costs of changing from one entry strategy where an exporter uses agents or distributors to a strategy based upon sales subsidiaries can take a significant toll on all involved parties. The agents and distributors have generally invested a considerable amount of time, money, and talent into building a significant market for the exporter's products, for which they are rightfully compensated according to the terms

Appropriate Entry Strategy

	Agent	Distributor	Subsidiary
The company expects a short product life cycle	X	X	
The product is a stock item		X	X
The product is custom-made for customers	X		X
The product is an expensive capital-good item	X		X
The expected sales are modest	X	X	
The company pursues a top-of-the-line strategy			X
The product is moderately priced		X	X
The product requires after-sale service		X	X
The product has substantial intellectual-property content			X
The company expects to become a major player in the market			X
The company anticipates a small market share	X	X	

Table 4.1: Criteria for Active Exporting Choices

of the original contract. If they are very successful, the exporter is often tempted to recover these expenses (the commissions paid to the agents or the profit opportunities given to the distributor) by establishing a sales subsidiary. This change of strategy should be avoided as much as possible, as it is traumatic for all involved parties and often results in reduced sales and profits for several years. This is because the customers' loyalties usually lie more with the agent or the distributor than with the exporter, and regaining the customers' confidence can take considerable effort. The slighted distributor can also be strongly tempted to counterattack, in court or otherwise: some companies can suffer greatly from this change of heart in strategy if the courts are sympathetic to the plight of the local firm,[8] as they often are.

4.3.6 Foreign Sales Corporation

foreign sales corporation
A subsidiary, created for tax-reduction purposes only, that handles an exporter's overseas sales.

Foreign sales corporations (FSCs) were created in the United States as tax breaks for exporters. It was not a method of entry at all, but rather a way for U.S.-based corporations to lower their income tax. The only conditions were that the corporation had to export products with a 50-percent U.S. content and had to incorporate a subsidiary in one of several pre-approved foreign locations, such as the U.S. Virgin Islands, Barbados, or Jamaica. By channeling its export sales through an FSC, a corporation was eligible for a reduction in its tax rate on profits earned on export sales of fifteen percentage points, from 45 percent to 30 percent.[9] It was essentially a tax incentive available to exporters, regardless of the method used for export.

The European Union brought a complaint to the World Trade Organization (WTO) that the FSC concept was a subsidy to exports, a practice that was prohibited by the agreement. The WTO ruled against the United States in August 1999. Subsequently, the U.S. Congress created the Extraterritorial Income Exclusion (ETI) Act, which offered roughly the same benefits to U.S. exporters, but under a different legislation.[10] The ETI was also found to be contrary to WTO rules in 2004 under the same argument; export sales were not taxed, and therefore the ETI was considered a form of export subsidy, contrary to WTO rules. In 2005, the U.S. Congress created a new provision to counter that setback, the Domestic Production Deduction; although it is available to all companies operating in the United States,[11] it is designed to provide favorable tax treatments to exporters.[12] The WTO had not ruled against that latest legislation as of June 2013.

Another tax incentive to U.S. exporters is the Interest-Charge Domestic International Sales Corporation [IC-DISC]. It allows exporters to create a separate subsidiary to which it pays a commission on its foreign sales. The tax rate that the subsidiary pays on these commissions is 15 percent, a much-lower rate than the 35 percent that corporations pay on ordinary income.[13] The WTO has not ruled on that tax strategy as well, and, actually, it looked like no foreign state had filed a complaint against this practice as of June 2013.

Regardless of the WTO's eventual rulings on these two tax incentives for exporters, the United States Congress is likely to keep on promoting the concept of a tax break for exporters. In 1984, Domestic International Sales Corporations (DISCs) were found to be in violation of the General Agreement on Tariffs and Trade, and Congress created FSCs in their place. Similarly, after the WTO ruled FSCs to be counter to free trade, the U.S. Congress passed the ETI Act. When that was found to not conform to WTO rules, the Domestic Production Deduction and IC-DISC were created.

4.4 Production Abroad

A company can also elect to start operations abroad rather than export. This strategy can be followed, for example, when the manufacturing costs are lower abroad, or when the shipping costs are prohibitive, or when domestic manufacturing capacity is reached, or when the product has a significant intangible content, as in services. Here again, the order in which the alternatives are introduced represents an increasing level of involvement for the company interested in penetrating a foreign market.

4.4.1 Contract Manufacturing/Subcontracting

The first alternative is contract manufacturing—also called subcontracting—which occurs when a company enters an agreement with a producer in the foreign market to manufacture its goods. For example, a publishing firm may contract with a printing facility to publish its books rather than ship them from its home printing plant. Another example would be a cement manufacturer contracting with local producers to make and package cement under its brand. Yet another would be a supplier to an automobile manufacturer (often called an Original Equipment Manufacturer, or an OEM) that contracts with a company to provide sub-assemblies for that manufacturer's plant in a foreign country.

contract manufacturing An arrangement between two companies where one manufactures goods for the other.

Contract manufacturing is not truly a method of entry. It is a way to get the product manufactured in a foreign country, and the marketing and distribution of the product remains to be organized. This distribution can be achieved through a distributor or a marketing subsidiary or, very occasionally, through the marketing channels used by the local contractor.

The "Pet Shop" bags

Firms frequently contract abroad to have a product manufactured and re-imported into their home country, taking advantage of lower production costs than at home. Nothing is particularly special about this. However, the case of the Scottish Pet Shop bags illustrates the possible unintended consequences of such an arrangement. Back in 1990, the Pet Shop in Glasgow, Scotland, decided to have its plastic bags printed in an Asian country. In many ways, the bags were very traditional, with the name of the store and its address appearing on them; however, they were also adorned with a drawing of a red parrot. For some unknown reason, the printing plant where the pet store owner had had the bags printed decided to print millions more, and these additional bags found their way throughout Central Asia. They have been found by tourists and diplomats in Pakistan, China, Uzbekistan, Russia, and Kyrgyzstan. Curious about the provenance of the bags, they sometimes contact the pet store in Glasgow to inquire about the mystery. The shop owner is as baffled as they are. Eventually, knock-offs of the Pet Shop bags started emerging in these countries as well, some with two parrots, some with made-up names, or some with the peculiar English found on counterfeit goods.[14]

While it is difficult to argue that there was much intellectual property in the design of a simple shopping bag, and that the pet store actually lost much in the process—actually, this notoriety may have increased its sales—this example makes it evident that it is difficult to control what a contract manufacturer will do when the initial order is completed.

Contract manufacturing is often sought as a strategy to enter a market in which there are significant barriers to entry, such as high tariffs and quotas, but there is always great difficulty to find a suitable manufacturing facility in such a country: if the country has a protectionist streak, it is unlikely to have domestic firms that are operating at world standards.

4.4.2 Licensing

licensing
An arrangement between two companies where one uses the other's intellectual property in exchange for a royalty.

royalty
The fee paid by a company so that it can use another party's intellectual property.

Licensing is the granting of rights to intellectual property owned by a company to another company for a fee. The intellectual property is either a patent on a specific technology, process, design, or product; a trademark; a brand; a copyright; a trade secret or other know-how, and it remains the property of the licensor—the firm granting the license. The company using the intellectual property—the licensee—has the right to use the property for a fee, or royalty, that it must pay for each use. Licensing is quite common in manufacturing, where companies license processes they have developed to other firms, or products such as chemical compounds and molecules.

In an international environment, the licensor is the exporting company and the licensee is the foreign company, and the range of intellectual property commonly licensed increases; several companies license their more visible intellectual property—trademarks, copyrights, or designs—to foreign firms. This strategy is followed when the access to the market is limited by high tariffs or non-tariff barriers, when the shipping costs are prohibitive, or when the licensor is uninterested in actively pursuing the market.

Licensing, as a strategy, can be quite beneficial to a firm. It does not have to lay out any capital and can generate worldwide income from its intellectual property fairly rapidly. The downside is that intellectual property is not always well protected in some countries, that piracy is rampant in several, and that these risks can be perceived as major deterrents for the owners of intellectual property. However, these are danger associated more with the ownership of intellectual property than with the strategy of licensing. An individual who decides to violate a patent or infringe a copyright certainly does not need a licensing agreement to start: patent information is available from all patent offices as a matter of course—the U.S. Patent Office has most of its seven million patents available online—and copyrights are by definition protecting publicly available products, such as this book, and software. To a certain extent, it is probably better to have a local firm enforce its license of a copyright than to attempt to enforce the copyright from abroad.

licensor
The company that grants to another company, the licensee, the right to use its intellectual property.

licensee
The company that obtains the right to use the licensor's intellectual property.

4.4.3 Franchising

Franchising is, in concept, quite similar to licensing, except that the franchisor is granting the rights to a large number of intellectual property items, all bundled in a business package, to a franchisee who pays royalties for using this business model. The business model includes trademarks, copyrights, and patents, as well as know-how, training, and methods of operation. Most franchises tend to be retail establishments, because consumers tend to value a uniform product and service and like to find retail names with which they are familiar.

Similarly, entrepreneurs abroad like to invest in a business concept with a proven track record, which most franchised businesses have. Finally, franchisors have the opportunity to gain market share without having to invest any capital. It has proven to be a fairly popular means of expansion both domestically and abroad.

Franchising is usually a very good option for a number of businesses seeking expansion abroad, but it certainly is inappropriate for many. The ones who can enter a market successfully are retail operations that involve a service requiring a fairly low level of employee skills, such as fast food restaurants, car repair shops, hotels, and car rental outlets. Franchising is inappropriate for high-skill consulting or advertising services, and nearly impossible for manufactured goods.

One of the consequences of the franchising strategy is that it generates a substantial amount of piggy-backing: as the franchisors demand that the franchisees use exactly the same equipment worldwide, the suppliers of those pieces of equipment end up selling worldwide as well. This is also true for items such as signage, furniture, and, in some cases, consumables: in 1997, for every dollar earned by franchisors in foreign franchising fees, $15 was spent on U.S. products by the franchisees to set up and run their franchised operations.[15] The proportion today is unlikely to be much different.

franchising
An arrangement between two companies where one licenses an array of related intellectual property items.

franchisor
The company that owns an array of related intellectual property items and lets another firm use them in exchange for a royalty.

franchisee
The company granted the right to use an array of related intellectual property items owned by the franchisor in exchange for a royalty.

McDonald's Franchising

McDonald's Restaurants is a corporation that has used franchising as its main method of expansion in the United States and abroad. As of December 2012, McDonald's had a total of 12,605 franchised restaurants in the United States,[16] owned by about 2,400 independent franchisees. Abroad, the company has also followed an aggressive development policy by using franchises. There were 15,277 franchised McDonald's restaurants in 119 countries, with several countries having more than 1,000 restaurants (Japan, China, Brazil, Germany, the United Kingdom, and France). Almost 81 percent of all 34,480 McDonald's restaurants are franchised. Worldwide, there were only 6,598 restaurants owned by the corporation.[17]

This foreign growth was not without some hitches; for example, in 1967, McDonald's Corporation divided Canada into two franchising territories, which it licensed to two individuals, George Tidball (Western Canada) and George Cohon (Eastern Canada). Realizing that this large market's potential could not be controlled by only two franchisees, McDonald's Corporation purchased these franchises in 1970 and 1971.[18]

The company is intent on expanding the percentage of its restaurants that are owned by franchisees, as it believes that they are best at gauging their local markets and key to the company's success: "[McDonald's Corporation sees itself] as a franchisor and believe[s] that franchising is important to delivering great, locally-relevant customer experiences and driving profitability."[19] McDonald's allows its franchisees to adapt its business model to the characteristics of the country. For example, McDonald's serves beer and wine in France and Germany, and it makes scooter deliveries in China (see Figure 4.2 on the next page)

The franchisees have been one of the greatest strengths of McDonald's development: several of the company's best-selling sandwiches were developed by franchisees, notably the Big Mac (1968) and the Egg McMuffin (1973). The same was true internationally. The former franchisee in Canada, George Cohon, now head of the corporate McDonald's Restaurants of Canada, opened the first restaurant in Moscow, on Pushkin Square, in January 1990. After selling more than 30,000 meals on its first day of operations, this restaurant was still the busiest McDonald's in the world twenty years later, and was only temporarily relegated to second-busiest after the McDonald's restaurant that served the London Olympic Park operated in the Summer of 2012.[20] As of June 2013, there were 358 restaurants in all of Russia.

In Japan, McDonald's used a slightly different strategy early on: it formed a 50-50 joint venture with Den Fujita in 1970, and soon opened its first restaurant on the glamorous Ginza in Tokyo.

Most of Japan's 3,600 restaurants are owned by the venture, but eventually McDonald's started to add franchised operations, and today 22 percent of the restaurants are franchises. System-wide, McDonald's restaurants' sales are roughly U.S. $69,687 million, 55 percent of which is generated by franchises in foreign countries. Each of the franchised restaurants grosses an average of just under U.S. $2,500,000 in sales every year, and each of the corporate-owned restaurant a little over U.S. $2,800,000.[21]

Figure 4.2: McDonald's delivery scooter in Beijing, China
Photo ©Tony Vingerhoets. Used with permission.

4.4.4 Joint Venture

With a joint venture (JV), the exporter invests in a facility abroad but finds one or more partners with which to share the costs of the venture. A joint venture is characterized by the creation of a new corporation in a foreign country, jointly owned by the venture partners in any combination of ownership percentages; most JVs involving two partners are owned 50 percent-50 percent or 51 percent-49 percent,[22] but they can be held 97 percent-3 percent. Some JVs include three or more partners, but these are less frequent.

joint venture
An overseas company that is jointly owned by two or more companies.

Entry strategies using JVs are generally created for one of several reasons:

1. The firm feels compelled to minimize its exposure in a foreign investment (*i.e.*, the amount of money it has at stake in a foreign country), and it achieves this objective by lowering the investment costs by half or two-thirds.

2. The firm finds a partner with a complementary line of products to offer to the same market. Both partners feel that a joint effort, with a complete line, is the appropriate strategy, and neither of them is ready to enter the market alone.

3. The firm wants a minority local partner to teach it the local ways of business and help smooth out the many obstacles that a firm is bound to experience in a foreign venture.

4. The firm is legally required to find a local partner by the host government. This requirement was popular until the mid-1990s and has become less of an issue recently. Generally, the local partner was a politically connected individual rather than a partner who brought in additional capital.

The JV strategy was frequently used until the early 1990s for several reasons. First and foremost, this strategy lowered the exposure of firms to the political risk presented by some countries. As early as the 1950s, some developing countries' governments decided that a good way to obtain means of production and create investment capital would be to nationalize plants owned by foreign investors. This policy also looked attractive politically, because the local perception was that the natural resources of a country should be managed and owned by its people. Libya, Egypt, Venezuela, and numerous others decided to seize, without compensation to their actual owners, all of the petroleum production facilities within their borders. Several other countries followed the same policy, nationalizing any type of foreign-owned facility, until the late 1970s; some did it with some form of compensation, most without. The end result of these expropriation policies was clear: not only did the countries have difficulties in running plants without the expatriate technicians who had been employed in the facility before it was nationalized, but they also scared away new foreign investors for decades. A JV with another firm was therefore a strategy developed to minimize the impact of a possible nationalization. In addition, a joint venture with a politically well-connected local partner was a good strategy for those firms that sought to minimize the probability of nationalization.

Countries that still wanted to create local ownership of capital and had not practiced nationalization found another effective strategy: their governments asked foreign enterprises that wanted to invest in their countries to take on local businessmen as JV partners. These local businessmen were always very well connected but often largely undercapitalized and therefore did not bring anything but their contacts to the venture. In effect, the requirement was a partial nationalization of sorts, as the 100 percent investment that the foreign corporation made was quickly diluted to a 50-percent ownership of the JV. Some of these partnerships ended up being extreme examples of nepotism, such as in Indonesia, where President Suharto's relatives were the only possible JV partners.[23] In other cases, the political partners were more of a hindrance than a help, even in dealing with the government, because they had been chosen more for their contacts than for their business acumen, and some ended up being dishonest.[24]

However, the greatest problem with joint ventures, and the main reason a large majority of them are unsuccessful, is that they are akin to marriages in which the spouses change over time. When the JV is first created, there is a good fit between all the partners' goals and strategies, and most JVs start well. However, as time goes on, the original management on each side changes. Some managers might retire or change positions within the firm, one of the original partners may be purchased by a conglomerate, corporate strategies can change, and gradually, the perfect strategic match that had created the JV in the first place is gone and partners squabble over the JV's objectives. Eventually, they accuse each other of all ills. The JV between

Ford and Volkswagen in Argentina—named Autolatina—failed because the partners' objectives changed as the venture progressed.[25]

Because of all these problems, the strategy of creating joint ventures has become less and less attractive to foreign investors. Some countries have actually retreated and no longer require foreign investors to create a JV with a local partner, at least partly because the existence of these policies deterred some highly sought investors from entering their markets: for example, Pepsico in India and 3M in China. These countries now routinely allow 100 percent ownership by a foreign entity.

4.4.5 Subsidiary

A subsidiary, also called a wholly owned foreign enterprise (WOFE, pronounced "WOO-fee"), is an investment of 100 percent in a foreign venture by a firm. This strategy is followed by firms that want total control of an investment and are willing to take the risk of such a venture. A WOFE is either a green-field operation, where a foreign firm builds a brand-new facility, or an acquisition of an existing firm. Greenfield operations represent more than 90 percent of all investments in Asia and Latin America, but the preferred method of entry in most European markets is a merger or an acquisition, representing more than 80 percent of all foreign investments.[26]

subsidiary
A company entirely owned by another company.

wholly-owned foreign enterprise
Another term for a subsidiary.

There is another alternative, which is still limited in scope but growing, particularly in the developing countries' markets: a firm will relocate an entire plant to a foreign location, usually to use cheaper labor and forgo the higher costs of a brand-new facility. The technology may not be the latest available, but the cost savings may be numerous, especially if the old plant no longer meets the environmental regulations of the exporting country. As the United States does not track export sales of used equipment—the Shipper's Export Declarations (see Section 9.3.1 on page 242) do not distinguish between old and new equipment—the extent of this practice is not fully known, but anecdotal evidence abounds.

The WOFE strategy allows the firm to retain complete control over its investment, which has become the main reason for a firm to choose this form of entry. The firm does not have to share its trade secrets or know-how, and no one is privy to any of its strategies or policies. The firm does not have to share its profits with anyone else, does not have to rely on anyone else for information on its customers, is free to pull out from a given market if the prospective sales do not become concrete, and so forth.

The WOFE strategy is also often very beneficial to the host country—it creates jobs, for one—and many countries offer substantial incentives to foreign companies willing to establish a facility within their borders: free land, tax abatements of all sorts, training programs, and infrastructure improvements. If the foreign firm considering the investment is willing to establish itself in a rural or economically depressed area, the incentives can make a WOFE extremely attractive. For example, Ireland put in place an extensive panoply of tax incentives in the 1980s and achieved unprecedented growth and employment in the following decade. Today, Ireland is no longer perceived as an essentially rural country, but as a booming, economically prosperous country with access to the entire European market; its incentive program convinced dozens of firms to invest there. The southern states of the United States followed a similar strategy in the 1990s and 2000s. The results of these strategies were quickly positive: BMW built in South Carolina, Mercedes-Benz and Honda in Alabama, Nissan in Mississippi, and Volkswagen in Tennessee.

The drawbacks of a subsidiary strategy are that there is a high cost of setting up a facility abroad, and all of it is borne by a single firm. However, the firm can use this facility to manufacture goods to be shipped back to the home country or to other markets; for example, having a facility within the European Union gives a firm duty-free access to the entire western European market and more favorable duty rates in eastern Europe than a facility in the United States. The costs can therefore be recovered fairly quickly. Similarly, a Japanese firm can get duty-free access to the United States and Canada by setting up a facility in Mexico, which also enjoys low labor costs.

A wholly owned subsidiary subjects the firm to a high exposure to the risks of investments, although it is evident that the risks that make a management team worry about its investments abroad are in decline: political risks are becoming less prominent, with yet a greater number of countries solidly in the democratic camp, and the economic risks are in decline as well. Except for countries in which there is no real market for many products, the prospects for a stable economy, a stable government, or at least a stable transition to a new government, are very good.

A WOFE also faces the relocation costs if a decision is made to move the production facility to another country. Cost may include significant compensation to employees who will be laid off during the relocation process. The expenses vary by country and must be considered in the relocation analysis. In 2006, Kraft Foods decided to move its subsidiary from Australia to China, and this decision resulted in several substantial costs.

Kraft Foods Australia

Kraft Foods is one of the world's largest food and beverage companies, with sales in more than 145 countries. Kraft was acquired in 1988 by Philip Morris Companies, which also purchased Miller Brewing in 1985 and Nabisco Holdings in 2000. Philip Morris changed its name to Altria Group in 2003 to reflect its more diversified business ventures.

In 2002, Kraft Foods Australia acquired a manufacturing plant in Broadmeadows, Australia, as a wholly owned subsidiary to manufacture its cookies. The Australian facility, which had been built in 1964, employed 151 people. Kraft then embarked on a strategy to improve the performance of the facility, reduce costs, and maintain quality; however, the cost reductions were not sufficient, and the older plant did not have the capacity to support an expanding market. On March 31, 2006, Kraft Foods Australia closed the cookie manufacturing facility and moved the manufacturing of cookies to a regional facility in Suzhou, China. Later in the year, Kraft Foods Australia announced that it would close its distribution center in Port Melbourne and a dairy plant in Strathmerton that manufactured cheese and Vegemite, a dark brown Australian food paste made from yeast extracts, a uniquely Australian product (see Figure below). However, all the product lines would continue to be sold in Australia, with a third-party-logistics provider taking responsibility for the distribution of these products.

The employment contracts that Kraft had negotiated with its unions and the laws of Australia required the company to provide substantial support to its laid-off workers in both locations: they had to be paid a severance package that included four weeks' pay for each year worked at the plant (a benefit called an "entitlement") and given access to outplacement services for a minimum period of eight weeks (called a "redundancy package").[27]

Kraft Foods vice president and area director for Australia/New Zealand Chris Bell said, "Kraft is especially mindful of the impact this decision will have on our employees, as we greatly value the support that all our employees give to Kraft Foods Australia. We will ensure that all affected [...] employees are given access to every support during this difficult period, and they are guaranteed to be paid their appropriate entitlements, including a redundancy package. Employees will also have access to comprehensive career transition support services."[28]

When it purchased the Broadmeadows plant in 2002 as a wholly owned Australian subsidiary, Kraft had undoubtedly anticipated the additional costs of its legal obligations to its new workforce and had considered the employees when it decided to close the plant. Not all companies who invest abroad take those factors into consideration.

Finally, a WOFE presents the disadvantage of having to manage in a foreign country without a very good understanding of local customs and regulations. As a firm invests in a foreign country, it oftentimes chooses to have an expatriate manager at its helm; this manager often runs into difficulties that may have been avoided, had the firm elected to have a local partner. For example, the European countries have countless customs that sound peculiar or even counterproductive to any foreigner but which local managers support heavily: thirty-five-hour workweeks in France, Mitbestimmung (co-determination) in Germany, late-night work hours in Spain, and so on. These drawbacks can easily be overcome by hiring a competent local general manager.

4.5 Parallel Imports

One of the greatest problems faced by a firm involved in several markets is the risk of parallel imports, which is particularly acute if the firm has relinquished some control over its goods' prices. That would be the case if it is using distributors, for example.

Parallel imports—or gray market goods—are goods that are sold outside the regular distribution channels of a company, usually because there is a discrepancy between the price charged in one country and the price charged in another. Gray

parallel imports
Goods purchased in one country by unauthorized intermediaries and sold to unauthorized retailers in another country.

gray market goods
Goods purchased in one country by unauthorized intermediaries and sold to unauthorized retailers in another country.

market goods are not counterfeit or shoddy goods: they are legitimate items but are sold outside the channel chosen by the company (see Figure 4.3). For example, an item such as shampoo may sell at different prices in Germany and in Spain: for whatever reason, the Spanish version of a brand is significantly cheaper. An entrepreneur buys some shampoo in Spain, ships it to Germany, and sells it through a discount store. The price paid by a consumer in Germany for the Spanish version of the product ends up being lower than the price of the German version; since the sale is "outside" of the regular channel of distribution, it is considered a parallel import. The legitimate retailer in Germany is not happy to be undersold and the shampoo manufacturer has lost some control over the marketing of its products.

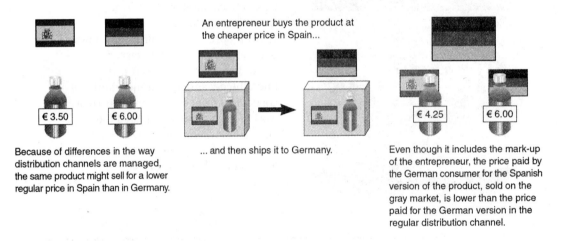

Figure 4.3: Parallel Imports between Spain and Germany

Parallel imports occur in all sorts of product lines, from shampoo to cars to spare parts; however, it is a particularly sensitive issue in luxury goods, such as watches, electronics, and high-end automobiles. While there are ways to combat parallel imports, which can be found in any good textbook in international marketing, the best strategy is to avoid having discrepancies in prices from one country to another, which usually means that the firm must have a coherent entry strategy.

On a final note, there is no legal recourse possible, as the product is a legitimate product, manufactured by an authorized plant. In the United States, the Supreme Court affirmed this point recently: once a firm has sold a product, it has no right to keep on controlling it. In Justice John Paul Stephens's words: "The whole point [...] is that once the copyright owner places a copyrighted material in the stream of commerce by selling it, it has exhausted its exclusive statutory right to control its distribution."[29] The U.S. Customs Service will not stop gray market goods unless they are different from the goods sold by the traditional distribution channel in the United States. That is the case, for example, for products sold under the same brand name, but with a different chemical composition to satisfy foreign requirements or consumer tastes abroad.[30] Other countries have taken similar stances.

4.6 Counterfeit Goods

One other significant issue that a firm encounters when it starts to expand abroad is the increased probability that unscrupulous competitors —and sometimes partners— will manufacture and distribute counterfeits of the original product. Counterfeit goods are copies of the original products sold under the same (or a very similar) brand name, are generally of lower quality, and are also generally sold at much lower prices than the original. Most of the time, the purchasers are well aware that they are not purchasing the genuine product, but do not feel that they are doing anything wrong; they are intent on saving money or are interested in obtaining the status that the brand conveys, but without paying for it.

counterfeit goods Goods manufactured to look like original products, but whose manufacturing was not approved by the brand owners.

Counterfeiting generally happen when there is a substantial discrepancy between the variable cost of manufacturing the product and the price at which it sells. Counterfeits are therefore abundant in the software and entertainment industries; a DVD of a movie or a CD of a software program can be reproduced for a few pennies but sell for much more. Most of the counterfeit goods that U.S. Customs and Border confiscated in 2012[31] were luxury goods (handbags, watches, clothing), pharmaceutical drugs, and cigarettes, all of which exhibit the same characteristics: low manufacturing costs and high selling prices. The probability increases further if the product is physically small and light enough that it can be sold easily and discreetly on the streets: sidewalk peddlers constitute the most common distribution channel for counterfeit goods.

The existence of such counterfeiting activity is not dependent on the method of entry chosen. Whether a firm enters a foreign market through licensing, contract manufacturing, or a wholly owned subsidiary does not matter. Counterfeit manufacturing is generally present in countries in which government authorities have other priorities than defending the intellectual property rights of (foreign) firms. China and India are often the countries that are most commonly accused of ignoring counterfeiting activities, but they are just the most visible targets. Counterfeiting happens in just about any country in the world.[32] The task remains daunting. Counterfeiting is difficult to prosecute, and most consumers—as well as local law enforcement officials who are also consumers—see counterfeiting as a crime that benefits them and hurts only the large foreign corporations, with whom they do not empathize.[33]

The tide seems to be turning, though. Since the beginning of the twenty-first century, many countries have cracked down seriously on counterfeiting, for several reasons. Their governments have realized that counterfeiting is not a crime that affects just the profits of foreign firms, it also affects the health of their citizens. The examples happen in China with unscrupulous local businesses selling counterfeit baby formula and adulterated milk. The problem is so wide spread that the Chinese government found 15,000 instances of tainted food products, and shut down 5,700 food businesses.[34]

4.7 Other Issues in Methods of Entry

Several other factors need to be considered to make an appropriate decision regarding a company's method of entry into a foreign market.

4.7.1 Foreign Trade Zones

Foreign trade zones (FTZs) are areas of a country that have acquired a special Customs status, with the specific purpose of encouraging foreign investments and exports. Effectively, a foreign trade zone—sometimes also called a free trade zone—is an area of a country that is, for Customs purposes, still "outside" of the country; goods can be shipped to the FTZ without being subject to duty and quotas. Once in the FTZ, the goods can be transformed, assembled, repackaged, and eventually shipped to customers. If the goods are re-exported, they never pay duty in the host country in which the FTZ is located; if they are sold in the host country, it is only after leaving the FTZ that they have to pay duty.[35]

FTZs exist in one form or another in just about every country. Some countries use them aggressively to encourage foreign investments by allowing just about any economic activity within the zone, including manufacturing; goods come in the trade zone duty-free; are transformed in the zone into a final product, creating jobs in the host country; and the product is then re-exported abroad or into the host country. In China, the Waigaoqiao Free Trade Zone, near Shanghai, is home to 104 of the world's 500 largest companies, employed 170,000 people, including 8,600 foreign workers, and had added RMB 67 billion (about U.S. $9 billion) to the Chinese economy.[36]

FTZs are particularly attractive to a manufacturer if the host country has an inverted tariff structure (*i.e.*, the tariffs charged on parts are higher than the tariffs charged on the final product).[37] FTZs can also be quite advantageous to hold a good in inventory until sold, or to wait for a numerical quota to open. However, in view of the progress made in the last few years by the WTO to lead countries to lower tariffs and increase trade, FTZs may have a limited future because their advantages are dwindling. Nevertheless, they remain attractive and should be considered as a possible alternative site for a foreign investment, whether a sales subsidiary, a joint venture, or a WOFE.

foreign trade zone
An area that is physically within the borders of a country, but that is considered outside of its borders for Customs' purposes.

4.7.2 Maquiladoras

Maquiladoras are companies in Mexico with a Customs status similar to that of an FTZ located both in Mexico and in the United States. They can import goods from the United States duty free, transform these goods by assembling them into products, and then re-export them to the United States, where the goods are assessed duty only on the value added in Mexico. Originally, maquiladora status could be obtained in only a geographic band located just south of Mexico's border with the United States, but it was expanded to the remainder of the country in the late 1980s. Today, with the completion of the North American Free Trade Agreement (NAFTA), maquiladoras have limited attractiveness to a foreign investor, but this alternative is still available, and many plants located in the Northern part of the country have retained that status.

maquiladora
A plant located in Mexico that have the same status as a foreign trade zone located both in the United States and Mexico.

duty
The amount of tax paid to Customs authorities in the importing country on imported goods.

4.7.3 Anti-Bribery Conventions

One of the last aspects of significant concern in the creation of a method of entry in a foreign country is the fact that business practices in some countries tend to include corruption and bribery. The Organisation for Economic Co-operation and Development (OECD) has tried to ban such practices by developing its Anti-Bribery Convention (ABC), which 40 countries had ratified by June 2013. One aspect of the convention is that it asks the developed countries' governments to cease the practice of letting firms deduct bribery as a business expense.

Eleven countries (Australia, Bulgaria, Finland, France, Hungary, Iceland, Italy, Luxembourg, Mexico, Norway, and Switzerland) incorporated measures outlined in the ABC in their penal codes, and five (Canada, Germany, Greece, Korea, and the United States) passed specific separate legislation. Two of the signatory countries (Japan and the United Kingdom) wrote specific statutes penalizing companies and officers of companies involved in the bribery of foreign officials.[38]

The United States implemented in 1977 a punitive Foreign Corrupt Practices Act (FCPA), which heavily fines companies that are caught using bribery to gain access to foreign contracts. The FCPA is far-reaching and prohibits "all officers and employees and anyone else acting on behalf of the firm and its subsidiaries [from] offer[ing] any payments, direct or indirect, or through a third party, to government officials in return for getting or keeping business."[39] This includes payments made by an agent to a foreign official, or "special incentives" given to a well-connected partner in exchange for having won a contract. Anything that is not contractual is deemed suspect. The U.S. government prosecutes the firms that it thinks has violated the law, and the officers of the firm, whether they knew of the practice or not, and fines can run in the millions of U.S. dollars.[40]

The FCPA is often understood to be aimed at preventing the bribery of high-level foreign officials; while this was originally the case, it was amended in 1998 and now targets attempts at influencing all levels of foreign officials, including such practices as asking for a favorable treatment of a Customs entry or a reduced tariff rate.[41]

The FCPA and the ABC are attempts by the developed countries' governments to clean up business practices abroad and prevent firms from being subject to extortion by corrupt foreign government officials. So far, there seems to be minimal evidence that these efforts have been effective, but they have taught foreign officials that it was useless to attempt to request bribes from developed countries' companies, and, in that respect, these efforts have worked. There is substantial grumbling, though, in the export community that the FCPA and the ABC have cost developed countries' exporters billions of dollars in lost business to foreign competitors that are unimpeded by these laws and can deduct bribes as a business expense.

From a practical standpoint, for any exporter, the rules are fairly simple: business abroad must be conducted aboveboard and remain within the boundaries set in the original agency or distributorship contracts.

Anti-Bribery Convention
An OECD convention that requires countries to penalize companies engaging in bribery.

Foreign Corrupt Practices Act
A U.S. law that punishes severely U.S. companies engaging in bribery outside of the borders of the United States.

Review and Discussion Questions

1. What are the principal differences between an agent and a distributor?

2. What are the different methods of entry regrouped under the term "indirect export"?

3. Using a product of your choice and a country of your choice, determine what would be the best method of entry for an exporter interested in that market. Justify your decision using the guidelines provided in the chapter.

4. Why would a company decide to franchise abroad?

5. What advantages would a foreign trade zone represent for an importer/exporter?

6. What are the advantages and disadvantages of using a subsidiary rather than a joint venture for a firm interested in manufacturing abroad?

Notes

[1] *Foreign Market Entry, Breaking into the Trade Game*, Small Business Administration, 3rd ed., http://www.sba.gov/idc/groups/public/documents/sba_program_office/oit_bitg4th_ch pt4.pdf, retrieved May 23, 2009.

[2] Root, Franklin R., *Entry Strategies for International Markets*, Revised and Expanded Edition. New York: Lexington Books, 1994.

[3] Phillips, Michael M., "Carving out an Export Industry, and Hope, in Africa," *The Wall Street Journal*, July 18, 1996, p. A10.

[4] Dugger, Celia, "Peace Prize to Pioneer of Loans to Poor No Bank Would Touch," *The New York Times*, October 14, 2006.

[5] Lacey, Marc, "US Trade Law Gives Africa Hope and Hard Jobs," *The New York Times*, November 14, 2003

[6] Bello, Daniel C., and Ritu Lohtia, "Export Channel Design: The Use of Foreign Distributors and Agents," *Journal of the Academy of Marketing Science*, Spring 1995, pp. 83Ű93.

[7] Root, Franklin R., *Entry Strategies for International Markets*, Revised and Expanded Edition. New York: Lexington Books, 1994.

[8] Shirouzu, Norihiko, "In Japan, Breaking Up Can Be Hard to Do," *The Wall Street Journal*, December 31, 1997, p. A7.

[9] Tirschwell, Peter, "The ABCs of FSCs," *The Journal of Commerce*, November 29, 1997, p. 1C.

[10] "Overview of the Foreign Sales Corporation/Extraterritorial Income (FSC/ETI) Exclusion," The Tax Foundation, January 2, 2002, http://www.taxfoundation.org/news/show/154.html, retrieved June 10, 2013.

[11] Losi, Ryan, "The Domestic Production Deduction: Does it apply to you?", Virginia International Trade, http://www.exportvirginia.org/newsletter/articles/archives/piascik.htm, retrieved May 23, 2009.

[12] "Comparison of Certain Provisions of H.R. 4520 as passed by the House of Representatives and as Amended by the Senate: Provisions relating to the Repeal of the Exclusion for Extraterritorial Income, Domestic Production, and the Corporate Income Tax Rates Applicable to

Small Corporations," Joint Committee on Taxation, September 29, 2004, http://www.house.gov/jct/x-61-04.pdf, retrieved June 10, 2013.

[13] Zerbe, Dean, "IC-DISC: The Big Tax Break for Exporters," *Forbes*, March 29, 2011, http://www.forbes.com/sites/deanzerbe/2011/03/29/ic-disc-the-big-tax-break-for-exporters/, retrieved June 10, 2013.

[14] Whalen, Jeanne, "Cool in Kyrgyzstan: a Scottish Pet Store and its Red Parrot," *The Wall Street Journal*, May 2, 2000, p. A1

[15] Martin, Josh, "Profitable Supply Chain," *The Journal of Commerce*, March 11, 1998, p. 1C.

[16] "McDonald's," *Entrepreneur*, http://www.entrepreneur.com/franchises/mcdonalds/282570-0.html#, retrieved June 10, 2013.

[17] *McDonald's 2012 Annual Report*, http://www.aboutmcdonalds.com/mcd/investors/annual_reports.html, retrieved June 10, 2013.

[18] Gibson, Richard, "Some franchisees say Moves by McDonald's hurt their Operations," *The Wall Street Journal*, April 17, 1996, p. A1

[19] "Management's Discussion and Analysis of Financial Condition and Results of Operations," *McDonald's 2012 Annual Report*, http://www.aboutmcdonalds.com/mcd/investors/annual_reports.html, retrieved June 10, 2013.

[20] Hennessy, Selah, "McDonald's Olympic Restaurant is Company's Busiest," *Voice of America*, August 7, 2012, http://www.voanews.com/content/temporary_olympic_park_mcdonalds_company_busiest/1475424.html, retrieved June 10, 2013.

[21] *McDonald's 2012 Annual Report*, http://www.aboutmcdonalds.com/mcd/investors/annual_reports.html, retrieved June 2013.

[22] Bianchi, Stefania, and Sabrina Cohen, "Libya Opens Doors to Foreign Banks," *The Wall Street Journal*, February 16, 2010.

[23] Engardio, Pete, and Michael Shari, "The Suharto Empire," *Business Week*, August 19, 1996, pp. 46-50.

[24] Garcia-Castro, Roberto, "Governing Joint Ventures In China: Lessons from Success and Failure," *The IFCAI [Institute of Chartered Financial Analysts of India] University Journal of Mergers and Acquisitions*, March 2009, http://www.iupindia.org/309/IJMA_Governing_Joint_Ventures_7.html.

[25] Bradsher, Keith, "After Latin Venture Fails, Volkswagen Succeeds and Ford Scrambles," *The New York Times*, May 16, 1997.

[26] "Global FDI Recovery Derails," *Global Investment Trends Monitor*, January 23, 2013, unctad.org/en/PublicationsLibrary/webdiaeia2013d1_en.pdf, retrieved June 10, 2013.

[27] Ross, Emily, "Sack with Care," *Business Management*, Compak 2006 Supplement, http://www.vcta.asn.au/files/2006%20files/compak06/May/BM206_2.pdf, accessed June 6, 2006.

[28] "Kraft Foods Cuts Australian Jobs, Moves to China," *China SCR: News & Views on Corporate Social Responsibility in China*, January 12, 2006, http://www.chinacsr.com/2006/01/12/kraft-foods-cuts-australian-jobs-moves-to-china.

[29] Greenhouse, Linda, "Court Ruling Helps 'Gray Market' in U.S. Goods," *The New York Times*, March 10, 1998.

[30] Chester, James, "Policing and Protecting U.S. Intellectual Property Rights at the Border," Chester and Associates, March 28, 2008, http://www.tradelawfirm.com/sitebuildercontent/sitebuilderfiles/protect_ip_at_border.pdf.

[31] "Intellectual Property Rights—Fiscal Year 2012 Seizure Statistics," January 1, 2013, U.S. Customs and Border Protection, http://www.cbp.gov/linkhandler/cgov/newsroom/publica-

tions/trade/fy_2012_final_stats.ctt/fy_2012_final_stats.pdf, retrieved July 6, 2013.

[32] Balfour, Frederik, "Fakes: The Global Counterfeiting Business is Out of Control, Targeting Everything from Computer Chips to Life-Saving Medicines. It's So Bad That Even China May Need to Crack Down," *Business Week*, February 7, 2005, pp. 54-64.

[33] Fishman, Ted C., "Manufaketure," *The New York Times*, January 9, 2005.

[34] McDonald, Mark, "From Milk to Peas, a Chinese Food-Safety Mess," *The New York Times*, June 21, 2012.

[35] Chester, James, "Foreign Trade Zones; Creating Profits through Savings," Chester and Associates, March 28, 2008, http://www.tradelawfirm.com/sitebuildercontent/sitebuilderfiles/FTZ_ppt.pdf.

[36] "Waigaoqiao: the First Free Trade Zone in China," *China Economic Review*, May 12, 2009, http://www.chinaeconomicreview.com/node/49471, retrieved June 10, 2013.

[37] Calabrese, Dan, "Business Guide to Tax Evasion (Relax, It's Perfectly Legal)," *Inbound Logistics*, January 2009, pp. 171-179.

[38] *Annual Report 2013*, OECD Working Group on Bribery, http://www.oecd.org/daf/anti-bribery/oecdworkinggrouponbribery-annualreport.htm, retrieved June 10, 2013.

[39] "Update of Country Descriptions of Tax Legislation on the Tax Treatment of Bribes," Organisation for Economic Co-operation and Development, October 1, 2007, http://www.oecd.org/dataoecd/42/43/37116153.pdf, retrieved June 10, 2013.

[40] "FCPA penalties for individuals and entities," World Compliance, http://www.fcpa-worldcompliance.com/resources/fcpa-penalties.html,
retrieved June 10, 2013.

[41] Chester, James, "Guide to the FCPA," Chester and Associates, April 17, 2007, http://www.tradelawfirm.com/sitebuildercontent/sitebuilderfiles/fcpa.pdf.

Chapter 5

International Contracts

5.1	*Lex Mercatoria*	120
5.2	International Sales Contracts and the CISG	121
5.3	Agency versus Distributorship Legal Issues	124
5.4	Elements of an Agency or Distributor Contract	126
5.5	Termination	134
5.6	Arbitration	136
5.7	Mediation	137

Whenever a firm gets involved in international business, it enters into a substantial number of contracts, either written or implied, with a number of partners, some of which are located abroad. Examples of such contracts would be:

- The contract of sale between the exporter and the importer

- The contract of insurance between the exporter or the importer (depending on the terms of sale, which will be covered in Chapter 6) and an insurance company

- The contract of carriage between the exporter or the importer and the shipping line

- The contract between an exporter and its agent or distributor

- The contract between an exporter or an importer and its bank, regarding payment arrangements such as documentary collection or letters of credit (concepts that will be covered in Chapter 7)

All of these contracts are formed under the precepts of a multitude of traditions, local laws, multilateral governmental agreements, and international treaties that are sometimes not ratified or only partially ratified by some countries. Frequently, these contracts are further complicated by a profoundly different understanding of what a contract represents. Nevertheless, international traders and logistics managers have learned to operate within this complex framework.

5.1 Lex Mercatoria

Whenever a contract is established between two parties in the same country, the law governing the execution of this contract is clearly determined by that country's legal system. In the United States, for example, it is the Uniform Commercial Code (UCC), in France, it is the *Code de Commerce Français*, and in Germany, it is the *Handelsgesetzbuch*. All domestic legal systems include ample jurisprudence and expertise to determine how this contract should be executed. However, when the contract is between two parties in different countries, there is no specific law governing this contract, except what is called *Lex Mercatoria*—trade law—a multitude of international agreements and international trade customs, all of which complement domestic laws.

Lex Mercatoria The body of laws and international agreements that govern the relationships and contracts between international parties.

Lex Mercatoria is complex because it includes a multitude of different sources of law and jurisprudence. There are United Nations treaties and other decisions; international agreements, such as the General Agreement on Tariffs and Trade (GATT), which has given rise to the World Trade Organization (WTO) with its own rules and court system; multilateral agreements on specific industry issues, such as the Warsaw Convention on international air transport or the textile Multi-Fiber Agreement; regional agreements, such as the European Union and the North American Free Trade Agreement (NAFTA); bilateral agreements, such as the Open Skies agreement between the United States and the Netherlands (see Chapter 12) and the special status granted to Hong Kong SAR by the People's Republic of China; International Chamber of Commerce rules, such as the Incoterms® rules for terms of trade (see Chapter 6) and the UCP-600 for bank documentary credits (see Chapter 7); arbitration decisions and jurisprudence, established by the International Chamber of Commerce Arbitration Court or private arbitrators; and so on. In addition, many states* pick and choose which treaties they will ratify and, on occasion, which articles of the treaties they will ratify. They can also choose to become signatories to a treaty, which means they do not make a full commitment to a treaty. In addition, states can decide to abide by the terms of a treaty but not ratify it. Finally, things get even more interesting when courts decide that some domestic principle cannot be violated by an international convention or custom, even if the country has ratified the agreement.

The United States is an exception in many ways regarding its compliance with *Lex Mercatoria*. The courts of the United States generally do not consider that jurisprudence established in other countries, or decisions made by international bodies, can be used in their decisions. The courts' position is that laws are the results of a democratic process and that neither foreign courts nor international bodies are elected by U.S. nationals, and therefore their decisions cannot be binding.[1] The counter-argument is that the United States, by following such policies, is isolating itself from the rest of the world. The debate is far from settled.[2]

Convention on Contracts for the International Sale of Goods A United Nations' treaty that acts as international sales law.

Vienna Convention Another name for the Convention on Contracts for the International Sale of Goods.

This chapter does not attempt to cover *Lex Mercatoria* in depth. Only an overview of three of its major aspects is presented here. The first part covers the issues regarding the contract of sale between an exporter and an importer, which, for most countries, are covered by the United Nations Convention on Contracts for the International Sale of Goods (CISG), also known as the Vienna Convention. The second part of the chapter covers the issues regarding contracts between exporters and

---

*It is important to note that, in an international context, the meaning of "state" is that of "country." Readers in the United States should be mindful of the distinction.

5.2 International Sales Contracts and the CISG

agents and contracts between exporters and distributors, as well as the resolution of eventual disputes through the arbitration system.

The specific aspects of contracts as they pertain to the terms of sale—the International Commerce Terms (Incoterms® rules) of the International Chamber of Commerce (ICC)—will be covered in Chapter 6. Contracts relating to banking and payments will be covered in Chapter 7, insurance contracts will be covered in Chapter 10, and contracts of carriage between shippers and carriers will be covered in Chapters 11 and 12.

5.2 International Sales Contracts and the CISG

Whether or not a sales contract is considered "international" is not always evident. Courts will generally look at two criteria to decide whether a contract is international: the economic criterion, that is, whether there was a transaction that involved a transfer of merchandise from one country to another, and its mirror image of a transfer of funds; and the judicial criterion, which is based on whether the transaction has links to the laws of different states.[3] For example, a sale of office supplies to a French company's subsidiary located in Germany by a German supplier is not considered international, because it does not involve two countries; however, the same sale to the company's headquarters, located just across the border, would be international. Whenever there is a sales contract between two parties in two different countries, the domestic laws no longer apply, and it is governed by the Vienna Convention.[4]

simple signatory
The first step in the acceptance of a treaty by a state. It signs it to indicate that it agrees with its premises, but it will need to ratify it before it is bound by it.

The Vienna Convention, or CISG, was born in 1980 of two other conventions, the Uniform Law for the International Sale of Goods (ULIS) and the Uniform Law on the Formation of Contracts for the International Sale of Goods (ULF). Both had been written in The Hague in 1964 but had been ratified by only a few countries because they were somewhat deficient.[5] In contrast, the CISG has been ratified by more than 79 countries,[6] whose export and import activities represent more than 80 percent of all world trade. The major exception to the list of developed countries that have signed the CISG is the United Kingdom, whose "[m]inisters do not see the ratification of the Convention as a legislative priority" and therefore have not taken the time to introduce legislation to ratify it in the last 33 years.[7] As often is the case, though, several countries, including the United States, have not ratified all of the Convention and have left out some provisions, some of which may have conflicted with domestic law. However, the CISG has become the law of international contracts, as traders will often elect to have their contracts governed by the laws of a contracting state, and therefore the CISG will apply.

full signatory
The acceptance of a treaty by a state. It signs it to indicate that it agrees with its premises, without further ratification.

ratification
The process by which a state fully accepts to be bound by an international treaty. It makes it part of its national legislation by having its Congress vote on it.

Because the United States is not a full signatory to the CISG, transactions between United States companies and their counterparts abroad fall under the Vienna Convention only if the country of the other party is a signatory to the CISG. In addition, U.S. companies have the right to "opt in" or "opt out" of the CISG by specifying in the contract that they choose a particular law to apply to the contract. This can be deceiving, though; by choosing to have "the laws of the State of Texas" apply to a particular contract, a company would actually elect to have the CISG apply, because the State of Texas operates within the U.S. federal system, which includes all treaties in force, including the CISG.[8] This would be correct as long as the foreign company is located in a country that is a signatory, such as Poland. It would be incorrect if the foreign company were located in a non-signatory country, such as the United

Figure 5.1: The United Nations Complex in Vienna, Austria
Photo ©Alexandra & Sharif El-Hamalawi. Used with permission.

Kingdom.

The CISG is substantially different from the UCC—the Uniform Commercial Code, or the commercial law of the United States—in a few of its aspects, notably the contract formation and remedies in the case of non-conforming goods or late delivery. It is likely to be different from a number of other countries' domestic laws as well, as evidenced by the number of countries that have not ratified specific articles of the CISG. Although these exclusions may make good political fodder, they may not be acceptable to the courts that will have to handle disputes between traders located in countries that have adopted different versions of the CISG or have amended it to include some other interpretation.[9]

5.2.1 Contract Formation

The CISG does not consider that a contract has been accepted until both parties agree to all of its terms. It is customary for a seller to make an offer. The buyer may respond positively but indicate that it wants a different schedule of delivery or term of payment, or some other aspect of the transaction to be handled differently. Under the UCC of the United States, such a response is construed as an acceptance of the offer. Under the CISG, it is understood as a rejection of the offer made by the seller and as a counteroffer by the buyer, unless the terms suggested do not materially

Uniform Commercial Code
The set of federal laws that govern commercial contracts in the United States.

offer
The first step in the formation of a contract. The contract is initiated when one of the parties makes an offer to the other.

5.2 International Sales Contracts and the CISG

affect the contract. The CISG specifies that changes to "price, payment, quality, and quantity of the goods, place, and time of delivery, extent of one party's liability to the other—most likely to be understood as Incoterms® Rule (see Chapter 6)—or the settlement of disputes are considered to alter the terms of the offer materially" and therefore that no acceptance is made in those cases.

Another area of difference between the UCC and the CISG regarding offer and acceptance of a sales contract is what is referred to by U.S. lawyers as the "Battle of the Forms." For most businesses, an offer or an acceptance is made on some standard business form, with a number of small-print statements preprinted on it, designed to protect the interests of the party writing the offer (or the acceptance). In most instances, these pre-printed clauses do not match. Under the UCC, the courts have determined that the differences do not matter in the formation of a contract, unless they significantly affect the terms of the contract, and regard these different terms as additions to the terms of the contract, to be sorted out by the court in case of conflict. Under the CISG, the requirement of a mirror image may signify a return to what, for Americans, would be the pre-UCC rules, where the terms of the contract are determined by the form of the party "firing the last shot." Then again, it may signify that there is no contract until all terms match, with little tolerance for differences.[10] There is little evidence that the second interpretation is likely to prevail, especially if both parties thought there was a contract and acted in consequence.

acceptance
The second step in the formation of the contract. After the offer is made, the other party accepts the terms offered.

rejection
An intermediary step in the formation of the contract. After the offer is made, the other party rejects the terms offered and makes a counter-offer.

counter-offer
An intermediary step in the formation of the contract. After the offer is made, the other party does not accept the terms offered, and proposes modifications ot the terms of the contract.

5.2.2 Creation of the Contract

The CISG treats the length of time during which the offer is considered outstanding in a significantly different manner than the UCC does. Most offers contain a clause stating that the offer is open until a certain date; under the UCC, however, the offer can be withdrawn at any time, without prejudice, for almost any reason. Under the CISG, the offer cannot be withdrawn by the seller (or the buyer) before its expiration date, and the other party can accept it at any time until that time. It is considered an irrevocable offer.

The CISG does not dictate that contracts of sale have to be written: any agreement between a seller and a buyer can form a contract. Obviously, the issues of the proof of the existence of a contract and of the terms of the contract then become quite thorny unless there are witnesses to the discussion between seller and buyer. Even in the event where a contract of sale is signed, the written terms of the contract can be superseded by an oral exchange between the two parties, as long as there is evidence that it was the intent of both parties. In one of the jurisprudence cases contained in the United Nations Commission on International Trade Law (UNCITRAL) database—called CLOUT, for the Case Law on UNCITRAL texts—two witnesses corroborated that the written terms of the contract had been modified orally by the seller and the buyer, and the modifications were used by the court in determining the case.[11] In contrast, the UCC requires that any sales agreement above U.S. $500 be in writing.

5.2.3 Breach of Contract

Finally, the CISG treats nonconforming goods and delays in shipments much differently than does the UCC. Whereas the UCC applies the "perfect tender" principle (*i.e.*, the goods must exactly conform to the goods contracted and be delivered within the framework specified in the contract), the CISG grants the seller more latitude. For example, the buyer cannot refuse delivery or cancel unless the nonconformity or the delay "substantially deprives the buyer of what it was entitled to expect under the contract and, even then, only if the seller foresaw, or a party in its position would have foreseen, such a result."[12] In other words, the buyer cannot avoid the contract unless the seller performs a fundamental breach of the contract. Therefore, those firms operating on a just-in-time basis should specifically notify their suppliers that they are following such a manufacturing policy, so that their suppliers can then "foresee" the problem that a delay in shipment would cause.

> **breach**
> In the event that one of the parties to a contract does not meet its obligation, that is in *breach* of the contract.

In counterbalance, the CISG allows the buyer to unilaterally apply a price reduction to the amount agreed upon in the contract for nonconforming goods. Such a price reduction should be proportional to the loss of value of the goods (percentage that is nonconforming) or to the loss of market incurred by the buyer, in the event of a delay. However, the burden placed on the buyer to notify the seller in a timely manner and to explain which remedy it will seek has a very high threshold. The notification must be made as soon as possible; it has to be clear and painstakingly detailed in the description of the problem, and it has to be extremely clear and specific in the remedies sought. Several cases in CLOUT (given by McMahon[13]) show that the burden placed on the buyer by the courts seems unduly harsh. In addition, this issue is somewhat moot for a buyer paying on a letter of credit (see Chapter 7), because it is committed to pay for the full amount in all cases. Finally, the notification by the buyer to the seller that a price reduction will unilaterally be applied must be made within two years; such a long upper limit is also of concern, because the statute of limitations for claims against a carrier may be shorter than two years in some countries, preventing the seller from recovering damages caused by a carrier.[14]

5.3 Agency versus Distributorship Legal Issues

The second type of contract of interest are the contracts between an exporter and its representatives in foreign markets; either an agent or a distributor. To briefly repeat ground covered in Chapter 4, an agent is a representative located abroad and earning a commission on the sales it makes on behalf of the exporter. An agent cannot negotiate prices, delivery, or other sales terms with the buyer, but only represents the decisions made by the exporter. In contrast, a distributor is also located abroad, but it purchases goods from the exporter, with the idea of reselling them in its country, earning a profit in the process. The distributor is setting its own prices and has an inventory of goods to sell. It is most often responsible for after-sale service as well.

> **distribution contract**
> A contract between an exporter and an overseas intermediary, whether an agent or a distributor.

It is difficult to generalize about agency and distributorship agreements: there is no international agreement on the way each of these relationships is governed. In most cases, the country of residence of the agent or of the distributor considers that it has jurisdiction over the agreement, and in many cases, despite the fact that the agreement may specify that the laws of another country apply to the contract (see Section 5.4.8 on page 130 and Section 5.4.9 on page 130 for specific information regarding the Choice of Law and the Choice of Forum in an international distribution contract). Because each country has its own laws and regulations regarding these agreements and because the jurisprudence of each country may differ even on similar statutes, it is very difficult to be specific without getting into tedious listings

5.3 Agency versus Distributorship Legal Issues

of countries. Therefore, only broader issues will be covered, to understand which aspects of a distribution contract should be examined.

5.3.1 Contract Law versus Labor Law

In the absence of specifics, agreements between an exporter and an agent and agreements between an exporter and a distributor will be called distribution contracts. One of the greatest differences among countries is whether they consider such distribution agreements as contracts between equals or as contracts between unequal partners.

In the first case, when considering that the contract is between two equal parties, courts will consider the terms of the contract when dealing in a dispute. This approach is referred to as contract law or case law, where the question is resolved by trying to interpret the meaning of the contract between the two parties. Both parties are considered to have equal sophistication in dealing with legal matters, and therefore neither of the parties would have entered a contract without understanding it. Most countries, but certainly not all, consider that agreements between an exporter and a distributor fall into this category. The contract between the two parties is the framework that courts will consider in dealing with a dispute between the two parties. When the contract is silent about the point in contention, then the courts will use jurisprudence on what other contracts of the same type have established.

contract law
A set of laws that govern relationships established by contracts between two parties.

In other cases, though, countries will equate an international distribution agreement as something akin to an employment contract, where the parties are considered unequal in their ability to interpret and understand a legal contract, and therefore where the weaker party has to be protected. This point of view calls for the application of labor law or for the application of special statutes, dealing specifically with the relationship between an exporter and an agent, or an exporter and a distributor. Such statutes cannot be overruled by the terms of the contract in any way. Therefore, the courts, in ruling in a dispute between the two contract parties, will ignore the terms of the contract and use the laws of the country in which the agent or distributor is located. Most countries that follow such an interpretation will tend to protect agents rather than distributors—Belgium being the lone country protecting its distributors but not its agents[15]—but several protect both. In addition, this point of view is often independent of the fact that the agent or the distributor is an individual or a corporation. Labor law has been used to supersede contracts between an exporter and an incorporated agent.

labor law
A set of laws that govern relationships between employees and employers.

5.3.2 Home Government Restrictions

The main reason some countries use specific statutes to regulate international distribution agreements is that they feel that they need to protect agents and/or distributors against contracts that may not be fair or equitable. Specifically, they want to protect agents or distributors against wrongful or abusive termination (more specific information on this aspect of international distribution contracts can be found in Section 5.5 on page 134).

registration
For an agent or a distributor, the process of notifying the importing country's government that it is entering a distribution agreement with an exporter.

In addition, those governments can also construct much more complicated systems to manage agents and distributors operating within their borders. They can require the agents and distributors to formalize and legally record their relationships with their principals. This process of registration is not unlike the process of joining a professional association, but it often doubles as a tax. Governments can require that the agents and distributors be nationals of the country in which they represent the exporter; such is the case in most Middle Eastern countries. They can also mandate that the terms of the contracts be inspected by their administration—in order to monitor the commissions paid to agents, for example—which they sometimes limit with a floor or a ceiling. Other governments will allow only exclusive agents or distributors—a single agent or distributor within a specific geographic area, usually the country itself—as do most South American countries. Finally, some governments will simply not allow agents at all—they mandate a distributor—or not allow any third-party representation, coercing exporters to establish a subsidiary, which they can then tax on income. Unfortunately, it is difficult to generalize about all of these different requirements, as they are very country specific. They even vary from one region of a country to another, as shown in the laws of the State of Louisiana, which are in contrast with the laws of just about any other area in the United States, or of the laws of the Alsace-Lorraine region, which are significantly different from those in the remainder of France. In addition, such regulations can change at any time. Specific legal expertise and advice is therefore necessary before writing a distribution contract in any country.

5.3.3 Other Issues in Agency and Partnership Agreements

There are two additional issues with which an exporter should be familiar in the context of an international distribution agreement, whether with a foreign agent or with a foreign distributor.

- The first is specific to U.S. exporters: because the agent or the distributor acts as a representative of the U.S. exporter, the Foreign Corrupt Practices Act applies (see Section 4.7.3 on page 114). Therefore, the exporter is liable for unlawful actions taken by the agent or distributor, even if the exporter had no knowledge of them and cannot control the agent's actions.[16] This places a particular burden on U.S. exporting companies that other countries governed by the OECD's Anti-Bribery Convention and their exporters do not have. Their courts do not recognize agents as a "directing mind" employed by the exporter.[17]

- The second is valid for all exporters: whenever an exporter enters an international distributorship agreement with an agent or a distributor, it must guard against the possible perception that the parties are entering into a partnership agreement, rather than a contract in which one party is committing to using the services of another. If the exporter and its agent or distributor are portraying themselves as partners to other parties, then they are also communicating that they are jointly assuming each other's liabilities. This can present substantial risks for both parties.[18]

5.4 Elements of an Agency or Distributor Contract

There are a number of points that must be covered in any contract, regardless of the country in which it will be used. This section explores a number of these mandatory contract elements. Some country-specific requirements can obviously still influence each one of them.

5.4 Elements of an Agency or Distributor Contract

5.4.1 Contract Language

Because distribution agreements are usually entered into by two parties who do not necessarily share a common language, it is often necessary to have these contracts written in two languages. However, as any speaker of a foreign language can attest, it is utterly impossible to translate accurately and precisely contract terminology from one language to another. It is therefore critical to include a clause that specifies that the contract written in Language A is the original contract and that the contract written in Language B is a translation, and that in case of dispute or problems of interpretation, the original contract should prevail.

contract language
The language in which a contract is written. If the contract exists in other languages, those versions are considered translations, and not the original contract.

There are exceptions to this practical rule, however. Most international agreements between countries, such as the CISG or the International Chamber of Commerce's Incoterms® rules, are written in several languages, all of which are given the same legal status; they are all "originals," which can sometimes present problems when translations cannot precisely duplicate the meaning of the framers of the agreement. These problems can be avoided in a distribution agreement by having one original and the other clearly labeled as a translation.

5.4.2 Good Faith

Another mandatory clause in a distribution agreement states that both parties enter into the agreement in good faith. A contract is entered in good faith when neither of the parties has any ulterior motive about the agreement. It's probably best to understand good faith as the prerequisite for a contract to be formed: both parties must want to fulfill the terms of the contract rather than pursue some other idea, using the contract agreement to dupe the other party into providing some necessary material toward that goal.

good faith
The assumption that both parties entering a contract do not have ulterior, undisclosed, motives.

The same interpretation of good faith applies to the terms of the contract as well; both parties agree that they will adhere to the terms of the contract in good faith (*i.e.*, interpret the terms without trying to distort them to their advantage). Both parties agree to deal fairly with each other and not to try to dupe the other by attempting to find, in the terms of the contract, loopholes or ways to interpret a clause to their advantage to the detriment of the other party.

5.4.3 *Force Majeure*

All contracts contain some sort of a *force majeure* clause. This is a French expression that translates loosely as "overwhelming power" but which refers to any event that cannot be avoided and for which no one is responsible, at least neither of the two parties entering the contract. Examples of such events would be a major storm that sinks the ship carrying products to the distributor, or a fire that prevents a firm from producing the goods on time, civil unrest, or a lengthy strike at a port that delays the delivery of the goods. Contracts always contain a clause that absolves either party from not fulfilling its responsibilities in case of *force majeure*, or a cause of non-performance beyond its control. Generally, there is also some statement that qualifies such exemption of liability to perform, "as long as the affected party resumes the performance of this agreement" after the *force majeure* statement.

force majeure
An event beyond the control if any of the parties in an agreement that prevents one of the parties from fulfilling its obligations.

Contracts may also contain another legal term, "Acts of God," to address events beyond the control of the parties. However, the concept of *force majeure* is broader. The term "Acts of God" defines only large-scale natural disasters, such as floods or volcanic eruptions, whereas the term *force majeure* defines all of the events beyond the control of the parties that would prevent the fulfillment of the terms of the contract.

5.4.4 Scope of Appointment

scope of appointment
The scope [products, territory, customers] to the contract applies.

The scope of appointment clause principally defines the function that the representative will perform; it is the clause that spells out whether the representative will be an agent or a distributor. It is generally the first clause in the contract.

It also indicates the products to which the contract applies, and defines the product lines that the agent or distributor is contracted to sell, spelling out which it is allowed to sell and which it is not allowed to sell. There is often language to the effect that the representative cannot "cherry-pick" the most profitable products and ignore the remainder of the lines; this latter requirement may be expressed in quantitative terms. In addition, a specific list of the products that are to be sold by the representative is often placed in an Appendix and made part of the contract.

The scope-of-appointment clause also refers to the territory of the agreement and to corporate accounts, both of which are defined later in the agreement.

5.4.5 Territory

territory
The geographical area in which the agent or distributor is restricted/expected to sell.

exclusive representative
An agent or a distributor that has been granted the right to be the sole representative of the exporter in a given territory.

The territory clause defines the geographical limits within which the agent or distributor is authorized (expected) to sell. It is generally the entire country in which the representative is located, with some possible exceptions. In very large countries, there may be a regional appointment, and for regions with limited sales potential, there may be several countries included. The clause also spells out whether the agreement makes the agent or distributor an exclusive representative in that territory, which essentially grants a monopoly to the representative.

There are many problems associated with the definition of an exclusive territory, specifically in the European Union (EU). While it is possible to write a contract limiting a representative to a single country's territory, the EU considers that a firm operating in one EU country can also legally sell in any other. It is therefore difficult for the exporter to limit the activities of a representative to a single country—it is contrary to the laws of the EU and has been construed as an antitrust violation[19]—and it is difficult to grant exclusive rights to a territory when neighboring representatives have the right to sell there as well.

In many South American countries, the issue is different: unless an international representation agreement specifically spells out that it is non-exclusive, it is always interpreted as an exclusive agreement in that territory.[20]

5.4.6 Corporate Accounts

corporate accounts
The customers to which the agent or distributor is not allowed to sell. These accounts are handled directly by the exporter.

Some agreements will specify which customers remain corporate accounts, or customers to which the representative is not allowed to sell, for whatever reason. Generally, corporate accounts are very large customers who have negotiated terms that will apply to all their purchases worldwide. The agreement always includes some provisions under which the list of corporate accounts can be amended.

It is important for an exporter to pay close attention to the number of corporate accounts that are included in a representation agreement, because too many of them may discourage the representative. An example of such a counterproductive agreement would be one that specifies that all accounts above a certain level of sales automatically become corporate accounts; consequently, a successful agent, after having developed an account and reached that critical level of sales, would see it removed from its commission basis, and therefore from its income. This is certainly not the way to reward a good representative intent on excelling and is likely to limit the sales of the exporter, as such a policy encourages the representative to limit efforts to stay just below the critical threshold. At least, accounts first developed by the agent should be exempt from this policy.

5.4.7 Term of Appointment

This clause determines the duration of the appointment of the representative. It must always be a definite period, with the possibility of renewal if certain performance criteria are met.

> **term of appointment**
> The initial duration of the distribution contract, and the duration of its eventual renewal periods.

It is critical to determine the original duration of the contract appropriately. Finding the balance between a sufficiently long appointment period, so that the representative has enough time to develop the market to the point where it is a sustainable venture, and a sufficiently short period, so that an ineffective representative may be removed and replaced without too much of an opportunity cost to the exporter, is a very delicate task. Most of the time, such an initial appointment period is dictated by the market conditions and by the type of product sold. If the representative is expected to do "pioneer sales," in which it has to sell a new product with little brand awareness and unique characteristics, a longer period is necessary than for a standard product with multiple competitors and a well-known brand. If the market is characterized by personal contacts and long-term relationships between customers and suppliers, then a longer period is necessary than in a market that is more competitive and fluid.

Once the initial appointment period is completed, the clause also specifies the renewal period and, very importantly, the conditions under which the contract will be renewed for that duration. Renewal periods can be similar in duration to the initial appointment period or can be shorter; there are no specific recommendations either way. What is important is to specify clearly the performance criteria for renewal: level of sales reached, market share obtained, number of customers contacted, amount spent on advertising, number of sales calls made, and so forth. The issue is to make sure that the contract is not renewed as a matter of course.

Should the representative not meet the criteria for renewal set in the contract at the end of the initial appointment period, then the principal has two alternatives. It certainly can terminate the contract, which is often a bad solution, unless the representative has done particularly poorly, as the exporter is now confronted with the task of finding another representative and providing training, possibly delaying the venture by a year or more. This decision also creates ill will: the slighted representative can always retaliate and create problems for the next appointed representative and alienate existing customers by giving them the impression that the firm is not committed to that market.

The other alternative is to renew the contract anyhow. The representative may have been unable to achieve the objectives set in the original agreement because of circumstances beyond its control, or because the difficulties of entering the market had been underestimated, or because the market potential had been overestimated. In any case, what is important is to renew the contract but to make clear to the representative, in a carefully worded communication, that the terms of the renewal had not been met, although the exporter was willing to renew because of the circumstances.

Should such a communication be omitted and the contract be renewed anyhow, it could then be construed by a court as an evergreen contract, that is, a contract with no determined duration, and a contract that can no longer be terminated for non-performance, as there was a precedent of non-performance and simultaneous renewal. Although generally a couple of instances are necessary before such a conclusion is reached, some overprotective court may not see it that way.

evergreen contract
A contract that, by design or by default, does not have a specified duration.

5.4.8 Choice of Law

Because an international contract is a contract that has links to the laws of two different countries, some different interpretations of specific clauses are quite possible. To avoid these problems of interpretation, every contract includes a clause that determines which of the two sets of laws should be used by a court or by an arbitration panel when a conflict arises between the parties. In general, the choice of law is made by the exporter rather than the agent or distributor; however, this does not preclude a possible resolution in the courts of the importing country, which may assume jurisdiction over the contract because of the country's statutes regarding agents or distributors, despite the clause. This is the case when the importing country determines that agency contracts are governed by labor law, for example. In such cases, the contract clause that assigns the choice of law to the exporter's country is ignored: the court will recognize it, but explain why it is not valid.

choice of law
The national laws that govern the terms of the contract.

The choice of law can make a substantial difference in the way a case is resolved. In a well-publicized case, individual American investors in Lloyd's of London insurance syndicates tried to sue the company in U.S. courts to circumvent an exemption from liability from negligence that the company enjoys in the United Kingdom. However, because the contract between the investors and Lloyd's clearly stated that the laws of the United Kingdom would prevail in case of dispute—the choice of law clause—the U.S. Supreme Court ruled that the U.S. courts had no jurisdiction over the dispute,[21] even though such an exemption is contrary to generally accepted principles of law in the United States. The peculiarities of Lloyd's insurance market and its functioning, as well as its problems with investors, are covered in Chapter 10.

The International Chamber of Commerce (ICC) model contracts for agency[22] and for distributorship[23] approach the issue of choice of law innovatively, by giving the contract writer two possibilities, the first being the traditional choice of a specific country's laws, and the second being the "principles of law generally recognized in international trade as applicable to international agency [distribution] contracts,"[24] or those principles that constitute the *Lex Mercatoria* mentioned earlier in this chapter. As more and more arbitration jurisprudence accumulates, this alternative may become the preferred way of wording choice of law clauses, as it shields both parties from unexpected outcomes.

5.4.9 Choice of Forum or Venue

choice of forum
The court in which disputes regarding the contracts will be resolved.

Strongly linked to the choice of law is the choice of forum—or choice of venue—clause. In it, both parties agree on the location of the court that will rule on an eventual dispute, using the laws chosen in the choice of law clause. In most instances, the choice of law somewhat dictates the choice of forum, as it makes logical sense

5.4 Elements of an Agency or Distributor Contract

to link both and benefit from a court experienced in the jurisprudence of the laws governing the contract.

One of the preferences of exporters—and of their legal representatives—is to choose courts with which they are familiar, and that generally means a court in the exporting country. While this has obvious advantages of convenience for the exporter, it may present more difficulties when it comes time to ask a foreign court to enforce the decision. It should be noted that in general, foreign courts will look more favorably upon enforcing the resolution of a dispute in another court if the terms of the contract are clearly international, that is, if the contract uses terminology and concepts that are specifically international—for example, the CISG, the ICC's Incoterms® rules, and/or arbitration under ICC rules.

choice of venue
The court in which disputes regarding the contracts will be resolved.

5.4.10 Arbitration Clause

An increasing number of contracts include a clause which does not call for a court to settle disputes, but for an arbitration panel. Either the arbitration panel is decided upon at the outset of the contract or a mention is made of the Rules of Conciliation and Arbitration of the International Chamber of Commerce to outline how the panel should be chosen. Generally speaking, the panel is made up of three arbitrators, with each of the parties choosing one and the third being chosen by the arbitration organization, such as the ICC.

arbitration panel
A group of arbitrators who are empowered by both parties to resolve a contract dispute. Their decision is binding on both parties.

In many instances, the clause states that the dispute will be "finally settled"[25] by the panel (*i.e.*, that the panel's decision is binding on both parties). If the country in which the arbitration takes place is one of the 130 signatory countries to the Convention on the Recognition and Enforcement of Foreign Arbitral Awards, also known as the New York Convention, then the ruling can be enforced just about anywhere;[26] unfortunately, China, although a signatory, has stood out as the only country where arbitration awards have to be reviewed by a local court, and that requirement makes it difficult to arrange for redress.[27] Foreign companies should be weary about arbitration solutions in that unusual environment.

arbitration
A process by which parties to a contract choose to settle a dispute. An arbitration decision is binding on both parties.

Altogether, though, there are several specific advantages to settling a dispute through arbitration rather than through the courts, many of which are outlined in Section 5.6.

5.4.11 Mediation Clause

For many contractual disputes, the possibility of mediation or conciliation is encouraged before arbitration or litigation is undertaken. A mediator is an individual who will encourage and facilitate the communication between both parties in a dispute so that they can reach a compromise satisfactory to both. A mediator will not reach a decision for the parties but will lead the parties toward a compromise.

mediation
A process by which parties to a contract choose to find a compromise in a dispute. A mediation recommendation is not binding.

Mediation is not binding, which means that the decision cannot be enforced and has to be agreed upon by both parties. Because mediation is also done in private, there are no public records of mediation, and it is an appropriate alternative to settling disputes when one of the parties is concerned about "saving face."[28] Mediation is sometimes initiated by the arbitration panel or the court for resolutions of disputes where both parties seem open to conciliation. (The advantages of mediation over arbitration and litigation are outlined in Section 5.7)

litigation
The final process by which parties to a contract have to settle a dispute, in a court of law.

5.4.12 Profitability or Commission

This clause is worded quite differently if it spells out the amount of commission that the agent will earn or, reciprocally, the price at which the distributor is expected to sell the product, or the margin that it is expected to add to its costs.

For agency agreements, the exporter spells out the commission that the agent will earn for sales in its territory. It may vary from product to product, so that the agent is given a financial incentive to sell a specific product, but it generally is around 5 percent of the selling price of a product, obviously depending on the type of industry in which the agreement takes place. A savvy exporter sometimes adds the possibility of negotiating the commission with its agent, in order to win a contract for which the price is critical. Agents usually go along with such reduced commissions on the philosophy that a lower commission is better than no commission at all, if the sale is not successful. For sales outside of the territory that the agent may generate accidentally—for example, by attending a trade show and meeting some prospect from a different country—the contract will often call for a lower commission.

Finally, the exporter will also spell out when the commission will be paid to the agent. As a matter of course, the commission is never paid until after the customer has paid the exporter to which the agent sold the product. Commissions can then be paid as they are earned, or monthly, quarterly, or even semi-annually or annually.

For distributorship agreements, the issue of price can be thorny; if the distributor is completely free to set its own prices, then there is always the possibility of having substantially different prices for the same product in different countries, thereby creating the possibility of parallel imports (see Section 4.5 on page 111) and risking the aggravation of customers and distributors alike.

However, if an exporter is attempting to limit the probability of parallel imports, for example by trying to control the price at which the distributor sells the product or the markup that the distributor can add to the cost of the product, then there is always the possibility that such a clause will be construed as price fixing and therefore an attempt at reducing competition. Nevertheless, several versions of such clauses exist: some companies bluntly set exactly the same price worldwide and argue that they do not want their distributors to compete on price, but rather on such other attributes as service, assortment, and repair facilities. Others make advertising support and other sales help conditional upon the distributor keeping the price in line with the exporter's guidelines. Some others do not contractually state anything but make explicit threats of possible delays in delivery for those distributors who do not respect guidelines. Obviously, all of these attempts can be struck down by courts as collusion, but such agreements evidently exist worldwide. Obtaining advice from an experienced lawyer in drafting such clauses would be money well spent.

5.4.13 Intellectual Property

Exporters who benefit from substantial advantages due to intellectual property items will also want to specify the handling of trademarks, patents, and copyrights particularly carefully when a contract between an exporter and an agent or a distributor is drawn.

While the exporter can protect its intellectual property by making sure that it follows the proper registration procedures in the importing country, it is often use-

trademark
An intellectual property item that refers to a brand, a commercial name, or a slogan.

5.4 Elements of an Agency or Distributor Contract

ful to specify and define the intellectual property issues in the contract, especially in countries where intellectual property protection is lax. By including an intellectual property clause in the contract, the exporter transforms the protection of patents, trademarks, and copyrights into contractual issues, which are more likely to be enforced by a court. There are countless instances, unfortunately, of distributors or agents who violate intellectual property items nevertheless, but a good contract can dissuade them from attempting to do so.

The contract should also include a confidentiality clause to determine how trade secrets and other strategic advantages are handled. The International Chamber of Commerce provides a model agreement for the international protection of confidential information.[29]

Finally, the contract should specify how improvements to existing products made by the agent or the distributor are handled. Although they traditionally become the property of the exporter, the compensation to which the agency or the distributor is entitled should be outlined. This is an important aspect of contracts for all parties involved. Chapter 4 shows that two of the most popular products sold by McDonald's Corporation were first created by franchisees: the Big Mac and the Egg McMuffin.

patent
An intellectual property item that refers to a process, material, or design.

copyright
An intellectual property item that refers to a musical piece, a piece of art, or a written product.

confidentiality
A promise by both parties to a contract to not disclose what they have learned about each other's business to other parties.

5.4.14 Miscellaneous Other Clauses

There are evidently many more clauses in a foreign distribution contract, whether with an agent or with a distributor, many of which are more managerial in nature and become much more specific to the industry, the strategy of the exporter, and its representatives than can be generalized.

For example, the **facilities and activities** clause spells out what the exporter and the agent or distributor have agreed with respect to the type of establishment that the representative will maintain, the size of the retail establishments it will build, the amount of inventory they will carry, the type of training that employees will receive, and the expectations of managerial policies toward customer complaints, all of which are specific to an industry or a corporate strategy. McDonald's has much more stringent requirements in that respect than would an exporter of agricultural by-products.

The same is true regarding the **advertising** clause, which spells out the obligations of both parties regarding promotional activities such as advertising, trade show attendance, ownership of ideas for advertising campaigns and sales promotion items, and, very importantly, how the costs of such promotional activities will be shared. For many consumer products, advertising costs are shared by the exporter and the representative in some varying percentages, but for industrial products, the spectrum can go from entirely the responsibility of the exporter to entirely the responsibility of the representative. This may also vary as a function of the country in which the representative operates. A word of caution, though: if there are large discrepancies among the cost burden of distributors in different countries, the sale price may be affected and parallel imports triggered, which is something that an exporter should attempt to avoid.

The clause regarding **competing lines** spells out how an agent or distributor will be allowed to handle products manufactured by competitors. In most instances, an agent is not allowed to represent firms that are competing directly with the exporter's products, but a distributor is allowed to do so. Both are encouraged to carry products that complement the product line of the exporter, with the under-

facilities and activities
The specific facilities and activities that each party to a contract is committing to maintaining.

advertising
The promotional activities that each party to a contract is committing to pursue.

competing lines
Products manufactured by a company other than the principal that compete directly with the principal's products.

standing that they would increase the attractiveness of the agent or the distributor's portfolio of goods. Some exporters, though, prefer that the agent or the distributor sell their products at the exclusion of all others, to ensure that the representative is concentrating its efforts on their products. Such decisions are made generally as a function of the bargaining strength of the parties: a Japanese *sogo shosha* will carry whatever it pleases, whereas a small dealer involved in distributing products manufactured by a large firm, such as Caterpillar, will have to abide by whatever its principal dictates.

Finally, the issue of the **ownership of the customers' list** has to be resolved for distributors. Because they sell for their own account, the exporter is usually not privy to the identity of these customers. In some cases, the exporter may find out who the distributor's customers are when they are requested to fill out some sort of warranty registration form, but in general, they are unknown to the exporter. Some exporters demand that the distributor report the names of its customers, while others prefer to leave this issue alone. Except for warranty issues, the only reasons an exporter would want to know the names of the distributor's customers are in expectation of poor performance of the distributor or in expectation of the creation of a sales subsidiary in the future, neither of which represent a good basis on which to start a contract. As far as agents are concerned, because the exporter is shipping and billing directly to the customers to whom the agent sold, the exporter is aware of the customers' identities, and therefore the issue is of much less significance.

customers' list
The list of the customers to which the agent or distributor sells the principal's products.

5.5 Termination

Most definitely, the most sensitive issue in an international distribution contract is the issue of termination, or the act of ending the relationship between the exporter and the agent or the exporter and the distributor. All contracts will contain a termination clause, which will include a pre-termination notice and specify termination compensation.

- A pre-termination notice spells out how many days the exporter must give to the agent or the distributor before the termination becomes effective. This duration usually is shorter for agents than it is for distributors, but country statutes can extend it far beyond the contractual agreement. Some contracts call for no pre-termination notice—the contract is canceled immediately upon notice[30] and some go as high as a year.

- Termination compensation, often called a "goodwill compensation," would be equivalent to the amount of income the agent or distributor would have earned for a certain period. This compensation can be as low as none, and as high as two years' worth of income. Again, this provision of the contract may also be rendered null by the importing country's statutes, which may mandate a specific compensation.

Both of these issues can be determined by the terms of the contract, but the terms are often superseded by the statutes of the country in which the agent or the distributor is located. Actually, there are so many disparities and criteria that it is very difficult to determine what will be the requirements of a particular country. The European Union has attempted to reduce the differences between its member states' requirements,[31] but has not been successful in that goal.

5.5 Termination

The specific elements of a termination clause are dependent upon the reason behind the termination of the contract, which can be for either just cause or convenience.

5.5.1 Just Cause

Termination for "just cause" is triggered when either of the parties (exporter, agent, or distributor) is not honoring the terms of the contract. Generally, the representative is not doing something that it is contractually obligated to do, such as meet the sales performance objectives, spend a certain percentage of sales on advertising, or maintain the type of establishment spelled out in the contract. Alternatively, the representative is doing something that it is contractually not allowed to do: for example, selling competitors' products, applying for patent protection on the improvements it has made to the products, or keeping the list of customers a secret. Only in a few cases is just-cause termination due to the exporter not performing its obligations, such as not providing the agent with prompt *pro forma* invoices or not shipping diligently. Most terminations for just cause are triggered by a problem with the representative's performance.

In any case, it is relatively easy to terminate a contract for just cause, as there is a reason to terminate it. In most instances, the party guilty of not fulfilling its part of the agreement is not entitled to much compensation or many days' notice. Nevertheless, national statutes may still supersede the agreement in such cases, and mandate a minimum notice period and a minimum compensation, even though there is breach of the contract.

> **termination for "just cause"**
> The unilateral decision, by one of the parties to a contract, to terminate the contract because the other party has not met the terms of the agreement.

5.5.2 Convenience

Termination for "convenience" can occur for any other reason than non-performance. It can be triggered by any of the parties, but generally, it is the exporter that is seeking to terminate the contract. One of the most egregious—but unfortunately very common—reasons is that the representative is very successful and the exporter realizes that it is earning too much in commissions and wants to replace it with a sales subsidiary. Another cause for termination is a change in the exporter's strategy that modifies how the exporter intends to penetrate foreign markets, or, worse, necessitates a complete retrenchment on the domestic market. In any case, the problem is that the termination is not linked to a lack of performance by one of the parties on the terms of the contract, but due to some extraneous reason.

> **termination for "convenience"**
> The unilateral decision, by one of the parties to a contract, to terminate the contract for reasons unrelated to the performance of the contract by the other party.

A termination for convenience should be handled with the greatest care, as the potential for damages to the spurned party can be substantial; in those cases, a lengthy termination notice, as well as a generous goodwill compensation package, is the only way to ensure no litigation and a smooth(er) termination. In particular, if there are issues to resolve, such as inventories of unsold merchandise or outstanding orders, every effort should be made by the exporter to compensate the distributor or the agent. If it is not done, the representatives can very easily ask courts to intervene. In most instances, courts look upon terminations for convenience very harshly, sometimes assimilating distributors to agents so as to give them the advantages that the statutes of their country give agents. These statutes usually mandate long notice periods and generous compensation packages. Belgian courts granted three months of income to a distributor in compensation for a contract that lasted only four months, and three years of profits in compensation to a distributor who was associated with a manufacturer for 22 years but had been fairly unsuccessful, with yearly sales of BFr. 1,400,000 or roughly U.S. $28,000 at that time.[32]

Unfortunately, in a termination for convenience, going to court can even be the best-case scenario, as several injured representatives took upon themselves to sabotage the efforts of the exporter later on, through all sorts of means, from mentioning to all of their customers the callous treatment they suffered at the hands of the exporter to attracting new competitors in the market.

5.6 Arbitration

arbitration
A process by which parties to a contract choose to settle a dispute. An arbitration decision is binding on both parties.

Arbitration is fast becoming the preferred way of resolving disputes between international partners. In 1960, the International Chamber of Commerce received about 50 requests for arbitration; in 1999, it received 529 requests,[33] and in 2012, 759 requests on which it rendered 491 awards.[34] The ICC developed its own *Rules of Conciliation and Arbitration* in 1988, and revised them in 2011, as *Arbitration ADR Rules*[35] (ADR stands for Amicable Dispute Resolutions) which are translated in thirteen languages. However, there are many alternative venues for arbitration: the London Court of International Arbitration, the Stockholm Chamber of Commerce, the World Intellectual Property Organization, the American Arbitration Association, and countless individual law firms that specialize in this function, a number of which are located in Switzerland.

The advantages presented by arbitration over litigation in court are many:

- Arbitration tends to be perceived as fair. Arbitration panels are not a court in either of the parties' countries and therefore are perceived as being more independent and even-handed. This is, of course, only a perception, because courts in any developed country using a modern commercial code are fair, but it is often a perception of importance in dealing with sensitive litigants.

- Arbitration tends to be much more expeditious than litigation. Arbitration panels are numerous and do not have the same backlog as traditional courts, which are generally understaffed and overworked. In some countries, commercial disputes can drag on for years: in India, probably one of the worst cases, there are more than 31 million backlogged civil cases—by the government's own admission—many of which have gone on for more than ten years! The High Court estimated in 2010 that it would take 320 years to clear the backlog.[36]

- Arbitration tends to be much more efficient. Because arbitration panels do not have to follow the same rules of evidence as courts, proceedings go much faster, and testimony can be given much more efficiently. Because other procedures are also simplified—there is no pre-trial discovery—an arbitration meeting generally lasts a few days, whereas a lawsuit can take weeks.

- Arbitration panels tend to be much more creative in the solutions. Arbitrators seek to resolve the dispute to the satisfaction of both parties and can find compromises that are impossible in a formal court, where one of the parties has to win, while the other loses. There is also the possibility of iterative negotiations between the parties and the arbitration panel, a process that can lead to an acceptable compromise. Courts do not have this freedom.

- Arbitration tends to be more effective. Arbitrators generally have a wealth of experience in international business matters and can very quickly understand the issues at stake, draw on their experience and knowledge of arbitration jurisprudence, and settle the dispute to the satisfaction of both parties more effectively than can a court with limited experience in international business matters.

- Arbitration is not open to the public. Whereas court decisions are generally published and available to all, arbitration decisions are private, and only the parties involved in the dispute know what steps were taken to resolve it.

- Probably most importantly, arbitration is cheaper. All of the advantages previously presented tend to lower the costs of the litigation. In addition, these lower costs are generally shared by the parties in dispute, whereas court costs are usually borne by the loser, a custom called "European rules"; however, in court disputes adjudicated in the United States, both parties pay their own costs.

The only step to ensure arbitration in the case of disputes between the exporter and its representatives abroad is to include a clause directing that "any dispute [...] shall be finally settled in accordance with the *Arbitration and ADR Rules* of the International Chamber of Commerce."

5.7 Mediation

Mediation is a process by which a third party attempts to find a middle ground between the parties that are having a dispute. The mediator will often shuttle between the two companies and seek to find a commonly acceptable solution to both parties. Most mediators are people with a legal background or who have knowledge of the particulars of an industry; they can be found through referrals and within the trade associations of most industries.

mediation
A process by which parties to a contract choose to find a compromise in a dispute. A mediation recommendation is not binding.

Mediation presents several advantages over litigation or arbitration in several cases:

- Mediation is less formal. The parties in a dispute are often reluctant to enter arbitration proceedings because it is a fairly formal process, taking place over a few days, involving meetings in a neutral venue, and restricted to a few individual managers. Litigation is even more formal. Mediation is often achieved over a longer period of time, each party having the opportunity to meet with the mediator in its own corporate environment, and the mediator meeting with many different people in both organizations, in order to get a better idea of the issue.

- Mediation is non-binding. It can be the first step in resolving a dispute and can help both parties assess how their positions are perceived by unrelated parties. In other words, it is an indicator for both parties of the strength of their respective positions and of their probabilities of winning an arbitration hearing or a court case.

- Mediation is more practical for smaller disputes and specifically when parties are interested in keeping a business relationship. Unfortunately, arbitration—and certainly litigation—is commonly perceived as resulting in the formal severing of all commercial relationships between both parties. Mediation allows both parties to resolve a dispute without affecting the remainder of their business.

- Mediation is often best for disputes that have arisen from misunderstandings. Both parties are unable to reach a compromise because they do not understand what the other was trying to accomplish, and the mediator can help them reach that middle ground.

Mediation is often the best approach when there is a genuine interest on the part of both parties to resolve the dispute in a manner that is fair to both parties and when both parties are interested in resuming normal business relationships as quickly as possible.

Review and Discussion Questions

1. What are the general provisions of the United Nations Convention on Contracts for the International Sale of Goods?

2. What are the issues brought about by the concept of labor law in an international distribution agreement?

3. Describe three of the elements generally found in an agency or distributorship agreement.

4. What are the differences between the "choice of law" and "choice of forum" clauses? How are they related?

5. What two possible forms of termination are there? How differently will they be handled by a court of law?

6. What are the differences between mediation and arbitration? How different are they from a proceeding in a court of law?

Notes

[1] Feldman, Noah, "When Judges Make Foreign Policy," *The New York Times*, September 25, 2008.

[2] Associated Press, "Supreme Court Justices Spar over International Law," Law.com, January 18, 2005, http://www.law.com/jsp/article.jsp?id=1105364112559, retrieved June 11, 2013.

[3] Gourion, Pierre-Alain, and Georges Peyrard, *Droit du Commerce International*, 1997, Librairie Générale de Droit et de Jurisprudence, 14, rue Pierre et Marie Curie, 75005 Paris, France.

[4] JBC International, "Think You Understand the Vienna Convention? Then Read This Sad Tale," *The Journal of Commerce*, June 24, 1998, p. 12C.

[5] Lookofsky, Joseph M., *Understanding the CIGS in the USA: A Compact Guide to the 1980 United Nations Convention on Contracts for the International Sale of Goods*, 1995, Klumer Law International, Boston, The Hague, London.

[6] Kritzer, Albert, "CISG: Table of Contracting States," Pace Law School Institute of International Commercial Law, http://www.cisg.law.pace.edu/cisg/countries/cntries.html, retrieved June 11, 2013.

[7] Moss, Sally, "Why the United Kingdom has not ratified the CISG," *Journal of Law and Business*, 25, 2005-2006, pp. 483-485.

[8] Chester, James, personal e-mail communication, January 19, 2009.

[9] Ziegler, Jacob, "Canada Prepares to Adopt the International Sales Convention," *Canadian Business Law Journal*, vol. 18, issue 3, Fall 1991.

[10] Gellman, Gila E., "Forming International Sales Pacts," *Marketing Management*, Winter 1994, pp. 60-62.

[11] Ferrari, Franco, "What Sources of Law for Contracts for the International Sale of Goods; Why One has to look beyond the CISG," *International Review of Law and Economics*, 25, September 2005, pp. 314-341.

[12] Walt, Steven, "The CISG Expansion Bias: A Comment on Franco Ferrari," *International Review of Law and Economics*, 25, September 2005, pp. 342-349.

[13] McMahon, John P., "Applying the CISG: Guide for Business Managers and Counsels," Pace Law School Institute of International Law, http://www.cisg.law.pace.edu/cisg/guides.html, accessed May 23, 2009.

[14] Huber, Peter, and Alastair Mullis, *The CISG: A new Textbook for Students and Practioners*, Munich: Sellier European Law Publisher, 2007.

[15] Heron, Karl G., and David D. Knoll, "Negotiating and Drafting International Distribution, Agency, and Representative Agreements: The United States Exporter's Perspective," *The International Lawyer*, Fall 1987, pp. 939-983.

[16] Deming, Stuart, *The Foreign Corrupt Practices Act and the New International Norms*, Chicago: American Bar Association, 2005.

[17] Carr, Indira, and Opi Outhwaite, "The OECD Anti-Bribery Convention Ten Years On,", *Manchester Journal of International Economic Law*, 5, Issue 1, 2008, pp. 3-35.

[18] Chester, James, personal e-mail communication, January 19, 2009.

[19] Heron, Karl G., and David D. Knoll, "Negotiating and Drafting International Distribution, Agency, and Representative Agreements: The United States Exporter's Perspective," *The International Lawyer*, Fall 1987, pp. 939-983.

[20]Dubberly, David E., "When Giving Your Rep the Boot: In Latin America, Labor Laws May Prove Surprisingly Costly, Unless You Plan Ahead," *Export Today*, May 1998, p. 26.

[21]"Lloyd's Revamp Won't Be Challenged," Associated Press News Release, June 23, 1997.

[22]*The ICC Model Commercial Agency Contract*, 2nd ed., 2002, publication No. 644 of the International Chamber of Commerce, ICC Publishing, 156 Fifth Avenue, New York, NY 10010, USA and ICC Publishing SA, 38, Cours Albert 1er, 75008 Paris, France.

[23]*The ICC Model Distributorship Contract*, 2002 ed., publication No. 646 of the International Chamber of Commerce, ICC Publishing, 156 Fifth Avenue, New York, NY 10010, USA and ICC Publishing SA, 38, Cours Albert 1er, 75008 Paris, France.

[24]*The ICC Model Commercial Agency Contract*, 2nd ed., 2002, publication No. 644 of the International Chamber of Commerce, ICC Publishing, 156 Fifth Avenue, New York, NY 10010, USA and ICC Publishing SA, 38, Cours Albert 1er, 75008 Paris, France.

[25]*The ICC Model Distributorship Contract*, 2002 ed., publication No. 646 of the International Chamber of Commerce, ICC Publishing, 156 Fifth Avenue, New York, NY 10010, USA and ICC Publishing SA, 38, Cours Albert 1er, 75008 Paris, France.

[26]Ulmer, Nicolas C., "Bullet-proofing Your International Arbitration: Part 2 of 2," *World Trade*, August 2000, p. 68.

[27]Howell, David, James Rogers and Matthew Townsend, "Chinese Arbitration—Still Distinctive," Harvard Business Law Review, April 2013, pp. 196-202.

[28]Connors, Kathleen, "Arbitration Taking Hold in Asia with Help of International Chamber," *The Journal of Commerce*, April 2, 1997, p. 8A.

[29]*The ICC Model Confidentiality Agreement*, 2006 ed., publication No. 664 of the International Chamber of Commerce, ICC Publishing, 156 Fifth Avenue, New York, NY 10010, USA and ICC Publishing SA, 38, Cours Albert 1er, 75008 Paris, France.

[30]Puelinckx, A. H., and H. A. Tielemans, "The Termination of Agency and Distributorship Agreements: A Comparative Survey," *Northwestern Journal of International Law and Business*, Fall 1981, 3:542, pp. 452-495.

[31]Miller, Edward, and Larry Coltman, "International Commercial Agency Agreements and Private International Law," July 8, 1999, m.reedsmith.com/files/Publication/23acd8f4-c3c3.../Comag3.pdf, retrieved June 11, 2013.

[32]*Ibid.*

[33]Ulmer, Nicolas C., "Bullet-proofing Your International Arbitration: Part 2 of 2," *World Trade*, August 2000, p. 68.

[34]"New Rules Attract International Arbitration Cases," International Chamber of Commerce, April 29, 2013, http://www.iccwbo.org/News/Articles/2013/New-rules-attract-international-arbitration-cases/, retrieved June 11, 2013.

[35]"ICC Rules of Arbitration," International Chamber of Commerce, http://www.iccwbo.org/Products-and-Services/Arbitration-and-ADR/Arbitration/ICC-Rules-of-Arbitration/, retrieved June 11, 2013.

[36]"Courts will take 320 years to clear backlog cases: Justice Rao," *The Times of India*, March 6, 2010, http://articles.timesofindia.indiatimes.com/2010-03-06/india/28143242_1_high-court-judges-literacy-rate-backlog, retrieved June 11, 2013.

Chapter 6

Terms of Trade or Incoterms® Rules

6.1 International Commerce Terms 142
6.2 Understanding Incoterms Rules 142
6.3 Incoterms Rule Strategy 143
6.4 Ex-Works (EXW) 146
6.5 Free Carrier (FCA) 148
6.6 Carriage Paid To (CPT) 150
6.7 Carriage and Insurance Paid To (CIP) 151
6.8 Delivered At Terminal (DAT) 152
6.9 Delivered At Place (DAP) 154
6.10 Delivered Duty Paid (DDP) 155
6.11 Free Alongside Ship (FAS) 156
6.12 Free on Board (FOB) 158
6.13 Cost and Freight (CFR) 161
6.14 Cost, Insurance, and Freight (CIF) 162
6.15 Summary of Incoterms® Responsibilities 163
6.16 Common Errors in Incoterms® Rules Usage 165
6.17 Incoterms Rules as a Marketing Tool 167

Whenever an exporter sells goods to a foreign company, whether through an intermediary such as an agent or a distributor or directly to an importer, there are many steps involved in getting the goods to the customer:

- The goods must be cleared for export
- The transport of the goods must be arranged between the exporter and the importer, often using several means of transportation—also known as means of conveyance—, including at least three distinct legs in that journey:
    - pre-carriage, the transportation that takes place in the country of export
    - main carriage, the international transportation between the country of export and the country of import

pre-carriage
The portion of an international shipment that takes place in the exporting country.

main carriage
The portion of an international shipment that takes place between the exporting country and the importing country.

○ on-carriage, the transportation that takes place in the country of import

- The goods must clear Customs in the importing country

on-carriage
The portion of an international shipment that takes place in the importing country.

The terms of trade used in the contract of sale determine which of these steps are the responsibility of the exporter and which are the responsibility of the importer. Often, the number of issues involved in an international shipment is substantial, and determining the way these tasks should be divided between the exporter and the importer for each shipment would be a daunting task. In addition, it would be virtually impossible to anticipate everything that could go wrong during transit and determine at the time of the contract which of the parties should be responsible for each incident.[1]

6.1 International Commerce Terms

International Chamber of Commerce (ICC)
The largest business organization in the world. Its goal is to champion international business growth and its members are the national chambers of commerce.

Fortunately, a set of standardized Terms of Trade was created in 1936 by the International Chamber of Commerce: they have evolved into eleven International Commerce Terms rules, from which the acronym Incoterms® is derived. These Incoterms® rules were revised in 1953, 1967, 1976, 1980, 1990, 2000, and most recently in 2010.[2]

It is of significant benefit to both parties to use one of these Incoterms® rules, because ample information is available for each, and substantial jurisprudence has accumulated for each through the International Chamber of Commerce arbitration system. These Incoterms® rules are used in all the documents used in an international transaction. For example, a *pro forma* invoice would read:

> FCA · 2300 Industrial Parkway, Milwaukee, WI 53223, USA, Incoterms® 2010.

to indicate which tasks the exporter would be willing to perform and which tasks would remain the responsibility of the importer. When faced with an Incoterms® rule, exporters and importers know precisely what tasks they have to complete, which costs they have to bear, and the exact point at which the responsibility for the goods transfers from the exporter to the importer.

6.2 Understanding Incoterms® Rules

Incoterms® Rules
A series of eleven international terms of trade standardized by the International Chamber of Commerce.

The Terms of Trade or Incoterms® rules that the exporter and the importer agree to use in a given transaction defines five aspects of an international sale:

- Which tasks will be performed by the exporter

- Which tasks will be performed by the importer

- Which activities will be paid by the exporter

- Which activities will be paid by the importer

- When the transfer of responsibility for the goods will take place

This last point is complicated: it is necessary to make the distinction between (1) the transfer of responsibility for the goods between the exporter and the importer and (2) the transfer of title between the exporter and the importer. The transfer of responsibility (transfer of risk) is dictated by the choice of the Incoterms® rule. The transfer of title (transfer of ownership) usually takes place when the importer has either paid the exporter—and obtained the original bill of lading (see Chapter 9)—, accepted to sign a draft (see Chapter 7), or performed some other event specifically outlined in the contract of sale between both parties. The transfer of responsibility coincides with the delivery of the goods, a point that is clearly outlined in each of the Incoterms® rules, and in most cases, a point that occurs chronologically much earlier than the transfer of title.

The transfer of responsibility of the exporter never extends beyond the services for which that company has paid. There are several Incoterms® rules, however, where the exporter is obligated to pre-pay a portion of the transportation costs—main carriage and on-carriage—even though it is no longer responsible for the goods. Such is the case for the so-called C-terms, the ones whose three-letter acronyms start with the letter C.

transfer of responsibility
In an international voyage, the point at which the exporter ceases to be responsible for the goods.

transfer of title
The point in time at which the ownership of the goods changes from the exporter to the importer.

delivery
In an international voyage, the point at which the responsibility for the goods switches from the exporter to the importer.

6.3 Incoterms® Rule Strategy

The proper choice of an Incoterms® rule is therefore contingent upon the strategy followed by the exporting firm, but is also somewhat constrained by the following parameters:

- The type of product sold: several industries (commodities in particular) prefer using some specific terms of trade rather than others.

- The method of shipment: goods shipped by ocean or barge are sold under different Incoterms® than cargo shipped by air or by ground transportation—rail or road.

- The package size: containerized goods, small packages, and large crates are transported under different Incoterms® rules and use different transportation modes.

- The ability of either of the parties to perform the tasks involved in the shipment.

- The amount of trust placed by either of the parties toward the other.

Nevertheless, the greatest criterion to be used in determining the proper Incoterms® rule for a transaction is the willingness of both parties to perform and pay for some of the tasks involved in the shipment. In some cases, an exporter can gain a strategic advantage and facilitate the sale of its products by assisting the importer in the shipment. In others, an importer can obtain a lower price if it performs all or most of the tasks involved in the shipment. However, a company generally does not determine which Incoterms® rule to use on a case-by-case basis, but will determine which strategy it would like to pursue and determine which Term of Trade should be used regularly, given its product line, its customers' expectations, and its trade volume. Sophisticated exporters will offer more than one Incoterms® rule choice to their customers (see Section 6.17 on page 167) to gain a tactical advantage over their competitors.

International Commerce Terms

Main Carriage by Any Means of Transportation

EXW	Ex Works
FCA	Free Carrier
CPT	Carriage Paid To
CIP	Carriage and Insurance Paid to
DAT	Delivered At Terminal
DAP	Delivered At Place
DDP	Delivered Duty Paid

Main Carriage by Ocean

FAS	Free Alongside Ship
FOB	Free On Board
CFR	Cost and Freight
CIF	Cost, Insurance and Freight

Table 6.1: International Terms of Trade Abbreviations

Another issue to understand clearly in this decision is that, regardless of the Incoterms® rule chosen, the importer is always paying for the transportation and other costs of shipping internationally. The fact that the exporter is pre-paying and arranging for certain aspects of the shipment is reflected in the invoice price; therefore, the importer ends up being charged for them. In addition, it is likely, although not always the case, that the exporter's invoice is going to include a charge that is higher than the actual cost of the service. Many exporters add a premium to these costs to reflect the fact that it took some time and effort to arrange for those services.[3]

Nevertheless, the choice of Incoterms® rule is often the exporter's decision: it is difficult for an exporter to adapt its Incoterms® rule strategy to accommodate the requirements of an importer, as it may require the exporter to be responsible for tasks that it has decided it would rather not perform. Should the importer feel that the exporter is not providing a service that is adequate, it can always purchase from another source. However, should the importer want to perform more tasks than what the exporter prefers, it is certainly possible for the exporter to do less than what it expected, and use a different Incoterms® rule on that transaction, one for which it is responsible for fewer aspects of the shipment.

Finally, the choice of the proper Incoterms® rule is a critical decision for a firm, as it is an integral part of its export strategy and linked to the level of customer service it is aiming to provide.[4]

In this chapter, all eleven Incoterms® rules are reviewed in depth. They are first divided into two groups; those Incoterms® that are appropriate for all forms of international transportation (the main carriage) and those that can only be used with ocean shipments. In each group, the Incoterms® rules are then reviewed in an order that reflects increased services provided by the exporter (see Table 6.1 on the facing page).

Changes from Incoterms 2000

The latest revision of Incoterms® rules was published in 2010. The Incoterms® rules were modified by the International Chamber of Commerce to reflect more accurately the trade practices followed by international shippers. For example, the 2010 Incoterms® rules mirror the process that ocean carriers follow for containerized cargo; shipments are accepted at a container terminal in the port of departure before being shipped abroad and delivered in a terminal in the port of destination. The International Chamber of Commerce created two brand-new terms (Delivered At Terminal [DAT] and Delivered At Place [DAP] to accommodate these practices.[5]

For the same reason, the International Chamber of Commerce eliminated four of the terms that had been in place for a number of years: (Delivered Ex Ship [DES], Delivered Ex Quay [DEQ], Delivered Duty Unpaid [DDU], and Delivered At Frontier [DAF]), as they were infrequently used or were replaced by the new DAT and DAP terms.

The 2010 Incoterms® rules also made some significant changes to several of the terms and the way they had been used. The International Chamber of Commerce designated some Incoterms® rules to be restricted to certain means of transportation (main carriage conducted by ocean), and some to be for all means of transportation. It also wanted certain Incoterms® rules to be restricted to certain types of cargo, a position it did not take until 2010. For example, the ICC is encouraging traders to use the Ex-Works [EXW] Incoterm® rule only for shipments conducted door-to-door, such as the time-defined shipments offered by FedEx or DHL.

Another modification made by the ICC is that the 2010 Incoterms® rules should be used with increased precision in the address used on the Incoterms® statement. Where a "FCA München, Deutschland" had been sufficient, it is now necessary to specify "FCA · Prinzregentenstrasse, 240, München, D-80538, Deutschland."

A significant change is the definition of the point at which the responsibility for the goods shifts from the exporter to the importer for maritime shipments. Where it had been the ship's rail for all previous Incoterm versions, the 2010 version now uses "on board," without defining it specifically. This distinction is explained further in the vignette on page 159.

The International Chamber of Commerce is also attempting to broaden the scope of Incoterms® rules. Since many multinational companies are operating in multiple countries, they are faced with different domestic terms of trade in each of these countries, with their own rules and definitions. To simplify this myriad of different terms, the ICC reasoned that it would make sense to use Incoterms® rules in domestic transactions as well. Time will tell whether companies follow that suggestion.

Finally, the International Chamber of Commerce wanted to change the way these international terms of trade should be addressed. It is now requiring a registered trademark (®) to be added to Incoterms, and it wants them to be addressed as Incoterms® rules. It is likely that this change will take some

time to take hold.
These modifications, coupled with the fact that Incoterms® rules had also been changed in 1990 and 2000, mean that a number of organizations have managers who have used multiple versions of the same Incoterms® rules. It is important to know which modifications were made between 2000 and 2010, to prevent confusion and possible misunderstandings. It is therefore imperative that a quote or invoice include the statement: "2010 Incoterms® ." Section 6.16.2 on page 166 covers some of the problems presented by having employees who have learned different Incoterms® versions.

6.4 Ex-Works (EXW)

The EXW Incoterms® rule can be used for any merchandise and for any means of transportation. It should be used with the following syntax:

EXW · 2400 Progress Drive, Poughkeepsie, New York 12601, USA, Incoterms® 2010.

where the address is the location at which the exporter will hold the merchandise available to the importer. It is located in the exporting country.

Ex-Works is the easiest of the Incoterms® rule for the exporter, and the most difficult for the importer. In an Ex-Works transaction, the exporter only has the obligation to "place the goods at the disposal of the buyer" and "render every assistance [...] in obtaining [...] any export license or other official authorization necessary for the export of the goods." [6] In addition, the exporter has to package the goods for export, but the exporter does not have to load the goods onto the importer's pre-arranged vehicle. It should be evident that this is not an advantageous Incoterms® rule from the importer's perspective: arranging to pick up goods in a foreign country is not easy, and neither is providing domestic transportation nor clearing goods for export in a foreign country.

Because of these restrictions, the International Chamber of Commerce is directing exporters to limit the use of EXW to international shipments that are transported by small-package companies, such as FedEx or DHL.[7] In that case, the goods are clearly placed at the disposal of the buyer, who can instruct the small-package carrier to collect them at the exporter's place of business. The goods are small enough that there is no concern about placing the goods on board the means of conveyance. The small-package company then transports them to their destination in the importing country, under a single bill of lading. Under these circumstances, an EXW Incoterms® rule is attractive to importer, since there is little effort extended to arrange for the collection and shipment of the goods.

6.4.1 Delivery under EXW

There is nothing specified in this Incoterms® rule regarding the delivery of the goods. It occurs at the time at which the importer (or the importer's agent) picks up the goods at the exporter's plant. This delivery has to take place at a mutually convenient time. The exporter has the obligation to notify the importer that the goods are available for pickup and the importer has the obligation to notify the exporter of the time at which the goods will be picked up.

There is no specific transportation document corresponding to the delivery of the goods under this Incoterms® rule, although, if a transportation company is picking up the goods, the exporter will generally be given a copy of the bill of lading or some form of receipt for the goods.

Figure 6.1: Small-Packet Delivery Vehicles in Tokyo, Japan, ready to pick up EXW shipments
Photo ©Marek Ślusarczyk. Used with permission.

6.4.2 Responsibilities of the Exporter and the Importer under EXW

The exporter's responsibilities are limited to the most basic functions: make the goods available to the buyer, package the goods for export shipment, assist in the export clearance procedures, and provide the documents to the importer so that the goods can clear Customs in the importing country or be insured. None of these requirements are trivial, though. The exporter has to package the goods in such a way that the goods are protected during their international voyage. That requirement means that the exporter should find out what the means of transportation will be and make sure that the goods are adequately packaged to make sure that they are not damaged. If the goods are damaged in transit due to improper packaging, the exporter is responsible and the insurance coverage contracted by the importer will not cover the costs of the damage. This requirement is, however, easy to meet for a small package traveling by air, since the packaging requirements would be similar to those for a small package traveling domestically.

The exporter also has to provide all of the documents necessary for the importer to clear Customs in the importing country; this means that the invoice has to be a good international invoice and include product description, Harmonized System numbers, weights, volume measures, unit price, total price, and so on (see Chapter 9 for further details and examples), that the other documents be prepared carefully and accurately (certificate of origin, packing list, and so on), and that the correct number of originals and copies be included. The exporter has to provide these documents, but can charge the importer for the costs of providing them. Because the importer is also the one in charge of exporting the products, the exporter has to provide the documents necessary to clear the goods for export in the exporting country.

At export, the United States handles EXW shipments in a way that is somewhat at odds with the Incoterms® rule. Under EXW rules, the importer is the party that clears the goods for export, and therefore is the exporter of record. However, in the United States Shipper's Export Declaration (SED) (an export document explained in Section 9.3.1), with which the Census Bureau records who the exporter is, the seller-exporter has to be listed as the "U.S. principal party in interest."[8] This terminology was specifically created to allow the U.S. Census to record who was the exporter of a specific shipment under an EXW sale, rather than record the importer of the goods: actually, the term "exporter" has been stricken from the SED. Because of this requirement, the United States government has placed the responsibility of providing the correct Export Commodity Classification Number (ECCN) and any information that could affect an export license on the exporter in the case of an EXW transaction.[9]

The importer is responsible for all other aspects of the shipment in an EXW transaction: arrange for main transportation, clear Customs in the importing country, purchase insurance, and provide on-carriage (transportation) in the importing country.

FCL shipment
An international shipment that uses, by weight or volume, the entire capacity of a container.

LCL shipment
An international shipment that is combined with other shipments in a single container.

6.5 Free Carrier (FCA)

The FCA Incoterms® rule can be used for any merchandise and for any means of transportation, but it was specifically created for goods shipped through multi-modal transportation (*i.e.*, merchandise that is shipped through multiple means of transportation—without being "handled" between means of transportation because it is containerized—and under one single bill of lading). This Incoterms® rule can be used for shipments of either full-container loads (FCL) or less-than-container loads (LCL). FCA has become one of the most popular Incoterms®rules as the number of multi-modal shipments increased. This Incoterms® rule should be used with the following syntax:

FCA · Bâtiment B, 46 Allée Corbière, F-81000 Castres, France, Incoterms® 2010

where the address is the location at which the delivery takes place. It is usually located in the exporting country or in a neighboring country.

The goods can be given to the carrier at the exporter's premises or they can be delivered by the exporter to the carrier's place of business. In the first case, it is common to refer to that transaction as an FCA "exporter's premises" and in the second case to an FCA "carrier's premises." The location depends on the agreement between the importer and the exporter, but the selection of the carrier is the responsibility of the importer. In either case, the exporter is responsible for loading the goods on the means of transportation.

Because FCA is a fairly recent Incoterms® rule—it was created in 1990—great care has been taken to define specifically what responsibilities are borne by the exporter, and which are borne by the importer. In the 2010 version of Incoterms® rules, the International Chamber of Commerce has made it clear that it would prefer international shipments of goods other than small packages to be conducted under FCA rather than under EXW when the exporter and the importer agree that the exporter's role in the international shipment should be minimal.

6.5.1 Delivery under FCA

Under FCA, the delivery takes place when either of two conditions is met:

- If the named point in the Incoterms® rule refers to the exporter's plant, then delivery takes place when the goods are loaded, by the exporter and at its expense and risk, onto the carrier's truck.

- If the named point in the Incoterms® rule refers to the carrier's premises, then delivery takes place when the goods are made available to the carrier (*i.e.*, when the goods have arrived at the carrier's dock). The goods are delivered even though they have not been unloaded from the exporter's truck. They are unloaded by the carrier and at the carrier's expense (*i.e.*, at the importer's expense), and at their risk.

The document that corresponds clearly to the transfer of responsibility for an FCA shipment is the receipt given by the carrier to the exporter; it is generally a multi-modal bill of lading.

6.5.2 Responsibilities of the Exporter and the Importer under FCA

The exporter is in charge of packing the merchandise for export, as under EXW. However, if the transaction is an FCA exporter's premises, its responsibilities increase to include loading the merchandise into a container provided by the carrier, and loading the container on the truck provided by the carrier, or loading the non-containerized goods onto the means of conveyance provided by the carrier. If the transaction is an FCA carrier's premises, then the exporter is responsible for loading the goods onto his own truck and delivering the merchandise to the carrier's facilities.

In addition, the exporter is responsible for clearing the merchandise for export, and has to provide whatever information and documents are needed by the importer to clear Customs in the importing country and to obtain insurance. In the United States, the exporter fills out the Shipper's Export Declaration and is the "U.S. principal party in interest." For shipments originating in countries where export authorities require a Pre-Shipment Inspection (see Chapter 16), the exporter has to pay for it.

The exporter also has to provide all of the documents necessary for the importer to clear Customs in the importing country; it can charge the importer for the costs of providing them.

The importer is responsible for arranging the main carriage and on-carriage (*i.e.*, finding a carrier between the exporter's town and the final destination) and communicating to the exporter which carrier has been selected. The importer is also responsible for arranging for insurance and for clearing Customs in the importing country. If the importing country requires a Pre-Shipment Inspection, the importer has to pay for it.

6.6 Carriage Paid To (CPT)

The CPT Incoterms® rule is an Incoterms® rule where the exporter and the importer agree that the exporter should pre-pay the main carriage for the goods. This Incoterms® rule is designed to be used for all cargo types and all means of transportation. It is most commonly used for goods transported by surface or air transportation, but it can be used for goods transported by ocean; however, it is rarely used for cargo that is directly handed by the exporter to an ocean carrier in a port. In addition, it is more likely to be used for cargo that is not containerized, such as roll-on/roll-off cargo or large crates. This Incoterms® rule should be used with the following syntax:

CPT · Graacher Straße 20, Köln, Deutschland D-50969,
Incoterms® 2010.

where the address refers to the location in the city of destination in which the importer takes control of the goods. It is generally located in the importing country or a neighboring country.

In a Carriage Paid To transaction, the delivery does not take place in the city of destination (at the address mentioned in the Incoterms® rule) but at the point where the exporter delivers the goods to the carrier in the exporting country. Unless unusual circumstances prevail, shipping charges do not include the unloading of the merchandise in the destination city.

6.6.1 Delivery under CPT

Delivery takes place when the exporter hands over the goods to the first carrier, in the exporting country. This is the case even though the exporter has pre-paid shipping charges to the city of destination (pre-carriage, main carriage and on-carriage) and the contract of carriage is in the exporter's name. Proof of delivery is obtained when the exporter is given a bill of lading or equivalent document (air waybill, sea waybill, multi-modal bill of lading) by the carrier.

6.6.2 Responsibilities of the Exporter and the Importer under CPT

The exporter is responsible for packaging the goods for export, shipping them to the carrier, and pre-paying the shipping costs to the city of destination. In the United States, the exporter fills out the Shipper's Export Declaration and is the "U.S. principal party in interest," or the exporter of record. In countries where export authorities require a Pre-Shipment Inspection, the exporter has to pay for it.

The exporter also has to provide all of the documents necessary for the importer to clear Customs in the importing country; it can charge the importer for the costs of providing them.

The importer assumes responsibility for the goods at the time the seller delivers them to the first carrier. The importer is responsible for unloading the goods from the carrier's truck in the importing country, clearing Customs, and for paying inland transportation (if any) beyond the city of destination. If the importing country requires a Pre-Shipment Inspection, the importer has to pay for it.

Figure 6.2: CPT Delivery: Cargo is Loaded in First Means of Conveyance
Photo ©Ragip Candan. Used with permission.

6.7 Carriage and Insurance Paid To (CIP)

The CIP Incoterms® rule is a modification of the CPT Incoterms® rule for which the exporter also purchases insurance for the cargo while it is in transit. It can be used for all goods and all means of transportation, but is mostly designed for non-containerized cargo that travels by surface or air. It is possible to use it for ocean cargo, as long as the cargo is not handed to an ocean carrier in a port. This Incoterms® rule should be used with the following syntax:

> **CIP · Ulitsa Poruchik Nedelcho Bonchev, Sofia, Bulgaria,
> Incoterms® 2010**

where the address refers to the location in the city of destination where the importer takes control of the goods. It is located in the importing country or a neighboring country.

In a Carriage and Insurance Paid To transaction, the delivery does not take place in the city of destination, but in the city where the exporter delivers the goods to the first carrier. In addition to the responsibilities it has under the CPT Incoterms® rule, the exporter must pre-pay for insurance until the city of destination.

Under the CIP Incoterms® rule, the amount insured must be at least 110 percent of the value of the goods, a custom that dates back to 1906, when Great Britain instituted the Marine Insurance Act[10] and introduced the maritime equivalent to the CIP Incoterms® rule (see 6.14 on page 162).

The insurance coverage required by the ICC is Coverage C of the Institute Cargo Clauses, and therefore minimum-cover insurance. Expectedly, a modification to the

Incoterm® rule variant
A modification to an Incoterm® rule, not sanctioned by the ICC, that changes one or more of its parameters.

CIP Incoterms® rule has emerged, called an Incoterms® rule variant, that requests that the exporter provide coverage A of the Institute Cargo Clauses, or maximum-cover insurance. The syntax must accommodate the fact that Incoterms® rule variants are not regulated by the International Chamber of Commerce and should therefore read:

CIP · Ulitsa Poruchik Nedelcho Bonchev, Sofia, Bulgaria, Incoterms® 2010, maximum cover

Certain countries (see Table 6.2 on page 164) do not allow their importers to purchase insurance abroad, and therefore prevent any import on a CIP basis.

6.7.1 Delivery under CIP

Delivery takes place when the exporter hands over the goods to the first carrier in the exporting country. This is the case even though the exporter has pre-paid shipping charges to the city of destination (pre-carriage, main carriage and on-carriage) and the contract of carriage is in the exporter's name. Proof of delivery is obtained when the exporter is given a bill of lading or equivalent document (air waybill, sea waybill, multi-modal bill of lading) by the carrier.

6.7.2 Responsibilities of the Exporter and the Importer under CIP

The exporter is responsible for export packing, transportation costs (pre-carriage, main carriage and on-carriage) to the city of destination, and for minimum insurance costs. In addition, the exporter is responsible for clearing the goods for export. In the United States, the exporter fills out the Shipper's Export Declaration and is the "U.S. principal party in interest" or the exporter of record. In countries where export authorities require a Pre-Shipment Inspection, the exporter has to pay for it.

The exporter also has to provide all of the documents necessary for the importer to clear Customs in the importing country; it can charge the importer for the costs of providing them.

The importer's responsibility starts when the exporter delivers the goods to the first carrier. The importer is responsible for unloading the carrier's truck, clearing Customs in the importing country, and for transportation costs beyond the city of destination. If the importing country requires a Pre-Shipment Inspection, the importer has to pay for it.

6.8 Delivered At Terminal (DAT)

container terminal
A location where containerized cargo changes mode of transportation.

The DAT Incoterms® rule is an Incoterms® rule that was created in 2010. It reflects the practice that containerized cargo often transits through a container terminal, whether in the exporting or importing country. It is intended to be used for all modes of transportation and all types of cargo, but fits closely with intermodal containerized shipments. A terminal, or more precisely an intermodal terminal, is a location where cargo shifts from one mode of transportation to another; from truck to rail, or from rail to ocean, for example. This Incoterms® rule should be used with the following syntax:

6.8 Delivered At Terminal (DAT)

> DAT · Paranaguá Container Terminal, Avenida Portuária, Paranaguá, Parana 83206-410, Brazil, Incoterms® 2010.

where the address refers to the terminal in which the importer takes control of the goods. It can be located in the exporting country, in which case the importer is responsible for the main carriage, or it can be located in the importing country, in which case the exporter is responsible for the main carriage. This Incoterms® rule is quite flexible.

6.8.1 Delivery under DAT

In a DAT transaction, the delivery takes place in the terminal, when the goods are unloaded from the means of transportation provided by the exporter. If the terminal is located in the port of origin, then the exporter delivers the goods when they are unloaded from the truck that took them to the terminal. If the terminal is located in the port of destination, the transfer of responsibility takes place when the goods are unloaded from the ship. Proof of delivery is generally provided by the terminal with a terminal receipt.

Figure 6.3: Cargo Container Staged before Loading onto Ship at an Intermodal Terminal in the Port of Santos, Brazil

Photo ©Pierre David. Used with permission.

6.8.2 Responsibilities of the Exporter and the Importer under DAT

The exporter is responsible for export packing and transportation costs to the terminal of destination. Depending on the location of the terminal, the transportation costs may include pre-carriage, main carriage and possibly on-carriage. The exporter is also responsible for the costs of unloading the goods at the terminal. In addition, the exporter is responsible for clearing the goods for export and, in the

United States, is the "U.S. principal party in interest," or the exporter of record. In countries where export authorities require a Pre-Shipment Inspection, the exporter has to pay for it.

The exporter also has to provide all of the documents necessary for the importer to clear Customs in the importing country; it can charge the importer for the costs of providing them.

The importer's responsibility starts when the exporter has delivered the goods at the terminal. The importer is responsible for clearing Customs in the importing country, and for transportation costs beyond the terminal. Depending on the location of the terminal, the transportation costs may include main carriage, on-carriage, and possibly pre-carriage. If the importing country requires a Pre-Shipment Inspection, the importer has to pay for it.

6.9 Delivered At Place (DAP)

The DAP Incoterms® rule is an Incoterms® rule that was created in 2010. It allows the exporter to provide a great level of service by delivering the goods at the importer's place of business—or some other location chosen by the importer. It is intended to be used for all modes of transportation and all types of cargo. This Incoterms® rule should be used with the following syntax:

> DAP · 97 Brisbane Street, Sydenham 8023, New Zealand, Incoterms® 2010.

The DAP Incoterms® rule was designed to replace a former Incoterms® rule called DDU—Delivered Duty Unpaid—which had been frequently used, but could not be used for domestic transactions, since there is no duty that a seller has to consider in a domestic transaction. The two terms—the former DDU and the new DAP—are essentially similar; for a manager accustomed to DDU, a change to DAP will be smooth and require few adjustments.

6.9.1 Delivery under DAP

In a DAP transaction, the delivery takes place when the goods arrive, still loaded on the means of transportation provided by the exporter, at their destination. Since the delivery generally takes place at a location that is the place of business of the importer, the proof of delivery is the arrival of the goods, ready to be unloaded.

6.9.2 Responsibilities of the Exporter and the Importer under DAP

The exporter is responsible for export packing and transportation costs to the destination mentioned on the Incoterms® rule statement. Generally, the transportation costs include pre-carriage, main carriage and on-carriage. The exporter is not responsible for the costs of unloading the goods at their destination, which are borne by the importer. The exporter is responsible for clearing the goods for export, and, in the United States, the exporter is the "U.S. principal party in interest" or the exporter of record. In countries where export authorities require a Pre-Shipment Inspection, the exporter has to pay for it.

The exporter also has to provide all of the documents necessary for the importer to clear Customs in the importing country; it can charge the importer for the costs of providing them.

The importer has to pay the costs of unloading the goods from the means of conveyance used for the on-carriage, and has to clear Customs in the importing country, using the documents provided by the exporter.

Incoterms®2010 Rules in Domestic Trade

The latest version of Incoterms® rules created a group of commerce terms that could be used for both domestic and international trade, as is clearly stated in the ICC document: Incoterms® rules are the "ICC rules for the use of domestic and international trade terms."

There are several reasons for this change; the first is that, in 2002, the American Law Institute and the National Conference of Commissioners on Uniform State Laws eliminated the definitions of shipping and delivery terms from the United States Uniform Commercial Code (FOB factory, FOB destination).[11] Even though none of the fifty states had incorporated these changes by 2010, it was expected that they would eventually be adopted and the ICC thought that the Incoterms® 2010 rules would fill the void. However, in May 2011, the American Law Institute withdrew that change, and reinstated the traditional shipping and delivery terms of the UCC.[12]

The second is that Incoterms® rules are revised and reviewed at periodic intervals. That single fact allows for the terms to reflect the trade practices and creativity of domestic and international shippers. Consider that the UCC's version of FOB had been written in 1941, before all of the major innovations of the past sixty years: containers, widespread air shipments, and computers. The Incoterms® rules are certainly more in tune with current shippers' practices.

The third is that companies and managers are increasingly multi-national, and operate in a large number of domestic markets in addition to their international activities. By following Incoterms® rules, managers have to learn only one set of rules, rather than a large number of domestic rules, several of which contradict one another. For example, the UCC's Free On Board is radically different from the *franco à bord* or from the *franco de port* of the French, from the *frei an Bord* of the German, and of the Free On Board of the Incoterms® rules.

It is unknown whether Incoterms® rules will eventually gain usage as domestic terms of trade. However, the modifications made by the International Chamber of Commerce would likely enhance that possibility.

6.10 Delivered Duty Paid (DDP)

The DDP Incoterms® rule can be used for any merchandise and for any means of transportation. This Incoterms® rule should be used with the following syntax:

> DDP · Kopparbergsgatan 226, Malmö 214 44, Sverige/Sweden, Incoterms® 2010.

where the address is the location at which the importer takes control of the goods. This location is generally the place of business of the importer, but can be any other location in the importing country or in a neighboring country that the importer selects.

Choosing the DDP Incoterms® rule provides the ultimate level of customer service on the part of the exporter. The exporter handles everything for the importer, including shipment to the customer's plant and Customs clearance in the importing country. For the importer, this type of transaction is exactly equivalent to receiving a domestic shipment from a domestic supplier: the only thing left to the importer's care is the unloading of the merchandise, something that is usually its responsibility under a domestic shipment.

In some cases, it may be advantageous for pragmatic reasons to use a variant of the DDP Incoterms® rule: in a number of countries, the Customs authorities collect not only duty on the goods imported but also Value Added Tax (VAT) on the value of the goods. Because of the peculiarities of VAT accounting, it is often much more convenient for the importer to pay the VAT than it is for the exporter. In those circumstances, the DDP VAT unpaid Incoterms® rule variant may be used. The syntax should be:

> DDP · Kopparbergsgatan 226, Malmö 214 44, Sverige/Sweden, Incoterms® 2010, VAT unpaid.

6.10.1 Delivery under DDP

Under the DDP Incoterms® rule, the delivery takes place when the exporter places the goods at the disposal of the importer at the address of delivery mentioned in the Incoterms® rule. The goods are delivered unloaded (*i.e.*, it is the responsibility of the importer to arrange and pay for unloading the goods). However, this is often a very minor point, as the destination of the delivery is often the importer's plant, which obviously has the ability to unload a truck.

Although there is no transportation document that corresponds to this delivery, a commonly used alternative is for the exporter to provide the bill of lading at the time of delivery.

6.10.2 Responsibilities of the Exporter and the Importer under DDP

The exporter assumes all responsibilities in a DDP shipment: clearing the goods for export, transporting them to the importer's facilities, and clearing Customs in the importing country. All costs and responsibilities are for the exporter.

The importer only has the responsibility to receive the goods at delivery and unload them.

6.11 Free Alongside Ship (FAS)

Although the FAS Incoterms® rule can be used for any merchandise, it is specifically designed for ocean transportation, and is not meant for any other means of transportation or for merchandise that is not destined to be handed to an ocean shipping

6.11 Free Alongside Ship (FAS)

line at the port of departure. The practices followed by international shippers make it an Incoterms® rule that should be used sparingly with containerized cargo, which should be best handled under a DAT Incoterms® rule. The FAS Incoterms® rule should be used with the following syntax:

FAS · Waalhaven Noordzijde 2089, Rotterdam, 3089KM, The Netherlands, Incoterms® 2010.

where the address refers to the dock in the port of Rotterdam in which the delivery takes place. This port is usually located in the exporting country or a neighboring country.

In a Free Alongside Ship transaction, the exporter is responsible to bring the goods to the port, on a quay "alongside" a ship designated by the importer, at which time the responsibility shifts to the importer.

Figure 6.4: Lumber Delivered Alongside the Ship in the Port of Paranaguá, Brazil
Photo ©Pierre David. Used with permission.

6.11.1 Delivery under FAS

The delivery officially takes place when the exporter has delivered the goods "alongside" a ship designated by the importer. The problem with this Incoterms® rule is that ports rarely keep merchandise "alongside" a ship, or keep merchandise on a quay waiting for a ship. The delivery takes place in a holding area, then the goods are cartaged (transported within the port area) from the holding area to the ship

stevedore
Historically, an individual, and today a company, that loads and unloads goods from a vessel.

before the stevedoring (loading onto the ship) takes place. However, there are some merchandise types that are delivered next to the ship, such as large crates or bulk cargoes.

Compounding this difficulty is the fact that there is no transport document that clearly corresponds to a delivery to a holding area or to the quay alongside the ship. The ICC recognizes that the exporter may not be able to obtain "a receipt or a transport document from the carrier"[13] since no ocean carrier will issue a bill of lading until the goods have been received in good condition on board the vessel. However, it adds that the exporter must then "provide some other document to prove that the goods have been delivered" [14] but does not suggest what it may be. A dock receipt from the port authorities may be sufficient; however, this lack of clear physical evidence of delivery could be a substantial deterrent to the use of the FAS Incoterms® rule. However, the use of Electronic Data Interchange (EDI) by the parties involved can remedy this problem: the exporter can notify the importer that the delivery has been made in the port of departure and the terminal operator can also do the same. However, the ICC did not list such notices as acceptable proofs of delivery.

It is for those reasons that the DAT Incoterms® rule was developed; there is a clear point at which the responsibility for the goods shift from the importer to the exporter.

6.11.2 Responsibilities of the Exporter and the Importer under FAS

The exporter is responsible for packing the goods for export, transporting them to the port, and unloading them onto the quay or holding area in the port. The exporter is responsible for clearing the goods for export, providing whatever documents and assistance the importer may need to clear Customs in the importing country and to obtain insurance. In the United States, the exporter fills out the Shipper's Export Declaration and is the "U.S. principal party in interest," or the exporter of record. In countries where export authorities require a Pre-Shipment Inspection, the exporter has to pay for it.

The importer is responsible for the shipment starting from the point of delivery. Therefore the importer is responsible for port handling charges, stevedoring (loading the goods in the vessel), and for ocean transportation costs, as well as insurance, if purchased, unloading in the port of arrival, and Customs duties in the importing country. If the importing country requires a Pre-Shipment Inspection, the importer has to pay for it.

6.12 Free on Board (FOB)

Although the FOB Incoterms® rule can be used for any merchandise, it is specifically designed for ocean transportation, and is not meant for any other means of transportation or for merchandise that is not destined to then be handed to an ocean shipping line at the port of departure. The practices followed by international shippers make it an Incoterms® rule that should be used sparingly with containerized cargo, which is best handled under a DAT Incoterms® rule. The FOB Incoterms® rule should be used with the following syntax:

> **FOB · Breakbulk Terminal, 660 Duncan Road, Cape Town, South Africa, Incoterms® 2010.**

6.12 Free on Board (FOB)

where the terminal indicated is the location in the port of Cape Town at which the goods are placed aboard the vessel and delivery takes place. This port is generally located in the exporting country or a neighboring country.

The Free On Board term, sometimes incorrectly called Freight On Board, is one of the oldest maritime Terms of Trade. The exporter is responsible for the goods until they are placed on the ship. The importer is responsible for them after that.

Unfortunately, because FOB is such an old Term of Trade, its meaning is somewhat dependent on the practices of the port in which the goods are loaded. These differences matter specifically in the way the loading costs are billed: some ports have the tradition to include loading, stowing, and securing the goods in the hold of the ship as part of the stevedoring costs. Some other ports will customarily bill for these services as part of the ocean cargo costs. The shipping line contracted by the importer obviously would be able to communicate what the practice is at a given port of departure. However, these differences in practices have triggered the need for a variant to the FOB Incoterms® rule to reflect which of the trade partners is responsible for handling costs on the ship; either "FOB stowed" or "FOB stowed, trimmed, and secured"[15] can be used to denote that the exporter is responsible for those specific costs. Here again, because the International Chamber of Commerce does not regulate Incoterm variants, the correct syntax should be:

> FOB · Breakbulk Terminal, 660 Duncan Road, Cape Town, South Africa, Incoterms® 2010, Stowed, Trimmed and Secured.

For these reasons, it may be preferable to use the DAT Incoterms® rule which outlines clearly the responsibilities of the exporter and those of the importer.

stowed
Goods are considered stowed when they are aboard the ship and placed in the position in which they will be transported.

trimmed
A ship is considered trimmed when the cargo aboard the ship is balanced side-to-side and front-to-back.

secured
Once goods are stowed and the vessel trimmed, the goods are tied to the vessel by means of ropes or chains.

The ship's rail is no longer

In an FOB transaction, the point of delivery had traditionally been extremely clear and had been governed by centuries of maritime tradition. There was a major change with Incoterms® 2010 rules.

The "FOB point," the point at which the responsibility shifted from the exporter to the importer, was the ship's rail, an imaginary line that circled the ship. Until the merchandise had cleared the ship's rail, it was the responsibility of the exporter. After that, it became the responsibility of the importer. If the merchandise fell while being loaded and was damaged, the responsible party was determined based on whether it had crossed the ship's rail and remained on the ship (importer) or fell back toward the quay (exporter).[16]

For the 2010 version of Incoterms® rules, the ship's rail is no longer the relevant concept. The responsibility for the goods shifts from the exporter to the importer when the goods are "on board" the ship. The ship's rail is dead.[17]

6.12.1 Delivery under FOB

The point at which the responsibility for the goods shift from the exporter to the importer is when they are "on board" the vessel. This interpretation of the delivery point is new with Incoterms® 2010 rules, and little jurisprudence has accumulated on what constitutes "on board." It is expected to mean that the goods are delivered when they are in the hold of the ship, but remain to be stowed—placed in the exact location on the deck.

The document associated with the FOB term is quite clear however: the proof of delivery is an ocean bill of lading or a sea waybill. Since the ocean bill of lading certifies that the goods have been received on board the ship, there is a perfect match between the documents available and the requirements of the Incoterms® rules. Only after receiving the goods will the shipping line issue this document, giving a copy to the exporter.

6.12.2 Responsibilities of the Exporter and the Importer under FOB

The exporter is responsible for packaging the goods for export, shipping them to the port of departure, and paying to have them loaded onto the ship by a stevedore. The exporter is responsible for clearing the goods for export, and has the obligation of providing whatever documents and assistance the importer may need to clear Customs in the importing country and to obtain insurance. In the United States, the exporter fills out the Shipper's Export Declaration and is the "U.S. principal party in interest" or the exporter of record. In countries where export authorities require a Pre-Shipment Inspection, the exporter has to pay for it.

The importer is responsible for arranging and paying for ocean transportation from the port of departure to the goods' destination, clearing Customs in the importing country, and eventually arranging and paying for insurance. If the importing country requires a Pre-Shipment Inspection, the importer has to pay for it.

Figure 6.5: Cargo Loaded but not yet Stowed, in Porto Marghera near Venice, Italy
Photo ©Luciano Miglietta. Used with permission.

6.13 Cost and Freight (CFR)

Although the CFR Incoterms® rule can be used for any merchandise, it is specifically designed for ocean transportation, and is not meant for any other means of transportation or for merchandise that is not destined to then be handed to an ocean shipping line at the port of departure. The practices followed by international shippers make it an Incoterms® rule that should be used sparingly with containerized cargo, which is best handled under a DAT Incoterms® rule. The CFR Incoterms® rule should be used with the following syntax:

> CFR · ENL Multi-purpose Terminal, Apapa Wharf, Lagos, Nigeria, Incoterms® 2010.

where the multi-purpose terminal operated by ENL in Lagos, the port of destination, is the location at which the importer takes physical control of the goods. This port is usually located in the importing country or in a neighboring country. In a CFR transaction, the delivery (the transfer or responsibility or the transfer of risk) does not take place in the port of destination, but in the port of departure.

The Cost and Freight term is also one of the oldest maritime Terms of Trade, and it was known until the 1990 version of Incoterms® rules as C&F or C+F, abbreviations which are now obsolete. The exporter is responsible for the goods until they are placed on board the ship in the port of origin in the exporting country, and the importer is responsible for them after that. However, the exporter pre-pays the ocean freight.

Unfortunately, because CFR is such an old Term of Trade, its meaning is somewhat dependent on the practices of the port in which the goods are unloaded. These differences matter specifically in the way the unloading costs are billed: some ports have the tradition to bill separately for the unloading of the goods as stevedoring costs, and others will ask shipping lines to bill for these services as part of the ocean cargo costs. The shipping line contracted by the exporter obviously would be able to communicate what the practice is at a given port of discharge. Nevertheless, in order to account for these differences in practices, variants to the CFR Incoterms® rule were created to reflect which of the trade partners was responsible for unloading costs. "CFR landed" explicitly states that the costs of unloading are borne by the exporter, and "CFR undischarged" notes unloading costs are borne by the importer.[18] In these cases, the correct syntax should be:

> CFR · ENL Multi-purpose Terminal, Apapa Wharf, Lagos, Nigeria, Incoterms® 2010, landed.

6.13.1 Delivery under CFR

In a CFR transaction, the point of delivery is the "FOB point," the point at which the responsibility shifts from the exporter to the importer in the port of origin. Until the merchandise is loaded aboard the ship, it is the responsibility of the exporter; after that, the responsibility shifts to the importer.

The document associated with the CFR term is the proof of delivery in the port of origin: an ocean bill of lading or a sea waybill. Only after receiving the goods will the shipping line issue this document, giving one of the originals to the exporter.

6.13.2 Responsibilities of the Exporter and the Importer under CFR

The exporter is responsible for packaging the goods, shipping them to the port of departure, loading them onto a ship "of a kind normally used for the transport of goods of the contract description,"[19] and pre-paying for the main carriage. Depending on the practices at the port of destination, this pre-paid contract of carriage may include the costs of unloading the goods. If it does not, then the importer has to pay for unloading the ship. The exporter is also responsible to clear the goods for export, assist the importer in providing the documentation necessary to clear Customs in the importing country and obtain insurance. In the United States, the exporter fills out the Shipper's Export Declaration and is the "U.S. principal party in interest" or the exporter of record. In countries where export authorities require a Pre-Shipment Inspection, the exporter has to pay for it.

The importer takes responsibility for the goods at the delivery point (*i.e.*, once the goods are aboard the ship in the port of departure), even though the exporter is the one who contracts for the ocean shipping of the goods. Depending on the practice at the port of destination, and the possible Incoterms® rule variant used, the importer may also have to pay for the unloading costs. It is also responsible for clearing Customs in the importing country and for inland on-carriage after that. If the importing country requires a Pre-Shipment Inspection, the importer has to pay for it.

6.14 Cost, Insurance, and Freight (CIF)

Although the CIF Incoterms® rule can be used for any merchandise, it is specifically designed for ocean transportation, and is not meant for any other means of transportation or for merchandise that is not destined to be handed to an ocean shipping line at the port of departure. It is also mostly designed for non-containerized cargo; containerized cargo is better handled through a DAT Incoterms® rule. The CIF Incoterms® rule should be used with the following syntax:

> **CIF · Naigai Lines, 176 Higashi-Machi, Chuo-Ku, Kobe 650-0031, Hyogo, Japan, Incoterms® 2010.**

where the point at which the importer takes control of the goods is a specific terminal in the Port of Kobe, in Japan. In a Cost, Insurance, and Freight transaction, the delivery does not take place in the port of destination, but in the port of departure, when the goods are placed on board the vessel.

The CIF Incoterms® rule is quite similar to the CFR term, with the exception that the exporter has the additional responsibility to pre-pay for marine cargo insurance until the port of destination. Unfortunately, the mandate of the International Chamber of Commerce is for "minimum cover," or Coverage C of the Institute Cargo Clauses, a practice that results in the creation of yet another Incoterms® rule variant,[20] CIF maximum cover—mandating Coverage A of the Institute Cargo Clauses—in addition to the predictable CIF undischarged and CIF landed, which are mirrors of their CFR equivalents. The syntax again must accommodate the fact that Incoterms® rule variants are not regulated by the International Chamber of Commerce and should read:

> **CIF · Naigai Lines, 176 Higashi-Machi, Chuo-Ku, Kobe 650-0031, Hyogo, Japan, Incoterms® 2010, maximum cover, landed.**

Finally, under the CIF Incoterms® rule, the amount insured must be at least 110 percent of the value of the goods, a custom that dates back to 1906 and the British Marine Insurance Act.

One aspect of CIF is also unusual: certain countries (see Table 6.2 on the following page) do not allow their importers to purchase insurance abroad, and therefore prevent any import on a CIF or CIP basis.[21] This restriction is in place to conserve foreign currency—it obligates importers to purchase insurance locally in local currency—and to subsidize the national insurance industry; all of the countries practicing this restriction are relatively small traders. Export restrictions generally prevent exporters from offering CPT or CFR if the importer is expected to purchase insurance.

6.14.1 Delivery under CIF

In a CIF transaction, the point of delivery is again the "FOB point," the point at which the responsibility shifts from the exporter to the importer, the ship's rail. Until the merchandise has cleared the ship's rail, it is the responsibility of the exporter; after that, the responsibility shifts to the importer. The document associated with the CIF term is also quite clear: the proof of delivery is an ocean bill of lading or a sea waybill. Only after receiving the goods will the shipping line issue this document, giving one of the originals to the exporter.

6.14.2 Responsibilities of the Exporter and the Importer under CIF

The exporter has to package the goods for export, and has to pay for shipping costs and minimum insurance costs to the port of destination. It is also responsible for clearing the goods for export. In the United States, the exporter fills out the Shipper's Export Declaration and is the "U.S. principal party in interest" or the exporter of record. In countries where export authorities require a Pre-Shipment Inspection, the exporter has to pay for it. The importer is taking responsibility for the goods at the ship's rail in the port of departure, even though the contract of carriage is between the seller and the ocean shipping line. The importer is responsible for clearing Customs in the importing country and for inland transportation after that. If the importing country requires a Pre-Shipment Inspection, the importer has to pay for it.

6.15 Summary of the Division of Responsibilities between Exporters and Importers

Table 6.3 on page 165 summarizes the responsibilities of the exporter and those of the importer for each Incoterms® rule. When the exporter is responsible for an aspect of a shipment, the column is marked with an X. When the importer is responsible, it is marked with an I. When it could be either of the two, then the column is marked with an asterisk. A dash signifies that there are no requirements to purchase insurance.

For example, under FCA, if the term "exporter's premises" is used, then the pre-carriage is the responsibility of the importer. If "carrier's premises" is specified, then the pre-carriage is the responsibility of the exporter. Similarly, under DAT, the main carriage can be the responsibility of the exporter if the delivery takes place

Countries with Restrictions on Insurance Purchases

Country	Import	Export	Country	Import	Export
Algeria	■		Laos	■	■
Angola	■		Libya	■	
Bangladesh	■		Malaysia	■	
Barbados	■		Mali	■	
Benin	■		Mauritania	■	
Burkina Faso	■		Morocco	■	
Burundi	■	■	Myanmar/Burma	■	■
Cameroon	■		Nicaragua	■	
Central African Republic	■		Niger	■	
Chad	■		Nigeria	■	
Congo (Brazzaville)	■		Oman	■	■
Congo (Kinshasa)	■	■	Pakistan	■	
Cuba	■	■	Papua New Guinea		■
Djibouti	■		Qatar	■	■
Dominican Republic	■		Russia	■	
Ecuador	■		Rwanda	■	■
Ethiopia	■		Senegal	■	■
Gabon	■		Serbia	■	■
Georgia		■	Sierra Leone	■	
Ghana	■		Solomon Islands	■	
Guatemala		■	Sudan	■	
Guinea	■		Syria	■	
Haiti	■		Tanzania	■	
Indonesia	■		Thailand	■	■
Iran	■		Togo	■	
Iraq	■		Tunisia	■	
Ivory Coast	■		Uganda	■	■
Jordan		■	Venezuela	■	■
Kenya	■		Yemen	■	■

Table 6.2: Countries with Restrictions on Insurance Purchases for Incoterms® Sales
American Institute of Marine Underwriters.

in a terminal in the importing country, or the responsibility of the importer if the delivery takes place in a terminal located in the exporting country.

Under CFR and CIF, the responsibility for unloading the goods in the port of destination is determined by the customs of that port. If the contract of ocean carriage includes the unloading of the goods, that expense is the responsibility of the exporter; if it does not, it is to the importer's account.

Division of Responsibilities under Incoterms® Rules

Task	All-methods-of-transportation Incoterms® rules							Maritime Incoterms® rules			
	EXW	FCA	CPT	CIP	DAT	DAP	DDP	FAS	FOB	CFR	CIF
Export Packing	X	X	X	X	X	X	X	X	X	X	X
Export Clearance	I	X	X	X	X	X	X	X	X	X	X
Pre-Carriage Loading	I	X	X	X	X	X	X	X	X	X	X
Pre-Carriage	I	*	X	X	X	X	X	X	X	X	X
Main Carriage Loading	I	I	X	X	*	X	X	I	X	X	X
Main Carriage	I	I	X	X	*	X	X	I	I	X	X
Insurance	—	—	—	X	—	—	—	—	—	—	X
Main Carriage Unloading	I	I	X	X	*	X	X	I	I	*	*
On Carriage	I	I	X	X	I	X	X	I	I	I	I
On Carriage Unloading	I	I	I	I	I	I	X	I	I	I	I
Import Clearance	I	I	I	I	I	I	X	I	I	I	I
Import Duty	I	I	I	I	I	I	X	I	I	I	I

Table 6.3: Summary of Incoterms® Responsibilities
X=exporter; I=importer; * =depends on point of delivery; —=undetermined.

6.16 Common Errors in Incoterms® Rules Usage

6.16.1 Confusion with Domestic Terms

Probably the most commonly made errors in international Terms of Trade is the substitution of domestic Terms of Trade for international Terms of Trade: an inexperienced exporter will use "FOB factory" rather than the correct corresponding Free Carrier, exporter's premises, or FCA Incoterms® rule; similarly, rather than the correct Delivered Duty Paid (DDP) Incoterms® rule, the same inexperienced exporter would use "FOB destination."

"FOB factory" (also known as "FOB origin") is a term of trade used in the United States (see vignette on page 155) for domestic sales that limits the responsibility of the seller to the loading of the merchandise onto a vehicle owned or hired by the buyer. At the time at which the merchandise is loaded onto the vehicle, the title of the merchandise transfers to the buyer. There are therefore several differences between the "FOB factory" concept and its closest Incoterms® equivalent, which is Free Carrier (FCA) exporter's premises. Firstly, it shows a transfer of title, which none of the Incoterms® rule does, rather than a transfer of responsibility, the only concept to which the Incoterms® rules refer. Secondly, "FOB factory" does not make reference to any form of documentation, which is critical to the international buyer, because these documents are needed to clear Customs. Thirdly, it applies to any form of transportation, and not only to ocean transportation, as the FOB Incoterms® rule does. Finally, "FOB factory" does not have any specific requirements regarding packaging, whereas FCA clearly requires packaging sufficient to withstand the international voyage.

"FOB destination" (also known as "FOB delivered") is also a term used in the United States for domestic sales that extends the responsibility of the seller to the delivery point, at the buyer's place of business; the seller pays for the carriage cost to the point of delivery. At the time at which the merchandise is unloaded from the vehicle, the title transfers to the buyer. The "FOB destination" term of sale is not equivalent to the DAP Incoterms® rule. For one, it also refers to the transfer of title, whereas the DAP Incoterms® rule does not. Second, it makes no reference to Customs clearance, which DAP excludes, but DDP requires.

Other terms that are also used incorrectly in international trade are "Freight Pre-Paid" and "Freight Collect," which are also former UCC terms and refer to the fact that the seller either includes the cost of shipment in the invoice or excludes it. Both of these terms do not work in an international environment for essentially the same reasons that "FOB factory" and "FOB destination" do not.

On occasion, there are some other terms used in international trade that have their roots in domestic trade, although they have become obsolete. For example, some invoices will reflect a *franco* price, which is conceptually equivalent to the "FOB factory" term; however, it does not specifically require the loading of the merchandise onto the vehicle provided by the buyer. There are no reasons to use this term of trade domestically, but a multitude of reasons not to use it internationally.

6.16.2 Confusion with Older Incoterms® Versions

The International Chamber of Commerce modified the Incoterms® rules in 1980, 1990, and 2000. It eliminated some Incoterms® rules, modified others and created some new ones. For a number of reasons, several exporters have failed to adapt to these changes.

Older ICC versions included several Incoterms® rules that have since disappeared: FOB rail (which eventually changed to FOR, "Free on Rail" in 1980, and eventually was abandoned altogether in 1990), FOB truck (which became FOT, "Free on Truck" in 1980, and which was also abandoned in 1990), and FOB airport (eliminated in 1990). On occasion, though, such older Incoterms® rules are still used on invoices. Although this is a practice that is allowed under ICC rules, it is most likely that the use of such obsolete Incoterms® rules is more due to carelessness than to a deliberate attempt at using an Incoterms® rule that has advantages over the current version. It is therefore preferable to use the Free Carrier (FCA) Incoterms® rule instead of the previous similar Incoterms® rules, as fewer and fewer people are familiar with the specific requirements of the former Incoterms® rules.

Another problem is the use of C&F or C+F rather than CFR to communicate that an ocean shipment is made under a Cost and Freight Incoterms® rule. Not only has the abbreviation changed, but the transfer of responsibility has changed from the point at which the goods crossed the ship's rail to the point at which they are on board the vessel. Therefore such older abbreviations should be avoided: they could confuse the importer and present challenges, should the shipment experience a mishap.

Another obsolete term is "Free Domicile," although there is no evidence that such a term was ever part of the recognized Incoterms® rules. This pricing term is used when the exporter pays all the applicable duties, all the transportation and other charges until the shipment is delivered to the importer's premises. Because this term is not recognized by the International Chamber of Commerce Arbitration

Panel, it should be replaced by the either of two Incoterm® rules: Delivered At Place (DAP) or Delivered Duty Paid (DDP).

Appropriate Incoterms® Rule per Type of Shipment

Task	All-methods-of-transportation Incoterms® rules							Maritime Incoterms® rules			
	EXW	FCA	CPT	CIP	DAT	DAP	DDP	FAS	FOB	CFR	CIF
Bulk Cargo	−	+	−	−	+	+	+	+	+	+	+
Breakbulk Cargo	−	++	+	+	++	+	+	++	+	++	++
Roll-on-Roll-off Cargo	−	++	+	+	++	+	+	+	+	+	+
Containerized Cargo	−	++	+	+	++	++	+	−	−	−	−
Small Packet	++	+	+	+	−	+	+	−−	−−	−−	−−

Table 6.4: Summary of Incoterms® Choice by Types of Cargo
−− inappropriate; − discouraged; +appropriate; ++best fit.

6.16.3 Improper Use of Correct Incoterms® Rules

Sometimes shippers use the correct Incoterms® rule, but for the incorrect commodity. Table 6.4 outlines the proper use of Incoterms® rules for specific shipments. For example, a containerized shipment should not be shipped EXW, could be shipped CIF or CFR, but should be shipped FCA, DAT or DAP.

The other misuse of Incoterms® rules is when a shipper uses FOB for an air shipment, even though FOB is an ocean-shipment term. The correct Incoterms® rule to use for an air shipment should be Free Carrier (FCA), to clearly outline the responsibilities of the exporter and of the importer. Table 6.5 on the next page outlines the proper use of Incoterms® rules by Mode of transportation.

6.17 Incoterms® Rules as a Marketing Tool

As mentioned earlier, the greatest criterion to be used in the choice of a particular Incoterms® rule is the willingness of both parties to perform and pay for some of the tasks involved in the shipment. In some cases, a strategic advantage can be gained by an exporter willing to facilitate the sale of its products by assisting a novice importer in the handling of a shipment. In other cases, a price advantage may be obtained by an experienced importer willing to perform all or most of the tasks involved in the shipment.

Generally speaking, an exporter does not determine which Incoterms® rule to use on a case-by-case basis. It adopts a "policy" to include in international quotes those services that it feels it can provide efficiently. It is difficult for an exporter to adapt its Incoterms® strategy to accommodate the requirements of an importer, as it may require the exporter to be responsible for tasks that it has decided it would rather not perform. However, should the importer want to perform more tasks than

Appropriate Incoterms® Rule per Main Carriage

Task	All-methods-of-transportation Incoterms® rules							Maritime Incoterms® rules			
	EXW	FCA	CPT	CIP	DAT	DAP	DDP	FAS	FOB	CFR	CIF
Ocean	−	+	−	−	+	+	+	+	+	+	+
Air	++	+	+	+	−	+	+	−−	−−	−−	−−
Rail	−	++	+	+	++	++	+	−	−	−	−
Road	++	+	+	+	−	+	+	−−	−−	−−	−−
Multi-modal (FCL)	−	++	+	+	++	+	+	++	+	++	++
Multi-modal (LCL)	−	++	+	+	++	+	+	+	+	+	+

Table 6.5: Summary of Incoterms® Choice by Means of Transportation
−− inappropriate; − discouraged; +appropriate; ++best fit.

what the exporter prefers, it is certainly possible for the exporter to do less than what it expected, and use a different Incoterms® rule on that transaction that allows the importer to do more.

The choice of the proper Incoterms® rule is a critical decision for a firm: it is an integral part of its export strategy and linked to the level of customer service it is aiming to provide. From this perspective, therefore, it makes most sense for an exporter to become as well-versed as possible in international logistics and be prepared to include as many of the transportation functions as possible in its quote.

An exporter intent on increasing its sales should therefore offer to provide the importer with the most customer-friendly Incoterms® rule quotes (either DAP or DDP), if only by using the services of a competent freight forwarder. Should the importer want to shoulder more responsibilities, it is always possible for the exporter to reduce its involvement and quote FCA or even EXW. The best type of quote would be one in which the exporter lists different prices for different Incoterms® rules, leaving the importer with the decision to choose which is best for its specific case.

For example, an exporter could submit a quote that reads:

FCA · 2500 Industrial Parkway, Cleveland, OH 44114, USA _____ $10,000

FCA · Terminal 5, Cincinnati Airport, Covington, KY 41048, USA _____ $11,000

CIP · CDG Cargo, route des badaux, 95700 Roissy, France _____ $15,500

DAP · 114 rue de Prat, 63100 Clermont-Ferrand, France _____ $16,500

DDP · 114 rue de Prat, 63100 Clermont-Ferrand, France _____ $17,800

and leave the customer to decide which of the Incoterms® rules it would like to choose.

Review and Discussion Questions

1. Describe two Incoterms® rules of your choice.

2. What is the Incoterms® rule that is most importer-friendly? Least importer-friendly? Justify your answer.

3. Which of the Incoterms® rules include a requirement of insurance by the exporter?

4. The Delivered Incoterms® rules (DAT, DAP, and DDP) do not include insurance. Why not?

5. Using a product of your choice as well as an importer and an exporter of your choice, determine what would be the ideal Incoterms® rule for a transaction. Make as many assumptions as necessary to justify your decision.

6. Explain why a developing country would want to prevent its importers from purchasing CIF or CIP and instead require CFR or CPT shipments.

7. A certain sogo shosha (a Japanese Trading Company) always requests its suppliers to provide an FCA exporter's premises quote. Knowing what you know about trading companies, why do you think this is the case?

Notes

[1] Debattista, Charles, Editor, *ICC Guide to Incoterms® 2010*, International Chamber of Commerce Publication No. 720E, ICC Publishing S.A., 38 Cours Albert 1er, 75008 Paris, France and ICC Publishing, Inc., 156 Fifth Avenue, Suite 417, New York, NY 10010, USA.

[2] *Incoterms® 2010, ICC Rules for the Use of Domestic and International Trade Terms*, International Chamber of Commerce Publication No. 715E, ICC Publishing S.A., 38 Cours Albert 1er, 75008 Paris, France and ICC Publishing, Inc., 156 Fifth Avenue, Suite 417, New York, NY 10010, USA.

[3] Kaye, Simon, "Using Incoterms to Simplify Global Sourcing," *Inbound Logistics*, January 2012, pp. 193-196.

[4] Freudmann, Aviva, "Traders get a Brand-new Bible," *Journal of Commerce*, September 9, 1999, p. 1.

[5] Johnson, Eric, "How do you Spell Trade?", *American Shipper*, November 2010, pp.12-15.

[6] *Incoterms® 2010, ICC Rules for the Use of Domestic and International Trade Terms*, International Chamber of Commerce Publication No. 715E, ICC Publishing S.A., 38 Cours Albert 1er, 75008 Paris, France and ICC Publishing, Inc., 156 Fifth Avenue, Suite 417, New York, NY 10010, USA.

[7] Reynolds, Frank, *Incoterms® for Americans (Completely rewritten for Incoterms® 2010)*, International Projects, Inc., Toledo, Ohio, USA.

[8] "U.S. Principal Party in Interest Overview," United States Census Bureau, https://www.aesdirect.gov/support/usppi_overview.html, retrieved May 18, 2013.

[9] Biederman, David, "New Rules for Exports," *JoC Week*, July 24-30, 2000, pp.10-12.

[10] Reynolds, Frank, "Seminar in Paris Yields Answers to Widely Asked Questions on Incoterms," *Journal of Commerce*, April 22, 1998, p. 2C.

[11] King and Spalding LLP, "UCC Article 2 (Sales of Goods)—Significant Changes on the Way," www.kslaw.com/Library/pdf/UCCArticle2.pdf, retrieved May 18, 2013.

[12] American Law Institute, "Recommendation of the Permanent Editorial Board for the Uniform Commercial Code to Withdraw the 2003 Amendments to UCC Articles 2 and 2A from the Official Text of the Uniform Commercial Code," http://www.theconglomerate.org/2011/05/-withdrawing-the-2003-amendments-to-ucc-articles-2-and-2a.html, retrieved May 18, 2013.

[13] Ramberg, Jan, *ICC Guide to Incoterms® 2010*, International Chamber of Commerce Publication No. 720E, ICC Publishing S.A., 38 Cours Albert 1er, 75008 Paris, France and ICC Publishing, Inc., 156 Fifth Avenue, Suite 417, New York, NY 10010, USA.

[14] *Ibid.*

[15] Raty, Asko, "Variants on Incoterms (Part 2)," in Debattista, Charles, Editor, *Incoterms in Practice*, International Chamber of Commerce Publication No. 505, ICC Publishing S.A., 38 Cours Albert 1er, 75008 Paris, France and ICC Publishing, Inc., 156 Fifth Avenue, Suite 417, New York, NY 10010, USA, 1995.

[16] Reynolds, Frank, "Tale of a Rail and Other Nuances of the Marine Cargo Insurance Experience," *Journal of Commerce*, November 18, 1998, p. 10A.

[17] Bergami, Roberto, "The ship's rail is dead; Incoterms 2010," *International Business Training*, www.ibt-articles.com/absnet/templates/trade_article.aspx?articleid=402&zoneid=2, retrieved May 18, 2013.

[18] Raty, Asko, "Variants on Incoterms (Part 2)," in Debattista, Charles, Editor, *Incoterms in Practice*, International Chamber of Commerce Publication No. 505, ICC Publishing S.A., 38 Cours Albert 1er, 75008 Paris, France and ICC Publishing, Inc., 156 Fifth Avenue, Suite 417, New York, NY 10010, USA, 1995.

[19] Ramberg, Jan, *ICC Guide to Incoterms® 2010*, International Chamber of Commerce Publication No. 720E, ICC Publishing S.A., 38 Cours Albert 1er, 75008 Paris, France and ICC Publishing, Inc., 156 Fifth Avenue, Suite 417, New York, NY 10010, USA.

[20] Mikkola, Kainu, "Variants on Incoterms (Part 1)," in Debattista, Charles, Editor, *Incoterms in Practice*, International Chamber of Commerce Publication No. 505, ICC Publishing S.A., 38 Cours Albert 1er, 75008 Paris, France and ICC Publishing, Inc., 156 Fifth Avenue, Suite 417, New York, NY 10010, USA, 1995.

[21] American Institute of Marine Underwriters, "A list of countries with restrictive measures in the field of marine insurance (August 2008)," http://www.aimu.org/cargoinsurancerestrict.-html, retrieved May 18, 2013

Chapter 7

Terms of Payment

7.1	International Payment Characteristics	172
7.2	Alternative Terms of Payment	174
7.3	Risks in International Trade	175
7.4	Cash in Advance	178
7.5	Open Account	178
7.6	Letter of Credit	180
7.7	Additional Types of Letters of Credit	190
7.8	Documentary Collection	192
7.9	Forfaiting	196
7.10	Purchasing Cards	197
7.11	TradeCard	198
7.12	Bank Guarantees	199
7.13	Terms of Payment as a Marketing Tool	200

One of the greatest concerns an exporting company has is to make sure that it will be able to collect payment from its foreign customers. Although this is also a legitimate concern domestically, an international transaction is generally perceived to involve a much greater non-payment risk than a strictly domestic sale, for many reasons.

There are a number of ways in which an exporting company can ensure that it will get paid and be paid on time; a company can always tailor its international terms of payment to the characteristics of its customers, the countries in which it does business, and its own tolerance for risk. Although these methods are more complex than the open-account arrangements traditionally found in all domestic sales, they are universally accepted, and there is ample jurisprudence to buttress them. It is therefore relatively simple to arrive at a choice of international terms of trade that will secure the interests of the exporter.

What is difficult in choosing an international term of trade is managing the delicate balance between protecting the interests of the exporter and offering good marketing practices that will engender good customer relations.

7.1 International Payment Characteristics

Exporters tend to prefer conservative measures in handling their foreign receivables. They tend to err on the side of caution for several reasons:

- **Credit information.** There is generally much less information available on the creditworthiness of a creditor in a foreign market than there is for a domestic customer. Although a few credit reporting agencies, accounting firms, and factoring houses do keep information, it is not always readily obtainable or is not always in existence for a specific customer, especially if the customer is a recently created firm or is in a developing country. Some improvements have been made recently, though, with the creation of centralized credit information portals, which offer links to access foreign countries' credit agencies. The task, though, is usually much more complicated for a foreign customer than for a domestic one, if only because the identity of a domestic firm is usually easier to establish. The paucity of information about certain countries is often coupled with an unfamiliarity with the diverse business organizations (different types of partnership and corporations) of a foreign country's legal system and with an inability to decipher businesses' names.

- **Lack of personal contact.** International transactions tend to be conducted in a more impersonal fashion (through fax, telex, e-mail) than are domestic transactions, which tend to be conducted at least initially with some sort of personal contact (in person or over the phone). This lack of contact tends to lead to a climate in which the exporter has no way to evaluate the character of the importer, and where the possibility of a greater risk is often assumed. Where there is personal contact, it is sometimes between people who are not always well versed in inter-cultural communication and can substantially misunderstand each other. This can foster the perception of a greater risk and encourages a more cautious approach.

- **Difficult and expensive collections.** Should a foreign customer renege on a payment, the collection of such a past-due account can be particularly difficult. Although there is a generally well structured system on the domestic side, there are few firms that have the capability of offering international collection services. Those that do tend to offer the service at a very high price. In some cases, relying on a foreign collection agency can lead a company to unwillingly employ some pretty unsavory characters, a situation that can eventually taint the image of the exporter, as Citibank discovered to its detriment when it used a "strong-arm" collection company in India.[1]

- **No easy legal recourse.** Unlike in a domestic setting, in which there is often a commercial code (of laws) and abundant jurisprudence, there is little of either in international trade. In addition, there is no court with jurisdiction over international disputes, and therefore a ruling by a court in the exporter's country cannot be easily enforced in the importer's country. The reciprocal is also true.

Convention on Contracts for the International Sale of Goods
A United Nations' treaty that acts as international sales law.

The creation of the United Nations Convention on Contracts for the International Sale of Goods (CISG) and its implementation in 1980 have helped establish a body of legal principles for the sale of goods between companies located in two different sovereign countries. As of June 2013, 79 countries had ratified this treaty, representing about 80 percent of the world's trade, but some countries, such as the United States, have ratified only part of it,[2] presumably those articles that do not conflict with their own code law (Uniform Commercial Code [UCC] for the United States). The United Kingdom has yet to ratify this convention at all.[3] The enforcement of the convention is left to the domestic courts' interpretation, and although there is some jurisprudence in this area, it is still fairly scant (all of the available jurisprudence is made accessible through a database created by the United Nations Commission on International Trade Law [UNCITRAL] called CLOUT, for Case Law On UNCITRAL Texts).

There are always concerns on the part of exporters that conflicts of law between domestic laws and the CISG and differences in interpretation by the courts make the prospect of a court battle much more daunting. Chapter 5, Section 5.2 outlined several of the differences between the CISG and the United States UCC. It is a common misconception that there is some sort of an international court of justice; although the International Court in The Hague, Netherlands (see Figure 7.1 on the following page), arbitrates disputes between governments and between governments and multinational corporations, it never interferes in disputes between corporations. In addition, its rulings are non-binding, as the International Court does not have the executive authority to enforce them.

- **Higher litigation costs.** The costs of international litigation, arbitration, or mediation are generally much greater than those of domestic litigation. Seeking a ruling against an importer in the importer's country is time consuming, can involve several trips abroad, and necessitates the hiring of foreign law specialists, a process that involves greater expenses than domestic disputes. In some countries, the backlog of civil and commercial cases in the court system is such as to render impossible the probability of a swift decision. In India, for example, a judgment takes five years on average (see Table 7.2 on page 177), and may not rendered for ten years, with some cases meandering through the system for much longer periods than that. Other countries, such as China, Russia, Indonesia, and Ukraine, are not much different.[4, 5]

    Suing a foreign customer for non-payment in the courts of the exporter's country could be perceived as a means to speed this process up and eventually lower its costs; however, it is followed only by the prospect of having to file suit in the importing country's courts as well, just to enforce the judgment rendered against the importer. Most exporters perceive that litigation should be an absolute last resort.

- **Mistrust.** Finally, there is the perception that the importing company is well aware of all these factors and knows that the exporter is unlikely to aggressively pursue an uncollected foreign receivable. This creates a climate of distrust on the part of the exporter, who could assume the worst intentions on the part of the importer.

litigation
The final process by which parties to a contract have to settle a dispute, in a court of law.

arbitration
A process by which parties to a contract choose to settle a dispute. An arbitration decision is binding on both parties.

mediation
A process by which parties to a contract choose to find a compromise in a dispute. A mediation recommendation is not binding.

Figure 7.1: The International Court in The Hague, Netherlands
Photo ©Uygar Sirin. Used with permission.

7.2 Alternative Terms of Payment

There are essentially four traditional payment methods in foreign transactions, all involving a different level of risk: cash in advance, open account, documentary collection, and letters of credit. Although there are variations in each of these methods, each designed to mitigate one or another aspect of the risks involved in the transaction, they have not changed much in the past fifty years. However, about twenty years ago, an interesting fifth alternative emerged, called TradeCard, and it promises to become a particularly effective means of securing payment from a customer abroad without involving as many fees or intermediaries as do some of the more secure traditional alternatives. However interesting this alternative is, though, it has not been particularly successful in gaining market share.

Each of these five general alternatives presents advantages and disadvantages and can be generally seen as a trade-off between the risk of non-payment and the risk of losing the business to a more aggressive competitor who is willing to accept a greater risk and therefore present the customer with a simpler alternative form of payment.

Table 7.1 gives an example of the most common perceptions in terms of this trade-off. It is an overly simplified summary of the different alternative payment methods. The ultimate choice of a term of sale should be carefully determined as a function of several objective and subjective factors, and each variant of the preferred method should be given careful consideration. Unfortunately, if only for the obvious reason of simplification of the process of selling, several exporting firms

Term of Payment	Probability of Losing The Business because of the Choice of Method of Payment	Probability of Loss due to Non-Payment
Cash in Advance	High	Nil
Letter of Credit	Fairly High	Almost Nil
Documentary Collection	Low	Low
Open Account	Nil	Relatively High
TradeCard	Low	Almost Nil

Table 7.1: Methods of Payment and Perceived Risks

do not have the inclination—nor do they have the time and personnel—to tailor terms of payment to specific customers or countries, and these firms have designed a foreign-sales policy to deal with all orders from importers, regardless of where these customers are located or who they are. Such a lack of flexibility tends to lead to exceedingly conservative policies. One exporter confessed to the author that it considered only cash-in-advance sales orders; undoubtedly this conservative stance never got the exporter's company in trouble, but it very likely yielded much lower sales than a slightly more aggressive approach. Ideally, the terms of sale of a particular transaction should be evaluated according to the risks attached to the transaction.

7.3 Risks in International Trade

There are three sources of risk in international trade that need to be considered. First is obviously the commercial risk, which is also encountered in domestic transactions and relates to the ability (and the willingness) of the importer to pay the invoice in time. However, there is also the country risk that encompasses all of the issues related to the country to which an exporter is shipping and that may affect payment, regardless of the creditworthiness of the importer. Finally, exporters also associate risk with exposure, which is the potential financial impact of non-payment or reduced payment on the exporter's business.

commercial risk
The probability of not being paid by a creditor, either because the creditor does not have the funds, or because it refuses to recognize the debt.

7.3.1 Country Risk

Country risk is made up of an aggregate of different issues, some political, and some strictly economic.

On the political side, the government's stability should be considered. For example, the possibility that a government may be changed (with a new election) may influence import policies, which, in turn, could mean that goods cannot clear Customs as easily, or that tariffs increase, or that other policies are changed to such an extent that the importer will refuse delivery. In a country in which such a political risk is perceived, the exporter would prefer a term of payment that is more secure. Similarly, a government that is in a weak position could also see its policies challenged by a strong public opposition, a situation that can lead to strong political unrest, as was the case in the French Caribbean islands of Martinique and Guadeloupe, where there was a massive general strike early in 2009.[6] When such general

country risk
The probability of not being paid by a creditor, because the importer's country does not have the foreign currency or does not allow the creditor to pay—political embargo.

strikes take place, just about all economic activity stops, and therefore importers do not pay their creditors until the situation is stabilized. The strike in Guadeloupe lasted more than a month. In 2011, the Arab Spring[7] certainly disturbed quite a few transactions.

Port personnel or other personnel critical to the timeliness of a shipment—such as Customs officers—strike often in some countries, and this fact should be factored into the decision of the terms of payment. A strike in U.S. West Coast ports lasted only a day in May 2008,[8] but a similar action in 2013 at the International Terminal in the Port of Hong Kong SAR lasted forty days and disrupted many shipments.[9] Sometimes, social movements are so commonplace that businesses have to learn to plan around them. The French government tallies an average of at least 2 million worker-days of strike every year, and many more are lost because of the strikes (when nonstriking employees cannot make it to work, for example).[10]

Finally, in some cases, the government chooses to delay payment of international obligations, including trade obligations, whenever it is found to make sense politically. However, although a few governments have reneged on their public debt, there has been no recent evidence of governments refusing to honor their commercial (trade) debt.

Secondly, the overall health of the economy should also be considered. If there is high unemployment, policies against "job-stealing" imports could be implemented. If there is high inflation, price controls may be initiated. Moreover, the balance of payments of the importing country may also be relevant: if it is badly in a deficit position, imports of goods that are deemed non-essential could be curtailed. Such would be the case when the import cover, or the amount of foreign currency that the country has to cover its imports, starts to become low; generally, the import cover is expressed in months (*i.e.*, foreign currency reserves can cover the next n months of imports).[11]

Finally, a quick survey of the social system of the country could be conducted. Some countries' societies foster a climate where fraud is commonplace, sometimes prevalent (*e.g.*, Nigeria),[12] a situation that is conducive to much caution on the part of an exporter. The fairness of the legal system should also be considered. An importer located in a country in which claims are handled professionally should be offered more lenient terms of payment than one located in a country where the administrative and justice systems are notoriously biased, inadequate, or agonizingly slow. Table 7.2 on the facing page outlines the number of days that it takes an importer to clear a product for import (once all documents are received), the number of days it takes to export a product, and the average duration of a commercial lawsuit. The World Bank has information on all countries of the world.[13]

Finally, it is important to note that expectations of currency exchange rate fluctuations do not affect the choice of the term of payment but will affect the choice of the currency of quote (see Chapter 8) and the strategy used to minimize this risk.

7.3.2 Commercial Risk

This is the area in which it is more difficult to obtain accurate and reliable information. If the potential customer is a distributor who does business with other exporting firms, it is often possible to obtain firsthand information from these other exporters. Actually, it is considered good commercial practice in the United States to share information on the creditworthiness of a common customer—and in some cases to monitor this customer's payments—with other suppliers.

	Days needed to			
Country	Import a Product	Export a Product	Settle a Lawsuit	Obtain a Construction Permit
Brazil	17	13	731	469
France	11	9	390	184
Germany	7	7	394	97
India	20	16	1,420	196
Japan	11	10	360	193
Singapore	4	5	150	26
United States	5	6	370	27
Zimbabwe	73	53	410	614

Table 7.2: Days Required to Perform Certain Tasks, by Country The World Bank.

Commercial risk can also be evaluated from private sources, including credit report companies, factoring houses, some accounting firms, insurance companies, and banks. However, these are usually fee-based services and tend to be focused on larger established firms in developed countries. These sources are reliable and unbiased, though they tend to be conservative in their evaluations.

Table 7.3 lists several companies offering foreign credit reports on overseas customers. Each of these firms usually issues a report on a foreign customer for about U.S. $150.[14]

Several International Credit Reporting Services

Name	Coverage	website
COFACE	worldwide	www.cofacerating.com
Dun & Bradstreet	worldwide	www.dnb.com
International Company Profile	Britain	www.icpcredit.com
Estimo Reports	Italy	www.estimoreports.com
Arab Business Information	Middle East	www.cedar-rose.com
Cristal Credit International	Latin America	www.cristalcredit.com
Unicredit Beijing	China	www.unicredit.com.cn
Graydon International	Britain	www.graydon-group.com
Rencom International	France	www.rencom.fr
Owens Online	worldwide	www.owens.com
AMS Inform Private Limited	Southeast Asia	www.amsinform.com

Table 7.3: Several International Credit Reporting Services

7.3.3 Exposure

The risk of non-payment is the probability of not getting paid or of getting paid late, and it therefore dictates the terms of payment chosen by the exporter.

However, another issue to be considered is the consequence of that loss on a company, or the exposure of a company. At equal probabilities of loss, a small

exposure
The impact of an unpaid receivable for an exporter and its effect on the exporter's financial well-being.

business would be much more careful in handling a U.S.$ 50,000 export transaction than a large company would be. The amount is a much greater percentage of its business, and the loss of this amount could be very significant. The greater the exposure, the more secure the terms of payment should be.

7.4 Cash in Advance

7.4.1 Definition

cash in advance
A method of payment in which an importer has to pay the exporter before the exporter ships the goods.

In a cash-in-advance transaction, the exporter requests that the customer provide payment in advance, before shipment of the goods can take place. Payment is usually made with an electronic SWIFT (Society for Worldwide Interbank Financial Telecommunication) fund transfer from the customer's bank to the exporter's bank.

This is the ultimate risk-free alternative for the exporter. The importer has to pay before the goods are released; therefore, there are no collection worries, no foreign-exchange fluctuation exposure, no cash-flow problem, and only nominal fees to pay to banks.

In a cash-in-advance transaction, the risk is completely transferred to the importer. It sends cash to the exporter with the expectation that the exporter will ship the goods that were requested, in the quantity that was ordered, in due time, and with the documents necessary to clear Customs in the importing country. In addition, this takes place in an atmosphere in which the exporter just demonstrated that it has no trust whatsoever in the importer because it is requesting cash in advance.

7.4.2 Applicability

Cash in advance is a recommended way of conducting international transactions in countries in which fraud is rampant, in which there is a substantial risk of political instability or the possibility of foreign exchange freezes, and in which there is no convertible currency. Transactions conducted in some of the republics of the former Soviet Union would probably best be conducted on a cash-in-advance basis.

However, this method is unsound for business conducted in developed countries and in countries in which there is a significant level of sophistication in international business. In these countries, the probability that an importer will place a cash-in-advance purchase is infinitesimally small if there are other comparable suppliers available, and insisting on this method of payment is likely to create resentment on the part of the importer rather than initiate an amicable business relationship. It should be avoided at all costs.

7.5 Open Account

7.5.1 Definition

In an open-account transaction, the exporter conducts international business in a manner similar to the way it conducts business domestically. The exporter just sends an invoice to the importer along with the shipment and trusts the customer to pay within a reasonable amount of time, commensurate with the credit usually granted in the country in which the importer operates, usually 30 to 90 days. It is essentially the conceptual opposite of cash in advance, as the exporter shows complete trust in the importer and ships the merchandise without any guarantee that it will be paid. The only recourse in case of non-payment is legal action in the importing country, a time-consuming and expensive process that exporters rarely undertake.

7.5.2 Applicability

This term of payment should be reserved to established customers, or customers with whom the exporter expects to have an ongoing relationship. It could possibly be extended to new orders from large companies and/or companies for which commercial credit data is available, and whose credit rating is excellent. At least, that's theoretically the way that this term of payment should be used.

In practice, however, this term of sale has become almost necessary in some markets if the exporter is to expect any sales. For example, in the European Union, it has become very difficult to conduct business on any other basis. It is to be expected that the trend will continue and expand to other markets as well. For example, European Union companies offer open-account terms of payment to 80 percent of their customers[15] outside of the EU. The main reason is that, historically, European exporters have often benefited from their government's support, and were often offered free (or substantially discounted) commercial insurance on their foreign receivables. Until 1994, for example, a French exporter could obtain insurance from COFACE (Compagnie Française d'Assurance pour le Commerce Extérieur), a government-run insurance company, at a greatly reduced cost; its risk of non-payment had therefore essentially been assumed by the government. Today, COFACE and other European-based companies constitute the largest providers of international commercial credit insurance and are present in many different countries, a position reached through many consolidations. Once exporters have learned that it is very simple to offer open-account terms to their foreign customers, they tend to continue selling on those terms.

open account
A method of payment in which the exporter sends an invoice to the importer along with the goods and expects the importer to pay within a reasonable amount of time.

7.5.3 Commercial Credit Insurance

In order to compete in those markets in which open-account has become the rule, companies must offer this term of payment in their quotes to new customers. However, the risks associated with an open-account transaction should entice an exporter to acquire credit insurance on those sales. Therefore a commercial policy covering credit risks should be contracted either on a blanket basis (*i.e.*, covering all export transactions, up to a certain overall amount) or on a per-sale basis (*i.e.*, each individual transaction is covered by a separate commercial insurance contract). Chapter 10 gives more detailed information on these types of coverage.

credit insurance
An insurance policy that the exporter can purchase to protect itself against the risk of non-payment by the importer.

7.5.4 Factoring

Factoring is a process used most frequently domestically (between two parties in the same country) by which the creditor uses an intermediary, called a factor or a factoring house, to finance a receivable. There are two cases: in the first, called factoring "without recourse," the creditor sells the receivable to the factor, who is then responsible for collecting from the debtor. If the latter does not pay, the factor assumes that responsibility, and the creditor keeps the proceeds of the sale of the receivable. In the second case, called factoring "with recourse," the factor attempts

factoring
A means of financing international receivable accounts, by which a firm asks a factoring company to advance funds on the receivable.

to collect the funds from the debtor but, if it is unsuccessful, can turn to the creditor for assistance. Ultimately, in a factoring transaction with recourse, the creditor is responsible for collecting the funds.

In an international transaction, it is possible that the importer wants credit terms that are beyond what the exporter is comfortable giving. For example, a 90-day credit is requested when the exporter can afford only a 30-day credit. The exporter can use international factoring as a means to extend this credit to the importer. When it involves two countries, factoring is much more complicated than in a domestic sale: the exporter would contact a factor in the exporting country that would in turn contact a factoring house in the importing country. Once both factors agree to the transaction, the sale is completed on an open-account basis. The exporter, once the invoice is sent, sells the receivable to the exporting country's factor and collects its face value, from which are deducted the fees and interest charges covering the period of time during which credit is extended.[16]

In an international transaction, the factoring is generally done without recourse and the factoring house is responsible for collecting the receivable and cannot turn to the exporter if it is unable to collect. This is the main reason for which factoring houses often involve a second factoring company located in the importing country; its responsibility is to check the creditworthiness of the importer and, in some cases, to act as a collection agent for the factoring company in the exporting country.[17]

If the exporter is unable to provide the importer with the type of credit terms that the importer requests, the importer can, on its end, find financing for its purchase by asking a financial institution to lend it funds based upon this incoming inventory. In the United States, for example, the United Parcel Service offers "capital cargo finance," which allows an importer to borrow money against an incoming in-transit shipment.[18]

7.6 Letter of Credit

7.6.1 Definition

letter of credit
A method of payment in which a bank promises to pay the beneficiary (the exporter) on behalf of the applicant (the importer), as long as the exporter has provided the documents requested in the letter of credit.

issuing bank
The bank that opens the letter of credit on behalf of the importer and pays the exporter if the exporter provides the documents requested in the letter of credit.

A letter of credit is a document in which the importer's bank essentially promises to pay the exporter if the importer does not pay. The creditworthiness of the bank is substituted for the creditworthiness of the importer. However, the concept is substantially more complex than this. The promise is not made upon the exporter meeting certain conditions (or the importer not meeting certain conditions), but it is made on the documents of the transaction. This is the reason why a letter of credit is often called a documentary letter of credit and the process is called documentary credit.

It is fundamental to understand that the documents are the critical elements to a letter of credit. The bank is under no obligation to pay if the documents do not conform to the letter of credit's requirements, even though delivery has been made and the importer has obtained control of the merchandise. Similarly, the bank is obligated to pay if the documents are in order, even though the merchandise may be shoddy or not fit for sale.

The letter of credit is a contractual agreement between the issuing bank and the beneficiary that is undertaken on behalf of the importer. This agreement is independent of the underlying business relationship between the exporter and the importer; only the documents relating to a particular transaction between the ex-

7.6 Letter of Credit

porter and the importer matter.[19] This obviously means that extreme care must be taken in handling the documents related to a letter of credit; otherwise, it triggers a very time-consuming and expensive process of amendments and corrections.

A transaction conducted on a letter-of-credit basis is almost as good as one made on a cash-in-advance basis in that the exporter will be paid, but it involves going through a lot more steps and paying a lot more banking fees. Figures 7.2 through 7 on page 171 in Section 7.6.2 explain the process followed by a letter of credit transaction from issuance to payment.

beneficiary
The party that will be paid by the letter of credit, the exporter.

7.6.2 Process

Issuance

Figure 7.2 describes the issuance of a letter of credit, or the steps that take place before the exporter ships the merchandise to the importer.

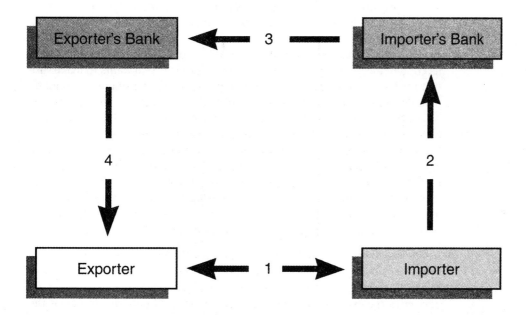

Figure 7.2: The Issuance of a Letter of Credit

- The first step in the process is the negotiation, which takes place between the exporter and the importer, in which it is agreed that the terms of payment will be by letter of credit. The exporter then sends a *pro forma* invoice to the importer, which estimates the terms of the transaction as closely as possible (see Chapter 9, Section 9.2.2 for further details on the elements of a *pro forma* invoice). The exporter also provides a series of instructions to the importer, detailing the terms of the transaction.

- The second step takes place when the importer (the applicant) requests its bank (the issuing bank) to open a letter of credit on the importer's behalf, naming the exporter as the beneficiary. The importer follows the instructions of the exporter regarding the terms of the sale and makes sure to include in

applicant
The firm whose payment is supported by the letter of credit, the importer.

issuing bank
The bank that opens the letter of credit, and that will pay the beneficiary, the exporter, if it presents the documents required in the letter of credit.

SWIFT-Society for Worldwide Interbank Financial Telecommunications
An interbank electronic network for the secure transfer of funds and documents.

advising bank
A bank that reviews the letter of credit on behalf of the beneficiary.

the application all of the documents that it will need to clear Customs in the importing country. The importer may also send a copy of the application to the exporter, to ensure that the terms listed on the application are acceptable to the exporter.

Because it is promising that it will pay if the importer does not pay, the issuing bank may request that the importer freeze a certain percentage (from 0 to 100 percent) of the amount of the letter of credit in an account or on a line of credit, essentially ensuring that the importer will pay the bank by obtaining the funds before the letter of credit is issued. This constraint on cash flow is one of the reasons why importers prefer other terms of payment to a letter of credit. Another is the fact that the issuing bank will request a fee that will vary between 0.5 and 3 percent of the amount of the letter of credit, although most of them request about 1.5 percent.

- In the third step, the issuing bank sends the letter of credit (generally electronically, using the SWIFT network; or by fax; or, rarely, by mail) to the exporter's bank, which then advises the letter of credit. In this simplified example, the exporter's bank is also the advising bank. The advising bank checks a number of things: first, that the letter of credit is drawn on a legitimate bank and that its content meets the requirements of the exporter. It also wants to make sure that the letter of credit is irrevocable: an irrevocable letter of credit cannot be modified without the express consent of both the issuer and the beneficiary. All letters of credit issued under the Universal Customs and Practice for Documentary Credit of the International Chamber of Commerce (UCP 600) are irrevocable unless specifically marked as "revocable." There are very few instances in which it would make sense for an exporter and an importer to agree to have a revocable letter of credit, or one that can be modified by either party without the approval of the other. The advising bank finally confirms that the letter of credit's information matches the *pro forma* invoice exactly and that the expiration date is appropriate for the transaction.

- In the fourth step, the advising bank notifies the beneficiary that the letter of credit is acceptable from the bank's perspective. By reviewing the letter of credit, the bank is not engaging its responsibility; it is only acting as an adviser to the exporter and will have no liability (will not have to pay) if the issuing bank does not honor its commitment.

The bank then forwards the letter of credit to the exporter (the beneficiary), who then determines that the terms of the letter of credit are consistent with what was agreed upon between the exporter and the importer. Once the exporter has determined that the letter of credit is acceptable, the exporter can then start the shipping process.

Shipment

Figure 7.3 describes the steps that take place once the exporter ships the merchandise to the importer and transmits the sale's documents to the advising bank.

- The fifth step in the process is composed of two parts.

    1. First the exporter ships the merchandise abroad. Most of the time, the exporter ships directly to the importer, but in some cases, it may be

7.6 Letter of Credit

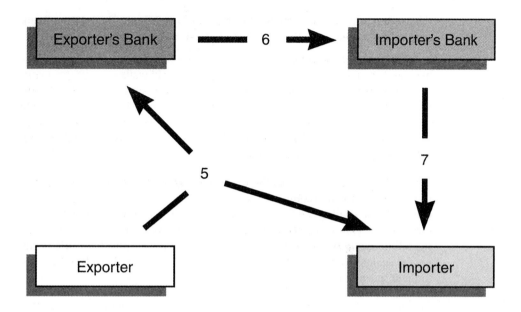

Figure 7.3: Shipment under a Letter of Credit

to another party, such as a wholesaler working with the importer. In all cases, the party to which the exporter ships the goods is called the consignee. In all cases, the exporter ships the goods according to the terms outlined in the letter of credit.

In the process of shipping the goods, the exporter generates a lot of paperwork (an invoice, a certificate of origin, an export license, a packing list, a Shipper's Export Declaration [U.S.], and so on) and collects a lot of paperwork as well, such as a bill of lading or an air waybill from the shipping company and miscellaneous certificates (certificate of insurance, certificate of inspection, and so on) from different suppliers (for more information on all of these terms, please see Chapter 9). Extreme care must be given to make sure that the paperwork matches precisely the requirements of the letter of credit, as the issuing bank's promise to pay is contingent upon presenting the proper documents. Any error or omission in the documents will trigger a discrepancy and will delay payment (see Section 7.6.3 on page 185).

2. After these documents are collected, the exporter will send them to its bank (the advising bank), which will check them against the terms of the letter of credit. This is the process that the exporter must follow in order to provide the importer with the documents that it will need to clear Customs in the importing country. No documents travel with the goods; they are sent to the the exporter's bank, and eventually are delivered to the importer through the banking system.

- The sixth step happens when the advising bank receives the documents sent by the exporter and sends them to the issuing bank if the documents conform to the requirements of the letter of credit. If they do not conform, then the advising bank will hold the documents until the issue is resolved. When everything eventually matches the terms of the letter of credit, the advising bank sends the documents to the importer's bank (the issuing bank).

In some cases, depending on the working relationship between the issuing bank and the advising bank, the advising bank could issue a credit (payment) to the exporter at that point. However, this payment is not final and is dependent on the issuing bank honoring the letter of credit. The simplest example illustrated in Figure 7.3 does not presume such a relationship and assumes that the advising bank will wait until it is actually paid by the issuing bank before it credits the exporter's bank account.

- The issuing bank then checks the documents again, and determines whether they conform to the requirements of the letter of credit. If the documents conform, the issuing bank notifies the importer that the documents are in order and it exchanges them (paying particular attention to the original of the bill of lading or the air waybill, which acts as the certificate of title to the goods) against payment by the importer. The importer can then clear Customs in the importing country.

Payment

The payment of a letter of credit is a fairly simple process: payment is first made by the importer to its bank, in exchange for the documents. In many cases, since the issuing bank has frozen a portion of the importer's bank account before issuing the letter of credit, the payment is simply processed from this account. The importers' bank then wires the payment to the exporter's bank, and finally the exporter's account is credited (see Figure 7.4).

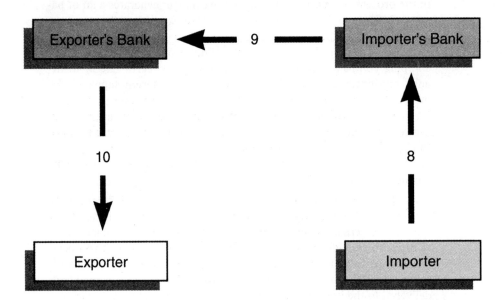

Figure 7.4: Payment under a Letter of Credit

The entire process of a letter of credit is shown in Figure 7.5 on the next page. The reason the process is labeled "simplified" is because a number of additional

7.6 Letter of Credit

parties can get involved in the process, as will be seen in the following section.

7.6.3 Additional Information

Advising Bank

It is not unusual for an exporter's bank to determine that it does not have the expertise to advise a particular letter of credit. It is the case when the letter of credit comes from a country with which the exporter's bank rarely conducts business, or when the letter of credit is issued by a bank with which the exporter's bank is unfamiliar or has not done business in the past.

In those cases, the exporter's bank will decline advising the letter of credit and will ask another bank to become the advising bank for that transaction. For that responsibility, the exporter's bank will generally seek the expertise of a large bank located in one of the world's international financial centers (New York, London, or Hong Kong SAR). Figure 7.5 would then include an additional bank, the advising bank, separate from the exporter's and the importer's banks, and through which the letter of credit would transit, on its way from the importer's bank to the exporter's bank. The documents would also transit through the advising bank, from the exporter's bank to the importer's bank.

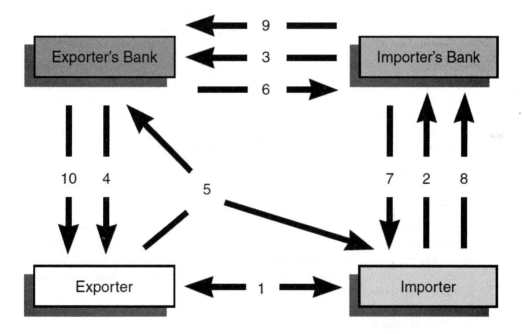

Figure 7.5: Complete, but Simplified Letter of Credit Process

Confirming Bank

In some cases, the exporting company may not be comfortable doing business with the issuing bank, which, after all, is an unknown foreign entity. It may not know the bank's creditworthiness, it may feel that the risk of relying on a foreign bank is too high, or it may simply be quite risk averse or new to the export business. In any case, the exporter can ask the advising bank to confirm the letter of credit; it then becomes a confirmed letter of credit.

A confirmed letter of credit signifies that, in the event the issuing bank does not honor its letter of credit, then the confirming bank will pay the exporter, as long as the documents submitted conform to the terms of the letter of credit. It is a way to substitute the creditworthiness of the domestic bank for that of the issuing bank. Because the confirming bank is often also the advising bank, the practice is that the confirming bank will issue a credit to the exporter upon presentation of the documents at the time of shipment. It therefore speeds up the process of collection by a week or so.

In most cases, confirming a letter of credit is not a wise choice, as banks are creditworthy. In addition, confirming a letter of credit is expensive, costing 0.5 to 1.5 percent of the amount of the letter of credit, a substantial cost considering that foreign banks rarely, if ever, fail. Some U.S. companies have a policy of always confirming letters of credit, generally because they prefer dealing with U.S. banks should there be difficulties in collection; nevertheless, this leads companies to confirm letters of credit drawn on extraordinarily solid banks, such as Crédit Suisse, using less-than-stellar U.S. banks as confirming banks. In addition, most bank failures, when they occur, tend to be rescued by their respective governments and their obligations are honored. The practice of confirming a letter of credit can only be justified on the grounds that it allows earlier payment.

Correspondent Bank

In some cases, yet another bank can get involved in the process. Most banks enter agreements with other banks in which they act as correspondent banks for each other. The purpose of these agreements is for each bank to have representation in a foreign market. The consequence of these agreements is that the banks favor their correspondent banks in financial transactions, and will generally direct some of the business they conduct in the correspondent bank's country to that bank. Correspondent banks also keep funds in one another's accounts.

For the sake of example, let's pretend that Bank A in Germany has an agreement with Bank Z in Thailand in which they are each other's correspondent bank. An exporter in Germany, doing business with German Bank B, requests a letter of credit from its Thai customer, which has an account with Bank Z. It is quite likely for Bank A to be part of the transaction and act as the "courier" between Bank Z and Bank B, or even for Bank Z to request that Bank A become the advising bank. In most cases, it would be advantageous for the German exporter to have Bank A involved, as Bank A may release the funds on behalf of the issuing bank, Bank Z (under the International Chamber of Commerce's URR 725 regulations). Payment would then be collected earlier.

UCP 600

UCP 600[20] is the Universal Customs and Practice for Documentary Credit, 2007 revision, Publication 600 of the International Chamber of Commerce. It is a publication that details the responsibilities of the banks involved in letters of credit, as well as the responsibilities of the applicant and the beneficiary.

---

confirmed letter of credit
When a letter of credit is confirmed, should the issuing bank not pay, the confirming bank does.

confirming bank
The bank that confirms a letter of credit. Should the issuing bank not pay, the confirming bank does.

correspondent bank
A foreign bank with which a domestic bank has a preferred business relationship.

7.6 Letter of Credit

```
RECEIVED FROM:    BTTT76XXX UNIVERSAL BANK, TAIWAN
TO:               TDOMCATTTOR TORONTO DOMINION BANK, TORONTO, CANADA

ISSUE OF A DOCUMENTARY CREDIT

40A: FORM OF DOCUMENTARY CREDIT          : IRREVOCABLE
20A: DOCUMENTARY CREDIT NUMBER           : 001/5845
31C: DATE OF ISSUE                       : 97/01/15
31D: DATE AND PLACE OF EXPIRY            : 97/02/20
                                           CANADA
50:  APPLICANT                           : A-TO-Z-IMPORT LIMITED
                                           77, EWE STREET
                                           TAIPEI, TAIWAN
59:  BENEFICIARY                         : EXPORT TRADING INC
                                           21 MAIN ST
                                           TORONTO, CANADA
32B: CURRENCY CODE, AMOUNT               : USD 50000.00
41D: AVAILABLE WITH...BY...              : YOURSELVES
                                           PAYMENT
42C: DRAFTS AT...                        : SIGHT
42D: DRAWEE                              : YOURSELVES
43P: PARTIAL SHIPMENTS                   : NOT ALLOWED
43T: TRANSHIPMENT                        : NOT ALLOWED
44A: LOADING ON BOARD/DISPATCH...        : VANCOUVER, CANADA
44B: FOR TRANSPORTATION TO...            : TAIPEI, TAIWAN
44C: LATEST DATE OF SHIPMENT             : 97/02/10
45A: DESCRIPTION OF GOODS AND/OR SERVICES :2 MOLDING MACHINES AS PER P.O
                                           NUMBER 26578 CIF TAIWAN
46A: DOCUMENTS REQUIRED
     1/FULL SET OF CLEAN ON BOARD MARINE BILLS OF LADING MADE OUT TO THE
     ORDER OF UNIVERSAL BANK, TAIWAN MARKED FREIGHT PREPAI AND NOTIFY
     APPLICANT
     2/COMMERCIAL INVOICE IN ORIGINAL AND TWO COPIES
     3/INSURANCE CERTIFICATE IN DUPLICATE FOR 110% OF INVOICE VALUE COVERING
     ALL RISKS
     4 PACKAGING LIST
71B: CHARGES                             : BANKING CHARGES OUTSIDE OF
                                           TAIWAN ARE FOR BENEFICIARY'S
                                           ACCOUNT
48:  PERIOD FOR PRESENTATION             : DOCUMENTS MUST BE PRESENTED
                                           NO LATER THAN 10 DAYS AFTER
                                           DATE OF SHIPPING DOCUMENTS
                                           FOR NEGOTIATION BUT WITHIN
                                           THE CREDIT VALIDITY
49:  CONFIRMATION INSTRUCTIONS           : WITH
53A: REIMBURSEMENT BANK                  : TDOMCATTTOR
72:  SENDER TO RECEIVER INFORMATION      : THIS IS THE OPERATIVE INSTRUMENT
                       * END OF MESSAGE*
```

Figure 7.6: A Letter of Credit Issued under UCP 600

Document ©Toronto Dominion Bank. Used with permission.

It also attempts to address most of the areas in which there could be misunderstandings between the issuing bank, the advising bank, the applicant, and the beneficiary. Because of the jurisprudence that has accumulated with the almost universal usage of UCP 600 (and its predecessor, UCP 500), it is greatly preferable to always follow its guidelines and to request that the letter of credit be issued "subject to" UCP 600.[21]

Whenever a letter of credit is transmitted through the SWIFT network—the Society for Worldwide Interbank Financial Telecommunications—it is by convention issued under UCP 600 guidelines unless otherwise noted. Because the immense majority of banks belong to the SWIFT network, almost all letters of credit are therefore issued under UCP 600.

Irrevocable Letter of Credit

irrevocable letter of credit
A letter of credit that cannot be altered without the consent of the issuing bank and the beneficiary.

An irrevocable letter of credit cannot be canceled by the issuing bank for any reason, unless the beneficiary agrees to it. A revocable letter of credit can be changed by the importer (or the issuing bank) without prior approval of the beneficiary. In very few cases does it make sense for a beneficiary to accept a revocable letter of credit. Almost all letters of credit are irrevocable.

Since letters of credit are almost all transmitted through the SWIFT network, they are following UCP 600 guidelines, and are therefore irrevocable. However, this is still a point of confusion: under the previous guidelines (UCP 500), all letters of credit were irrevocable as well. However, before 1993, under the UCP 400 rules, the opposite was true, and all letters of credit were revocable, unless specifically marked as irrevocable. There seems to still be some confusion regarding this important distinction, even though it is more than 20 years old, and exporters are still told to make sure that Letters of Credit are irrevocable. If they are issued under UCP 600, they are irrevocable.

URR 725

The International Chamber of Commerce has also published a document entitled Uniform Rules for Bank-to-Bank Reimbursements under Documentary Credits, which is called URR 725 and was implemented in October 2008.[22]

These rules outline the responsibilities of the banks involved in an international transaction conducted under UCP 600 and in which payment to the exporter is made directly by the advising bank (or by the correspondent bank of the issuing bank). The paying bank is then reimbursed by the issuing bank. This practice is becoming more and more common as a means to expedite the process of a letter of credit. The International Chamber of Commerce felt that uniform rules were necessary in this matter and created the URR 725 rules to direct banks into the proper way of implementing the UCP 600 rules. Although these rules apply to banks rather than exporters, it might be advisable to refer to them before requesting payment from the advising or the correspondent bank of the issuing bank.

Discrepancies and Amendments

Unfortunately, and for a number of reasons, there are often discrepancies between the requirements outlined in the letter of credit and the documents presented by the exporter. Since no payment will be made to the exporter (and no document will

7.6 Letter of Credit

be released to the importer) if they do not match, the exporter and the importer must resolve any discrepancy that arises so that the transaction can be completed.

Such discrepancies can be on shipping dates, changes in the number of packages, changes in part numbers, suppliers' costs (insurance, shipping charges), and a host of different reasons (see Table 7.4)[23]. It is estimated that around 50 percent of all letters of credit have some sort of discrepancy. Given these potential problems, it is crucial for the exporter to pay close attention to the terms of the letter of credit and to attempt to adhere to them as closely as possible.

discrepancy
A difference between the documents required by the letter of credit and the documents provided or obtained by the exporter.

Source of Discrepancy	Percentage of all Discrepancies
Inconsistent data	25.1%
Absence of documents	8.4%
Late presentation	7.9%
Carrier not named	8.8%
Incorrect goods description	4.1%
Incorrect data	7.1%
Incorrect BOL Endorsement	3.8%
Incorrect Insurance Cover	1.8%
Other discrepancies	33.0%

Table 7.4: Leading Sources of Discrepancies in Documentary CreditsSitpro.

Great care should be given to the preparation of the *pro forma* invoice, as this is the document upon which the issuing bank relies to issue the letter of credit. In those few cases in which the letter of credit does not reflect exactly the *pro forma* invoice (misspellings, for example), it is wise to issue an invoice that matches the letter of credit. While this is obviously difficult to do with an automated invoice processing system, it may save a considerable amount of aggravation later on. Many bankers have "horror stories" of issuing banks refusing payment on a letter of credit because there was a typo on it. Many letters of credit are typed by clerks with no knowledge whatsoever of the exporter's language.

In those cases in which there is a discrepancy between the requirements of the letter of credit and the documents presented by the exporter, the exporter and the importer must request their respective banks to negotiate an amendment to the letter of credit. The process is initiated by the advising bank, which requests an amendment to the letter of credit from the issuing bank. Since the amendment is a change to an irrevocable letter of credit, it must be authorized by both parties; the beneficiary and the importer (through the issuing bank) must agree to it. There is usually a fee attached to an amendment, and in some cases it can be difficult to obtain because the importing country's government gets involved (the import license may have to be changed) or because the change is not to the advantage of the importer (a delay in shipping date, for example). In the overwhelming majority of cases, though, the problem can be solved to the satisfaction of both parties; one personal banking acquaintance could recall only one deal "gone bad"—unpaid— in 20 years of letter of credit management.

amendment
A change to a letter of credit to which all parties have agreed, from the applicant to the beneficiary.

Yet More Complications

Things get a lot more complicated in a letter of credit transaction as yet more parties can get involved. For example, the exporter's bank may feel that it is unqualified to advise the letter of credit and will request that another, larger or more experienced bank become the advising bank. In those cases, there would then be at least three banks involved; the importer's bank, the exporter's bank, and the advising bank.

In the worst case, there are six banks involved: the exporter's bank, the importer's bank, an advising bank (to help the exporter's bank), a confirming bank (to reassure the exporter), and the correspondent banks of the latter two (to "simplify" the exchange of documents). When so many banks are involved, it can quickly become quite confusing, and it may be difficult to ascertain where the documents are at any point in time. Amendments to letters of credit in such cases can be extremely protracted, as several of the banks will intervene.

Drafts

draft
A promissory note in which the importer formally recognizes its debt to the exporter.

It is possible to add a draft (see Section 7.8.3) to a letter of credit. The draft is an instrument that legally binds the importer to pay within a certain period of time. This allows the exporter to grant commercial credit to the importer whenever it is deemed necessary. If no draft is attached to a letter of credit, the assumption is that the importer is not granted any credit (*i.e.*, that the letter of credit is payable at sight; in other words, immediately). The different types of drafts available in an international transaction are explained in Section 7.8.3.

7.6.4 Applicability

A letter of credit used to be the instrument of choice in international transactions, especially in those cases in which the exporter had no pre-existing business relationship with the importer, or when the importer was located in a country that was considered to be risky. It still is an outstanding means of making sure that the exporter will be paid, and is recommended in situations in which the exporter is risk averse, new to the business of exporting, has substantial exposure in the transaction in question, or has some uneasiness regarding the creditworthiness of the importer.

However, it is often a disadvantage to request a letter of credit because of the costs (and the cumbersome process) associated with it. It is also unwise to demand payment on such restrictive terms when other competitors can offer open-account terms. Therefore, it may be a more sensible alternative, especially in western Europe, to offer terms that are more favorable to the importer and to use commercial insurance to cover the commercial risk.

7.7 Additional Types of Letters of Credit

In addition to ordinary letters of credit that cover one single transaction, a few types have been designed to handle specific cases.

7.7.1 Stand-By Letters of Credit

A stand-by letter of credit is similar to an ordinary letter of credit, with a few exceptions. First, it generally has a much longer validity period, sometimes longer than a year. Second, it usually applies to more than one shipment from the exporter to the importer. Under such a system, the exporter will make shipments on an open-account basis and will "call" on the letter of credit only if the importer is not meeting its obligations;[24] for example, if it is not paying on time. These qualities make stand-by letters of credit a tool of choice for handling business with a distributor, for example, or making a series of shipments to a customer.

stand-by letter of credit
A letter of credit that is valid for multiple shipments and allows for bills of lading issued on multiple dates.

The stand-by letter of credit is an instrument that was created by U.S. banks as a substitute for bank guarantees, because U.S. banks are prohibited from offering them. Therefore, stand-by letters of credit are often also used to secure the obligations of the seller/exporter (as in a performance bond) (see Section 7.12 on page 199). The sums secured by stand-by letters of credit are vastly superior to the amount secured by traditional letters of credit, as they involve long, large-scale contracts.

The rules for stand-by letters of credit are regulated by the International Stand-By Practices ISP98, a series of eighty-nine rules governing the language, documentation, and practices of this type of letters of credit.[25]

7.7.2 Transferable Letters of Credit

A distributor may be interested in exporting products that it has to first purchase from a manufacturer. In that case the exporter may have to be able to demonstrate to the manufacturer that it will be able to pay. He can do that with a transferable letter of credit, with which the beneficiary of a letter of credit (the exporter) asks the issuing bank to allow the letter of credit to be used to secure the payment of the beneficiary toward others. Generally, banks will not allow a transferable letter of credit to be made transferable to further than one intermediary. A transferable letter of credit must be issued as transferable, and the issuing bank is the only party that can allow this transferability.

transferable letter of credit
A letter of credit that the beneficiary can use as a means to insure its creditors that they will be paid.

Because of the number of export trading companies in some parts of Asia, transferable letters of credit are used extensively in China, Taiwan region, and Singapore.[26]

7.7.3 Back-to-Back Letters of Credit

In a case where the exporter purchases the goods from a manufacturer and needs to re-assure the manufacturer of the goods that it will be paid, it is possible to use a back-to-back letter of credit rather than a transferable letter of credit, although the concept is rather similar.

back-to-back letter of credit
A letter of credit issued using another letter of credit as a payment guarantee.

In that type of transaction, the exporter obtains a letter of credit from its bank, with which the payment to the manufacturer is secured. This letter of credit is a secondary letter of credit that uses the letter of credit that was issued in the importing country on behalf of the importer—and is therefore called the primary letter of credit—as collateral. To a great extent, the secondary letter of credit is not as secure as a transferable letter of credit, because there is the possibility that the primary letter of credit will not be paid because of some non-performance by the exporter, over which the manufacturer has no control. Nevertheless, back-to-back transactions are relatively common when intermediaries do not have the financial capability to handle large sales.

7.8 Documentary Collection

7.8.1 Definition

documentary collection
A method of payment in which an exporter enlists the help of a bank in the importer's country to collect payment from the importer.

Documentary collection is a process by which an exporter asks a bank located in the importer's country to safeguard the exporter's interests. The exporter asks the bank not to release the documents—specifically the bill of lading, which is the certificate of title to the goods (see Chapter 9)—until the importer satisfies certain requirements, most often paying the exporter or signing a financial document (called a draft or a bill of exchange) promising that it will pay the exporter within a given amount of time. This allows the exporter, should the importer decide not to take delivery of the goods, to have them shipped back to the exporting country and to lose only the costs of shipment rather than the total value of the goods. Another possibility is to find another customer for these goods.

7.8.2 Process

remitting bank
In a documentary collection, the remitting bank collects the documents from the exporter and sends them to the presenting bank. It has no other involvement.

Although the process can conceivably be done with the exporter sending the documents directly to the bank in the importer's country, the process generally starts (see Figure 7.7) with the exporter sending the documents to its own bank, which acts as a conduit for sending the documents to the importer's bank. The exporter's bank is the remitting bank, and it acts only as an intermediary; it has no responsibility in the process but the safe transmittal of the documents. The reason a remitting bank is used is to help the foreign bank ascertain the legitimacy of the exporter; the bank is not dealing with an unknown exporter, it is dealing with a bank with which it has dealt in the past, and which it trusts.

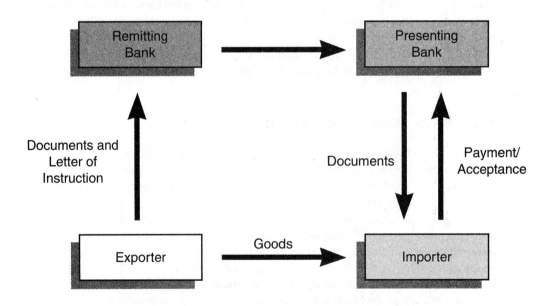

Figure 7.7: The Documentary Collection Process

The remitting bank then forwards the documents, as well as an instruction letter

7.8 Documentary Collection

from the exporter, to the presenting bank. The presenting bank can be the importer's bank or another bank in the importing country, but it is most often the correspondent bank of the remitting bank in the importer's country. The presenting bank then follows the instruction letter and alerts the importer that the documents have arrived. It notifies the importer that it will have to either pay for the goods or sign a draft in order to obtain the documents. Since the importer needs the documents in order to clear Customs in the importing country, it complies with the requirements of the presenting bank. If the importer decides not to collect the documents, the bank retains them and follows the exporter's instruction letter to determine what its next steps should be.

Once the presenting bank has obtained payment from the importer, it forwards the funds to the remitting bank, which then notifies the exporter that the funds have arrived.

presenting bank
In a documentary collection, the presenting bank interacts with the importer and withholds the documents until payment is received or a draft signed.

7.8.3 Drafts

The exporter has several alternatives in deciding what it wants the presenting bank to request in exchange for delivering the documents to the importer. It can request immediate payment or it can grant the importer some time to make the payment, and uses a draft in order to do so. A draft is a promissory note, signed by the importer in the presence of a representative of the presenting bank, in which the importer commits to pay the invoice amount to the exporter on a given date.

A draft (or a bill of exchange) is a legal document in the importing country in which the importer officially recognizes a commercial debt toward the exporter. This makes it easier to collect payment if the importer decides not to honor its commitment, as the default is now a domestic issue rather than an international one—a dispute over which a domestic court would have no problem ruling. Specifically, in the instructions to the presenting bank, it is possible to request a protest in case of non-payment on a draft, which is a legal process that can have serious consequences for an importer; it may be difficult (if not impossible) for the importer to obtain credit after it has been recorded that it does not honor its debt. In some countries, such defaults are even published prominently in the local business press, tarnishing the reputation of a business.

bill of exchange
Another term for a draft. A promissory note with which the importer formally recognizes it debt to the exporter.

Although drafts are introduced in the section dealing with documentary collections, it is not unusual for a draft to accompany a letter of credit as well. When they accompany a letter of credit, they fulfill exactly the same role; the documents held by the issuing bank are not given to the importer until the importer signs the draft.

Sight Draft

The exporter can request that the presenting bank release the documents only upon payment of the invoice by the importer. Such a transaction is called "documents against payment" (D/P) or a sight draft transaction, meaning that the draft (a promissory note) is payable "at sight" (*i.e.*, immediately). In this case, the exporter retains the title to the goods, embodied in the bill of lading or air waybill, until payment is made and the bill of lading or air waybill is given to the importer.

sight draft
A draft in which the importer promises to pay the exporter immediately, "at sight."

Time Draft

time draft
A draft in which the importer promises to pay the exporter 30, 60 or 90 days after the importer has signed the draft.

In some cases, the exporter may want to grant some credit terms to the importer but still want some means to ensure it will be paid. In that case, it can request that the bank exchange the documents against a time draft: the importer has to sign (endorse) a document promising it will pay within a certain time after the draft is endorsed. Credit is generally extended for durations that are multiples of thirty days: 30, 60, 90, and 180 days are the most common credit terms. The presenting bank should specifically be instructed to remit the documents when the draft is signed ("documents against acceptance" [D/A]), or to remit them against payment (D/P), in which case the importer will not take title to the goods until after payment is made, a requirement that mostly defeats the purpose of granting credit. Specifically because of problems associated with the custody of the goods between their arrival in the importing country and the time they become the property of the importer, the International Chamber of Commerce advises that "collections should not contain bills of exchange [drafts] payable at a future date with instructions that commercial documents are to be delivered against payment."[27]

Date Draft

date draft
A draft in which the importer promises to pay the exporter 30, 60 or 90 days after the shipment date of the goods, regardless of the date on which importer has signed the draft.

A date draft is another way of granting credit to the importer. The difference is that the credit is extended to the importer for 30, 60, or 90 days from the shipment date rather than from the endorsement of the draft. The shipment date is determined by the main contract of carriage, generally the date at which the ocean bill of lading or the air waybill is issued.[28] The advantage of the date draft over the time draft is that the exporter has control over the date at which shipment is initiated (and therefore over the date at which the payment is due), whereas it has no control over the date at which the importer will endorse the draft.

A date draft transaction therefore alleviates one of the problems of documentary collection in general: the date at which the importer will endorse the draft. Under the Uniform Rules for Collection of the ICC,[29] the bank must notify the importer as soon as it receives the documents. However, the importer has no incentive to come to the bank to collect them—if the draft is a sight or time draft—because delaying endorsement delays payment as well.

7.8.4 Instruction Letter

instruction letter
In a documentary collection, a document prepared by the exporter that instructs the presenting bank on the steps to take before releasing the documents to the importer.

In addition to the documents (*e.g.* invoice, bill of lading, certificates, licenses) and the draft, each documentary collection includes an instruction letter in which the exporter, through the intermediary of the remitting bank, specifies what the presenting bank is expected to accomplish.

The instruction letter is a document in which the remitting bank instructs the presenting bank on the procedures it should follow in its dealings with the importer. For example, the instruction letter will specify whether the documents should be exchanged against payment (D/P) or against an acceptance of the draft (D/A). It also indicates what the procedure should be if the importer refuses to sign the draft, if the importer refuses to pay for the fees (if any), or if the importer does not honor its signature. The presenting bank could be asked to file a protest, for example.

This instruction letter is the only document that the presenting bank will follow in a documentary collection. The bank does not need to find its instructions among

7.8 Documentary Collection

the other documents that accompany the documentary collection. The International Chamber of Commerce is quite clear about this issue in its Uniform Rules for Collections (URC 522). Despite this *caveat*, it is nevertheless preferable to mention in the instruction letter that the collection is subject to URC 522, for it outlines rules for the timeliness of presentations and information reports.

7.8.5 Acceptance

Trade Acceptance

The responsibilities of the presenting bank generally stop at notifying the importer that the documents have arrived and at requesting that the importer endorse the draft (D/A) or at requesting payment (D/P) before releasing the documents. In those cases, this process is called trade acceptance—sometimes "trader's acceptance"—as the importer has control over the decision to accept or reject the draft and over the timing of the endorsement.

> **trade acceptance**
> In a documentary collection, trade acceptance takes place when the importer signs the draft.

This could be somewhat inconvenient for the exporter, as the importer could delay acceptance of the draft for an inordinate amount of time—a problem that can be solved with a date draft—or even refuse to sign the draft. In such a case, the exporter still has title but over merchandise that is warehoused in a foreign country. The costs associated with warehousing goods in an unknown location, as well as the risks of pilferage and the exporter's difficulties in arranging for such storage, can lead unscrupulous importers to take advantage of the situation by extorting better terms from the exporter (*e.g.* a discounted price, given the costs of repatriating the goods) before signing the draft. This is a strategy that would work only once, but an unscrupulous importer could attempt to follow it.

Banker's Acceptance and Aval

The problems presented by a trade acceptance can be solved by requesting a banker's acceptance. In this case, it is the presenting bank that endorses the draft on behalf of the importer. The bank will usually endorse the draft immediately upon receipt of the documents, and the endorsement of the bank engages the responsibility of the importer: it signs on behalf of the importer. The presenting bank is unlikely to offer a banker's acceptance unless it feels in a position to aval the draft.

> **banker's acceptance**
> In a documentary collection, banker's acceptance takes place when the bank signs the draft on behalf of the importer.

An aval is a promise by the presenting bank that the importer will honor the draft and that, should the importer default, the bank will make the payment. The bank therefore acts as a co-signer of the draft.

Although an aval is theoretically independent and different from a banker's acceptance, in practice the latter is often used as a substitute for aval. Therefore the remitting bank will often offer credit to an exporter based upon a banker's acceptance, as it understands that the credit risk is now based upon the creditworthiness of the presenting bank, which is a situation almost as good as that of a letter of credit, but at a lower cost.

> **aval**
> In a documentary collection, the promise by the presenting bank that the importer will honor the draft and that, should the importer default, the bank will make the payment.

7.8.6 URC 522

The International Chamber of Commerce publishes guidelines for documentary collections in its Uniform Rules for Collections (URC 522).[30] The main benefit of these rules is that they outline specifically the responsibilities of the remitting bank and the responsibilities of the presenting bank, as well as the limits of their responsibilities. For example, the presenting bank has to make sure that it promptly notifies the importer to come in to sign the draft (D/A) and is responsible for making sure that the draft is signed properly (according to local laws), but it has no obligation to determine that the person has the authority to sign. All of these obligations (and limitations) are very well described and explained in the Commentary on URC 522.[31]

The URC 522 mandates the inclusion of an instruction letter to the presenting bank, which clarifies what the presenting bank has to do with the documents. Because URC 522 is becoming the international standard for documentary collection—although it has not reached the universal nature of UCP 600—it is advisable to always state in the instruction letter that the collection is subject to the Uniform Rules for Collections (URC 522) of the International Chamber of Commerce.

7.8.7 Applicability

Documentary collections are a good way to conduct international sales because they are clearly less cumbersome (and less expensive) than letters of credit and provide a good amount of safety. The title remains in the hands of the exporter until the importer accepts the draft (D/A) or makes payment (D/P). This risk is further reduced if a banker's acceptance is requested.

However, documentary collections represent more risk for the exporter than a letter of credit because payment is dependent upon the primary transaction (the contract of sale); the importer could refuse to sign the draft (invoking poor-quality merchandise, for example) or delay signing the draft (until it has resold the merchandise), in which case the exporter retains title but does not get paid. A letter of credit, however, is not dependent on the primary transaction, but only on the documents; it will ensure payment as long as the documents are in the proper form.

A documentary collection could be used for customers in which there is a fair amount of trust but for which an open-account transaction is out of the question for whatever reason. A banker's acceptance could be used for customers who refuse to conduct business on a letter of credit basis and about whose creditworthiness the exporter is uncertain.

7.9 Forfaiting

forfaiting
A means of financing an international sale in which an exporter collects a series of drafts from the importer, and then sells them.

In those cases where the importer wants credit terms that are beyond what the exporter is comfortable giving—for example, a five-year term is requested on a piece of machinery when the exporter can extend only a 180-day credit—there is the possibility of using international forfaiting as a means to extend this credit. In an international transaction, forfaiting is generally achieved with the help of a series of drafts from the importer, which have been given an aval by the importer's bank. Forfaiting is used for longer credit terms than factoring, which tends to be used for credit terms of up to 180 days. In contrast, forfaiting can be used for terms as long as seven years.

The exporter, once it has obtained an agreement from the forfaiting firm, will obtain this series of drafts, all with different due dates from the importer. It will then sell this series of drafts to the forfaiting firm at a discount. The forfaiting firm purchases them without recourse, which means it cannot hold the exporter responsible for non-payment by the importer. Forfaiting is an arrangement that usually satisfies the credit requirements of the importer at no risk—and at a fairly moderate cost—to the exporter.

7.10 Purchasing Cards

A number of banks are offering a system of credit cards for their corporate accounts. The product originates from the observation that companies purchase myriad small items, from office supplies to small maintenance parts. In the past, the traditional process to purchase these parts was through a centralized purchasing department that issued a purchase order, processed a significant amount of paperwork, and then paid an invoice. More recently, companies have been using purchasing cards, also know as procurement cards or P-cards. These cards allow each department to make certain purchases directly from a vendor, a much more expedient process. The P-cards are similar in concept to consumers' credit cards; they have a certain credit limit, they are billed directly to the department (or at least can provide an itemized billing statement showing which department is responsible for a specific purchase), and most importantly, they allow transactions to be conducted extremely rapidly. in addition, their usage can also be restricted to specific vendors, allowing the purchasing department to restrict purchases to pre-approved suppliers. Moreover, the supplier is paid immediately—minus a certain transaction percentage, in the neighborhood of 2 percent—and the customer is billed at the end of the month.[32]

purchasing cards Credit cards used by companies to make small purchases, and that can be used in international transactions.

Most P-cards are used for domestic purchases, but there are several advantages to using them for international purchases. The first is that the exporter is essentially paid in advance, because it is paid almost immediately after the goods have been shipped. The second is that the exchange rate on the transaction is essentially the best one can get: because banks process thousands of foreign transactions worth millions of dollars on the same date, the exchange rate is the one that large transactions can earn. Finally, the importer has some sort of recourse (in a way similar to a consumer using a Visa or American Express card) if the merchandise is defective. It should be expected that this type of transaction will increasingly take place in international business, particularly for small items (maintenance parts) and will facilitate the handling of rush orders, which will increase the level of customer service a company can offer from its home country.

This product seems to present only advantages, and the number of banks currently offering such a service is increasing rapidly. However, one issue that has recently affected negatively the use of P-cards is the way that banks have modified their foreign exchange procedures. In 2005, many of the banks offering P-cards changed their policies on currency exchange and added a fee on foreign currency transactions that can vary from 1 to 3 percent of the value of the transaction. This additional cost negates the advantageous exchange rates that procurement cards can offer. Another slight disadvantage is that the exchange rate in effect on the processing date may differ from the rate on the date used for the transaction, resulting in a slightly different currency exchange rate than was initially anticipated. As of June 2013, there was still one notable exception: Capital One in the United States and Britain did not charge a foreign transaction fee.

7.11 TradeCard

TradeCard
A proprietary process that combines payment and documents and facilitates international transactions.

Created by the World Trade Centers Association in 1994, TradeCard is a proprietary electronic system that is gaining greater acceptance in the trade community and is an alternative that combines the advantages of letters of credit and of procurement cards:

- No payment is made until all the documents are in order and there are no discrepancies.

- The buyer is obligated to pay if the documents are in order.

- The system is expedient (payment is received quickly).

TradeCard also has two advantages over both of these methods of payment in that it is extremely inexpensive—charging only $150 for a transaction up to $100,000, in contrast to 1 to 3 percent for letters of credit and 2 to 3 percent for procurement cards—and combines document handling as well as payments.

TradeCard encompasses several electronic tools. First, it has a secure system for the transmission of documents, from the *pro forma* invoice to the bill of lading, packing list, and other transportation documents. It also has a system that checks the creditworthiness of the customer and, should the importer be deemed creditworthy, guarantees payment to the exporter if the documents conform. This service is offered through a partnership with COFACE. Finally, TradeCard has a system that automatically settles invoices once the documents have been found to be in order and without discrepancies.

Unfortunately, TradeCard has still not achieved a critical mass of customers (a significant enough number of customers to make it a standard form of payment), and therefore, as of 2013, despite its gains, it remains an unusual form of payment in international trade, far behind letters of credit, documentary collections, and open accounts. When an exporter suggests a payment on TradeCard, it is unlikely that the importer already has an account with TradeCard, and therefore it is unlikely that the transaction will be completed under this term of sale. The reciprocal is also true: a savvy importer may have a TradeCard account, but the exporter may not have one. As they do business more frequently, the TradeCard customer may eventually convince the other of the advantages of such a system.

Add to this issue the fact that importers and exporters often ask their bankers for advice in such matters, and that the latter are generally quite conservative in their recommendations, and it becomes clear why this method of payment has not gained as much momentum as was originally anticipated. Nevertheless, TradeCard presents such advantages over the other forms of international payment that it should be expected to become the dominant method of payment in the 2020s.

In early 2013, TradeCard merged with GT Nexus, a cloud-based business network that provides supply-chain solutions to multinational companies, and this development may help that method-of-payment alternative develop a greater market share.

7.12 Bank Guarantees

7.12.1 Definition

A bank guarantee is another instrument used in international trade, but in different situations. A bank guarantee is usually requested to secure the performance of the seller (exporter), rather than to ensure that payment will be made by the buyer (importer). This requirement happens in cases in which the exporter is a company contracting to build a plant, establish a drilling platform, or install a sewer system; for example, companies like Bechtel and Bouygues are often asked to provide bank guarantees.

A bank guarantee is applicable to all long-term contracts in which the importer wants to ensure that the work will be brought to completion. Frequently, the bank guarantee is offered by a group of banks rather than a single bank, because of the amounts involved. Finally, a bank guarantee is usually for an amount that is only a fraction of the total amount of the contract. By law, U.S. banks are not allowed to offer bank guarantees, so those are always provided by banks based outside of the United States.

Like a letter of credit, a bank guarantee is an independent contract between the bank giving the guarantee (guarantor) and the beneficiary.

bank guarantee
A contract from a bank in which the bank guarantees that the exporter will perform as required by the importer.

guarantor
The bank that provides the bank guarantee.

7.12.2 Guarantee Payable on First Demand

A bank guarantee payable on first demand—at first request— is one in which the beneficiary does not have to provide any evidence that the terms of the underlying contract between the contractor and the beneficiary have not been met; the issuing bank has to pay at the first request of the beneficiary, solely upon the presentation of a request for payment, sometimes accompanied by a statement from the beneficiary stating that the contractor is not meeting its obligations. No other proof is necessary. This type of bank guarantee is the most common one.

7.12.3 Guarantees Based upon Documents—Cautions

In some cases, a guarantee can be made conditional upon presentation of certain documents rather than on first demand. The beneficiary must present documents that demonstrate that the contractor is not meeting its obligations; such a document may be a ruling by a court, or some other evidence as agreed upon in the terms of the guarantee.

The International Chamber of Commerce has issued a series of conventions regarding documentary bank guarantees in Publication No. 325, Uniform Rules for Contract Guarantees. These rules are not widely used,[33] primarily because documentary guarantees are rarely used.

7.12.4 Stand-By Letters of Credit

Because U.S. law prohibits bank guarantees, American banks offer an alternative to bank guarantees with stand-by letters of credit. The only difference between a stand-by letter of credit and a bank guarantee is that the stand-by letter of credit is always documentary (*i.e.*, the beneficiary must present a document before collecting from the bank). A simple statement that the contractor is not performing is usually considered sufficient.[34]

7.12.5 Types of Bank Guarantees

Several types of bank guarantees—or stand-by letters of credit—are available:

- The tender guarantee or bid guarantee is one that is requested by a beneficiary to ensure that the contractor is bidding in good faith and will enter the contract if awarded.

- The performance guarantee is the most commonly used type of guarantee and is used to ensure that the contractor finishes the project.

- The maintenance guarantee is used to ensure that the contractor performs the services necessitated by the contract after the completion of the project (*i.e.*, maintenance and after-sale service).

- The advance-payment guarantee or repayment guarantee is used to ensure that payments made by the beneficiary in advance of the work (to enable the contractor to purchase supplies or machinery) would be reimbursed if the contractor fails to start the project.

- The payment guarantee is used in a very different context. It covers the obligations of the buyer (often a distributor) toward the exporter, and is essentially a stand-by letter of credit.

7.13 Terms of Payment as a Marketing Tool

An exporter has several alternatives from which to choose in negotiating terms of payment with the importer. Although the choice of the term of sale is dependent on the level of experience of both the exporter and the importer as well as on the level of confidence that the exporter has in the ability of the importer to make the payment, there are some alternatives that are definitely preferable and will increase an exporter's probability of clinching the sale.

An importer, in most situations, obtains several possible quotes from several exporters located in different countries. For example, a Brazilian newspaper looking to replace a printing press will seek bids from a number of suppliers, who could very well be located in the United States, Germany, Japan, Switzerland, Taiwan region, and Canada. Although the alternative bids are likely to be evaluated on a large combination of criteria (price, specific capabilities, after-sale service, delivery terms, credit terms, financing, and so on), one of the issues will be the ease with which the purchase transaction will take place. From the importer's perspective, the easiest alternative—and the one that does not demand that cash flow be affected—is to purchase on an open-account basis. It is likely that at least one of the potential suppliers will offer such terms, and that others will ask for a letter of credit. Therefore, the supplier offering an open-account transaction has an advantage over the others and, if it has purchased credit insurance, has not affected its probability of getting paid.

There are some regions of the world in which letters of credit are still playing a significant role (see Table 7.5 on the facing page).[35] However, in just about all

7.13 Terms of Payment as a Marketing Tool

Percentage of Transactions Conducted on Letters of Credit
(based on the location of the importer)

European Union [15]	9%
Rest of Europe	20%
North America	11%
Latin America	27%
Middle East	52%
Asia-Pacific	43%
Africa	49%
Asia	46%
Australia-New Zealand	17%

Table 7.5: Percentage of Transactions Conducted on Letters of Credit_Sitpro_.

cases, more than half of international transactions, and more than 90 percent of the transactions in which the importer is located in the fifteen original European Union countries or North America, are conducted using some other means of payment.

Although no specific information is known, it is likely that the rank order of the other methods of payment are:

1. Open account (with or without credit insurance)

2. Documentary collection

3. Procurement cards (for smaller purchases)

4. TradeCard (for larger purchases)

5. Cash in advance

An exporter intent on increasing its sales should choose to display that it is confident in the ability of the importer to pay for the goods by using an open account. After all, this is the way its domestic sales are conducted—and generally the way many other competing exporters are intent on selling. If the exporter is unsure about the ability of the importer to pay, it should consider purchasing a credit insurance policy.

Review and Discussion Questions

1. Why is it more difficult and riskier to collect receivables from a foreign purchaser?

2. What are the differences between political risks and commercial risks of non-payment?

3. Describe the concept of cash in advance.

4. Describe the process of documentary collection.

5. Describe the mechanism of a letter of credit, from the exchange of the pro forma invoice to final payment.

6. What is credit insurance? Why is it associated with open-account transactions?

7. Several people claim that letters of credit will soon be replaced by the concept of TradeCard. What is this product, and why do those people think it has such a bright future?

8. Describe the concept of bank guarantees. What are the different types of bank guarantees?

Notes

[1] Stecklow, Steve and Jonathan Karp, "Citibank in India Used Collectors Accused of Strong-Arm Tactics," *The Wall Street Journal*, May 5, 1999, p. A1.

[2] Kritzer, Albert, "CISG: Table of Contracting States," Pace Law School Institute of International Commercial Law, http://www.cisg.law.pace.edu/cisg/countries/cntries.html, retrieved June 11, 2013.

[3] Moss, Sally, "Why the United Kingdom has not ratified the CISG," *Journal of Law and Business*, 25, 2005-2006, pp. 483-485.

[4] Freedman, Michael, "Judgment Day: U.S. Companies Complain They Can't Get a Fair Shake from America's Plaintiff-Friendly Juries. Try Resolving a Dispute in Russia, Indonesia, or Ukraine," *Forbes*, June 7, 2004, pp. 97-98.

[5] Dolven, Ben, "Foreign Investors Find that China's Legal System Resolves Few Disputes," *The Wall Street Journal*, April 7, 2003, p. A14.

[6] Chrisafis, Angelique, "France faces revolt over poverty in its Caribbean Islands," *The Guardian*, February 12, 2009, http://www.guardian.co.uk/world/2009/feb/12/france-revolts-guadeloupe-martinique, retrieved February 12, 2009.

[7] Goldberg, Jeffrey, "The Modern King in the Arab Spring," *The Atlantic*, April 2013, pp. 17-24.

[8] Yardley, William, "Union's War Protest Shuts down West Coast ports," *The New York Times*, May 2, 2008, http://www.nytimes.com/2008/05/02/us/02port.html.

[9] Foxman, Simone, "Hong Kong port strike ends with 9.8% raise for dockworkers—plus potty breaks," *Quartz*, May 6, 2013, http://qz.com/81552/40-day-hong-kong-port-strike-finally-ends-with-a-deal-in-writing/, retrieved May 23, 2013.

[10] Ministère du Budget, des Comptes Publics et de la Fonction Publique, Rapport Annuel sur l'Etat de la Fonction Publique: Faits et Chiffres 2007-2008, Volume 1, p. 591, http://lesrapports.ladocumentationfrancaise.fr/BRP/084000616/0000.pdf, accessed May 24, 2009.

[11] "Total Reserves in Months of Import," The World Bank, http://data.worldbank.org/indicator/FI.RES.TOTL.MO, retrieved June 11, 2013.

[12] Shoenmakers, Y. M. M., E. De Vries Robbé, and Anton Van Vijk, *Mountains of Gold: An Exploratory Research on Nigerian 419 Fraud: Backgrounds.* Amsterdam: SWP Publishers, 2009.

[13] "Doing Business: Trading Across Borders," International Finance Corporation, The World Bank, http://www.doingbusiness.org/data/exploretopics/trading-across-borders, retrieved June 16, 2013.

[14] "International Credit Reports," Kansas Department of Commerce—Trade Development, http://kdoch.state.ks.us/KDOCHdocs/TD/CofaceInternationalCreditReportsFlier.pdf, retrieved May 24, 2009.

[15] Banham, Russ, "Credit Clout: Export Credit Insurance Offers Low-Cost Insurance that Protects Shippers from Non-Payment," *International Business*, March 1997, pp. 8-44.

[16] Pereira, Ray, "International Factoring: The Viable Financing Alternative," *World Trade*, December 1999, pp. 68-69.

[17] *Trade Finance Guide: a Quick Reference for U.S. Exporters*, U.S. Department of Commerce, International Trade Administration, April 2008, http://www.ita.doc.gov/media/Publications/pdf/tfg2008.pdf, retrieved June 16, 2013.

[18] "UPS Capital Cargo Finance," United Parcel Service, http://www.upscapital.com/solutions/cargo_finance.html, accessed October 13, 2008.

[19] Wood, Jeffrey, "Drafting Letters of Credit; Basic Issues under Article 5 of the Uniform Commercial Code, UCP 600 and ISP 98," *Banking Law Journal*, February 2008, pp. 103-149.

[20] *Uniform Customs and Practices for Documentary Credits*, UCP 600, 2007 Revision, Publication No. 600 of the International Chamber of Commerce, ICC Publishing S.A., 38 Cours Albert 1er, 75008 Paris, France and ICC Publishing, 156 Fifth Avenue, New York, NY 10010.

[21] *User's Handbook for Documentary Credits under UCP 600*, Publication No. 694 of the International Chamber of Commerce, ICC Publishing S.A., 38 Cours Albert 1er, 75008 Paris, France and ICC Publishing, 156 Fifth Avenue, New York, NY 10010.

[22] *Uniform Rules for Bank-to-Bank Reimbursements under Documentary Credits*, URR 725, 2008, publication No. 725 of the International Chamber of Commerce, ICC Publishing S.A., 38 Cours Albert 1er, 75008 Paris, France and ICC Publishing, 156 Fifth Avenue, New York, NY 10010.

[23] Adapted from "Report on the Use of Export Letters of Credit 2001/2002," dated April 11, 2003, Sitpro, Simplifying International Trade, http://sitpro.org.uk/reports/lettcredr, accessed May 25, 2009.

[24] Tyler, Joseph, "Financing Exports," in *Export Practice: Customs and International Trade Law*, Terence P. Stewart, ed., New York: Practicing Law Institute, 1994.

[25] *International Standby Practices*, ISP98, Institute of International Banking Law and Practice, Inc., Publication No. 590 of the International Chamber of Commerce, ICC Publishing S.A., 38 Cours Albert 1er, 75008 Paris, France and ICC Publishing, 156 Fifth Avenue, New York, NY 10010.

[26] Borcky, Ron, "Understanding and Using Letters of Credit: Part II," Credit Research Foundation, http://www.crfonline.org/orc/cro/cro-9-2.html, retrieved June 17, 2013.

[27] *Uniform Rules for Collection*, URC 522, 1995, publication No. 522 of the International

Chamber of Commerce, ICC Publishing S.A., 38 Cours Albert 1er, 75008 Paris, France and ICC Publishing, 156 Fifth Avenue, New York, NY 10010.

[28] Reynolds, Frank, "Use Caution with Semi-Secured Terms," *The Journal of Commerce*, October 20, 1999, p. 10.

[29] *Uniform Rules for Collection*, URC 522, 1995, publication No. 522 of the International Chamber of Commerce, ICC Publishing S.A., 38 Cours Albert 1er, 75008 Paris, France and ICC Publishing, 156 Fifth Avenue, New York, NY 10010.

[30] *Ibid.*

[31] *Commentary on the ICC Uniform Rules for Collections*, 1995, Publication No. 550 of the International Chamber of Commerce, ICC Publishing S.A., 38 Cours Albert 1er, 75008 Paris, France and ICC Publishing, 156 Fifth Avenue, New York, NY 10010.

[32] "Purchasing Card Introduction: What, Why, How, Who," Professional Association for the Commercial Card and Payment Industry, http://www.napcp.org/?page=PCardIntro, retrieved June 17, 2013.

[33] Bertrams, R. I. V. F., *Bank Guarantees in International Trade*, Kluwer Law and Taxation Publishers, Deventer, The Netherlands, 1990.

[34] *Ibid.*

[35] "Ninth Survey of International Services Provided to Exporters," commissioned by the Institute of Exporters, and reproduced in the *Report on the Use of Export Letters of Credit 2001/2002*, April 11, 2003, Sitpro, Simplifying International Trade, http://sitpro.org.uk/reports/lettcredr, accessed June 1, 2006.

Chapter 8

Managing Transaction Risks

    8.1 Currency Used in the Sales Contract 206
    8.2 The System of Currency Exchange Rates 210
    8.3 Theories of Exchange Rate Determinations 220
    8.4 Exchange Rate Forecasting 224
    8.5 Managing Transaction Exposure 227
    8.6 International Banking Institutions 231
    8.7 Currency of Payment as a Marketing Tool 233

The previous chapters have shown that, for each international sale, the exporter and the importer must agree on two particular points:

- The terms of trade under which the sale is conducted (*i.e.*, the costs the exporter should pay, the costs the importer should pay, and the point at which the responsibility for the cargo shifts from one to the other). These responsibilities are determined by the Incoterms® Rule chosen.

- The terms of sale under which the transaction is performed (*i.e.*, at what point in the transaction the exporter wants to be paid, and what its level of confidence is in the ability of the importer to pay). The exporter and the importer can choose any number of alternatives, from Cash in Advance to an Open Account transaction to a TradeCard.

However, there is still one more issue for the exporter and the importer to consider: the currency that will be used in the transaction. While the exporter and the importer have several options, they have to agree on one, based on the advantages and disadvantages of each of these alternatives.

Once the currency of the transaction has been determined, at least one of the parties is left with a potential currency-fluctuation risk, since there is always a time lag between the time at which the amount of the transaction is set and the time at which payment is made. The party at risk has to determine how it will manage that risk.

term of trade
An element of the contract of sale that specifies the responsibilities of the exporter and those of the importer in the shipment of the goods.

term of sale
An element of the contract of sale that specifies the method of payment used in an international transaction.

currency
The monetary unit used to settle economic transactions in a given country.

8.1 Currency Used in the Sales Contract

The exporter and the importer have three possible alternatives in determining the currency that will be used in an international transaction. The sale can be conducted using the exporter's currency, the importer's currency, or a third country's currency. When considering these options, the exporter and the importer should weigh two factors:

exchange rate risk
The risk presented by the fluctuations in exchange rates between the time at which the sale is made and the time at which it is paid.

- **The risk of currency fluctuation.** This is a speculative risk, that is, one for which there is the possibility of a gain or a loss, depending on which way the exchange rate fluctuates, and depending on whether the exporter or the importer is holding the currency risk. If the transaction is conducted in the exporter's currency, then the importer is the one carrying the exchange rate risk. If the transaction is conducted in the importer's currency, it is the exporter who assumes the exchange rate risk. The two vignettes on pages 208 and 209 illustrate this point.

hard currency
A currency that can be easily converted into another currency.

convertible currency
A currency that can be converted into another currency.

- **The convertibility of the currency.** This is a pure risk that reflects the degree to which a currency can be converted into other currencies. Major countries' currencies are fully convertible—they are called hard currencies—and these currencies can be freely exchanged, at a moment's notice: they are also called convertible currencies.

The ability to convert a currency into hard currency is generally measured in "months of foreign exchange cover" or an approximation of the size of the hard

Figure 8.1: Foreign Exchange Quotes of Convertible Currencies
Photo ©Brian Jackson. Used with permission.

8.1 Currency Used in the Sales Contract

currency stock a given country has, expressed in months of import activities this stock can cover. The World Bank publishes these data and most countries have two to four months' cover.[1]

However, some developing countries' currencies are not readily convertible into hard currencies, because the country has few exports and its government controls which imports get paid first. Those countries have little foreign currency cover. In most cases, the lack of convertibility of the currency just delays the date at which it can be exchanged for hard currency. All currencies that are difficult to convert into hard currencies are called soft currencies. In some rare cases, the currency is not convertible at all (*i.e.*, the currency cannot be exchanged for any other currency, at any time), or more commonly, the currency has a different exchange rate for purchases and for sales. Finally, some currencies can be purchased, but not sold. All of these currencies are collectively called inconvertible currencies.

> **soft currency**
> A currency that cannot always be converted into an other currency.
>
> **inconvertible currency**
> A currency that cannot be converted into an other currency.

8.1.1 Exporter's Currency

In this first case, the exporter and the importer agree that the currency of the transaction will be the currency of the exporter's country. For example, if the exporter is located in Germany and the importer is located in Colombia, then the transaction takes place in euros (EUR),* the currency of (most of) the European Union.

In this case, the exchange rate risk is nil for the exporter; all of the risks are borne by the importer, and it has to determine how it will handle its transaction risks. In addition, the possible convertibility problems of the currency are to be resolved by the importer. In this particular case, because the Colombian peso (COP) is fully convertible, this is not an issue.

8.1.2 Importer's Currency

In this case, the exporter and the importer determine that the currency of the transaction will be the currency of the importer's country. For example, if the exporter is located in Jordan and the importer is located in the United States, then the transaction takes place in U.S. dollars (USD), the currency of the United States.

In this case, the exchange rate risk is nil for the importer; all of the risks are borne by the exporter, and it has to determine how it will handle its transaction risks. It is also ultimately responsible for converting the currency so any convertibility problem will have to be resolved by the exporter. In this particular case, there is no issue as the Jordanian dinar (JOD) is fully convertible.

8.1.3 Third Country's Currency

Finally, the exporter and the importer can agree that the currency of the transaction will be a third country's currency. For example, if the exporter is located in Thailand and the importer is located in India, they may decide to use the U.S. dollar as the currency of the transaction.

This alternative presents several advantages for both the exporter and the importer: for example, they each bear the risks of currency fluctuation of their respective country's currency against the currency of the transaction. In this example, the

---

*All currencies are abbreviated with a string of three letters, with the first two letters being the abbreviation of the country's name, and the third being, generally, the first initial of the currency's name

exporter is responsible for the fluctuations of the baht (THB) against the dollar, and the importer is responsible for the fluctuations of the rupee (INR) against the dollar.

In some cases, the exporter and the importer choose an artificial currency (a non-circulating currency) for a transaction, such as the Special Drawing Rights (SDR) of the International Monetary Fund, which are sometimes used for international contracts; such is the case of the Liability Conventions of the ocean shipping industry (see Section 11.5 on page 301).

Special Drawing Rights
An artificial currency whose value is determined by the the value of a basket of currencies.

All three of these alternatives present challenges and call for some form of management of the risks presented by exchange rates.

8.1.4 The Special Status of the Euro

euro
The common currency of 17 of the 27 countries in the European Union.

The euro was first created as an artificial currency; in its early years, when it was known as the European Currency Unit (ECU), its value was determined by the value of a basket consisting of the various currencies of the European Union.

When the Exporter Carries the Exchange Rate Risk

The choice of a currency is a fundamental aspect of the sale: it can substantially affect the profitability of a sale for an exporter. Take for example a sale for U.S. $ 1,000,000 on which an exporter was expecting to generate a 10 percent profit margin; its total costs are therefore U.S. $ 900,000 and its expected profits are $ 100,000.

Suppose the exporter and the importer agree to conduct this transaction in the importer's currency, the European euro. The exporter will then be the one assuming the exchange rate risk. Assuming that the exchange rate at the time of the sale is $ 1.2761/€; the exporter bills the importer for € 783,637.65.

If the value of the euro declines by 2 percent by the time the actual payment is made, about a month later, then the exchange rate at that time will be $1.2506/€. When the customer pays the invoice for € 783,637.65, the U.S. exporter converts that amount of money into U.S. dollars, and collects $ 980,017.24, assuming, for the sake of this example, that there are no banking fees collected. The importer pays exactly what had been agreed, and carries no currency fluctuation risk whatsoever.

The $ 100,000 profit that the exporter was anticipating has been reduced to $ 80,017.24 [$ 980,017.24 − $ 900,000], which is about 20 percent less than what it had anticipated.

The reverse can also happen: the profitability of the exporter can be drastically affected by an increase in the value of the currency that it uses to pay for its merchandise. For example, if the exchange rate had changed the other way, and the euro had increased in value by 2 percent, the new exchange rate would have been $ 1.3016, which means that the U.S. exporter, after collecting his € 783,637.65, would have been able to convert the currency into $ 1,019,982.77, for a profit of $ 119,982.77, an increase of roughly 20 percent.

When the Importer Carries the Exchange Rate Risk

The textbox on the left was an example of a sale for which the exporter assumed the currency fluctuation risk. If the exporter and the importer had agreed to conduct the transaction in the exporter's currency (U.S. dollars) rather than in the importer's currency (euros), then the importer would have assumed the exchange rate risk.

For the sake of simplification, take the same sale: the exporter is selling the goods for $ 1,000,000, its total costs are $ 900,000 and its expected profits are $ 100,000.

Suppose also that the exchange rate at the time of the sale is still $ 1.2761/€, the same as it was in the previous example: the exporter bills the importer for $ 1,000,000, and the importer equates this amount to a payment of € 783,637.65.

If, as in the previous example, the value of the euro declines 2 percent by the time the actual payment is made, about a month later, the exchange rate at that time will be $ 1.2506/€. When the customer pays the invoice for $ 1,000,000, the U.S. exporter collects exactly what he had anticipated, but the importer needs to supply its bank with € 799,616.18, assuming, for the sake of this example, that there are no banking fees collected.

The importer had anticipated to pay € 783,637.65 for these goods, but it actually has to pay € 799,616.18, which is about 2 percent more. Assuming that the importer was anticipating selling the goods at a price of € 950,000, a markup of approximately 21 percent, its profits are reduced from € 166,262.35 to € 150,383.82, a reduction of almost 9.6 percent.

The reverse can also happen: the cost for the importer can be lower if the value of his country's currency increases. For example, if the euro had increased 2 percent, the exchange rate would have been $ 1.3016/€, which means that the importer, in order to pay the $ 1,000,000 that it owes the exporter, would have needed to convert only € 768,285.19, a 2 percent decrease. That would have increased its profits from € 166,262.35 to € 181,714.81, or approximately 9.3 percent.

Since the creation of the euro, there were at least 129 instances in which the exchange rate between the U.S. dollar and the euro changed by more than 2 percent over a month's time, when that determination is calculated on a week-by-week basis.

When it was officially unveiled as the euro in 1999, its value was fixed in terms of each of the eleven (later twelve, with the inclusion of Greece) currencies of the participating EU countries. Only in January 2002 did it become a circulating currency, losing its status as an artificial currency. When five other countries joined the euro, their legacy currency's value was also translated using a fixed currency exchange rate with the euro.

The euro is a unique case as a truly international currency; not only has it become the official domestic currency of seventeen of the European Union countries, but it is also used for all of the intra-European trade in the Eurozone and is therefore a currency used extensively to settle international debts. The stated goal of the

Eurozone
The seventeen countries of Europe in which the euro is the currency.

Value of the Euro and Date of Conversion

Country	Currency	Value	Date
Austria (schilling)	ATS	13.7603	December 31, 1998
Belgium (franc)	BEF	40.3399	December 31, 1998
Finland (markka)	FIM	5.94573	December 31, 1998
France (franc)	FRF	6.55957	December 31, 1998
Germany (mark)	DEM	1.95583	December 31, 1998
Ireland (punt)	IEP	0.787564	December 31, 1998
Italy (lira)	ITL	1,936.27	December 31, 1998
Luxembourg (franc)	LUF	40.3399	December 31, 1998
The Netherlands (guilder)	NLG	2.20371	December 31, 1998
Portugal (escudo)	PTE	200.482	December 31, 1998
Spain (peseta)	ESP	166.386	December 31, 1998
Greece (drachma)	GRD	340.750	June 19, 2000
Slovenia (tolar)	SIT	239.640	July 11, 2006
Cyprus (pound)	CYP	0.585274	July 10, 2007
Malta (lira)	MTL	0.429300	July 10, 2007
Slovakia (koruna)	SKK	30.126	July 8, 2008
Estonia (kroon)	EEK	15.6466	June 13, 2010

Table 8.1: Value of the Euro in Legacy National Currencies European Central Bank.

European Union is to eventually transform the euro from a challenger to the U.S. dollar to the preferred third-country currency.

Table 8.1 lists the rate at which the legacy currencies of the European Union countries were converted to the dollar and Table 8.2 on the next page lists the status of the conversion for the thirteen countries of the European Union that have not yet adopted the euro.[2]

8.2 The System of Currency Exchange Rates

In order to manage exchange rate risks (the risks presented by currency exchange rate fluctuations), it is necessary to have a good understanding of the functioning of the system of exchange rates. Unfortunately, this section can only be a cursory review of the current knowledge in this area; the reader interested in obtaining a greater understanding of the field of international corporate finance should refer to any number of excellent textbooks in this field.[3,4,5,6]

8.2.1 Types of Exchange Rate Quotes

The exchange rate of two currencies is the value of one currency expressed in units of the second. For example, on June 10, the exchange rate for the euro against the U.S. dollar was $1.3257/€ (*i.e.*, one euro was worth U.S. $1.335).[7] As the *Wall Street Journal* defines it, the exchange rate is the midpoint between the bid and offer rates for exchanges of a value greater than $1,000,000 between banks. The *Financial Times* published the midpoint, as well as the bid-offer spread.[8] The actual exchange rate offered to a company seeking to purchase euros would be different: it would

8.2 The System of Currency Exchange Rates

European Countries That Have Not Yet Adopted the Euro

Bulgaria (lev)	BGN	Bulgaria plans to adopt the euro in 2015. The lev is not part of the ERM-II system, so this introduction is likely to be delayed.
Czech Republic (koruna)	CZK	The Czech Republic will probably not adopt the euro until 2019. The koruna does not participate in the ERM-II system.
Denmark (krone)	DKK	Denmark rejected the euro by referendum on September 28, 2000. The krone is part of the ERM-II system (semi-pegged to the euro).
Hungary (forint)	HUF	Hungary may adopt the euro in 2016. The forint does not participate in the ERM-II system.
Latvia (lats)	LVL	Latvia plans to adopt the euro on January 1, 2014. The lats is part of the ERM-II system (semi-pegged to the euro).
Lithuania (litas)	LTL	Lithuania will adopt the euro on January 1, 2015. The litas is part of the ERM-II system (semi-pegged to the euro).
Poland (złoty)	PLN	Poland has plans to introduce the euro on January 1, 2016. The złoty is not part of the ERM-II system, so this introduction is likely to be delayed.
Romania (leu)	RON	Romania has plans to adopt the euro on January 1, 2016. The leu is not part of the ERM-II system, so this introduction is likely to be delayed.
Sweden (krona)	SEK	Sweden rejected the euro by referendum on September 13, 2003. The krona is not part of the ERM-II system.
United Kingdom (pound)	GBP	The United Kingdom is officially no longer in favor of adopting the euro. There are no plans to change over.

Table 8.2: European Countries and Adoption of the Euro European Community.

have to pay more, say $1.35, for every euro purchased. Reciprocally, the exchange rate offered to a company seeking to sell euros would be lower: it would collect less, say $1.30, for every euro sold.

Traders in foreign exchange consider two ways to quote a currency:

- The first way to value a currency is the direct quote, in which the value of the foreign currency is expressed in units of the domestic currency. For example, the direct quote for the euro in U.S. dollar terms would be $1.3257/€, as of June 10, 2013. This is the preferred way of quoting the euro, the British pound, the Australian dollar, and the New Zealand dollar.

direct quote
The value of a foreign currency expressed in units of the domestic currency.

- The second way to value a currency is the indirect quote, in which the value of the domestic currency is expressed in units of foreign currency. For example, the indirect quote for the Japanese yen against the U.S. dollar would be ¥98.74/$ as of June 10, 2013. Most currencies are traditionally expressed as indirect quotes: the Canadian dollar, the Swiss franc, and the Japanese yen, for example.

indirect quote
The value of the domestic currency expressed in units of a foreign currency.

It should be self-evident that there is an inverse relationship between the two ways of quoting a currency exchange rate between two currencies:

$$\text{Direct quote} = \frac{1}{\text{Indirect Quote}}$$

Spot Exchange Rates for Selected Currencies

Country/Region	Currency	Direct Quote (in U.S.$)	Indirect Quote (per U.S.$)
Argentina	Peso [ARS]	0.1885	5.3037
Australia	Dollar [AUD]	0.9465	1.0565
Brazil	Real [BRL]	0.4656	2.1478
Canada	Dollar [CAD]	0.9811	1.0193
Chile	Peso [CLP]	0.001986	503.50
China	Yuan [CNY]	0.1631	6.1329
Czech Republic	Koruna [CZK]	0.05154	19.401
Denmark	Krone [DKK]	0.1778	5.6242
Hong Kong	Dollar [HKD]	0.1288	7.7640
Hungary	Forint [HUF]	0.004431	225.68
India	Rupee [INR]	0.01720	58.155
Indonesia	Rupiah [IDR]	0.0001019	9811
Israel	Shekel [ILP]	0.2749	3.6374
Japan	Yen [JPY]	0.010128	98.74
Jordan	Dinar [JOD]	1.4115	0.7085
Kuwait	Dinar [KWD]	3.5179	0.2843
Lebanon	Pound [LBP]	0.0006616	1511.45
Malaysia	Ringgit [MYR]	0.3196	3.1286
Mexico	Peso [MXN]	0.0774	12.9143
New Zealand	Dollar [NZD]	0.7904	1.2652
Norway	Krone [NOK]	0.1737	5.7577
Pakistan	Rupee [PKR]	0.01013	98.695
Peru	New Sol [PEN]	0.3646	2.743
Philippines	Peso [PHP]	0.0233	42.927
Russia	Rouble [RUB]	0.03098	32.275
Saudi Arabia	Riyal [SAR]	0.2667	3.7499
Singapore	Dollar [SGD]	0.7952	1.2575
South Africa	Rand [ZAR]	0.0982	10.1837
Republic of Korea	Won [KRW]	0.00088864	1128.14
Sweden	Krona [SEK]	0.1521	6.5763
Switzerland	Franc [CHF]	1.0709	0.9338
Taiwan	Dollar [TWD]	0.03353	29.823
Thailand	Bhat [THB]	0.03249	30.783
Turkey	Lira [TRY]	0.5259	1.9014
United Kingdom	Pound [GBP]	1.5571	0.6422
	SDR	1.51423	0.660402
European Union	Euro [EUR]	1.3257	0.7543

Table 8.3: Spot Exchange Rates of Selected Currencies *The Wall Street Journal.*

Spot Exchange Rate

The first type of exchange rate is the spot exchange rate, or the exchange rate for a foreign currency for immediate delivery. This "immediate delivery" is somewhat subject to interpretations that vary from country to country and, within one country, from one currency to another; however, it is (roughly) the price of a foreign currency to be delivered within forty-eight hours.

This is the exchange rate with which most international travelers are familiar: it is the one used by foreign exchange kiosks and banks all over the world (see Table 8.3 on the facing page)[9]. Comprehensive spot currency exchange rates are published daily in *The Wall Street Journal* and many dailies. The *Financial Times* is the most comprehensive of all periodicals in that respect quoting daily the spot currency exchange rates for more than 150 currencies against the U.S. dollar, the British pound, the European euro, and the Japanese yen.[10] These quotes are available for free.

spot exchange rate
The exchange rate of a foreign currency for immediate delivery (within 48 hours).

Forward Exchange Rates

The second type of exchange rate is the forward exchange rate, or the exchange rate for a foreign currency to be delivered any number of days in the future. Financial newspapers such as *The Wall Street Journal* often publish forward exchange rate quotes for 30 days, 90 days, 180 days, or one year in the future. The party entering into a forward currency contract is committing to purchasing one currency with another at a certain price on a certain date. The quoted exchange rate quotes given are the mid-points for transactions of U.S. $1,000,000 or more that take place between banks; the actual exchange rate obtainable by a company involved in international trade would be less favorable.

forward exchange rate
The exchange rate of a foreign currency for delivery in 30, 60 or 180 days from the day of the quote.

In the United States, *The Wall Street Journal* only publishes the forward rates for four currencies: the British pound, the Japanese yen, the Swiss franc, and the Australian dollar. Surprisingly, as of June 2013, it was still not publishing forward rates for the European euro, and had abandoned publishing the forward rates for the Canadian dollar, even though this country is the United States' largest trade partner, by far. However, there is a forward market for almost all currencies, and most forward rate quotes are published in the *Financial Times*, including the forward exchange rates for the Czech krona as well as the Indian rupee and the Thai baht. Another difference between these two periodicals is that *The Wall Street Journal* publishes rates for 30, 90 and 180 days, but does not publish a one-year forward rate, and that the *Financial Times* publishes 30 and 90 days and one-year rates, but not a 180-day rate (see Table 8.4 on the next page).[11,12]

There are two ways in which a forward rate can be quoted. The first is the outright rate, which is the rate at which a commercial customer purchases or sells a foreign currency forward. It is the exchange rate quote shown in Table 8.4. However, in the interbank market, there is another way of quoting forward exchange rates, called the swap rate. Such a forward rate is expressed in points that must be subtracted or added to the spot rate in order to arrive at the forward exchange rate. A point is the unit of the last digit quoted: for example, if the spot exchange rate for the Japanese yen was $0.010546/¥ on a given date, and the forward swap rate for 180 days was expressed at a 22 points premium on the same day, then the 180-day forward exchange rate would be $0.010546 + 0.000022, for a forward exchange rate quote of $0.010568/¥ for a delivery 180 days from that date.

Forward Exchange Rates for Selected Currencies

Country	Currency		Direct Quote (in U.S.$)	Indirect Quote (per U.S.$)
Canada	Dollar [CAD]	Spot	0.9811	1.0193
		Forward 30 days	0.9810	1.0194
		Forward 90 days	0.9803	1.0201
		Forward 180 days	0.9758	1.0248
Japan	Yen [JPY]	Spot	0.010128	98.74
		Forward 30 days	0.010129	98.73
		Forward 90 days	0.010132	98.69
		Forward 180 days	0.010139	98.63
Switzerland	Franc [CHF]	Spot	1.0709	0.9338
		Forward 30 days	1.0712	0.9335
		Forward 90 days	1.0719	0.9329
		Forward 180 days	1.0731	0.9319
United Kingdom	Pound [GBP]	Spot	1.5571	0.6422
		Forward 30 days	1.5568	0.6423
		Forward 90 days	1.5562	0.6426
		Forward 180 days	1.5555	0.6429
Europe	Euro [EUR]	Spot	1.3257	0.7543
		Forward 30 days	1.3197	0.7577
		Forward 90 days	1.3201	0.7575
		Forward 180 days	1.3224	0.7562

Table 8.4: Forward Exchange Rates of Selected Currencies
The Wall Street Journal and *The Financial Times*.

A foreign-currency swap refers to the practice of a simultaneous purchase of one currency on the spot market and the sale of the same currency, in the same amount, on the forward market. A foreign-currency swap can also refer to the practice of purchasing and selling the same currency forward, but with two different maturity dates. That is, a swap transaction is either a spot transaction and a forward transaction, or two forward transactions.[13] The swap market is much larger than either the spot market or the forward market. This technique is used by banks and companies that have funds readily available in one currency, and temporary needs in another currency; they exchange the currencies on the spot market, and know at what exchange rate they will be able to change them back, at some pre-determined time in the future.

Currency Futures

currency future
The value of a fixed quantity of a foreign currency, to be delivered at a fixed date in the future.

Finally, some currencies are also traded in the currency futures' market as commodities: in the United States, futures for six currencies are traded on the Chicago Mercantile Exchange.

A futures' contract is an agreement between two parties: the seller (called the "short") who promises to deliver the currency on a certain date, and the buyer (called the "long") who agrees to buy the currency at a price that is agreed upon ahead of time.

8.2 The System of Currency Exchange Rates

Futures' contracts were first created for commodities other than currencies (such as corn or wheat) and fulfill very different purposes for the parties that use them. Generally, the contract takes place between a party that wants to limit its risk and a party that is speculating. For example, a farmer anticipates that he will be able to harvest a certain amount of corn; in order to limit his uncertainty regarding the price at which he will be able to sell this commodity, he enters into a futures contract, which obligates him to deliver a specified amount of corn on a certain date, at a set price. The other party to the contract is a speculator who is not interested in the corn at all, but is intent on reselling it immediately to another party and speculates that the corn, on that date, will fetch a higher price than what he promised to pay the farmer.

Similarly, a company that uses wheat for a particular purpose may enter into a futures' contract to make sure it can purchase a certain amount of that commodity on that date at a set price. The other party to the futures' contract is a speculator who thinks that he can obtain the wheat on that date for less than what he can sell it to the company.

In the first case, the farmer is intent on minimizing his risk (for example, a bumper crop lowers the value of his corn), and in the second case, the company is looking to minimize its uncertainty regarding the price of one of its raw materials. In both cases, the speculator is taking the risk; if the corn supply is lower than what the market anticipated, he will be able to take delivery from the farmer at a price lower than the spot price and make money. In the second case, he makes money if the supply of wheat is larger than what the market anticipated, and he will make money. If he is incorrect, he loses money, but he nevertheless must make good on his promise to purchase the corn or sell the wheat.

There are two major differences between a forward contract and a futures' contract as they apply to currency exchange rates:

1. The amount of the foreign currency for which a company can purchase futures is fixed; in the United States, they are only available in increments of 100,000 Australian dollars, 62,500 British pounds, 100,000 Canadian dollars, 125,000 euros, 12.5 million Japanese yen, and 500,000 Mexican pesos. This is in contrast with the forward market, in which any given amount can be purchased or sold.

2. The date at which the future has to be settled (purchased or sold) is fixed: in the United States, it is always the third Wednesday of the months of March, June, September or December. This is in contrast with the forward market, in which any given date can be chosen in advance.

Because of this lack of flexibility, companies involved in international trade do not use futures' contracts for currencies as frequently as they use forward contracts.

Currency Options

In addition to the futures market, there is also a currency options' market, which takes place, in the United States, at the Philadelphia Stock Exchange's United Currency Options Market.

An option contract is quite different from a futures' contract. In a futures' contract, both parties are obligated to deliver (or buy) the currency on the date at which the futures' contract is settled. In contrast, in the options' market, the buyer of the

currency option
The right—but not the obligation—to purchase (or sell) a currency at a certain price some time in the future.

call option
A currency option with which a firm buys the right to buy a currency at a given price some time in the future.

put option
A currency option with which a firm buys the right to sell a currency at a given price some time in the future.

strike price
The price at which a currency option is exercized.

option is purchasing the right (the option) to buy or sell a particular currency at a predetermined price. However, the buyer of the option does not have the obligation to exercise that option; it can decline to purchase or sell at that price. If the buyer of the option elects to exercise the option, however, the seller of the option is obligated to comply.

There are two types of options: call options and put options. A call option is the right to buy—but not the obligation to buy—a predetermined amount of foreign currency at a predetermined price (called the strike price) on a predetermined date. A put option is the right to sell—but not the obligation to sell—the same. If the buyer of the option decides not to exercise its option, it only loses the amount that it paid for that option. The seller of the option keeps the amount that it charged for the option, regardless of what the buyer decides to do.

To add to the complexity, there are two styles of options: the U.S.-style option gives a company the right to exercise its option at any time until the expiration date, while a European-style option only allows it to exercise that option on that date. Options are priced by the market, the aggregate of companies wanting to purchase options and speculators and other companies selling options. Several mathematical models can be used in determining the pricing of options, but their complexity is beyond the scope of this textbook.

How Does the Options Market Work?

Call Options: A U.S. firm purchases a call option—the right to buy—British pounds on November 1, at a predetermined exchange rate of £ 1.00/U.S. $1.88; that price is called the strike price. The firm has to pay U.S. $4,000 for that option.

On November 1, it can exercise its call option and tell the seller of the option that it wants delivery of the currency, and the seller of the option has to comply. The buyer of the option only does that if the spot exchange rate of that currency on November 1 is higher that the agreed-upon strike price, say £ 1.00/U.S. $1.90, because buying British pounds on the spot market on that date would be more expensive than exercising the option.

If the spot exchange rate is lower, say £ 1.00/U.S. $1.84, the buyer of the option would not exercise its option and purchase the currency on the spot market instead; it would willingly forego what it had paid for the option or U.S. $4,000.

Put Options: A German firm purchases a put option—the right to sell—European euros on December 1, at a predetermined exchange rate of € 1.00/U.S. $1.26; that price is called the strike price. The firm has to pay € 3,000 for that option.

On December 1, it can exercise its put option and tell the seller of the option that it wants the money for the currency, and the seller of the option has to comply (buy the currency from the German firm). The buyer of the option only does that if the spot exchange rate of that currency on December 1 is lower that the agreed-upon strike price, say € 1.00/U.S. $1.24, because selling the euros on the spot market on that date would be more attractive than exercising the option.

If the spot exchange rate is higher, say € 1.00/U.S. $1.30, the buyer of the option would not exercise its option and sell the currency on the spot market instead; it would willingly forego what it had paid for the option, or € 3,000.

8.2.2 Types of Currencies

In determining the exchange rate risks carried by a specific transaction, it is helpful to determine the type of currency with which the exporter (or importer) is dealing. There are three types of currencies.

Floating Currencies

Floating currencies are foreign currencies whose value changes (or can change) continuously against other currencies. For example, the U.S. dollar continuously changes in value as it is traded between companies having dollars and companies wanting dollars; only the market determines its value. Figure 8.2 illustrates the exchange rate between the U.S. dollar and the European euro since its placement in circulation in January 2001.[14] The countries representing the greatest percentage of world trade all have floating currencies.

floating currency
A currency whose value is determined by market forces. A floating currency's value changes frequently.

The fact that a currency is floating does not always represent unpredictability for a company involved in international trade; most currencies are relatively stable in their values in the short term. However, those currencies that are considered volatile (*i.e.*, currencies that can experience a great deal of variation in their exchange rates from one day to the next) can present a significant risk. Even though the euro has

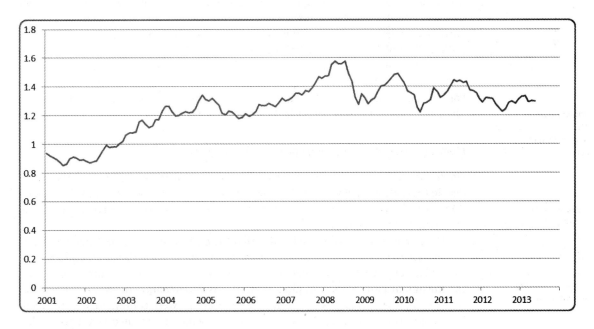

Figure 8.2: The Euro-U.S. Dollar Exchange Rate, January 2001-May 2013
Federal Reserve System.

fluctuated substantially against the U.S. dollar—almost 100 percent, from a low of € 1.00/U.S.$ 0.8270 on October 25, 2000, to a high of € 1.00/U.S.$ 1.601 on April 22, 2008—in the fifteen years since its inception, neither the euro nor the U.S. dollar are considered volatile currencies.

In order to squelch some of this volatility, currencies are sometimes supported by their country's government, which intervenes in the foreign exchange markets in order to sustain the value of a currency. Such policies can be quite onerous for countries: in order to support the value of a currency, the government must purchase it on the open market, and that is only achieved by selling foreign exchange, or the proceeds of export sales. George Soros made a fortune (more than U.S. $1 billion) by betting against the British pound in September 1992, at a time when the British government was intent on shoring up its value.[15]

Most of the developed countries have currencies that are stable, that is, currencies for which it is reasonable to expect a predictable exchange rate. It's only under those conditions that an international firm will accept payment—or agree to pay—in that country's currency.

Pegged Currencies

pegged currency
A currency whose value is determined by a fixed exchange rate with a more widely traded currency, such as the dollar or the euro.

A number of countries have been plagued with very volatile currencies. There are several reasons for this situation, most notably the lack of a sustained level of trade, giving rise to substantially varying demands on the currency from one month to the next. Pegging a currency makes it worth a fixed exchange rate relative to another, stronger currency. The exchange rate is therefore entirely predictable at any time. In most instances, the currency chosen is that of the greatest trading partner, and therefore it is often the United States dollar or the European euro; for example, the Lithuanian litas was pegged to the U.S. dollar until February 2002, and then it became pegged to the European euro. Some currencies are pegged for a period of time, often to weather a turbulent economic period, and then become floating currencies; such is the case of the Argentine peso, which was pegged to the dollar until 2002, and has been a floating currency since.

dollarization
The decision by a country to replace its domestic currency with the dollar.

In some rare cases, the country can elect to completely eliminate its currency and replace it with the currency of another country altogether. This occurred in Panama and Ecuador, which both have adopted the U.S. dollar as their currency, a phenomenon dubbed the "dollarization" of these economies.

Floating Currency Blocs—European Monetary System

Finally, there is the case of countries that trade so much with each other that they decide to create a currency bloc. Such was the case of the European Monetary System (EMS), which eventually gave rise to the creation of the common currency of the European Union, the euro.

currency bloc
A group of currencies whose values fluctuate in a parallel fashion with other currencies and whose values vary within a small percentage among themselves.

The EMS was designed in such a way that the currencies of the member countries would have to stay within a few percentage points of each other's value, a policy that was called the Exchange Rate Mechanism (ERM). In the beginning of this experiment, the maximum percentage variation allowed was 5 percent, and toward the end of the system, it was as low as 1 percent. Such variations were continuously controlled by the governments of the European countries, which intervened routinely in the foreign exchange markets. Such a system allowed the EMS currencies to float as a bloc against other non-EMS currencies, while maintaining a very stable foreign exchange environment within the European Union, a situation that greatly promoted trade among the Union members.

Eventually such a bloc can evolve into a fixed exchange rate between all the internal currencies. In Europe, the fixed exchange rates were established in terms of an artificial currency, the European Currency Unit (ECU), which was created in January 1999, and whose value was determined by the value of a basket of the internal currencies. The European Currency Unit was named the euro soon thereafter. Finally, on January 1, 2002, all internal currencies were eliminated and the European euro became the only circulating currency for twelve of the European countries (see Table 8.1 on page 210). When the European Union was expanded on June 1, 2004, the original ERM was resurrected as ERM-II and many of the new countries' currencies will eventually be replaced by the euro (see Table 8.2 on page 211) after they meet certain requirements for admission, and have been part of the ERM-II system for at least two years.

There are other currency blocs and common currencies in the planning stages as of June 2013. The Gulf Cooperation Council, encompassing Bahrain, Kuwait, Oman, Qatar, Saudi Arabia, and the United Arab Emirates, has proposed the creation of a common currency, tentatively called the *Khaleeji*, but Oman withdrew from the project in 2006 and the U.A.E. in 2009, threatening the most advanced of these projects.[16] In addition, since the GCC countries' currencies are all pegged to the U.S. dollar (with the exception of Kuwait), this new currency was more symbolic than substantial.

artificial currency
A currency that does not circulate. After the euro was changed into a circulating currency in 2002, the only artificial currency in the world is the Special Drawing Rights of the International Monetary Fund.

The 2009 Chinese Proposal

Since the 1980s, including during the worldwide recession years of 2008-2009, China had run a very large yearly trade surplus with the United States, reaching two consecutive record-high years with U.S. $ 262 billion in 2007 and U.S.$ 290 billion in 2008. This recurring trade deficit had allowed the Chinese government to accumulate as much as U.S.$ 2.5 trillion in foreign currency reserves, 82 percent of which it had invested in U.S. Treasury bonds.[17] Part of the reason behind such large trade deficits was that the Chinese government had refused to let the value of the yuan float during the 1990s: if it had, the large deficit would have shrunk as the value of the yuan increased, erasing some of the competitive position of the country's manufacturers.

The Chinese were earning a very modest income on these bonds, as the interest rates in the United States were relatively low, but the Chinese government was apparently satisfied with the arrangement, because the investment was safe. However, the 2007-2009 fall of the value of the dollar against all major world currencies presented the Chinese with a major challenge; as the value of the dollar went down, so did the value of their investments in U.S. dollars;[18] if the value of the dollar decreased by 5 percent, so did the value of their investments. For the Chinese, a decrease of 5 percent equated with a capital loss equivalent to U.S.$ 102 billion, or one third of the trade surplus it had earned in 2008, and about half of what it earned in 2009.

In order to protect this investment, the Chinese were faced with a conundrum. If they diversified into other currencies, including the euro or the British pound, they would have had to sell dollars and purchase those other currencies.

However, doing so would have further depressed the value of the dollar, as any large influx of dollars on the world markets would have affected its value. In March 2009, at the G20 meeting in London, the governor of the Chinese Central Bank, Zhou Xiachuan, proposed the creation of a "super-sovereign reserve currency,"[19] not unlike the Special Drawing Rights [SDR] of the International Monetary Fund, which would be independent of a particular country's currency. This new currency would wean the world economies from their dependence on the dollar and its exchange rate fluctuations, many of which are due to domestic political choices (the huge government deficits of 2008-2010, for example). It would also make the international currency system more stable and more predictable, leading a number of U.S. economists to cautiously endorse the proposal. There was also however hostility in the United States about this particular idea, with much of the opposition stemming from the realization that the dollar would lose its dominant role in international governmental reserves.[20] Nevertheless, the proposal had some definite advantages, and the creation of a worldwide new currency was no more unrealistic than the creation of a pan-European currency; the euro was first greeted with the same type of concerns.

Sensing that the hostility to this idea was too much to overcome, the Chinese quietly abandoned this strategy. In order to reduce their dependence on the U.S. dollar and investments in U.S. Treasury bonds, the government started to let the value of the yuan increase further against the U.S. dollar. From a historical (pegged) exchange rate of ¥ 8.28/$ that had been in place until July 2005, to a gradual decrease to ¥ 6.8/$ that the currency reached in June 2008 and maintained until June 2010, the currency appreciated further to ¥ 6.1/$ by June 2013.[21]

8.3 Theories of Exchange Rate Determinations

In order for a company to determine what its risks are in an international currency transaction, it is imperative to understand how exchange rates are determined. Once a company's management understands the theories behind the exchange rate fluctuations, it can then forecast them, and therefore determine what would be its best strategy for a specific transaction.

There are a total of five different, complementary theories that help explain the variations between two countries' exchange rates.

8.3.1 Purchasing Power Parity

purchasing power parity An economic theory that holds that exchange rates should reflect the price differences paid by consumers.

In its absolute form, the Purchasing Power Parity theory holds that exchange rates should reflect the price differences of each and every product between countries. The idea is that exchange rates should fluctuate in such a way as to equalize the price differences of similar products between countries, so that a set amount of currency would purchase the same goods in any country of the world.

However, this is essentially impossible to achieve (and measure), given the disparity of goods and services that are purchased worldwide. Even for a perfectly

8.3 Theories of Exchange Rate Determinations

uniform good, there are wide discrepancies in its price from one country to the next.

Price of the Big Mac in Selected Countries/Regions

Country/Region	Price in the Local Currency	Price in U.S.$	Percentage of U.S. price
United States	USD 4.33	4.33	100%
Argentina	ARS 19	4.16	96%
Australia	AUD 4.56	4.68	108%
Brazil	BRL 10.08	4.94	114%
Britain	GBP 2.69	4.16	96%
Canada	CAD 3.89	3.82	88%
Chile	CLP 2050	4.16	96%
China	CNY 15.65	2.45	57%
Czech Republic	CZK 70.33	3.34	77%
Denmark	DKK 28.5	4.65	107%
Egypt	EGP 16	2.64	61%
Euro area	EUR 3.58	4.34	100%
Hong Kong	HKD 16.50	2.13	49%
Hungary Forint	HUF 830	3.48	80%
India	INR 89	1.58	36%
Indonesia	IDR 24200	2.55	59%
Israel	ILS 11.9	2.92	67%
Japan	JPY 320	4.09	94%
Lithuania	LTL 7.8	2.74	63%
Malaysia	MYR 7.4	2.33	54%
Mexico	MXN 37	2.70	62%
Norway	NOK 43	7.06	163%
Pakistan	PKR 285	3.01	70%
Philippines	PHP 118	2.80	65%
Poland	PLN 9.1	2.63	61%
Russia	RUB 75	2.29	53%
Singapore	SGD 4.40	3.50	81%
South Africa	ZAR 19.95	2.36	55%
Republic of Korea	KRW 3700	3.21	74%
Sri Lanka	LKR 290	2.21	51%
Sweden	SEK 48.4	6.94	160%
Switzerland	CHF 6.5	6.56	152%
Taiwan	TWD 75	2.48	57%
Thailand	THB 82	2.59	60%
Turkey	TRY 8.25	4.52	104%
Ukraine	UAH 15	1.86	43%
Venezuela	VEF 34	7.92	183%

Table 8.5: The Big Mac Index in Selected Countries/Regions in June 2013 *The Economist.*

This inconsistency is illustrated very well with the Big Mac Index, published by *The Economist* (see Table 8.5 on the previous page),[22] which observes that the price of one of McDonald's Big Mac sandwiches can vary from 36 percent (in India) to 183 percent (in Venezuela) of the U.S. price. In effect, the price of a Big Mac is 5.1 times as much in Venezuela as it is in India.

Practically speaking, Purchasing Power Parity is determined by using a basket of goods and calculating how much domestic currency an average person would have to spend to purchase it. The World Bank uses this version of the Purchasing Power Parity to determine the GDP per capita (PPP adjusted) of all the nations of the world.

In its relative form, as used in international finance as a determinant of changes in exchange rates, Purchasing Power Parity is calculated using inflation rates, which is only a slightly different methodology, because in each country, inflation rates are determined by taking the level of prices of a basket of goods. Therefore, the only differences between the Purchasing Power Parity determined by the World Bank and Purchasing Power Parity determined through inflation rates is that the basket of goods of the World Bank attempts to be identical in each country, whereas the inflation rate is calculated using different baskets of goods in each country, and that the basket of goods used for inflation determination tends to include a wider number of items.

The Purchasing Power Parity Theory holds that exchange rates should reflect the differences in inflation rates between countries. In other words, if the inflation rate is higher in one country, then its currency should decrease in value relative to other currencies. This can be illustrated mathematically as:[23]

$$\frac{\text{Spot value of currency F at time } t \text{ in Country D}}{\text{Spot value of currency F at time } 0 \text{ in Country D}} = \frac{(1 + \text{inflation rate in Country D})^t}{(1 + \text{inflation rate in Country F})^t}$$

and symbolically as:

$$\frac{S(e_t)}{S(e_0)} = \frac{(1 + \inf_D)^t}{(1 + \inf_F)^t}$$

8.3.2 Fisher Effect

The Fisher Effect is the observation that a country's nominal interest rate (what a borrower actually has to pay for a loan) is comprised of both the inflation rate in that country and the real interest rate that borrowers are paying.

The real interest rate is the rate that borrowers have to pay to borrow money anywhere in the world and it is expected to be uniform throughout the world. This expectation is only partially realistic; while large corporations have access to many financial markets, most businesses and individuals are restricted to one. However, the theory asserts that people expect to pay the same real interest rate in every country, at all points in time.

In consequence, individuals in countries with high inflation rates should expect to have to pay high nominal interest rates, and individuals in countries with low inflation rates should expect low nominal interest rates.

The mathematical representation of this phenomenon is:

$$(1 + \text{real interest rate}) \times (1 + \text{inflation rate}) = 1 + \text{nominal interest rate}$$

Fisher effect
An economic theory that holds that interest rates that businesses pay should be uniform throughout the world.

and symbolically as:

$$(1 + \text{rir}) \times (1 + \text{inf}) = 1 + \text{nir} \iff \text{nir} = \text{rir} + \text{inf} + (\text{nir} + \text{inf}) \approx \text{rir} + \text{inf}$$

8.3.3 International Fisher Effect

The International Fisher Effect is the observation that spot exchange rates reflect the differences between nominal interest rates in different countries. It posits that, if nominal interest rates are higher in country F than in country D, then country F's currency should be expected to decrease in value relative to country D's currency.

Conceptually, the expected spot rate reflects the fact that an investor would get the same yield on an investment, whether it is made in country D or country F.

Mathematically, this can be described as:

$$\frac{\text{Spot value of currency F at time } (t+1) \text{ in Country D}}{\text{Spot value of currency F at time } (t) \text{ in Country D}} =$$

$$\frac{1 + \text{nominal interest rate in Country D}}{1 + \text{nominal interest rate in Country F}} =$$

and symbolically as:

$$\frac{S_{e_{t+1}}}{S_{e_t}} = \frac{1 + \text{nir}_D}{1 + \text{nir}_F}$$

international Fisher effect
An economic theory that holds that spot exchange rates between two currencies should reflect the differences in nominal interest rates between these two countries.

8.3.4 Interest Rate Parity

The Interest Rate Parity Theory links the forward exchange rate of a foreign currency to its spot rate, using the differences in nominal interest rates between the foreign country and the domestic country. The principle is that the forward exchange rate should be expressed as a discount if the foreign country is experiencing higher nominal interest rates than the domestic country, and should reflect a premium if the foreign nominal interest rates are lower.

In other words, at time t, the forward exchange rate $F_{t+1}(e_t)$ for delivering currency F n days from t (that is, at time $t + 1$) reflects the difference between the nominal interest rate in country D and the nominal interest rate in country F, adjusted for the length of n days. This relationship always holds in the real world unless prevented by government action.

This relationship translates mathematically as:

$$\frac{F_n(e_t) - S(e_t)}{S(e_t)} \times \frac{360}{n} = \text{nir}_D - \text{nir}_F$$

interest rate parity
An economic theory that holds that the forward exchange rate between two currencies should reflect the differences in nominal interest rates between these two countries.

8.3.5 Forward Rate as Unbiased Predictor of Spot Rate

This theory holds that forward exchange rates for currencies are good predictors of the future spot exchange rates of that currency. In other words, if the forward rate for a currency shows a discount of 2 percent for a maturity date of n days, then the spot rate in n days should be 2 percent lower than it is today.

Conceptually, the relationship is that the forward exchange rate of currency F at time t in Country D for delivery at time $t + 1$ is the expected (average) spot value of currency F at time $t + 1$ in country D.

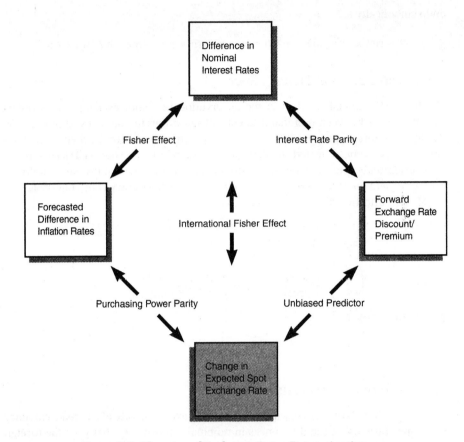

Figure 8.3: Theories of Exchange Rates Determination

This can be expressed mathematically as:

$$F_{t+1}(e_t = S(e_{t+1})$$

8.3.6 Entire Predictive Model

The five relationships can be combined to understand how each can be used to forecast expected spot exchange rates, as shown in Figure 8.3.[24]

8.4 Exchange Rate Forecasting

It should now be evident that forecasting exchange rates is difficult. In addition to the five theories mentioned in the preceding section, there are always political changes, unpredictable economic variations, and the occasional natural catastrophe that influence the exchange rate of a given currency. Figure 8.4 on the next page illustrates the exchange rate of the Japanese yen with the U.S. dollar over the past forty-two years;[25] it has been altogether very unpredictable, although reasonably stable in the short run. In addition to the U.S. Federal Reserve System,[26] historical exchange rates can easily be obtained, for any currency, from the Bank of Canada[27] and from the Pacific Exchange Rate Service at the University of British Columbia.[28]

Figure 8.4: The Yen-U.S. Dollar Exchange Rate, January 1971-May 2013
Federal Reserve System.

There are three general methods that can be utilized for forecasting exchange rates, and, again, the reader should refer to textbooks dealing with forecasting specifically in order to understand these techniques better. Only a cursory review is made here.

8.4.1 Technical Forecasting

The so-called technical forecasting methods are essentially all based upon time-series analysis, from simple moving averages (something that can be done easily on a spreadsheet) to sophisticated ARIMA (Auto-Regressive Integrated Moving Average) methods and neural-network models that require dedicated software packages and pretty powerful computers. Several possible sources on technical forecasting exist.[29,30,31,32]

Technical forecasting is based on the premise that future movements in the value of a currency are mathematically linked to its past movements, and use techniques that extract patterns in the historical data. These patterns are then duplicated with very recent data to forecast the future exchange rates of the currency.

Such technical forecasts are valuable in determining the possible variations of a currency's exchange rate in the short run. In the long run, they tend to accumulate errors fairly quickly, as they ignore the economic fundamentals of exchange rate determination.

8.4.2 Fundamental Forecasting

The idea behind fundamental forecasting is to integrate all of the theories presented in Section 8.3 into a mathematical, causal model that would use the exchange rate of a specific currency as the dependent variable and the expected inflation rates, nominal interest rates, forward interest rates, and real interest rates as the independent variables.

Fundamental forecasting is the use of a large multiple linear regression model and of ANOVA—Analysis of Variance—techniques, and it can be done with any good spreadsheet program, such as Microsoft® *Excel*. However, there are several pitfalls with causal models, and a good survey of such models should be undertaken before they are used. A large number of sources can be consulted to learn about these linear models.[33,34]

The problem with causal models in general, and especially in the case of foreign exchange forecasting, is the difficulty in accounting for all of the possible influences on a given currency's exchange rate—it is impossible to isolate its movements to a single pair of currencies—and, at the same time, limit the inevitable collinearity of the independent variables. Novices tend to increase the number of independent variables, as it increases the coefficient of determination (R^2), but often overlook the problem of collinearity that this strategy brings along.

8.4.3 Market-Based Forecasting

Market-based forecasting is based on the premise that "the market knows best" and that, therefore, the forward exchange rate of a given currency is the best unbiased predictor of the future spot rate of a particular currency.

Because it is very likely that speculators have conducted their own analytical and mathematical forecasts for a given currency, it is quite logical to conclude that the forward exchange rate includes the entire wisdom of the market, and that, therefore, it is the best predictor of the future value of a currency. This observation is called the Efficient Market Hypothesis.

However, this assumption may be incorrect, as forward rates often reflect the futures' contract rates, which are set by speculators who may include people motivated by entirely different motives than the actual purchase and delivery of a currency. Such was the case with George Soros in 1992 when he decided to bet against the British pound, driving the government of the United Kingdom to spend a large amount of foreign currency to sustain its value, and eventually forcing the pound out of the Exchange Rate Mechanism (ERM) of the European Union.[35]

Moreover, the forward rates do not account for possible government interventions, which can wreak havoc on the actual spot rates of currencies. For example, in the spring of 2002, the Japanese government consistently kept the value of the yen down, in order to boost the Japanese economy through undervalued exports. The forward rates also do not reflect the possibility of an unexpected change or a currency crisis; such was the case when the Argentinean peso, which was pegged to the U.S. dollar at the rate of $1.00 per peso, suddenly was allowed to float on January 6, 2002, and reached $0.25 on March 25, 2002. It stabilized relatively quickly at around U.S. $ 0.35 in 2002, but slowly declined thereafter; it stood at U.S. $0.19 in June 2013,[36] at the official rate, but the unauthorized "black market" rate was considerably lower. The Chinese currency, the yuan (also known as the renminbi [RMB]), was also artificially kept at a pegged rate against the U.S. dollar at the rate of RMB 8.28/$ from 1994 until July 2005, when it was changed to "better reflect market conditions" and appreciated to ¥8.11/$ almost immediately. The yuan has progressively appreciated since, and stood at ¥6.13/$ in June 2013.[37] Nevertheless, there is a consensus that the yuan is still considered undervalued, helping Chinese exports while making imports to China more expensive.

8.5 Managing Transaction Exposure

Whenever a company is engaged in an international transaction and agrees to use a foreign currency to conduct this transaction, it is then exposed to a certain amount of risk, due to possible fluctuations in currency exchange rates. Such risk is called transaction exposure and can be handled in one of two ways: it can be retained by the firm, or it can be hedged, or reduced, by using one of three possible techniques, which will be presented in this section.

transaction exposure The impact of a change in a currency exchange rate for a company involved in international trade and its effect on the company's financial well-being.

Under these general guidelines, firms can pursue one of two strategies:

1. Determine what its decision should be on an invoice-by-invoice basis, depending on the currency at stake, the amount of the invoice, and its forecast of the currency's exchange rate.

2. Set a policy that the firm follows for all of its foreign currency receivables and payables.

In either case, the choice of the strategy should be dependent on the forecast that the company makes of the exchange rate at stake; it also depends on the size of the firm—and of its ability to weather a currency risk—on the size of the invoice relative to the total sales of the firm—what is called the exposure—and on the company's degree of sophistication in terms of international finance. In general terms, it is almost always better for a firm to hedge its foreign exchange risks, with only a few exceptions; however, certain firms choose to retain their exchange rate risks instead.

risk retention A risk management strategy in which a company decides to retain a risk and not insure or hedge against it.

8.5.1 Risk Retention

The strategy of risk retention is fairly simple: the company decides that it is best to retain the risk of currency fluctuation. There are three different types of companies that will decide to systematically retain their currency risks:

- Very large traders—importers and exporters, often in the same currency—that simultaneously carry risks on the "up" side, where they can earn additional income because of a favorable exchange rate change, and on the "down" side, where they can lose money for exactly the same reason. Overall, for these firms, transaction exchange rate risks are a zero-sum game, and it is not necessary to hedge, as the positions they hold offset each other. Nevertheless, those firms tend to be very sophisticated in international finance, and they would actually hedge their positions, and even speculate in the currency markets.

- Exporters or importers that have little exposure (*i.e.*, which are shipping or buying goods of relatively small value, in fairly small shipments, and therefore for which a currency loss would not have substantial financial consequences).

Often, for these firms, the costs of hedging, or of determining whether they should hedge, exceed the benefits that they would accrue.

- Firms that do not evaluate the international currency transaction risks clearly. They are not following a specific policy; they have no policy, or have a management that is not well versed in the intricacies of international trade. Those firms are also often the ones that generally cannot afford not to hedge, as they tend to be smaller, and therefore more susceptible to a partial loss due to exchange rate fluctuations.

8.5.2 Forward-Market Hedges

forward-market hedge
A technique to reduce exchange rate fluctuation risk that uses forward market exchange rates.

The first of the strategies that a company can follow to protect itself from currency fluctuations is a forward-market hedge. This strategy involves selling forward a future receivable in a foreign currency, or purchasing forward the currency necessary to cover a foreign payable. This strategy varies in its implementation for each situation.

Two examples will make this strategy much clearer:

An Exporter Selling in the Importer's Currency

A U.S.-based company is selling a product to an Italian firm on March 2, 2013; the invoice is payable in euros on June 2, 2013 (ninety-day credit). The amount that the firm wants to collect is U.S.$ 200,000.

The company could use the spot exchange rate on March 2, 2013, which was U.S.$ 1.2988/€, and bill the customer for € 155,279.50.[38] However, as of March 1, 2013, the ninety-day forward exchange rate for the euro is U.S.$ 1.2830/€, indicating that the market is expecting a decrease in the value of the euro against the U.S. dollar. The firm therefore decides to invoice its customer for $200,000/1.2830 = € 155,884.65.

In this case, a forward-market hedge consists of the U.S. firm entering a forward contract with a bank, in which it would promise to sell € 155,884.65 to the bank on June 2, 2013, at the predetermined (forward) exchange rate of U.S.$ 1.2830/€.

On June 2, 2013, the U.S. company presents € 155,884.65 to the bank and exchanges these funds for the U.S.$ 200,000 it wanted to collect. The U.S. firm is unconcerned about the spot exchange rate of the euro on June 2, 2013.

An Importer Buying in the Exporter's Currency

A German firm purchases a product from a British firm for £ 250,000.00. The machine is delivered on April 4, 2013, and payment is expected (in pounds) on July 6, 2013.

On April 4, 2013, this amount was equivalent to € 294,475.00 because the spot exchange rate between the UK pound and the euro was € 1.1779/£.[39]

However, on April 4, 2013, the pound is expected to rise in value and the 90-day forward exchange rate with the euro is € 1.1920/£. The German firm wants to make sure it knows how much it will spend on the machine, and can use a forward-market hedge by entering into a contract with a bank from which it promises to purchase £ 250,000 on July 4, 2013, at a predetermined (forward) exchange rate of € 1.1920/£. On July 4, 2013, the German firm hands € 298,000.00 to the bank and obtains in exchange the £ 250,000 that it needs to pay its British supplier.

8.5 Managing Transaction Exposure

The German firm could determine on April 4, 2013 exactly how much it had to pay for the machine and is unconcerned about the spot exchange rate of the British pound on July 4, 2013.

In either of these cases, the firm has eliminated its exchange rate risk by using a forward-market hedge; it knew, with total certainty, at the time it entered the forward contract with the bank how much it would collect (U.S. firm) or how much it would have to pay (German firm). For both of those firms, the forward-market hedge removed the exchange rate risk.

8.5.3 Money-Market Hedges

money-market hedge
A technique to reduce exchange rate fluctuation risk that uses the banking institutions of the foreign currency's country.

A money-market hedge consists of using the banking system of the country of the currency in which the receivable or the payable is going to be paid. The firm that is hedging its exposure either borrows from a bank in the foreign country or deposits money in a bank in the foreign country.

This can again be explained best with two illustrations:

An Exporter Selling in the Importer's Currency

A firm located in Switzerland sells a piece of machinery to a firm located in Japan, for the equivalent of CHF 150,000.00; in order to be competitive with Japanese competitors, though, it decided to bill the customer in Japanese yen.

The transaction takes place on January 16, 2013, with a payment date of March 16, 2013. The transaction amount is expressed in Japanese yen, for a total of JPY 14,277,240.00 because the exchange rate on January 16, 2013 is JPY 95.1816/CHF.[40]

To protect itself from currency fluctuations, the Swiss firm can use a money-market hedge, by borrowing from a Japanese bank the present value (as of January 16, 2013) of JPY 14,277,240.00 on March 15, 2013. Supposing that the commercial lending rate in Japan on January 16, 2013, was 3 percent *per annum*, or about 0.5 percent for two months. The amount the Swiss firm would borrow would be then be JPY $(1 - 0.005) \times 14,277,240.00 = 14,205,853.80$; it will pay the bank back on March 15, 2013, using the payment of JPY 14,277,240.00 made by its customer.

On January 16, 2013, the Swiss firm would exchange the proceeds from the loan (JPY 14,205,853.80) for CHF 149,250.00 (the exchange rate on January 16, 2013 is JPY 95.1816/CHF), and get an amount roughly equal to the payment of CHF 150,000.00 it had expected, although decreased by the cost of getting the money two months earlier. The Swiss firm is unconcerned about the spot exchange rate of the yen on March 15, 2013.

An Importer Buying in the Exporter's Currency

On May 2, 2013, a firm located in Denmark purchases raw materials from a firm located in Australia, which asks to be paid in Australian dollars. The amount of the invoice is AUD 20,000,000, payable six months later, on November 1, 2013.

The Danish firm can eliminate its exposure to exchange rate fluctuations between the Danish krone and the Australian dollar by using a money-market hedge. It can invest a sum in an Australian bank that will mature to AUD 20,000,000 on November 1, 2013. Assuming an annual interest rate of 4 percent paid on deposits in Australia, the Danish firm would have to invest AUD $20,000,000/(1 + 0.02) = 19,607,845$ to have enough to cover its obligation on November 1, 2013.

On May 2, 2013, the Danish firm converts DKK 114,531,804.91 into Australian dollars (the exchange rate is AUD 0.1712/DKK on May 2, 2013),[41] and deposits that amount into a bank account in Australia. The Danish firm is unconcerned about the spot exchange rate of the Australian dollar on November 1, 2013.

The money-market hedging strategy is effective because it allows the firm to use the exchange rate as of the date of the transaction rather than speculate on the value of the exchange rate at the date of payment. In that respect, it is a strategy that eliminates the risks of currency fluctuations; the only cost to the Swiss firm is the interest it has to pay to the Japanese bank, in addition to the fees that will be charged for the foreign exchange transactions. However, the amount of interest it pays should be the same as what it would have paid by borrowing the same amount in Switzerland, at least if the Interest Rate Parity Theory holds. Similarly, the only cost to the Danish firm—in addition to the fees—is the opportunity cost of the investment, from which the interest earned in Australia must be deducted. Both of these should offset each other approximately as well.

8.5.4 Options-Market Hedges

options-market hedge
A technique to reduce exchange rate fluctuation risk that uses options for a particular currency.

It is also possible to hedge a foreign currency fluctuation risk with options. An options-market hedge is a more sophisticated alternative yet, because it amounts to remaining unhedged—retaining the risk—if the exchange rate turns favorable and to purchasing an option, which acts as an insurance policy, to protect against unfavorable exchange-rate fluctuations. If the exchange rate turns unfavorable, the firm can exercise its option—its insurance policy—and is covered. If the exchange rate turns favorable, the firm can still benefit from this situation by not exercising its option, even though it will lose the cost of the option.

This strategy involves purchasing put or call options, or the option to sell or purchase certain currencies at a certain exchange rate on (European-style options) or before (U.S.-style options) a certain date. This agreed-upon exchange rate is called the strike price. Here again, two examples will illustrate the concepts better than an abstract description:

An Exporter Selling in the Importer's Currency

A company located in the United States sells a large piece of equipment to a firm located in the United Kingdom, and agrees to be paid in pounds. The invoice, for £ 1,000,000, is issued on December 10, 2012, but is not payable until March 10, 2013.

The exporting firm can minimize its currency fluctuation risk by using an option hedge; on December 10, 2012, it purchases a put option—the right to sell £ 1,000,000 on March 10, 2013—at an agreed-upon exchange rate of U.S.$ 1.3615/£. If the spot exchange rate on March 10, 2013, is lower than U.S.$ 1.4615/£, then the American firm will exercise its option and sell the currency at that price. If the spot rate is higher than U.S.$ 1.3615/£, the firm will let its option lapse and will sell the currency it received at the spot market rate.

Because the exchange rate on March 10, 2013 is U.S.$ 1.4908/£,[42] the firm sells its pounds without using its option.

The firm still incurs the cost of the option, which is approximately 1.25 percent of the contract amount, or about U.S.$ 18,268.75; however, this cost is offset by the fact that it sells its British pounds for U.S. $29,300 more than it had anticipated. The net profits on this financial transaction are U.S. $11,031.25.

An Importer Buying in the Exporter's Currency

A company located in Spain purchases a plant located in Canada. The contract is signed on June 28, 2012, and the firm has agreed to make three installment payments of Can$ 1,000,000 each on December 28, 2012, March 28, 2013, and June 28, 2013 (six months, nine months and twelve months after purchase).

In order to minimize its currency risks, the Spanish firm can use an options hedge by purchasing the right to buy Can$ 1,000,000—call options—at exchange rates of Can$ 1.3348/€ for December 28, 2012, Can$ 1.2871/€ for March 28, 2013, and Can$ 1.2743/€ for June 28, 2013.

Because the spot exchange rate was Can$ 1.3177/€ on December 28, 2012,[43] the Spanish firm did not exercise its option, purchased the Canadian dollars on the spot market, and sent them to the Canadian supplier.

On March 28, 2013, the spot market was Can$ 1.3020/€,[44] and therefore the Spanish firm exercised its option and purchased the Canadian dollars at Can$ 1.2871/€ (the strike price of its option), because it was a more favorable exchange rate than the spot market.

As for its future June 28, 2013 payment, the firm still has the possibility of saving money if the spot rate is more favorable than its option rate; if not, it will exercise its option.

The cost of these successive options for the Spanish firm was approximately 0.75 percent, 1.25 percent, and 1.5 percent of the contract amounts for November, February, and August, respectively, for a total of approximately € 27,000.00. However, the costs were reduced by the fact that the firm saved € 9,722.17 in December by not having to spend as many euros as it had anticipated.

The main problem with option hedging is that options are very expensive, which is somewhat understandable as they are only covering the "down" side. The second issue is that options are only commonly traded for a limited number of currencies, and that the amounts are not as flexible as in forward markets. Nevertheless, some banks will write options that are tailored to their customers' needs. For the sophisticated firm involved in international trade, this strategy has great potential.

For further information on this hedging strategy, the other hedging strategies described in this section, as well as additional strategies, the reader is referred to a number of textbooks in international finance[45] or to textbooks on options and futures.[46]

8.6 International Banking Institutions

There are several institutions that are involved in international banking; however, only a few of these have a function that is linked to international payments. A brief synopsis of each of these institutions is given in this section. The reader interested in gaining more information on these institutions should consult a textbook in International Economics or International Banking.[47,48]

8.6.1 Central National Banks

central bank
The entity that controls the money supply of a nation and functions as a clearinghouse for inter-bank exchanges.

In every country in the world, there is a Central Bank, or some institution that acts as a Central Bank: Great Britain has its Bank of England, the European Union has its European Central Bank (ECB), and the United States has the Federal Reserve System that, although not technically a Central Bank, fulfills the role of one. Each of the countries of the European Union has also retained its Central Bank, because only the control of the monetary supply is in the hands of the ECB; France has its Banque de France and Germany has its cherished BundesBank.

Central Banks provide several services to the domestic banks of their respective countries. Their first role is the creation and control of the monetary supply, through market operations and the control of currency. This role can be one of maintenance or a more active role, such as executing monetary policy operations. Their second role is their function as a check clearinghouse where accounts regarding checks written on different domestic banks' accounts are settled. In some countries, they also manage the exchange rate of the national currency and the national foreign exchange reserves.

8.6.2 International Monetary Fund

International Monetary Fund
The international organization created in 1945 to oversee exchange rates and develop an international system of payments.

The International Monetary Fund (IMF) was created in 1944 at the Bretton-Woods Conference; it was designed to oversee the fixed exchange rate system that the Conference had started. When exchange rates started to float in 1971—the end of the gold standard—the IMF changed its focus to helping countries manage their balance of payments. In particular, the IMF lends money to countries that experience difficulties with their balance of payments. These loans are usually accompanied by a number of conditions to which the country has to agree; inflation control and money supply growth are often on the list. The funds necessary for those loans are collected from the countries that become members of the IMF; they are assessed a quota that is determined by the country's economic size.

The IMF is also the curator of an artificial currency called the Special Drawing Rights (SDR), which was designed to supplement the U.S. dollar in its role as the international currency. The SDR's value is determined by a basket of four currencies: the U.S. dollar for 41.9 percent, the European euro for 37.4 percent, the British pound for 11.3 percent, and Japanese yen for 9.4 percent. Although the SDR is not often used by businesses, it is often used by governments to settle their debts with each other. It is also used in the settlement of disputes under the liability conventions of ocean cargo shipping (see Section 11.5 on page 301).

8.6.3 Bank for International Settlements

Bank for International Settlements
The bank that advises central banks and provides a clearinghouse for exchanges between central banks.

The Bank for International Settlements was created after World War I to manage Germany's war reparation payments. Since then it has evolved into a major international institution, providing support to Central Banks—which constitute its membership—and particularly recently providing guidance to the new Central Banks of the former Eastern Bloc Countries. Although membership was originally limited to European Central Banks, the United States' Federal Reserve System joined in 1994.

8.6.4 World Bank

The International Bank for Reconstruction and Development—known as the World Bank—was created in 1945 after the Bretton-Woods Conference. Its purpose was to help countries rebuild their infrastructure after World War II, and it has slowly evolved to become the bank in charge of financing large infrastructure projects. The government that is borrowing the funds must be a member of the IMF and the loan is usually repaid as a long-term loan.

World Bank The bank that was created at Bretton-Woods in 1944 and finances large-scale infrastructure projects in the world.

8.6.5 Ex-Im Bank

The Export-Import Bank (Ex-Im Bank) is a federal agency of the United States' government. Its purpose is to provide assistance to U.S. exporters in the form of loans (only available to large exporters), loan guarantees (available to banks who finance exporters), or in the form of political risk insurance policies available through the Foreign Credit Insurance Association (FCIA). See Chapter 10 for further details.

Ex-Im Bank An agency of the U.S. federal government that provides financial assistance to U.S. exporters.

8.6.6 Society for Worldwide Interbank Financial Telecommunication (SWIFT)

The Society for Worldwide Interbank Financial Telecommunication (SWIFT) is a corporation supporting an Electronic Data Interchange network that was created by banks to obtain a secure and reliable means of transferring financial information internationally. In particular, it allows the communication of Letters of Credit and miscellaneous international fund transfers. Because of the high level of security that the network enjoys, documents transferred through the network have the same value as original paper documents.

Society for Worldwide Interbank Financial Telecommunication An interbank electronic network for the secure transfer of funds and documents.

8.7 Currency of Payment as a Marketing Tool

In an international transaction, the choice of the currency exposes the exporter (or the importer) to the risk of currency exchange rate fluctuation. Rather than consider this risk to be a drawback in an international sale, a good exporter should consider it an opportunity.

There are four main tactics that the exporter can pursue to eliminate this foreign exchange risk:

- Elect to quote in the exporter's currency. Although this is the easiest of the alternatives for the exporter, it only shifts the risk onto the importer, who is likely to consider this risk to be a burden. In addition, if the exporter's quote is being evaluated against other quotes, including some domestic proposals, a quote that is presented in a foreign currency is going to be less attractive to the importer.

- Elect to quote in the importer's currency and minimize the risk of exchange rate fluctuation with a forward-market hedge. In that case, the importer has no currency fluctuation risk and the exporter knows exactly what its foreign exchange cost is going to be at the time of the transaction. The only drawback is that the exporter may not have easy access to the forward market of some currencies that are not commonly traded in the forward markets (a currency other than the European euro, the Japanese yen, the British pound, or the Australian dollar for a U.S.-based exporter). Nevertheless, these other currencies are traded in the forward market in London and, with some help from a savvy international banker, an exporter can hedge just about any receivable in any currency.

- Elect to quote in the importer's currency and minimize the exchange rate risk with a money-market hedge. In that case, the importer has no currency fluctuation risk; the exporter also knows exactly what its foreign exchange cost is going to be, although it requires knowing what the interest rates are in the importing country. However, the exporter has to be quite experienced—and have an international presence—to be able to borrow from a bank in a foreign market; only a few companies have this option available, although a savvy international banker can provide substantial help in this regard.

- Elect to quote in the importer's currency and minimize the exchange rate risk with an options-market hedge. In that case, the importer has no currency fluctuation risk and the exporter benefits in two ways. If the exchange-rate fluctuation is favorable, the exporter benefits from it. If the exchange-rate fluctuation is unfavorable, the exporter has minimized its risk. The main issue with options-market hedges is the same as with the forward-market hedges: not all currencies are readily available in the home country of the exporter, and the help of a savvy international banker may be required to purchase options on the London market, for example.

Because of the intense competition that an exporter faces in international markets, it is very likely that a significant percentage of its competitors will offer quotes in the importer's currency. Because it is easier for the importer to handle a purchase in its own currency, it would place an exporter at a strategic disadvantage not to quote in that currency.

An exporter intent on increasing its sales abroad should therefore consider very seriously offering quotes in the importer's currency and discuss with its banker which of the three hedging tactics would be most appropriate.

Review and Discussion Questions

1. What are three of the possible choices that an exporter can make (in terms of currency) for a specific transaction?

2. Explain the three different types of exchange rates. Find the three exchange rates for a currency of your choice and explain the values you find.

3. Explain the three different types of currencies. Give an example of each.

4. Choose two of the theories of exchange rate determination and explain them.

5. What does it mean for a firm to retain its currency fluctuation risk in a transaction?

6. There are three types of hedges that a firm can use to protect itself against transaction exposure. Choose one of them and explain it.

Notes

[1] "Total Reserves in Months of Import," The World Bank, http://data.worldbank.org/indicator/FI.RES.TOTL.MO, retrieved June 11, 2013.

[2] Multiple sources, but Wikipedia has generally a series of continuously updated webpages covering the status of all of these countries and their progress toward their accession to the euro.

[3] Eiteman, David K., Arthur I. Stonehill, and Michael H. Moffett, *Multinational Business Finance*, 2012, Thirteenth Edition, Pearson-Addison-Wesley Publishing Company, Reading, Massachusetts.

[4] Madura, Jeff, International Financial Management, 2011, Eleventh Edition, South-Western Publishing, Cincinnati, Ohio.

[5] Shapiro, Alan C., *Multinational Financial Management*, 2009, Ninth Edition, John Wiley & Sons, Hoboken, New Jersey.

[6] Sercu, Piet, *International Finance: Theory into Practice*, 2009, Princeton University Press, Princeton, New Jersey.

[7] "Currencies," *The Wall Street Journal*, June 11, 2013, p. C6.

[8] "Currencies," *Financial Times*, June 12, 2013.

[9] "Currencies," *The Wall Street Journal*, June 11, 2013, p. C6.

[10] "Currencies," *Financial Times*, June 10, 2013.

[11] "Currencies," *The Wall Street Journal*, June 11, 2013, p. C6.

[12] "Currencies," *Financial Times*, June 10, 2013.

[13] "Foreign Exchange Swap Transactions," *The Learning Center*, Allied Irish Bank, http://www.fxcenterusa.com/us/learning/FX%20Swaps.pdf, retrieved May 30, 2009.

[14] "Foreign Exchange Rates. H.10," Board of Governors of the Federal Reserve System, http://www.federalreserve.gov/releases/h10/hist/, retrieved June 12, 2013.

[15] Mallaby, Sebastian, *More Money than God*, Penguin Press HC, New York, New York, 2010.

[16] Reuters, "U.A.E. Quits Gulf Monetary Union," *The Wall Street Journal*, May 21, 2009, p. C2.

[17] Bradsher, Keith, "China Grows More Picky About Debt," *The New York Times*, May 21, 2009.

[18] Krugman, Paul, "China's Dollar Trap," *The New York Times*, April 3, 2009.

[19] Batson, Andrew, "China Takes Aim at the Dollar," *The Wall Street Journal*, March 24, 2009, p. A1.

[20] Slater, JoAnna, "Beijing Faces Big Barriers in Effort to Supplant Dollar," *The Wall Street Journal*, March 24, 2009, p. A10.

[21] "Foreign Exchange Rates. H.10," Board of Governors of the Federal Reserve System, http://www.federalreserve.gov/releases/h10/hist/, retrieved June 12, 2013.

[22] "The Economist Big Mac Index," *The Economist*, July 2012, http://www.scribd.com/doc/102253973/big-mac-index-july-2012, retrieved June 11, 2013.

[23] Shapiro, Alan C., *Multinational Financial Management*, 2009, Ninth Edition, John Wiley & Sons, Hoboken, New Jersey.

[24] Peck, Earl, "Prices, Interest Rates, and Exchange Rates in Equilibrium," unpublished research paper, Baldwin-Wallace College, Berea, Ohio.

[25] Board of Governors of the Federal Reserve System, http://research.stlouisfed.org/fred2/series/EXJPUS/downloaddata, retrieved June 13, 2013.

[26] "Economic Research and Data," Board of Governors of the Federal Reserve System, http://www.federalreserve.gov/econresdata/default.htm, retrieved June 13, 2013.

[27] "10-Year Currency Converter," Bank of Canada, http://www.bankofcanada.ca/rates/exchange/10-year-converter/, retrieved June 13, 2013.

[28] Antweiler, Werner, "Pacific Exchange Rate Service," http://fx.sauder.ubc.ca/data.html, retrieved June 13, 2013.

[29] Bowerman, Bruce L., Richard L. O'Connell, and Anne Koehler, *Forecasting, Time Series, and Regression*, 2005, Fourth Edition, Southwestern Publishing, Cincinnati, Ohio.

[30] Box, George E., Gwilym M. Jenkins, and Gregory C. Reinsel, *Time Series Analysis: Forecasting and Control*, 2008, Fourth Edition, John Wiley, Hoboken, New Jersey.

[31] Makridakis, Spyros, Steven C. Wheelwright, and Rob Hyndman, *Forecasting: Methods and Applications*, 1998, Third Edition, John Wiley and Sons, Inc., New York, New York.

[32] McNelis, Paul, *Neural Networks in Finance: Gaining Predictive Edge in the Market*, 2005, Academic Press Advanced Series in Finance, Elsevier, New York, New York.

[33] Kutner, Michael, Christopher Nachtsheim, William Wasserman and John Neter, *Applied Linear Statistical Models*, 2003, Fourth Edition, McGraw-Hill, New York, New York.

[34] Seber, George, and Alan Lee, *Linear Regression Analysis*, 2003, John Wiley, Hoboken, New Jersey.

[35] Weiss, Gary, "George Soros, All Warm and Cuddly," *Business Week*, March 4, 2002, p. 68, reporting on Michael T. Kaufmann's *Soros: The Life and Times of a Messianic Billionaire*, 2002, Alfred A. Knopf, New York.

[36] "Currencies," *The Wall Street Journal*, June 11, 2013, p. C6.

[37] *Ibid.*

[38] "U.S./Euro Foreign Exchange Rate," Federal Reserve Bank of St. Louis, http://research.stlouisfed.org/fred2/series/DEXUSEU/, retrieved June 13, 2013.

[39] "British Pound (GBP) to Euro (EUR) Exchange Rate History," Exchange Rates, http://www.exchangerates.org.uk/GBP-EUR-exchange-rate-history.html, retrieved June 13, 2013.

[40] "Swiss Franc (CHF) to Japanese Yen (JPY) Exchange Rate History," *Ibid.*

[41] "Danish Krone (DKK) to Australian Dollar (AUD) exchange rate history," *Ibid.*

[42] "British Pound (GBP) to US Dollar (USD) exchange rate history," *Ibid.*

[43] "Euro (EUR) to Canadian Dollar (CAD) exchange rate history," *Ibid.*

[44] "Euro (EUR) to Canadian Dollar (CAD) exchange rate history," *Ibid.*

[45] Eiteman, David K., Arthur I. Stonehill, and Michael H. Moffett, *Multinational Business Finance*, 2012, Thirteenth Edition, Pearson-Addison-Wesley Publishing Company, Reading, Massachusetts.

[46] Hull, John C., *Options, Futures, and Other Derivatives*, 2011, Eighth Edition, Prentice-Hall, Englewood, New Jersey.

[47] Krugman, Paul and Maurice Obstfeld, *International Economics: Theory and Policy*, 2011, Ninth Edition, Prentice-Hall, Englewood, New Jersey.

[48] Smith, Roy, and Ingo Walter, *Global Banking*, 2012, Third Edition, Oxford University Press, New York, New York.

Chapter 9

International Commercial Documents

9.1　Documentation Requirements 237
9.2　Invoices 238
9.3　Export Documents 242
9.4　Import Documents 250
9.5　Transportation Documents 261
9.6　Electronic Data Interchange 270
9.7　Document Preparation as a Marketing Tool 272

A very large number of documents are involved in international transactions, many more than in a purely domestic exchange. Some of these documents are required by the exporting country, some by the importing country, some by the banks involved (especially if the shipment is made under a letter of credit), some by the shipping (transportation) company, and some by the importer of the goods.

Under each of the Incoterms® rules outlined in Chapter 6, the exporter is responsible for generating and collecting all—or almost all—of the documents linked to an international transaction. Any error or omission in the creation of these documents can create difficulties for both the exporter and the importer, as the goods will be detained by Customs in the importing country, the bank will request amendments in order to process payment, or the carrier will load the goods improperly.

It is therefore imperative for international logistics managers to exert special care and follow best practices in generating the documents linked to every international transaction.

9.1　Documentation Requirements

Most international trade transactions require numerous documents, each of which must be filled out in a very specific fashion, depending on the country of destination for the goods, the type of goods, the method of transportation, the method of payment chosen by the exporter and importer, the bank(s) involved, and so on. Each of these documents must also contain very detailed information and specific statements, and must often be filed in a certain time frame with a specific administration. Such are the difficulties of generating these documents that a multitude of software packages exist to help the international logistics manager complete the task. Most of them promise that they can help an exporter complete an entire set in "as little as two hours."

In addition, it is a common requirement to issue more than one original for some of these documents, as well as a multitude of copies—one for just about every possible intermediary involved. For some transactions, the number of originals and copies can be staggering: a particularly egregious case was a letter of credit from Ethiopia for U.S.$ 1,067 that called for "15 original invoices, five of them certified by a chamber of commerce."[1] In many cases, the thickness of the export documentation necessary for an international transaction reaches more than 1.5 centimeters (0.5 inch), even for a simple export.

Finally, most countries still require all of these documents to be issued on paper. Although there has been a recent increase in the number of countries that accept electronic submissions of paperwork, most still prefer paper. For many of them, it is required to file everything on paper; for others, only documents that are in paper form have legal status. This is the case in countries that have a legal system based on the old Napoleonic Code and have not updated their laws. Italy, for example, formally started to give an equivalent legal status to electronic documents only in February 2002.[2]

9.2 Invoices

One of the documents common to both international and domestic transactions is the bill (invoice) that the exporter sends to the importer. However, the content of an international invoice is more complex and should be prepared substantially differently for a foreign customer than for a domestic one.

9.2.1 Commercial Invoice

commercial invoice The document sent by the seller to the buyer that lists the goods purchased and the amount due.

The invoice that accompanies the shipment is called the commercial invoice. Depending on the terms of payment to which the exporter and the importer agreed (see Chapter 7), the commercial invoice may be sent directly to the importer (with the merchandise) or indirectly, through the banking channels.

This invoice should present precisely what the importer is being billed for. This seems obvious, but it is a much greater challenge to fulfill this requirement for an international transaction than it is for a domestic transaction. Several areas of the invoice must be very carefully written in order to avoid problems later on (see Figure 9.1 on page 241):

- A very precise description of the product should be given. In domestic marketing, it is common to just print a part number, a number of units, a per-piece price, and a total. This is highly insufficient in international trade, as the invoice is one of the documents that will be used by the importer (or the exporter, depending on the terms of trade or Incoterms® rule used; see Chapter 6) to clear Customs in the importing country. Because the tariff paid is a function of the classification (type) of the product imported (see Chapter 16, Section 16.1.1), a clear and accurate description of the product should be written on the invoice, including the Harmonized System Number. In addition, because tariff rates are determined using a multiplicity of criteria—the number of units in the shipment, their dimensions, weight, and total value—such information should also be included.

However, it is not possible to assume that tariffs will be calculated on the same basis everywhere; Switzerland, for example, uses weight to calculate duty for a number of products, including computers.

- The terms of trade (or Incoterms® rule used) should be made quite clear and should indicate that the seller intends to follow the guidelines proposed by the International Chamber of Commerce. This information is crucial to clarify whether the exporter or the importer is responsible for the payment of a number of ancillary services and fees: shipping, stevedoring, insurance, dock fees, terminal fees, duty, and so on. A misunderstanding in this area can cause countless problems and cost a substantial amount of money. The use of non-traditional terms of trade or the use of domestic terms of trade in an international transaction, which no one understands, should be avoided at all costs.

- A detailed list of the items that the exporter has prepaid for the importer should be noted; for example, the amount paid by the exporter for international insurance should be clearly indicated in the case of a CIF or CIP shipment, as some importing countries—such as the United States—will exclude this amount when duty is calculated. Stevedoring charges in the port of departure should be spelled out for the same reason. There are probably countries for which it would make sense to spell out what amounts were prepaid for domestic transportation in the exporting country as well.

- The terms of payment (see Chapter 7) should also be clearly detailed; they are the conditions under which the invoice should be paid. The invoice may be accompanied by a letter of credit or a bank draft. It could also indicate that the merchandise has already been paid for (as in a cash-in-advance, a purchasing card, or TradeCard purchase) or just show a due date (as in the case of a sale conducted on an open-account basis).

- The currency in which the payment is to be made should be clear. The issues regarding the choice of the currency and ways to manage the risk of currency fluctuations are presented in Chapter 8.

- The shipping information should also be presented; it includes the ports of departure and destination, the name of the shipping company(ies), the dates of the shipment, the number of boxes or containers, their weight (gross and net), and their size.

- Finally, the customary information should be provided: the name of the seller-exporter, the name of the buyer-importer, the persons to be contacted, addresses, and so forth. The telephone access codes should be eliminated, so as to not confuse the foreign customer.*

---

*In the United States, it is necessary to dial the digit "1" before making a phone call to another state. In Great Britain and in France, it is necessary to dial the digit "0" before making a domestic call. These access digits should be omitted from the letterhead.

9.2.2 *Pro forma* Invoice

***pro forma* invoice**
A quote provided by the exporter to the importer for the purpose of obtaining a letter of credit or an import license.

A *pro forma* invoice is a very common international document; despite its name, it is not an invoice at all, but a quote.

An international transaction includes so many variables that it is sometimes difficult for an importer to have a good grasp of what its final costs will be; for example, the cost of the goods is increased by the costs of shipping, insurance, and so forth. In order to determine these costs, the importer may request a *pro forma* invoice, literally an invoice "as a matter of form" (*i.e.*, an invoice in advance or an accurate and precise preview of what the actual invoice would be like if the transaction were to take place). The importer can then compare this invoice to the other quotes it receives.

In those cases in which the exporter requests payment on a letter-of-credit basis, the information contained on the *pro forma* invoice is used by the issuing bank to open the letter of credit. Because the letter of credit dictates that the documents submitted for payment must match exactly those outlined in the letter of credit, whatever information is included in the *pro forma* invoice will be present in the letter of credit. Therefore, it is actually against the information contained in the *pro forma* invoice that the actual documents will be reviewed. Extreme care should therefore be given to the writing of a *pro forma* invoice, as the final commercial invoice should not vary from it. If it does, it is likely that this situation will be considered a discrepancy between the letter of credit and the actual documents, and amendments will have to be made, and paid for. It is therefore imperative for the exporter to have a very accurate *pro forma* invoice, including exactly the same type of information as the final commercial invoice would have, in the same amount, with exact quotes from the other suppliers involved (shipping, insurance, and the like).

It also should include an expiration date, or the date after which the quote is no longer valid. The expiration date in an international transaction is treated very differently than in a domestic transaction. Whereas under the Uniform Commercial Code of the United States (UCC) and under the domestic laws of many other countries, where the offer can be withdrawn at any time, without prejudice, for almost whatever reason, it is not the case in an international transaction conducted under the United Nations Convention on the International Sale of Goods (CISG). Under the CISG, the offer cannot be withdrawn by the seller (or the buyer) before its expiration date, and the other party can accept it at any time until then; it is an irrevocable offer. Most countries have now adopted this convention for international sales contracts (see Section 5.2 for further details).

Casual handling of a *pro forma* invoice may cause countless problems later on. As *A Basic Guide to Exporting* wisely points out, "problems [...] are more easily avoided than rectified after they occur."[3]

9.2.3 Consular Invoice

consular invoice
An invoice printed on stationery provided by the importing country's Consulate.

For exports to some countries—specifically a decreasing number of Latin American countries—a consular invoice may be necessary. A consular invoice is nothing more than a regular commercial invoice, but printed on stationery (paper) provided by the importing country's consulate, and made "official" (stamped, embossed, given a visa, or whatever other procedure is used to legalize it) by the consulate before the invoice can be sent to the importer. The process of obtaining a consular invoice

EBERT PIPE ORGANS, INC.

INVOICE: 072313-001   **Date:** July 23, 2013

Sold By: **Shipped By:**
Ebert Pipe Organs, Inc.   Ebert Inc. Warehouse
1234 Carnegie Avenue   7200 Industrial Parkway
Cleveland, OH 44111   Cleveland, OH 44111
USA   USA

Sold To: **Shipped To:**
Australian Importers   St. John's Methodist Church
4/2 Wilson Avenue   76 Ewing Road
Brunswick, Victoria 3089   Brunswick, Victoria 3095
Australia   Australia

Crates: 3   **Weight:** 57.55 kg net each   **Volume:** 1.2 x 0.6 x 0.4 m each
                        65.00 kg gross each   0.288 m³ each
                       195.00 kg total   0.864 m³ total

Purchase Order: 062083

Quantity	Description	Unit Price	Total
3	Catalog Item # 095673. Pipe organ blower. HS 8414.59.1000 Insurance paid to Brunswick, Australia Airfreight Costs to Brunswick, Australia US Domestic Transportation Costs	USD 975.00 USD 128.70 USD 585.00 USD 87.00	USD 2,925.00
	Total:		USD 3,725.70

Shipped via: Trans-Air   CIP 76 Ewing Road Brunswick,
                                        Australia, Incoterms 2010
Country of Origin: USA

Terms: 1.5% 10 days / net 30 days

Figure 9.1: A Sample Commercial Invoice

is often time-consuming, as it involves at least one exchange (by mail or in person) with the consulate. Because consulates for most countries are rarely located in a city convenient to the exporter, there are a number of messenger service companies that provide couriers who will pick up the invoice, wait in line at the consulate, have it legalized, and return it to the exporting company.

This process is usually favored by countries that want to accurately forecast their needs for foreign currency. From these consular invoices, they can determine their foreign currency outflows and therefore accurately manage their needs for foreign currency. However, this process also has the added benefit of generating additional revenues, as the stationery sold by the consulate and the officialization procedure are usually quite expensive. All of these fees are also obviously generated in hard currency, another added benefit.

Fortunately, this type of requirement is slowly disappearing, as it is often viewed as a non-trade barrier by exporters. As of June 2013, consular invoices were still required in half a dozen countries, mostly in Latin America.

9.2.4 Specialized Commercial Invoices

Some countries require that all commercial invoices be printed on a standard form, which is usually easily available at a low cost from specialized printers of international stationery, such as Unz & Co. These countries include Canada, Mexico, New Zealand, Brazil, and Israel.[4] In general, these requirements are not considered trade barriers, and it is understood that their purpose is to simplify the work of Customs employees.

9.3 Export Documents

A country's government may require a number of documents before a product can be exported. These requirements are primarily motivated by the desire to keep accurate data on what is exported from that country. Such is the case for the Shipper's Export Declaration (SED) in the United States, for example. In some cases, though, the government also wants to control the outflow of certain types of merchandise, or does not want to trade with certain countries for political reasons (embargoes). In those cases, the country will require the exporter to obtain an export license.

9.3.1 Shipper's Export Declaration

Shipper's Export Declaration (SED) A document collected by U.S. Customs detailing the type and value of goods exported, as well as their destination.

The Shipper's Export Declaration (SED) (see Figure 9.2) is a data collection document required by the U.S. government for all exports valued at more than $2,500 per item category, as determined by the Harmonized System Number ($500 for parcels sent through the postal system), and for all shipments that require an Individual Validated Export License. The SED is not required for exports to Canada, but it is required for shipments to Puerto Rico, the U.S. Virgin Islands, and Guam, even though those shipments are not exports. The SED must be sent electronically to the U.S. Customs Service.

This form (see Figure 9.2 on the facing page) allows the U.S. government to tabulate what products are exported from the United States and to determine where these products are sold. The data are available for all commodities and for all countries in the National Trade Data Bank, available on the website of the International

U.S. DEPARTMENT OF COMMERCE – Economics and Statistics Administration – U.S. CENSUS BUREAU – BUREAU OF EXPORT ADMINISTRATION

FORM **7525-V** (7-18-2003) **SHIPPER'S EXPORT DECLARATION** OMB No. 0607-0152

1a. U.S. PRINCIPAL PARTY IN INTEREST (USPPI)(Complete name and address) ZIP CODE	**2.** DATE OF EXPORTATION / **3.** TRANSPORTATION REFERENCE NO.
b. USPPI'S EIN (IRS) OR ID NO. / **c.** PARTIES TO TRANSACTION ☐ Related ☐ Non-related	
4a. ULTIMATE CONSIGNEE *(Complete name and address)*	
b. INTERMEDIATE CONSIGNEE *(Complete name and address)*	
5a. FORWARDING AGENT *(Complete name and address)*	
5b. FORWARDING AGENT'S EIN (IRS) NO.	**6.** POINT (STATE) OF ORIGIN OR FTZ NO. / **7.** COUNTRY OF ULTIMATE DESTINATION
8. LOADING PIER *(Vessel only)* / **9.** METHOD OF TRANSPORTATION *(Specify)*	**14.** CARRIER IDENTIFICATION CODE / **15.** SHIPMENT REFERENCE NO.
10. EXPORTING CARRIER / **11.** PORT OF EXPORT	**16.** ENTRY NUMBER / **17.** HAZARDOUS MATERIALS ☐ Yes ☐ No
12. PORT OF UNLOADING *(Vessel and air only)* / **13.** CONTAINERIZED *(Vessel only)* ☐ Yes ☐ No	**18.** IN BOND CODE / **19.** ROUTED EXPORT TRANSACTION ☐ Yes ☐ No

20. SCHEDULE B DESCRIPTION OF COMMODITIES *(Use columns 22–24)*

D/F or M (21)	SCHEDULE B NUMBER (22)	QUANTITY – SCHEDULE B UNIT(S) (23)	SHIPPING WEIGHT (Kilograms) (24)	VIN/PRODUCT NUMBER/ VEHICLE TITLE NUMBER (25)	VALUE (U.S. dollars, omit cents) (Selling price or cost if not sold) (26)

27. LICENSE NO./LICENSE EXCEPTION SYMBOL/AUTHORIZATION	**28.** ECCN *(When required)*
29. Duly authorized officer or employee	The USPPI authorizes the forwarder named above to act as forwarding agent for export control and customs purposes.

30. I certify that all statements made and all information contained herein are true and correct and that I have read and understand the instructions for preparation of this document, set forth in the **"Correct Way to Fill Out the Shipper's Export Declaration."** I understand that civil and criminal penalties, including forfeiture and sale, may be imposed for making false or fraudulent statements herein, failing to provide the requested information or for violation of U.S. laws on exportation (13 U.S.C. Sec. 305; 22 U.S.C. Sec. 401; 18 U.S.C. Sec. 1001; 50 U.S.C. App. 2410).

Signature	**Confidential –** Shipper's Export Declarations (or any successor document) wherever located, shall be exempt from public disclosure unless the Secretary determines that such exemption would be contrary to the national interest (Title 13, Chapter 9, Section 301 (g)).
Title	Export shipments are subject to inspection by U.S. Customs Service and/or Office of Export Enforcement.
Date	**31.** AUTHENTICATION *(When required)*
Telephone No. (Include Area Code)	E-mail address

This form may be printed by private parties provided it conforms to the official form. For sale by the Superintendent of Documents, Government Printing Office, Washington, DC 20402, and local Customs District Directors. The **"Correct Way to Fill Out the Shipper's Export Declaration"** is available from the U.S. Census Bureau, Washington, DC 20233.

Figure 9.2: The United States Shipper's Export Declaration (SED)

Trade Commission[5] with a subscription. However, when the procedure was done in paper form, it did not ensure that all exports were properly counted. As late as 1998, it was estimated that up to 50 percent of the SEDs had defective entries, from the value of the goods to their classification.[6] In addition, many SEDs were filed very late, and several shipments that would have been inspected or seized had already left the United States. The results were fines for the shipping lines that accepted such shipments.[7] For that reason, the SED must now be submitted to Customs before the shipment is allowed to leave the United States.

In 1999, the U.S. Census Bureau, the entity that eventually collects all of this information through Customs, decided to fight another issue with SEDs; many of them were filled out by hand, and then faxed, and some of those were literally illegible. The Census Bureau started to entice exporters to use a new electronic system for filing SEDs, one that would no longer allow errors or incomplete entries as the old system did. The Automated Export System (AES) became the only way exporters could submit SEDs on September 30, 2008.[8]

Several other recent changes in the SED include its definition of "exporter." Because errors in classifications can sometimes be attributable to a lack of understanding of the products being shipped, the exporter of record—now called euphemistically the "U.S. principal party in interest," or PPI—is now always the manufacturer of the goods, even on an EXW shipment, where the goods are actually owned by the importer when they leave the United States. With this move, the Census Bureau has effectively forced the seller to provide accurate and timely information to the importer, who is still responsible for filling out and filing an SED. These policy changes have increased the reliability of the export statistics of the United States.

9.3.2 Export Licenses

export license
The express authorization, granted by the exporting country's government to the exporter, to export a particular product.

An export license is an express authorization by a given country's government to export a specific product before it is shipped. There are many reasons for a government to require an export license, but they are usually triggered by one of the following two viewpoints:

- The government is attempting to control the export of national treasures or antiques. This is the case in India, which prohibits the export of any object older than 100 years old; with Britain and with France, which both control the export of antiques and works of art; with Russia, which prohibits the export of cultural artifacts;[9] and with Turkey, which was recently involved in a high-stakes fight over a trove of antique coins that were discovered in 1984 and eventually smuggled into the United States.[10] Several countries have been successful in repatriating such artifacts: Italy convinced the Metropolitan Museum of Art in New York City to return some 15 objects,[11] Greece repatriated several objects from the Getty Museum in Los Angeles, and the Boston Museum of Fine Arts returned the coins to Turkey.[12,13]

- The country's government is controlling the export of some raw materials, generally to conserve natural resources and promote domestic industry. In 2011, China restricted the export of rare earths—chemical elements critical to the manufacturing of some electronic components—of which it controls 90 percent of the world's production.[14] Vanuatu—an island country in the middle of the South Pacific—controls the export of phosphates, the only source of export for the country, and the primary industry on the island.

9.3 Export Documents

No. BX 57894

FORM 2

THE WILD LIFE PROTECTION (EDIBLE BIRDS' NESTS) RULES, 1998

LICENCE TO *IMPORT/EXPORT EDIBLE BIRDS' NESTS
(Issued under rule 6(2))

Licence No: BC 03322

Licence is hereby granted to GOLDENEST TRADING COMPANY of No. 20, Court House, 93000 Kuching, Sarawak
(address)

to *import/export the quantity/weight of 200gm [Processed] edible birds' nests specified below *from/to ....
(place)

subject to the Wild Life Protection Ordinance, 1998, and these Rules, and to the following special conditions, namely—

....
....
....

2. This licence is not transferable and shall not be sub-let, sub-licensed, assigned nor any benefit hereby granted be conferred on any other person.

Date of issue: 18.05.2010

Quantity/weight of edible birds' nests imported/exported 200gm [Processed]

Fees RM 10.00 (paid)

Signature: ....
Name of Wild Life Officer: Ngui Siew Kong
Designation: For Controller of Wildlife

*Delete where inapplicable.

Figure 9.3: an Export License from the State of Sarawak, in Malaysia

- The country can also implement export controls for political reasons. Following an internal struggle between the president-elect and the outgoing president of the Ivory Coast, the country banned the export of cocoa in January 2011.[15] Belarus stopped the export of butter, cheese and macaroni in 2011, in an attempt to maintain lower consumer prices in the country.[16]

- The government is trying to exert some control over foreign trade for political or military reasons: this is mostly the way the United States government manages its export licensing program; the process it follows is described further in the next section. Some other countries also pursue similar objectives: China seized and prohibited from export a book published by an American firm but printed in China.[17] The European Union prohibits the export of personal data gathered on customers or consumers.[18]

Many countries have export restrictions: an OECD study tallied a comprehensive list of items that cannot be legally exported without an export license, and found more than 50 countries with some form of export restrictions or controls.[19]

9.3.3 U.S. Export Controls

The U.S. government's policy regarding export controls is anchored in several milestones: the existence of a (once secret) agreement between Western countries to deny access to certain military technologies (nicknamed CoCom), which ceased to exist in 1994;[20] the Export Administration Act, which controlled the type of goods that could be exported to certain "unfriendly" countries, but that lapsed in 1992; the Fenwick Anti-Terrorist Amendment of the Export Administration Act, written to prevent exports to nations supportive of international terrorism; and the Comprehensive Anti-Apartheid Act, which created a number of regulations for exports to South Africa. These documents brought into existence the current Commerce Control List, which details which commodities and products can and cannot be shipped to certain countries. The list is updated regularly and published in the U.S. Export Administration Regulations (EAR).[21] In 1996, the EAR was completely revised to reflect a major shift from a policy of "everything that is not explicitly authorized needs an export license" to a policy of "everything is authorized unless specifically prohibited." Finally, in April 2002, the Bureau of Export Administration, which was in charge of administering the EAR, changed its name to the Bureau of Industry and Security.

For some products, therefore, the U.S. government wants to ascertain that the goods are purchased for a legitimate commercial purpose (and not a military or a criminal one) and that there is no risk of diversion (sale to another, unfriendly company or country). This is particularly true of products that have a dual use (*i.e.*, that can be used for several purposes, one of which is commercial, the other military in nature). For example, Polaroid employees need to use night-vision goggles to assemble some instant cameras. When sales of the product surged in Japan, the company tried to expand its manufacturing facility in Mexico and attempted to ship more night-vision goggles there, but was rebuffed by the Bureau of Export Administration (BXA), the predecessor of the BIS, because these instruments have a dual use.[22]

The U.S. export control policies are focusing on three elements: the product considered for export, the entity abroad that is buying the product or an intermediary

9.3 Export Documents

(abroad or in the United States) involved in the sale of the product, and finally, the ultimate country of destination for the product.

Internet Encryption

The Internet is a growing area of interest for companies that expect to be able to conduct business by using this international network. However, conducting business transactions through a computer network necessitates a means to keep certain data, such as credit card information, confidential.

It is quite possible to keep data secure with encryption software, a type of computer program that scrambles data in such a way that it cannot be read intelligibly by anyone but the intended recipient equipped with the same software. However, the United States government has long regarded encryption technology as sensitive—it could be used for military purposes—and therefore has kept it on its Commerce Control List.[23]

For years, it steadfastly refused to allow companies to use encryption software on the Internet, as it considered its use to be an export because the network is essentially borderless. Only banks, subsidiaries of U.S. firms, health and medical facilities, and certain online merchants were allowed to have access to U.S. encryption technology abroad. It is only recently that the Bureau of Industry and Security (BIS) has allowed low-level encryption to be sold freely outside of the United States; the terminology used by BIS is "mass-market encryption," or encryption items available to the public that cannot be easily modified beyond their original intent. However, software products containing high-level encryption are still listed in the Commerce Control List, and each and every potential export must be reviewed by the BIS.[24]

The Product Exported

To determine which products fall under the possible control of the EAR, the BIS publishes a Commerce Control List (CCL) on which it lists all products for which the BIS has deemed that exports should be of concern to the United States. Each product on the CCL is given an Export Control Classification Number (ECCN)—which is different from the Harmonized System Number used by Customs—and determines whether it will necessitate an export license.

Commerce Control List (CCL)
A list of products that cannot be exported from the United States without an export license.

All of the products that do not fall on the CCL list are given the classification "EAR99" by the BIS. However, a few of the EAR99 products can still require an export license, if they fall under the jurisdiction of another government entity that controls export. For example, the Drug Enforcement Administration controls the export of pharmaceuticals under the authority of the Controlled Substances Act and can require an export license for some products.

The BIS gives the reason for the inclusion of all products listed on the CCL. Items are listed for reasons of national security, anti-terrorism, crime control, chemical and biological weapons control, nuclear non-proliferation, regional stability, encryption, short supply, United Nations embargo, or "significant item."

Depending on the reason for which they were listed, ECCN commodities do not require a license for some countries, but do for others. The BIS maintains a Product/Country License Determination Matrix to help the exporter in determining its obligations.[25]

The Purchaser of the Product

In those cases where the ECCN classification does not require a license, or when the product is classified as EAR99, the exporter is still required to determine whether the importer or an intermediary involved in the sale is on one of several lists:

- **The Entity List**. This list identifies people, companies, and organizations engaged in weapon proliferation, drug smuggling, or terrorism, and to which the U.S. government wants to control exports. Sales to persons or organizations on the Entity List require an export license. That list is maintained by the BIS.

- **The Unverified List**. This list identifies individuals, companies, and organizations that are suspected of engaging in activities that the BIS considers illegal. Before making a sale to a person on that list, the exporter is required to inquire with the BIS about possible issues. That list is also maintained by the BIS. In addition, the exporter is required to report a suspect transaction when the transaction has elements that the BIS considers "red flags," such as when a cash sale is made for a product that is generally purchased on credit terms, or when a product is sold to a company that does not appear to be in the exporter's main line of business.

- **The Specially Designated Nationals and Blocked Persons List**. On this list are the names of persons located abroad with whom exporters are expressly warned not to do business. These persons have been deemed to represent countries to which the United States does not want to export, or they represent companies or organizations engaged in terrorism or trafficking. That list is maintained by the Department of the Treasury.

- **The Denied Persons List**. This list identifies U.S. persons, companies, or organizations "whose export privileges have been revoked." Some of these companies are located in the United States. That list is maintained by the BIS. An exporter is expressly prohibited to sell to a person on that list, and a company that is contacted (even for a domestic sale) by one of these companies must notify the BIS.

The Country of Import

The Commerce Control List determines whether a given product, for which an ECCN exists, can be sold to a specific country. There are substantial differences in an exporter's ability to export to countries that the United States considers friendly and to countries that it considers unfriendly.

In addition, though, the United States has embargoes on sales of certain products to several countries. Exporters cannot sell any of these products and will never be able to obtain an export license. Finally, the United States has a total embargo on five countries; no products whatsoever can be exported to Cuba, Iran, D.P.R Korea, Sudan, and Syria. It has limited embargoes on a number of other countries, including Burma/Myanmar, the Democratic Republic of the Congo, Iraq, the Ivory Coast, Liberia, Libya, Somalia, Yemen, and Zimbabwe.[26]

In any of the cases in which a license is deemed necessary, the U.S. government requires an exporter to obtain an Individual Validated Export License, or an express authorization to ship that particular product to a particular country, and to write the following Destination Control Statement on the commercial invoice and the Shipper's Export Declaration: "This merchandise licensed by U.S. for ultimate destination [country]. Diversion contrary to U.S. Law prohibited." An Individual Validated Export License is generally granted with very specific terms and conditions to which the exporter is required to adhere.

Individual Validated Export License The express authorization, given by the U.S government, to export a particular commodity.

Deemed Export

The U.S. Bureau of Industry and Security determines that the export of products that could be used against the United States must be controlled. However, the BIS also considers that products that are sold to foreign nationals in the United States are "deemed exports," and therefore fall under its jurisdiction. For example, companies should carefully monitor the access of their foreign employees to technology (computers that have access to certain databases, or hold certain programs) and apply for an export license to allow them access. All foreign employees are subject to this rule, except those who are permanent residents of the United States.[27]

deemed export A product sold in the United States to a non-U.S. citizen.

Fines

The fines levied by the BIS can be staggering and are meant to strongly enforce compliance. Here are a few cases from a BIS booklet called *Don't Let This Happen to You! Actual Investigations of Export Controls and Anti-Boycott Regulations*:[28]

- The Balli Aviation Limited, a U.S. subsidiary of a United Kingdom company exported three used Boeing 747 aircrafts from the United States to Iran without a Validated Export License. The company was fined $15,000,000.

- Prime Technology Corporation exported high-modulus carbon fiber material to China without a Validated Export License. The president of the company was sentenced to 46 months in prison.

- Novamet Specialty Products Corporation exported nickel powders without the required licenses to the People's Republic of China, Singapore, Taiwan region, Thailand, India, Israel, the Dominican Republic and Mexico. The company was fined $700,000.

- FMC Technologies, Inc., headquartered in Houston, Texas, exported and reexported to a variety of countries butterfly and check valves without the proper license. The company was fined $ 610,000.

- J. Reece Roth, a Professor Emeritus at the University of Tennessee, and princi-pal of Atmospheric Glow Technologies, Inc., engaged in a conspiracy to trans-mit export controlled technical data to foreign nationals from Iran, a deemed export. He was convicted and sentenced to 48 months in prison.

9.3.4 End-Use Certificates

In some cases, and in particular for shipments of military equipment, an importer will be required to provide the exporter with an End-Use Certificate, or a document that certifies that the product is going to be used for a legitimate purpose, such as military training, and that the product will not be diverted to another, less acceptable task, such as police ammunition against a civil unrest. Most of these certificates are provided by the governments of the importing country.

end-use certificate
A certificate, required by the exporting country, that attests that the goods are purchased for a legitimate purpose.

9.3.5 Export Taxes

Several countries require exporters to pay an export tax on certain commodities.[29] While this appears at first sight to be quite counterproductive—discouraging exports prevents a country from earning foreign currency with which it could import other products, and is likely to affect negatively its balance of trade—it can make sense in the case where the goods are minerals in short supply, or when the product has been heavily subsidized by the government. This was the case for the European Union when it decided to tax the export of wheat in 1996.[30] However, although export taxes may seem attractive to some governments to raise funds quickly, they can be politically difficult to implement: in 2008, after the Kirchner government in Argentina implemented an export tax increase on agricultural products from a fixed 35 percent to a floating rate as high as 44 percent, farmers rebelled and the measure was defeated in the Argentinean Parliament.[31]

export tax
A tax collected on the value of the goods exported.

9.3.6 Export Quotas

In the same spirit, several countries have export quotas, which physically limit the amount of a certain category of goods that can be exported from the country. This strategy can be followed in an attempt to control scarce resources, such as in Vietnam, which has had an export quota of 5 million metric tonnes of rice, which it increased to 5.2 million metric tonnes in 2009 because of a large crop, and eventually completely abandoned.[32] An export quota can also be used to attempt to control the prices of a commodity on which the country has a monopoly. Such was the case with Russia, which imposed strict export quotas on platinum, palladium, rhodium, and ruthenium, commodities for which it is one of the very few world suppliers. After its application to join the World Trade Organization (WTO) was denied in part because of these export quotas, Russia lifted them in 2008.[33] Russia acceded to WTO membership in August 2012.[34]

export quota
A limit on the quantity of a particular commodity that can be legally exported.

9.4 Import Documents

A very large number of documents are required by countries in which goods are imported. There are several reasons for these requirements. These documents:

- ensure that no goods of shoddy quality are imported,
- help determine the appropriate tariff classification,
- help determine the correct value of the imported goods,
- protect importers from fraudulent exporters, and

9.4 Import Documents

CERTIFICATE OF ORIGIN

The undersigned _____
(Owner or Agent)

for _____ declares
(Name and Address of Shipper)

that the following mentioned goods were shipped on
on the date of _____ consigned to _____
are products of **NEW ZEALAND**
(Country of Origin)

Marks and Numbers	Number of Packages Boxes or Cases	Weight in Kilos Nett / Gross	Description of Merchandise Material or Goods
			Volume (m3)
TOTAL	Packets	0.000 / 0.000	Total Volume: 0.000 m3

Sworn to before me

this 08th day of August 2005
(Day) (Month) (Year)

(Signature)

The **ROTORUA CHAMBER OF COMMERCE**
NEW ZEALAND

Dated at **ROTORUA**

this 08th day August 2005
(Day) (Month) (year)

(Signature of Owner or Agent)

a recognized Chamber of Commerce under the laws of
has examined the manufacturer's invoice or shippers
affidavit concerning the origin of the merchandise and, according to the best of its knowledge and belief, finds that the products named originated in the country shown above. This certificate however is solely based on the information provided by the shipper/exporter/manufacturer, and the chamber expresses no opinions regarding its accuracy and assumes no responsibility for inaccuracies or errors in the statements affidavits or any other document.

Secretary _____

Figure 9.4: A Blank Certificate of Origin from New Zealand

DEPARTMENT OF HOMELAND SECURITY
U.S. Customs and Border Protection

OMB No. 1651-0098
Exp. 03-31-2012

NORTH AMERICAN FREE TRADE AGREEMENT
CERTIFICATE OF ORIGIN

19 CFR 181.11, 181.22

1. EXPORTER NAME AND ADDRESS	2. BLANKET PERIOD
	FROM
	TO
TAX IDENTIFICATION NUMBER:	
3. PRODUCER NAME AND ADDRESS	4. IMPORTER NAME AND ADDRESS
TAX IDENTIFICATION NUMBER:	TAX IDENTIFICATION NUMBER:

5. DESCRIPTION OF GOOD(S)	6. HS TARIFF CLASSIFICATION NUMBER	7. PREFERENCE CRITERION	8. PRODUCER	9. NET COST	10. COUNTRY OF ORIGIN

I CERTIFY THAT:

- THE INFORMATION ON THIS DOCUMENT IS TRUE AND ACCURATE AND I ASSUME THE RESPONSIBILITY FOR PROVING SUCH REPRESENTATIONS. I UNDERSTAND THAT I AM LIABLE FOR ANY FALSE STATEMENTS OR MATERIAL OMISSIONS MADE ON OR IN CONNECTION WITH THIS DOCUMENT;
- I AGREE TO MAINTAIN AND PRESENT UPON REQUEST, DOCUMENTATION NECESSARY TO SUPPORT THIS CERTIFICATE, AND TO INFORM, IN WRITING, ALL PERSONS TO WHOM THE CERTIFICATE WAS GIVEN OF ANY CHANGES THAT COULD AFFECT THE ACCURACY OR VALIDITY OF THIS CERTIFICATE;
- THE GOODS ORIGINATED IN THE TERRITORY OF ONE OR MORE OF THE PARTIES, AND COMPLY WITH THE ORIGIN REQUIREMENTS SPECIFIED FOR THOSE GOODS IN THE NORTH AMERICAN FREE TRADE AGREEMENT AND UNLESS SPECIFICALLY EXEMPTED IN ARTICLE 411 OR ANNEX 401, THERE HAS BEEN NO FURTHER PRODUCTION OR ANY OTHER OPERATION OUTSIDE THE TERRITORIES OF THE PARTIES; AND
- THIS CERTIFICATE CONSISTS OF _____ PAGES, INCLUDING ALL ATTACHMENTS.

11.	11a. AUTHORIZED SIGNATURE		11b. COMPANY	
	11c. NAME		11d. TITLE	
	11e. DATE	11f. TELEPHONE NUMBERS	(Voice)	(Facsimile)

CBP Form 434 (04/11)

Figure 9.5: A NAFTA Certificate of Origin—Certificate of Manufacture

- limit (or eliminate) imports of products that the government finds inappropriate for whatever reason.

However, there is also the possibility that the country is trying—not so subtly—to hinder imports and therefore adopt a protectionist stance. In Russia, for example, it takes an average of 36 days to clear Customs, and shipments require 11 documents before clearance is given. The Doing Business database of the World Bank gives this information for all countries of the world, and Russia is far from being the worst offender; it takes 17 documents to enter the Central African Republic and 101 days to clear Customs in Chad. In contrast, it takes 2 documents for France and 4 days in Singapore.[35]

9.4.1 Certificate of Origin

The most common type of required document is a Certificate of Origin, which the exporter must have signed by its Chamber of Commerce (see Figure 9.4 on page 251). In most instances, the Chamber of Commerce delegates that responsibility to the exporter and allows the exporter to sign the Certificate of Origin on its behalf. Some importing countries do not allow that substitution.

The Certificate of Origin is a statement that the goods originated in a particular country; it is important to note that it does not attest to the location where the product was manufactured, but only that the goods were shipped from a specific locale. This situation sometimes leads to abuses (fraud), in which merchandise is shipped from a different country than the one in which it was manufactured, often to avoid numerical quotas or higher tariffs. In order to prevent these practices, the Certificate of Manufacture was instituted.

The Certificate of Origin is used by importing countries to determine the tariff applied to the goods, as most countries apply a multi-column tariff system—different groups of countries pay different tariffs (see Chapter 16)—and to compile trade statistics. As in the case of commercial invoices, some countries require a specialized Certificate of Origin; for example, there is a specific Certificate of Origin for the North American Free Trade Area (see Figure 9.5 on the facing page).

In most countries, more than one original copy of the Certificate of Origin must be provided; in the countries that were formerly part of the Soviet Union, three copies are required, but, in addition, all of these copies must be notarized—embossed—and signed.[36]

certificate of origin
A certificate, signed by the exporter's chamber of commerce, that attests that the goods originated in the country in which the exporter is located.

9.4.2 Certificate of Manufacture

A Certificate of Manufacture is quite similar to a Certificate of Origin, except that it attests to the location of manufacture of the exporting products. The Certificate of Manufacture must also be signed by the Chamber of Commerce of the exporter. Because of the requirements that goods must contain at least 50 percent of regional content (made in Canada, the United States or Mexico), the NAFTA Certificate of Origin is actually a Certificate of Manufacture.

certificate of manufacture
A certificate, signed by the exporter's chamber of commerce, that attests that the goods were manufactured in the country in which the exporter is located.

9.4.3 Certificate of Inspection

In some cases, an importer will request a Certificate of Inspection, which is a document signed by an independent company—a third party—which attests to the au-

certificate of inspection A certificate, provided by an independent company, that attests that the goods conform to the description contained in the exporter's invoice.

pre-shipment inspection The inspection, conducted by an independent company, that allows the determination that the goods conform to the description contained in the exporter's invoice.

thenticity and accuracy of the shipment. The company determines that the product being shipped is actually the product shown on the invoice, that the quantity shipped is actually the one for which the importer is invoiced, that the product is in the same condition as the importer expects (new rather than used, for example), and so forth.

A Certificate of Inspection is useful to the importer in several situations; for example, in a purchase conducted on the basis of documentary collection, or with a letter of credit, the documents are the only items that the bank will inspect before making payment on behalf of the importer, or before committing the importer to pay (see Chapter 7). There is no possible way of withdrawing payment if there is a problem with the merchandise, and often no way to inspect the merchandise without first taking delivery. A Certificate of Inspection provides evidence that there were no problems with the merchandise when they left the country of export.

Some countries require pre-shipment inspections (PSIs) and the submission of a Certificate of Inspection for all or some of their imports (see Table 9.1)[37], and they generally have this requirement for reasons similar to the motivations of the importers. They want to protect their importers from unscrupulous exporters, but they also find it a convenient way to ensure the correct classification and valuation of the goods upon entry. Once classification and valuation are established by an independent inspection company in the exporting country, it prevents the potential corruption of local Customs officials and generally speeds up the process of Customs clearance and the collection of duties.[38]

Countries Requiring PSIs

Angola	Indonesia
Bangladesh	Iran
Benin	Kenya
Burkina Faso	Kuwait
Burundi	Liberia
Cambodia	Madagascar
Cameroon	Malawi
Central African Republic	Mali
Comoros	Mauritania
Republic of Congo (Brazzaville)	Mexico
Democratic Republic of Congo (Kinshasa)	Mozambique
Cote d'Ivoire	Niger
Ecuador	Senegal
Ethiopia	Sierra Leone
Guinea	Togo
India	Uzbekistan

Table 9.1: Countries Requiring Pre-Shipment Inspections

There are several companies that provide PSI services; the largest—with an estimated 60 to 70 percent of the world's business—is the Société Générale de Surveillance (SGS) of Switzerland.[39] In some cases, the SGS has an agreement with a country that all shipments made to that country must have a Certificate of Inspection signed by SGS (this is the case, for example, for Indonesia).

9.4 Import Documents

Arasto Pharmaceutical Chemicals Inc.

CERTIFICATE OF ANALYSIS

Product: Amitriptyline Hydrochloride	Batch NO: AMI(136)02-12
Manufacturing Date: February, 2012	Retest Date: May, 2013
Analysis Number: AMI-F4-22-90	Release Number: R-D-478-90

Test Method: USP34

Tests	Specifications	Results
Appearance	White or practically white, odorless or practically odorless, crystalline powder or small crystals.	Conforms
Solubility	Freely soluble in water, in alcohol, in chloroform, and in methanol; insoluble in ether.	Conforms
Identification	A: IR spectrum	Conforms
	B: R.T in assay chromatogram corresponds to that of RS	Conforms
	C: Test of Chloride	Conforms
Melting range	195 -199°C	197 -198 °C
PH	5.0-6.0	5.73
Loss On Drying	Max.0.5%	0.1%
*Organic Volatile Impurities	Meets the requirements	0ppm
Residue On Ignition	Max.0.1%	0.06%
Heavy Metals	Max.0.001%	Conforms
Chromatographic Purity(HPLC)	known impurities:	
	Dibenzosuberone(RCA) Max:0.05%	Not Detected
	Hydroxy Amitriptyline(RCB) Max:0.15%	Not Detected
	Nortriptyline. HCl Max:0.15%	Less Than 0.05%
	Cyclobenzaprine HCl Max:0.15%	Less Than 0.05%
	Each unknown impurities: Max:0.1%	Not Detected
	Total known and unknown impurities: Max:1.0%	0.1%
Residual Solvents	Toluene Max. 890 ppm (Class II)	Not Detected
Assay	98.0-102.0%	99.8%

Analyst: J.Borozmand, B.Sc.Chem.

Checked: M.Zarei, B.Sc.Chem.

Release ☑   Reject ☐

Approved by: H.Safari, B.Sc.Chem.

*Halogenated solvents and 1,4- dioxane are not used in our process of production of Amitriptyline.HCl.

Arasto Pharmaceutical Chemicals Inc.
No. 8 , 23th St.,Jahan Ara St., Asad Abadi Ave.Tehran 1438933743 Iran Tel: +98(21) 8833-227
Fax: +98(21)8863-0677
E-Mail: info@arasto.com

Figure 9.6: A Certificate of Analysis from Iran

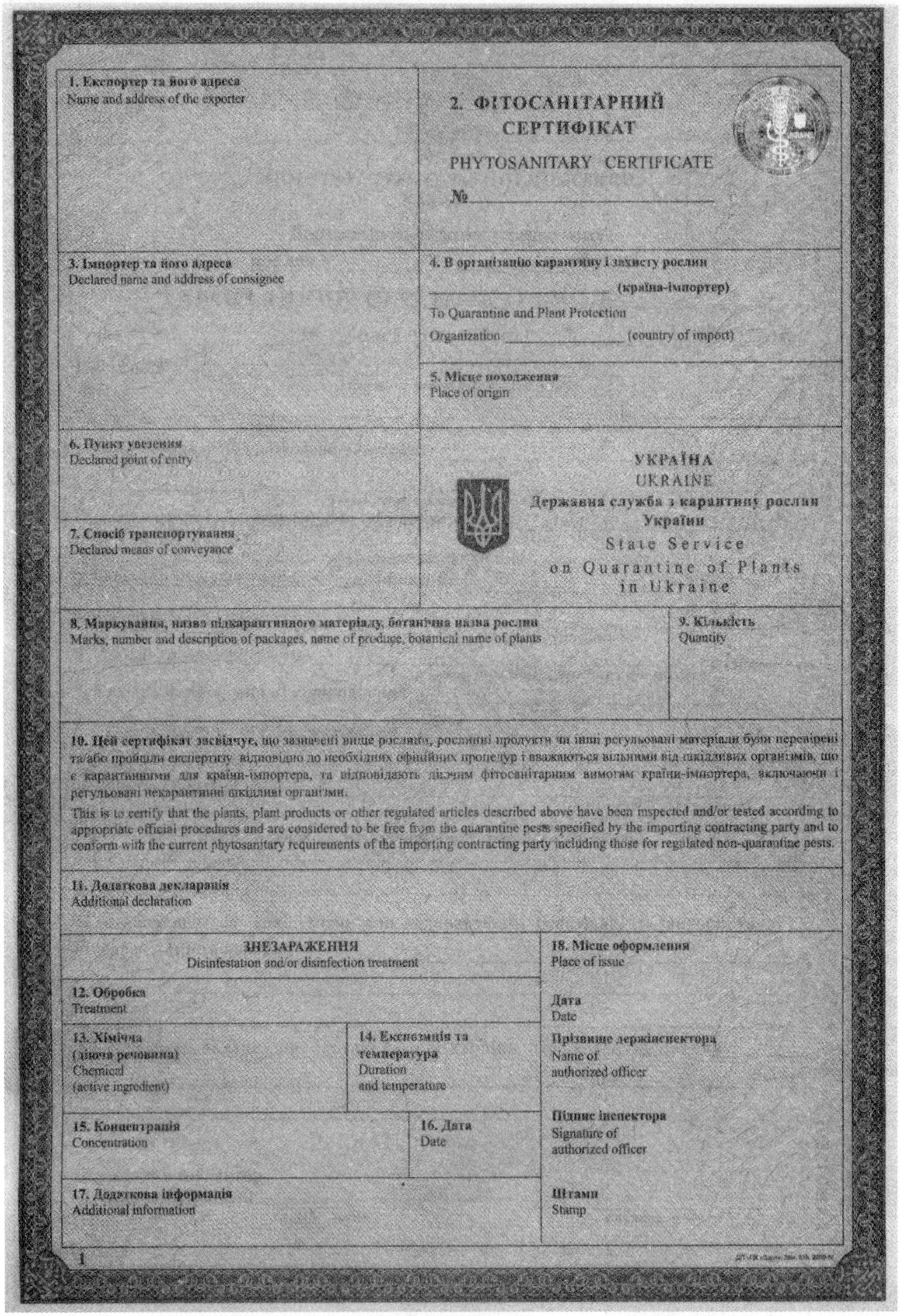

1. Експортер та його адреса
Name and address of the exporter

2. ФІТОСАНІТАРНИЙ СЕРТИФІКАТ
PHYTOSANITARY CERTIFICATE
№ ____________

3. Імпортер та його адреса
Declared name and address of consignee

4. В організацію карантину і захисту рослин ____________ (країна-імпортер)
To Quarantine and Plant Protection Organization ____________ (country of import)

5. Місце походження
Place of origin

6. Пункт увезення
Declared point of entry

УКРАЇНА
UKRAINE
Державна служба з карантину рослин України
State Service on Quarantine of Plants in Ukraine

7. Спосіб транспортування
Declared means of conveyance

8. Маркування, назва підкарантинного матеріалу, ботанічна назва рослин Marks, number and description of packages, name of produce, botanical name of plants	9. Кількість Quantity

10. Цей сертифікат засвідчує, що зазначені вище рослини, рослинні продукти чи інші регульовані матеріали були перевірені та/або пройшли експертизу відповідно до необхідних офіційних процедур і вважаються вільними від шкідливих організмів, що є карантинними для країни-імпортера, та відповідають діючим фітосанітарним вимогам країни-імпортера, включаючи і регульовані некарантинні шкідливі організми.

This is to certify that the plants, plant products or other regulated articles described above have been inspected and/or tested according to appropriate official procedures and are considered to be free from the quarantine pests specified by the importing contracting party and to conform with the current phytosanitary requirements of the importing contracting party including those for regulated non-quarantine pests.

11. Додаткова декларація
Additional declaration

ЗНЕЗАРАЖЕННЯ
Disinfestation and/or disinfection treatment

12. Обробка
Treatment

13. Хімічна (діюча речовина)
Chemical (active ingredient)

14. Експозиція та температура
Duration and temperature

15. Концентрація
Concentration

16. Дата
Date

17. Додаткова інформація
Additional information

18. Місце оформлення
Place of issue

Дата
Date

Прізвище держінспектора
Name of authorized officer

Підпис інспектора
Signature of authorized officer

Штамп
Stamp

1

Figure 9.7: A Phyto-Sanitary Certificate from the Ukraine

PSIs are often considered by exporters as a major annoyance, because inspection companies delve into information that exporters feel should not be divulged to a third party. In addition, because the inspection companies have the responsibility to make sure that the shipment is valued correctly, they can—and sometimes do—recommend a change in the value of the merchandise on the invoice. This generally infuriates sellers, justifiably, especially when they feel that the inspection company inflates the value of the goods to increase tariff revenues in the importing country.[40]

Inspection companies provide a valuable service to the importer; had Daewoo used their services, it would have discovered that its Chinese supplier shipped 15 containers of cement blocks rather than the expected plastic videocassette holders. Because the shipment was made on a letter of credit and because the documents were in perfect order, Daewoo had to pay for the shipment.[41]

9.4.4 Certificate of Analysis

A Certificate of Analysis is a document attesting to the composition of certain products; for example, it is used to determine the purity of certain chemicals (for example, the exact percentage of alcohol in a pure-alcohol shipment, which always has some amount of water) or the exact composition of certain mixtures (cement, steel alloys, plastic polymers) or the purity of a pharmaceutical chemical, as seen in Figure 9.6 on page 255.

A Certificate of Analysis is usually provided by an independent laboratory or another independent inspection company, such as SGS. In some cases, the exporter's laboratory is accredited and can provide its own certificate of analysis.

certificate of analysis A certificate, provided by an independent company, that attests that the goods conform to the physical description contained in the exporter's invoice.

9.4.5 Phyto-Sanitary Certificate

In the cases of transactions involving agricultural products and foodstuffs, the importing country often requires a Phyto-Sanitary Certificate along with the paperwork. Such a certificate is used to ensure that the product being shipped is free of (certain) diseases, that it is fit for human (or animal) consumption, that it is free of pests, and so forth.

This certificate is often written by the governmental agency in charge of agricultural and food services in the exporting country (such as the U.S. Department of Agriculture [USDA] or the U.S. Food and Drug Administration [FDA]), but it also can be obtained from a commercial third party. Figure 9.7 on the facing page shows a blank Phyto-Sanitary Certificate from the Ukraine.

phyto-sanitary certificate A certificate, provided by the agricultural authorities of the exporting country, that attests that the agricultural products exported are free of disease and pests.

9.4.6 Certificate of Certification

A number of countries have industrial standards that define quite clearly the technical characteristics that a part or product must possess before being allowed for sale in that country. For example, Germany has the *Deutsche Industrie Normen* (DIN), Japan has the Japanese Industrial Standards (JIS), and France has the *Normes Françaises* (NF). The United States has several of its own as well, including the American National Standard Institute (ANSI), the American Petroleum Institute (API), the Society of Automotive Engineers (SAE), the American Gas Association (AGA), all of which have developed performance standards for the products their member companies use.

certificate of certification A certificate, issued by an independent company, that attests that the goods conform to the industrial standards of the importing country.

CERTIFICATE

No: 50028/M/2011

Futura Surgicare Pvt. Ltd.

Office: No. 29, Balanjaneya Temple Street, Opp. M.S. Ramaiah Hospital, KGE Layout, RMV II Stage, Bangalore - 500 094 India

Factory: 86/C2, 3rd Main, 8th Cross, Industrial Suburb 2nd Stage, Yeshwanthpur, Bangalore - 560 022, India

Certification body of management systems hereby confirms that management system of above-mentioned organization has been assessed and certified as meeting requirements of

ISO 13485: 2003

for

Manufacture and Supply
of
Absorbable and Non Absorbable Surgical Sutures and Surgical Mesh.

Nova Dubnica, July 11th, 2011
The certificate is valid until July 10th, 2014

Marek Hudák

EVPÜ a. s., Trenčianska 19,
018 51 Nová Dubnica, Slovak Republic
www.evpu.sk
Page 1/1

SNAS
Reg. No. 010/Q-052

Figure 9.8: A Certificate of Certification from the Czech Republic

9.4 Import Documents

Food and Drug Administration
Ministry of Public Health, Thailand
CERTIFICATE OF FREE SALE

Ref. No. 1-5-03-99-10-00326   15 February 2010

It is hereby certified that the cosmetic product(s), listed herein, in compliance with the Cosmetic Act B.E. 2535 (1992 A.D.) of Thailand, manufactured by

SABOO (THAILAND) CO.,LTD,
39/108 OSATIS 1 VILLAGE, CHOCKCHAI 4 SOI 31/1,
LAD PRAW 53, LAD PRAW ROAD, BANGKOK, 10230 THAILAND,

may/can be freely sold in Thailand.

Product Listing : 104 Item(s)
1. SABOO NATURAL SOAP - AMERICANO COFFEE
2. SABOO NATURAL SOAP - APPLE
3. SABOO NATURAL SOAP - APRICOT

VALID UNTIL : 14 February 2012

(Pochanee Sinsomboon)
Pharmacist Cosmetic Control Division For Secretary-General
Food and Drug Administration

ห้ามนำเอกสารนี้ หรือ Ref. No. แสดงบนฉลากหรือประกาศโฆษณา
Cosmetic Control Group, Bureau of Cosmetic and Hazardous Substances Control
Food and Drug Administration, Ministry of Public Health 88/24 Tiwanon Road, Nonthaburi 11000, Thailand
Tel. : 66 2590 7244 , Fax. : 66 2591 8468

Figure 9.9: A Certificate of Free Sale from Thailand

certificate of conformity
Another name for a certificate of certification.

An importer may require a Certificate of Certification in order to ascertain that the product purchased meets the requirements of the standard and that the product can "pass" whatever certification procedures are required by the standard. In some countries, this certificate is called a Certificate of Conformity. Figure 9.8 on page 258 shows a Certificate of Certification issued by an independent company in the Czech Republic on behalf of a textile plant in India.

Although there are no well-defined procedures for a Certificate of Certification, it is often assumed that it is written by an independent company or by a trade association's representative. However, there are some cases in which the exporter writes and signs the certificate and has it countersigned by its Chamber of Commerce, in a way similar to the manner a Certificate of Origin is obtained.

9.4.7 Certificate of Free Sale

certificate of free sale
A certificate, issued by the exporter, that attests that the goods can be legally sold in the exporting country.

A Certificate of Free Sale attests that the product sold by the exporter can be sold legally in the country of export. Such a certificate is usually written and signed by the exporter and is countersigned by the local Chamber of Commerce or the regulatory agency that is responsible for this type of product. In the United States, that could be the United States Department of Agriculture or the Food and Drug Administration. Figure 9.9 on the preceding page shows a Certificate of Free Sale delivered by the Food and Drug Administration of Thailand.

A government or an importer concerned that the exporter might attempt to send some defective or second-rate products that it could not sell in its home country might require a Certificate of Free Sale to protect itself from this possibility. Neither the importing government nor the importer wants to be perceived as possible dumping grounds for products that could not legally be sold in the exporting country. This is a common fear if the requirements of the importing country are in some way less stringent than the ones of the exporting country.

This type of certificate has become relatively common for pharmaceutical imports. Because of stringent regulations, medical supplies have a relatively short shelf life in most developed countries, and some pharmaceutical firms sell or donate expired or soon-to-expire drugs to relief agencies in order to generate tax write-offs and generate goodwill.[42] While some may perceive this behavior as unethical, the companies argue that most drugs are equally useful beyond their arbitrarily determined expiration dates. Nevertheless, the governments of countries where these products are sold are requiring Certificates of Free Sale with increasing frequency.

In commercial transactions, a possible example of the use of a Certificate of Free Sale would have been when Coca-Cola introduced its Dasani purified water in the United Kingdom. By adding calcium to its purified water, the company also inadvertently added bromates, at a level that exceeded the standards of the United Kingdom, but not those of the remainder of the European Union and of the United States.[43,44] A concerned importer may have wanted to get a Certificate of Free Sale to make sure that it was not sold these sub-standard products.

9.4.8 Import License

Some countries, notably developing countries, will require the importer to obtain an import license, or an express authorization to import a given product or commodity. Often, this requirement is instituted to prevent the import of items considered luxurious or nonessential, especially in countries in which there is a short supply of foreign currency, which the government would rather spend on imports that enhance the country's economic position.

The process by which an importer obtains an import license varies from country to country, but it is often assumed that it is the responsibility of the importer. In that regard, the importer will probably need a *pro forma* invoice before requesting an import license.

import license
The express authorization, granted by the importing country's government to the importer, to import a certain product.

9.4.9 Consular Invoice

In some cases, an importing country can require the exporter to provide a consular invoice. A consular invoice is a regular commercial invoice, but printed on stationery provided by the country of import and officialized by its consulate in the exporter's country. For more details, see Section 9.2.3 on page 240.

9.4.10 Certificate of Insurance

Depending on the terms of trade of a specific shipment—and particularly on whether contracting insurance for the shipment is the responsibility of the exporter or of the importer, a responsibility determined by the Incoterms® rule chosen—the importer or the importing country can require a Certificate of Insurance with the shipment. This certificate is easily obtainable from the insurance company that insures the cargo. The insurance policy can be contracted for a single shipment or can be an umbrella policy, covering all of the shipments of a particular exporter. Figure 9.10 on the following page shows an example of umbrella coverage. For further details on the content of insurance policies in international shipments, see Chapter 10.

certificate of insurance
A certificate, issued by the exporter's insurance company, that attests that a particular shipment is insured.

9.5 Transportation Documents

9.5.1 Ocean Bill of Lading

An ocean bill of lading is a fundamental international shipping document used in ocean transportation. Its (almost) equivalent for shipments by air is called the air waybill (see Section 9.5.4). A bill of lading (see Figure 9.11 on page 264) is the contract of carriage used for the shipment of containers, automobiles, crates, and any form of cargo that does not requisition the capacity of the entire ship; when a shipment requires the use of the entire capacity of a ship—generally a bulk shipment of oil or other commodities—another document, called a charter party, is used (see Section 9.5.5).

ocean bill of lading
The contract of carriage between an ocean carrier and the shipper.

The ocean bill of lading when issued by an ocean carrier (a steamship company) is also frequently called a master bill of lading. When the bill of lading is issued by a Non-Vessel-Operating Common Carrier (NVOCC), it is often called a house bill of lading. A house bill of lading indicates the name of the ocean carrier and the master bill of lading.

non-vessel-operating common carrier
A shipment consolidator or freight forwarder that does not own means of transportation, but issues its own bills of lading, and therefore acts as a carrier.

The bill of lading is extremely important because it fulfills three roles in an international transaction:

shipper
The party in an international transaction-exporter or importer-that is responsible for arranging the main carriage.

- It is a contract. The shipping company agrees with the shipper—either the exporter or the importer, depending on the terms of trade (or Incoterms® rule) of the shipment, see Chapter 6—to transport the merchandise from one port to another for a given amount of money; it is a contract of carriage.

Associated MARINE INSURERS Agents Pty. Ltd. (ABN 41 006 104 007)

Agents for and owned by
CGU Insurance Limited (ACN 004 478 371 and Zurich Australian Insurance Limited (AC 000 296 640)

Victoria Branch
459 Collins Street, Melbourne 3000
GPO Box 1337L, Melbourne 3001
DX 135 Melbourne
Telephone: (03) 9629 2081
Facsimile: (03) 9614 6929
International + 61 3 9614 6929

Certificate of Marine Insurance — ORIGINAL

CGU Insurance Limited, Melbourne and Zurich Australian Insurance Ltd, Melbourne (the Insurers, each for its own equal proportion) through their agents Associated Marine Insurers Agents Pty. Ltd. hereby agree to insure against loss damage liability or expense in the manner hereinafter provided

SCHEDULE

Assured	ABC EXPORTING CO
Certificate No.	CASSIE012 Dated at MELBOURNE on 13TH AUGUST 2002

Marks and Numbers	Number and Kind of Packages / Description of Goods Insured	Insured Value (Figs.)
XYZ IMPORTS 2922.30	1 PCS STC SAMPLES	US$

Total Insured Value (in words)   US$ TWO THOUSAND NINE HUNDRED & TWENTY-TWO DOLLARS & THIRTY CENTS

Shipped per   CSCL FUZHOU V21   and conveyances on 13TH AUGUST   2002
From (commencement of transit)   MELBOURNE
to (final destination)   OSAKA
via

Conditions:
Institute Cargo Clauses (A)
Institute Radioactive Contamination Exclusion Clause
Institute Replacement Clause (Applicable only to Machinery)
Institute War Clauses (Cargo)
Institute Strikes Clauses (Cargo)
Institute Classification Clause
ISM Code Endorsement
On new machinery shipped uncontainerised or in open top containers or used machinery cover excludes rust, oxidisation and discolouration howsoever caused. Excess 0.50% of sum insured or A$250 whichever the greater in respect of machinery shipments.

(The Institute Clauses Referred to are those current at the date of this Certificate)

Claims Payable By   COMMERCIAL UNION ASSURANCE CO PLC TEL: 351 2 6068170

In the event of loss or damage which may give rise to a claim under this Insurance, immediate notice of such loss or damage should be given to and a survey report obtained from   ASSOCIATED MARINE INSURERS AGENTS PTY LTD
before submitting documents in accordance with the procedure stated over.

On Behalf of the Insurers..

M3451

Figure 9.10: A Certificate of Insurance from Australia

- It is a receipt for the goods. When the shipping company signs the bill of lading, it is acknowledging that it has received the goods in good condition and that everything seems in proper order. The document acts as a receipt for the goods; the shipping company accepts responsibility for the goods until their port of destination.

  However, in some cases, the shipping company finds that something is wrong with the merchandise it is picking up (*e.g.*, the drums in which the merchandise is contained are rusty, there are some damaged crates, the merchandise was loaded when it was raining, the merchandise was packaged in crates that are too weak to sustain an ocean voyage) and it does not want to assume responsibility for that condition. In those cases, the shipping company will make a note about the issue or write an exception on the bill of lading of what it has observed. The bill of lading then becomes a soiled bill of lading or a foul bill of lading.

  In the opposite situation (*i.e.*, when the shipping company finds everything in proper order at the time of loading and does not record any reservations at the receipt of the goods), the bill of lading is considered clean.

  In general, letters of credit and documentary collection transactions require a clean bill of lading; should the bill of lading be soiled, it would require an amendment to the letter of credit. Carriers may not accept goods for transportation if loading them would result in a soiled bill of lading.

- It is a certificate of title. The document that the shipping company will need to see to authorize the release of the goods in the port of destination will also be the bill of lading. It is commonly considered that the company that has the original of the bill of lading is the one to which the goods belong, or that the bill of lading is a Certificate of Title.

  There are two types of bills of lading in this respect: the straight bill of lading is one on which the name of the consignee (the person or company that will pick up the goods at the port of destination) is specified. On the other hand, a to-order bill of lading is one in which the name of the consignee is left blank or the term "to order" is written. This means that the bill of lading is negotiable; in other words, it allows the sale of the cargo while it is at sea. This is a common occurrence in certain industries, notably in the oil business, in which it is not unusual to see a specific cargo change hands several times during a given voyage. In some cases, the cargo is sold to a company that wants it delivered to a different port, and the shipping company is asked to arrange for that alternative.

soiled bill of lading
A bill of lading that reflects the fact that the carrier did not receive the goods in good condition.

foul bill of lading
A bill of lading that reflects the fact that the carrier did not receive the goods in good condition.

clean bill of lading
A bill of lading that reflects the fact that the carrier received the goods in good condition.

carrier
The company that transports the goods on its vessel, truck, or train.

straight bill of lading
A bill of lading on which the name of the consignee has been entered.

consignee
The party to whom the goods should be surrendered at destination.

to-order bill of lading
A bill of lading on which the name of the consignee is marked "to order." A negotiable bill of lading.

negotiable bill of lading
A bill of lading on which the name of the consignee has been left blank.

9.5.2 Uniform Bill of Lading

The uniform bill of lading is a document that fulfills the same functions as an ocean bill of lading but is used either for inland transportation between the exporter's place of business and the port of departure, or for land transportation (rail or road) between the exporter and a foreign customer. In the immense majority of cases, the uniform bill of lading is a straight bill of lading. The uniform bill of lading also acts as a receipt for the goods and as a contract between the shipper and the carrier.

uniform bill of lading
A bill of lading used for transportation by truck or train, domestically or internationally.

Shipper MATEXIM COMPANY HOANG QUOC VIET STR., CAU GIAY DIST., HA NOI CITY, VIETNAM		Document No. VN/ 02459	Bill of Lading No. **SHINING LINES** VN 919242
		Export references Shipper's Ref. 987654	
Consignee (not negotiable unless consigned to order) OOO "KORVET TEKHKOR" LIT. A 10 BLDG, GONCHARNAYA STR. 193036 SAINT PETERSBURG RUSSIAN FEDERATION		Forwarding agent – references (complete names and addresses) Shining Ocean Lines 345 Strumond Street Hong Kong	
Notify party (see Clause 19) OOO "KORVET TEKHKOR" LIT. A 10 BLDG, GONCHARNAYA STR. 193036 SAINT PETERSBURG RUSSIAN FEDERATION		Unless marked "NON NEGOTIABLE/EXPRESS BILL", one original BILL of Lading must be surrendered endorsed in exchange in for the goods or delivery order. For the release of goods apply to: Shining Ocean Lines Warehouse Complex No. 3 Port of Saint Petersburg 193036 Saint Petersburg Russian Federation Tel. : 00132 628990 Fax : 00132 628991	
Pre-carriage by	Place of receipt by pre-carrier Hai Phong Vietnam		
Vessel/Voy. No. V.90 MV Shining Star	Port of loading Hai Phong	On carriage to	
Port of discharge Saint Petersburg	Place of delivery by on-carrier Saint Petersburg		

Marks and Numbers	Number of Container(s) or pkgs	Kind of packages – description of goods	Gross weight (kilos)	Measurement (cubic metres)
See attached list	30	Containers	26,000 net each 27,000 gross 810,000 total	72.5 each 2175 total

Total number of Container(s) or Pkgs 30	Freight payable by Origin	Excess Value Declaration: Refer to Clause 13 and 14 on reverse side. N/A			
Freight and charges		Quantity based on	Rate	Per	Prepaid	Collect

Freight and charges	Quantity based on	Rate	Per	Prepaid	Collect
USD 25,500 Stevedoring	30	850	Cont.	X	
USD 6,000 Document Prep.	30	200	Cont.	X	
USD 350 Storage Fees					
USD 2,000					
TOTAL: USD 33,850					

| RECEIVED by the carrier from the shipper in apparent good order and condition (unless otherwise noted herein) the total number or quantity of containers or other packages or units indicated stated by the shipper to comprise the goods specified for carriage subject to all the terms hereof (INCLUDING THE TERMS ON PAGE 1 HEREOF AND THE TERMS OF THE CARRIER'S APPLICATION TARIFF) from the place of receipt or the port of loading, whichever is applicable to the port of discharge or the place of the delivery, whichever is applicable. In accepting this Bill of Lading the merchant expressly accepts and agrees to all its terms, conditions and exceptions whether printed, stamped or written, or otherwise incorporated, notwithstanding the non-signing of this Bill of Lading by the merchant | IN WITNESS whereof the number of the original Bills of Lading stated below all of this tenor and date has been signed, one of which being accomplished, the other(s) to stand void.
Number of original B(S)/L

These commodities, technology or software were exported from the U.S in Accordance with the Export Administration Regulations. Diversion contrary to U.S. law Prohibited. | Place of B(S)/L issue
Cleveland

SHINING OCEAN SERVICES
As Agents for the Carrier
SHINING OCEAN LINES | DATE
07/24/13

COPY
Not Negotiable |

Figure 9.11: An Ocean Bill of Lading from Hong Kong SAR

9.5 Transportation Documents

Doc No.	Destination Airport Code MEL (Melbourne)	Flight 5698	Date 2013-07-24	**AIR WAYBILL** NON-NEGOTIABLE **TRANS-AIR, INC.**	
Consignee Account No. MEL 341	Consignee Order No.				
Consignee Name and Address Australian Importers 4/2 Wilson Avenue Brunswick, Victoria 3089, Australia				Carrier / Agent TRANS-AIR, Inc., Cleveland	
				The shipper certifies that the particulars on the face hereof are correct, agrees to the Conditions on Reverse hereof, accepts that carrier's liability is limited as stated, and accepts such value unless a higher value for carriage is declared.	
Shipper Account No.	Shipper's Reference No. 072306-001				
Shipper Name and Address Ebert Pipe Organs, Inc. 1234 Carnegie Avenue Cleveland, OH 44111, USA				These commodities, technologies or software were exported from the United States in accordance with the Export Administration regulations. Diversion contrary to U.S. Law prohibited.	

No of pieces or packages	Dimensions			Weight		Carrier certifies goods described herein were received for carriage subject to the conditions on the reverse thereof, the goods then being in apparent good order and condition except as noted hereon.	
	Length	Width	Height	lbs	kg	Quantity, Description and Marks	
3	1.2 m	0.6 m	0.4 m	429.00	195.00	Pipe organ blowers (3) Boxes marked "Ebert Pipe Organs, Inc" FRAGILE Each crate sealed with seals No: 158062, 158063 and 158064.	
Total Pieces 3	Cubic Content 86,400 cm³			Total Dimensional Weight 14.4 kg			
Shipper's Declared Value USD 2,925.00				Total Gross Weight 195.00 kg			
Total Freight Charge USD 585.00				Chargeable Weight 195	Commodity No. 8414	Rate 3/kg	Air Carriage To MEL Qantas To LAX United
Inbound Freight Advance							
Origin Handling Fees USD 57.00		FSH	Detail of all origin and handling fees USD 22.80		SSF	USD 43.20	
USD 128.70	Shipper's Requested Insurance Fee	Amount USD 3,217.50		Rate USD 0.04		If the shipper has requested insurance as provided for, shipment is insured in the amount specified by the shipper, recovery being limited to actual loss.	
USD 30.00	Pickup Charge					Remit to: TRANS-AIR, Inc. 3450 United Avenue St Louis, MO 63011	
USD 800.70	TOTAL DUE CARRIER					Carrier's Air Waybill No. CLE 23012013-0007	

1. SHIPPER (ORIGINAL). THIS COPY FOR YOUR FILES. THIS IS NOT AN INVOICE.

Figure 9.12: An Air Waybill from the United States

9.5.3 Intermodal Bill of Lading

intermodal bill of lading
A bill of lading used for transportation that uses more than one mode of transportation, domestically or internationally.

The intermodal bill of lading is a document that reflects the substantial increase in the number of international shipments in which the exporter delivers the goods to a carrier who will arrange for the transportation and delivery of the shipment until its final destination. Because the shipment is likely to take more than one mode of transportation, it is called an intermodal shipment.

Intermodal bills of lading cover several legs of an international shipment. They are straight bills of lading in the majority of cases. Intermodal bills of lading are also receipts for the goods and evidence of a contract of carriage between the shipper and the carrier.

9.5.4 Air Waybill

air waybill
A bill of lading used for transportation by air, domestically or internationally.

An air waybill is a document that fulfills the same function as an ocean bill of lading, but applies only to airfreight. An air waybill is always a straight air waybill and is therefore non-negotiable (see Figure 9.12 on the preceding page). This can be easily understood because, in most cases, the documents and the merchandise arrive approximately at the same time in the country of destination, and there is literally no time to sell the cargo while it is in transit. As the other bills of lading, it is also a receipt for the goods and a contract between the shipper and the air carrier.

9.5.5 Charter Parties

charter party
A type of contract of carriage, in which the shipper uses all or most of the carrying capacity of the ship to transport commodities.

wet lease
A type of leasing contract in which an airplane is leased, along with a crew, maintenance services, insurance, and fuel.

ACMI lease
A type of leasing contract in which an airplane is leased, along with a crew, maintenance services, and insurance.

dry lease
A type of leasing contract in which only the airplane is leased.

damp lease
A type of leasing contract in which an airplane is leased, with maintenance and insurance, but no crew.

Whenever it is shipping bulk commodities (oil, ores, grains, polymers, sand, cement, sugar, and so on), an exporter does so in such large quantities that an entire ship is often necessary to accommodate the goods. In those cases, the ocean bill of lading is not the document used as the contract of carriage; the contract between the carrier and the shipper is called a charter party.

Charter parties are fairly complex, as they can be negotiated for a single shipment (a voyage charter party) or for a period of time (a time charter party); charter parties that cover more than one voyage but do not demand the exclusive use of the ship for a specific period of time (for example, one shipment every other month) are called contracts of affreightment. Moreover, some shippers negotiate charter parties that only include the use of the ship, exclusive of the boat's crew, as the shipper provides the captain and the crew (a bareboat charter party). Finally, because there are different requirements for different commodities, most charter parties are industry specific (oil, grain, gas, and so forth).

The owner of a freight aircraft can lease its equipment under four types of leases, whether for a single voyage or for a duration of time: (1) A wet-lease agreement under which the owner of the aircraft provides the airplane, a flight crew, maintenance services, insurance, and fuel. (2) An ACMI lease that includes aircraft, crew, maintenance and insurance, but not fuel. (3) A dry lease, under which the owner provides only the aircraft. (4) A damp lease under which the owner provides fewer services than in a wet lease, but more than in a dry lease. For example, a damp lease could include the aircraft, maintenance, and insurance, but not the crew, which would need to be hired by the lessee. In all cases, the lessee has to cover the additional costs of operating the aircraft, from simply paying landing fees in a wet lease, to obtaining a crew, securing insurance and providing maintenance in a dry lease.

9.5.6 Packing List

A packing list always accompanies the shipment. It is a detailed document provided by the exporter that spells out how many containers there are in the shipment and which merchandise is packaged in each container (see Figure 9.13 for an example). Because of the recent emphasis placed by the International Maritime Organization and world governments on security, packing lists have become more precise; while at one time it was acceptable to mention "freight all kinds," often abbreviated FAK, it is now necessary to clearly list all items in a shipment, in as detailed a manner as possible. Whenever authorities determine that a shipment presents some risks and should be inspected, a detailed packing list can prevent the inspection and avoid further delays.

packing list
A detailed list of the contents of a shipment.

Baking Technologies, Inc. – Packing List			
Shipper/ Exporter: Baking Technologies, Inc. 45 South 7th street Minneapolis, MN 55402 USA	Ultimate Consignee: Mendez Panaderias S.A. Col Roma Mexico D.F., C.P. 0670 Attention: Carlos Mendez	Bill To: Mendez Panaderias S.A. Col Roma Mexico D.F., C.P. 0670 Attention: Carlos Mendez	Intermediate Consignee Galfiro Montemayor brokers Avenida de Colombia 1025 Veracruz, Mexico
Commercial Invoice No.: BT-1638 Order No.: M3652 AWB/BL Number: MXVZ9707503 Date Of Shipment: 18Feb03 Currency: USD Freight: Prepay	Total number of Packages: 4 Total Gross Weight (Lbs): 6,000 Total Gross Weight (Kgs): 2,724 Total Net Weight (Lbs): 4,000 Total net Weight (Kgs): 1,816 Total Cubic Feet: 1,680 Total Cubic Meters: 47.57	Transportation: Truck via Yellow Freight to Houston, from Houston Ocean Carrier Via President Lines. Conditions of Sale and Terms of Payment: CPT Veracruz, Mexico per Incoterms 2000 Payable by letter of Credit	

Shipment Line No.	Item Number	Item Description, Sales Order No., Customer PO No.	Shipped Quantity	Packaging Type	Dimensions Inches			Dimensions centimeters			Per package gross weight	
					L	W	H	L	W	H	LBS.	KGS.
1	BT002043	Baking/Kneading Equipment Tariff Classification 8438.10	1	Crate	96	90	84	37	35	33	1,500	681
2	BT002043	Baking/Kneading Equipment Tariff Classification 8438.10	1	Crate	96	90	84	37	35	33	1,500	681
3	BT002043	Baking/Kneading Equipment Tariff Classification 8438.10	1	Crate	96	90	84	37	35	33	1,500	681
4	BT002043	Baking/Kneading Equipment Tariff Classification 8438.10	1	Crate	96	90	84	37	35	33	1,500	681

Country of Origin: USA
Marks: addressed and numbered 1 of 4, 2 of 4....

Figure 9.13: A Packing List from the United States

9.5.7 Shipper's Letter of Instruction

A Shipper's Letter of Instruction is delivered to the shipping company when the shipper—again, either the exporter or the importer, depending on the terms of trade, or Incoterms® rule chosen for the transaction—wants specific steps taken during the transport of the merchandise. For example, the shipper may request that the cargo be stowed below deck (if the cargo is susceptible to become wet) or stowed at the "water line" (*i.e.*, the location in the ship that experiences the least movement), or even above deck (if the cargo is dangerous). When the cargo is livestock, the Shipper's Letter of Instruction explains what to do in most situations.

shipper's letter of instruction
A document in which the shipper spells out how it wants the carrier to handle the goods while they are in transit.

9.5.8 Shipments of Dangerous Goods

International shipments of dangerous goods are regulated by either the International Maritime Organization's International Maritime Dangerous Goods Code,[45] by the International Air Transport Association's Dangerous Goods Regulations,[46] by the International Civil Aviation Organization's Technical Instructions for the Safe Transport of Dangerous Goods by Air,[47] or by local shipment codes, such as the United States Code of Federal Regulations, Title 49 (abbreviated 49CFR).[48]

There are such an extensive number of regulations that can affect a shipment of hazardous goods that it is always best to entrust a specialized shipper to handle the paperwork associated with such a shipment. This statement is also true for the packing and the labeling of the goods. There are often very specific forms to be filled out; in the case of an air shipment, a Shipper's Declaration for Dangerous Goods must be provided, and a specific mention must be made on the air waybill that the shipment contains dangerous goods. In some cases, the air waybill must also specify that the cargo cannot be shipped on a passenger airplane, but only on a cargo airplane. Similar restrictions must also be observed for ocean, road, and railroad cargoes.

The complexity of the rules is such that in an audit conducted by the Canadian Coast Guard in 1995, 66 percent of hazardous shipments inspected were found to have some rule violation: 41 percent did not have the correct markings, 31 percent did not have the correct documentation, 19 percent were incorrectly stowed (secured in the containers or on the ship), and so on.[49]

Shipping Live Animals

The business of shipping live animals is quite substantial: each year, many racehorses fly from one track to another,[50] and many exotic animals fly from one zoo to another. In 2011, the Chicago Shedd Aquarium shipped seven whales and two dolphins from Chicago to Connecticut and back during the renovation of its oceanarium.[51] It is also the part of international shipping in which the Shipper's Letter of Instruction is critical, as every shipment is different because every animal has its own requirements regarding temperature, humidity, and its tolerance for shipment delays.

As he related it in a lengthy article,[52] Barry Lopez spent days accompanying airfreight cargo pilots on 40 flights, totaling 110,000 nautical miles, to report on this part of international lore.

In some legs of his journey, the cargo included Vietnamese potbelly pigs, a killer whale, racehorses, and ostriches. In these situations, the shipper can ask for very specific considerations. Lopez reports that on his flight from Chicago to Tokyo, during which he traveled with sixteen horses, "[t]he pilot made a shallow climb out of Chicago to lessen the strain on the horses' back legs." (It has since become common practice to ship horses facing the rear of the plane to lessen the strain on their necks and front legs.) When the plane hit some turbulence, the pilot changed altitude and a handler went in the cargo hold to soothe the animals.

Actually, the business of shipping live animals by air is so difficult to manage that the International Air Transport Association created a set of Live Animal

9.5 Transportation Documents

Regulations[53].

Live animals are also shipped by ocean. Australia, New Zealand, and Argentina ship a large number of sheep to the Middle East, and live cattle travels from Australia to Southeast Asia. These shipments of animals require much care while they travel thousands of miles to their destination. The World Organisation for Animal Health (OIE) has developed guidelines for the transport of animals by sea,[54] but here again, the shipper communicates its requirements for the handling of the live cargo with precise instructions in its Letter of Instruction.

Figure 9.14: Horses Shipped by Air Require a Detailed Letter of Instruction
Photo ©José Ramón Valero, courtesy of MyAviation.net. Used with permission.

9.5.9 Manifest

The manifest is a shipping document that is quite dissimilar to the documents seen so far in this chapter. The manifest is a document created by the carrier, or shipping company—the operator of the ship or the aircraft—that lists the exact makeup of the cargo, its ownership, its port of origin and its port of destination, whether there are specific handling instructions, and so forth. Although officially an internal document of the shipping company, it is often used by public authorities to verify that rules and regulations are respected. The following example may clarify this point.

manifest
A document, internal to the shipping company (carrier), that lists all cargoes onboard the transportation vehicle.

A number of Middle Eastern countries—Jordan, Saudi Arabia, the United Arab Emirates, Syria, Kuwait, Iraq, Iran, and Libya—engaged in what was referred to as the Arab embargo of Israel; no ship that delivered goods to these Arab nations could have stopped (or be planning to stop) in any Israeli port or have cargo coming from or going to Israel. The manifest is used by authorities in those countries to determine whether the ship or its cargo has had any "unlawful" contact with Israel.[55] American firms dealing in that region were prohibited from honoring this embargo, a situation that made for complicated arrangements, which both Israel and its neighbors conveniently chose to ignore—business is business, after all. In its heyday, the boycott was somewhat bothersome, but was widely derided as ineffective; in 2013, the boycott has essentially disappeared, with Jordan having signed a peace treaty with Israel, and the Gulf Cooperation Council countries no longer honoring it, and having called for an end to it.

9.6 Electronic Data Interchange

9.6.1 Proprietary Commercial Electronic Data Interchange

electronic data interchange (EDI) A method to send documents from one company to another, using electronic means.

The alternative way to send documents overseas is through Electronic Data Interchange (EDI) rather than by airmail. The best way to define EDI is to determine what it is not: first, it is not a fax, which transmits only a reproduction of a paper document. A fax is essentially a copy machine where the original is in one location and the copy is in another location. Second, EDI is not e-mail (electronic mail). E-mail is only the electronic transmission of text, as in a letter or a memo, for which there is no need to have a specified format ahead of time.

EDI is an electronic exchange of documents, from computer to computer, following a format to which both the sending and the receiving parties have agreed. There are two areas in which the agreement to a common format is crucial:

- First, the sender and the recipient have to agree to a technical EDI understanding; for example, the choice of a computer protocol, the determination of a standard outline—which electronic field corresponds to which information on the document (sender, consignee, product description, purchase order number, invoice number, and so forth)—and the possible use of a third-party intermediary to translate one electronic format into another or archive the transmissions between the parties. Such translating service providers are called Value-Added Networks (VANs). They also archive whatever transmission takes place between the two parties.

  Currently, there are only a few international agreements on EDI formats; they tend to be company, industry, or country specific. The most likely to prevail internationally is the standard developed by the United Nations Working Party on the Facilitation of International Trade Procedures of the Committee on Trade of the Economic Commission for Europe (nicknamed WP4, for short), called the United Nations Electronic Data Interchange for Administration, Commerce, and Transport (UN-EDIFACT), which has been accepted by a significant number of countries, including the United States. Actually some U.S. firms have adopted EDIFACT for all of their EDI communications with their suppliers; however, the prevailing EDI standard in the United States is the ANSI X12 format.

- The second issue is the existence of a legal agreement between the parties; not only should the definition of responsibilities (acknowledgment of an EDI transmission, procedure to follow when there is a defective transmission, confidentiality of the data) be specified, but legal issues have to be addressed, such as the timing of the contract formation, liability for errors in the communication, and the evidentiary value of messages—whether and how they can be introduced in a court proceeding.

To date, there have been several efforts made to create a universal EDI agreement; the International Chamber of Commerce has Uniform Rules of Conduct for Interchange of Trade Data by Teletransmission (UNCID), and several EDI associations have created their own versions. Nevertheless, there is yet no agreement that has international acceptance, and courts still tend to rely on laws designed for written documents whenever there are problems.

9.6.2 Network Electronic Data Interchange

Another well-developed EDI system is the one that was developed by the Society for Worldwide Interbank Financial Telecommunication (SWIFT) to facilitate the exchange of banking documents such as letters of credit. Since banks are essentially all members of the SWIFT system, they can exchange secure messages with each other. Because of a large number of safeguards in the network, banks can rely on the data transmitted over the network, and a letter of credit transmitted by SWIFT is considered genuine (as good as a paper original). In addition, the SWIFT network adds new services regularly, such as Interbank File Transfers (in free form such as database files, graphs, spreadsheets) over a secure network, a requirement that is of paramount importance to the banks. The security and reliability of the network is ascertained by the protocols that the computers in the network must follow. Each login is recorded and must be cleared, messages must first be stored before they are sent, there must be positive confirmation of each message by the recipient, there are redundant links, there is a double backup of each file, and so forth.

Because of the reliability of its system—and its experience in that area—SWIFT created the Bolero network. Bolero is similar to the SWIFT banking network, but it allows the transmission of all sorts of documents (specifically logistics documents) such as invoices, bills of lading, certificates, and so on; however, Bolero does not support payment through the network. Bolero became active in September 1999.

Such an EDI network is shared by several hundreds of customers worldwide, which makes it very different from proprietary EDI systems because communications between member parties are authenticated and there is a common standard. Therefore, both of the issues of proprietary EDI are overcome. It is a much more efficient way of exchanging information.

Bolero is currently competing with TradeCard on many points; Bolero has the distinct advantage that it is supported by a company with which bankers have dealt for a long time and trust. TradeCard has the advantage of offering payment options through its network; time will tell whether both of these systems will remain or whether one will start dominating the business. One thing is certain, though: paper documents are in jeopardy.

9.7 Document Preparation as a Marketing Tool

It should be relatively clear by now that accurate and timely documents are an essential part of international logistics and of the smooth transfer of goods from an exporter to an importer:

- The *pro forma* invoice must be a perfect preview of the actual invoice. Otherwise, payment through the letter of credit can be affected (*i.e.*, the actual invoice does not match the requirements of the letter of credit and both parties have to pay for amendments) or Customs clearance can be delayed because the actual invoice does not match the import license.

- The commercial invoice must be clear, detailed, and precise. It must include all the information that is necessary for the importer to clear Customs and minimize the duty that it has to pay (*i.e.*, description, Harmonized System number, weight, size, number of packages, domestic transportation costs, insurance costs, terminal charges, stevedoring charges, international transportation costs, and so on). It also minimizes the probability of an inspection.

- Certificates of many kinds have to be provided. They have to be properly prepared, signed, and occasionally stamped and notarized to facilitate the goods' Customs clearance in the importing country.

- The correct number of originals and copies of a multitude of documents must be prepared (invoices, certificates, and so on) or collected (bill of lading). A discrepancy in the number of originals can delay Customs clearance until another original is express mailed to the importer.

- The packing list must be prepared carefully and precisely. An incomplete or imprecise packing list increases the probability of a Customs inspection.

- The export paperwork must be prepared and filed correctly and in a timely manner. Several countries, including the United States, will not allow goods to be loaded if there are issues with the export paperwork (SED).

Any failure to provide these documents or to provide complete and accurate documents in a timely manner is likely to delay a shipment, generate additional costs by requiring last-minute mailings of critical documents, or create "headaches" for one or more of the parties involved in the transaction. Unfortunately, problems with documents are common, although they are clearly avoidable in most instances.

Because the responsibility of proper document preparation falls mostly on the exporter, regardless of the Incoterms® rule used in a transaction, an exporter can turn its ability to do a good and thorough job in this aspect of international logistics into a marketing advantage. An exporter intent on increasing its sales should therefore be thorough and meticulous in the way it prepares the documents that it provides to the importer. This should be reflected in the first contact, the *pro forma* invoice, and be communicated to the importer by emphasizing the experience of the company at providing accurate and thorough documents.

NOTES

Review and Discussion Questions

1. There are three types of invoices mentioned in this chapter. Explain each one of them and tell which is truly an invoice and which is not.

2. Explain why a country could consider having no deficit in its balance of trade even though the value of its exports represents only 98 percent of the value of its imports.

3. What documents are necessary for exporting from the United States?

4. There are many different types of certificates that can be requested by the importing country or the importer. Describe three of them.

5. A pre-shipment inspection certificate can be requested by the importing country or by the importer. Why would a country request one? Why would an importer request one?

6. The ocean bill of lading has three general functions. Explain each one in detail and tell what alternative "types" of ocean bills of lading there are.

7. What are the advantages of conducting international trade using electronic document transmissions, such as EDI, Bolero, and TradeCard?

Notes

[1] Mehta, Ravi R. Singh, "Freak and Faulty L/C's from Third World and Eastern Europe," *The Exporter*, September 1997, pp. 15-17.

[2] Scannicchio, Tommaso, "Important Decision of the Italian Supreme Court of Cassazione in the Matter of Electronic Documents," *Electronic Law Journals*, JILT 2002, http://www2.warwick.ac.uk/fac/soc/law/elj/jilt/2002_2/scannicchio/#a3, retrieved May 27, 2009.

[3] *A Basic Guide to Exporting*, Export.gov, http://export.gov/basicguide/eg_main_017244.asp, retrieved June 17, 2013.

[4] *Ibid.*

[5] "Interactive Tariff and Trade DataWeb," United States International Trade Commission, http://dataweb.usitc.gov/, retrieved July 10, 2013.

[6] Lelyveld, Michael S., "Electronic Export Filings Triple, Boosting Census," *Journal of Commerce*, April 20, 1998, p. 6A.

[7] Tirschwell, Peter, "The New Cost of Exporting," *JoC Week*, August 14-20, 2000, p. 4.

[8] Kulish, Eric, "Mandatory AES debuts," *American Shipper*, July 2008, pp. 38-45.

[9] Schwirtz, Michael, "Tourist in Russia Stumbles into Legal Predicament," *The New York Times*, August 27, 2007.

[10] Meier, Barry, "The Costly, Bitter Case of the Coins of Elmali," *The New York Times*, September 24, 1998.

[11] Eakin, Hugh, and Elizabetta Povoledo, "Ceding Art to Italy, Met Avoids Showdown," *The New York Times*, February 21, 2006.

[12] Eakin, Hugh, "Getty Museum Will Return 2 Antiquities to Greece," *The New York Times*, July 10, 2006.

[13] "Elmalı Treasure Finally on Display at Home," *Hurriyet Daily News*, October 2, 2009, http://www.hurriyetdailynews.com/default.aspx?pageid=438&n=elmali-sikkeleri-ait-oldugu-topraklarda-2009-10-27, retrieved June 17, 2013.

[14] Bradsher, Keith, "Specialists in Rare Earths Say a Trade Case Against China May Be Too Late," *The New York Times*, March 13, 2012.

[15] Blas, Javier, "Cocoa Soars as Traders back Ivory Coast Ban," *Financial Times*, January 25, 2011, p. 23.

[16] Kramer, Andrew, "Restrictions on Exports Ignite Protests in Belarus," *The New York Times*, June 13, 2011.

[17] Kirkpatrick, David, "China Seizure Halts Delivery of U.S. Book," *The New York Times*, August 28, 2000.

[18] Clayton, Gary E., "Eurocrats Try to Stop Data at Border," *The Wall Street Journal*, November 2, 1998, p. A34.

[19] Kim, Jeonghoi, "Recent Trends in Export Restrictions," *OECD Trade Policy Papers*, No. 101, OECD Publishing, 2010. http://dx.doi.org/10.1787/5kmbjx63sl27-en.

[20] Litman, Gary V., and John M. Breen "Overview of Federal Export Restriction Programs," in *Export Practice: Customs and International Trade Law*, Terence P. Stewart, ed. New York: Practicing Law Institute.

[21] U.S. Export Administration Regulations Database, Bureau of Export Administration, http://www.access.gpo.gov/bis/ear/ear_data.html, retrieved June 18, 2013.

[22] Klein, Alec, "The Techies Grumbled, but Polaroid's Pocket Turned into a Huge Hit," *The Wall Street Journal*, May 2, 2000, p. A1.

[23] Gallacher, David, "Encryption Export Restrictions Loosened under New Rules that Reduce Pre-Review and Reporting Requirements," Government Contracts Blog—Sheppard-Mullin, November 17, 2008, http://www.governmentcontractslawblog.com/2008/11/articles/export-controls/encryption-export-restrictions-loosened-under-new-rules-that-reduce-prereview-and-reporting-requirements, retrieved June 18, 2013.

[24] U.S. Export Administration Regulations Database, Bureau of Export Administration, http://www.access.gpo.gov/bis/ear/ear_data.html, retrieved June 18, 2013.

[25] *Introduction to Commerce Department Export Controls*, March 2007, Bureau of Industry and Security, http://www.bis.doc.gov/licensing/bis_exports2.pdf, retrieved May 28, 2009.

[26] "OFAC Sanctions Programs and Country Information," U.S. Department of the Treasury, Office of Foreign Asset Control, http://www.treasury.gov/resource-center/sanctions/Programs/Pages/Programs.aspx, retrieved June 18, 2013.

[27] "Deemed Exports: Questions and Answers," Bureau of Industry and Security, United States Department of Commerce, http://www.bis.doc.gov/deemedexports/deemedexportsfaqs.html, retrieved June 18, 2013.

[28] *Don't Let This Happen to You! Actual Investigations of Export Controls and Anti-Boycott Regulations*, December 2010 Edition, Bureau of Industry and Security, United States Department of Commerce, http://www.bis.doc.gov/complianceandenforcement/dontletthishappentoyou-2010.pdf.

[29] Kim, Jeonghoi, "Recent Trends in Export Restrictions," *OECD Trade Policy Papers*, No. 101, OECD Publishing, 2010. http://dx.doi.org/10.1787/5kmbjx63sl27-en.

[30] Wilson, William, D. Demcey Johnson, and Bruce L. Dahl, "Transparency and Export Subsidies in International Wheat Competition," *Agricultural Economic Reports*, No. 415, May 1999, http://ageconsearch.umn.edu/bitstream/23208/1/aer415.pdf.

[31] Barrionuevo, Alexei, "Argentina Blocks Farm Export Tax," *The New York Times*, July 18,

2008.

[32] Nguyen, Tri Khiem, "Vietnam Rice Trade, Policy and Future Outlook," Agri Benchmark Project, www.agribenchmark.org/fileadmin/...rice/rice_trade_VN_130319.pdf, retrieved June 18, 2013.

[33] "Quota Removal Secures Russia Platinum Exports," Reuters, January 17, 2007, http://uk.reuters.com/article/businessIndustry/idUKL1532931620070117, retrieved June 18, 2013.

[34] Rose, Scott, "WTO Admits Russia as 156th Member to Cap 18-Year Talks: Economy," Bloomberg News, August 22, 2012, http://www.bloomberg.com/news/2012-08-22/wto-admits-russia-as-156th-member-after-two-decades-of-talks-1-.html, retrieved June 18, 2013.

[35] "Doing Business: Trading Across Borders," International Finance Corporation, The World Bank, http://www.doingbusiness.org/data/exploretopics/trading-across-borders, retrieved June 16, 2013.

[36] Rao, N. Vasuki, "Indian Customs System Stuck in Miles of Thick, Red Tape," *The Journal of Commerce*, January 7, 1998, p. 4A.

[37] "When Is Pre-Shipment Inspection Required?", http://www.export.gov/logistics/eg_main_018120.asp, retrieved June 18, 2013.

[38] Wilmott, Peter, "Pre-Shipment Inspection—A Force for Good?", *American Shipper*, November 2006, pp. 24-27.

[39] Freudmann, Aviva, "Top Provider Alters Its Approach," *The Journal of Commerce*, April 7, 2000, p. 1.

[40] Green, Paula, "U.S. Exporters Slam Inspection Companies," *The Journal of Commerce*, December 31, 1997, p. 1A.

[41] Mottley, Robert, "Shippers' Case Law: Consignee, NVOs Clash Over Sealed Shipments," *American Shipper*, April 2000, p. 69.

[42] Russell, Timothy, *The Humanitarian Relief Supply Chain: Analysis of the 2004 South-East Asia Earthquake and Tsunami*, Master's of Engineering in Logistics thesis, Massachusetts Institute of Technology, June 2005, http://ctl.mit.edu, August 1, 2006.

[43] Jones, Chris, "Coke Admits Defeat in Dasani Rollout," *Food and Drink Europe*, March 26, 2003, http://www.foodanddrinkeurope.com/Products-Marketing/Coke-admits-defeat-in-Dasani-rollout, retrieved May 23, 2009.

[44] "Dasani UK Delay Cans Europe Sales," *BBC News*, March 24, 2004, http://news.bbc.co.uk/1/hi/business/3566233.stm, retrieved May 23, 2009.

[45] *2012 International Maritime Dangerous Goods Code*, International Maritime Organization, 4 Albert Embankment, London SE1 7SR, United Kingdom, http://www.imo.org/publications/imdgcode/Pages/Default.aspx, retrieved June 19, 2013.

[46] *Dangerous Goods Regulations*, 2013, 54th Edition, International Air Transport Association, 33 Route de l'Aéroport, Case Postale 672, CH-1215 Genève 15 Aéroport, Switzerland and 800 Place Victoria, Montréal, Québec, Canada H4Z 1M1, http://www.iata.org/publications/dgr/Pages/manuals.aspx, retrieved June 19, 2013.

[47] *2013-14 Technical Instructions For The Safe Transport of Dangerous Goods by Air* (Doc 9284), International Civil Aviation Organization, 999 University Street, Montréal, Québec H3C 5H7, Canadahttp://www.icao.int/safety/DangerousGoods/Pages/technical-instructions.aspx, retrieved June 19, 2013.

[48] *Electronic Code of Federal Regulations—Chapter 49*, U.S. Government Printing Office, http://www.ecfr.gov/cgi-bin/text-idx?c=ecfr&tpl=/ecfrbrowse/Title49/49tab_02.tpl, retrieved June 19, 2013.

[49] Compton, Mike, "Saying and Doing," *Cargo Systems*, March 1996, pp. 77-78.

[50] Sowinski, Lara, "A Flying Barn," *World Trade 100*, January 2011, p. 50.

[51] "Precious cargo; Transporting Animals by Air," *Air Cargo World*, May 2011, pp. 27-28.

[52] Lopez, Barry, "On the Wings of Commerce," *Harper's*, October 1995, pp. 39-54.

[53] *2012 Live Animal Regulations Manual*, Live Animals and Perishables Board, http://www.iata.org/publications/Pages/live-animals.aspx, retrieved June 19, 2013.

[54] Section 7, *Terrestrial Animal Health Code*, Organisation for Animal Health (OIE), http://www.oie.int/fileadmin/Home/eng/Health_standards/tahc/2010/en_titre_1.7.htm, retrieved June 19, 2013.

[55] Lelyveld, Michael S., "Peace Dividend: Easing in Arab Boycott of Israel," *The Journal of Commerce*, February 17, 1997.

Chapter 11

International Ocean Transportation

11.1 Types of Service	278
11.2 Size of Vessels	278
11.3 Types of Vessels	284
11.4 Flag	298
11.5 Liability Conventions	301
11.6 Non-Vessel-Operating Common Carriers	303
11.7 Security Requirements	305

In order to manage international logistics, it is fundamental to have a good understanding of the transportation alternatives open to an international shipper. The next three chapters provide an overview of the many options given to an exporter or an importer interested in making transportation arrangements for a given shipment.

The first chapter (Chapter 11) deals with the alternatives available in ocean transportation and the complexities of the international framework of rules that enable shipping lines to operate. The second chapter (Chapter 12) deals with air transportation and its rules and regulations. The third chapter (Chapter 13) deals with land transportation—rail and road—but also covers multimodal transportation, which is not really a mode of transportation, but a shipping alternative that simplifies the work of the shipper—exporter or importer—by allowing it to send its freight with only one carrier (shipping company). It also covers pipelines, which can only transport a limited range of products, and several other less-frequently used modes of transportation, mostly used in limited domestic markets.

The ocean shipping industry plays a key role in the fulfillment of world trade. There are more that 50,000 merchant ships operating in the world, registered to more than 150 nations, and operated by more than a million seafarers of virtually every nationality. Merchant ship operations generate an estimated annual revenue of over U.S.$ 380 billion in freight within the global economy, and transport over 7.7 billion tons of cargo.[1] Primarily because it transports all heavy cargoes, the ocean shipping industry is responsible for the carriage of 90 percent of the world's trade when measured by weight. Modern ships are technically sophisticated, high-value assets: large ships have capital costs in excess of U.S.$ 100 million, and the latest Triple-E containerships purchased by Maersk Lines have an estimated building cost of U.S.$ 190 million.[2]

11.1 Types of Service

The first differentiation to be made among ocean vessels is between liner ships and tramp ships.

liner ship
A ship that operates on a regular schedule, traveling from one group of ports to another group of ports.

Liner ships travel on a regular voyage, following a pre-established schedule, and with determined ports of call. A scheduled voyage may include only two ports (Santos, Brazil, to Miami, USA, and back) or, more commonly, a series of ports in one region of the world (*e.g.*, Bremerhaven, Germany; Rotterdam, Netherlands; Felixstowe, Great Britain) to another (*e.g.*, Boston, USA; Baltimore, USA; Nassau, Bahamas). Quite a few liners follow round-the-world (RTW) schedules, either eastbound or westbound, passing through the Panama Canal and/or the Suez Canal. There are many types of liner ships, a large number of which are adapted to specific routes, their size and equipment dependent on the ports of call they visit and on the specific types of cargo that their trade route entails. Liners are common carriers in that they offer their services to any shipper that will pay the freight rate.

tramp ship
A ship that does not operate on a regular schedule and is available for charter for any voyage, from any port to any port.

Unlike liners, tramp ships operate wherever and whenever the market dictates. They do not operate on a regular schedule but travel wherever the company that has contracted (chartered) the vessel wants the cargo delivered. Because of the way they operate, tramp ships usually carry only one type of cargo at a time, for one exporter or importer. Most tramp ships therefore are designed for one type of cargo exclusively, even if they carry several dry cargoes or several grades of petroleum products.

A possible analogy is that a tramp vessel is a taxicab, whereas a liner ship is a public bus.

11.2 Size of Vessels

The second principal differentiation to be made is the size of the vessel. Vessel size dictates trade routes, economies of scale, and ports of entry. Ships are often categorized by their size, which is expressed in "tons." Unfortunately, there are several types of tons and several ways of evaluating the tonnage of a vessel, and the tonnage of a vessel can be used for very different purposes, a situation that can lead to some substantial confusion.

Under the English system of measurements, tons are generally used as units of weight and may be "short," or equal to 2,000 pounds (907 kilograms), or "long," equal to 2,240 pounds (1,016 kilograms). However, tons can also be units of volume, equal to 100 cubic feet (2.83 cubic meters), and vessel size can be expressed in those units. Under the metric system, a tonne is only a measure of mass (weight), equal to 1,000 kilograms (2,204.6 pounds).

11.2.1 Deadweight Tonnage and Cubic Capacity

The deadweight tonnage (dwt) is the total weight capacity of the ship (*i.e.*, the maximum weight of the cargo that a vessel can carry) expressed in long tons (2,240 pounds) or in metric tonnes (2204.6 pounds). It is the measurement used by companies interested in shipping cargo and is often just called "tonnage." It is measured using the weight of the difference in water displacement when the ship is empty and when it is fully loaded to its maximum. The deadweight tonnage of a ship includes the fuel that the ship needs to travel—called bunker—and the supplies that it needs to function—called stores—and any ballast that the vessel may carry. Therefore, it is the theoretical capacity of the ship more than its actual capacity.

Vessels also have volumetric capacity for cargo that is called grain or bale cubic capacity. The grain cubic capacity is the cargo space available for loading a flowing cargo such as grain. The bale cubic capacity represents the total volume of space available for loading solid cargoes such as bales or boxes. The grain cubic capacity is always a larger figure. A vessel, when loaded with a very dense material—such as iron ore—can utilize its weight capacity before it reaches its cubic (volume) capacity; conversely, it can reach its volume capacity before it reaches its weight capacity if it is loaded with a light but voluminous cargo, such as timber or corn. A vessel that uses all of its cubic capacity and is also loaded down to its maximum draft is said to be "full and down."

deadweight tonnage
The maximum weight that a ship can carry.
bunker
The fuel that a ship carries onboard and that it needs to operate.
stores
All the supplies that a ship needs to carry in order to operate.
grain
An agricultural commodity, such as wheat, corn or sugar, that is loaded directly onboard, without packaging, like a liquid.
bale
The package bundle created by compressing cotton or wool when these commodities are tightly wrapped and bound with string or metal bands.

11.2.2 Gross and Net Tonnage

The gross tonnage is the total volume capacity of the ship, expressed in tons, which are in this case equal to hundreds of cubic feet (2.83 cubic meters). The gross tonnage measures only the capacity of the ship below its deck, so this measurement is not appropriate for determining the cargo-carrying capacity of a ship, because a good number of vessels also carry cargo above deck, particularly containerships. This measurement is used to determine how much a ship owner will have to pay in taxes to the country in which the ship is registered, or tolls to the authorities of the ports it visits or the canals it uses; that measure is also used for regulatory purposes. In that case, gross tonnage is referred to as gross registered tonnage (GRT), which takes into account the specific way a canal authority (such as Suez or Panama) determines gross tonnage. Once the volume occupied by the engine room, the crew, and other space necessary for the good operation of the ship is removed, the net tonnage is obtained. Net tonnage is further complicated by the fact that canal authorities calculate net tonnage differently; a ship will have a Panama Canal/Universal Measurement System (PC/UMS) net tonnage and a Suez Canal Net Tonnage (SCNT) as well.

Gross tonnage is commonly used when assessing the size of fleets for statistical purposes. Because different organizations set the cutoff for ship size at different gross tonnage levels (for example, in increments of 300 or 1,000 gross tons), this difference in baseline often is the principal cause of fleet size discrepancy between reports.

gross tonnage
The volume capacity of a ship, expressed in hundreds of cubic feet.
gross registered tonnage[GRT]
The volume capacity of a ship, calculated in a way that meets the requirements of a specific authority, such as the Suez Canal or the Panama Canal Authorities.
net tonnage
The volume capacity of a ship, after subtracting the space used for the operation of the ship.

11.2.3 Displacement

The displacement tonnage is the total weight of the ship, when fully loaded, measured by the weight of the volume of water it displaces. The light tonnage is the weight of the ship, measured the same way, but when the vessel is empty, which means that it is the displacement of the vessel after it was built but before any ballast, cargo, fuel, or supplies were put aboard. Both are generally measured in long

displacement tonnage
The total weight of a fully loaded ship, measured by the weight of the water displaced.

light tonnage
The total weight of an empty ship, measured by the weight of the water displaced.

tons and are used for naval architecture purposes in order to determine the vessel's stability, the stress it endures, and other engineering issues.

The relationship between the different vessel tonnages can be expressed mathematically, and Table 11.1 shows the different measurements of an actual 35,000-dwt (deadweight tonnage) Handysize bulk vessel ready for a 3,500-nautical-mile voyage (6,500 kilometers).

Dimensions of a 35,000-DWT Vessel

Measurements	Metric	U.S.
Length overall (LOA)	186.31 meters	611 feet, 3 inches
Beam (width)	28.40 meters	93 feet, 2 inches
Summer draft (amount of water needed to float)	10.73 meters	35 feet, 2.5 inches
Freeboard (distance between the water line and deck)	4.59 meters	15 feet, 0.75 inches
Winter draft (47/48 of the Summer draft)	10.50 meters	34 feet, 5.75 inches
Freshwater draft	10.96 meters	35 feet, 11.5 inches
Net tonnage (NT)	55,222 cubic meters	19,513 tons
Gross tonnage (GT)	69,007 cubic meters	24,384 tons
Suez gross registered tonnage (GRT)	69,607 cubic meters	24,596 tons
Displacement	44,828 tonnes	44,122 long tons
Light ship displacement	7,768 tonnes	7,646 long tons
Deadweight tonnage (dwt) at summer loadline	37,059 tonnes	36,476 long tons
Bunker (varies with voyage length)	610 tonnes	600 long tons
Potable drinking water (varies with voyage length)	244 tonnes	240 long tons
Constant (allowance for crew and consumable stores)	152 tonnes	150 long tons
Ballast (carried for trim if needed)	102 tonnes	100 long tons
Cargo deadweight (deadweight available for cargo)	35,952 tonnes	35,386 long tons

Table 11.1: Relationships Between the Measurements of a Vessel
source: Richard Stewart, PhD.

11.2.4 Plimsoll Mark and Load Lines

load lines
Marks on the side of the ship that indicate how low a ship can be in the water, depending on the season and conditions.

Plimsoll mark
A mark on the side of the ship that indicates the classification society that inspects the ship.

One more difficulty arises when one understands that ships are considered fully loaded at different drafts (how deep they sit in the water) in function of the season in which they are operating, of the latitudes under which they ply their trade, and of the density of the water. The deepest draft a ship can sit in is called the "tropical line" (T), followed by the "summer line" (S), the "winter line" (W), and the "winter North Atlantic line" (WNA). A "freshwater line" (F) is also present, as well as a "tropical freshwater" (TF) as freshwater density is lower—a ship will sit lower in freshwater than it would in saltwater with the same quantity of cargo. Those lines are clearly marked on the side of a ship with weld lines and painted with a contrasting color. At the same height as the vessel's summer deadweight draft, there is another diagram called the Plimsoll mark: a circle bisected by a horizontal line, which identifies the classification society that determined the vessel's load lines. Figure 11.1 shows the

11.2 Size of Vessels

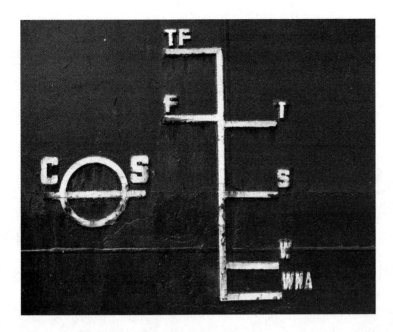

Figure 11.1: Plimsoll Mark and Load Lines on the Side of a Ship
Photo ©Jamie Serenko. Used with permission.

Plimsoll mark and load lines for a ship classified by the Bureau Veritas, a Belgian Classification Society.

The deadweight tonnage is generally determined at the summer line or at the line that represents accurately the conditions under which a ship is used. For example, a vessel used consistently in the Caribbean would have its deadweight tonnage calculated with the tropical load line. The load lines correspond to geographical regions of the globe, and a vessel must be at the appropriate load line when it arrives in the geographical region. For instance, a vessel that loads in Matadi, Congo, in January and sails for Antwerp will load to the tropical load line (T) but must consume enough fuel to be at the winter North Atlantic load line (WNA) when the vessel arrives in that geographical region. A vessel that exceeds appropriate load lines is subject to heavy fines and may also be considered to be in an unseaworthy state.

11.2.5 Size Categories

One of the biggest distinctions made in ships' sizes is between the ships that can travel through the locks of the Panama Canal and those that cannot. A ship of the maximum size that can possibly fit through these locks is called a Panamax ship; such a ship can have up to 75,000 long tons of deadweight tonnage, and its outside dimensions allow it to barely fit within the locks, with only a few inches of clearance between the locks' walls and the ship (see Figure 11.2). The locks are 304 meters long (1,000 feet) and 33 meters wide (110 feet). The longest ship to cross the Panama Canal is the *Marcona Prospector*, which is 296 meters long (973 feet) and 32 meters wide (106 feet), and the widest is the *USS New Jersey*, which is 32.4 meters wide (106 feet).[3] All ships built that are larger than this size are called post-Panamax ships.

Panamax ship
A ship of the maximum size that can enter the locks of the Panama Canal.

post-Panamax ship
A ship whose size is too large to enter the locks of the Panama Canal.

Figure 11.2: A Panamax Ship in the Miraflores Locks. Note the 13 Containers Abreast
Photo ©Andrés Balcázar de la Cruz. Used with permission.

Other terminologies used are:

- **Handysize ship.** A term commonly used in the dry-bulk trade and which refers to ships in the 10,000 to 50,000 deadweight ton range. Such ships tend to be used for tramp service.

- **Suez-Max ships.** This term is used to describe ships sized at roughly 150,000 deadweight tons and which are of the maximum size that can fit through the Suez Canal (about 285 meters long, 35 meters wide, and 23 meters of draft; that is 935 feet long, 115 feet wide, and 75 feet of draft). In 1996, the Suez Canal was deepened and widened, so the Suez-Max terminology is losing some of its validity.

- **Capesize ships.** This term is used to describe large dry-bulk carriers of a capacity greater than 80,000 deadweight tons that cannot transit through the Suez Canal and must pass by the Cape of Good Hope in South Africa.

- **Very large crude carrier (VLCC).** This term is used to describe an oil tanker of up to 300,000 deadweight tonnage, which is about 350 meters long and 55 meters wide and has 28 meters of draft. These dimensions correspond to 1,150 feet long, 180 feet wide, and 92 feet of draft.

11.2 Size of Vessels

Figure 11.3: A Very Large Crude Carrier at an Offshore Oil Terminal
Photo ©Kevin Tierney. Used with permission.

- **Ultra-large crude carrier (ULCC).** This term describes an oil tanker of more than 300,000 deadweight tonnage. The largest ULCC ever built, the *Knock Nevis*—formerly called the *Seawise Giant* and the *Jahre Viking*—had a deadweight tonnage of 565,000 tonnes, is 458 meters long and 69 meters wide and has a draft of 26.4 meters.[4] That represents a deck surface of 2.5 hectares. These dimensions translate to 556,000 long tons, 1,527 feet long, 230 feet wide, a draft of 88 feet, and an area of 6.25 acres. The current largest ULCC, the *Hellespont Alhambra* is smaller: 380 meters long, 68 meters wide, and a draft of 24.5 meters. Such ships generally are unable to go into traditional ports, and they remain in deep sea at all times. Their cargo is removed using a process called lightering, which consists of transferring the cargo onto smaller ships (see Section 11.3.5 on page 291), or using offshore oil terminals (see Figure 11.3).

deck
A permanent cover over the ship's hull.

For comparison purposes, the largest containership in use as of 2013, the *Maersk Mc-Kinney Møller*, is a much smaller vessel, even though it is gigantic. This ship is 398 meters long and 58 meters wide and has a draft of 14.5 meters (1,306 feet long, 190 feet wide, and a draft of 48 feet). Its deadweight tonnage is 165,000 tonnes (162,290 long tons). It can carry 18,000 twenty-foot equivalent units (TEUs) (*i.e.*, 20-foot containers).[5] As of June 2013, there were 842 Post-Panamax containerships in use, and 236 Post-Panamax containerships on order. There were 175 mega-containerships (larger than 10,000 TEUs) in use and 111 on order (see Table 3.1 on page 53). The largest cruiseship in the world, the *Allure of the Seas* is 362 meters long (1,187 feet), 60.5 meters wide (198 feet), and draws 9.3 meters (31 feet). Its displacement is 19,750 tonnes (19,430 long tons).[6]

TEU
Twenty-foot Equivalent Unit. The equivalent of a twenty-foot container. A forty-foot container is two TEUs.

11.3 Types of Vessels

hold
In a ship, a portion of the inside volume designed to hold cargo.

The third principal differentiation to be made is based on the type of cargo carried by the vessels, and those cargoes are used to classify merchant ships into many different categories (see Figure 11.4).[7] First, a distinction is made between cargo ships that carry wet-bulk (liquid) cargoes and those vessels that carry dry-bulk cargoes. Second, wet and dry cargoes can either be shipped in bulk (where the cargo is loaded as a liquid would be, directly in the hold of a ship) or unitized (shipped in units that are unloaded one at a time, such as boxes, crates, or containers).

There are more than 46,000 commercial vessels worldwide with an individual capacity greater than 500 gross tonnes. The total cargo carrying capacity of the world's commercial fleet exceeded 1.5 billion deadweight tons in 2013 (see Figure 11.5).[8] Almost every single one of these ships is designed differently. It is therefore difficult to classify them much better than in broad-based groups, with many ships not fitting neatly into one category.

11.3.1 Containerships

containership
A ship designed to exclusively carry containers, both below its deck and above it. A containership's size is expressed in TEUs.

The containerized trade is growing rapidly. Approximately 60 percent of world trade (in value) is containerized, and container transportation volume has been growing by 7.5 percent per year since 1990 (see Figure 11.6 on the next page). Even in trade lanes where containers are solidly implanted, such as Asia-North America or Europe-North America, the growth in the volume of shipment is estimated at 5 percent. Given the fact that goods that traditionally traveled in bulk are now shipped using containers—for example, forestry products and grain—and given the fact that intermodal transportation is responding well to customer needs, it seems that the container, which was created in 1956, will dominate international trade yet further.

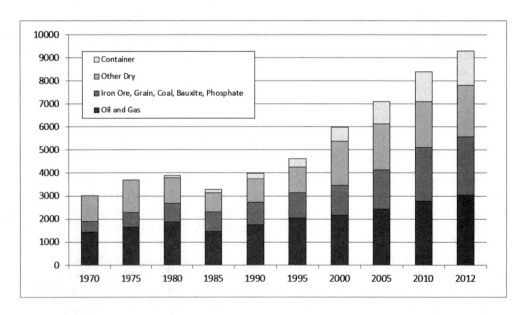

Figure 11.4: Ocean Worldwide Trade by Cargo Type (in millions of tons)
Review of Maritime Transport 2012.

11.3 Types of Vessels

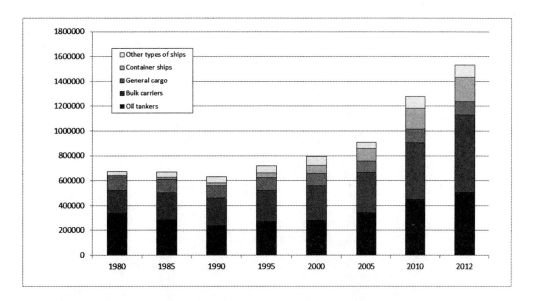

Figure 11.5: Worldwide Vessel Capacity by Cargo Type (in millions of DWTs)
Review of Maritime Transport 2012.

Containerships, also known as "box ships," carry containerized cargo on a scheduled voyage. Vessels dedicated to the container trade can carry up to 18,000 TEUs—20-foot equivalent units, or the space equivalent of a 20-foot container—but there are many mixed-cargo ships that can also carry containers, sometimes as few as 100 TEUs. Most containerships rely upon the port cranes to unload their cargo, but some

box ship
Another, more casual, name for containerships.

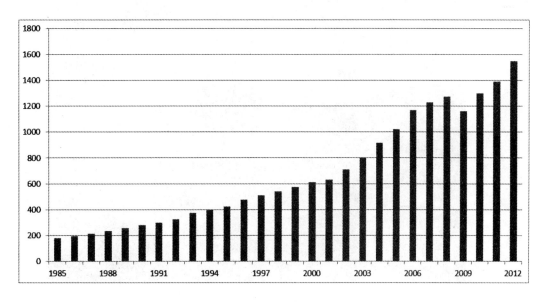

Figure 11.6: Growth in Worldwide Containerized Cargo (in millions of tons)
Review of Maritime Transport 2012.

Figure 11.7: A Post-Panamax Ship, with 16 Containers Abreast
Photo ©Jun Takahashi. Used with permission.

Figure 11.8: Containers Lashed with Twistlock on a Containership Deck
Photo ©Ole Tange. Used with permission.

11.3 Types of Vessels

Figure 11.9: A Hatchless Containership. Photo ©Shaun Lowe. Used with permission.

do have cranes on board. All containerships used to be capable of going through the Panama Canal and carried around 4,500 TEUs. When the first post-Panamax containerships were delivered, they carried more than 6,000 TEUs and forced some substantial changes in ports. For example, they were so wide and so high (see Figure 11.7 on the facing page) that some ports had to upgrade their crane equipment. Moreover, some ports became entirely inaccessible; some of the post-Panamax ships cannot enter some of the ports on the East Coast of the United States, because their air drafts do not allow them to fit under the bridges that span the port access channels, or their water drafts do not allow them to enter the ports, since they are not deep enough (for example, Port Elizabeth of the Port of New York-New Jersey).

As larger ships, as big as 18,000 TEUs, are coming into service, there will be additional demands made on port infrastructure, and it will certainly reduce the number of ports in which these giant ships can berth to a handful worldwide. The trend in the industry is therefore seen as the creation of a system of large hubs, to and from which the mega-containerships would travel, coupled with a number of smaller ships, called feeder ships, which would travel between these giant hub ports and smaller ports. Those feeder ships would essentially be the existing fleet of traditional containerships. Although a hub system would cause trans-shipments to occur, it is estimated that it would lower transportation costs.

Traditional containerships hold containers under deck as well as on deck. Some containers are first loaded in the holds of the ship, then the hatch covers (the deck) are put in place, and the remainder of the containers are placed on top of them. Containers placed under deck are usually held in place by vertical guides, along which the crane operator slides them. On-deck containers are usually stacked on top of each other and latched to each other with metal bars and twistlocks (see

Figure 11.8).

Since the early 1990s, several shipping lines have tried to speed up the process of loading containers by equipping their ships with vertical guides for on-deck containers as well, and some have eliminated the deck hatches altogether (see Figure 11.9), simply choosing to equip the vessel with much larger bilge pumps (the pumps that remove the water from the inside of a ship). Eventually, it is conceivable that the concept of "deck" will no longer exist in the container trade.

11.3.2 Roll-On/Roll-Off Ships

RORO
Roll-On/Roll-Off. A type of ship in which cargo is rolled on board rather than carried by crane.

Roll-on/roll-off (RORO) ships were created to accommodate cargo that was self-propelled, such as automobiles or trucks, or cargo that could be wheeled into a ship, such as railroad cars or excavation equipment. They are essentially floating parking garages (see Figure 11.10).

Figure 11.10: A Roll-On/Roll-Off Ship for Vehicles Photo ©Lisa-Blue. Used with permission.

The concept is fairly straightforward. Because it takes a long time to load such vehicles over the rail of a ship by using a crane, it is preferable to load them by rolling them onto the ship. RORO ships therefore have a portion of their hulls that opens up and acts as a ramp on which the vehicles are driven before being parked on the many decks of the ship and secured with chains. The hull opening is either on the side of the ship or on its stern (rear).

RORO ships have an advantage in that specialized lifting equipment is not required, even for the heaviest of loads, because the cargo rolls under its own power or is pulled by a tractor. It therefore needs only some docking space and a substantial number of dock workers to load or unload its cargo. There are distinctions between a pure car-carrier (PCC) ship, which loads only cars and has decks with only 5 feet (1.5 meters) of overhead clearance, and other, more versatile, so-called "true"

11.3 Types of Vessels

RORO ships that can accommodate larger cargo. Many RORO ships are equipped with adjustable decks, which allow them to transport any sort of rolling cargo.

As the number of cars manufactured worldwide increases, it seems that the future of the RORO concept is secure. However, there are several companies that are selling specialized equipment that can be used in traditional 40-foot containers and can handle six automobiles (on two levels) at once with equipment that can be collapsed and placed into another container for the return trip. This concept is attractive, as it overcomes some of the drawbacks of the RORO ships. There is no need to hire expensive stevedore labor to drive the vehicles onto the ship—it is replaced with cheaper inland labor to load and unload the containers—and it makes the loading and unloading faster, as it requires only one cargo movement for every six vehicles. This alternative also eliminates the cost of modifying the configuration of the decks so that regular bulk cargo can be loaded in the now-empty RORO ship on the return trip. The latter issue is significant for trades with countries that import a lot of vehicles but export far fewer, such as the United States.

The concept of RORO has been expanded to another variation, designed for the transport of livestock, which are led aboard the ship rather than hoisted over its rail. Therefore, the ships are given the moniker of trot-on/trot-off ships. Such ships are used mainly to transport sheep between Australia or New Zealand and the Middle East. Some are also used to transport cattle between Argentina or Brazil and the Middle East. The TOTO ships also return empty to their ports of origin.

Trot-On/Trot-Off
A type of ship designed to carry livestock. Animals use a ramp to walk on board and exit the ship.

11.3.3 Breakbulk or General-Merchandise Ships

Breakbulk ships (also called general-merchandise ships) constitute the least homogeneous category of vessels. There are all sorts of breakbulk ships, which are often created for a specialized trade or a given shipping lane. Altogether, though, breakbulk cargo ships are multipurpose ships that can transport shipments of unusual sizes, unitized on pallets, in bags, or in crates (see Figure 11.11). Because of the increase in the percentage of international cargo shipments that are containerized, including the containerization of some goods that are larger than what can normally fit in a regular container, and because of the increasing role of RORO ships, breakbulk ships' share of international trade is decreasing but is still the single largest fleet in number of ships.

breakbulk
A type of cargo that is unitized—boxes, crates, or bales—and placed directly in the holds of a ship.

breakbulk ship
A type of ship designed to carry breakbulk cargo.

general-merchandise ship
Another name for a breakbulk ship.

The main problem with general-merchandise ships stems from their labor-intensive loading and unloading; each unitized piece must be handled separately, with several stevedores in the hull of the ship and several stevedores on the quay, in addition to the crane operators. Because the cargo is of different sizes, each piece may require different equipment (a different number of hooks, shorter or longer slings, and so on) and in some cases demand "problem solving," which may involve a few attempts before it is loaded or unloaded successfully. In addition, the securing of the loads on the decks is just as labor intensive, because pieces of cargo have odd sizes. Consequently, breakbulk ships stay in port much longer, especially because they cannot load or unload in the rain, and their schedules can be erratic.

stevedore
A person who loads and unloads goods from a vessel in a port.

Since a large percentage of breakbulk ships are equipped with an onboard crane, which allows them to load and unload without relying on port equipment, they can call at just about any port to load different kinds of cargo loads, giving them a flexibility that containerships do not have. Although decreasing in percentage, the breakbulk trade has a significant future in that it will always carry odd-sized shipments and always carry heavy cargoes that cannot be containerized. Nevertheless, it

Figure 11.11: A Breakbulk Ship with a Removable Deck
Photo ©Dan Barnes. Used with permission.

is likely that there will be fewer general-merchandise ships in the future—very few breakbulk ships have been built in the last 15 years—although it is likely that there will be a corresponding increase in the number of combination ships, which will carry breakbulk cargo, but also some bulk, some RORO cargo, and a few containers.

11.3.4 Combination Ships

combination ship
A type of ship that is versatile and can carry different types of cargo.

tweendeck
A deck located below the main deck and used to carry smaller cargo.

The ultimate multipurpose ships are combination ships, which are designed to carry all sorts of different loads in a single voyage. A typical combination ship has several holds in which bulk cargo, such as timber or grain, can be placed. Those holds can also be used for breakbulk cargo, especially oversized and heavy cargo, such as machinery, and sometimes containers. It also has a tweendeck, or a deck below the main deck, which accommodates smaller breakbulk cargo as well as vehicles that are loaded through the RORO access door. On its main deck, the typical combination ship can carry several containers as well (see Figure 11.12 on the facing page).

Finally, a combination ship can have one or more onboard cranes, to increase its versatility and allow it to unload its cargo in any port. Because of their versatility, combination ships thrive in shipping lanes that have a low volume of trade, such as the trade between developed countries and developing countries, or the trade to and from small island nations, such as those in the South Pacific or the Caribbean.

11.3 Types of Vessels

Figure 11.12: A Combination Ship Photo ©Losinjska Plovida. Used with permission.

11.3.5 Product, Chemical, and Crude Carriers

Petroleum transported in bulk by ships are broken down into three principal trades: product, chemical, and crude. products

Product vessels transport refined products such as gasoline, diesel oil, or other refined products. These products need to be carefully segregated and kept from contamination. The vessels range in size from small coastal vessels (about 1,000 dwt) to large product carriers, roughly 60,000 dwt in size. The vessels may carry up to six different products if the vessel's tank and piping system allow segregation.

product carrier
A liquid-bulk ship that carries refined oil products.

Chemical carriers are specially designed ships in the 1,000 to 40,000 dwt range that carry chemicals (see Figure 11.13). Some may transport as many as 40 different chemicals and are referred to as "drugstore" ships. The hazardous nature of some chemicals, such as benzene, and the handling requirements of other chemicals that require special tanks, dedicated piping systems, and complex safeguards limit the vessels to the chemical trade.

chemical carrier
A liquid-bulk ship that carries liquid chemicals.

Crude carriers are the bulk ships dedicated to the transport of unrefined (crude) oil. The largest ships in the world are crude carriers; there is a distinction made between Panamax crude carriers of up to 80,000 dwt, AfraMax tankers with a capacity between 80 and 120,000 dwt, named after the Average Freight Rate Assessment system; very large crude carriers (VLCC), of up to 300,000 dwt; and ultra-large crude carriers (ULCC) beyond this tonnage. There were 589 VLCCs and ULCCs in 2013, a figure that is far larger than what is needed to transport the current oil production

crude carrier
A liquid-bulk ship that carries unrefined oil.

Figure 11.13: A Chemical Carrier with its Network of Tanks and Pipes
Photo ©Zennie. Used with permission.

of the world.[9]

After many oil spills, including the infamous *Exxon Valdez* into Alaskan waters in March 1989, all VLCCs and ULCCs are now equipped with double hulls, which makes them less likely to spill their cargoes if they accidentally run aground. The additional hull (and the space between the hull of the ship and the part of the ship that contains the petroleum oil) is believed to provide some protection in the case of groundings, but the design reduces the carrying capacity of vessels by as much as 15 percent and adds to the cost of construction and maintenance.

VLCCs and ULCCs are such large ships (see Figure 11.14) that they can call on only a few ports in the world; because their draft, when loaded, can reach 30 meters (100 feet), they need very deep ports and, because they are so long and wide, a very large docking area. In a number of cases, the VLCCs and ULCCs do not enter a port but stay at anchor outside of the port in deep waters. The oil cargo of the large crude carrier is then transferred into smaller crude carriers that subsequently transport it and unload it into the port. This process is called lightering and is also occasionally used for traditional breakbulk or dry-bulk ships. On other occasions, the VLCCs and ULCCs are connected to an artificial island, or a "floating island," which is a pipeline terminal in deep waters (see Figure 11.3 on page 283). Some countries have transformed natural islands into deepwater oil terminals for such ships, such as in the case of the Mina-al-Bakr oil terminal in Iraq.

11.3 Types of Vessels

Figure 11.14: A Very Large Crude Carrier Photo ©William Stevens. Used with permission.

Masters Unlimited

Maneuvering an ultra-large crude carrier is a job that few people can handle, but it is the daily responsibility of captains who have reached the prestigious title of "Master Unlimited." There are about 3,000 of them worldwide and they are the only captains accredited to command ships of more than 5,000 tons GRT.[10]

Handling such large ships can be quite a hair-raising experience. Consider that a ULCC can be as long as four football fields and that, at cruising speed and fully loaded, it stops in a mere six miles if its engine is stopped. If put in full reverse, the distance "shrinks" to two miles. When fully loaded, the ship takes more than 30 minutes to come to a full stop.[11]

In order to learn how to pilot these behemoths, captains either practice on computer simulations or travel to the unusual training camp of Port Revel in the foothills of the Alps in France, where they are placed in models of large ships. A similar model training program is operated by the Massachusetts Maritime Academy in Buzzards Bay, Massachusetts. Like their real-life equivalent, these model ships are extremely underpowered, at least relatively speaking. A ship of this size is "like a large lorry [truck] with a moped engine and no brakes," says an instructor at Port Revel, noting that the 40-foot-long model *Europe* that weighs 41,000 pounds, has a motor of less than one horsepower.[12] Real-life ULCCs weigh 600,000 tonnes and have engines of 30,000 kW—40,000 HP—which is actually a higher weight-power ratio than the models.[13]

After a few days on the pond at Port Revel, these gifted sailors are capable of maneuvering these ships so well that they can squeeze a 700-foot behemoth into the 750-foot space left between two other ships in port without the help of a tug. In other words, simple parallel parking.

11.3.6 Dry-Bulk Carriers

dry-bulk carrier
A dry-bulk ship that carries grain, ores, dry chemicals, or minerals directly in its holds.

Dry-bulk carriers operate on the same basis as oil tankers in that they are chartered for a whole voyage. Dry-bulk ships (see Figure 11.15) have several holds in their hull, in which non-unitized cargo is loaded through hatches (openings on deck). There are many types of dry-bulk ships, and because of the trade in which they are engaged—the type of merchandise that they carry and the ports on which they call—dry-bulk ships can have specialized configurations or equipment. Generally speaking, dry-bulk ships carry agricultural products, such as cereals, as well as coal, ores, scrap iron, dry chemicals, and other commodities that behave as liquids, since they take the shape of the hold of the ship. Some of those ships, because of the

Figure 11.15: A Bulk Carrier Being Loaded with Coal
Photo ©Dan Prat. Used with permission.

11.3 Types of Vessels

versatility of the cargoes that they can carry, are called oil-bulk-ore (O-B-O) carriers, as they can transport oil during one leg of the voyage and then on the next leg, after cleaning the tanks/holds, carry dry-bulk products.

In terms of size, dry-bulk ships are generally classified into three types: Capesize, which are ships that are too large to fit through the Suez Canal and must go around the Cape of Good Hope on the southern tip of Africa; Panamax ships, which are small enough to fit through the Panama Canal; and Handysize bulkers, which are from 10,000 to 45,000 deadweight tons. Many of these Handysize tramp bulkers are somewhat older vessels.

A good portion of the trade in commodities in the world transits through a myriad of these Handysize vessels, carrying cargoes of sugar, rice, and other staples from small ports to other small ports. These ships are chartered primarily through the Baltic Exchange, which is a meeting place for brokers representing the ship owners and the cargo owners to meet and conduct business. The business is initially done verbally, and the word of the brokers is their bond.[14]

Baltic Exchange
The world market for maritime cargo transport services, located in London, where ship owners and cargo owners negotiate the cost of moving cargo.

As seen in Chapter 9 three types of charters are typically used for bulk vessels. A voyage charter hires the ship with all functions provided by the ship owner, such as crew, management, and fuel, to deliver cargo to one or more ports in the world. A time charter is a vessel hired to deliver cargo with the ship owner providing all services over a fixed period of time, which may vary from a few months to several years. A bareboat or demise charter is a vessel hired and run by another party. The ship owner provides a vessel that is bare of crew and supplies. The vessel charterer operates the vessel in all respects and returns the bareboat to the ship owner after the end of the demise charter, which can last months or years. Both dry and wet trade vessels are chartered.

There is a specific group of dry-bulk carriers that serve the ports of the Great Lakes, between the United States and Canada, called lakers (see Figure 11.16). Their characteristics are determined by the size of the canal locks of the Welland Canal, which gives them long and narrow hulls. Lakers trade mostly in three commodities: iron ore and iron ore pellets, coal, and finished steel. They are not ocean-going

laker
A dry-bulk ship designed to operate on the Great Lakes between the United States and Canada.

Figure 11.16: A Great Lakes Freighter—A Laker Photo ©Ellis Veech. Used with permission.

vessels, but they fit the general description of dry-bulk carriers. These vessels have self-unloading gear that allows for the rapid (10,000 short tons per hour) unloading of bulk cargoes. The design of the self-unloading booms allows the vessels to place cargo up to 150 feet (45 meters) off the side of the vessel. A number of the self-unloading lakers are over 1,000 feet in length (304 meters) and can trade only in four of the five Great Lakes, as they cannot fit through the Welland Canal into Lake Ontario.

Although not altogether the same as dry-bulk carriers, there are also a large number of ships that carry specialized cargoes that can be considered as dry bulk. Examples are refrigerated ships—also called "reefer" ships—which are slowly being replaced by refrigerated containers aboard containerships with the possible exception of specialized refrigerated ships called banana ships; liquid food carriers, which therefore carry liquid bulk cargoes such as molasses, orange juice, and vegetable oils; lumber carriers; and cement carriers.

11.3.7 Gas Carriers

LNG-LPG carrier
A ship designed to transport liquefied—compressed—natural gas or petroleum gas.

Another important bulk trade is the transportation of liquefied natural gas (LNG) and of liquefied petroleum gas (LPG). These types of carriers have a very distinctive shape. These ships hold several spheres of compressed gasses, only part of which are visible above their main deck (see Figure 11.17).

The LNG and LPG trades tend to be slightly different than the average bulk transport, as they are used in a particular trade for long periods of time, on long-term contracts—called time charter parties (see Chapter 9)—and therefore nearly have a sailing schedule, not unlike liner ships. They carry cargo on only half of their voyage and return empty.

Figure 11.17: A Liquefied Natural Gas Carrier
Photo ©Oleksandr Kalinichenko. Used with permission.

The Baltic Exchange

Located in London, the Baltic Exchange was once the location where traders and ship owners would meet to arrange for the maritime transportation of commodities. Through a process not unlike that of a commodities exchange, the cargo owners and the ship owners would negotiate the cost of moving bulk cargo from one port to another.

Today, the Baltic Exchange is the world's only independent source of maritime market information, obtained through the same process of negotiation. Its more than 550 members, representing the vast majority of the world's shipping companies, help determine the costs of shipping cargo through a series of indices, called the Baltic Exchange Indices, which are published daily.

The indices reflect the average costs per day (expressed in U.S. dollars) for an end customer to have a shipping company transport a certain commodity in a certain type of ship. The exchange calculates the indices by averaging the daily costs of shipping dry-bulk cargo on different routes.

The most frequently used indices are the Baltic Exchange Capesize Index (BCI), which is the average daily cost of utilizing a vessel capable of carrying 172,000 metric tonnes of cargo, calculated over ten routes; the Baltic Exchange Panamax Index (BPI), which is the daily cost of utilizing a Panamax ship capable of carrying 74,000 metric tonnes of cargo, averaged over four routes; the Baltic Exchange Supramax Index (BSI) for ships capable of carrying 52,454 metric tonnes averaged over six routes; and the Baltic Exchange Handysize Index (BHSI) for ships capable of carrying 28,000 metric tonnes calculated over six routes. These indices are then combined to form the Baltic Exchange Dry Index (BDI).[15] For oil-related cargoes, the Baltic Exchange publishes the Baltic Exchange Dirty Tanker Index (BDTI), which reflects the costs of shipping unrefined petroleum oil, calculated on the average costs of 17 different routes, and the Baltic Exchange Clean Tanker Index (BCTI), which reflects the costs of shipping oil-based refined products, such as gasoline or naphtha, averaged over seven routes. Both of these indices are combined into the Baltic Exchange International Tanker Route Index (BITR). Finally, there is a Baltic Exchange Palm Oil Route Index (BPOIL) and a Baltic Exchange Liquefied Petroleum Gas Index (BLPG).

The Baltic Exchange Dry Bulk Index is widely considered a leading economic indicator. Since ships are hired (chartered) only when there is a cargo to be moved as a result of primary demand, the costs of shipping reflect the derived demand of transportation services. The worldwide demand for raw materials drove the Baltic Exchange Dry Index to reach a record high level of 11,793 points on May 20, 2008. On December 5, 2008, less than six months later, the index had dropped by 94 percent, to 663 points, the lowest since 1986.[16] At the end of June 2013, it had recovered and was at 890,[17] still below its long-term average of 1,700.

11.4 Flag

By international convention, each vessel engaged in international trade must be registered in a specific country, and therefore flies a specific country's flag. In many ways, the vessel is an extension of the territory of this country, and all its laws and regulations apply on board the ship. In exchange, the naval forces of the flag of registry will protect those flagged merchant ships in time of conflict. In addition, the vessel must pay the taxes that this country imposes. There is one significant caveat to this situation: with very few exceptions, a ship owner can choose the country in which its ship is registered, or choose the flag that it flies.

flag
The flag of the country in which a ship is registered. By extension, the country in which the ship is registered.

The flags of developed countries tend to impose very substantial regulations on the way a ship is operated, in such areas as the composition of the crew on board, its minimum training requirement, its nationality (because it is a country's extension of its territory, its immigration rules apply), the work rules on board (such as the number of hours worked per day and week before overtime pay is earned), the vacation time earned by the crew, and so on. In addition, taxation can be significantly higher. In contrast, regulations and taxes for some developing countries are minimal. It is estimated that flying an American flag rather than a developing country's flag can multiply costs by a factor of 2.7—i.e. the operating costs of the U.S. ship are 2.7 times the operating costs of a foreign-flagged vessel. A 2011 Maritime Administration study showed that the operating costs of a cargo ship flying the U.S. flag were U.S.$ 20,053 per day, whereas the same ship flying a developing country's flag were U.S.$ 7,454 per day. The crew sizes were similar (22.9 crew members for U.S.-flagged ships and 21.7 for foreign-flag ships), but the crew costs were considerably different. The U.S.-flagged ships had to pay $ 13,655 per day but the foreign-flag ships only paid $ 2,590.[18]

The National Defense Transportation Administration determined that the taxes that a U.S.-flagged ship would have to pay would be approximately U.S.$ 700,000 per year. In contrast, the same vessel, operating under the flag of Panama would have to pay U.S.$ 10,497, and under the flag of the Isle of Man, only U.S.$ 680.[19]

open registry
A flag—country of registration—that is open to all ship owners, regardless of their nationality.

flag of convenience
A flag—country of registration—that is open to all ship owners, and imposes few requirements—regulations or taxes—on ship owners. A derogatory term.

To take advantage of their much lower fiscal costs, a small number of countries have created what is called an open registry, which means that any ship owner can choose to have its vessel fly this country's flag. There are no requirements regarding the citizenship of the owners of the ship. Because these countries tend to have minimal onboard requirements and taxes, many ship owners decide to fly such countries' flags, which have been deridingly called "flags of convenience." Most of these open registries emanate from developing countries, but, fairly recently, some developed countries established their own versions of open registries, which are called secondary registries, with much less stringent requirements than their normal registries in order to prevent their merchant fleets from being entirely registered under flags of convenience. Norway, Denmark, and France are three notorious examples.

Table 11.2 on the facing page[20] shows the 25 largest fleets in the world (by flag), and Table 11.3 on page 300[21] shows the percentage of a country's fleet that is registered in a number of selected registry, mostly flags of convenience.

It should be noted that the choice of a flag regulates the qualifications of the crew, its compensation, and the amount of taxes that the ship owners pay. It does not influence the seaworthiness of the vessel, which is evaluated by classification societies and determines the insurance premiums (hull insurance and P&I insurance) that the vessel owners have to pay (see Chapter 10). A competent crew and a seaworthy vessel are guaranteed if the vessel is registered in a developed country, if it

Merchandise Fleet by Flag of Registry

Country/Region	Number of Ships	Tonnage (000s dwt)
Panama	8,127	214,760
Liberia	3,030	121,519
Marshall Islands	1,876	76,054
Hong Kong	1,935	70,206
Singapore	2,877	53,830
Bahamas	1,409	52,390
Malta	1,815	45,117
Greece	1,386	41,276
China	4,148	37,924
Cyprus	1,022	20,993
United Kingdom	1,965	19,807
Italy	1,667	18,492
Japan	5,619	17,423
Norway	2,004	16,512
Germany	868	15,320
Isle of Man	410	13,341
Korea	2,916	12,084
Denmark	981	11,901
United States	6,461	11,601
Bermuda	164	11,323
Antigua & Barbuda	1,322	11,163
Indonesia	6,332	10,430
India	1,443	9,762
Malaysia	1,449	8,197
Russia	3,362	7,591

Table 11.2: Merchandise Fleet by Flag of Registry *Review of Maritime Transport 2012.*

is operated by a reputable shipping company, or if it is classed with one of the major classification societies; however, problems are more likely to arise with vessels registered under a flag of convenience.

Countries attempt to influence, as much as possible, the flags of the ships that enter their ports. Although they cannot outright ban certain nationalities, they can prevent ships not registered in the country from carrying certain freight. For example, the Cargo Preference Act of the United States requires that at least 50 percent of U.S. government cargo be carried by U.S.-flagged ships. The Jones Act requires that cargo transported from one port in the United States to another port in the United States—a trade called cabotage—must be carried exclusively on U.S.-flagged ships. This is the case for cargo going from the West Coast to Hawaii, for example. Finally, all cargo in trades supported by the Ex-Im Bank must be shipped through U.S.-flagged ships. A study by the Maritime Administration of the United States found that over 50 maritime countries had some form of cabotage or flag protection laws of one form or another.[22]

cabotage
An ocean trade consisting of shipping goods between two ports located in the same country.

Countries Fleet by Flag of Registry

Country	Bahamas	Cyprus	Liberia	Malta	Marshall Islands	Panama	Other Registry	Own Registry
Germany	0.7%	6.6%	31.8%	2.7%	6.2%	0.6%	40.8%	10.6%
Japan	2.7%	0.5%	2.9%	0.1%	1.8%	60.9%	13.1%	18.1%
China	0.1%	0.2%	0.4%	0.2%	0.4%	14.7%	27.3%	56.8%
Greece	7.4%	6.0%	16.3%	14.6%	13.6%	11.6%	8.3%	22.2%
United States	5.6%	0.6%	3.9%	1.8%	13.0%	6.6%	56.3%	12.2%
Norway	11.4%	1.7%	1.9%	5.5%	4.2%	4.2%	49.2%	21.9%
Korea	0.1%	0.0%	0.2%	0.2%	4.4%	32.2%	2.9%	59.9%
Denmark	7.1%	0.8%	0.9%	3.3%	0.8%	3.9%	47.7%	35.6%
Italy	1.2%	0.7%	5.4%	5.6%	0.1%	2.5%	11.5%	72.9%
United Kingdom	4.8%	1.0%	5.5%	4.4%	0.1%	5.8%	46.1%	32.4%

Table 11.3: Percentage of a Country's Fleet by Flag of Registry
Review of Maritime Transport 2012.

requisition
demand the use of an asset.

The U.S. situation is yet more complicated. Its government compensates the ship owners who elect to fly the stars-and-stripes flag to the tune of several million per year per vessel,[23] but not just because it is more expensive to run a U.S.-flagged ship. The reason is purely military. Because of its geographical situation, the United States would need a lot of ship transport capacity to ship troops and military materials abroad in the case of a conflict, and the current program was developed in response to military sealift issues.[24] In that eventuality, the U.S. government can then requisition all merchant ships registered with the U.S. flag that are under the subsidy program. In order to ensure that it does have some ships to requisition, the U.S. government subsidizes ship owners who choose this alternative.

Flying Flags

The choice of a flag has many consequences beyond the crew's training and the taxes that the ship owners have to pay:

• Cabotage rules require that American flags and crews be used for ships traveling from one port in the United States to another port in the United States. Cruise ships, none of which flies the U.S. flag, therefore cannot travel between two U.S. ports. Cruise ships destined for Alaska leave from Vancouver, Canada, and cruise ships destined for Hawaii leave from Ensenada, Mexico.

• Many of the cruise ships fly flags of convenience, such as that of the Bahamas, or secondary registries, such as that of Norway. Because those registries do not exert much oversight over working conditions on their vessels, working cruise ship crews are generally employed for sub-standard wages and in miserable jobs. Very low wages are commonplace, and so are 12- to 15-hour days. U.S. court decisions have determined that because these cruise vessels are based in U.S. ports,

select U.S. labor laws can apply.[25].
- When Hong Kong became part of the People's Republic of China (PRC) in July 1997, a flag issue surfaced. Because it is common practice to fly a host port's flag on a ship, it meant that the ships of the shipping company Evergreen of Taiwan region would have had to fly the PRC's flag when they called on the port of Hong Kong, and that Hong Kong ships would have had to fly the flag of Taiwan region when they were in Taipei. Neither alternative was welcome; the issue was finally resolved when both sides decided not to fly any flag in each other's ports.[26]
- During the conflict between Iran and Iraq in the Persian Gulf, several Kuwaiti ships were temporarily placed under the U.S. flag so that they could gain the protection of the U.S. Navy, a protection refused to U.S. owners of tankers flying flags of convenience. The U.S. Navy finally relented, and all crude carriers were temporarily re-flagged as American while they were in the Persian Gulf.[27]
- When more than a hundred merchant ships were attacked by pirates in the Gulf of Aden in 2008-2009, the U.S. Navy was empowered to intervene to protect only the *Maersk Alabama*, because it was the only ship that was flying the U.S. flag.[28] It was flying the U.S. flag because it was carrying a cargo of relief supplies for USAID, which mandates that its cargo be carried on U.S.-flagged ships.

11.5 Liability Conventions

In 1924, the International Convention for the Unification of Certain Rules of Law Relating to Bills of Lading was adopted by 26 participating countries. This convention, known as the Hague Rules, limited the liability of a ship owner to the cargo owners to U.S.$ 500 per package or "customary freight unit," and it allowed ship owners to escape liability in 17 specified cases—called the 17 "defenses"—including the infamous nautical fault, or errors of the crew of a ship in its management or navigation. In 1936, the United States adopted the Hague Rules by incorporating them into the Carriage of Goods by Sea Act (COGSA).

Hague Rules
A 1924 international liability convention for ocean cargo that restricts the liability of the carrier to U.S.$ 500 per package or per customary freight unit.

The Hague Rules' U.S.$ 500 limit per package became a problem with the advent of containers, when shipping lines began claiming that they were "customary freight units" and attempted to limit their liability to U.S.$ 500 per container. Surprisingly, some courts actually agreed with that interpretation, and essentially granted shipping lines immunity from liability.[29] The Hague Rules were therefore revised in 1968 to clarify the definition of package to the units listed on the bill of lading. It also increased the liability of the carrier to U.S.$ 666.67 or U.S.$ 2 per kilogram, whichever was higher. These revised rules are known as Hague-Visby Rules. The United States has not ratified this treaty, although it has been ratified by all of its major trading partners. In 1979, the Hague-Visby Rules were amended to reflect the declining value of the U.S. dollar, and the liability limits were expressed in Special Drawing Rights (SDRs), the artificial currency of the International Monetary Fund, and set at SDR 666.67 per package or SDR 2 per kilogram, whichever was higher.

Hague-Visby Rules
A 1968 international liability convention for ocean cargo that restricts the liability of the carrier to SDR 666.67 per package or per customary freight unit.

The advent of better navigational equipment and the annoyance of shippers at the continuous existence of the nautical fault defense triggered yet another round of international negotiations led by the United Nations Commission on International Trade Law (UNCITRAL), which abolished the 17 defenses of the Hague and Hague-Visby Rules and replaced them with only three: damage that the carrier took all

Hamburg Rules
A 1978 international liability convention for ocean cargo that restricts the liability of the carrier to U.S.$ 833 per package or per customary freight unit.

reasonable steps to avoid, damage by fire, and damage due to an attempt by the carrier to save life or property at sea. It also increased liability limits to SDR 835 per package and SDR 2.5 per kilogram. These rules are known as the Hamburg Rules and have been ratified by only a small number of countries, only a handful of which are significant international traders. A complete list of which countries have adopted which rules is available on the Internet.[30]

Because the United States has not ratified either the Hague-Visby Rules or the Hamburg Rules, the COGSA is still in effect for goods shipped from the United States, even though it is grossly outdated with its limit of U.S.$ 500. Several efforts have been made to attempt to revise COGSA, but none of them have been successful to date. In 1999, with the creation of the Ocean Shipping Reform Act (OSRA), the United States brought one additional level of complexity to the conventions regulating the liability of shipping lines by allowing private, confidential contracts between shippers and shipping lines, where traditional liability constraints are replaced by negotiated ones. OSRA allowed private contracts between shippers and shipping lines, and it is likely that the liability limit of carriers was lifted in many of these agreements and that all but a handful of defenses have been eliminated. Therefore, the revision of COGSA may become moot in the near future.

However, there is still a problem with liability in intermodal freight; that is, freight that is shipped through several means of transportation using only one bill of lading and for which one of the legs is carriage by sea. The liability limits are different for domestic transport in the exporting country, international transport by ocean (and depend further on the nationality of the carrier, which governs which liability convention will apply), and domestic transport in the importing country. When cargo is damaged in transit without the possibility of tracing where specifically in the voyage the peril occurred, which liability limit is applicable?

Rotterdam Rules
A 2008 international liability convention for intermodal cargo that restricts the liability of the carrier to U.S.$ 875 per package or per customary freight unit.

In June 2000, the United Nations Commission on International Trade Law (UNCITRAL) started the process of creating a formal multimodal liability framework. UNCITRAL finished its work in July 2008, and the General Assembly of the United Nations voted to accept the Rotterdam Rules in February 2009. In September 2009, the United States and 15 other countries signed the convention, heeding the recommendations of the International Chamber of Commerce, which had strongly advocated its ratification.[31] Another handful of countries have signed the convention, but only two had ratified it as of June 2013: Spain and Togo.[32] The remainder of the signatories have to ratify it, and each of the countries still has to complete its own legislation to implement the rules. The Rotterdam Rules will not enter into force until one year after the twentieth country ratifies the treaty;[33] nevertheless, there is optimism that a single liability convention may finally govern international shipments of goods, regardless of the method of transportation. The Rotterdam Rules have their critics, though, who are concerned that they are too complex, allow too many exceptions, and are just trying to cover too much under one agreement.[34]

The main aspects of the Rotterdam Rules are that it is a convention with higher liability limits for the carrier: SDR 875 per package and SDR 4 per kilogram for items that are not considered packages, such as automobiles and machinery. The convention eliminates several of the 17 defenses of the Hague Rules, including the "errors in navigation" defense, which has become unsupportable in an era of inexpensive Global Positioning System devices. Finally, the convention applies "door-to-door," which subjects the legs of the voyage that are in the exporting and importing countries to the same liability limits. In order to mirror the private agreements of the U.S. Ocean Shipping Reform Act, it allows private contracts between shippers and

11.6 Non-Vessel-Operating Common Carriers

carriers—contracts that could raise or lower the liability limits. While large shippers are likely to be able to negotiate higher liability limits, small shippers are concerned that they will be subjected to lower liability limits by boilerplate bills of lading offered by the carriers.[35]

Not only are these issues of interest to insurance companies, but they also are of interest to any shipper that decides to retain its shipping risks and decline insurance coverage. As the liability of the carrier is very difficult to engage, even in the case of navigational errors or negligence, it may make more sense to purchase insurance coverage (see Chapter 10) and let the insurance company interact with the carrier in determining the carrier's responsibility under these international conventions.

11.6 Non-Vessel-Operating Common Carriers

Non-Vessel-Operating Common Carriers (NVOCCs) make up another type of shipping company, but with the *caveat* that they do not own and operate ships. Nevertheless, NVOCCs are regulated by the Federal Maritime Commission (FMC). The way an NVOCC operates is by purchasing space on a ship on a given voyage and by selling this space to companies that need to ship cargo. The shipping line gets paid for the space—and weight—whether or not the NVOCC fills its allocation. The NVOCC makes money only by reselling the space at a higher rate than the one at which it purchased it. In most instances, an NVOCC also acts as a freight consolidator and aggregates less-than-container-load (LCL) freight from several customers into a full container. This allows small shippers to benefit from the protection of a container and allows them to ship without the extra packing protection that breakbulk demands.

The NVOCC system was the basis for the model followed by consolidators in the air passenger business. These consolidators purchase blocks of seats on airplanes and resell them to individuals, generally through discount travel agencies.

Freight Charges

Shipping lines will charge for container shipping either by following published tariff rates or by negotiating contract rates with large volume shippers. All tariff rates can be negotiated, and shipping lines will negotiate rates for as few as 12 containers shipped at once. Rates are determined per package or by weight, including cargo shipped in containers on a less-than-container-load (LCL) basis. In addition to the freight rate, there are additional charges of which the international logistics professional must be aware:[36]

• **ARB**—Arbitrary charge. This charge is for added expenses, such as transshipment in an intermediary port, ice-breaking, cleaning of returned containers that are not ready for the next cargo, electrical power to refrigerated containers, and monitoring of refrigerated containers.

• **BAF or FAF**—Bunker adjustment factor, also known as fuel adjustment factor or surcharge. This is an extra charge applied by shipping to reflect fluctuations in the cost of bunker fuel. This surcharge is expressed either as an amount per freight ton or as a percentage of the freight charge.

• **CAF**—Currency adjustment factor. This is a surcharge applied to freight rates by shipping lines. It is to ensure that the revenue of the shipping lines is unaffected by movements in the currencies in which transactions are carried out by the lines in relation to the freight rate currency. It is normally expressed as a percentage of the freight and may be negative as well as positive.

- **CY/CY**—Container yard to container yard movement of cargo. This is a charge added to the freight rate to reflect the cost of moving cargo from one yard in the port to another yard, a function that is fulfilled by a cartage company.
- **CFS/CY**—Container freight stations to container yard movement of cargo. This is a charge added to the freight rate to reflect the cost of moving cargo from outside of the port to a yard inside the port, a function that is fulfilled by a cartage company.
- **Chassis charge.** This is a charge imposed by container shipping lines for providing customers with a truck chassis at the harbor terminals. A chassis is a truck trailer on which the container will be placed before it is loaded onto the ship or after it is unloaded from the ship.
- **THC**—Terminal handling charge, also known as container yard charge. This is a charge payable to a shipping line either for receiving a full container load at the container terminal, storing it, and delivering it to the ship at the load port or for receiving it from the ship at the discharge port, storing it, and delivering it to the consignee.

Determining the correct charge for a container can be challenging and can amount to much more than the published or negotiated freight rate. Here is an example of the calculation of the cost of a full container shipment from Oakland, California, to Singapore. The container is filled with paper products.

Freight Charges Calculation

Base Container rate		U.S. $2,000
Additional charges:		
· CAF—Currency adjustment factor	5%	
· BAF—Bunker adjustment factor	15%	
· THC—Terminal handling charge	U.S.$ 125	
· ARB—Arbitrary charge: cleaning fee	U.S.$ 40	
Total additional charges:		
[container rate× (CAF+BAF)]+ THC+ARB=		
[$2,000× (0.05+0.15)] + $125 + $40 =		U.S.$ 565
Total Container Charges		**$2,565**

Table 11.4: Calculation of a Container's Freight Charges

NOTE: Container-based rates may at times be calculated by weight or by package, especially if the shipment is less-than-container load (LCL).

11.7 Security Requirements

After the terrorist attacks that took place in the beginning of the twenty-first century, a number of measures were taken worldwide to limit the probability of terrorist attacks carried out by sea. The countries that felt that they could be targets reasoned that an easy way for a terrorist to smuggle a dangerous weapon was to bring it in using the traditional import channels, mixed with traditional ocean cargo. Several initiatives to limit the probability of a terrorist attack through ocean imports were started within a few years, most by the United States and the European Union, but several others by other countries and the International Maritime Organization. More information on these different approaches can be found in Chapter 15, but there are two main measures that affect ocean cargo.

11.7.1 Cargo Inspections

Most countries have a program under which their Customs Service inspects cargo when it arrives in the port of importation. For example, a percentage of all shipments entering the United States are inspected upon arrival; this percentage varies from 1 to 5 percent, depending on the port. Such inspections have traditionally been conducted to prevent fraud—the import of products that were not correctly identified or valued on the import documentation—but they are now much more focused on terrorism prevention.

For the past decade, inspections have also happened in the port of exportation, either through non-invasive measures, such as a X-rays, or through physical investigation of the contents of a shipment. For example, the United States has implemented a Container Security Initiative, through which Customs and Border Protection (CBP) inspectors are temporarily assigned to foreign ports where they inspect containers bound for the United States. Such containers are either pulled at random or are flagged as suspicious because of their specific characteristics. A World Customs Organization initiative encourages ports abroad to purchase container-scanning equipment and agree to inspect cargo when such inspection is requested by the country of importation. In exchange, cargo shipped from these ports get preferential treatment when they enter the country that requested the inspection.

11.7.2 Advance Shipping Notifications

Many countries have implemented a process by which shippers have to notify the importing country's Customs authorities of the particulars of a shipment before cargo is loaded onto the carrier's ship. Such notification has to be made at least 24 hours in advance, and must include information on the shipper, the type of cargo, the consignee, and the carrier.

The first program that required such advanced notification was the 24-hour rule implemented by the United States and administered by the CBP of the Department of Homeland Security. That rule required that all importers (and carriers) provide a copy of the manifest of an ocean shipment bound for the United States, including shipments that were just transiting through a U.S. port and were bound for another country, 24 hours before that shipment was loaded onto the vessel bound for the United States.

The U.S. program has been superseded since January 26, 2010, by a program called the Importer Security Filing, which follows the guidelines of the World Customs Organization's SAFE initiative of June 2007 (see Chapter 15), which mandates that importing countries make uniform the type of information that can be required of shippers. The requirements of the Importer Security Filing expand the number of points of information that the shipper must provide, and it has become better known in the United States as the 10 + 2 rule, which somewhat mirrors the number of items required.

The purpose of these advanced notification rules is that the importing country's Customs authorities are able to inspect the paperwork, and eventually warn the carrier that something may be inappropriate with the shipment. When a shipment is identified as problematic, it is not loaded, and is inspected in the port of departure before it is loaded onto the next available ship. In some cases, the inspection is conducted by Customs inspectors from the importing country assigned to the foreign port.

Review and Discussion Questions

1. What two different types of ocean cargo services are there?

2. Describe three different types of ships used in international ocean transportation. What type of cargoes are they used for?

3. Explain the concept of a flag. Why does a ship need a flag? Why would an owner choose to fly a flag of convenience?

4. What is the Baltic Exchange? What is the purpose of publishing the Baltic Exchange indices?

5. What are the differences between the Hague Rules, the Hague-Visby Rules, the Hamburg Rules, and the Rotterdam Rules?

6. What are the major initiatives of the world governments in terms of cargo security?

Notes

[1] Shipping Key Facts, Maritime International Secretariat Services, http://www.ics-shipping.org/shippingfacts/worldtrade/volume-world-trade-sea.php, retrieved June 22, 2013.

[2] "Triple-E Class Container Ships, Denmark," Ship Technology, http://www.ship-technology.com/projects/triple-e-class/, retrieved June 24, 2013

[3] *The Panama Canal*, November 1996, a publication of the Panama Canal Commission Office of Public Affairs, APO Miami 34011-5000.

[4] "Knock Nevis," http://www.ships-info.info/mer-Knock-nevis.htm, accessed June 24, 2013.

[5] "Maersk claims new 'mega containerships' could cut shipping emissions," *The Guardian*, February 21, 2011.

[6] "MS Allure of the Seas," Wikipedia, http://en.wikipedia.org/wiki/MS_Allure_of_the_Seas, retrieved June 24, 2013.

NOTES

[7] Review of Maritime Transport 2012, United Nations Conference on Trade and Development, New York, USA and Geneva Switzerland, 2013, http://unctad.org/en/pages/Publication Webflyer.aspx?publicationid=380, accessed June 24, 2013.

[8] Ibid.

[9] Sheridan, Rob, "VLCC Market Will Take At Least 3 More Years to Recover Says Maersk Tankers CEO," Bloomberg News, http://gcaptain.com/vlcc-market-years-recover-maersk/, retrieved June 25, 2013.

[10] Sullivan, Allanna, "A 700-ft Tanker Just Does Not Handle Quite Like a Honda," *The Wall Street Journal*, April 14, 1989, p. 1.

[11] Wells, Ken, "Captain's Course: Life on a Supertanker Mixes Tedium, Stress for Kenneth Campbell," *The Wall Street Journal*, September 11, 1986, p. 1.

[12] McPhee, John, "The Ships of Port Revel," *The Atlantic Monthly*, October 1998, pp. 67-80.

[13] "Propulsion Trends in Tankers," MAN Diesel, mandieselturbo.com/.../Propulsion%20trends%20in%20tankers.htm.pdf?, retrieved June 28, 2013.

[14] "The Baltic Code," The Baltic Exchange, http://www.balticexchange.com/default.asp?action=article&ID=4, accessed June 27, 2009.

[15] "A History of Baltic Indices," The Baltic Exchange, June 2013, http://www.balticexchange.com/default.asp?action=article&ID=558, accessed June 25, 2013.

[16] Wright, Robert, "Collapse in Dry Bulk Shipping Rates Unprecedented in Its Severity," *Financial Times*, December 01, 2008.

[17] "Baltic Exchange Dry Index (BDI) & Freight Rates," Investment Tools, http://investmenttools.com/futures/bdi_baltic_dry_index.htm, retrieved June 26, 2013.

[18] *Comparison of U.S. and Foreign-Flag Operating Costs*, September 2011, United States Maritime Administration, http://www.marad.dot.gov/documents/Comparison_of_US_and_Foreign_Flag_Operating_Costs.pdf, retrieved June 25, 2013.

[19] Gillis, Chris, "Changing U.S.-Flag Vessel Economics," *American Shipper*, October 2004, pp. 72-76.

[20] Review of Maritime Transport 2012, United Nations Conference on Trade and Development, New York, USA and Geneva Switzerland, 2013, http://unctad.org/en/pages/Publication Webflyer.aspx?publicationid=380, accessed June 24, 2013.

[21] Ibid.

[22] *By the Capes Around the World: A Summary of World Cabotage Practices*, U.S. Maritime Administration, 1995.

[23] Bloom, Murray, "Notice of Open Season for Enrollment in the Voluntary Intermodal Sealift Agrement (VISA) Program," Federal Register, October 15, 2009, http://www.gpo.gov/fdsys/pkg/FR-2009-10-15/html/E9-24788.htm.

[24] David G. Harris and Richard D. Stewart, "U.S. Surge Sealift Capabilities: A Question of Sufficiency," Parameters, *U.S. Army War College Quarterly*, Spring 1998.

[25] *Dahingo v. Royal Caribbean Cruises, Ltd.*, 99 CIV 12774, 312 F. Supp. 2d 440 442 S.D.N.Y. 2004, United States District Court Southern District of New York

[26] Bangsberg, P. T., "Shipowners Tackle Asia Flag Question," *The Journal of Commerce*, May 29, 1997, p. 8B.

[27] Carrington, Tim, "U.S. Owners of Foreign-Registry Ships Want Navy to Rally Round the Flag their Vessels Don't Fly," *The Wall Street Journal*, December 29, 1987, p. 44.

[28] McFadden, Robert, and Scott Shane, "In Rescue of Captain, Navy Kills Three Pirates," *The

New York Times, April 13, 2009.

[29] Still, Craig, "Thinking Outside the Box: the Application of COGSA's $500 per Package Limitation to Shipping Containers," *Houston Journal of International Law*, Fall 2001, Vol. 24, No. 1.

[30] "International Conventions Membership List," InforMARE, www.informare.it/dbase/conv-uk.htm, accessed June 27, 2013.

[31] Edmonson, R. G., "ICC Endorses Rotterdam Rules," *Journal of Commerce*, June 2, 2009.

[32] "Status of the 2008 United Nations Convention on Contracts for the International Carriage of Goods Wholly or Partly by Sea—the 'Rotterdam Rules'," http://www.uncitral.org/uncitral/en/uncitral_texts/transport_goods/rotterdam_status.html, retrieved June 25, 2013.

[33] Hooper, Chester, "Ratification of the Rotterdam Rules and their Implications for International Shipping," February 2012, www.skuld.com/Documents/Library/Beacon/Beacon_2_2012_rotterdam_rules.pdf, retrieved June 25, 2013.

[34] Tetley, William, "Summary of Some General Criticisms of the UNCITRAL Convention (The Rotterdam Rules)," McGill University School of Law Internal Document, http://www.mcgill.ca/files/maritimelaw/Tetley_Criticism_of_Rotterdam_Rules.pdf, November 5, 2008, accessed June 27, 2009.

[35] Hailey, Roger, "Freight Forwarders Step Up Attacks on Rotterdam Rules," *Lloyd's List*, June 2, 2009, http://www.lloydslist.com/ll/news/freight-forwarders-step-up-attack-on-rotterdam-rules/1243872041051.htm.

[36] Brodie, P., *Dictionary of Shipping Terms*. London: Lloyd's of London Press, Ltd. 1994.

Chapter 12

International Air Transportation

> 12.1 Cargo Airlines, Airports, and Markets 310
> 12.2 Types of Service 312
> 12.3 Types of Aircraft 316
> 12.4 Airfreight Tariffs 327
> 12.5 International Regulations 328
> 12.6 Environmental Issues and Sustainability 328
> 12.7 International Air Cargo Security 329

The scale and scope of international air cargo transportation has grown steadily over the past four decades, driven by globalization and the increasing expectations of business and consumers worldwide. Today, even though airfreight may represent only 1 percent of world trade by weight, it accounts for approximately 40 percent of world trade by value. The demand for airfreight is also highly correlated with world GDP, and more than 75 percent of the world's airfreight is carried by non-U.S. airlines.[1] The slow but steady growth in this premium mode of transportation has been driven, in part, by the advent of time-definite shipments, a concept that was implemented with military-like precision by Federal Express in the United States market in the 1970s, and which has been adopted by just about all cargo airlines in the international arena. Figure 12.1 illustrates the growth in airfreight in revenue tonne kilometers (RTKs) from 1997 through 2011.[2] (A measurement used by the industry; one Revenue Tonne Kilometer corresponds to one metric tonne of goods transported for one kilometer). One RTK is equal to 0.68 ton-mile.

Prior to 2007, many experts felt that the airfreight industry had no alternative but to grow further, and its annual growth rate was 9 percent per year. However, high fuel prices and financial turmoil took a toll on air cargo traffic in 2008, resulting in a drop in airfreight in 2008 and 2009, but the industry recovered strongly in 2010, to soften further in 2011. At the end of 2012, both Boeing and Airbus were still optimistic on the long-term prospects for airfreight, but the prospects for growth were more moderate, in the 5 to 7 percent range,[3] which still would lead to a tripling of the worldwide freight traffic by 2035.[4]

time-definite shipments
Cargo or package shipments that must be delivered by a guaranteed, predetermined time and day.

revenue tonne kilometer(RTK)
A unit designed to express total airline activity. It is equal to the number of tonnes of cargo, passengers, baggages and mail shipped multiplied by the number of kilometers they were shipped.

12.1 Cargo Airlines, Airports, and Markets

freight tonne kilometer(FTK)
A unit designed to express cargo volume shipped. It is equal to the number of tonnes of cargo shipped multiplied by the number of kilometers they were shipped.

FedEx (previously called Federal Express) is the largest airfreight company in the world, serving more than 375 airports worldwide.[5] As can be seen in Table 12.1, FedEx also won the top spot for international cargo volume in 2012 with 16.1 billion freight tonne kilometers (FTKs)—11 billion ton-miles—followed by UPS (United Parcel Service) and Emirates, the fastest growing airline in the world, for both cargo and passenger traffic.[6] The top ten cargo carriers in the world account for about 45 percent of the world's freight transportation volume of 200 billion RTKs[7]—137.1 billion ton-miles.

The top fifteen cargo airports in the world for 2012 are listed in Table 12.2.[8] Each of the largest cargo airports is dominated by one or several large cargo airlines, either because it is headquartered in that city or it uses that airport as a major base for its operations. In the United States, Memphis is FedEx's main hub and headquarters; Anchorage is a major trans-Pacific transit point between the Asian continent and the United States, Canada, and the rest of the Americas; Louisville is the main hub for UPS; and Miami is a major gateway for traffic between the United States and Latin America. In Europe, Frankfurt is the main cargo hub for Lufthansa, and Paris is the main hub for Air France, FedEx, and La Poste. In Asia, Tokyo is the major hub for Japan Airlines; Incheon (Seoul) is the major hub for Korean Air; Shanghai is a major hub for Great Wall Airlines, China Eastern, and UPS; while Hong Kong SAR is the major Asian hub for DHL and a main hub for Cathay Pacific. Finally, it should be noted that, in that list, only Memphis and Louisville have a significant domestic cargo traffic. All of the others handle essentially only international cargo.

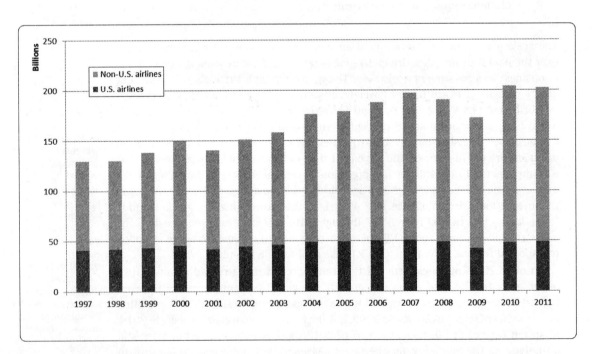

Figure 12.1: Growth in Air Cargo Volume in billions of RTKs
Boeing *World Air Cargo Forecast 2012-13*.

12.1 Cargo Airlines, Airports, and Markets

Top Ten Cargo Airlines, 2012

Rank	Airline	Millions of FTKs
1	FedEx	16,108
2	UPS Airlines	10,416
3	Emirates	9,319
4	Cathay Pacific Airways	8,433
5	Korean Air Lines	8,144
6	Lufthansa	7,175
7	Singapore Airlines	6,694
8	British Airways	4,732
9	China Airlines	4,538
10	EVA Air	4,470

Table 12.1: The Ten Largest Cargo Airlines (in millions of FTKs)
IATA *World Air Transport Statistics.*

Top Fifteen Cargo Airports, 2012

Rank	Airport	Metric Tonnes
1	Hong Kong SAR	4,062,261
2	Memphis	4,016,126
3	Shanghai	2,939,157
4	Incheon/Seoul	2,456,724
5	Anchorage	2,449,551
6	Dubai	2,267,365
7	Louisville	2,168,365
8	Paris	2,150,950
9	Frankfurt	2,066,432
10	Tokyo	2,006,173
11	Miami	1,929,889
12	Singapore	1,841,858
13	Beijing	1,787,027
14	Los Angeles	1,771,907
15	Taipei	1,577,728

Table 12.2: Fifteen Largest Cargo Airports (in metric tonnes loaded)
ACI *World Airport Traffic.*

Regionally, and as illustrated in Figure 12.2,[9] air cargo volume is expected to grow most between the People's Republic of China (PRC) and North America, which is expected to eventually surpass the internal North American market, and between PRC and Europe. Other trade lanes in which flows are expected to show substantial growth are in domestic PRC market, between North America and Europe, and in the domestic United States market. Airfreight traffic between Europe and Asia, North America and Asia, and between Europe and South America is expected to grow as well, but at a more moderate pace.

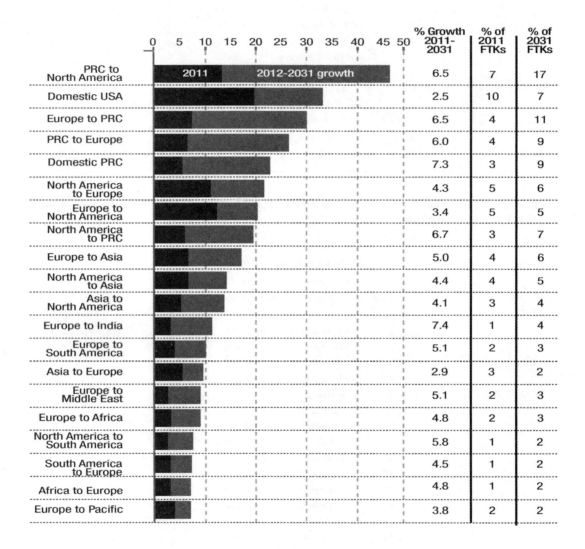

Figure 12.2: Cargo Volume Forecast by Region, in billions of FTKs
Airbus *Global Market Forecast 2012-2031*, used with permission.

12.2 Types of Service

The types of service offered by the airfreight industry are defined by the nature of the demand and type of commodity. Airfreight is particularly well suited for commodities that have a high value-to-weight ratio, or are perishable, quickly obsolete, required on short notice, or expensive to handle or store. Shipping by air is also attractive when demand is unpredictable, infrequent, exceeds local supply, or is seasonal. Shippers also choose air when the risk of pilferage, breakage, or deterioration is great, when the cost of insurance is high for long periods of transit, when heavy packaging is required for surface transportation, or when there is need for special handling. In some circumstances, shipping by air can be used to avoid warehousing costs that would otherwise be required if other, slower modes of transportation were used, such as ocean transportation.[10] Difficult terrain or the lack of rail, port, or road infrastructure are also valid reasons for shipping by air. Finally, the risk of losing a customer or halting production due to the lack of an urgently-needed repair part can also justify the expense of moving goods by air.[11]

Although the types of products shipped vary by region, in general, air transportation lends itself to the movement of industrial equipment, computers and office machines, consumer products, work-in-process goods, apparel, perishables, small packages, documents, and other manufactured goods. To meet the demand for these products, various types of service have evolved, including air mail services, express airfreight services, scheduled airfreight services, charter airfreight services, leasing, and airfreight forwarder services.

12.2.1 Air Mail Services

Air mail was the first type of cargo service offered and "an important factor in the formation of air transportation in the United States."[12] Today, air mail services are still important but represent a little under 3 percent of airline revenue and about 4 percent of air cargo carried, measured by RTKs.

12.2.2 Express Airfreight Services

Although DHL, FedEx, and UPS were not the first carriers to offer express air cargo services, these carriers and their services have continued to grow ever since FedEx deployed 14 small aircraft to deliver its first 186 packages on the night of April 17, 1973. Within the United States, FedEx and UPS now dominate the air express cargo market and are still competing for DHL's share following its withdrawal from the U.S. domestic market in late 2008. As the volume of domestic express services has grown, international express air cargo services have also continued to grow and now represent over 13 percent of international air cargo traffic, even as the distinction between express air cargo and regularly-scheduled air cargo services continues to blur.[13]

express cargo
Cargo shipped with a guaranteed predetermined delivery date.

Today, FedEx employs over 300,000 people and maintains the world's largest all-cargo airline, operating over 650 aircraft in more than 220 countries and territories. Through its hub in Memphis, Tennessee, FedEx Express operates more than 5,000 flights a month and serves 95 percent of the global economy on a 24- to 48-hour basis.[14] In addition to multiple hubs in the United States, FedEx operates major hubs in Paris (France), Subic Bay (The Philippines), Toronto (Canada), Guangzhou (China), and Cologne/Bonn (Germany).

While FedEx entered the market with a new and distinct business model, UPS evolved over time from a messenger service and common carrier into a leader in global supply chain management. Today, UPS owns 233 aircraft (and leases another 300) to provide express airfreight service to over 200 countries.[15] In addition to its major hub at Worldport in Louisville, Kentucky, UPS operates major hubs in

Cologne/Bonn (Germany), Taipei (Taiwan,China), Pampanga (The Philippines), Ontario (California), Hong Kong (China), Singapore, and Shanghai (China)—and is developing an intra-Asia hub in Shenzhen (China). Worldport has been expanded several times and now occupies a 48-hectare distribution center (5.2 million square feet) with the capacity to sort over 300,000 packages per hour.[16]

Outside the United States, Belgium-based DHL, a subsidiary of Deutsche Post, is the leader in many European and Asian markets, claiming 41 percent of the European market for courier, express, and parcel services, 40 percent of the Asian express market, and 40 percent of the eastern European, Middle Eastern, and African express market in 2012.[17] The company has been gaining in the North and South American market, with a new hub in Cincinnati serving international markets only. As of 2012, DHL operated a fleet of 250 aircraft serving over 220 countries and territories. Another Belgium-based airline is TNT Airways, the fourth largest consolidator in the world, and a very strong presence in Europe and China.

One of the major factors leading to the continued growth and long-term success of the express air cargo industry has been the shift in focus from carrying cargo to providing a bundle of services to meet the needs of customers who are willing to pay for the convenience of one-stop shopping. Over time, FedEx, UPS, DHL, TNT, and others have continued to expand their services to the point of offering supply chain solutions versus package delivery. As a result, these firms are often referred to as integrators, where the scope of integrated services has been continuously expanding.

integrator
An air cargo carrier that offers its customers complete door-to-door service.

12.2.3 Scheduled Airfreight Services

As the name implies, this category of service refers to flights that are offered on a published schedule. Scheduled airfreight services have many advantages. Since these services are offered on a routine basis, they tend to be highly reliable and efficient, resulting in relatively low-cost airfreight delivery. Scheduled airfreight services make up the bulk of international air cargo traffic. However, it is interesting to note that, even though the overall volume of international air cargo has increased over the years, the percent of world air cargo carried by U.S. carriers has declined as the U.S. domestic market has matured (see Figure 12.1).

Today, passenger airlines, integrators, and airfreight companies offer scheduled airfreight services. Although passenger airliners hold cargo in the belly of the aircraft, such cargo is often considered secondary to their focus on serving passengers. As a result, many of the all-cargo airliners and integrators, such as Cargolux and FedEx respectively, operate airfreighters on both a scheduled and non-scheduled basis. Some of the leading international scheduled airfreight service providers include Korean Air, Lufthansa, Cathay Pacific, Singapore Airlines, FedEx, China Airlines, Air France, Emirates, Cargolux, JAL, UPS, British Airways, KLM, United Airlines, Northwest Airlines, Quanta, El Al, and DHL.

12.2.4 Charter Airfreight Services

Charter airfreight services are those that are based on demand and do not operate on a published schedule. Although this alternative can be more expensive than scheduled service, charter airfreight services offer shippers more flexibility. Charter services can be tailored to meet the individual shipper's needs for specialized cargo, emergencies, or delivery to destinations that are not normally served by scheduled airlines or freight carriers. For example, charter aircraft can be used to meet the demands of seasonal traffic, such as the shipment of cherries from the Northwest of the United States to Japan in July, or roses from Colombia to the United States in February.[18] A large increase in demand for a new product, such as the shipment of a new Beaujolais Nouveau from France to the United States and Japan in November, can also cause a carrier to supplement its capacity through the use of charter airfreight services. Some of the world's largest air charter cargo providers include Air Charter Services, Lufthansa Cargo Charter, and Polar Air Cargo.

charter airfreight
A type of cargo that can only be shipped on a charter aircraft because it is too heavy, too bulky or its destination is not serviced by a scheduled airfreight service.

In addition to meeting emergency needs or the demand for products that exceed plans, there are also times when shippers need to ship products that do not fit in the cargo bay of a traditional cargo aircraft. Often referred to as "project cargo" (see Chapter 13), such items exceed the volume or weight restrictions of traditional aircraft and require special handling and carriage by aircraft designed to meet these special needs. Airbus's A-300 Beluga (see Figure 12.13 on page 325), Boeing's 747 Dreamlifter (see Figure 12.14 on page 325), and the Antonov 124 Ruslan (see Figure 12.11 on page 324) and its even larger cousin, the Antonov 225 Mriya (see Figure 12.12 on page 324) certainly fit that category. It is also interesting to note that, in at least three of these cases, these aircraft were originally developed to meet the outsize cargo needs of the aviation and aerospace industry itself. For example, the Beluga was originally designed to meet the complex logistics challenges of shipping parts across Europe to support the production and assembly of the Airbus series of aircrafts from Hamburg, Germany, to Toulouse, France. Similarly, the Dreamlifter was designed to meet the just-in-time assembly needs of Boeing's worldwide network of suppliers for the 787 Dreamliner. Finally, the Mriya was originally designed to transport the Russian space shuttle.

12.2.5 Leased Cargo Aircraft Services

As in other industries which involve large capital expenditures, leasing is also an option for the major carriers and other providers of airfreight services. There are a variety of leasing options available, but most leases take the form of a "dry" lease, "damp" lease, "wet" lease, or "aircraft, crew, maintenance, and insurance" [ACMI] lease.

wet lease
A type of leasing contract in which an airplane is leased, along with a crew, maintenance services, insurance and fuel.

In the past, a wet lease referred to a short-term lease which usually included the aircraft, crew, maintenance, insurance, and fuel. Today, the most common cargo aircraft leases include only the aircraft, crew, maintenance, and insurance (ACMI) and are therefore called ACMI leases. Damp leasing is similar to ACMI, but without the flight crew. Finally, a dry lease is a form of leasing where the lessor provides an aircraft without any crew, maintenance, insurance, services, or fuel.

ACMI lease
A type of leasing contract in which an airplane is leased, along with a crew, maintenance services, and insurance.

damp lease
A type of leasing contract in which an airplane is leased, along with maintenance services and insurance, but no crew.

According to Boeing's *World Air Cargo Forecast for 2012-2013*, about 6 percent of the world's air cargo is now transported by ACMI providers.[19] Although the demand for ACMI services does tend to vary with the economy, the market for large, long-haul international airfreight aircraft has increased over the years, since the new wide-body freighters are more efficient than most conversions—a former passenger aircraft converted into a freighter aircraft—and older airfreight aircraft.

dry lease
A type of leasing contract in which only an airplane is leased.

Both UPS and FedEx lease aircraft to supplement their core capacity, especially during the November-December holidays. FedEx, for example, leases almost 100 large jets to supplement its own fleet and approximately 50 smaller piston-driven and turbo-prop aircraft to deliver packages to and from airports served by its larger aircraft.[20]

12.2.6 Airfreight Forwarder Services

Like other modes of transportation, airfreight forwarders provide the link between shippers of airfreight and consignees at the destination. Freight forwarders contract with air carriers, consolidate shipments, buy space on flights, and arrange intermodal surface transportation needs. Some freight forwarders provide a full range of supply chain management services, while others specialize in performing specific tasks. Today, many of the integrators, such as DHL, UPS, and FedEx, offer international freight forwarding services and compete directly with traditional freight forwarders such as Schenker, Kuehne & Nagel, Panalpina, and numerous others.

12.3 Types of Aircraft

Although many types of aircraft are used to meet the growing demand for fast and efficient air transportation, in general these aircraft can be broken down into four categories: passenger aircraft, combination or "combi" aircraft, quick-change aircraft, and large cargo aircraft that are designed to serve as airfreighters.

Figure 12.3: The Largest Passenger Aircraft. The Airbus A380
Photo ©Chris Hepburn, used with permission.

12.3 Types of Aircraft

12.3.1 Passenger Aircraft

Just about every passenger aircraft transports cargo in addition to the passengers carried on its main deck. The "belly" of the aircraft is designed to accommodate the passengers' luggage and additional airfreight. Some of this airfreight cargo is loose freight (*i.e.*, not palletized) and is shipped piece by piece; the packages are not secured to the aircraft and are shipped in a manner that is similar to passenger luggage.

Figure 12.4: Cargo on a Wide-Body Passenger Aircraft (Boeing 747)
Photo ©Matthias Clausen, used with permission.

In larger, wide-body aircraft (see Figure 12.3), the freight is palletized or containerized (see Figure 12.4) and secured to the aircraft. International cargo services on passenger aircraft are somewhat unreliable, as airlines sometimes "bump" freight, creating more capacity to carry additional passengers and their luggage. Therefore, only the most urgent of cargo makes it on passenger aircraft, and it is often made up of machine or computer parts necessary for the repair of a critical piece of equipment, or small shipments of fresh produce, such as vegetables or fish.

The biggest constraint on a shipper regarding the use of passenger airplanes for shipping freight is the maximum weight or volume of the shipment. The issues to consider are the size of the hold, the weight capacity of the floor of the cargo hold, the overall weight limitations of the aircraft, and the size of the door used to

Figure 12.5: A Canadian North Combination Aircraft (Boeing 737)
Photo ©Kevin Wachter, courtesy of www.airliners.net, used with permission.

access the cargo hold. Most freight forwarders have a good grasp of the maximum sizes of packages that can be shipped in passenger airplanes and are quite helpful in determining whether or not the cargo will be allowed on a passenger flight. The second constraint is that there are some items that are not allowed on passenger aircraft but may be transported on cargo aircraft. Such hazardous material must be labeled Cargo Aircraft Only (CAO) and can be shipped only in airfreighters.

onboard courier (OBC)
A passenger on a regularly scheduled flight who relinquishes his or her baggage allocation to allow cargo in its place.

Another alternative way of using passenger airplanes for cargo is to use an onboard courier (OBC) service. A courier is often a student or a retiree who will fly to a city and take cargo as his or her luggage. This is often the fastest way for cargo to get anywhere and is a service used for delivery of critical parts and documents. It also presents the advantage of the cargo always making the plane, as passengers' luggage has priority over all other freight. The OBC business is substantial, but unfortunately there are no aggregate statistics for this activity. One OBC company in San Francisco shipped 2,000 metric tonnes of freight by courier.[21] That's a lot of document pouches.

12.3.2 Combination Aircraft

Combination aircraft, or combis, are passenger airplanes that are designed to carry freight on the main deck as well as in the belly hold. The main deck is split at

12.3 Types of Aircraft

some point in the middle of the aircraft, with one portion of the plane reserved for passengers and the other portion reserved for freight. Some aircraft are designed in such a way that this partition is somewhat mobile, depending on the demand for passenger seats (a decision usually based on seasonal fluctuations).

Some of the more common combi aircraft include the Airbus 330 and 340; the DC-10; and the Boeing 737, 747, and 757. Many of the larger wide-body combis, such as the Boeing 747 and DC-10, are used to fly passengers and cargo nonstop to remote areas of the world, such as the islands of the South Pacific, where the volume of passenger traffic by itself is not sufficient to justify such flights. In another example, Alaskan Airlines uses modified Boeing 737-400 combis to meet the needs of the seafood industry, as well as to transport passengers to and from the northern and western parts of Alaska.[22] Canadian North (see Figure 12.5) operates similar flights.

For shippers, combis present an advantage over passenger aircraft. The main deck has a greater weight capacity and a much larger door, and can accommodate palletized and containerized cargo. Moreover, the cargo can be secured to the plane to prevent damage caused by movement within the aircraft. However, the restrictions on what is allowed to be shipped with passengers aboard remain.

combi aircraft
A type of airplane that is designed to carry both cargo and passengers at the same time on the main deck.

main deck
The largest deck on an aircraft, the one on which passenger travel in a passenger aircraft.

lower deck
A deck designed to carry cargo and luggage, located underneath the main deck of an aircraft.

Figure 12.6: An Airfreighter, the Boeing 747-F
Photo ©Mark Abbott, courtesy of www.airliners.net, used with permission.

12.3.3 Quick-Change Aircraft

quick-change aircraft
A type of airplane that can be quickly converted from all-cargo service to all-passenger service, with the use of palletized seat sections.

As the name implies, quick-change aircraft are those which can be reconfigured from passenger to cargo configurations and vice-versa in a matter of hours. Airlines that operate quick-change aircraft use palletized sections of seats that can be easily added or removed from the main deck. Although limited in demand, the Boeing 737 200/300 series aircraft have had some moderate success in that configuration. Of the 1,731 airfreighters included in Airbus's computation of the world's airfreighter size in 2009, 59 were quick-change aircraft.[23]

12.3.4 Airfreighters

airfreighter
A type of airplane dedicated to carrying cargo.

Over the past decade, the amount of cargo carried has been equally split between airfreighters and the lower decks of passenger aircraft, with only slightly more than half of all air cargo carried by airfreighters. However, both Boeing and Airbus project that the demand for new freighters is going to grow. There are several reasons for this, including the increasing demand for air cargo, a decreased number of wide-body passenger aircraft available for conversion, and the fact that older airfreighters are reaching the end of their useful lives. In addition, the new airfreighters (see Figure 12.6) are much more fuel efficient, larger, and have lower maintenance costs.[24]

Figure 12.7: The Roller Deck of an Airbus A300F
Photo ©EDDL, courtesy of www.airliners.net, used with permission.

12.3 Types of Aircraft

Most airfreighters are "liners" (*i.e.*, they operate on a regular schedule) traveling between two airports, one of which is usually a hub, the location at which the cargo will be transferred to another flight. Most airfreighters are also variations of aircraft used for passenger service, with the exception that the freighter is equipped with a roller deck (see Figure 12.7). A roller deck is a main deck equipped with rollers that allows the palletized or containerized cargo to be pushed into or off the aircraft, either through an oversize side door or through the nose of the airplane, which, in some cases, can be lifted (see Figure 12.8). The cargo is then secured to the aircraft floor and walls using locks, hooks, and slings.

roller deck
A deck designed to carry cargo, and equipped with rollers and bearings that allow the cargo to be moved in any direction without much friction.

Figure 12.8: The Boeing 747-F can be Loaded through the Nose
Photo ©Ronén Björkquist, courtesy of www.airliners.net, used with permission.

In the past, most airfreighters were older passenger airplanes that were retrofitted for cargo service by specialized firms. Today, passenger-to-freighter conversions are still popular, but both Boeing and Airbus now offer freighter versions for almost every aircraft they build. For example, Boeing's 777-200F has done quite well as a new-built airfreighter, and Airbus offers the popular A330-200F. However, Airbus has temporarily postponed the introduction of its A380F, following the cancellation of orders by FedEx and UPS, with no new introduction date specified.[25] The A380-800F presents the advantage of having two main decks which can be loaded simultaneously, a fact that overcomes one of the pitfalls of a single-deck freighter, for which the loading sequence must be done very carefully, so as to not upset the balance of the aircraft on the ground. It is such a problem that most airfreight companies add a tail stand to prevent "nose up" situations during loading operations (see Figure 12.9).

Figure 12.9: A Tailstand Keeps an Airfreighter from Going "Nose up"
Photo ©Ben Wang, courtesy of www.airliners.net, used with permission.

Just as the ocean shipping industry has its own way of characterizing vessels, the air cargo industry has its own way of classifying freighters. The airfreighter fleet, for example, is often described in terms of standard body, medium wide-body, and large wide-body.

- The standard body category includes aircraft such as the McDonell-Douglas DC-8 and DC-9, the Boeing 727, 737, and 757, and the Airbus 320.

- The medium wide-body category includes the McDonell-Douglas DC-10, the Boeing 767 and 787, and the Airbus 300, 310, 330, and 340.

- The large wide-body category includes aircraft like the McDonell-Douglas MD-11, the Boeing 747 and 777, the Airbus 340-600SF, 350, and 380, and the Antonov 124.

Each of these aircraft was designed to meet specific air transportation needs. Figure 12.10 on the next page[26] illustrates how they vary by payload and range. As can be seen in this diagram, a Boeing 757 freighter would be well suited to carry 30 metric tonnes (66,140 pounds) over 2,500 nautical miles (4,630 kilometers), while a Boeing 777-200 could carry three times that payload twice as far. As of

12.3 Types of Aircraft

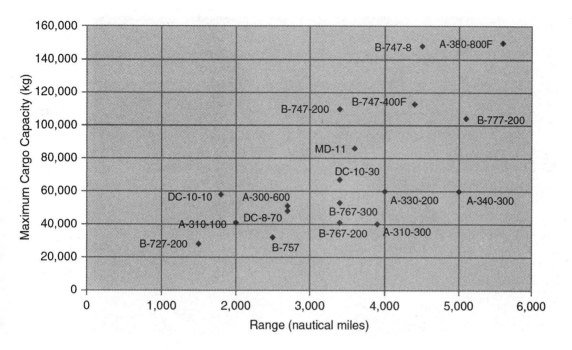

Figure 12.10: Freighter Payload and Range. *American Shipper*, Boeing and Airbus.

2013, the largest airline freighter is the Boeing 747-400F, but the likely introduction of the freighter version of the Airbus 380 will jeopardize this standing, since it is designed to carry 150 metric tonnes (330,693 pounds) over 5,600 nautical miles (10,371 kilometers).[27]

Airfreighters can also be aircraft that do not have passenger versions and are constructed exclusively for the purpose of moving freight. The Antonov 124 Ruslan (see Figure 12.11 on the following page) was built primarily for military use, but has found a niche in the civilian transport of cargo. The Antonov 124 can take off and land from poorly-maintained and short runways, despite a payload of 150 metric tonnes (330,693 pounds) and a range of 2,900 nautical miles (5,370 kilometers). It was the largest aircraft ever built until the Antonov 225 Mriya (see Figure 12.12 on the next page) took that distinction, with a payload of 250 metric tonnes and a range of 8,500 nautical miles (15,742 kilometers). The Antonov 225 was designed to transport the Russian Space Shuttle: it now specializes in the transport of very heavy airfreight.

Other aircraft designed exclusively for the purpose of transporting freight include the Airbus 300-600 ST Beluga (see Figure 12.13 on page 325) and the Boeing 747-400 Dreamlifter (see Figure 12.14 on page 325), both of which were transformations of traditional aircraft, designed to transport pieces of other aircraft from one assembly plant to another. The Beluga is used by Airbus to shuttle fuselage and wings from its plants in the U.K., Spain, and Germany to their final assembly location in Toulouse, France, and the Dreamlifter fulfills the same function for Boeing, transporting parts from Japan and Italy to Everett, Washington.

Figure 12.11: The Antonov *Ruslan* Designed to Handle Project Cargo
Photo ©Turker Hasimoglu, courtesy of www.airliners.net, used with permission.

Figure 12.12: The World's Largest Airfreighter, the Antonov 225 *Mriya*
Photo ©Dennis Muller, courtesy of www.airliners.net, used with permission.

12.3 Types of Aircraft

Figure 12.13: The A300-600ST *Beluga* Operated by Airbus
Photo ©Michael Lutz, courtesy of www.airliners.net, used with permission.

Figure 12.14: The B747-4J6 *Dreamlifter* Operated by Boeing
Photo ©S.L. Tsai, courtesy of www.airliners.net, used with permission.

Roses, Carnations and Cherries

In 2009, exports of cut flowers from Colombia totaled 205,407 metric tonnes, and 79 percent of these flowers were shipped to the United States,[28] utilizing the air services of FedEx and UPS, and LAN, a Chile-based airline, which slowly have replaced the specialized airfreight services that once dominated this trade route, such as Aeroflora. Improvements in the techniques used to chill and handle the flowers allow them to stay fresh for more than a week, until they are delivered to flower retailers. Most of the exports enter the United States through the Miami airport, and enter the European market through Schiphol Airport in the Netherlands.[29] Roses account for 33 percent of that volume—by value—carnations 18 percent, and chrysanthemums another 8 percent. A normal day will see from seven to ten flights from Bogotá to Miami, loaded with flowers.[30]

However, it is during the week preceding the Valentine's Day holiday that this business becomes crazy, with U.S. sales of roses reaching 40 million dozens. In 2012, each day of the week preceding the holiday, there were 32 flights from Colombia to Miami, each a large wide-body, packed tightly with literally millions of flowers.[31] A Boeing 747, packed to the gills, can hold 3.6 million roses.[32]

Figure 12.15: Cherries Being Loaded on an Airfreighter Bound for China
Photo ©Don Wilson, used with permission.

Cut flowers are not the only unusually seasonal business handled by airfreighters, though. From late May until late June, it is "cherry season" on the West Coast of the United States. In 2012, more than 1.2 million cartons (cardboard boxes of 8.2 kilograms [18 pounds]—see Figure 12.15) of cherries leave the United States for the Japanese market—that is a total of 10,350 metric tonnes.[33] These cherries all travel by airfreighters or in the bellies of passenger flights, at sometimes prohibitive rates because all West-bound capacity during that period is taken by these fruits (U.S.$ 1.95 per kilogram, whereas cargo normally fetches no more than U.S.$ 1.00 per kilogram on that route). It is the most profitable period of the year for the airlines involved in that trade because Narita Airport operates at full capacity and cannot accommodate any more flights.

12.4 Airfreight Tariffs

The tariff structure of international air cargo is not nearly as complicated as that of the ocean cargo industry, with its innumerable categories. Airfreight is priced as a function of two things: weight and volume.

In order to arrive at the freight cost of a particular shipment, airlines calculate two alternatives: the first is based on the actual weight of the shipment, and the other is based on its volume, a computation that uses the volume of the cargo to determine its "equivalent" weight, which is called either the volume-weight of a shipment or its dimensional weight—which many call simply the "dim weight" of a shipment. The airline will then charge the higher of the volume-weight or the actual weight of the cargo. On international shipments, the volume-weight conversion traditionally used 6,000 cubic centimeters per kilogram (166 cubic inches per pound), although some airlines had calculated this ratio slightly differently. In 2011, both FedEx and UPS introduced a significantly different ratio,[34] and started using 5,000 cubic centimeters per kilogram (139 cubic inches per pound).

volume weight (dimensional weight) An artificial weight, determined in function of the dimensions of a shipment, used by airlines to determine the tariff to be paid for a light shipment.

To illustrate, using FedEx's international airfreight calculator in June 2013, the cost to fly a cargo of 200 kilograms (440 pounds) would vary greatly in function of its volume. If the shipment comprised five containers, each measuring 90 × 90 × 50 centimeters (36 × 36 × 20 inches), each weighing 40 kg, the cost from Atlanta to Abu Dhabi (in priority airfreight) was approximately $3,700. However, the cost to ship the same weight in five larger containers with four times the volume (five 180 × 100 × 90-centimeter containers [71 × 39 × 36 inches]) was over $6,000. Thus, one can readily see how the volume of an air shipment can vastly affect its shipping costs.

The difficulty for a shipper using airfreight for lightweight products is to make sure that it does not pay too much for shipping by using packaging that is too voluminous. The trade-off is relatively simple. The shipper must decide between using packaging that satisfactorily protects but reduces the overall dimensions of the cargo and therefore reduces its volume-weight, and using more traditional packaging, which is likely to be less expensive but increases the freight costs by increasing the volume weight. The decision to decrease packaging should never be made without a thorough analysis, since improper packaging is one of the primary reasons insurance companies deny claims.

12.5 International Regulations

In terms of regulations, the international airfreight business is dominated by the International Air Transport Association (IATA) and the International Civil Aviation Organization (ICAO). International regulation of air traffic started with the Paris Convention of 1919, which established the concept of sovereignty of a country over its airspace. In 1929, the Warsaw Convention was signed, limiting the liability of international airlines toward passengers and freight in case of accidents. Both liability limits were eventually increased in 1955 with the Hague Protocol; in 1966 with the Montréal Agreement; in 1971 with the Guatemala City Protocol; in 1995 with the IATA Intercarrier Agreement on Passenger Liability; and finally in 1999, the Montréal Convention, which is also know as Montréal Protocol No. 4. As of 2013, for those countries that had ratified the Montréal Protocol, the liability limits for death or bodily injury had been removed, and the liability for lost cargo was limited to SDR 17 per kilogram.

Under IATA and ICAO rules, a country can restrict the number of airline flights in and out of its airspace. Generally, the limit is set to favor national airline companies; however, in 1992, the United States and the Netherlands agreed to remove limits on the number of flights that each country's airlines could fly into the other's territory, creating an "open-skies" agreement. Since 1992, numerous additional bilateral agreements have been signed. By late 2012, the United States had 110 open-skies partners,[35] including agreements with the 27 European countries that are part of the U.S.-European Union Trade Agreement that was signed on April 30, 2007.[36] Open-sky provisions apply to passenger and cargo flights as well as scheduled and charter air transportation services.

Even though open-skies agreements have removed many of the restrictions placed on international routes and carriers, flights in and out of specific airports are still restricted by the number of landing slots available at that airport. For example, the United States and Japan have an open-skies agreement,[37] but Narita Airport was constrained by having only one international-length runway until 2009[38] and therefore no additional flights could be scheduled until that constraint had been lifted.

Both the IATA and ICAO are also starting to assume a more active role in establishing industry standards for environmental protection. In 1983, ICAO established the Committee on Aviation Environmental Protection (CAEP). This committee now includes a number of groups that focus on both the technical and operational aspects of noise reduction and aircraft emissions.[39] The IATA has been equally aggressive and has established a vision of becoming a carbon-free mode of transportation in the next 50 years.[40]

12.6 Environmental Issues and Sustainability

Over the past ten years, the aviation industry has seen an enormous increase in concern for the environment and the adoption of sustainability practices. This shift is affecting the design and operation of passenger and cargo aircraft, as well as the airports and infrastructure that support them. The IATA, for example, is attempting to reduce greenhouse emissions by focusing on new technologies, changes in operations, infrastructure changes, and various economic incentives to encourage the industry to adopt more environmentally-friendly and sustainable aviation-related standards. Innovations in technology have already led to more fuel efficient air-

---

International Air Transport Association (IATA)
A trade association comprising almost 230 airlines, representing 93 percent of all scheduled air traffic.

International Civil Aviation Organization (ICAO)
An agency of the United Nations whose mission is to establish safety and security standards for civil aviation.

Warsaw Convention
A 1929 Convention that established the first liability limits for air carriers.

Montréal Protocol 4
A 1999 protocol that limits the liability of air carriers to SDR 17 per kilogram. There is no limit for death or bodily injury.

open-sky agreement
An agreement between two countries, in which the airlines of one country are allowed to serve any of the other country's airports.

craft engines, lighter airframes, more efficient wing designs, and new biofuels; while changes in operations have led to reduced toxins and waste in ground operations.[41] In fact, today's aircraft are 75 percent cleaner and 70 percent quieter than they were 40 years ago.[42]

In 2008, Virgin Atlantic conducted the world's first commercial aircraft flight, powered in part by biofuel, to demonstrate the potential of clean jet fuels.[43] Other more extensive tests have since been conducted using various blends and types of biofuels, suggesting that there are, in fact, environmentally-friendly alternatives to traditional jet fuels.[44]

The major aircraft manufacturers are equally committed to producing eco-friendly and more efficient aircraft. As stated in Airbus's *Global Market Forecast for 2007-2026*, "the need for an increasingly eco-efficient industry, which creates economic and social value with less environmental impact, is well understood by the millions of people involved in aviation. Aircraft manufacturers have an intrinsic requirement to be technological pioneers and to develop increasingly eco-efficient aircraft."[45]

Changes in air traffic control routing and other technology-enabled process changes are also expected to reduce fuel consumption, emissions, and noise pollution. Airfreighters, for example, often operate at off-hours, as their noise can create problems with airport neighbors. Some airports have considered banning night flights altogether. Brussels (Belgium) and the European Union have enacted some very stringent noise regulations, mostly aimed at older airfreighters. Frankfurt bans night flights between the hours of 23h00 (11:00 p.m.) and 5h00 (5:00 a.m.).[46] The future is likely to hold yet more regulations for other heavily-used metropolitan airports, leaving room for the creation of other hubs in less urbanized centers, such as Prestwick in Scotland, Hahn in Germany, and Chateauroux in France.[47] To some extent, this development mirrors that of the Memphis airport, which has become the largest cargo airport in the world, even though it is not located in a large metropolitan center.

The same motivation was behind the development of the Mid-America Airport near St Louis, Missouri, although it has not certainly not been as successful. Once believed to be able to become a geographically central hub for many passenger and freight flights in the United States, because of its ideal location and unencumbered airspace, the airport has been nevertheless essentially unused for the past decade, with very or no scheduled passenger airlines at all.[48]

In addition to the actions noted above, two relatively new approaches have recently been introduced to reduce the impact of aviation carbon emissions on the environment: carbon trading and voluntary carbon offset programs. These two unique programs allow owners and operators to purchase credits in organizations that absorb or offset carbon in an effort to mitigate total emissions.[49]

12.7 International Air Cargo Security

Beyond fuel prices and the overall state of the world's economy, security requirements represent the biggest challenge to the air cargo industry today, and the challenge is overwhelming. Within the United States, for example, over 640 million people traveled on commercial aircraft in 2012, and more than 170 million traveled from the United States to foreign destinations.[50] That represents more than 700 million pieces of baggage screened for explosives every year. There are also approximately 61 million tons of cargo transported by air domestically, and 3 million shipped internationally.[51] Of the 13 million tons of cargo transported domestically in the United States by air, 3 million are shipped on passenger aircraft and the remaining 10 million are moved on cargo aircraft.

One of the difficulties is that the security requirements are different for cargo shipped on passenger aircraft and for cargo shipped on freighters. In addition, because of the evolving state of technology and the dynamic and unpredictable nature of terrorism, the security guidelines and safety processes followed in the air cargo industry are continuously changing.

12.7.1 Transportation Security Administration

Within the United States, the Transportation Security Administration (TSA) has overall responsibility for transportation security for the air cargo industry. To meet this challenge, TSA, with the help of U.S. Customs and Border Protection (CBP), relies on several methods to enhance security. For air cargo transportation, the TSA uses:

- Advance information on shipments by demanding the electronic submission of manifests before a flight is allowed to leave the airport of departure or before the flight is allowed to land in the United States.

- An Automated Targeting System (ATS) that screens U.S.-bound shipments prior to their arrival to determine the level of risk they represent, using a risk-analysis algorithm.

- Mandatory security inspections using non-intrusive inspection technology (NII) for all high-risk shipments. These efforts include large-scale imaging and radiation technologies, as well as canine detection teams.

- A partnership with the trade community designed to strengthen air cargo security by giving shippers an incentive to strengthen their internal security systems. One example of such cooperation is the Customs-Trade Partnership against Terrorism (C-TPAT) (see Chapter 15).

12.7.2 Advance Manifest Rules for Air Carriers

The Trade Act of 2002 requires that cargo manifests for all freight shipments that transit the United States be submitted electronically prior to arrival to Customs and Border Protection through its Automated Manifest System (AMS). For flights originating outside North America, electronic manifests must be received at least four hours prior to arrival at their first U.S. airport. For Mexico, Canada, and other locations that are less than four hours away, manifests must be transmitted to CBP prior to the time of the aircraft's departure.

The U.S. Customs and Border Protection has launched a Web-based Automated Commercial Environment (ACE) that enables multimodal manifest processing and allows importers, exporters, brokers, and transportation providers to use one single integrated system to expedite shipping.

12.7.3 Certified Cargo Screening Program

Another key component in TSA's approach to security is the Certified Cargo Screening Program (CCSP). The CCSP mandates 100 percent screening of all air cargo transported by passenger aircraft, whether shipped within the United States or coming from abroad into the United States. This inspection is to be conducted at the "piece" level, which means that every item in a shipment needs to be inspected.[52]

The Certified Cargo Screening Program selects and approves Certified Cargo Screening Facilities (CCSFs) and monitors and maintains the security of shipments throughout the supply chain. The concept is that security is achieved with an inspection at the CCSF and with the continuous monitoring of the goods between the time they are inspected and the time at which they are loaded onto the aircraft. Such efforts are called chain-of-custody security methods. Once approved, a CCSF must adhere to increased TSA-directed security standards, share responsibility for supply chain security, employ chain-of-custody methods, permit onsite validations, submit a facility security plan, and be subject to transportation security inspections.[53]

It should also be noted that the United States built its air cargo Certified Cargo Screening Program based, in part, on best practices adopted from other countries such as the United Kingdom and Ireland.[54] It is also clear that many of the concepts now associated with the CCSP are being adopted by other foreign entities, in partnership with TSA, to validate and maintain the security of airfreight across international boundaries.

12.7.4 Air Carriers and C-TPAT

As is the case for all companies involved in international logistics, the U.S. Customs and Border Protection is looking for air carriers to join the Customs-Trade Partnership Against Terrorism (C-TPAT) to enhance existing security practices and reduce the threat of terrorism to international air shipments. Air carriers enrolled in C-TPAT are required to meet minimum-security criteria in order to achieve certification. To be eligible, air carriers must meet the following requirements:[55]

- Be an active air carrier transporting cargo shipments to the United States

- Have an active IATA code

- Possess a valid continuous international carrier bond registered with CBP

- Have a designated company officer who will be the primary cargo security officer responsible for C-TPAT

- Commit to maintaining the C-TPAT security criteria for air carriers

- Create and provide CBP with a C-TPAT supply chain security profile, which identifies how the air carrier will meet, maintain, and enhance internal policy to meet the C-TPAT security criteria for air carriers.

As indicated above, air carriers must conduct a comprehensive assessment of their security practices using C-TPAT criteria. These criteria include meeting business partner requirements, as well as the requirements for container or unit load devices (ULD) security, physical access controls, personnel security, procedural security, security training and threat awareness, physical security, and information technology security.

12.7.5 Air Cargo Security Requirements for Other Countries

Numerous countries have developed and implemented air cargo security standards similar to those established by the United States following the terrorist acts of the beginning of the twenty-first century. The United States and the European Union (EU), for example, signed an agreement in late 2008 to harmonize cargo screening standards for passenger aircraft. This agreement, signed between the TSA and the EU's Directorate General for Energy and Transport, is expected to provide a foundation for other bilateral security agreements based largely on the standards set by the 9/11 Commission Act of 2007. There is still room for greater harmonization between countries, however, and substantial concern among practitioners about multiple conflicting standards. As stated by Harald Zielinski, director of security for Lufthansa Cargo, "It is not possible to have 15 processes for 15 different security standards," and there is much work to be done.[56]

Review and Discussion Questions

1. Briefly describe the different types of air cargo services available.

2. Do you think that the demand for air cargo will increase or decrease over the next three years? Why?

3. How does an air carrier determine how much a shipment will cost? What can a shipper do to reduce the costs of shipping a light but voluminous package?

4. What is project cargo? Use the Internet to find and describe at least one example of the use of air transportation to ship project cargo internationally.

5. Using the freighter/payload range chart (Figure 12.10 on page 323), what type of airfreighter would you expect to use to ship 60,000 kilograms over 3,500 nautical miles?

6. What is the purpose of an open-skies agreement?

7. What are some of the environmental challenges facing the air cargo industry today? What is the industry doing to deal with these issues?

8. What is the purpose of the Certified Cargo Screening Program?

9. What are the Advance Manifest Rules and how do they apply to air shipments bound for the U.S.?

Notes

[1] Crabtree, Thomas, James Edgar, Thomas Hoang, Russell Tom, and Bradley Heart, *The World Air Cargo Forecast 2012-2013*, Boeing Corporation, http://www.boeing.com/commercial/cargo, accessed June 21, 2013.

[2] *Ibid.*

[3] Mecham, Michael, and Guy Norris, "Soft Freighter Market Dampens 747-8 Demand," *Aviation Week & Space Technology*, December 3, 2012.

[4] "Boeing Predicts Coming Wide-Body Surge," *Air Cargo World*, October 2012, pp.51-61.

[5] "About FedEx," http://about.fedex.designcdt.com/our_company/company_information/fedex_corporation, retrieved June 25, 2013.

[6] *World Air Transport Statistics*, International Air Transport Association, 57th Edition (2013), (http://www.iata.org/publications/Pages/wats.aspx, retrieved June 25, 2013.

[7] Crabtree, Thomas, James Edgar, Thomas Hoang, Russell Tom, and Bradley Heart, *The World Air Cargo Forecast 2012-2013*, Boeing Corporation, http://www.boeing.com/commercial/cargo, accessed June 21, 2013.

[8] "Preliminary 2012 World Airport Traffic and Rankings—Mar 26, 2013," Airport Council International, http://www.aci.aero/News/Releases/Most-Recent/2013/03/26/Preliminary-2012-World-Airport-Traffic-and-Rankings, retrieved June 25, 2013.

[9] "Global Market Forecast 2012-2031," Airbus, http://www.airbus.com/company/market/forecast/, retrieved June 25, 2013.

[10] Wensveen, John, *Air Transportation: A Management Perspective*, Seventh edition, 2011, Ashgate Publishing, Burlington, Vermont.

[11] *Ibid.*

[12] *Ibid.*

[13] *Ibid.*

[14] "About FedEx," http://about.fedex.designcdt.com/our_company/company_information/fedex_corporation, retrieved June 25, 2013.

[15] "UPS Fact Sheet," UPS Inc., http://pressroom.ups.com/Fact+Sheets/UPS+Fact+Sheet, accessed June 25, 2013.

[16] "UPS Worldport Facts," UPS Inc., http://pressroom.ups.com/Fact+Sheets/UPS+Worldport+Facts, accessed June 25, 2013.

[17] Deutsche Post - DHL World Net Annual Report 2012, Bonn, Germany: Deutsche Post, http://www.dp-dhl.com/en/investors/financial_reports/annual_reports.html, retrieved June 25, 2013.

[18] Solomon, Adina, "Flowers' Fantastic Voyage," *Air Cargo World*, June 2013, pp.36-40.

[19] Crabtree, Thomas, James Edgar, Thomas Hoang, Russell Tom, and Bradley Heart, *The World Air Cargo Forecast 2012-2013*, Boeing Corporation, http://www.boeing.com/commercial/cargo, accessed June 21, 2013.

[20] *FedEx Corporation Annual Report (10K)*, Item 2. Properties, FedEx Corporation, http://fedex.com/us/investorrelations/financialinfo/2008annualreport/corp_info.html, accessed February 16, 2009.

[21] Kayal, Michele, "Couriers on Board: Crucial Links Between You and Your Packages," *Journal of Commerce*, November 3, 1997, p. 1A.

NOTES

[22] "Alaska Airlines Introduces Two 737-400 'Combi' Aircraft to Fleet," RedOrbit News, February 1, 2007, http://www.redorbit.com/news/business/823041/alaska_airlines_introduces_two_737400_combi_aircraft_to_fleet/index.html.

[23] *Airbus Global Market Forecast 2009-2028*, Airbus, September 2009, http://www.airbus.com/en/gmf2009/data/catalogue.pdf, accessed October 29, 2009.

[24] Crabtree, Thomas, James Edgar, Thomas Hoang, Russell Tom, and Bradley Heart, *The World Air Cargo Forecast 2012-2013*, Boeing Corporation, http://www.boeing.com/commercial/cargo, accessed June 21, 2013.

[25] Solon, Daniel, "Aircraft Makers See Rosier Skies," *The New York Times*, July 8, 2012.

[26] "Merge Global. End of an Era?", *American Shipper*, August 2008, p. 45.

[27] Andriulaitis, Robert. "B747-8F v. A380F," *InterVISTAS*, December 2005, retrieved September 29, 2012.

[28] "Colombian Floriculture: 2009 Statistics," Asociación Colombiana de Exportadores de Flores, http://www.asocolflores.org/asocolflores/servlet/Download?idExternalFile=924&name=-HOJA-DATOS-2010+final+INGLES.pdf, retrieved June 28, 2013.

[29] Solomon, Adina, "Flowers' Fantastic Voyage," *Air Cargo World*, June 2013, pp.36-40.

[30] "Roses are ... Brown? Flower Imports Showcase International Logistics," *Compass Online*, UPS, http://compass.ups.com/goingglobal/article.aspx?id=1649, retrieved July 2, 2009.

[31] Schmidt, Blake, "Colombia's cargo expansion is coming up roses for Avianca," *Business Report*, February 13, 2012, http://www.iol.co.za/business/business-news/colombia-s-cargo-expansion-is-coming-up-roses-for-avianca-1.1232397#.Uc3QG9jxn4s, retrieved June 28, 2013.

[32] Sharepe, Rochelle, "Hearts of Gold: All Romance Aside, Valentine's Day can be Frantic—and Lucrative," *The Wall Street Journal*, February 15, 1996, p. A1.

[33] Ito, Kenzo, and Jennifer Clever, "Japanese Cherry and Peach Farmers Get Creative to Counteract Labor Shortages," August 15, 2012, USDA Foreign Agricultural Service, gain.fas.usda.gov/Recent%20GAIN%20Publications/Stone%20Fruit%20Annual_Tokyo_Japan_8-15-2012.pdf, retrieved June 28, 2013.

[34] "Changes in 'dim weight' formula proving a windfall for parcel carriers," *DC Velocity*, July 2011, p.20.

[35] "Open Skies Partners," United States Department of State, http://www.state.gov/e/eb/rls/othr/ata/114805.htm, retrieved June 28, 2013.

[36] "U.S.-EU Air Transport Agreement of April 30, 2007," United States Department of State, http://www.state.gov/e/eb/rls/othr/ata/e/eu/114768.htm, retrieved June 28, 2013.

[37] Wald, Matthew L., "U.S., Japan to Remove Air-Traffic Restrictions," *The New York Times*, January 31, 1998.

[38] "Runway extension at Narita finally opens," *Japan Times*, October 23, 2009, http://www.japantimes.co.jp/news/2009/10/23/news/runway-extension-at-narita-finally-opens/#.Uc1_Ntjxn4s, retrieved June 28, 2013.

[39] "Committee on Aviation Environmental Protection," International Civil Aviation Organization, http://www.icao.int/env/caep.htm, retrieved March 12, 2009.

[40] *Building a Greener Future*, 3rd ed., International Air Transport Association, October 2008, http://www.iata.org/nr/rdonlyres/c5840acd-71ac-4faa-8fee-00b21e9961b3/0/building_greener_future_oct08.pdf.

[41] Gardner, T., "Aviation Goes Green from the Ground on Up," *Chicago Tribune*, March 9, 2008, p. 2.

[42] *Airbus Global Market Forecast 2007-2026*, Airbus, December 2007, http://www.airbus.com

/fileadmin/documents/gmf/PDF_dl/00-all-gmf_2007.pdf, accessed June 29, 2009.

[43] "Virgin Atlantic Flies Biofuel-Powered Jumbo Jet," MSNBC News, February 24, 2008, http://www.msnbc.msn.com/id/23321510.

[44] Warwick, Graham, "Bio-fueled Jet Flies Cross-Country," *Aviation Week*, November 10, 2008.

[45] *Airbus Global Market Forecast 2009-2028*, Airbus, September 2009, http://www.airbus.com/en/gmf2009/data/catalogue.pdf, accessed October 29, 2009.

[46] "German Court Nixes Frankfurt Night Flights," *Air Cargo World*, November 2011, pp.6-7.

[47] Barnard, Bruce, "Night flights to be Banned in Brussels," *Journal of Commerce*, January 5, 2000, p. 3.

[48] Imbs, Christine, "Gateway to the World," *St. Louis Commerce Magazine*, March 2006.

[49] Essler, David, "The Greening of Business Aviation, Part III," *Aviation Week*, July 22, 2008.

[50] "Passengers—All Carriers, All Airports," Research and Innovative Technology Administration, Bureau of Transportation Statistics, http://www.transtats.bts.gov/Data_Elements.aspx?Data=1, retrieved June 29, 2013.

[51] "Passenger Boarding (Enplanement) and All-Cargo Data for U.S. Airports," Federal Aviation Administration, http://www.faa.gov/airports/planning_capacity/passenger_allcargo_stats/passenger/, retrieved June 28, 2013.

[52] "Certified Cargo Screening Program," May 29, 2013, Transportation Security Administration, http://www.tsa.gov/certified-cargo-screening-program, retrieved July 4, 2013.

[53] *Ibid.*

[54] "TSA/CBP Air Cargo Security Workshop," U.S. Customs and Border Protection, http://www.cbp.gov/linkhandler/cgov/trade/trade_outreach/trade_symposium_archive/symposium08/event_materials/air_cargo_ccsp.ctt/air_cargo_ccsp.pdf, retrieved July 4, 2013.

[55] "Air Carrier Eligibility Requirements,", U.S. Customs and Border Protection, http://www.cbp.gov/linkhandler/cgov/trade/cargo_security/ctpat/ctpat_application_material/ctpat_security_guidelines/air_carriers/ac_eligibility_requirements.ctt/ac_eligibility_requirements.pdf, retrieved July 2013.

[56] Conway, Peter, "Air Cargo Security Screening Deadline Draw Near," *Airline Business*, October 29, 2008, http://www.flightglobal.com/articles/2008/10/29/318023/air-cargo-security-screening-deadlines-draw-near.html.

Chapter 13

International Land and Multimodal Transportation

13.1 Truck Transportation 338

13.2 Rail Transportation 341

13.3 Intermodal Transportation 347

13.4 Freight Forwarders 359

13.5 Project Cargo 359

13.6 Alternative Means of Transportation 360

13.7 Ground Transportation Security 362

This chapter is the last of a series of three covering the means of transportation available to an international shipper. The preceding two chapters covered ocean and air transportation. This chapter presents the remaining alternatives.

First, it will present the two main land-based shipping methods available to an international shipper: road and rail transportation. Both are much more frequently used in Europe for international freight, where they represent more than 80 percent of the total intra-European freight traffic (see Figure 13.1),[1] than they are in Asia and North America. However, practices differ, and a savvy international logistics manager should be familiar with the issues presented by road and rail transportation.

In its second part, the chapter will cover the specifics of international intermodal transportation, which is not a transportation alternative properly speaking, but is the practice of shipping a product under a single bill of lading that covers more than one mode of transportation. For many shippers, that practice is often associated with container shipping.

Finally, two additional alternative methods of transportation are covered: inland waterway barges and pipelines. Although both represent a large percentage of the volume of the international shipments of some specific commodities (agricultural raw materials and crude oil), they are quite limited in their capabilities.

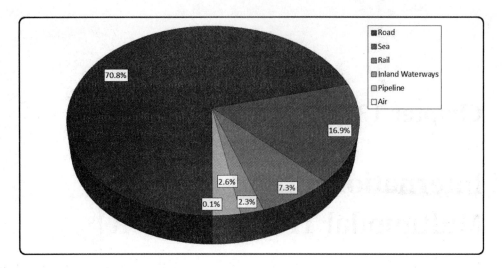

Figure 13.1: Intra-European Freight Transport, by Mode (in millions of tonnes)
Eurostat.

13.1 Truck Transportation

Trucking, from a North American perspective, is primarily a domestic means of transportation, with the exception of the significant amount of trade between Canada and the United States and some limited trade between the United States and Mexico. However, the latter is still mostly trade to and from the U.S.-Mexico border, as a large percentage of the trade between those two countries was conducted on a DAF Incoterm (Delivered At Frontier) basis —which is progressively changing to DAT (Delivered At Terminal) since DAF was eliminated under Incoterms® rules 2010 (see Chapter 6)— and because Mexican trucks are, for all intents and purposes, not yet authorized on American highways.

For the rest of the world, though, trucking is a vital way of shipping goods internationally. More than 85 percent of merchandise shipped by truck within the European Union is shipped to a destination in a foreign country,[2] and this share is increasing as the countries that are joining the Union are landlocked and even more reliant on road transport.

Worldwide, trucking is still dominated by a patchwork of domestic rules and regulations, which greatly influence the way the industry is organized. There are limits on the number of axles a truck may have, on the weight it can carry per axle, on its total weight, on its length and width, as well as requirements regarding its mandatory equipment, and the training of drivers and the number of consecutive hours they can drive. All of these constraints generate fleets of trucks that are different from country to country. Altogether, though, trucks carrying international cargo tend to be semi trucks. These are made up of two distinct units: a tractor pulling a trailer, both of which take on characteristics that are country specific (see Figures 13.2 and 13.3).

The biggest challenge in shipping goods internationally by trucks is to abide by all these rules and regulations, the complexity of which should not be underestimated. Case in point: European countries, even the smallest ones, like Luxembourg,

semi truck
An articulated truck that is made up of a tractor and a trailer.

tractor
The part of an articulated truck that is in the front and pulls the trailer.

trailer
The part of an articulated truck that is in the rear and pulled by the tractor.

13.1 Truck Transportation

have driving bans on certain days—generally Sundays—but none of these bans are coordinated or harmonized. There are hundreds of different driving bans or restrictions in the European Union, if the special holiday restrictions are included,[3] which can create havoc on a company's ability to ship goods just-in-time, or for a shipper to reach a port before a sailing. Poland, for example, prohibits trucks from driving when temperatures reach 30 degrees Celsius (86 degrees Fahrenheit), and Switzerland amended its constitution to prohibit trucks weighing more than 28 metric tonnes from going farther into Switzerland than 10 kilometers (6 miles), relegating all large trucks crossing the country to piggy-back on railroad cars[4] (see Figure 13.4); in 2012, the Rollende Landstrasse (rolling highway) carried a total of 100,000 tractor-trailers through the Alps.[5] The Freight Transport Association publishes an annual *Yearbook of Road Transport Law* to keep its members informed of all of the different laws and road regulations within the European Union.[6]

piggy-back
A technique that consists of placing semi trucks or trailers on railroad cars.

Such constraints often have the effect of creating giant parking lots of trucks at the entry points into a country and at highway exits. The enforcement of this myriad of rules and regulations also creates delays. Although there are officially no longer any border controls for trucks within the European Union, police routinely stop truckers in order to enforce rules regarding driving times, speed limits, and so on, few of which are the same from one country to the next.

The second challenge regarding shipping by truck is the state of the infrastructure. Load limits, height limits, and speed limits (road conditions) hinder the smooth transportation of goods and have an impact on packing. For example, the E-30 highway, one of the key links between western Europe (Berlin) and Russia, is so crowded and in such a state of disrepair that traffic is very slow, making it one of the most dangerous highways in Europe. Its replacement is under construction, but only about 60 percent of it is completed and usable, leaving long stretches of the East-West itinerary to be completed under less than ideal conditions.[7]

Figure 13.2: A European Semi-Truck, Limited to 18.75 meters overall (61.5 feet)
Photo ©Pierre David. Used with Permission.

Figure 13.3: A North American Semi-Truck (Limited to a 53-foot Trailer—16.1 meter— but with no limit on the Tractor)

Photo ©Denis Desmond. Used with Permission.

However, that is not all: the prohibitive taxation of diesel fuel in some countries influences the power of trucks, the size of the trailers, and the speeds at which cargo moves. The high tolls of some European highways lure truckers into driving on secondary roads that are not as cargo friendly. Some companies are "flagging out" their trucks—registering them in other countries—to take advantage of lower taxation and regulations,[8] bringing the same kind of concerns that flags of convenience have triggered for the marine industry (see Chapter 11).

overloaded
A means of transportation that carries cargo in excess of its stated capacity.

Another factor is the cultural aspect of the industry. While overloaded trucks are rare in North America and Europe, they are strikingly commonplace in Africa and in some parts of Asia, where, seemingly, a truck is not full until one more piece of cargo will fit (see Figure 13.5).

Finally, the complementary infrastructure of railroads influences the way that some goods are shipped. In North America, for example, a large fleet of railroad cars capable of carrying truck trailers enables trucking companies to load trailers onto trains rather than drive them across the country. In Australia, however, the seemingly complete lack of railroads in some areas, and a mismatch of different gauges, has pushed trucking companies to develop road-trains, which are tractors pulling three to five full-size semi trailers (see Figure 13.6).

road train
An Australian trucking technique, consisting of one tractor pulling three to five semi trailers.

The last challenge regarding trucking, specifically in Europe, is the fact that road transport is often delayed by social unrest. In the first six months of 2013, there were no fewer than ten instances during which some group or another blocked truck traffic somewhere in the European Union. Farmers protesting high gas prices, truckers protesting low wages, ecologists worried about pollution—just about every pretext was used to block entrances to highways, harbors, refineries, Alpine routes, or whatever else, causing lengthy delays, up to seven days, for truck shipments. Because governments routinely cave in to these demands, it is unlikely that the number of such protests will diminish in the future.

13.2 Rail Transportation

Another contrast between North America and the rest of the world is the extent to which railroads are used for freight movements. In the United States, for example, 2.84 trillion freight tonne kilometers [FTKs] (1.73 trillion ton-miles) were shipped by rail in 2011, or a market share of more than 40 percent of all ton-miles shipped long-distance in the country.[9,10] The growth of intermodal freight accounted for almost 40 percent of the total number of carloads transported, a total of just under 12 million trailers or containers.[11] Although there are no figures available for international freight within North America, it is likely that the percentages are similar.

In contrast, European railroads carried only about 400 billion FTKs of freight traffic (about 225 billion ton-miles) in 2011,[12] even though the 27 countries of the European Union have a cumulative economy and territorial size that are larger than those of the United States—representing less than 18 percent of all FTKs shipped within the European Union.[13] In addition, only a small percentage of those were intermodal, with a great percentage of the cargo transported in traditional railroad cars, each designed for its own specific purpose (see Figure 13.7). Intermodal transport (or co-modality, as it is called within the European Union) grew from 28.5 billion FTKs in 1999 to 37.4 billion FTKs in 2012 (about 10 percent of the total rail traffic), and the number of trailers transported grew from 1.8 million to 4.8 million TEUs during the same period.[14]

intermodal
A shipment that takes more than one mode of transportation under a single bill of lading.

co-modality
A shipment that takes more than one mode of transportation under a single bill of lading.

container
A large metallic box used in international trade that can be loaded directly onto a truck, a railroad car or an ocean-going vessel. The most common dimensions of a container are $8 \times 8.5 \times 20$ feet and $8 \times 8.5 \times 40$ feet.

Figure 13.4: The Swiss "Rolling Highway" in the Alps
Photo ©Josef Petrák. Used with Permission.

single-stack
The practice of placing containers on a railroad car on only one height. It contrasts with the practice of placing them two high.

double-stack
The practice of placing containers on a railroad car on top of one another.

freight corridor
A section of a railroad network dedicated to freight traffic.

In Australia, of the total 410 billion FTKs carried in the country in 2008—the last year for which data were available—railroads carried 54 percent of freight, and roads 46 percent.[15] Most of the Australian freight traffic is made up of ores and grain over long distances. In Canada, the mix was 70 percent railroad and 30 percent road of a total 311 billion FTKs in 2011,[16] with essentially the same characteristics; ores and grain for very long distances to ports of export.

The railroad infrastructure in Europe is still focused mostly on passenger traffic, and freight traffic is mostly neglected, with little investment in railroad cars and facilities designed to facilitate intermodal cargo. In addition, because all railtracks are electrified, and therefore catenaries—overhead electric lines—are present on all railways, all European intermodal cargo must be transported on single-stack railroad cars (cars carrying a single container, see Figure 13.8). European practice is also to build very short trains of 20-25 cars, as well, mostly because passenger trains are shorter and the signaling equipment has been designed for them. In contrast, most of the United States infrastructure is not electrified, and has been modified to accommodate double-stack cars (see Figure 13.9), with trains of three or four locomotives and as many as 100 cars.

In the last few years, the European Community has introduced the idea of "freight corridors" that would carry freight from northern Europe's major ports (Antwerp, Belgium, and Amsterdam, the Netherlands) to Milan, Italy, and Vienna, Austria—

Figure 13.5: An Overloaded Truck in Mali, Africa
Photo ©Roberto Neumiller. Used with Permission.

13.2 Rail Transportation

Figure 13.6: An Australian Road Train Photo ©Ryan and Nada Clontz. Used with Permission.

and eventually to other cities as well—bypassing the requirements to change to a national locomotive and a national crew at every border crossing and allowing private freight companies to compete with the state-owned enterprises.[17] Nevertheless, as these "rail freight freeways" are going to utilize currently existing lines, and

Figure 13.7: European Railroad Cars, Each Designed for a Particular Type of Merchandise

Photo ©Stanislav Matyashov. Used with Permission.

because passenger trains have priority over all other traffic, there are widespread doubts about the feasibility of this initiative. Only a few of these corridors have been implemented.

To date, a single rail project involving a new rail corridor has been built, from the port of Rotterdam to the Netherlands-Germany border: it is called the Betuweroute. It connects to the network of the Dutch and German railways and relieves congestion in the port. It carries only freight trains and has reached a volume of 433 trains per week, carrying 80 percent of the cargo volume between the Port of Rotterdam and Germany.[18] Although successful, there has been much opposition, mostly because of the environmental impact of track construction, to its expansion.[19]

Another attempt at linking ports has been conducted by the Société Nationale des Chemins de Fer Français (SNCF), the French national railroad company. It created a subsidiary, Naviland Cargo,[20] that offers services between the large French ports and the large Belgian ports. However, there are only one or two departures per day, and not every day. Nevertheless, the company reports having transported 283,000 TEUs in 2012.[21]

Another aspect of the railroad industry is the change in the mix of cargo it has experienced over the past twenty years. In the U.S. particularly, railroads had traditionally transported three primary types of cargoes until the 1980s:

- Bulk freight, not only grain, coal, lumber, steel, ores, chemicals, and oil, but

Figure 13.8: Single-Stack Container Cars under Electric Catenaries
Photo ©Stanislav Matyashov. Used with Permission.

13.2 Rail Transportation

also molasses, vegetable oils, and other heavy items. Each of these bulk cargoes tends to have its own type of railroad car.

- Breakbulk freight placed in boxcars, either palletized or simply in its packaging
- Automobile freight, placed on specialized car carriers

In the last three decades, the advent of intermodal transportation has radically changed this mix and dramatically altered the railroad business. Railroads are now carrying an increasing number of containers placed on container carriers (see Figure 13.9) and of truck trailers on piggy-back cars (see Figure 13.10).

First, these container carriers were designed to be only one container high, but then double-stacks were introduced, which eventually doubled the capacity of each train but forced railroads to update their infrastructures—tunnels and overhead bridges in particular—so that these cars would fit. In 2012, the U.S. railroads carried a total of 12 million trailers or containers,[22] an estimated 25 percent of which were transiting on a land bridge between Asia and Europe (see Section 13.3.2).

As much as the future of rail transportation in the United States was bleak in the 1970s, it has transformed itself into a customer-oriented vibrant industry—despite some serious disturbances when Union Pacific bought Southern Pacific—with substantial expected growth emerging from its traditional cargoes, such as grain and

Figure 13.9: North American Double-Stack Container Cars
Photo ©Jim Mills. Used with Permission.

automobiles, moving to containers. The European railroads appear to have noticed this trend and are attempting to embrace it; however, the national railroads are such bloated bureaucracies that progress is slow and success is elusive. In November 2000, EU railroad companies passed a resolution that they will open their networks to each other's crews and engines; however, as of 2013, little progress had been made. Moreover, France opposes opening its network despite the agreement, so a large, geographically necessary swath of the network may not be available at all. Add to this information the discrepancies of at least two railroad gauges, five electrical systems, and 16 signaling systems, and the task seems daunting. The creation of the European Association for Railway Interoperability in 1996, charged with creating a trans-European network of high-speed passenger trains, has spurred cooperation between the national railroad companies, and such effort should eventually be extended to freight transport.

Another possible development is the replacement of some ocean trade with rail transportation, notably between the Far East (China, Korea) and Europe; such a possibility would seriously shorten transit times between the two areas and relieve some of the congestion in southern China's ports. After being extensively studied,[23] such a landbridge was pioneered by DB Schenker, the logistics subsidiary of Deutche Bahn, which now offers a daily train from Shanghai to Hamburg and Duisberg.[24,25]

Figure 13.10: North American Piggyback Railcars
Photo ©Chad Hewitt. Used with Permission.

13.3 Intermodal Transportation

Probably the best way to introduce intermodal transportation is to define the concept:

> Intermodal describes a shipment that takes several different means of transportation—road, rail, ocean, air—from its point of departure (seller/exporter) to its point of destination (buyer/importer). The meaning has evolved recently to limit the use of this term to freight for which a single bill of lading covering more than one of these alternatives is issued.

intermodal
A shipment that takes more than one mode of transportation under a single bill of lading.

Intermodal transportation is therefore not a means of transportation *per se*, but instead is the practice of utilizing a single bill of lading to cover several means of transportation for a single shipment. For that reason, it is also called multimodal transportation, or co-modality in Europe). To use a recent cliché, the changes in means of transportation are "transparent" to the user, which means that the shipper does not know which specific itinerary and carrier the cargo will use. The responsibility of arranging for all of the means of transportation falls onto the shipping company. Nevertheless, the shipper needs to be aware of the alternatives, so as to pack accordingly.

Shipping companies have had to change their perspectives from that of simple transportation providers to that of providers of a multiplicity of services, one of which is transportation in their core competency, such as ocean shipping. However, they also have to provide transportation services in other modes, such as trucking or rail. In addition, shipping companies now interact with their customers directly and offer such ancillary services as tracking of shipments online. Most important of all, intermodal service created the possibility for an exporter (or an importer) to have a single interlocutor in a complex international shipment involving more than one mode of transportation. This one-stop shopping is probably what has made intermodal transportation so popular with shippers.

Because of the ubiquitous use of the seagoing container in multimodal shipments, the term intermodal has also been strongly associated with this transportation concept. The container idea is fairly recent. It was created in 1956 by Malcom McLean in an attempt to eliminate the large number of handlings to which ocean cargo was subjected, and to speed up the loading and unloading of ships. This concept of container has been a smashing success, with more than 10.7 million TEUs (twenty-foot equivalent units) in use worldwide.[26]

Certainly, the use of containers allowed the concept of intermodality to develop, but the two concepts are not entwined. It is quite possible to have an intermodal shipment that is not packaged in a container, and it is possible to use only one mode of transportation to ship containerized cargo. Nevertheless, the two are strongly tied together, and probably 95 percent of all intermodal cargo is shipped in containers, of which there are many different types. In addition, that percentage is growing, as more container types have been created to allow nonstandard cargo to be containerized.

Movable Boxes

International commerce was completely changed by the arrival of the container. Before containers, the traditional method for loading and unloading a ship was a very time-consuming and labor-intensive process. Goods, in boxes small enough to be handled by humans, were loaded by cranes onto breakbulk ships. Gangs of longshoremen were responsible for stowing them into the ship and making sure that they would not be damaged during the ocean voyage. They had to make sure that heavy goods were lower in the hold than lighter goods, that the weight of the cargo was distributed evenly through the ship, and that every piece of cargo was wedged solidly against the others. Containers revolutionized this system; containers are loaded, once, in the plant that manufactured the product, and unloaded, once, in the plant of the customer. There is no intermediary handling, no chance for pilferage, no possible damage from mishandling. The labor costs are lower, since the laborers are inland and not part of the strong (and costly) longshoremen's unions. Containers of different sizes had been proposed several times before, but it was Malcom McLean, the owner of a trucking company, who eventually made the first investment in movable boxes of a size similar to a truck trailer and shipped them from Newark to Houston in April 1956. He eventually expanded this concept to other U.S. routes: the West Coast to Hawaii, Miami to Puerto Rico.

In the late 1950s, containers were of different sizes. As McLean had expanded its concept, others had copied him and chosen different standard sizes. It was eventually determined, after long negotiations between truckers, ship owners, railroads, and port authorities, both in the United States and in Europe, that containers should be 8 feet wide (2.44 meters), 8.5 feet high (2.59 meters) and either 10, 20, or 40 feet long (3.05, 6.10, or 12.19 meters). This standardization effort took the better part of a decade. Today, seagoing containers are only 20 or 40 feet long, so that they can fit in the holds of containerships. A few exceptions to these lengths exist, but they are rare. Since it was possible to modify their height without affecting the compatibility of containers, high-cube containers with a standard height of 9.5 feet high (2.90 meters) were added to the standard.

The composition of the 2010 worldwide fleet of containers, the latest year for which information is available, is shown in Figure 13.11.

13.3.1 Types of Seagoing Containers

The greatest number of containers in the seagoing trade are the standard 20-foot and 40-foot units (6.1 and 12.2 meters, respectively); these containers are 8 feet wide (2.44 meters), 8.5 feet tall (2.59 meters), and fully enclosed in steel (see Figure 13.12). They are equipped with a double door at one end (called the front of the container) and have a wooden floor; some have wooden sides as well. These standard containers are referred to ISO boxes, and are named after the International Organization for Standardization.

13.3 Intermodal Transportation

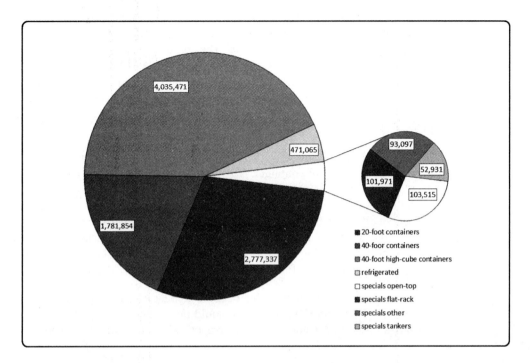

Figure 13.11: Worldwide Fleet of Containers, by Type (2010 data)
Institute of International Container Lessors.

Seagoing containers can be stacked on top of one another. Below deck, they can be stacked up to nine high, but above deck, it is generally fewer that that, but can be as many as six.

There are a large number of variants that were designed around this common platform measuring $8 \times 8.5 \times 40$ feet. Each of these alternatives is called a "special," and its availability may be limited to certain routes and/or shipping lines.

- **The liquid-bulk container.** In (see Figure 13.13) this container, a tank designed to hold liquids is placed inside a frame that has the same outside dimensions as a 20-foot unit. Containers holding liquid bulk actually have different designs depending on the type of cargo carried and can be made of a variety of materials as well. Nevertheless, the frame is built to standards of the International Organization for Standardization (ISO), and liquid-bulk containers can be stacked with traditional containers.

- **The dry-bulk container.** This container is designed to hold dry-bulk products, such as grain or polymer pellets. This method of shipping dry bulk is becoming more common, as it allows for fewer handlings than when the cargo is strictly bulk or packaged in drums or bags (see Chapter 14). Because some bulk cargo is quite heavy (grain, for example), a shorter container was created—about 5 feet tall—so that three containers can fit where two traditional ones normally do. This design greatly facilitates rail transport, as three containers fit on a double-stack train. Those containers can also be stacked with traditional ISO boxes as well.

standard container
A large metallic box used in international trade that can be loaded directly onto a truck, a railroad car or an ocean-going vessel. The most common dimensions of a container are $8 \times 8.5 \times 20$ feet and $8 \times 8.5 \times 40$ feet.

liquid-bulk container
A 20-foot container used to transport liquid loads.

dry-bulk container
A container used to transport bulk loads that are not unitized.

open-top container
A container designed so that cargo can be loaded from the top, and that is covered by a tarpaulin.

- **The open-top container.** This container (see Figure 13.14) is designed to hold cargo that is too large to be placed in the container through its doors and therefore must be loaded from the top. The container is then covered with a tarpaulin. Open-top containers can also be used to hold cargo that is taller than 8 feet, and the cargo then protrudes through the top of the container. Because it is then impossible to stack another container on top of that tall cargo, these containers are always considered "top of stack," whether placed under deck or on deck.

extended-length container
A container whose length extends beyond the traditional 40-foot length of standard containers.

- **The extended-length container.** This container is designed to hold cargo that does not fit in a 40-foot container. The enclosed extended-length containers are 45 feet long (see Figure 13.15). Some others are designed so that the cargo "sticks out" of the container itself: they are difficult to pack, as the center of gravity still has to be within the box itself. Extended-length containers are difficult to load aboard ships, and must be placed on top of stacks, but must have the next stack's slot empty as well. These containers probably represent a utilization of containers for what otherwise would be breakbulk cargo.

flat-rack container
A container designed to hold cargo whose width does not fit inside a standard container.

- **The flat rack.** This container(see Figure 13.16 on page 354) is designed to hold cargo that is less than 8 feet wide but would not fit in a standard container, which has inside dimensions of 92.5 inches (2.35 meters). Sometimes the flat

Figure 13.12: 20-foot and 40-foot Containers in the Port of Hamburg
Photo ©Frank Gärtner. Used with Permission.

13.3 Intermodal Transportation

Figure 13.13: A Liquid-Bulk Container Unloaded with A Stacker in Adelaide, Australia
Photo ©John Kirk. Used with Permission.

rack has corners or two end walls, giving it a shape that allows a flat rack to be part of a stack. Sometimes it does not, which then forces it to be a top of stack as well. Flat racks are used for shipments of pleasure boats, trucks, and military vehicles.

- **The refrigerated container.** These containers (see Figure 13.17 on page 355) are also called "reefers." This type of container is designed to hold cargo at a constant temperature during the voyage. It needs an outside power source (electricity) to function and must be plugged in during all the legs of its intermodal journey and while they are in port. Some of the refrigerated containers can maintain their temperatures with a refrigeration unit that is independent of shore—or ship—power, but these units must be refueled during their voyage, which can be quite difficult. Today, most containerships can accommodate quite a few refrigerated container units.

- **The high cube container.** This container is 9.5 feet (2.9 meters) tall and therefore can hold slightly more cargo. Such containers are designed to hold cargo that "cubes out" before it "weighs out"—*i.e.*, it fills the volume of the container before it reaches the maximum weight limit of a container, which is 24 metric tonnes (52,910 pounds) for a 20-foot container and 30.5 metric tonnes

refrigerated container (reefer)
A container designed to hold cargo that must be maintained at a constant temperature. It generally needs an outside power supply.

high-cube container
A container designed to hold cargo that is is voluminous and light. Its height is 9.5 feet.

(67,200 pounds) for a 40-foot container.

- **The hanger container**. This container is designed to hold garments "on hanger" (*i.e.*, it is equipped with steel bars on which clothes are hung). The hanger container is a relatively new device, but it seems to fulfill the need for a more convenient way to ship hanging clothes, which may be damaged when they are shipped flat in boxes or may be difficult to fold. Garment containers seem to be all high cube containers as well.

hanger container
A container designed to hold cargo that cannot be laid flat in a box, and must remain on hangers during the international voyage.

ISO box
Another term for a standard container.

A myriad of other specialized containers are available. They have been designed to ship automobiles, livestock, and other unusual cargo that could not otherwise be shipped in a standard ISO box. One aspect of importance in these modifications made to the standard, though, is that they all can accommodate the rigors of ocean shipping and fit within the existing ocean vessel and port infrastructure. In that, they are still all intermodal containers.

One of the difficulties of the development of specials is the fact that they are not multipurpose: while a traditional ISO box that holds a cargo of automobile parts from the United States bound for Malaysia can be used on the way back to ship garments or toys, such is not the case with a livestock container. If it is designed for cattle, it is unlikely that it can be used for anything else but cattle, and will come back empty, forcing its owner to pay for the return trip.

To a much lesser extent, a similar problem exists with all ISO boxes because of the imbalance of trade between ports. For example, much more trade arrives in

Figure 13.14: An Open-Top Container Before Loading
Photo ©Korean National Railroad. Used with Permission.

13.3 Intermodal Transportation

Figure 13.15: An Extended Length Container [45 foot] on Top of Two 20-foot Containers

Photo ©Jay Lazarin. Used with Permission.

the Ports of Los Angeles and Long Beach in the United States from Asia than leaves the ports for Asian destinations. There is therefore an accumulation of so-called "empties" in the United States, while there is a shortage of boxes in most Asian ports.

In the United States, the imbalance is further exacerbated by the fact that most containers are shipped to large population centers, such as New York, Washington, and Chicago, which can be far away from the manufacturing centers that export goods back to the Far East.

Finally, for some trade routes, there is another reason for the shortage of boxes in one direction: a substantial portion of empty containers shipped to some destinations disappear, as they are used for storage or housing. Such is the case in some of the republics of the former Soviet Union and some African countries.

Shippers returning empty containers are charged freight for transport. Empty containers entering the United States are considered "implements of international trade" and do not require a Customs Entry Processing form. However, U.S. Customs requires that empty containers be manifested and clears them as entry-exempt items. Empty containers must be completely empty: no blocking, bracing, or securing equipment, materials, or residual products of any kind can be found inside them. Because they can be inspected by U.S. Customs, the shipper is subject to being fined for illegal entry of goods if they are not completely empty.

Figure 13.16: A Flat-Rack Container That Must Be Top of Stack
Photo ©Robert Crallé, Chick Packaging. Used with Permission.

13.3.2 Land Bridges

The intermodal environment created several new ways of shipping goods internationally. One of the striking changes made was the concept of land bridges. Via a land bridge, cargo traveling on ocean liners can cross a land obstacle by being unloaded in one port, transferred to a train, carried across the land obstacle by rail, and reloaded onto another ship.

land bridge
A term coined to describe the practice of shipping goods from Asia to Europe through the United States by using railroads.

The use of a typical land bridge would involve cargo going from the Far East to Europe. A few years ago, breakbulk cargo loaded onto a ship would have crossed the Pacific, gone through the Panama Canal, and crossed the Atlantic before reaching its destination. (It could also have gone westward, through the Suez Canal, but then it would be a different story.) Today, the same cargo would be containerized and could use a land bridge: the cargo is shipped by ocean from the Far East to the West Coast of the North American Continent—Ports of Prince Rupert, Los Angeles/Long Beach, or Ensenada—after which it is unloaded and placed on a train that takes it to the East Coast of the Continent—Ports of Virginia, Halifax, or Baltimore. It is then reloaded onto another ship and sent to its destination in Europe. Using a land bridge is the penultimate in intermodal shipment; such changes in modes of transportation are so transparent to the shipper that it generally has no idea that its international cargo traveled through the Arizona desert on its way from Kobe, Japan, to Rotterdam, the Netherlands.

Such land bridges emerged because of several factors. The first is that the time

13.3 Intermodal Transportation

Figure 13.17: Refrigerated Containers or "Reefers" in the Port of Paranaguá, Brazil
Photo ©Gilberto de Oliveira Souza. Used with Permission.

spent by a ship traveling the Panama Canal route was greater than the time necessary to unload the cargo, cross the United States, and reload the cargo. The second is that it was equivalent in costs, or cheaper. The third was that economies of scale could be achieved with larger ships, which would not fit through the Canal. The fourth was the concern, expressed by a few shipping lines, regarding the reliability of the Canal when it became the responsibility of the Panamanian government, a concern that fortunately did not materialize.

There are several possible other locations for land bridges outside of the United States. The African continent is an obvious one, but at this time land bridges do not exist and are not planned. Another is the traffic from the Far East to eastern Europe, which can transit faster through Russia than by vessel: the port of Vostochny on the eastern shore of Russia was developed in the mid-1970s using Japanese funds to provide such a service. From having conveyed a high of 143,000 containers in 1983 to only 55,000 in 2000, this land bridge is but a speck in the transit from Japan and Korea to Europe.[27] However, the development of a seriously important land bridge is possible if D.P.R. Korea were to re-open its railway system, which would allow cargo from Republic of Korea to link with the Russian trans-Siberian railway and Europe. Finally, another quite ambitious idea was developed at a 2007 conference in Canada. It outlined the possibility of a Eurasian land bridge, which would cross Canada, Alaska, the Bering Strait, and connect the North American continent with Russia and Europe.[28] As of summer 2013, it was only an idea; however, the construction of a bridge spanning the Bering Strait has been considered several times.[29]

There are two trends with land bridge use in the United States that are likely to bring contradictory results:

- **The increased demand for domestic intermodal service.** Domestic intermodal service increasingly competes for resources and capacity with international container service (see Figure 13.18).[30] Specially designed 53-foot-long, high-capacity containers have been built and put into use by the trucking companies in the United States, which now own about 205,000 of them.[31] The 53-foot containers now account for a majority of the intermodal domestic traffic of the United States. These domestic intermodal movements add strain to a rail system that is already at or near capacity on key corridors, the primary routes for international intermodal cargo, some of which are still single-track (see Chapter 3).

- **The completion of the expansion of the Panama Canal.** The canal locks of the Panama Canal—and its overall capacity—have been the major reasons for some shipments being diverted to landbridges. However, with the completion of the new locks in 2015, and with the Canal's increased capacity, it is likely that a greater number of carriers will offer all-water service from East Asia to the East Coast of the United States.

The potential for higher freight rates exists if the capacity of the rail network is strained; however the possible competition with the Panama Canal may also bring some lower rates. It is difficult to predict the outcome of these two trends.

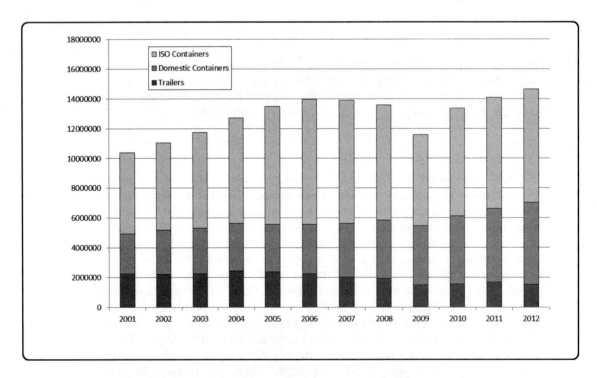

Figure 13.18: United States Intermodal Traffic by Type of Cargo
Adapted from IANA data.

13.3.3 Liability Issues

One aspect of intermodal shipping that has yet to be resolved is the liability of the carrier toward the shipper when the goods are damaged while in the carrier's care. As goods travel from one mode of transportation to another, the legal or regulatory liability limits change. The limits are different for the trucking leg of the trip, the rail leg, and the ocean leg. In many cases, they are also different from one carrier to another, if such carrier has negotiated a different limit under the U.S. Ocean Shipping Reform Act (OSRA). To add further complexity, the flag under which the carrier operates also matters. This issue is relevant mostly for shippers who elect to not insure their cargoes and for insurance companies. Nevertheless, it is one of the few issues left to be determined in intermodal transportation.

As mentioned in Chapter 10, the United Nations Commission on International Trade Law (UNCITRAL) has designed a multimodal liability framework, called the Rotterdam Rules, that governs the liability of carriers when a multimodal bill of lading is used. The General Assembly of the United Nations voted to accept the Rotterdam Rules in February 2009, and in September 2009, the United States and 15 other countries signed it, heeding the recommendations of the International Chamber of Commerce, which had strongly supported the new convention.[32] Each of the countries still has to ratify the treaty and complete its own legislation to implement the rules. A year after the twentieth country ratifies the treaty the Rotterdam Rules will enter into force; as of June 2013, only two had—Togo and Spain—but there is optimism that a single liability convention may finally govern international shipments of goods, regardless of the method of transportation. The fact that the Convention applies to door-to-door shipments, which subjects all of the legs of a multimodal voyage to the same liability limits, makes it particularly attractive to shippers, which will no longer have to determine on which leg of a voyage damage occurred. The Rotterdam Rules place liability limits of SDR 875 per package and SDR 4 per kilogram for items that are not considered packages, such as automobiles and machinery.

Rotterdam Rules
A 2008 international liability convention for intermodal cargo that restricts the liability of the carrier to U.S.$ 875 per package or per customary freight unit.

13.3.4 Aircraft Containers

The types of containers used in air transport are more specifically called Unit Load Devices (ULDs) and are quite different from the types used in ocean shipping. The major differences in the way they are built and used are:

- They are used to aggregate small individual packages rather than to form a whole shipment. Freight consolidators and airlines bundle together several different freight packages going to the same destination and unbundle them at the destination airport, sometimes to re-bundle them in another container for shipment to their final destination. In that regard, containers are used to speed up the loading and unloading of aircraft by shifting the task of loading and unloading small packages from the airplane to airport facilities. It also allows airfreight companies to use space more efficiently. For example, they can build shelves in the containers, which allow more freight to be carried.

- Although there have been some standardization attempts, most containers are designed to fit a specific aircraft. There are at least 20 different ULD sizes, all identified by a code such as L-2 or EH, and some variants within the same size can be used as well. For example, L-2 can be used only in the

unit load device (ULD)
The term used to describe the containers used in airfreight transport.

belly of a Boeing 767, but EH can be used on any aircraft's main deck. Most aircraft containers, therefore, cannot be conveniently transported from one airplane to the next, and cargo must be de-containerized and re-containerized at airport facilities. This certainly removes the advantage of being able to securely pack a container and leave it undisturbed until it is unpacked by the consignee.

- Aircraft containers are made of lightweight materials and are not designed to protect the cargo in any significant way. Most containers are made of aluminum, Plexiglas, or sometimes plywood, with "doors" that can be made of the same material, or of fabric, or even be nonexistent, with the cargo being simply held by a net. These containers offer little protection against the elements and against theft (see Figure 13.19).

- Aircraft containers are not intermodal by intent. They are designed to be used only in aircraft and, possibly, for very short truck routes to shuttle goods to and from a freight forwarder's facilities. They are rarely used outside of the immediate vicinity of an airport.

Figure 13.19: Unit Load Devices [ULD] About to Be Loaded in the Belly of a Passenger Aircraft

Photo ©Gatsenko Alexander. Used with Permission.

13.4 Freight Forwarders

This complex array of alternatives is often bewildering to an occasional shipper; in those cases, it makes sense for the shipper to use the services of a freight forwarder, or a firm specializing in handling freight, particularly international freight.

freight forwarder
A company specialized in shipping cargo on behalf of shippers—importers or exporters.

A freight forwarder is, in layman's terms, a travel agent for freight. It knows what alternative routes are available, it knows how to determine the cost of shipping goods between two points, and it can arrange all of the paperwork necessary to ship the goods, from the exporting country's requirements to the importing country's Customs clearance.

Freight forwarders are different from Customs brokers, who specialize in clearing Customs for freight and who have to take, at least in the United States, a rigorous examination to be allowed to fulfill this role. Freight forwarders are also different from Non-Vessel-Operating Common Carriers, who buy space on liner ships or airfreighters and resell it to less-than-container-load customers, and they are regulated by the Federal Maritime Commission. Nevertheless, it is not uncommon for all three functions to be present in the same firm.

The business of freight forwarders is highly fragmented, including a large number of firms. Some are very large, with operations in just about every country. Others are quite small and, to distinguish themselves from others, end up specializing in a specific market, such as moving hazardous cargo, moving live animals, or moving what is known as project cargo.

13.5 Project Cargo

The term project cargo is used to characterize cargo that is outside the normal realm of what shipping companies handle, specifically in terms of weight, volume, or destination. Most often, it encompasses all of the pieces of machinery or equipment required by a single project, such as the building of a dam or power plant, but can be an entire plant as well, which is being moved from a developed country, where its technology is outdated, to a developing country, where it will finish its useful life.[33] Project cargo also includes anything that requires some extra planning, such as the shipping of locomotives, railroad cars, large trucks, pleasure boats, large engines, electric generators, and so on.

project cargo
Cargo that is much larger, heavier, or more complex to handle than regular cargo. Project cargo generally requires specialized means of transport.

In general, project cargo needs careful planning in order to reach its destination. The trucks used to transport it to the port need to trace their itineraries very carefully, not only to avoid low bridges and tunnels, but also to make sure that the proper permits can be secured. Port cranes have to be checked to make sure they can handle the load, or else floating cranes have to be rented. The ship carrying the cargo has to be selected carefully, to make sure it can accommodate the cargo. Roll-on/roll-off and breakbulk ships are the most commonly used means of getting project cargoes to their port of destination. Finally, the final road trip has to be planned thoroughly as well. It is not unusual for such shipments to be planned more than a year in advance and to cost several million dollars because of their complexity.[34]

Such project cargo also moves quite slowly; it is difficult to make a 250-tonne piece of equipment (550,000-pounds) move quickly, especially when it involves using all lanes of a highway at once, or taking down and replacing all overhanging electric, telephone, and other utility wires.[35] In late 2005, a 1.5-million-pound (680.4

metric tonne) hydro cracker for Canada's oil-sands project in Long Lake, Alberta (Canada), was moved by a heavy-lift ship to the Port of Duluth, Minnesota (U.S.). From the port, the unusual cargo traveled by rail on the world's largest rail car, the 36-axle German-made Schnabel car, that itself had to be shipped in advance to the United States so that it could carry that special load. The planning for the transportation of such a massive piece of equipment took two years. Ed Clarke, the logistician in charge of the move, said, "It's all about preplanning. At every step along the way you have to check weights, dimensions, clearances. And you have to know everything about the environment in which the equipment will be handled."[36] On a typical oversize, heavy-lift project, the logistics manager has a long list of items to check: the cargo itself, generally where it is manufactured; the docks and cargo-handling equipment (cranes) in the ports in which the cargo will be handled; the vessel on which the oversize piece will be shipped; the rail cars, the rails, and the bridges and tunnels along the trip; and even the rail beds on which the cargo will be hauled.

13.6 Alternative Means of Transportation

Despite the preponderance of the traditional means of transportation of ocean shipping, airfreight, trucking, and railroads for moving cargo internationally, a few alternative ways are used on a regular basis.

13.6.1 Pipelines

pipeline
A mode of transportation consisting of a long pipe and used for the transportation of liquid cargo.

Probably the most easily overlooked of the alternative means of transportation are pipelines, which carry a substantial percentage of the world's petroleum oil and natural gas. Many of these pipelines are international. For example, Gazprom, the state-owned producer of gas in Russia, ships 525 billion cubic meters (18.5 trillion cubic feet) of gas to Europe in a single pipeline (see Figure 13.20), which meanders through Belarus, Ukraine, Poland, Slovakia, and the Czech Republic before stopping in Germany, and provides fully 20 percent of the European Union's gas needs. A second pipeline is being planned, that would serve Southern Europe, and would cross the Black Sea rather than the Ukraine.[37] Many other pipelines crisscross the Persian Gulf area and the North American continent.

Pipelines can also be used to replace ships for some areas of the world where it is particularly hazardous to navigate. One such planned pipeline would allow oil shipped from the oil fields of southern Russia to bypass the Bosporus, a particularly congested area located in the middle of a very densely populated city, Istanbul. More than 50,000 ships travel its waters every year. The people of Istanbul and their government have been advocating such a pipeline, as they cannot control what goes through the strait—it is considered international waters—and they fear a catastrophic accident. Given the condition of some oil tankers, the treacheries of the currents in the narrow passage, and the fact that dozens of ships run aground or collide in the Bosporus every year, it is not an unfounded fear. An oil and gas pipeline would remove some of this hazardous traffic.

Pipelines can be used for transporting coal as well, in the form of "slurry," a mix of water and pulverized coal that is then shipped as a liquid. Such a method can, in some cases, present some economic advantage over traditional railroad and truck transportation.

13.6.2 Barges

River barges are also commonly used to carry international cargo and are often significant sources of transportation services on certain routes and for certain merchandise. For example, 35 percent of all the containers shipped to and from Rotterdam, the eleventh largest container seaport in the world—and the largest in Europe—travel by barge, with 54 percent traveling by truck and 11 percent traveling by rail.[38] The latter is a growing percentage, expected to increase with the European emphasis on low-emission means of transport. Much of the bulk cargo (ores, agricultural commodities, and petroleum-related products) travels by barges; 62 million metric tonnes traveled to and from the port by barge in 2012.[39]

More than 2.3 billion short tons (mostly commodities such as coal, petroleum products, and grain) were carried on U.S. waterways in 2011.[40] Sixty three percent of that volume was bound for international destinations and traveled mainly on the Mississippi, the Ohio River, and the Gulf Intracoastal Waterway to the ports of New Orleans, Baton Rouge, Mobile, and Houston. Theses barges can easily be delayed, though, by natural variations in the weather: whenever the river is in flood stage, and the currents too strong, or when there is a drought, and the river water level is lower than normal. Although they are much slower, river barges offer a very economical alternative to trucks and railroads.

The barges on the North American rivers are not self-propelled. They are moved

barge
A flat-bottom ship designed to transport cargo on the inland river network. A barge can be pushed or pulled, or be self propelled.

Figure 13.20: The Russian-European Union Gas Pipeline
Photo ©Vladimir Kolobov. Used with Permission.

in groups of five to ten, pushed by a tugboat, and take considerable skill to maneuver (see Figure 13.21). The European and Asian barges (mostly found in China) are self-propelled, with crews living aboard them (see Figure 13.22 on the facing page).

Ocean barges are also commonly used for shipping, although it is unclear how much of this mode of transportation is used for international shipping. Nevertheless, most of the traffic between the continental United States and Puerto Rico is done by barge, as is some of the traffic with small Alaskan towns.

13.7 Ground Transportation Security

In the aftermath of the terrorist attacks of the early part of the twenty-first century, additional security efforts in ground transportation involved primarily thorough inspections by Customs and Immigration officials and other means of increased scrutiny. The strategies were similar in the European Union and in the United States.

At the U.S. border crossings, the early stages of implementation of those increased inspection levels caused substantial additional delays, as there was relatively little capacity to increase the number of inspection stations. As mentioned in Chapter 3, there are only three large border crossings between the United States and Canada: (1) the Ambassador Bridge and a small tunnel between Detroit, Michigan, and Windsor, Ontario, with a combined 10 truck lanes of Customs clearance in the

Figure 13.21: A U.S. Barge on the Black Warrior River, in Alabama
Photo ©Edward Todd. Used with Permission.

13.7 Ground Transportation Security

Figure 13.22: A European Barge on the Rhine River, in Germany
Photo ©Firina. Used with Permission.

United States; (2) the Peace Bridge between Buffalo, New York, and Fort Erie, Ontario, with 3 Customs clearance truck lanes; and (3) the Lewiston-Queenston Bridge north of Niagara Falls, with 3 truck lanes. Altogether, these 16 truck lanes must clear about 15,000 trucks each day. That is an average of about two minutes per truck, and therefore any additional inspections beyond a very cursory review of paperwork causes delays. While there is a significantly larger number of land border crossings between the European Union and its external trading partners, as well as a smaller volume of international trade, the consequences of increased inspections were similar. Long delays and substantial frustrations were the norm at border crossings between the European Union and Albania, Belarus, Croatia, Macedonia, Russia, Serbia, Turkey, and Ukraine.

The United States and the European Union addressed these issues in similar fashion; in order to identify the shipments that could present risks, they required an advanced shipping notification of the manifest for the shipment. In the United States, since May 2008, the notification must be made at least one hour before the expected crossing of the border, and in electronic form through the Automated Commercial Environment (ACE). For the European Union, since July 2009, the notification must be made two hours in advance and electronically as well.

In addition, the United States implemented the Free and Secure Trade (FAST) program with Canada and Mexico, in which companies that are part of the Customs-

Trade Partnership Against Terrorism (C-TPAT) can enroll. To recognize that these firms have implemented security measures in their supply chains, the U.S. Customs and Border Protection agency gives them access to a dedicated FAST lane at the border crossings, allowing them to clear Customs faster. It also allows them to send the manifest information as late as 30 minutes before crossing the border. However, in order for a shipment to benefit from the FAST program, all parties involved in the transaction and the logistics of the shipment must be part of the FAST program, including the driver of the truck, who must possess a FAST card. As of June 2013, more than 78,000 commercial truck drivers had been cleared by U.S. Customs and Border Protection.[41]

Review and Discussion Questions

1. How different are the ground transport alternatives in different areas of the world? What constraints does a shipper face when shipping with ground transport?

2. What is the concept of a land bridge? What effect will such a concept have on the frequency of use of containers in shipping cargo?

3. Choose three different types of ocean containers and explain how they are used.

4. In what ways are oceangoing containers and aircraft containers different?

5. Comment on the opinion that "the number of cargo handling points is not diminished by the use of aircraft containers."

Notes

[1] *Energy, Transport and Environment Indicators*, European Statistical Agency, http://epp.eurostat.ec.europa.eu/portal/page/portal/product_details/publication?p_product_code=KS-DK-12-001, retrieved June 29, 2013.

[2] *Ibid.*

[3] "Driving Restrictions in Europe on Specific Days and Times," Trans Sib logistics, http://www.transsib-logistics.de/en/drivingbans, accessed June 29, 2013.

[4] Mariani, Daniele and Christian Raaflaub, "Shifting Freight Traffic to Rail Proves Daunting," June 24, 2012, Swissinfo.ch, http://www.swissinfo.ch/eng/swiss_news/Shifting_freight_traffic_to_rail_proves_daunting.html?cid=32968240, retrieved June 29, 2013.

[5] Siegenthaler, Peter, "Truck Drivers Hit the Rails and Take a Break," August 27, 2012, Swissinfo.ch, http://www.swissinfo.ch/eng/swiss_news/Truck_drivers_hit_the_rails_and_take_a_break.html?cid=33367284, retrieved June 29, 2013.

[6] *Yearbook of Road Transport Law*, Freight Transport Association, Tunbridge Wells, Kent, UK, http://www.fta.co.uk.

[7] Autostrada Wielkopolska, http://www.autostrada-a2.pl/en, retrieved June 29, 2013.

[8] Koenig, Robert, "Danes Planning to 'Flag Out' Their Trucks," *Journal of Commerce*, January 10, 2000, p. 3.

[9] "Class I Railroad Statistics," Association of American Railroads, January 10, 2013, www.aar.org/StatisticsAndPublications/Documents/AAR-Stats-2013-01-10.pdf, retrieved June 30, 2013.

[10] *National Transportation Statistics 2013*, Bureau of Transportation Statistics, Department of Transportation, http://www.rita.dot.gov/bts/sites/rita.dot.gov.bts/files/publications/national_transportation_statistics/index.html, retrieved June 30, 2013.

[11] *Ibid.*

[12] "Trends in the Transport Sector," 2012, International Transport Forum, http://www.internationaltransportforum.org/statistics/trends/index.html, retrieved June 30, 2013.

[13] *Ibid.*

[14] "European Road-Rail Combined Transport 2012-13," 2013 UIRR Annual Report, International Union of Combined Road-Rail Transport Companies, May 21, 2013, http://www.uirr.com/en/media-centre/annual-reports/annual-reports/mediacentre/575-annual-report-2012-13.html, retrieved June 30, 2013.

[15] "Trends in the Transport Sector," 2012, International Transport Forum, http://www.internationaltransportforum.org/statistics/trends/index.html, retrieved June 30, 2013.

[16] *Ibid.*

[17] "The Rail Freight Sector Needs EU Action Now!", *Railway Insider*, June 9, 2009, http://rinsider.clubferoviar.ro/en/afiseaza_stire.php?id=4202.

[18] "Betuweroute loopt opnieuw achter op verwachtingen," June 4, 2013, Logistiek, http://www.logistiek.nl/Distributie/multimodaal-transport/2013/6/Betuweroute-loopt-opnieuw-achter-bij-verwachtingen-1273772W, retrieved June 30, 2013.

[19] "DNHK concerned about the Betuwe Route track expansion," November 23, 2012, Port of Rotterdam, http://www.portofrotterdam.com/en/News/pressreleases-news/Pages/dnhk-concerned-betuwe-route-track-expansion.aspx, retrieved June 30, 2013.

[20] http://www.naviland-cargo.com/?lang=en

[21] "Naviland Cargo," http://www.sncf.com/en/partners/naviland-cargo, retrieved June 30, 2013.

[22] "Class I Railroad Statistics," Association of American Railroads, January 10, 2013, www.aar.org/StatisticsAndPublications/Documents/AAR-Stats-2013-01-10.pdf, retrieved June 30, 2013.

[23] "The Northern East-West (N.E.W.) Freight Corridor," International Union of Railways, Executive Project Office, Transportutvikling AS, Narvik, 2004, http://www.transportutvikling.no/-NEW_report_2004.pdf, retrieved October 29, 2009.

[24] "Hitching a Ride on the Eurasian Express," *Inbound Logistics*, October 2008, p. 24.

[25] "DB Schenker to launch daily freight train to China," *Railway Gazette*, September 30, 2011, http://www.railwaygazette.com/news/single-view/view/db-schenker-to-launch-daily-freight-train-to-china.html, retrieved June 30, 2013.

[26] "2010 IICL Annual Leased Container Fleet Survey," Institute of International Container Lessors, April 5, 2010, http://www.iicl.org/news/fleet.cfm, retrieved June 30, 2013.

[27] Working, Russell, "Port Offers Shippers a Siberian Shortcut," *The New York Times*, December 3, 2000.

[28] Witzsche, Rolf, "The Global Dimensions of the Eurasian Land-bridge," http://www.rolf-witzsche.com/peace/landbridge/global-eurasian.html, retrieved July 5, 2009.

[29] Ricci, Tom, "Connecting Two Continents: The Ultimate Engineering Challenge," January 2012, American Society of Mechanical Engineers, ASME, https://www.asme.org/engineering-topics/articles/arctic-engineering/connecting-two-continents-the-ultimate-engineering, retrieved June 30, 2013.

[30] Casey, Joanne, "CCIB Intermodal Seminar," March 14, 2013, Intermodal Association of North America, http://www.theccib.com/files/3_Joanne_Casey_.2013_Intermodal_Association_of_North_America_and_Industry_Overview.pdf, retrieved June 30, 2013.

[31] Miller, Ken, "Supply Chain Trends in Intermodal," JB Hunt presentation, March 4, 2013, www.joc.com/sites/default/files/u48783/TPM2013_Presentations/Ken_Miller_Presentation_3-4.pdf, retrieved June 30, 2013.

[32] Edmonson, R. G., "ICC Endorses Rotterdam Rules," *Journal of Commerce*, June 2, 2009.

[33] Baldwin, Tom, "Carriers Move the Immovable," *The Journal of Commerce*, October 26, 1998, p. 1C.

[34] Zeller, Tom, Jr., "Big Loads on a 2-Lane Byway," *The New York Times*, October 22, 2010, p. B1.

[35] Millman, Joel, "Idaho Shortcut Stalls Global Treck," *The Wall Street Journal*, October 22, 2010, p. A6.

[36] Marciniak, Lisa, "Making the Big Jobs Look Easy," *North Star Port*, Duluth Seaway Port Authority, Winter 2005-2006 Issue.

[37] Kanter, James, "Gazprom Seeks a Pipeline to Bypass Ukraine," *The New York Times*, April 23, 2009.

[38] "Modal Split Containers," Port of Rotterdam, http://www.portofrotterdam.com/en/Port/port-statistics/Documents/Modal splitcontainers E 2012-2009.pdf, retrieved June 30, 2013.

[39] *Amsterdam Ports Statistics 2012*, Port of Amsterdam, http://www.portofamsterdam.com/-Eng/statistics, retrieved June 30, 2013.

[40] "The U.S. Waterway System—Transportation Facts," November 15, 2012, Navigation and Civil Works Decision Support Center, U.S. Army Corps of Engineers, www.navigationdatacenter.us/factcard/factcard12.pdf, retrieved June 30, 2013.

[41] "FAST Fact Sheet," May 2013, U.S. Customs and Border Protection, http://wwwcbp.gov/xp/cgov/travel/trusted_traveler/fast/fast_driver/, retrieved June 30, 2013.

Chapter 14

Packaging for Export

14.1 Packaging Functions	368
14.2 Packaging Objectives	369
14.3 Ocean Cargo	370
14.4 Air Transport	385
14.5 Road and Rail Transport	387
14.6 Security	389
14.7 Hazardous Cargo	391
14.8 Refrigerated Goods	392
14.9 Domestic Retail Packaging Issues	393
14.10 Packaging as a Marketing Tool	395

One of the challenging practical areas of international logistics is the packaging of goods for international shipment. This is a responsibility that always falls on the exporter, regardless of the terms of trade, or Incoterms® rule, chosen (see Chapter 6). Unfortunately, it is a function that is oftentimes just left to the shipping department, with few guidelines other than to make sure it gets to the customers without problems, and quite often with pressures to control costs; there is rarely a strategy developed for packaging, even though it is an area that certainly has strategic implications.

This chapter makes distinctions between primary, secondary, and tertiary packaging, as seen in Figure 14.1.

Primary packaging is consumer packaging, or what the consumers see when they purchase and handle the product. It is part of the marketing function of the firm and is traditionally covered in marketing management textbooks as part of the promotional efforts of the firm; primary packaging is only occasionally mentioned in this chapter. Secondary packaging is the packaging that usually groups several of the consumer goods into one unit. It is made up of one of two alternatives:

- The first is a cardboard box. Since the term used more frequently in the industry is corrugated paperboard box, it will be the one used in this chapter. Paperboard is categorized on several criteria, including thickness, the type of flutes used—the way the layer of paper sandwiched between the faces of the board is folded—and the number of layers: paperboard is available in single-, double-, and triple-wall versions.

corrugated paper
Two flat sheets of brown paper, in between which a sinusoidally shaped sheet is glued.

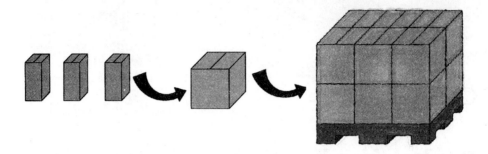

Figure 14.1: Primary, Secondary and Tertiary Packaging
Diagram courtesy of Jeff Post and Bob Iben. Used with permission.

- The second is a plastic wrap that is either stretched (stretch-wrap) or heat-shrunk (shrink-wrap) over several units of the primary package. The purpose of either method is to consolidate multiple units into one and to protect them from water. The two techniques differ in the thickness of the wrap, with shrink-wrap generally much thicker than stretch-wrap, and much more resistant to multiple handlings. The term "shrink-wrap," whenever used in this chapter, will refer to either of these two techniques.

Secondary packaging is what the retailer sees and handles before the goods are placed on the shelves. In discount retail stores, this secondary packaging may be seen by the consumer.

Tertiary packaging, or transportation packaging, includes all of the additional protection given to the goods to ensure their safe and efficient delivery, in sound condition, at the lowest possible cost, to their foreign purchaser.[1] Tertiary packaging for consumer goods is therefore the packaging placed around the secondary retail packaging units. For industrial goods, because there is generally no primary or secondary packaging of the products, the tertiary packaging encompasses all the packaging activities aimed at protecting them during shipment.

14.1 Packaging Functions

The first function of correct packaging for export is obviously the protection of the goods from the hazards of international shipping by ocean or by air. Proper packaging has direct cost implications. On one hand, it is certain that the costs of packaging generally increase as the protection of the goods increases; however, on the other hand, the costs of losing part of the cargo to improper packing are generally much higher[2] and cannot be insured against (see Chapter 10 for further details), and no real trade-off exists. It is generally in the best interest of the exporter to ensure that goods are properly packaged so that they arrive undamaged to their destination. This chapter will expand on this aspect of packaging, explaining the alternatives available and their advantages and disadvantages.

The second function of correct packaging is to facilitate the handling of goods while they are in transit; well-designed packaging will allow the stevedores, the ship-

improper packing
Packing that is not sufficient to protect the goods during their international voyage. Improperly packed goods will not be covered under any insurance policy.

ping line, and the trucking companies to handle the goods without difficulties, but mostly without having to improvise an inappropriate handling method. The capabilities of the equipment likely to be used in the handling of the goods must be respected (*i.e.*, the dimensional constraints and weight constraints they place on the package, as well as the different standards and regulations used in the countries through which the goods will travel). Finally, all the handling and care instructions must be clearly marked on the package.

The third function of correct packaging, and one that is often overlooked, is that it is part of the customer service strategy of the firm. While a customer expects to receive the goods in sellable or usable condition in all cases, it also expects to be able to quickly unpack the goods and not spend considerable time and money preparing them to be used or sold. This objective is often much more difficult to achieve than just protecting the goods for transport and facilitating their handling while in transit. The packaging has to be simple enough to be opened without using specialized tools or exerting much effort, but most of all, it has to be designed so that it can be opened without damaging the goods. To a great extent, the packaging used by a firm should also reflect the image it is trying to project to customers. A well-conceived and well-constructed package is a positive reflection on the ability of a company to manufacture quality products. Similarly, more and more customers are sensitive to a packaging alternative that is easily reused or placed in the waste stream. In some cases, it is legally mandatory.

14.2 Packaging Objectives

The objective of proper packaging is to make sure that goods are protected from the three major losses that can occur in international transit:

- Protecting the goods from mechanical damage: breakage, crushes, nicks, and dents (these perils represent roughly 43 percent of all claims made by shippers to their insurance companies)[3]

- Protecting the goods from water damage: seawater, rain, floods, and container sweat (15 percent of claims made)

- Protecting the goods from theft and pilferage (21 percent of claims made)

The remaining 21 percent of the claims are linked to fire, strandings, sinkings, collision, overboard losses, and jettison.

Each of these perils can be prevented to a great extent by the proper use of packaging techniques and by the correct design of the protective systems around the cargo.

However, that's not all: another objective of packaging is to provide good customer service to the recipient of the goods. This is achieved by paying attention to the smaller details of the packaging process and designing a "smarter" package. While it is difficult to give specific guidance, a few examples may illustrate the concept better:

- Instead of gluing—and then nailing—the plywood panels onto a crate, a customer-focused exporter would just nail them or, even better, attach them with screws, so that they can be more easily taken apart by the receiving department of the importer. The boards can then be reused internally by the importer or by its employees rather than discarded. An exporter shipping to countries where packaging materials may end up as housing materials would be even more empathetic if it considered using a slightly better grade of boards and plywood, and making sure that they have been heat-treated rather than fumigated with chemicals.

- Another way of displaying customer focus would be to include a packaging list in the recipient's language and to clearly mark all of the packages within a shipment; for example, by color-coding or letter-coding each pallet and its corresponding manifest.

- Yet another way of showing customer concern is to utilize unitized packages that match the size of the ones used by the customer, so that goods can be placed directly in its warehouse, without having to be reloaded onto the proper pallet size.

While it takes only a few extra minutes (and only a bit more money) to pack a shipment in a smarter manner, the importer will appreciate the attention; it may actually become a strategic advantage over a competitor whose shipping department is inattentive to details. In addition, it helps prevent claims of shortages when the customer cannot locate items within a shipment.

Finally, packaging should reflect the increasing sensitivity to recycling and energy conservation present in many countries. The focus in this case should be for the exporter to use recyclable and reusable materials rather than disposable materials; for example, it should use starch "peanuts" (packaging pellets) or recycled paper cubes rather than Styrofoam,[4] or inflatable dunnage rather than scrap pallets, and it should load the goods on pallets of the size used by the customer.

14.3 Ocean Cargo

Ocean cargo can be shipped using a large number of alternative packaging alternatives. Because an increasing percentage of cargo shipped by ocean is now containerized, this particular mode will be covered first, followed by breakbulk cargo and its packaging alternatives.

14.3.1 Full-Container-Load (FCL) Cargo

full container load (FCL) A shipment whose volume or weight is close to the container's limits, or for which the shipper requests that it be the only shipment in the container.

While it is true that containers protect the cargo well against most damages, the choice of the proper container is important when shipping a full-container-load (FCL) shipment. An FCL shipment utilizes the entire capacity of a container, whether by weight or by volume.

Choice of Container

After having determined the correct type of container (see Chapter 13) in which the cargo will be shipped, the exporter should, as much as possible, inspect the container before using it for a particular shipment. It is a particularly important step if the cargo is not be unitized on pallets or in crates, but will simply be placed in corrugated paperboard boxes or in their retail packaging directly inside the container.

The container should first be inspected from the outside for possible structural damage: a structurally unsound container could collapse under the weight of the several containers that will eventually be placed on top of it. Containers are designed to withstand the weight of up to eight other containers; a slight structural problem could weaken it enough to collapse under this kind of weight and a heavy sea. Hundreds of them do every year. The frame should look straight, the fittings used for lifting it and securing it on the ship or on a truck should be in place and not damaged, the doors should close properly, the repairs—if any—should appear to have been done competently, and there should be no visible structural rust. Surface rust is not pretty, but it usually does not affect the cargo carried; nevertheless, it may be a sign that the container is not very carefully maintained.

The container should also be inspected from the inside, with the doors closed, for possible light leakage, which would indicate a water infiltration risk during shipment. Sometimes, such leakage also indicates a structural problem. The container should have a wooden floor (plywood sheathing) and ideally wooden sides as well, so as to prevent condensation damage inside the container (container sweat) and protect the cargo from direct contact with the metal sides. The container should also have all of its inside hardware in place (tie-down rings and cleats), to allow for good securing of the cargo. The container should be inspected for foul and persistent odors. Several cargoes have been damaged by the content of a preceding shipment. Protruding nails or other fasteners should be removed to prevent an accidental puncture to the cargo. Finally, the container should be clean of grease, dirt, and other foreign material so as to keep the cargo clean.[5]

Palletization

It is always better for goods in a shipment to be unitized (assembled in a single larger unit) so that they can be manipulated more efficiently by using a forklift or other means of material handling. This can be done by placing the goods on pallets, or by building boxes in which they are placed. In either case, the unitized package includes one more layer of protection for the goods, which is better than when they are left in their original secondary package, which is often only some corrugated paperboard boxes.

The fact that the goods are placed on pallets and shrink-wrapped protects them better from water infiltration (by placing them a few inches above the floor) and from condensation in the container. It also facilitates handling and protects the goods once they have arrived at the importer's warehouse; the lower the likelihood that the goods are manipulated by hand, the greater the probability that they will be unloaded in good condition. Unitizing prevents the primary package from being crushed and therefore allows the goods to be immediately sellable; in those cases where the boxes have cosmetic damage, it is costly to repackage the goods into a new box, and therefore it is generally much cheaper to properly unitize them. Some shippers will include additional (empty) boxes, so that the goods can be re-packaged by the customer if the boxes are damaged. This is a way to overcome the problem, but it is best to prevent it.

Another advantage of a palletized unit is that the secondary packaging may then be sufficient to protect the goods, as long as the pallets are protected on the corners, as seen in Figure 14.2, and the pallets are properly stacked by adding a rigid support between the lower and upper pallets. This support could be heavy corrugated multi-wall paperboard or plywood.

unitized
Cargo in which smaller packaging units are assembled into a single larger unit, to facilitate handling.

pallet
A wooden (plastic) platform on which goods can be placed. A pallet necessitates mechanical equipment to be moved.

shrink/stretch wrap
A polymer film that is stretched over palletized cargo to protect it from water damage.

box
A wooden container designed to unitize the goods and protect them. In a box, the walls are an integral part of its structural strength.

Figure 14.2: A Unitized, Stretch-Wrapped Pallet, with its four Corners Protected
Photo ©Pierre David. Used with permission.

When unitizing the boxes onto pallets, there is another issue to take into consideration: most pallets are built by alternating the boxes so that they constitute a "brick" pattern, as such patterns are generally believed to be stronger. However, the stronger parts of the boxes are their corners, and therefore corners should support

Figure 14.3: An Incorrectly Loaded Pallet, Left, and a Correctly Loaded One, Right

most of the weight of the boxes on top of them. By alternating corners, as in a brick pattern, the weaker part of the box supports the greatest weight. Such a pattern results in a greater likelihood of crushed boxes and therefore should be avoided. It is generally better to build pallets in columns, where boxes fit directly on top of one another, as such a practice results in fewer crushed or damaged boxes (see Figure 14.3).*

Goods that are shipped in corrugated boxes that are not protected with reinforced corners or held together with stretch or shrink-wrap are much more likely to be damaged in shipment. The corners and shrink-wrap help keep the boxes together and make the unit much stronger. In the absence of corner protectors, slight damage to one of the lower-level boxes can cause the entire stack to collapse, causing further damage to all of the boxes on that pallet (see Figure 14.4).

Figure 14.4: An Incorrectly Loaded Pallet Can Result in Crushed Boxes
Photo ©Pierre David. Used with permission.

Although unitized cargo is preferable, it can also present challenges. For one, the standardized size of pallets in Europe has been 80 × 120 centimeters (31.5 × 47.25 inches) since 1959. Pallet sizes in the United States are, for all intents and purposes, not standardized, even though a great percentage of them are 36 × 48 inches

---

*The author is indebted to Professor Bud Cohan from Columbus State Community College for this point.

(91.5 × 122 centimeters). This presents difficulties, as pallets of one standard do not fit neatly into containers designed for the other. In addition, there are problems when corrugated-paper boxes that were designed to fit a pallet's footprint do not conveniently fill another size; for example, a European exporter may have boxes that have a base of 40 × 40 centimeters, and while such boxes fit nicely on a European pallet, they leave a good portion of a U.S. 36-inch pallet unused. Unfortunately, a dimension that is compatible with both standards is a difficult compromise.

Non-unitized Cargo

If the goods inside the container are not unitized, for whatever reason, it is preferable that they be somewhat protected from crushing and moisture by being packaged in a higher grade of corrugated paperboard, double- or triple-walled; regular secondary packaging is generally insufficient and its use should be avoided. If the goods are to be stacked, layers of strong corrugated paperboard or sheets of plywood should be used between the layers to protect the lower levels from collapsing and to prevent crushed boxes. If the goods are to be shipped from (or to) a high-humidity area, a layer of plywood on the floor of the container or a layer of pallets should be considered, to insulate the cargo from possible water at the bottom of the container, due to condensation. In addition, paperboard should be avoided as much as possible, as it loses up to 60 percent of its strength under humid conditions.[6] Figure 10-5 illustrates the differences in relative humidity levels for an ocean container shipment from China to the United States. It varied from 15 to 90 percent.

Blocking Materials

dunnage
Packing material designed to prevent cargo from moving when in transit.

When loading a container, it would be ideal if the goods could fill out the space as completely as possible, leaving no room for the cargo to shift. Unfortunately, that is generally unrealistic. Therefore, a number of blocking materials have been developed, collectively called dunnage.

The first method is to secure the goods to the container itself, if that is possible. This is normally done with hooks and straps, or wood braces, a system that is particularly good at keeping the cargo from moving inside the container (see Figure 14.5).

The second is to insert some sort of spacer in between the pallets or the packages. Some companies use old pallets, some use bracing contraptions made with wooden beams (in American measurements, "4 × 4s," which actually measure 3.5 × 3.5 inches, or roughly 9 × 9 centimeters), and some use inflatable bags (see Figure 14.6). Before closing the door of the container, similar bracing material must be inserted between the cargo and the door to prevent shifting. Insurance claim handlers "frequently come across cargo poorly secured in a container, perhaps because void spaces are not filled, or because heavier items are not lashed down."[7] As a reminder, insurance policies do not cover claims for improperly packaged cargo (see Chapter 10).

lashing
The process of attaching cargo to the means of transport. On a ship, containers are lashed onto the deck, in a container, goods are lashed to the container walls and floor.

The critical part is that the entire floor space in the container must be occupied, so that none of the cargo may move. However heavy the cargo may be, it will move and eventually be damaged if it is not braced securely. The costs of replacing damaged cargo will undoubtedly exceed whatever savings there were in not using proper dunnage.

14.3 Ocean Cargo

Figure 14.5: A Cargo Box Correctly Braced and Blocked in a Container
Photo ©Robert Crallé, Chick Packaging. Used with permission.

Stuffing the Container

If there are different types of goods to be placed in the same container, the heavier ones should always be placed on the bottom to lower the center of gravity of the load. Similarly, great care should be taken to make sure that the center of gravity is somewhat in the center of the container. This is achieved by making sure that the goods are loaded in symmetrical fashion in the container and that the blocking material is placed between the goods, as shown in Figure 14.6 on the next page. Many software packages have been designed to help exporters load mixed cargoes into containers in the most efficient manner, accounting for their volume and weight.

14.3.2 Less-than-Container-Load (LCL) Cargo

Single shipments that are too small to be shipped as full containers, called less-than-container-load (LCL) shipments, are consolidated by a freight forwarder or a Non-Vessel-Operating Common Carrier (NVOCC) with other freight and then shipped in a full container. Because of the greater number of instances during which the freight is handled, it is mandatory that these goods be unitized on a pallet or placed in a crate or box, as well as extremely well protected from water damage. Because the nature of the freight with which the shipment is placed is never known, the greatest amount of care should be exercised in packaging such goods. In addition to the risks normally associated with a shipment by ocean, there is also the possibility

less than container load (LCL)
A shipment that takes less than the full weight and volume capacity of a standard container and is therefore shipped with other LCL cargo in the same container.

consolidated
A shipment that is made up of several small shipments from different shippers.

non-vessel-operating common carrier
A shipment consolidator or freight forwarder that does not own means of transportation, but issues its own bills of lading, and therefore acts as a carrier.

of damage caused by other cargo in the container; a heavy load can inadvertently be placed on top of the pallet, or another can be poorly braced in the container and move in heavy seas. An LCL shipment can also be subjected to other cargoes' leakage, odors, and other hazards. Although the consolidator is almost always quite good at packaging a container properly, with proper dunnage and protection, the owners of other cargo on board the consolidated container may not be as careful, and that represents a hazard.

14.3.3 Breakbulk Cargo

breakbulk cargo
A type of cargo that is unitized—boxes, crates, or bales—and placed directly in the holds of a ship.

Breakbulk cargo is cargo that cannot be containerized because it is too large and will not fit in a traditional container (see Figure 14.7 on the facing page), or because it exceeds the maximum weight of a container load. Great efforts have been expended to containerize as much cargo as possible, with the creation of special container sizes (see Chapter 13). However, a substantial proportion of cargo is still shipped as breakbulk.

Breakbulk cargo is placed directly in the hold of the ship and therefore has to be packaged differently than containerized cargo, which enjoys the all-around protection of the metal box. In addition, breakbulk cargo (in its tertiary packaging) is handled more frequently than containerized cargo; for example, it is loaded onto a truck or rail car on its way to the port, then unloaded in the port, loaded onto

Figure 14.6: An Inflatable Dunnage Bag in a Container
Photo ©Robert Crallé, Chick Packaging. Used with permission.

14.3 Ocean Cargo

the ship, unloaded from the ship, and so on. Therefore, breakbulk cargo should be packed in such a way as to be well protected to reflect both the rigors of the journey and the extra handling.

Finally, the company responsible for shipping breakbulk cargo should ensure that the weight and dimensions of the cargo can be handled by all the facilities through which the cargo will travel; if the breakbulk cargo weighs more than the maximum capacity crane in a given port, an alternative route should be found, or arrangements should be made to rent specialized or larger equipment. If the cargo's weight exceeds the port cranes' capacity, there is a great risk that the breakbulk cargo will be taken out of its crate and dismantled so that it can be handled by the port's equipment. There is also the risk that the port personnel will try to move the cargo with the existing equipment (using it beyond its rated capacity) and damage the cargo in the process. Very heavy and cumbersome cargo, called "project cargo" is usually handled by specialized freight forwarders (see Chapter 13) that have an excellent knowledge of all of these limitations and can advise an international shipper accordingly.

Crates and Boxes

Boxes and crates—as shown in Figures 14.7 and 14.8—are very appropriate containers for either breakbulk cargo or LCL cargo to be handed to a freight consolidator. The crate or box should be built in a size that accommodates the goods without allowing them to shift. It should be very solidly built and be reinforced at those points where the crate is likely to be lifted. If the cargo needs to be kept in an upright posi-

Figure 14.7: An Oversize Box Being Loaded on a Flatbed Truck
Photo ©Robert Crallé, Chick Packaging. Used with permission.

tion, the best alternative is to mount the box or crate on a pallet or to equip it with hooks or straps that allow the goods to be handled in only one direction. In order to gather evidence of mishandling, it is often a good idea to include (inside as well as outside of a box or crate) a device that records whether a shipment was handled too roughly or whether it was not kept upright during handling (See Figure 14.9 on the next page).

Figure 14.8: A Wooden Crate on a Flat-Rack Container
Photo ©Pierre David. Used with permission.

box
A wooden container designed to unitize the goods and protect them. The walls are an integral part of a box's structural strength.

crate
A wooden container designed to unitize the goods and protect them. In a crate, the structural strength is provided by a web of wooden cross members.

Boxes and crates are built somewhat differently. While boxes are containers made of wood where the sides are an integral part of the structure of the container, crates are containers built on a wooden frame and are either open or enclosed with plywood. In general terms, well-built crates are stronger than boxes, because the wood used for the frame of the crate is of a larger size. Well-built crates are constructed with three-way corners (see Figure 14.10 on the facing page), which is the strongest possible corner design. Unfortunately, this technique appears to be an "art" that is disappearing, even though it makes a substantial difference in the ability of the crate to resist shocks and crushing. Both crates and boxes should always be reinforced with corner strapping and metallic bands (see Figure 14.8).

Open crates are obviously not appropriate for cargo that is not impervious to water. Boxes and enclosed crates protecting a shipment that is sensitive to water or moisture should be lined with a waterproof material such as polyethylene. Some packaging specialists prefer leaving the bottom of the boxes and crates free of waterproof material, while others prefer placing small holes in it to allow drainage should some water infiltration occur. To further protect crated machinery and metallic

 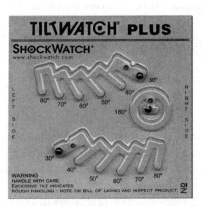

Figure 14.9: Recording Whether a Box was Mishandled in Transit
Photo ©ShockWatch. Used with permission.

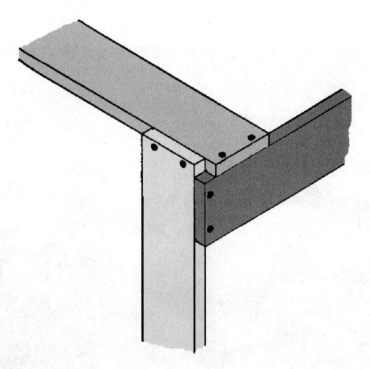

Figure 14.10: The Three-Way Corner Design is Very Strong
Diagram courtesy of Jeff Post and Bob Iben. Used with permission.

parts from water damage, it is common practice to simply spray them with oil before placing them in crates.

Since some crates and boxes are light enough to be handled by hand and are likely to be manipulated many times during an international shipment, they are sometimes mishandled despite the instructions of the shipper and the markings that they display. It is sometimes wise to determine whether rough handling occurred, and several monitoring systems have been designed to that effect. Figure 14.9 on the preceding page shows two such systems, one monitoring whether the goods were subjected to shocks, the other whether they were kept upright during the shipment.

Bags

Bags can also be used to transport breakbulk merchandise. The multi-wall shipping bag (which can hold around 25 kilograms [50 pounds]) is designed to be used with chemicals, plastics, and other powdered materials that are somewhat unaffected by water and unlikely to be pilfered.

The bag is made up of several layers of kraft paper, fabric, and/or light polymers, and is not very good at withstanding numerous manipulations. It is recommended to add about 3 percent additional empty, slightly larger bags to contain those bags that may be damaged during an international shipment. Shipping bags are quite sensitive to rough handling by dockhands (see Figure 14.11), including damage by

bag
A paper, plastic, or fabric container designed to unitize dry-bulk cargo and unitize it. A bag can generally be handled by a single stevedore.

Figure 14.11: Bags of Wheat Being Loaded in Port Sudan, The Sudan
Photo ©USAID. Used with permission.

Figure 14.12: Flexible Intermediate Bulk Containers
Photo ©Codefine. Used with permission.

accidental contact with mechanical equipment or other cargo with sharp angles such as boxes, crates, or pallets. The integrity of these bags is increased by palletizing and shrink-wrapping them, because mechanical equipment must then be used to handle them.

The second type of bag is a very large bag called a flexible intermediate bulk container (FIBC). FIBCs are constructed of woven polymer fibers, such as polyethylene or polypropylene (see Figure 14.12). They are usually of a capacity of about 1 cubic meter and can weigh up to 1 metric tonne, but many different sizes and types exist. They are used for transporting granular cargo, such as plastics, grains, and chemicals.

flexible intermediate bulk containers (FIBC)
A large polymer bag designed to contain dry-bulk cargo and to be handled by mechanized equipment.

Drums

Drums are used in three forms: metallic drums (steel drums), polymer drums, and fiber drums. Steel drums, shown in Figure 14-14, can be used for wet or dry cargo, and are pretty resilient containers that can withstand a good amount of abuse. They present great resistance to water damage and pilferage and have been used for a long time in ocean shipping. Their main disadvantage is their cost and their individual weight. Polymer drums, also shown in Figure 14.13, present the advantage of being able to carry liquid and wet cargo, but they are much less resistant to rough

drum
A cylindrical metal, plastic, or fiber container designed to unitize dry-bulk or liquid-bulk cargo.

Figure 14.13: Three Different Types of Drums: Steel, Polymer, and Fiber
Photo ©Pierre David. Used with permission.

handling. They should be palletized to minimize damage. Finally, fiber drums, also shown in Figure 14.13, can be used for only dry cargo, such as plastic pellets or fertilizers. They are usually lined with a polymer bag to contain the cargo.

Fiber drums are slightly more resistant to water damage than bags and are more resistant to pilferage. However, they are often damaged when port personnel handle them in the same manner as they do steel drums, such as rolling them on their sides, a practice which they are not designed to handle. Fiber drums are also somewhat sensitive to mechanical damage, such as that caused by careless forklift truck drivers or sharp corners.

14.3.4 Wood Requirements

International Plant Protection Convention (IPPC)
An international convention that mandates that wood used in packaging be fumigated or heat-treated against pests.

Since March 2005, all wood products used in packaging or dunnage must conform to International Phytosanitary Measure 15, a convention that was signed by 144 countries and which is designed to further prevent the threat of wood pests, specifically the Asian long-horned beetle that attacked hardwood forests in North America and Europe, and the North American pinewood nematode, which attacked softwood forests in Europe and Asia. All wood products used in international trade must be marked with the International Plant Protection Convention (IPPC) symbol or face heavy fines.

The IPPC mark identifies the country in which the wood product was treated with the first two letters. Figure 14.14 shows several examples. The marking also identifies the plant at which the process was conducted with an alphanumeric code. Finally, the process used in treating the product is identified; for example, HT indicates that the wood was heat-treated, and MB means that the product was treated with methyl bromide. These are the only two allowable treatments to date, and although MB is a gas that the U.S. Environmental Protection Agency phased out in 2007, it continues allowing its use for IPPC purposes only.[8] Three other abbreviations are used in Figure 14.14: DB stands for "debarked," and KD for "kiln-dried," which are used in many countries. The British IPPC mark also includes the abbreviation FC for the British Forestry Commission. Any wood product that has been marked with the IPPC symbol can be reused indefinitely in the international supply chain.

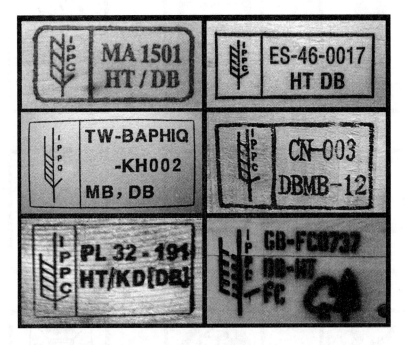

Figure 14.14: International Plant Protection Convention Marks from Morocco, Spain, Taiwan region, China, Poland, and Great Britain
Photo ©Pierre David. Used with permission.

14.3.5 Markings

There are two reasons to properly mark the cargo as it is shipped: it has to be protected from poor handling, and it has to be protected from theft and pilferage.

To protect the cargo from poor handling, it is necessary to use as many of the international pictorials for cargo handling as are relevant. A number of these pictorials, as standardized by the International Organization for Standardization (ISO), are shown in Figure 14.15. If at all possible, they should be accompanied by their translations in the languages of the ports through which the cargo is expected to transit. Both the net weight (the weight of the cargo alone) and the gross weight (the cargo plus the weight of the packaging) should be clearly displayed in metric units and so-called English units on the outside of the package. The outside dimensions of the goods should also be clearly displayed, both in English and in metric units. This is to prevent, as much as possible, inappropriate equipment from handling the goods at any point.

To protect breakbulk or LCL cargo from being lost or shipped to the wrong consignee, it should be clearly marked with the consignee's name—the name of the company that will pick it up at the port of the destination—as well as the shipment number. It is always a good idea to write that information on several of the sides of the load; that way, the information is never hidden from view. If at all possible, the name of the consignee should not include information that could indicate the brand

markings
Symbols printed on boxes or crates that help stevedores and terminals determine the proper way to handle, stow, or store a breakbulk shipment.

Figure 14.15: International ISO Handling Markings
Photo ©International Organization for Standardization [ISO]. Used with permission.

or the type of the goods in the shipment, for security reasons. Such markings only increase the probability of theft or pilferage.

All the units belonging to the same shipment should be marked as such, that is, as "1 of 4," "2 of 4," and so on. Another useful practice is to mark all the units in a given shipment with a particular color—for example, on the corners of the boxes—so that they are clearly designated as parts of one shipment and so that none of them are left behind. The temptation to use a color associated with a particular company should be avoided, however, to prevent jeopardizing the firm's security efforts. For the same reason, the color should be changed regularly.

There are a number of alternatives meant to determine whether a shipment has been the victim of theft. Some shippers paint the outside of their shipments with a uniform color in order to determine whether a shipment has been tampered with. Some use shipping tape of a specific design—while avoiding using a tape marked with their company logo—and others use a shrink-wrap of a particular color. All of these attempts have the added benefit of keeping the shipment uniform and therefore clearly identifiable.

Finally, it should be reiterated that markings that reveal the identity of the shipper and/or the content of the package should be avoided at all costs. Communicating to potential thieves the content of the cargo is foolish and can only lead to problems. Many companies use codes rather than brand markings to identify their shipments and change the code on a regular basis, without patterns, in an attempt to avoid security problems.

14.4 Air Transport

Because air transport is, by nature, less hazardous than ocean transport, packaging as a protection against damage is of lesser importance. Nevertheless, some perils still exist, such as water condensation and air pressure changes; still, the biggest problem for air cargo, by far, is theft and pilferage.

14.4.1 Containers

Containers used in air transport—Unit Load Devices (see Figure 13.19 on page 358)—are much different than the ones used in ocean cargo and are not intermodal (*i.e.*, they cannot be used conveniently in other modes of transportation, with the possible exception of one size: a 20-foot container that can be used in cargo planes and on trucks). The consequence of this situation is that cargo is usually placed (consolidated) in containers at the airport of departure, then manipulated again at the airport of arrival and placed into trucks. This additional handling should be taken into consideration when packaging goods for export by air. It is also likely that the goods will be unloaded from a container and reloaded into another at a connecting airport.

unit load device (ULD) The term used to describe the containers used in airfreight transport.

Containers used in air transport are lightweight, made of wood, Plexiglas, or aluminum, and are generally clean. As some containers are not fully enclosed, or are enclosed with netting rather than solid walls, some damage may occur in the voyage when cargo shifts. Nevertheless, most damage occurs in the handling before and after the flight; for example, while the container waits on the tarmac, the goods in the container could easily become wet from rain or snow. Such exposure should be considered when deciding on a proper package.

14.4.2 Packaging Materials

While many air cargo shipments are shipped by air in their secondary packaging, it is generally not an appropriate method for two reasons:

- Secondary packaging is not sufficient to protect the goods from the hazards of manipulation before and after the flight. In many cases, the airline operates on a hub-and-spoke model, and the goods are unloaded and manipulated at one or more hub airports. Goods in secondary packaging can be handled carelessly by hurried airport personnel, and boxes can fall from conveyor belts traveling at very high speeds (45 kilometers [30 miles] per hour).

- Secondary packaging often includes markings including the brand name of the goods, as well as model numbers and/or illustrations, which make them very tempting targets for thieves.

Appropriate shipping packaging would therefore be tertiary in nature and include one additional layer of corrugated paperboard, preferably double-walled, and a shrink-wrap. The United Nations established rules regarding the resistance of air packages to drops and crushes, especially for dangerous goods; these minimum requirements were last updated in 2007.[9] Nevertheless, a number of shippers still do not follow these rules.

For shipments that are fragile, the best strategy is to use a box within a box; the primary package is placed in a much larger box, which is then filled with packing material around the smaller, fragile product. While this is relatively simple, the cost of packaging in such a way can be substantial, as airlines charge a shipper on the higher of two alternatives; the actual weight of the product or its volume weight— dimensional weight— which is a weight calculated on the basis of the volume of the shipment. There can therefore be a substantial cost to using a box that is slightly too large.

For cargo sensitive to humidity, a possible way of avoiding condensation damage is to add small packets of desiccant material in the box with the goods, as they are designed to absorb ambient humidity. An additional layer of shrink-wrap is always advisable, as well, to protect against other condensation, rain, or leakage caused by other cargo on the plane.

For shipments susceptible to leakage if its primary packaging breaks, such as glass or plastic bottles, the U.S. Federal Aviation Administration regulations (and United Nations rules) require that the secondary or tertiary package be capable of containing an accidental leak. Most secondary packaging is not designed for such a contingency, so adequate additional absorbent material must be packed with the goods. Importantly, the risks associated with improper packaging resulting in a leak in an aircraft are substantial: violations of the U.S. regulations call for up to five years in prison and a U.S.$ 250,000 fine.[10]

14.4.3 Markings

Markings in international air shipments should be handled in much the same way as markings on ocean shipments. The use of the pictorials shown in Figure 14.15 on page 384 is quite appropriate.

14.5 Road and Rail Transport

In the case of international road and rail transportation, a policy of protecting the cargo in much the same way as for shipment by ocean container is most appropriate. It is always best to unitize the cargo into pallets so as to facilitate handling at the point where the goods are loaded and unloaded. The cargo pallets should be protected on all four corners, banded with nylon or steel straps, and shrink-wrapped for protection against rain and ambient humidity. As much as possible, the cargo should be blocked and braced in the truck trailer and, if applicable, in the railroad car to avoid all damage due to the cargo shifting and sudden accelerations and decelerations. Railroad companies issue very specific rules regarding the bracing of cargo in containers or truck trailers that will be carried on railroads; in particular, they mandate a very strong bracing of the cargo[11] to prevent stress against the container or trailer doors (see Figure 14.16).

Figure 14.16: Container Cargo Braced for Railroad Transport
Photo ©Robert Crallé, Chick Packaging. Used with permission.

Domestic shipments in the United States are almost all by truck or rail; the cargo is loaded onto a trailer that is then either driven to its destination or loaded on a railroad car (piggy-backed) to an intermediary destination and then driven to its final destination. Although it may appear that light-weight secondary packaging is sufficient to protect these goods, that is often not the case. In a 2008 study, the Grocery Manufacturers Association determined that the costs of goods damaged in domestic transportation were approximately U.S.$ 4 billion, or approximately 1.1 percent of gross domestic sales before 2004. After 2005-2006, the GMA noticed an improvement, down to less than one percent, which it attributed to "improvements in packaging."[12] Such improvements may include the use of heavier corrugated paper boxes, better pallet loading practices, or the addition of heavy corrugated paperboard between pallets.

In shipping consumer goods, close attention should be paid to the possibility of theft, and the goods should be packed in unmarked boxes to prevent the possibility of pilferage. Goods that are most frequently stolen are identifiable by their packaging. According to a study of freight theft by Freight Watch International, the most targeted products are food, drinks, and electronics in Asia and North America, but pharmaceuticals in Europe.[13] Anonymous packaging may reduce some of that risk.

Shipping Computers to China

The Chinese market for personal computers has always appeared very attractive to U.S. corporations because of the vast potential for sales it represents. However, there have been many difficulties for the companies involved in manufacturing personal computers in China, particularly in the last portion of these products' trip: the distribution to the final consumer. IBM faced charges that it was selling used machines when it was actually shipping brand new products. It turns out that the confusion arose over a packaging problem: the computers were wrapped in two layers of plastic and then shipped in paperboard boxes. However, this was not enough to protect them from the pervasive dust that floats around many Chinese cities—Beijing in particular—and the goods arrived dirty in the consumers' hands. An additional layer of shrink-wrap on the paperboard retail package solved the problem. Packaging has to solve other problems in China. A large percentage of personal computers are delivered to their final destinations strapped on the luggage racks of tricycles (see Figure 14.17), and most deliveries to retailers and wholesalers are made in flatbed trucks, barely protected from the elements by a tarpaulin. As for units shipped to distant cities, they go by railroads. Extremely sturdy packaging should be used in this case, as an IBM manager observed "the [cargo handlers] virtually throw[ing computer] cartons into trains."[14] A recently revealed video of such poor handling was a hit on YouTube®.[15]

Although those examples single out China, careless handling by individual workers in the supply chain can happen any time that boxes are light enough to be handled without mechanized equipment. It is therefore in the best interest of shippers to determine under which conditions their goods will be handled and package them appropriately. A few cents more spent on packaging can save quite a few dollars in damaged products and unhappy customers' claims.

Figure 14.17: Computers Delivered on Tricycles in China
Photo ©Hui Lu. Used with permission.

14.6 Security

The issue of theft and pilferage is becoming an increasing problem for cargo shippers. It is estimated that cargo theft represents losses of at least U.S.$ 10 billion per year in the United States,[16] €8 billion in the European Union,[17] and more than U.S.$ 40 billion worldwide. The problem is that there is very little reliable data on the incidence of this type of crime, but it is a substantial concern to international shippers. Many methods have been developed to foil theft attempts against cargo; unfortunately, none has proven completely effective, but a combination of several should cover most shippers and prevent theft and pilferage.

As much as possible, the cargo should not bear the name of the shipper, especially if it is a brand that has street appeal; this issue is crucial for goods that are shipped in their secondary packaging and for which the primary packaging and the secondary packaging are one and the same, as for electronics or appliances. Such a practice jeopardizes the safety of the cargo. A possible way to prevent this problem would be to ship exclusively in full container loads (FCLs) or full truck loads (FTLs), so as to hide the cargo from anyone other than the exporter or the importer. Another is to place the goods in an additional blank paperboard box, which would be recommended for goods shipped as LCL or less-than-truck load (LTL) goods, to

seal
A lock placed on a container door or truck trailer door that must be broken in order to access the cargo.

protect them from handling damage.

A plethora of different methods exists to place seals on containers, and all present advantages and disadvantages; however, all show whether the container has been opened. One critical aspect of seals is that the seal number should be written on the bill of lading so that the importer can check, upon arrival, that the seal on the container is the same as the seal with which the container left the exporter's premises.[18] Since October 2008, all containers shipped to the United States must be sealed with a tamper-proof seal, such as the one shown in Figure 15.5 on page 417.

Altogether, though, the aspect that security experts insist is critical when shipping internationally or domestically is the personnel involved. Most thefts seem to take place with some form of insider involvement.[19] All attempts should therefore be made to limit the number of people who know the content of the shipment by making sure that the bill of lading and packaging lists are given to trusted employees only, by keeping track of non-employees on the premises, by making sure that managers are present during loading and unloading operations, and so on. Some companies keep their docks under constant video surveillance to deter crime.

Trade in Precious Stones and Valuables

Trade in precious goods and valuables is an entire branch of logistics that, although not officially calculated separately from other data, is worth millions of U.S. dollars—in the United States alone, it is estimated at U.S.$ 50 million. There is a substantial business in shipping precious stones internationally, such as diamonds and emeralds, because the stones are often produced, cut, set, and sold in different countries. Artwork travels from museum collections to museum exhibits (and back). Antiques and collectibles travel to and from dealers and auction houses. Cash travels to where tourists flock.

The crash of Swissair 111 on September 2, 1998, exposed some of the extent of its international scale: the airplane was carrying 50 kilograms(110 pounds) of cash, 1.8 kilograms (4 pounds) of diamonds, 1.8 kilograms (4 pounds) of watches, 5 kilograms (11 pounds) of jewelry, and an artwork by Picasso entitled "The Painter."[20] Lloyd's of London, through which this cargo was insured, has never disclosed the value of these cargoes, although there are speculations that it exceeded U.S.$ 300 million.

Another notable shipment of precious stones was revealed when it resulted in the theft of U.S.$ 350,000,000 of diamonds from a parked airplane at the Brussels airport. The thieves were done in "barely five minutes", [21] which indicated an job performed by a well-informed group, which is the greatest threat for shippers of goods with very high value.

Altogether, there are few firms specializing in the shipment of precious and valuable goods, and these firms emphasize discretion—they do not advertise, do not display their names on their vehicles, and operate out of anonymous office buildings and warehouses. The additional security measures they take are many: they do not ship more than a certain amount on a specific airplane or ship, they use ever-changing consignee names, and they have created a whole series of specialized packaging technologies. Artex is such a firm. It is located in Washington, D.C., and specializes in the business of moving artwork, antiques, and jewelry collections. It employs a crew of 75 employees, most of whom are artists or art experts with museum experience. Each piece of work is moved in a crate that is specifically designed for that work of art and fitted with foam to the exact dimensions and shape of the artwork. When Artex was selected to move an African American burial site from New York City to Howard University, it took the firm's employees three months to pack the 20,000 objects this move represented.[22]

In addition, Artex's warehouse and trucks are equipped with air conditioning to keep humidity to a minimum. Each of its trucks is tracked with satellite transmitters and Global Positioning System; this way, the firm knows at all times where the art is located. Finally, each of the trucks is driven by a team of at least two drivers equipped with cellular phones and sometimes accompanied by armed guards. Nevertheless, the best security is when no one knows that a move is occurring.

14.7 Hazardous Cargo

Hazardous cargo can be shipped by ocean and by air, but, generally speaking, most dangerous goods that are flammable, explosive, or toxic are shipped by sea, and, if these shipments are containerized, they are shipped on deck rather than under deck.

The shipment of dangerous goods by sea is regulated by the International Maritime Organization (IMO), which publishes an *International Maritime Dangerous Goods Code* (IMDG) every other year, in order to keep up with the rapid expansion of the types of materials created. In October 2012, the IMO's Maritime Safety Committee released its 36th amendment, valid for 2013-2014.[23] The two-volume document is quite complex; in addition to the two volumes, there is a 2013-2014 IMDG Code Supplement for additional information. Although large, the IMDG Code was significantly reduced in size in 2000; prior to that amendment, it was a four-volume code. As its name indicates, the IMDG Code governs the packaging of all hazardous cargo, as well as their labeling, handling, and emergency responses that carriers are supposed to implement. The IMDG Code is followed by just about every country in the world, and is a *de facto* world standard.

The shipment of dangerous goods by air is regulated by a similar set of standards published by the International Air Transport Association (IATA). The IATA *Dangerous Goods Regulations* manual was developed in collaboration with the International Civil Aviation Organization (ICAO) and the standard-setting authorities of several countries and is revised every year. As of 2013, the IATA *Dangerous Goods Regulations* are in their 54th edition.[24] As could be expected, the shipment of hazardous cargo by air is no less complicated and cumbersome than by sea.

In addition to these international requirements, a shipper must abide by the requirements set by domestic regulatory agencies as well, as there often are two domestic legs to any international shipment, one in the exporter's country, the other in the importer's country. The complexity of such requirements, and their contradictory statements on occasion, makes it an obligation to contract with a specialized freight forwarder or a specialized consultant before undertaking any international shipment of hazardous goods. Shipments of products containing radioactive components are even more complicated.

14.8 Refrigerated Goods

Goods requiring refrigeration make up another category of cargo that demands particular care and specialized packaging services. It is difficult to generalize about refrigerated goods, as every commodity usually requires very specific handling; therefore, most refrigerated goods travel "alone" (*i.e.*, different refrigerated goods are not mixed with one another, as they require different temperatures and different humidity settings). In addition, some fresh produce simply cannot be mixed together as they emit odors and other gases that would spoil the rest of the cargo. For example, a load of cucumbers should not be mixed with apples, as cucumbers are sensitive to the ethylene that the apples produce,[25] and for obvious reasons, onions and strawberries do not travel well together.

refrigerated container (reefer)
A container designed to hold cargo that must be maintained at a constant temperature. It generally needs an outside power supply.

When goods needing refrigeration travel by ocean, they usually travel in a refrigerated container—also known as a reefer (see Figure 13.17 on page 355). Great care should be taken in ensuring that the temperature is kept at its correct setting throughout the voyage, which is achieved with temperature-sensitive indicators. Because containers are not very effective at cooling goods—but are effective at keeping them cool—several shippers make sure that the goods are well refrigerated before they are loaded to prevent possible damage. It should also be understood that reefers cannot possibly have a completely uniform temperature: temperatures within the box can vary by as much as five degrees Celsius (ten degrees Fahrenheit) just because air circulation cannot be made completely uniform. Finally, another common problem with refrigerated cargo coming in or out of the United States is the confusion between Fahrenheit and Celsius temperature settings and the errors they cause.[26]

With refrigerated cargo, the loading of the refrigerated container must allow air circulation around the cargo; this requirement means that the goods must be loaded in the center of the container, with sufficient space in between the walls of the container and the cargo for circulation, and that the goods must be braced with a frame rather than with inflatable dunnage, which would prevent air circulation. In addition, some goods need to travel in controlled atmospheres—mixtures of oxygen and nitrogen in different percentages than ambient air—to prevent spoilage. Some experiments are being conducted to determine whether a controlled atmosphere can also be effective against some pests, and whether the right mix of humidity, temperature, and correct gas mix can divert some of the cargo that normally travels by air because of its perishable nature to ocean transport, which is much cheaper.[27]

Fresh produce must also be kept at humidity levels of 95 to 100 percent to maintain its freshness as well as prevent weight loss due to evaporation. Most produce is made up of at least 80 percent water and is quite sensitive to water loss; for example, grapes will wrinkle and soften, and stems will turn brown with a weight loss of only 4 percent, making them more difficult to sell. In addition, because produce is sold by weight, a small weight loss can translate into a substantial decrease in revenue for the importer.

For air shipments of refrigerated cargo, the challenges are different, because the cargo is not placed in refrigerated containers but in cargo holds that have different temperature settings. For example, some cargo carriers offer multiple cargo holds, kept at different temperature settings, to keep perishables in their optimum environments. However, because of the possibility that incompatible cargo might be mixed together—such as the onions and strawberries mentioned earlier—great care should be extended to protect sensitive goods from this eventuality by keeping them in solid-wall corrugated paperboard boxes and possibly in shrink- or stretch-wrap, if applicable.

Banana Trade

In 2012, the United States imported a record 413,640 TEUs of bananas, an increase of 13.4 percent over 2010.[28] The top countries of origin for U.S. banana imports in 2012 were Guatemala, with a 30.2-percent share of imports, Costa Rica, with 21.2 percent, Ecuador, with 19. percent, and Honduras, 17.4 percent.[29]

Bananas are harvested green and hard, and immediately refrigerated. During their trip, the bananas are kept in a controlled atmosphere environment. At their arrival, they are then placed in a ripening environment where they acquire their yellow color before being shipped to retail stores.

Bananas are transported by dedicated banana ships. About half of these ships are completely containerized, while the others transport bananas on pallets as breakbulk cargo in refrigerated holds and in containers on deck. An increasingly large portion of banana imports are shipped with refrigerated containers, as they are easier to handle. For example, in 2012, containerized imports from Panama doubled to 7,322 TEUs in 2012, and imports from Mexico via ocean container nearly doubled with 16,089 TEUs imported. The banana trade now accounts for about 20 percent of the worldwide usage of refrigerated containers.[30]

Wilmington, Delaware, is by far the largest port of entry for bananas, and it handles almost 1 million tons of bananas every year.[31] One company, Chiquita of Cincinnati, Ohio, imports 117,000 TEUs per year.

14.9 Domestic Retail Packaging Issues

In dealing with consumer products specifically, several packaging issues are also greatly influenced by primary packaging, or the design of the packaging in which the final consumer purchases the goods, as well as by secondary packaging, or the packaging designed to facilitate handling in the retail environment. Collectively, these constraints tend to be domestic in nature (*i.e.*, they are specific to a single country or possibly a group of countries).

Adapting a firm's strategy to the different market requirements of a particular country adds substantially to the costs of manufacturing, as well as to inventory and logistical expenses. A firm has to determine whether it makes economic sense to adapt its approach to these different markets and incur those additional costs or decide to ignore them at the risk of losing potential sales. This is the same strategic dilemma faced by a firm involved in international marketing: should it adapt or standardize?

Some of the factors that may affect primary and secondary packaging are explored in the following sections.

14.9.1 Size

Consumer packages vary by country because of consumer preferences. They are generally smaller in those countries in which retail shopping is done frequently, and larger in those in which consumers shop at greater intervals. However, consumer packaging is complicated; consumers may demand smaller or larger packages based on preferences and customs, as well as packages of different shapes and materials.

For example, sugar is sold in some countries in paper bags weighing five pounds (2.5 kilograms), in others in paperboard boxes weighing 1 kilogram (2.2 pounds), and yet in others in tin cans of 1 pound (0.45 kilograms). Even products that are held to be great examples of international standardization, such as Coca-Cola® soft drinks, are sold in a large number of sizes and therefore a myriad of primary and secondary packaging units.

Consumer packaging may also be seriously influenced by the layout of the shelves in the stores, such as their depth and the linear space allocated, constraining manufacturers to use different retail packaging.

Secondary packaging—the unit that holds several consumer packages—is influenced by the size of the retail stores and their configuration, as well as the size of the delivery trucks; the tertiary packaging unit, such as the pallet; or even the configuration of the storage area. In addition, it is influenced by the frequency and the volume of sales of the retail units.

14.9.2 Legal Issues

Consumer packaging is also influenced by legal requirements. Some countries regulate sizes to be a multiple of simple metric units (1 kilogram or 1 liter), while others do not, allowing packages of any size and weight. However, the greatest requirements are in the legal constraints on handling: many countries regulate the maximum weight an employee may carry, which influences the weight of the secondary packaging unit and, consequently, of both consumer packaging and tertiary packaging as well.

The legal constraints placed on the distribution channels can also influence consumer packaging. For example, the United States allows retail sales of some medicines over the counter—without a doctor's prescription—which means that consumers buy them in drugstores, most often in a self-service environment. In France, in contrast, all drugs, including drugs not prescribed by a medical doctor, are sold exclusively through specialized stores called pharmacies. The primary package in a drugstore is often a blister pack or some variation of it, as the goods are sold hanging from aisle racks, and need to attract the attention of the shopper. Primary packages from French pharmacies are usually cardboard boxes, as the pharmacist keeps them on small shelves or in large but very shallow drawers. In addition, the drugstore may purchase goods in larger quantities than the pharmacies. In any case, the primary packaging is different and therefore the secondary and tertiary packaging will also be different.

14.9.3 Storage and Transportation Environment

Finally, there are a number of environmental influences on packaging, such as the dusty conditions under which transportation takes place, mentioned in the vignette on page 388 about IBM's packaging of personal computers in China. There are similar constraints triggered by high humidity, heat, or cold.

There are also constraints placed by the lack of refrigeration resources. The best example is probably the existence of long-conservation milk, which is sold unrefrigerated with expiration dates six or seven months after its production in a large number of European countries. Not only does this packaging alternative allow the use of non-refrigerated shelving in the store, but it also requires no refrigeration at all in the rest of the supply chain, from warehouses to transportation. It can also be transported safely quite far from its production location, including internationally.

All in all, several domestic issues in the importing country will affect the packaging of goods. Companies should develop appropriate strategies to account for the possible diversity of consumer and retail packaging alternatives present in their export markets.

14.10 Packaging as a Marketing Tool

It should be relatively clear by now that good handling of the packaging requirements by the exporter will help considerably in the smooth transfer of goods from the exporter to the importer.

The most important way of looking at packaging is to prepare for the worst. The exporter should truly imagine the worst-case scenarios and the roughest possible journey when it is considering the way in which it will package its goods for export. It is only under this premise that it will adequately serve the needs of the importer to receive goods in sellable and usable condition.

The exporter should make sure that the goods are protected from physical damage by ensuring that they are packaged in sturdy cartons and loaded correctly on pallets, that the pallets are separated by appropriate dunnage such as plywood and inflatable bags, and that all goods are protected from humidity and rain by protecting them with a plastic film and by outfitting the container with desiccant strips. The container should be cleaned and inspected before it is loaded, and the seals used on the container should be of good quality. The procedures in place should be effective in keeping the paperwork in the hands of appropriate personnel only.

Although such procedures are more expensive than a more casual attitude, the benefits are substantial. Consider a hypothetical case where, from the use of an inexpensive plywood sheet spread over three pallets (a plywood sheet is 4×8 feet, or 122×244 centimeters), several boxes are slightly crushed, and the importer has to repackage the goods to make them sellable. The costs of repackaging these few boxes (labor, new boxes, calling the importer to resolve the issue) far exceed the original cost of the plywood sheet. Identical benefits can be drawn from using good pallets that do not break when the goods are unloaded, making sure that the container is watertight, and so on. In addition, because poor packaging can be used by insurance companies to deny a claim, it is to the exporter's advantage to have a track record of stellar packaging.

However, the greatest benefits from such a good packaging policy are the goodwill that it generates with the importer and the marketing benefits that can be derived from it. Because the importer is obviously not interested in having to challenge invoices or having to ask for allowances for goods that were damaged in transit, it welcomes shipments that arrive packaged carefully enough that it does not have to worry about anything. This confidence enhances the relationship between exporter and importer, and builds trust.

Finally, the exporter should make sure that the packaging is friendly to the employees who will unpack the goods: that the packing list is written in their language, that shipments are identified with colors that identify pallets that belong together, that the wood dunnage is assembled in a way that it can easily be taken apart, and so on. When shipping to countries in which the dunnage and packaging materials are likely to be recycled as housing materials, an exporter would be even more empathetic if it considered using a slightly better grade of board and plywood, and making sure that they have been heat-treated rather than fumigated with methyl bromide, so that the importer's employees can recycle or repurpose the wood without harm.

Review and Discussion Questions

1. What are the consequences of improper packaging for the exporter? Does your response depend on the Incoterms® rule used? Does it depend on the insurance policy in force?

2. What are the different alternative means of packaging products that are not containerized?

3. What are some of the issues and risks that international packaging faces and that are not present in a domestic shipment?

4. Use a product of your choice and ship it from one country to another in a multimodal shipment. What packaging methods would you use? Why?

Notes

[1] "Packaging Technology and Development," Lund University, Department of Packaging Logistics, Lund, Sweden, http://www.plog.lth.se/about_us/background_and_description/, retrieved July 1, 2013.

[2] Hensel, Bill, Jr., "A Loaded Problem," *JoC Week*, August 14-20, 2000, p. 13.

[3] *Ports of the World*, 15th ed., Cigna Insurance Corporation, available from Publisher, Ports of the World, Cigna Companies, P.O. Box 7716, Philadelphia, Pennsylvania 19192, USA.

[4] Harps, Leslie Hansen, "Popcorn! Peanuts! Bubble Wrap! Thinking Inside the Box," *Inbound Logistics*, November 2000, pp. 40-46.

[5] "Container Matters" and "Any Fool Can Stuff a Container," videos published by the Thomas Miller P&I Ltd, International House, 26 Creechurch Lane, London, EC3A 5BA, United Kingdom.

[6] Mottley, Robert, "Chilling out," *American Shipper*, June 2000, pp. 43-51.

[7] Porter, Janet, "Insurer Warns of the Dangers of Incorrectly Packed Containers," *Journal of Commerce*, August 4, 1997, p. 16A.

[8] Brindley, Chaille, "Fumigation 101," *Pallet Enterprise*, February 2004.

[9] *United Nations Recommendations on the Transport of Dangerous Goods—Model Regulations*, 15th ed., 2007, United Nations Economic Commission for Europe, http://www.unece.org/trans/danger/publi/unrec/rev15/15files_e.html, retrieved July 16, 2009.

[10] "Electronic Code of Federal Regulations," http://ecfr.gpoaccess.gov/cgi/t/text/text-idx?c=ecfr&rgn=div5&view=text&node=49:2.1.1.3.10&idno=49, retrieved July 16, 2009.

[11] BNSF Intermodal Loading Guide, March 2005, BNSF Railway, Load and Ride Solution Team, http://www.bnsf.com/tools/lars/intermodal_loading_guide.html, retrieved July 1, 2013.

[12] Grocery Manufacturers Association, 2008 Joint Industry Unsaleables Report: The Real Causes and Actionable Solutions, written in collaboration with the Food Marketing Institute and Deloitte, September 2008, http://www.gmabrands.com/publications/UnsaleablesFINAL-091108.pdf.

[13] "FreightWatch Annual Global Cargo Theft Assessment Shows Theft Rates Climbing in Europe and Asia; No Decline in the Americas," April 29, 2013, Freight Watch International, http://www.freightwatchintl.com/announcements/04292013-0800/freightwatch-annual-global-cargo-theft-assessment-shows-theft-rates, retrieved July 2, 2013.

[14] Hamilton, David, "Untamed Frontier: PC Makers Find China Is a Chaotic Market Despite Its Potential," *The Wall Street Journal*, April 8, 1996, p. A1.

[15] http://www.youtube.com/watch?v=Gu09aaZqwVE, retrieved July 2, 2013.

[16] "National Commercial Vehicle and Cargo Theft Prevention Initiative," April 16, 2008, National Commercial Vehicle and Cargo Theft Prevention Task Force, https://www.nationalcargothefttaskforce.org/ncttf/app/doc/Context_preview.action?documentId=NAT.

[17] Cargo Theft Report: Applying the Brakes to Road Cargo Crime in Europe, 2009, Europol, http://www.europol.europa.eu/publications/Serious_Crime_Overviews/Cargo_Theft_Report.pdf.

[18] "Container Matters" and "Any Fool Can Stuff a Container," videos published by the Thomas Miller P&I Ltd, International House, 26 Creechurch Lane, London, EC3A 5BA, United Kingdom.

[19] Anderson, Bill, "Prevent Cargo Theft," *Logistics Today*, May 23, 2007.

[20] Estrin, Robin, "Swissair 111 Went Down with Millions in Valuables, Including Picasso Painting," Associated Press News Release, September 4, 1998.

[21] Higgins, Andrew, "Brazen Jewel Robbery at Brussels Airport Nets $50 Million in Diamonds," *The New York Times*, February 19, 2013.

[22] Hull, Dana, "How a Moving Company Capitalizes on Valuable Secrets," *Washington Post*, May 5, 1997, p. F12.

[23] *International Maritime Dangerous Goods Code*, 2013 IMDG Code, Amendment 36-12, International Maritime Organization, available from IMDG Publications/Regulations, ICC Compliance Center, http://imdgpublications.com, retrieved July 2, 2013.

[24] *Dangerous Goods Regulations 2013-2014*, 54th edition, International Air Transport Association, available from http://www.iata.org/publications/dgr/Pages/index.aspx, retrieved July 2, 2013.

[25] Mottley, Robert, "Chilling Out," *American Shipper*, June 2000, pp. 43Ű51.

[26] *Ibid.*

[27] Seemuth, Mike, "The Ocean Alternative (Transport of Perishable Cargo by Sea)," *Journal of Commerce*, April 16, 2007.

[28] "U.S. Banana Imports Rise Sharply," April 2, 2013, PIERS, http://pierstransportation.wordpress.com/2013/04/02/u-s-banana-imports-rise-sharply/, retrieved June 30, 2013.

[29] *Ibid.*

[30] Rodrigue, Jean-Paul, "Main American Banana Import Ports, 2011," The Geography of Transport Systems, http://people.hofstra.edu/geotrans/eng/ch5en/appl5en/map_banana_ports.html, retrieved July 2, 2013.

[31] *Ibid.*

Chapter 15

International Logistics Security

15.1 The Impact of a Significant Disruption in International Logistics . 401
15.2 International Organizations 402
15.3 The United States' Approach 406
15.4 The European Union's Programs 414
15.5 Other Countries' Approach 415
15.6 Corporate Efforts 415

The terrorist attacks of September 11, 2001 in New York and Washington tragically illustrated the vulnerability of open economies to acts of terrorism. While a large number of terrorist attacks had preceded the destruction of the New York World Trade Center towers, the scale and symbolism of their destruction made it a turning point in the way governments addressed terrorism threats. Their strategies shifted from mostly reactive attempts to a decidedly preventive and systematic approach. The response to the September 11 attacks was therefore unprecedented; within a few years, the United States, its trading partners, and a large number of international organizations implemented a series of measures designed to prevent further occurrences of acts of international terrorism. These measures have greatly influenced the way international business is now conducted.

The creation of these security measures, as well as efforts by corporations to reduce the vulnerability of their international supply chain to more traditional criminal activities, have triggered the creation of a number of corporate management functions, collectively called security management. This chapter outlines the way security measures imposed by governments and international organizations can be integrated with the security activities of a firm involved in international trade.

While none of these measures taken in isolation can be considered significantly effective in reducing the threat of terrorist activities, their collective implementation has resulted in a much higher level of security in international logistics, and certainly a greater focus on these efforts.

security management
A corporate function that manages all of a security efforts of a company.

one-hundred-percent inspection
A security strategy that consists of inspecting every single shipment.

The Fallacy of One-Hundred-Percent Inspections

Whenever the topic of international security is debated, there are always proponents of a one-hundred-percent inspection alternative, in which all imported cargo is inspected, regardless of its origin, destination, or means of transportation used. This is often touted as the safest method: since all cargo is inspected, nothing dangerous can be shipped into the country. The proponents of one-hundred-percent inspection justify their point of view with two logical reasons: the first is that everything that is dangerous will be caught by the inspection process, and the other is that the fear of being caught will act as a deterrent for criminals. While a thorough inspection process may act as a deterrent, it is actually an ineffective way to increase the security of a country's borders, for several reasons. First, it would consume an extraordinary amount of resources. Considering that each container, in order to be physically inspected, has to be opened and its cargo unloaded, inspected, and then reloaded, it is safe to assume that it takes a minimum of three hours to ensure that a container is carrying safe cargo. Assuming that paperwork has to be completed for each container and that the officer conducting the inspection is particularly efficient and can work alone, an average of three containers can therefore be inspected by a single inspector every day. Given a work-year of 250 days, a single inspector would be able to handle 750 containers in a year. In 2012, there were more than 10 million ocean containers that crossed the borders of the United States, and a similar number that crossed into the European Union. Just for these two economic entities, and just for ocean cargo, 20 million containers would need to be inspected, and therefore a total of 27,000 inspectors would need to be hired. Add air and road cargo, the remainder of the world's economies, and the number of inspectors would easily reach 100,000, at a cost of multiple billions of dollars.

Second, it would result in incredible delays in ports. A single port crane can handle between 15 and 40 container movements per hour. There are often three or four cranes unloading a containership. There is therefore a need for a space sufficiently large to store and inspect approximately 120 newly unloaded containers every hour. Meanwhile, the containers from the preceding two hours are still being inspected, since it takes about three hours for each, assuming that none are isolated because they are believed to be carrying dangerous goods. Ports would then need to have enough room to inspect all the containers in addition to the space needed to accommodate container movements from the ship to the inspection area, and from the inspection area to the secondary means of transportation (truck or rail). This lack of infrastructure would force ships to have to wait to unload their cargoes. Finally, a one-hundred-percent inspection program is a fallacy. Since it is not possible to hire the required number of inspectors, nor is it to find the necessary room in the ports of the world, the inspection process would have to be less thorough. Each container would be inspected, but in such a rushed fashion that it would not be inspected very well. There would be a perception that the system would work (after all, all containers are inspected), but inspection would never be able to uncover carefully hidden dangerous goods. There is strong evidence that such a system does not work effectively; the TSA operates a system that is based on one-hundred-percent inspection of all passengers and all pieces of luggage. In reviews of the TSA's progress toward its interdiction mission, the U.S. Government Accountability Office (GAO) found that "TSA oversight of checked baggage screening procedures could be strengthened"[1] and "more work remains."[2] These reports are charitable; many others are much more critical and note that GAO's testers were able to bring all sorts of unauthorized items onboard aircraft, undetected.[3,4]

Figure 15.1: Luggage Explosive Detection System
Photo ©Fraport AG. Used with permission.

15.1 The Impact of a Significant Disruption in International Logistics

The extent to which world trade can be seriously disrupted by a single instance of a catastrophe should not be underestimated. The closing of the U.S. ports located on the Gulf of Mexico after Hurricane Katrina delayed shipments of grain and other commodities for months.[5] The fires around Los Angeles in 2003 and the three-day power outage of August 2003 in the Midwest and Northeast of the United States cost billions of dollars in manufacturing delays and shipment disruptions.[6]

However, the greatest impact is that of a terrorist act. All North American international and domestic airline traffic was completely stopped after September 11, 2001, for 3 days; it took one complete day to reposition all of the aircraft and a couple of weeks to clear the logjam of air cargo shipments. Thirteen months later, in October 2002, the Booz-Allen-Hamilton firm conducted a "war game" simulation in which the players were told that a dirty bomb—a bomb containing radioactive materials that are spread by the force of the explosion—had been found in the Port of Los Angeles; they were then told that another bomb had been found in Minneapolis and that a third one had exploded in Chicago. The initial response of the 85 game participants (all from the U.S. government) was to shut down two ports for 3 days and, as the crisis worsened, to shut down all U.S. ports for 12 days.[7] The Booz-Allen-Hamilton report estimated that this single decision would have engendered a backlog of containers in U.S. ports that would have taken three months to clear, and the delays would have cost the U.S. economy U.S.$ 58 billion in 2002.[8] The corresponding costs in 2013 would likely be much higher, probably closer to U.S.$ 75 to 80 billion.

Similar disruptions could be anticipated in other parts of the world, whether they are the results of natural or man-made catastrophes. In order to prevent those occurrences, governments and international agencies have collaborated to establish security measures that address possible weaknesses in the international supply chain.

15.2 International Organizations

The first groups to implement large-scale security efforts were the international organizations that monitor agreements and treaties, such as the International Maritime Organization (IMO) and the Customs Cooperation Council.

15.2.1 International Maritime Organization

International Maritime Organization (IMO)
A United Nations agency responsible for improving maritime safety and preventing pollution from ships.

One of the first international organizations to implement enhanced security measures was the International Maritime Organization (IMO), when it voted to create the International Ship and Port Facility Security (ISPS) Code in December 2002. In order to implement this code quickly, the IMO made it a part of the International Convention for the Safety of Life at Sea (SOLAS), in a section that addresses "Special Measures to Enhance Maritime Security." Since the code had already been signed by 148 countries, these changes had to be implemented by all signatory countries, and they did so relatively quickly, with most ports and ships in compliance with the ISPS Code by June 2004. As of 2013, there were 159 countries that had signed on to the ISPS code.[9]

International Ship and Port Facility Security (ISPS) Code
A series of security requirements placed by the International Maritime Organization upon ports and ships.

To enhance port security, the code contains two sections: one specifies the required measures that a port has to put in place (Part A), and the other is a series of recommendations for the implementation of these measures (Part B). Because ports face different threats due to their location, the types of cargo they handle, and their physical layout, the implementation of the ISPS Code has been quite different from port to port, and the costs of implementation have varied widely.[10,11] This discrepancy is also caused by the fact that the mandatory requirements are somewhat ill-defined, worded mostly in terms of questions that need to be addressed rather than specific requirements.[12] Nevertheless, the consensus of the research reports

15.2 International Organizations

is that implementation of the ISPS Code has improved the situation everywhere and that it has many benefits in addition to the increase in the level of security. It has led to a decrease in the incidence of theft and pilferage, a substantial decline in the number of stowaways, and much smoother operations in loading and unloading ships—all of this at a cost of a few cents to a few dollars per container handled.[13]

Ports have implemented the ISPS Code in three specific ways. First, they monitor tightly who has access to the port facilities. This is achieved by mandating that workers carry identification cards, by allowing access to only authorized persons, and by requiring visitors to provide identification. Second, the ports also monitor the activities taking place in the port, by recording them on video cameras (see Figure 15.2) and keep these records for a period of a few weeks. Finally, the ports have secure systems of communications, designed to raise the alarm whenever a threat is detected. The alarm systems must be redundant, so that they cannot be easily rendered ineffective by an intruder.

Figure 15.2: Monitoring of Port Facilities by Video Cameras
Photo ©Volodymyr Kyrylyuk. Used with permission.

As it applies to ships, the ISPS Code involves the creation of a company security officer for each carrier and a ship security officer for each ship, whose responsibilities are the development of a Ship Security Assessment, as well as several ship security plans to respond to possible threats against the ship, all of which are also dependent on the type of ship and the type of cargo it carries. Ships are also required to possess certain types of equipment and to restrict onboard access. Ship owners must adhere to additional standards, such as conducting background checks before the hiring of crew members, ensuring the security of paperwork on board, training employees in security procedures, and so on.

Unfortunately, since the research on ISPS has concentrated mainly on port facilities and since the ships' implementations of the ISPS Code are private, corporate decisions, little is known about the ways these measures were enacted. Nevertheless, the IMO has issued countless International Ship Security Certificates, which indicates that most ships are in compliance with the ISPS Code requirements.

15.2.2 World Customs Organization

World Customs Organization (WCO)
An international body whose mission is to improve the administration of Customs. Its members are the national Customs administrations.

Another international institution involved in security improvements in the international shipping of goods is the Customs Cooperation Council, better known as the World Customs Organization (WCO). Despite the fact that the primary role of the WCO has traditionally been the "simplification and harmonization of Customs' procedures,"[14] it has been involved in a number of initiatives designed to enhance security.

Early on, the WCO saw its role as complementing the efforts of the IMO by helping importing countries and importers identify, before the goods leave the country of export, the cargoes that should be scrutinized before they should be allowed on their international trip to the importing country. The WCO achieved that objective by encouraging the standardization of documents, by identifying the data characteristics of high-risk shipments, and by establishing guidelines that allowed Customs authorities to have access to the documents of a particular shipment before it is loaded on board the carrier's vessel or aircraft. This particular emphasis is called the Advanced Cargo Information guidelines,[15] which mirrors one of the initiatives of the U.S. Customs and Border Protection agency.

Security and Facilitation in a Global Environment (SAFE)
A set of guidelines to increase the cooperation of national Customs administrations in fighting security threats.

In June 2005, the WCO implemented its SAFE (Security and Facilitation in a Global Environment) initiative, a program it revised further in June 2007. The SAFE initiative further coordinates the efforts of Customs authorities worldwide in their efforts to combat terrorism. The SAFE requirements are fourfold:

- All Customs authorities have to adhere to a set of advance electronic information standards for all international shipments. What is required of shippers should be identical, regardless of country of export and country of import.

- Each country must have consistent risk management approaches to address security threats.

- Exporting countries' Customs authorities must comply with a reasonable request from the importing country's Customs authorities to inspect outgoing cargo, preferably by using non-intrusive technology (X-rays) if possible (see Figure 15.3).

- All Customs authorities must provide benefits to companies that demonstrate that they meet minimum standards of security. Such companies are called Authorized Economic Operators, and benefit from faster processing of Customs clearance and lower inspection rates.[16]

15.2.3 International Chamber of Commerce

The International Chamber of Commerce (ICC) also weighed in on the issues related to security initiatives in the domain of international logistics, in a policy statement

15.2 International Organizations

Figure 15.3: Mobile X-Ray Scanner for Cargo Containers
Photo ©Gerald Nino. Used with permission.

dated November 2002;[17] in it, the ICC emphasized that security initiatives should be the domain of international agreements between countries, rather than initiatives imposed unilaterally by some governments. The ICC also emphasized that businesses involved in international trade have already invested considerable amounts in security initiatives and that, therefore, the rules and regulations imposed by international agreements should capitalize on these investments.

The recommendations made by the ICC reflect the organization's goals of facilitating international trade; its concerns were that country-specific requirements would place undue burdens on businesses and hamper trade. It also was concerned about the widespread dissemination of information among a number of law enforcement authorities and counseled that great care should be taken in the handling of the business information collected by security initiatives, so that no "sensitive confidential company information" would be released.[18]

International Chamber of Commerce (ICC) The largest business organization in the world. Its goal is to champion international business growth and its members are the national chambers of commerce.

15.2.4 National Governments' Involvement

Despite the efforts undertaken by the international organizations to make international trade more secure, and the admonitions of the ICC that unilateral requirements would hinder trade, as well as the efforts of the WCO toward a common set of requirements, many governments unilaterally implemented a number of different measures in the wake of the terrorist attacks of the past two decades. While the attacks on the World Trade Center and the Pentagon in 2001 tend to be at the forefront of most Americans' consciousness, the list of tragedies is unfortunately much longer, as shown in Table 15.1. The frequency of those attacks, as well as the increasing diversity of groups intent on disrupting democratic societies, led many governments to create and enforce a number of security measures, many of which have had a substantial impact on international trade.

Each government implemented those security measures because they felt that their country was specifically targeted. Unfortunately, this is not the case, as is shown in Table 15.1; terrorists, from groups to individuals, are indiscriminate in their activities, attacking multiple targets in many different countries. It has truly become a worldwide concern, and very few countries have escaped this plague. Some of the terrorists are foreign, but most are citizens of the countries they target.

Major Terrorist Attacks 1990-2012

Terrorist Act	Date	Location
World Trade Center bombing	February 26, 1993	New York, United States
Sarin gas subway attack	March 20, 1995	Tokyo, Japan
Oklahoma City bombing	April 19, 1995	Oklahoma City, United States
Métro bombings	Summer-Fall 1995	Paris, France
Omagh bombings	August 15, 1998	Omagh, Northern Ireland
World Trade Center attacks	September 11, 2001	New York, United States
Anthrax mailings	September-October 2001	United States
Bali bombings	October 12, 2002	Bali, Indonesia
Istanbul bombings	November 15 and 20, 2003	Istanbul, Turkey
Moscow Metro bombing	February 6, 2004	Moscow, Russia
Beslan School Hostages	September 2004	Beslan, Russia
Madrid train bombings	March 11, 2004	Madrid, Spain
London subway bombings	July 7, 2005	London, United Kingdom
Mumbai train bombings	July 11, 2006	Mumbai, India
Mumbai hotel attacks	November 26, 2008	Mumbai, India
Peshawar bombings	October 28, 2009	Peshawar, Pakistan
Lahore bombings	March 8 & 12, 2010	Lahore, Pakistan
Kampala attacks	July 11, 2011	Kampala, Uganda
Utoya Island massacre	July 22, 2011	Utoya Island and Oslo, Norway
Monterrey Casino attack	August 25, 2011	Monterrey, Mexico
Borno State church attacks	January 2012	Nigeria
Sana'a bombings	May 21, 2012	Sana'a, Yemen

Table 15.1: Worldwide Terrorist Attacks 1990-2012

15.3 The United States' Approach

The U.S. government implemented a large number of measures to limit the country's vulnerability to terrorist attacks, focusing initially on interdiction, a strategy

15.3 The United States' Approach

that the country had already been pursuing in its war against contraband street drugs and illegal immigration, and eventually moving to a system of partnership with importers.

15.3.1 Interdiction

Interdiction is a strategy that attempts to eliminate all imports of a particular type of good and all entries of a specific group of persons into a country. The reasoning is relatively simple: if no terrorist can enter the country, and if no materials that can be used to cause widespread harm can be imported, then no terrorist acts are possible. The United States started to follow this approach almost immediately after the terrorist attacks of September 11, 2001, with a very strict monitoring of the flying public and of the luggage transported on airliners.

interdiction
A security strategy that consists of preventing all imports of potentially dangerous goods and potentially dangerous persons.

The Transportation Security Administration (TSA) was created in November 2001 by consolidating a large number of small private security firms, a move that was quite controversial at the time, as many employees of these firms did not meet federal hiring standards.[19] The interdiction policy implemented by the TSA involves a systematic inspection of all passengers and of their checked luggage, a policy which is plagued with a number of failings, as described in the following three boxes.

Because of these issues, the TSA policies have increasingly been characterized as "theater," ineffective at achieving their stated goals, but presenting a reassuring presence in airports that demonstrates that "something is being done" to combat terrorism.[20,21]

The United States formalized further the creation of its interdiction strategy on November 25, 2002, by creating the Department of Homeland Security (DHS), consolidating 22 services that had so far operated somewhat independently. The goal was that these departments would be more effective if they were able to cooperate around a shared mission. The DHS reinforced the visibility of its mission of interdiction by renaming or regrouping many of these agencies to reflect their role in terrorism prevention: The U.S. Customs Service became Customs and Border Protection, and the investigative bureaus of the former Immigration and Naturalization Service and Customs became Immigration and Customs Enforcement. This newest department of the U.S. government counts more than 200,000 employees, third in size to the Department of Defense and the Department of Veterans Affairs, and three times larger than the Social Security Administration.

Understanding Type I and Type II Errors

The implementation of security measures is predicated on a correct understanding of the two types of errors that can be made in statistics, called Type I error and Type II error. Although these concepts are relatively complex mathematically, they can be understood relatively easily through an illustration, using airport procedures for handling passenger luggage.

Suppose that there is a machine (see Figure 15.1 on page 401) designed to determine whether an explosive device (a bomb) is present in a piece of luggage. Although this machine can be made particularly well, the fact that it has to process hundreds of pieces of luggage a day means that it cannot investigate thoroughly each and every piece that is loaded onto an aircraft and that it has to rely on some method that is less time-consuming and less invasive. Most of these machines take a sample of the air that surrounds a bag and analyze it to detect the presence of certain chemical molecules. If a particular type of molecule is present in a minimum concentration, the machine alerts the operator that there is the possibility of a bomb. At that time, the operator then opens the piece of luggage and conducts a more thorough, physical investigation of the piece of luggage. However, the machine can commit two types of errors, as illustrated in Figure 15.4:

- The machine can erroneously detect a bomb where there is none; this can happen because it has to be calibrated to be extremely sensitive. After all, it has to detect minute levels of certain chemicals in a fraction of a second. Since some of these chemical molecules can be on the luggage for a number of reasons, the machine sounds the alarm even though there is actually no bomb in the luggage. Further investigation by the operator confirms that the bag is fine, and the piece of luggage is then cleared. This is called a Type I error. Another terminology, more commonly used in medicine, calls this type of error a "false positive:" The medical device concludes that the patient has a certain disease when in reality that patient does not have it.

- The machine can erroneously clear a piece of luggage when it actually contains a bomb; this may be due to the fact that the terrorist has done a particularly good job of packaging the bomb or because the sample that the machine used did not contain, by chance alone, enough of the trace chemicals it needed to sound an alarm. In that case, the machine does not ring the alarm even though the piece of luggage is dangerous. This is called a Type II error. In medicine, it is called a "false negative:" the medical device concludes that the patient does not have a particular disease when in reality the patient does have it.

Suppose that the bomb-sniffing machine in this example is designed and calibrated in such a way that it experiences a 5 percent error rate for both Type I and Type II errors. Which of the two error rates is most worrisome?

	The piece of luggage does not contain a bomb	The piece of luggage does contain a bomb
The machine does not give an alarm		Type II error
The machine gives an alarm	Type I error	

Figure 15.4: Type I and Type II Errors

When asked to evaluate a bomb-sniffing machine with equal Type I and Type II error rates of 5 percent, most people conclude that the Type II error rate is most worrisome; after all, a machine that misses 5 percent of all bombs is very scary indeed. However, this is an incorrect position; the Type I error rate is the problem. This is known as the paradox of Type I and Type II errors. Suppose that there is an incidence of one bomb per one million pieces of luggage. For simplicity's sake, suppose that the total volume of luggage that the system processes every year is also one million pieces of luggage. The rate is 0.0001 percent, which is actually much higher than the actual rate. There are, thankfully, fewer bombs and far many more pieces of luggage; however, restricting the analysis to one million pieces of luggage, inspected at the rate of approximately 2,750 pieces a day, makes the paradox more understandable.

Let's assume that on a given day, a terrorist places a bomb in a piece of luggage. With a Type II error rate of 5 percent, there is a 95 percent chance that the machine will correctly detect the piece of luggage with the bomb and sound the alarm, which makes it a quasi-certainty. However, over the past year, the machine also inspected 999,999 other pieces of luggage, none of which contained a bomb; nevertheless, for approximately 50,000 of them (exactly 49,999 of them), the machine rang the alarm (because it committed a Type I error) and the operator had to inspect the piece of luggage manually.

Out of the 50,000 pieces of luggage that the operator has inspected up until that day, none contained a bomb. The operator had been very vigilant, looking for all possible ways a bomb could be hidden in the midst of someone's belongings, but had not found one. However, he had only a few minutes to do the work, since the luggage had to be sent to its destination with the plane on which the passenger is ticketed.

The single piece of luggage that does contain a well-concealed bomb will not escape scrutiny; the operator will handle it with much care. However, it is also likely that the operator will assume that it is a false alarm; after all, 100 percent of the ones inspected so far were. The dangerous piece of luggage will then be cleared, even though the bomb-sniffing machine identified it correctly as dangerous. Consider that only 0.002 percent of the luggage physically inspected by the operator will contain a bomb; 99.998 percent of the inspected bags are perfectly fine.

Human nature prevents most of us from paying much attention to a phenomenon that is that infrequent;[22] facing a probability of 0.002 percent is equivalent to meeting a U.S. national for the first time and assuming that this person is an undergraduate student at the University of Chicago (the ratio is roughly identical: 6,000 students in a population of 300 million); we know it's possible, but that is certainly not our first assumption.

15.3.2 Customs-Trade Partnership Against Terrorism

The United States complemented its interdiction approach with the creation of the Customs-Trade Partnership Against Terrorism (C-TPAT) in 2001; however, only a handful of companies were involved in this program in 2001 and 2002. By 2003, 137 companies joined, and in 2012, there were over 10,500 importers and logistics services providers enrolled in the program.[23] About 55 percent of the shipments

Customs-Trade Partnership Against Terrorism (C-TPAT) A voluntary partnership program of the U.S. CPB. Participating companies obtain priority processing and reduced inspection rates.

entering the United States—by value—were entered by C-TPAT participants and 100 percent of the shipments made by C-TPAT participants were in compliance with U.S. Customs and Border Protection security guidelines. [24]

The program is a shift away from interdiction and one-hundred-percent inspection; it is designed to recognize that the immense majority of the shipments that travel internationally are innocuous and, therefore, that they should not be the targets of law enforcement. The only concerns with these shipments should be the possibility that they are intercepted by criminals and the merchandise that they contain is substituted for dangerous goods. The goal of the program is therefore to encourage corporations involved in international trade to enact security measures that would prevent tampering with the shipments at any point in the supply chain; corporations are asked to evaluate their levels of security in the supply chain, determine their vulnerability, and remedy any issues.

The program is a voluntary program in which companies elect to participate. Corporations must first apply for participation in the C-TPAT program, and after their applications have been accepted, they become "Tier I" members. Tier I members are also called certified corporations. After their supply-chain security has been analyzed by Customs and Border Protection and the firms' security measures have been found to be "reliable, accurate, and effective,"[25] the firms' applications are validated, and the firms become "Tier II" members. In 2012, U.S. Customs and Border Protection validated or re-validated 2,448 companies.[26] Corporations that go beyond the minimum requirements of Customs can reach the level of "Tier III" members. As of December 2008, there were about 8,000 corporations that had Tier II status, and a little over 300 had reached Tier III status.[27]

In order to encourage corporations to participate in the C-TPAT program, Customs and Border Protection offers companies several advantages:

- **A lower inspection probability**. At the port of entry, U.S. Customs and Border Protection assigns a security score to a shipment. If a shipment's score exceeds a given threshold, an inspection is deemed necessary. For C-TPAT participating companies, the targeting score is lowered. Tier I companies have an inspection rate that is 15 to 20 percent the inspection rate of non-C-TPAT companies. The targeting score is lowered further for Tier II companies, and Tier III companies' shipments are not subjected to security inspections, only random compliance inspections.[28]

- **Priority inspections**. For Tier II companies, if an inspection is deemed necessary for their shipment, it receives priority, and is moved to the front of the line.

- **Priority processing**. Both Tier I and Tier II companies have access to FAST lane at the land borders of the United States, allowing them to process shipments faster. Tier III companies have access to a true "green lane," which speeds up the processing on an import considerably.[29] That "green lane" was what had been promised in the beginning of the implementation of the C-TPAT program, and what Tier II companies had hoped to obtain. As of 2013, it is not anticipated that this benefit would be extended to companies that have not achieved Tier III.

- **Customs assistance**. All C-TPAT participating companies can obtain assistance from Customs' supply-chain security specialists to resolve security challenges.

Although the program was originally instituted as a voluntary program for companies involved in international trade, it has evolved into a mandatory program for all importers, carriers, and third-party logistics providers; participation is not encouraged, it is essentially expected.

The C-TPAT program operates very much within the guidelines established by the SAFE initiative enacted by the WCO. In addition, by concentrating on the analysis of shipments that can be presumed to present some level of risk (determined by their characteristics, often the fact that they are unusual in some fashion), the C-TPAT program also meets the requirements of the ICC to be least disruptive to international commerce.

In May 2012, the United States and the European Union signed an agreement that grants mutual recognition to each other's program of security compliance. A U.S.-validated (Tier II) C-TPAT company is recognized as an Authorized Economic Operator (see Section 15.4.1 on page 414) in the European Union, and *vice versa*.[30] Similar agreements were signed with New Zealand, Canada, Jordan, Japan, Korea, and Taiwan region.[31]

15.3.3 Maritime Transportation Security Act

In addition to the C-TPAT program, the United States has also created a number of other initiatives, all designed to improve security: in 2002, the U.S. Congress passed the Maritime Transportation Security Act (MTSA), which has been made part of the Code of Federal Regulations, 33-CFR-101 through 107.

The MTSA is the U.S. implementation of the IMO's International Ship and Port Facility Security Code (ISPS), although there are a few minor differences. The MTSA is slightly more encompassing: it applies to cargo vessels of more than 100 DWT, and to any structure, "any structure of any kind located in, on, under, or adjacent to any waters subject to the jurisdiction of the United States," both of which are more encompassing than the ISPS, which only covers vessels of more than 500 DWT and port facilities. The MTSA is also different from the ISPS in that it applies to passenger vessels of more than 150 passengers, whereas the ISPS applies to all passenger ships.[32]

Marine Transportation Security Act (MTSA)
The U.S. legislation that implemented the recommendations of the International Maritime Organization's International Ship and Port Facility Security Code.

The MTSA requires ports to have a security plan, monitored by a Port Security Officer. It mandates that the port security plan be approved by the U.S. Coast Guard Captain of the Port before the port can operate. The plan must contain information on access to the port, on training programs, on drills, on record keeping, and on the existence and maintenance of emergency communication equipment.[33]

For vessels, the MTSA requires a security plan as well, managed by a Vessel Security Officer, and the plan must be submitted and approved by the U.S. Coast Guard Marine Safety Center. This requirement applies to all vessels calling a U.S. port, whether the ship flies a U.S. or a foreign flag.

15.3.4 Security and Accountability for Every Port

In 2006, the U.S. Congress passed an additional piece of legislation called the Security and Accountability For Every Port (SAFE Port) Act, which modified some aspects of the Container Security Initiative (CSI), and of the Customs-Trade Partnership Against Terrorism (C-TPAT), and created the Transportation Workers' Identification Credential (TWIC) program. The primary effect of the legislation was to empower the U.S. Coast Guard to enforce the implementation of the MTSA.

Security and Accountability For Every Port (SAFE) A U.S. piece of legislation that created a number of security-related programs.

The bill's existence was mostly due to a reaction to the Dubai Ports World's purchase of the P&O company, which was under contract to manage several terminals in ports of the United States, including New York, Miami and New Orleans. Since the Dubai company was state-owned, a number of politicians objected to the possibility of a Middle-Eastern company running a port in the United States, and passed the SAFE Port Act. Because of this opposition, Dubai Ports World relinquished the management of the terminals to a U.S. company.

Although this law shares the same name as the WCO's initiative, it is not related.

15.3.5 The Transportation Workers' Identification Credential

Transportation Workers' Identification Credential (TWIC) A U.S. program designed to limit access to ports to persons without a serious criminal background.

The Transportation Workers' Identification Credential (TWIC) program is a requirement that all persons who have access to U.S. ports must carry an identification card. The identification card is based on biometric information and is obtained after the worker has completed a background check. There are 2.5 million transportation workers who have acquired their TWIC credentials. [34]

Very few criminal offenses disqualify people from obtaining a card (espionage, sedition, treason, or terrorism), and a number of criticisms regarding the reliability of the cards, the ease with which they might be counterfeit, and their overall ability to prevent terrorist acts have been made. The program has been branded as essentially ineffective,[35] a position that was confirmed by a scathing Government Accounting Office report.[36]

Originally, the TWIC program was conceived to be extended to other transportation modes—beyond truck drivers having access to ports—including airports and public transportation. As of July 2013, these plans seem to be on hold.

15.3.6 Container Security Initiative

Container Security Initiative (CSI) A U.S. Customs and Border Protection program that consists of inspecting overseas the shipments that are bound for the United States.

The Container Security Initiative (CSI) is an initiative that addresses the threat posed by the terrorist use of a container to deliver a weapon. It attempts to identify containers before they are placed onboard vessels headed for the United States. U.S. Customs and Border Protection has stationed teams of U.S. officers from both U.S. Customs and Border Protection (CBP) and Immigration and Customs Enforcement (ICE) in foreign ports to identify, target, screen, and eventually inspect containers before they are loaded. The CSI requirements demand cooperation from foreign officials, since U.S. Customs do not have the authority to conduct searches in non-U.S. territories.

CSI is the United States' implementation of the World Customs Organization's SAFE (Security and Facilitation in a Global Environment) initiative, and it is careful to operate within the constraints of this program; containers should be screened through a non-invasive method, such as X-rays, and the process should not delay the shipping of goods.

As of 2011, CSI was operational in 58 ports in North America, Europe, Asia, Africa, the Middle East, and Latin America, and screened over 80 percent of all maritime containerized cargo imported into the United States.[37]

15.3.7 Free and Secure Trade

The Free and Secure Trade (FAST) program is a joint initiative between the Canada Border Services Agency (CBSA) and U.S. Customs and Border Protection (CBP) and

15.3 The United States' Approach

CBP and Mexican Customs. It is designed to allow cargo and carriers to cross these borders more expeditiously. Three entities must have been cleared to obtain the benefits of the program: the exporter/importer, the carrier of the goods, and the driver. The clearance process involves a background check for the driver, and a review of the security measures in place for the importer and the carrier.

If all three entities are FAST members, they can gain access to dedicated lanes at the border crossing point, for faster and more efficient border clearance. At the crossing, the driver presents three bar-coded documents to the border services officer (one for each of the participating parties: the driver, the carrier and the importer). The officer can quickly scan the bar codes while all trade data declarations and verifications are done at a later time, away from the border. If there is no dedicated FAST lane, the process is the same, but the driver does not enjoy priority handling.

FAST is a voluntary program that Customs officials in all three countries are encouraging shippers to join. As of 2013, there were 78,000 drivers enrolled in the program.[38]

Free And Secure Trade (FAST) A joint Canada-U.S.-Mexico voluntary program. Participating companies enjoy dedicated fast lanes when crossing the Canada-U.S. border or the Mexico-U.S. border.

15.3.8 Importer Security Filing

The United States first implemented in 2002 a program called the "24-hour rule" that required that all importers (and carriers) provide a copy of the manifest of an ocean shipment bound for the United States, including shipments that were just transiting through a U.S. port and were bound for another country, 24 hours before that shipment was loaded onto the vessel bound for the United States.

This program has been superseded since January 26, 2010, by a program called the Importer Security Filing, which follows the guidelines of the World Customs Organization's SAFE initiative, which mandates that importing countries make uniform the type of information that can be required of shippers. The requirements of the Importer Security Filing expand the number of points of information that the shipper must provide, and it has become better known in the United States as the 10 + 2 rule, which mirrors the number of items required.

Importer Security Filing A U.S. program that implements the Security and Facilitation in a Global Environment (SAFE) guidelines of the World Customs Organization.

The Importer Security Filing requires that the importer provide U.S. Customs and Border Protection with the following data:

- The 10 items required from the importer

    1. The identification number of the importer of record (Employer Identification Number [EIN] or Social Security Number [SSN])
    2. The identification number of the consignee (EIN or SSN)
    3. The manufacturer (name and address)
    4. The seller of the goods (name and address)
    5. The buyer of the goods (name and address)
    6. The name and address of the business to which the shipment is going
    7. The stuffer's name and address (the party that filled the container)
    8. The location where the container was stuffed
    9. The country of origin of the goods
    10. The six-digit Harmonized System number for the goods

- The 2 items required from the carrier

  1. The vessel stow plan (the way the containers were organized onboard the vessel)
  2. The container status message (container number, location, condition—full/empty—, events—loading/unloading—, and event times)

The importer must provide U.S. CBP with the data contained in the Importer Security Filing at least 24 hours prior to the goods arriving in the United States port.

15.4 The European Union's Programs

The European Union has approached security in a significantly different way: while it recognizes that there are new security issues with the increase in terrorism and the availability of weapons of mass destruction in the hands of criminals, its primary focus has been prevention. In a paper outlining its security strategy, the European Union emphasized that the reduction of poverty, the enforcement of international agreements against arms proliferation, the restoration of democratic governments in areas of regional conflicts, and an increase in international cooperation for criminal investigations would be most effective in dealing with security threats.[39]

Nevertheless, the European Union has implemented a number of programs in response to international organizations' guidelines, first the International Ship and Port Facilities Security Code of the IMO, and then the SAFE framework of the WCO. Although there were some unilateral interpretations of these guidelines, the European Union, by and large, has responded to security threats in a relatively uniform fashion.

15.4.1 Authorized Economic Operator

Authorized Economic Operator (AEO)
An E.U. program that implements the Security and Facilitation in a Global Environment (SAFE) guidelines of the World Customs Organization.

The Authorized Economic Operator (AEO) program is designed to respond to the WCO mandate that Customs organizations provide benefits to businesses that meet minimal supply chain security standards and best practices.

A company involved in the international movement of goods—importer, exporter, carrier, port, airport, or other trade intermediary—can become an AEO after demonstrating that it has a number of security measures in place, and having had these measures reviewed and approved by a national Customs administration. It is a standard similar to Tier II of the United States C-TPAT; however, the EAO has requirements regarding financial viability[40] that are not found in the C-TPAT requirements.

An Authorized Economic Operator benefits from simplifications in Customs procedures and reductions in Customs controls,[41] but those benefits tend to be country specific rather than be similar in all European countries.

The AEO status is granted by one of the Customs authorities of the European Union, and the other Customs authorities "should grant" the same simplified processes that their own AEOs are given.[42] Similarly, the status of AEO should be granted to companies that have been validated (Tier II) under the Customs-Trade Partnership Against Terrorism (see Section 15.3.2 on page 409).

15.4.2 Customs Security Programme

The European Union's Customs Security Programme (CSP) was designed to develop and implement measures that enhanced the security of its borders. It achieved this through improved Customs controls. Importers are required to provide Customs authorities with information on goods prior to their arrival in the European Union (pre-arrival declaration), and Customs use this advance electronic information to perform a risk analysis of every shipment, which enables Customs to identify high risk cargo bound for Europe.

In a way that is encouraged by the WCO, European Customs cooperate with other Customs authorities worldwide to identify cargo that may present a threat, and inspect cargo prior to shipment when requested.

Customs Security Programme (CSP) An E.U. program that implements the Security and Facilitation in a Global Environment (SAFE) guidelines of the World Customs Organization.

15.5 Other Countries' Approach

Countries outside of Europe and North America reacted with policies that mirrored those of the European Union, by implementing the ISPS Code and SAFE framework, mostly in the spirit of international cooperation rather than as a response to a perceived threat of terrorism. The prevalent viewpoint was that terrorists were targeting mostly the United States and possibly the European Union and that this was a U.S. problem, from which they could remove themselves.

This attitude was further reinforced by actions of the United States that often imposed additional measures on its trade partners, who were asked to implement them under the scrutiny of U.S. enforcement agencies, whether Customs and Border Protection, Immigration and Customs Enforcement, or the Coast Guard.

Many countries engaged in these changes reluctantly, as they had much more significant domestic problems and did not want to spend their resources on a "foreign" problem. The subsequent bombings in Bali, Moscow, Madrid, London, and Mumbai changed this perspective relatively quickly, and most countries today agree that terrorism is a worldwide problem, although they often see it as less significant than widespread poverty and its associated risks of significant crime and potential social unrest.

15.6 Corporate Efforts

Although governments frame the issue of supply chain security in terms of the risk of terrorism, most companies see security in a much narrower way, focusing principally on the risk of theft and other criminal activities, such as tampering, vandalism, and counterfeit products. Companies comply with requests to reduce terrorism by participating in governmental programs and other efforts to secure the international logistics' environment, but they see the benefits of such increased security mostly in terms of reduced cargo losses.

Nevertheless, the surge in government programs designed to eliminate terrorism was the impetus for many companies to engage in Total Security Management (TSM), a management philosophy based on the Total Quality Management concepts developed by W. Edwards Deming in the 1970s,[43] which encourages every employee, at every level, to recognize the importance of security within the corporation and suggest improvements in processes and procedures. By having a commitment to security that permeates all levels of responsibility within the company, security is

Total Security Management (TSM) A management philosophy that posits that security is better achieved if every member of the organization is vigilant and pro-active in identifying security issues.

increased greatly and becomes an essential part of the culture of the firm. Even though there are costs to making these improvements, the idea behind TSM is that these costs will be offset by the corresponding reductions in theft, damaged goods, and lost productivity, in the same way as Crosby once determined that "quality is free."[44]

In order to be comprehensive in their security efforts, companies have to secure four areas in their supply chains: (1) their fixed assets (plants, warehouses, distribution centers), (2) their inbound and outbound shipments while they are in transit, (3) the information on which they rely to manage their operations, and (4) their workforce, to ensure that it is reliable and trustworthy.

In order to protect their fixed assets, companies install physical barriers designed to prevent entry by unauthorized persons. Fences are built along the perimeter of the facilities, the doors to the buildings are locked (emergency exit doors are locked from the inside so that they cannot be opened from the outside), all other points of access (*e.g.*, roof hatches) to the buildings are secured, the number of outside lights is increased, a backup electric generator is added to prevent interruptions to lights and communication systems, and a public-address and an alarm system are installed. Companies also build gates at the entrance to the facilities, with a security guard ensuring that no unauthorized person is allowed to enter. Companies install security cameras to monitor all activities on the premises, and the videos are monitored by trained security personnel. Finally, emergency security procedures are established and training is provided for all employees, so that they know what their responsibilities are in the event of a security breach. These measures mirror the requirements of the ISPS Code for port facilities.

seal
A lock placed on a container door or truck trailer door that must be broken in order to access the cargo.

In order to protect their shipments while they are in transit, companies implement a different set of measures. They make sure that all cargo containers are sealed before they leave any facility, with a seal that is a good deterrent to a potential thief (see Figure 15.5), and that the seal numbers are carefully monitored. They make sure that the information on the identity of the cargo is released to as few people as possible. Companies also instruct their truck drivers to continuously monitor their surroundings and make sure that they do not stop at a rest area soon after leaving a plant, as most cargo thefts occur within a few miles of the cargo's point of origin.

geo-fencing
A technique based on Global Positioning System that alerts management when a shipment is diverted from its intended itinerary.

Many U.S. companies have put in place a "geo-fencing" system, which alerts security officials when the cargo departs from a pre-determined itinerary. Such a system is based on the Global Positioning System (GPS) and allows only slight variations in itinerary (such as a detour for construction or an accident) but sends a warning if the cargo strays more than 25 miles (40 kilometers) from the highway that the truck is supposed to take. The truck driver is then immediately contacted for further information, and the local police authorities are dispatched if there is a problem. Finally, an emergency plan should be developed and all employees should be trained in its application.

It is also very important for companies to guard their corporate information. While the techniques used to safeguard electronic data are quite complex, and are the subjects of a number of books,[45] a good system of procedures must ensure that information reaches only those people who need to know what is transported or what is currently in inventory. Procedures should be in place to monitor the dissemination of information (electronic and paper) within the firm.

Finally, good security measures are fundamentally predicated on good human resources practices. For instance, if employees are intent on violating the security measures put in place by a corporation, they likely will achieve their goals, as it

Figure 15.5: Two Container Seals: A Bolt Seal (Top) and a Wire Seal (Bottom). Only the Bolt Seal is Accepted in International Shipments
Photo ©Pierre David. Used with permission.

is impossible to defend against all possibilities without affecting the normal conduct of business. It is therefore very important to verify employees' backgrounds, monitor their activities, train them to recognize security violations, and provide an anonymous system to report their concerns.

Review and Discussion Questions

1. What are the different main international logistics security programs, implemented either by international agencies or national governments?

2. What are the main differences between the alternative approaches taken by the United States and the European Union in terms of security?

3. What are the problems of a security policy that is based on one-hundred-percent inspection?

4. What are the four areas in which a corporation must enact security measures to protect itself against theft and terrorism?

5. Suppose a particular disease has an incidence of 1 percent in the population. The test used to detect this disease has a 5 percent Type I error rate; there is no Type II error rate. A physician sees test results from a patient that indicates that the patient has that disease; the probability that the patient actually has that disease is 0.01/0.0595, or about 17 percent. Explain this result.

Notes

[1] "TSA Oversight of Checked Baggage Screening Procedures Could Be Strengthened," Government Accountability Office, July 2006, http://www.gao.gov/new.items/d06869.pdf.

[2] "Screener Training and Performance Measurement Strengthened, but More Work Remains," May 2005, Government Accountability Office, http://www.gao.gov/new.items/d05457.pdf.

[3] Hsu, Spencer, "TSA Minimizes Failure to Detect Threats," *Washington Post*, November 16, 2007.

[4] Frank, Thomas, "Most Fake Bombs Missed by Screeners," *USA Today*, October 22, 2007, http://www.usatoday.com/news/nation/2007-10-17-airport-security_N.htm.

[5] Peige, John, "Gulf Coast Hurricanes Have Huge Impact on Shipping Flows," *MM&P Wheelhouse Weekly*, October 27, 2005, p.43.

[6] Ritter, Luke, J. Michael Barrett, and Rosalyn Wilson, *Securing Global Transportation Networks* 2007, McGraw-Hill, New York, New York.

[7] Gerencser, Mark, Jim Weinberg, and Don Vincent, "Port Security War Game: Implications for U.S. Supply Chains," Booz-Allen-Hamilton, 2003, http://www.boozallen.com/media/file/128648.pdf, retrieved September 21, 2009.

[8] *Ibid.*

[9] "Introduction to The Maritime Transportation Security Act (MTSA) and The International Ship and Port Facility Security Code (ISPS)," February 1, 2013, U.S. Coast Guard, Office of Port and Facility Compliance, https://homeport.uscg.mil/mycg/portal/ep/home.do, retrieved July 4, 2013.

[10] *Maritime Security: ISPS Code Implementation, Costs and Related Financing*, Report by the UNCTAD Secretariat, March 14, 2007, United Nations Conference on Trade and Development, http://www.unctad.org/en/docs/sdtetlb20071_en.pdf.

[11] Boske, Leigh, *Port and Supply-Chain Security Initiatives in the United States and Abroad*, Lyndon B. Johnson School of Public Affairs, University of Texas at Austin, Policy Research

Project Report 150, 2006, http://www.utexas.edu/lbj/pubs/pdf/prp_150.pdf, retrieved September 22, 2009.

[12] Kruk, C. Burt, and Michel Luc Donner, *Review of Cost of Compliance with the New International Freight Transport Security Requirements: Consolidated Report of the Investigations Carried Out in Ports in the Africa, Europe and Central Asia, and Latin America and the Caribbean Regions*, World Bank, Transport Paper 16, February 2008, http://siteresources.worldbank.org/INTTRANSPORT/Resources/tp_16_ISPS.pdf.

[13] *Ibid.*

[14] "About Us," World Customs Organization, http://www.wcoomd.org/home_about_us.htm, accessed September 22, 2009.

[15] "The Role of Customs and the World Customs Organization in Border Management," United Nations Counter-Terrorism Committee, March 2004, http://www.osce.org/documents/sg/2004/03/2196_en.pdf.

[16] "WCO SAFE Framework of Standards," June 2007, World Customs Organization, http://www.wcoomd.org/files/1.%20Public%20files/PDFandDocuments/SAFE%20Framework_EN_2007_for_publication.pdf.

[17] "Supply Chain Security," November 18, 2002, Policy Statement, International Chamber of Commerce's Commission on Transport and Logistics, http://www.iccwbo.org/policy/transport/id518/index.html.

[18] *Ibid.*

[19] Roots, Roger, "Terrorized into Absurdity: the Creation of the Transportation Security Administration," *Independent Review*, March 22, 2003.

[20] Stross, Randall, "Theater of the Absurd at the T.S.A.," *The New York Times*, December 17, 2006.

[21] Goldberg, Jeffrey, "The Things He Carried," *Atlantic Monthly*, November 2008.

[22] Johnson, Eric, John Hershey, Jacqueline Meszaros, and Howard Kunreuther, "Framing, Probability Distortions, and Insurance Decisions," *Journal of Risk and Uncertainty*, August 1993, pp. 35-51.

[23] "C-TPAT Conference Draws Record Numbers," January 11, 2013, Customs-Trade Partnership Against Terrorism, U.S. Customs and Border Protection, http://www.cbp.gov/xp/cgov/newsroom/highlights/-ctpat_record_numbers.xml, retrieved July 3, 2013.

[24] *Performance and Accountability Report—Fiscal Year 2012*, April 9, 2013, U.S. Customs and Border Protection, http://www.cbp.gov/xp/cgov/newsroom/publications/admin/, retrieved July 3, 2013.

[25] Boske, Leigh, "Port and Supply-Chain Security Initiatives in the United States and Abroad," Lyndon B. Johnson School of Public Affairs, University of Texas at Austin, Policy Research Project Report 150, 2006, http://www.utexas.edu/lbj/publications/3986, retrieved July 3, 2013.

[26] *Performance and Accountability Report—Fiscal Year 2012*, April 9, 2013, U.S. Customs and Border Protection, http://www.cbp.gov/xp/cgov/newsroom/publications/admin/, retrieved July 3, 2013.

[27] "What is C-TPAT?", SSI Global Compliance LLC, http://www.ssi-gc.com/C-TPAT.html, retrieved July 3, 2013.

[28] "Customs-Trade Partnership Against Terrorism (C-TPAT)," Samuel Shapiro and Company, Inc., http://www.shapiro.com/html/ctpat.html, retrieved July 3, 2013.

[29] *Ibid.*

[30] "Frequently Asked Questions EU—US Mutual Recognition Decision," January 31, 2013, Taxation and Customs Union, http://ec.europa.eu/taxation_customs/resources/documents/common/whats_new/13_01_31_eu-us-questions-answers.pdf, retrieved July 4, 2013.

[31] *Ibid.*

[32] "Introduction to The Maritime Transportation Security Act (MTSA) and The International Ship and Port Facility Security Code (ISPS)," February 1, 2013, U.S. Coast Guard, Office of Port and Facility Compliance, https://homeport.uscg.mil/mycg/portal/ep/home.do, retrieved July 4, 2013.

[33] *Ibid.*

[34] "Welcome to the TWIC Deployment Website," Transportation Workers' Identification Credential, http://www.twicinformation.com/twicinfo, accessed July 4, 2013.

[35] Bryant, Dennis, "Maritime Security and the Useless TWIC," *Maritime Reporter & Engineering News*, May 2012.

[36] *Transportation Workers' Identification Credential: Card Reader Pilot Results Are Unreliable; Security Benefits Need to Be Reassessed*, May 8, 2013, Government Accounting Office report GAO-13-198, www.gao.gov/assets/660/654431.pdf, retrieved July 4, 2013.

[37] "CSI in Brief," October 7, 2011, U.S. Customs and Border Protection, http://www.cbp.gov/xp/cgov/trade/cargo_security/csi/csi_in_brief.xml, retrieved July 4, 2013.

[38] "FAST FAct Sheet," U.S. Customs and Border Protection, May 2013, http://wwwcbp.gov/xp/cgov/travel/trusted_traveler/fast/fast_driver/,
retrieved June 30, 2013.

[39] Solana, Javier, "A Secure Europe in a Better World: European Security Strategy," December 12, 2003, http://www.consilium.europa.eu/uedocs/cmsUpload/78367.pdf.

[40] "Authorised Economic Operator (AEO)," Taxation and Customs Union, http://ec.europa.eu/taxation_customs/customs/policy_issues/customs_security/aeo, retrieved July 4, 2013.

[41] "Customs-related security initiatives of the EU," Taxation and Customs Union, http://ec.europa.eu/taxation_customs/customs/policy_issues/customs_security/security_initiatives/index_en.htm, retrieved July 4, 2013.

[42] *Ibid.*

[43] Ritter, Luke, J. Michael Barrett, and Rosalyn Wilson, *Securing Global Transportation Networks*, 2007, McGraw-Hill, New York, New York.

[44] Crosby, Philip, *Quality Is Free*, 1980, Mentor/Penguin-Putnam, New York, New York.

[45] Merkow, Mark, and James Breithaupt, *Information Security: Principles and Practices*, 2005, Prentice-Hall, Englewood Cliffs, New Jersey.

Chapter 16

Customs Clearance

16.1 Duty 421
16.2 Non-Tariff Barriers 435
16.3 Customs Clearing Process 440
16.4 Foreign Trade Zones 446

Another aspect of international trade is the process that an importer must follow when it brings goods into a country. This process is dictated by Customs, the government office in charge of collecting taxes on imports and of enforcing a number of rules and regulations regarding what can and cannot be admitted into the country. It is generally a complex process, fraught with pitfalls and loaded with paperwork. Most countries, with very few exceptions, do not like to import goods, and they act accordingly. This chapter explains how the Customs system works in general but draws most of its examples from the process followed to import goods into the United States.

16.1 Duty

Duty is the tax that an importer must pay in order to bring goods into a country. Such duty is calculated in a number of different ways, generally based upon three criteria:

1. The type of goods imported, which is determined according to a number of rules of classification that essentially have been standardized worldwide.

2. The value of the goods imported, which is determined not only by the invoice value, but also according to a number of rules that differ from country to country, collectively called valuation rules.

3. The country from which the goods are imported; this determination is made according to the rules of origin, a process recently simplified but still quite cumbersome for manufactured products with components made in multiple countries.

duty
The amount of tax paid to the importing country on an imported good.

classification
The process of determining what is the correct Harmonized System number for an import.

valuation
The process of determining the value of an import, specifically the amount on which the duty is calculated.

rules of origin
The rules used to determine the country of origin of an imported product.

tariff rate
The rate at which an import is taxed. The rate depends on classification and origin. Also called the duty rate.

Harmonized System of classification
A system of classification for goods, developed by the World Customs Organization, and followed by 179 countries.

From these three elements, Customs calculates what tariff will be charged on the import, or the tax that the importer will have to pay on the imported goods. It is generally a percentage of their value, but it can also be calculated with some other method, based on the number of units shipped or their weight, for example.

16.1.1 Classification

The classification of goods follows a coding scheme that is essentially the same worldwide, as most countries have adopted the Harmonized Commodity Description and Coding System—also called the Harmonized System (HS) of classification—developed by the Customs Cooperation Council (also known as the World Customs Organization [WCO]).

The Harmonized System is used by 179 countries, representing 98 percent or more of world trade, to classify both exports and imports.[1] The fact that a trader can use the same code when it is exporting a product from one country and importing it into another is a great simplification. At one time, almost every country had its own classification and coding system.

According to the HS, each product can have a code that uses up to ten digits. An example, taken from the tariff schedule of the United States, would be:

6402.19.05		**golf shoes**
	30	for men
	60	for women
	90	for other persons

where the first six digits represent the "root" of the international coding (*i.e.*, the code that will be identical in all the countries that have adopted the Harmonized System for this product). Since "golf shoes" are not specifically listed in the 6-digit system, they fall under "other," which is the 6-digit code 6402.19. The last four digits are country specific (*i.e.*, every country can use them to differentiate between different subcategories of the main product, as the United States does). For the United States, the 8-digit code 6402.19.05 represents golf shoes, and a further differentiation is made between golf shoes for men, for women, and for "other persons," presumably children rather than aliens).

The Harmonized System of classification is accompanied by a series of six General Rules of Interpretation, which detail how an importer should arrive at the correct HS code for an entry:[2]

rules of interpretation
A series of six rules developed to help importers and Customs determine the correct HS classification of a good.

1. The section, chapter, and heading serve only as guides, and the correct classification may be in a different section, chapter, and heading altogether.

2. The classification of an incomplete or unfinished product is that of the finished product. For example, shipments that contain all of the subassemblies for a final product should be classified as the final product rather than as individual parts. This is true of chemical compounds as well.

3. When in doubt between two classifications, the one with the most specific description is the correct one. However, if the product is made up of several parts, each of which would lead to a different classification, then the classification that lends it its "essential character" is the correct one.

Details on the Classification of Golf Shoes

The Harmonized System is divided into 21 sections, logically determined by the type of product and material, each divided into one or more chapters, with a total of 97 chapters for the entire HS nomenclature. The chapter in which the golf shoes are classified is Chapter 64, entitled "Footwear, gaiters, and the like; parts of such articles."

Each chapter is then divided into headings, which make up the first four digits of the HS number.

The heading 6401 is *Waterproof footwear with outer soles and uppers of rubber or plastics, where the uppers of which are not assembled to the sole by means of stitching, riveting, nailing, screwing, plugging or similar process*. That remark means that the soles and the uppers are "one" or welded together, like rubber boots and downhill ski boots.

Each heading is then divided into subheadings, and this six-digit code is common to all countries that have adopted the Harmonized System. For example, heading 6401 has these two subheadings (among others):

○ 6401.10 is *footwear [of the type defined in 6401] that includes a protective metal toe-cap*.

○ 6401.92 is *other footwear [of the type defined in 6401] covering the ankle but not the knee*. (for example, downhill ski boots).

The next heading is 6402, *Other footwear with outer soles and uppers of rubber or plastics*. Since it is a different heading than 6401, it is easy to conclude that shoes whose uppers are stitched, riveted, nailed, or screwed to the soles would be classified under this heading. They would not be considered waterproof either. Heading 6402 has five subheadings:

○ 6402.12 is *ski-boots and cross-country ski footwear and snowboard boots*. This classification would apply to boots that are not considered to be waterproof and for which the uppers are stitched or glued to the soles.

○ 6402.19 is *other footwear [of the type defined in 6402] where 90 percent or more of the external surface area is rubber or plastics*, where most golf shoes are classified.

○ 6402.20 is *footwear with upper straps or thongs assembled to the sole by means of plugs (zoris)*, which are likely to be thongs, flip-flops or zoris.

○ 6402.91 is *other footwear [defined in 6402] that covers the ankle*.

○ 6402.99 is *other footwear [defined in 6402] and that does not cover the ankles*.

Worldwide, golf shoes are classified as 6402.19, since they are made with rubber soles, their uppers are attached to the soles by some mechanical method, and 90 percent of the external surface area is rubber or plastics. The United States defines golf shoes yet further, with a specific subheading for golf shoes, 6402.19.05, and a differentiation made between men's, women's, and children's shoes.

4. When there is no category under which a specific product can be classified, then the classification that should be used is that of a product that would be most like it.

5. Containers and packaging materials are classified with the products with which they enter. Such would be the case for camera cases, for example. However, if the container has usage beyond the product itself, then it must be entered and classified separately.

6. When comparing classifications, only descriptions at the same level should be compared; it is not appropriate to compare a heading to a subheading, for example.

Nevertheless, the correct classification is always subject to some interpretation on the part of the importer and Customs officers. Because the classification of a specific article determines at which tariff rate it will be taxed and whether it will be subjected to numerical quotas (as are some textile articles in developed countries, such as the United States; see Section 16.2.1), it can be a nontrivial issue. In those cases where a U.S. importer is in doubt about a correct classification, the Customs Office will issue, prior to the entry of the goods, a binding ruling where it will determine the correct classification of a specific product, a decision that will be binding on both parties.[3]

binding ruling
A determination, made by Customs prior to the importation of a good, of the correct classification of a good. The ruling is binding on the Customs administration of the country that issued it.

In early 2000, there were efforts undertaken to simplify the ten-digit classification used by the United States and to model it after some other countries' system, which uses only the six-digit subheadings of the HS.[4] However, as of 2013, the U.S. Customs tariff schedule was still using a ten-digit-based classification system, and there were no plans to change that method.

The correct classification of an imported good is generally made by the importer and then verified by the Customs Office; however, each country has different standards, and a few put the entire classification responsibility on Customs. In any case, it is critical to have a complete description of the goods on the commercial invoice, and not just a part number or an item number. When in doubt, Customs can ask to see the merchandise before it is released, and this inspection can create substantial delays.

Classification Quirks

Given the multitude of products imported into the United States—and given the eclectic tastes of the U.S. population—a large number of unusual products have to be classified by importers following the Harmonized System, with some decisions that can be amusing:

• A novelty item called a "necktie in a bottle" was classified by Customs as a necktie—no surprise here—and therefore was made subject to numerical quotas. However, because its bottle package was unusual, it also had to be classified separately, according to General Rule of Interpretation 5.[5]

• Some Halloween costumes are classified as "articles of clothing" rather than as toys by Customs, and are therefore made subject to higher tariffs and some numerical quotas. This decision has obviously brought jeers

from importers, who argue that children are unlikely to wear Dracula disguises to school, with the possible exception of a single holiday: Halloween.[6]
- A novelty item consisting of a cloth pocket that can be wrapped on a couch's armrest to hold a TV remote control or a few magazines, and sold under the trade name "TV Duck," was classified by Customs as a bedspread—Rule of Interpretation 4—which subjected it to high tariffs and numerical quotas. The importer disagreed, and this protracted fight went all the way to the U.S. Court of Appeals: "You had to be in the courtroom to appreciate the looks of disbelief that the judges directed toward [the Customs lawyer]."[7]
- Canadian exporters have drilled holes in boards to allow their construction lumber to be classified as "finished products"—because homebuilders can fit wires and plumbing lines through them—and therefore avoid the high tariffs placed by the United States on lumber,[8] which it considers subsidized by the provincial governments of Canada. U.S. Customs and the Canadian authorities fought over this issue for four years. The U.S. even suggested to Canada that it impose an export tariff on all lumber rather than face U.S. antidumping duties.[9]
- A company importing plastic action figures of the X-Men superheroes argued that the figures were not reproductions of human beings, which would have classified them as dolls, but rather were simply "creatures," which would classify them as toys and make them eligible for a lower tariff rate. It won its case against U.S. Customs and Border Protection. [10]

16.1.2 Valuation

Because most duty is collected *ad valorem* (on the value of the goods imported in a country), a correct valuation amount must be determined by the importer, following a number of valuation rules governed by the Customs Office of the country in which the goods are imported.

For all member countries of the World Trade Organization (WTO), the valuation of the goods is based on the transaction value of the sale. Therefore, the valuation of the goods must start with the value presented on the invoice sent by the exporter to the importer. For most countries, the value used is the "landed" value, or the CIF/CIP value of the goods (see Chapter 6), that is, the invoice value including packaging costs, transportation costs in the exporting country—pre-carriage—international transportation costs to the country of destination—main carriage—and international insurance costs. For other countries, including the United States, the value used is the FCA or FAS value (see Chapter 6), that is, the invoice value of the goods as well as packaging costs and transportation costs in the exporting country, but excluding the costs of international shipping and insurance.

There are obvious difficulties in reaching the correct valuation unless the commercial invoice is detailed enough to include all of these different costs in a clear, itemized fashion, regardless of the terms of trade (Incoterms® rule) used in the transaction. For example, a CIF sale to an American importer should spell out the costs of international freight and international insurance, so that they can be deducted from the invoice value for Customs purposes.

The valuation process can be much more complicated than what has been outlined so far. Some countries used to determine value based upon the Brussels Definition of Value (BDV), or the "usual" price of a commodity, based on the price at which a product would sell in a free market between an unrelated buyer and seller. However, since 1994 and the conclusion of the Uruguay Round of the General Agreement on Tariffs and Trade, BDV has slowly been replaced by the transaction value.[11] In those cases where Customs suspects that valuation based on the invoice would result in undervaluation—or, possibly, overvaluation—it can legitimately decide that valuation can be determined through other methods:

- **Comparative method.** Customs determines the value of the goods based upon the value of identical or similar goods imported in similar quantity into the same country. Note that the determination of the value of the goods is made based upon importing data and that differences in exporting countries' costs are not taken into consideration.

- **Deductive method.** Customs determines at what price identical or similar goods are sold within 90 days of importation into the importing country and determines an entry value based upon normal markups in the distribution channel.

- **Computed or reconstructed value method.** Customs determines the value of the goods by computing their manufacturing costs and adding "an amount for profit and general expenses equal to that usually reflected in the sales of goods of the same class or kind."[12]

- **Method of last resort.** Customs uses well-trained and well-informed Customs officials to determine the value of the goods imported. No specific guidelines are given, other than that the valuation cannot be "arbitrary." It is unlikely to be anything else, though.

assist
An item provided by the importer to the exporter so that the exporter could manufacture the imported goods. The value of the assist should be included in the valuation of the imported goods.

The valuation of the goods imported can be increased by some items not included on the invoice: for example, it can be a royalty to be paid by the importer to the exporter, a commission to be paid by the importer to a purchasing agent in the exporting country, or a percentage of the price at which the importer sells the goods to their final purchaser. The valuation can also be affected by the presence of what Customs calls an assist, or an item that the importer provided to the exporter in order to produce the goods: for example, a mold or a die that the exporter used in manufacturing the product. The value of such an assist must be added, on a per-item basis, to the value of the goods imported.

Finally, the issue of exchange rates is relevant. Customs must arrive at the value of the goods in the importing country's currency, even though the invoice can be written in a different currency. Each national Customs Office therefore has rules to determine what exchange rate will be used to convert an invoice issued in a foreign currency. U.S. Customs and Border Protection uses the exchange rate of the date of export of the merchandise.

16.1.3 Rules of Origin

The third element necessary to determine the duty that will be applied to a specific import is the country of origin of the goods. Goods are given a country of origin based upon the rules of origin, which follow one or the other of two methods, neither of which has yet been adopted universally, despite the fact that the WTO has been a committee working on this project since 1995.[13] So far, the committee has agreed that countries must make their rules of origin "transparent" and unbiased to importers,[14] and provide a ruling on a country of origin within 150 days.

- **Substantial transformation.** The country of origin of a product is the country in which it acquired its most substantial transformation. The determination of the "substantial transformation" is fraught with pitfalls and can lead to widely different interpretations. For example, consider a computer assembled in Mexico from parts originating in Taiwan region (memory chips), the United States (CPU), China (board and hard drive), Brazil (monitor), and so on. Where did the substantial transformation take place, and what is the country of origin of the product? Although vague, this is still the method followed by the United States—with the exception of textiles—and it can lead to fairly interesting decisions (see the box "Made in ... Where?" on page 428).

- **Change in HS classification.** The country of origin is the country in which the last change in Harmonized System classification occurred. This method is the one currently followed by the United States for textile products, and it has proven to be much easier to implement. Nevertheless, the decision can sometimes lead to a product's country of origin being a country in which a fairly inconsequential transformation took place and where little value was added. Already several exceptions have been made to this rule.

Unfortunately, there seems to be no easy way to determine the country of origin of a complex product. The determination of a country of origin—and the markings that are associated with it—is probably one of the most difficult issues facing firms engaged in international trade today, as different duty rates are used for different countries and as numerical quotas exist for some countries but not others. An importer can be charged very different duty rates and, in some cases, be fined substantially for having hidden the actual country of origin:

A Hong Kong clothing manufacturer was fined U.S.$ 388,000 for fraudulently seeking to export Chinese-made garments to the United States. The firm pleaded guilty to ten counts of lying about the origin of 14,400 dresses. They carried Hong Kong labels but were actually made in China. The maximum penalty for such cases is U.S.$ 500,000 and two years in jail.[15]

U.S. Customs keeps and publishes a list of all the firms that it has found guilty of transshipping, the practice of attempting to hide the country of origin of certain products by making them transit through another country. Because of the very different conditions under which textile products from China and from Hong Kong SAR are imported into the United States, many of these firms have been Hong Kong based.[16]

In addition, the country of origin of a good can have substantial marketing consequences, as most countries require that the goods be marked with their country of origin. For obvious reasons, importers of luxury clothing items prefer to have them marked *Made in Italy* rather than marked as made in a country not known for its designers. However, the issue is of consequence for all sorts of products, as consumers everywhere are sensitive to what international marketers call country-of-origin effects,[17] the perceptions that the country of origin imparts on the product.

Finally, the rules of origin can be affected by bilateral or multilateral agreements. For example, the North American Free Trade Agreement (NAFTA) between Canada,

Made In...Where?

Under the substantial-transformation rule of origin, U.S. Customs determined that transforming steel rods into steel wire was not substantial enough to warrant changing the country of origin but that the assembly of photo album pages into a binder was.[18]

- Similarly, ostrich chicks hatched in Great Britain from eggs laid in South Africa had not been subjected to "a process so substantial as to transform them into new and different articles of commerce" and therefore were coming from South Africa and subject to the then-existing embargo on imports from that country; however, ostrich feathers coming from South Africa and placed on hats made in China were considered transformed enough that their entry was permitted: they had originated in China.[19]

- Under the change-in-HS-number rule, though, there were similarly difficult situations. Underwear made for Victoria's Secret, assembled into final product in a Jordanian plant from panels cut in Israel, and shipped back across the border to Israel is officially *made in Israel*, as General Rule of Interpretation 2 dictates, and benefits from the free-trade agreement between Israel and the United States.[20]

- Silk scarves that are finished, dyed, and handpainted in Italy, and which used to be considered *made in Italy* under the substantial-transformation rule, are now considered to be originating in China, because the HS classification for a raw silk scarf and a painted one is the same.[21] Under pressure from the European Union, the United States relented, and those scarves are once again allowed to be *made in Italy* and fetch U.S.$ 200 prices,[22] a price difficult to obtain for a scarf labeled as made in China.

- Sometimes, the rules are followed to the letter, but the results are disconcerting. The olive harvest in Italy is not sufficient to cover the Italian domestic needs for olive oil. Nevertheless, Italy exports a large amount of olive oil worldwide, clearly labeled as *imported from Italy*. Most of the olives used in this oil come from Spain, Greece, and Tunisia. However, under both the change-in-HS-number rule and the substantial-transformation rule, olive oil can be sold as *made in Italy*, even though Italian companies report that as little as 20 percent of the oil comes from Italian olives.[23] In addition, under a universal rule that anything under 7 percent of a product does not affect its country of origin, the Italian olive oil can contain as much as 7 percent of oil not even processed in Italy.

All in all, even for simple products, it is often difficult to determine where a product is truly "from." Is chocolate made in Belgium from Ivory Coast cocoa beans *made in Belgium* or *made in the Ivory Coast*? Is espresso coffee made in the country in which the beans were roasted, ground, and steamed, or is it made in the country in which those beans were grown?

---

the United States, and Mexico has its own rules of origin, and such rules differ from commodity to commodity. In general, a product qualifies to enter duty free into any of the three NAFTA countries if its regional content (the percentage of its value that it acquired in any of the three countries) is at least 50 percent. For some goods, though, the maximum percentage of their value that can be outside of NAFTA is 7 percent.[24] Other free-trade agreements have their own rules of origin: the Canada-Chile Free Trade Agreement has its own rules, and so does the European Union in those agreements designed to provide EU market access to developing countries.[25] Because there are over 300 free-trade agreements worldwide, most of which have their own rules of origin, a uniform system is sorely needed.[26]

16.1.4 Tariffs

An importing country usually manages its imports under an n-column tariff system, with n, the number of columns, corresponding to the number of different classes of countries that the importing country considers. The tariff rates are the same for all of the countries in a given class. Most tariff schedules are known as two-, three-, or four-column schedules. For example, the United States operates under a two-column tariff schedule, with the countries with which the United States has normal trade relations (NTR) subject to Column 1 tariffs, and others to Column 2 tariffs. In 2000, what had been the "most favored nation" (MFN) designation was officially changed to the NTR classification.

tariff schedule
A document listing all the possible Harmonized System categories and their associated duty rates for different countries.

However, the number of columns is often quite an oversimplification of the actual tariff system. Because the number and complexity of multilateral trade agreements has increased, this terminology can sometimes be confusing, as there can be many more than n classes. Nevertheless, the terminology has remained.

For the United States, there are only two trading partners that do not have NTR status, both of which are, at best, minor trading partners: Cuba and North Korea.[27] However, among the NTRs, there are trading partners with which the United States has free-trade relations (Canada, Mexico, Israel, Chile, Colombia, Jordan, Korea, Singapore, Australia, New Zealand, as well as all Caribbean countries, all Central American countries, and all sub-Saharan African countries), and several that have a special status on specific products. Add to these several bilateral agreements on specific products, and the system is much more than a two-column system. Therefore, in the United States, the first column is actually split into two sub-columns, one labeled "General" for all NTR countries, and the other "Special" for all countries for which, for a given HS number, there is a special negotiated rate.

The United States also grants most developing countries duty-free access to the U.S. market under the Generalized System of Preference (GSP).[28] However, the GSP is a piece of legislation that has become a source of political disagreements in the United States. As of this writing, it is set to expire in July 2013, and although there is no indication that it will not be renewed, it may be changed to exclude the countries that have made much economic progress—such as Brazil, India, and Thailand—but maintained for countries that are less developed.[29]

Figure 16.1[30] shows the layout of the Tariff Schedule of the United States, with a total of 21 special tariffs. (Only three are not present in the table: the codes **C** for the Agreement on Trade in Civil Aircraft, **K** for the Agreement on Trade in Pharmaceutical Products, and **L** for the Uruguay Round Concessions on Intermediate Chemicals and Dyes.) Each product category has its own negotiated specific treatment, and the Harmonized Tariff Schedule of the United States is replete with exceptions of this nature.

Tariffs are generally calculated *ad valorem* or as a percentage tax on the value of the goods imported. Nevertheless, other methods exist, such as a fixed amount

***ad valorem* duty rate**
A duty rate based on the value of the imported item.

Harmonized Tariff Schedule of the United States (2013) (Rev. 1)
Annotated for Statistical Reporting Purposes

XVIII

Heading / Subheading	Stat. Suf- fix	Article Description	Unit of Quantity	Rates of Duty General	Rates of Duty Special	2
9114		Other clock or watch parts:				
9114.10		Springs, including hairsprings:				
9114.10.40	00	For watches............................	No.	7.3%	Free (A+, AU, BH, CA, CL, CO, D, E, IL, J, J+, JO, KR, MA, MX, OM, P, PA, PE, R, SG)	65%
9114.10.80	00	Other...................................	No.	4.2%	Free (A+, AU, B, BH, CA, CL, CO, D, E, IL, J, JO, KR, MA, MX, OM, P, PE, SG)	65%
9114.20.00	00	Jewels.................................	No.	Free	Free (A+, AU, B, BH, CA, CL, CO, D, E, IL, J+, JO, KR, MA, MX, OM, P, PE, R, SG)	10%
9114.30	00	Dials:				
9114.30.40	00	Not exceeding 50 mm in width...............	No..	0.4¢ each + 7.2%		5¢ each + 45%
9114.30.80	00	Exceeding 50 mm in width.................	No.	4.4%	Free (A+, AU, B, BH, CA, CL, CO, D, E, IL, J+, JO, KR, MA, MX, OM, P, PE, R, SG)	50%
9114.40		Plates and bridges:				
9114.40.20	00	Watch movement bottom or pillar plates or their equivalent..............	No.	12¢ each	Free (A+, AU, BH, CA, CL, CO, D, E, IL, J, J+, JO, KR, MA, MX, OM, P, PE, R) 3¢ each (SG)	75¢ each
9114.40.40	00	Any plate, or set of plates, suitable for assembling thereon a clock movement.................	No.	10¢ each	Free (A+, AU, B, BH, CA, CL, D, E, IL, J, J+, JO, MA, MX, OM, P, PE, R, SG)	38¢ each
9114.40.60	00	Other: For watches...........................	X	7.3%	Free (A+,AU, BH, CA, CL, D, E, IL, J, J+, JO, MA, MX, OM, P, PE, SG)	65%
9114.40.80	00	Other.................................	X	4.2%	Free (A+,AU, B, BH, CA, CL, D, E, IL, J, JO, MA, MX, OM, P, PE, SG)	65%
		.../...				

Legend:

A+: Generalized System of Preference
AU: United States – Australia Free Trade Agreement
B: Automotive Product Trade Act
BH: Bahrain Free Trade Agreement
CA: NAFTA Agreement with Canada
CO: United States – Colombia Free Trade Agreement
CL: United States Chile Free Trade Agreement
D: African Growth and Opportunity Act
E: Caribbean Basin Economic Recovery Act
IL: United States – Israel Free Trade Area
J: Andean Trade Preference Act
J+: Andean Drug Eradication Act
JO: United States – Jordan Free Trade Area Implementation Act
KR: United States – Korea Free Trade Agreement
MA: United States- Morocco Freee Trade Agreement
MX: NAFTA Agreement with Mexico
OM: Oman Free Tree Agreement
P: Dominican Republic – Central America US Free Trade Agreement
PE: Peru Free Trade Agreement
R: United States - Carribean Basin trade Partnership Act
SG: United States – Singapore Free Trade Agreement

Figure 16.1: United States Tariff Schedule United States International Trade Commission.

per unit imported. Some others are calculated with a mixed system, such as a fixed amount per unit in addition to a percentage of the value of the goods imported; such a tariff is called a compound duty rate. Figure 16.1 illustrates all these alternatives:

compound duty rate A duty rate based on a combination of value, number, or some other measurement of the imported item (weight, dimensions,...).

- A company importing springs for watches (9114.10.4000) would have to pay 7.3 percent duty on the FCA value of the goods if they came from an NTR country—for example, Japan. If the springs came from one of the eighteen different countries for which imports would be duty-free, such as India (Generalized System of Preference), Australia (U.S.-Australia Free Trade Agreement), Canada (NAFTA), Haiti (Caribbean Basin Initiative), Israel (U.S.-Israel Free Trade Agreement), Peru (U.S.-Peru Trade Promotion Agreement Implementation Act), or Mexico (NAFTA), the importer would have no duty to pay. If the springs came from D.P.R. Korea, the duty rate would be 65 percent.

- A company importing small watch movement bottoms (9114.40.2000) from an NTR country, such as Germany, would have to pay U.S.$ 0.12 per movement, regardless of the FCA value of the movements. The same product coming from some other countries could be imported duty free, while the importer would have to pay $ 0.03 per movement if the shipment came from Singapore. An importer obtaining the bottoms from Cuba would be saddled with a U.S.$ 0.75 duty per movement.

The complexity of the tariff rate schedule in most countries is baffling, and the level of detail that is imparted to the rates of duty is simply impossible to justify. Figure 16.1 shows that the U.S. duty rate for watch springs (classified as 9114.10.4000) is reduced from 7.3 percent to zero if the country of export is in the Caribbean [code R] or in sub-Saharan Africa [code D]. However, for other clock parts (items classified as 9114.10.8000, and not springs, jewels, or plates), those coming from the Caribbean country would have to pay the 7.3 percent duty rate, and the African country's products would be imported duty free. Similarly, it is hard to explain why dials smaller than 50 millimeters pay a compound duty rate of $0.004 per dial in addition to 7.2 percent duty, when those larger than 50 millimeters pay a duty of 4.4 percent. It is highly unlikely that it was the intent of the U.S. Congress to tax small dials at roughly twice the rate of the larger ones. Many other examples exist for this level of detail in the Harmonized Schedule of the United States and most countries. Such level of differentiation simply cannot be defended, and makes the work of international traders particularly complex.

Fortunately, this situation is likely to change, at least in the United States. Several importers of clothing products have filed lawsuits against the U.S. government, accusing it of engaging in gender discrimination. The companies are fighting the fact that bathing suits are taxed at 28 percent for men and 12 percent for women, that overalls are taxed at 9 percent for men and 14 percent for women, and that wool shirts are taxed at 18 percent for men and less than 9 percent for women.[31] The first complainant to file a lawsuit was Totes-Isotoner, an importer of gloves, which charged that the government was discriminating by charging 14 percent duty for men's gloves and 12.6 percent for "other persons." In July 2008, Totes-Isotoner's lawsuit was dismissed by the Court of International Trade. The court notified Isotoner that it needed to "allege that the government has engaged in gender-based discrimination without an exceedingly persuasive justification" in order to get relief. The court dismissed the lawsuit without prejudice, which allowed Totes-Isotoner to re-file. In May 2010, the Court ruled against the company.[32] A similar lawsuit was filed, and lost, by Forever 21, an apparel chain. The February 2012 decision stated that the company needed to "connect the tariff provisions and congressional action in a way to suggest with plausibility the existence of a governmental intent to discriminate."[33] In May 2013, Ann Taylor, another apparel company, filed a lawsuit alleging discrimination on a gender basis.[34] It is likely that these efforts will eventually lead to a reduction in the number of tariffs and classification alternatives.

Web Exercise

Some countries can have very unique ways of determining tariffs. Switzerland's tariff schedule stands out in that most of its tariffs are based on the gross weight of the goods imported (per 100 kilograms) rather than their value,[35] even for products such as computers or textiles. Most countries' tariff schedules are now published electronically and can be accessed through the International Customs Tariff Bureau's website:

http://www.bitd.org/Search.aspx

Find two (simple) products with which you are familiar, and calculate what the tariff would be for these two products if they were exported from Kenya and imported into the United States, the European Union, Switzerland, and India.

16.1.5 Dumping

In some cases, Customs can determine that the invoice value is lower (in some rare cases, higher) than the actual value of the goods. This is generally uncovered by comparing the value of a given invoice with a database of import entries with the same Harmonized System number made in preceding year(s). For example, in the United States, the invoice value is systematically compared to existing valuations. This is one of the purposes of the column labeled "unit of quantity" in Figure 16.1 that represents the units under which the Customs computer database keeps the values of other entries under a specific HS number to determine whether a given entry is within the bounds of "normal." Should the invoice give a value outside of these bounds, a Customs import specialist will scrutinize the entry before liquidating it.

dumping
A strategy, followed by some exporters, that consists of selling the goods at a price considered "too low" by the importing country's Customs authorities.

When the invoice's value is much below what Customs has historically accepted and when a much higher valuation is reached with one of the alternative valuation methods (see Section 16.1.2), Customs can determine that the exporter is dumping the goods in the importing country (*i.e.*, selling the goods at a price that is below their commercial value). The exact definition of "dumping" varies from country to country, but the most prevalent definition is that a price is set below the wholesale price of the goods in the exporting country and that this causes injury to competitors (or some other group, such as a labor union) located in the importing country. For some countries, such as the United States, there must be a complaint from an injured party before Customs considers that the under-valuation is a case of dumping. In addition, an organization independent of Customs—in the United States, the International Trade Commission—is asked to determine whether there is actual injury to competitors and to ascertain whether the goods are sold below their commercial value before an exporter is found guilty of dumping.

In those cases, Customs can add an additional duty to the regular duty rate of the commodity, and this duty rate is called an anti-dumping duty, which can range from 1 percent to several times the value of the goods imported. Unfortunately, dumping accusations have been one of the most commonly used tools of certain countries to restrict imports, and it is still one of the most commonly used methods of protectionism. In addition, Customs can use a countervailing duty to tax products that the exporting government is found to have subsidized. In that case again, it will only act after an allegation of injury by an affected competitor. However, although there is strong support for such countervailing duties in some industries, the U.S. Commerce Department has declined to impose them on products coming from countries in which non-market economies prevail.

In the United States, there was a rash of anti-dumping duty requests in the early and mid-2000s, due to the Byrd Amendment, named for Senator Robert Byrd of West Virginia. The Byrd Amendment directed Customs to give the anti-dumping duty it collected from importers to the U.S. companies that were harmed by the dumping. In 2003, U.S. Customs and Border Protection distributed U.S.$ 190 million to U.S. companies, U.S.$ 885 million in 2004, and an estimated U.S.$ 3.85 billion after 2005.[36] The Timken Company, one of the largest beneficiaries of the Byrd Amendment, reported anti-dumping income of U.S.$ 66 million in 2003, which was an amount equal to 67 percent of its operating income of $ 98 million.[37] Although the WTO ruled against the Byrd Amendment by finding that it violated the rules of international trade in August 2004,[38] the U.S. Congress did not repeal the amendment until October 2007.

16.1.6 Other Taxes

In addition to duties, several countries will assess additional taxes based on the value of the goods; these additional taxes are a disguised way of creating additional revenues from imports while remaining within the boundaries of the General Agreement on Tariffs and Trade (GATT) and the rules of the WTO, which mandate systematic reductions in tariffs.

Such additional taxes can be labeled very creatively:

- **Punitive duty.** The United States, unhappy about a decision by the European Union to give preferential treatment to bananas imported from former European colonies in the Caribbean and Africa, retaliated by placing a 100 percent duty on certain items coming from any of the 15 EU countries: cashmere, blue cheese, "handbags covered in plastic sheeting," and so on.[39]

- **Border traffic tax.** Russia, in order to "make a more accurate tally of border flows of people, cargo, and means of transportation," imposes a 1 percent tax on all goods crossing its borders. Russian travelers are taxed at 0.8 percent of their monthly income.[40]

- **Safeguard tax.** Argentina, after being chastised by the WTO for having increased its duty rate on footwear, reduced them, then immediately re-imposed them through an emergency "safeguard tax" designed to protect its footwear industry against foreign competition, a method it has used many times since.[41]

- **Temporary protection tax.** The United States imposed a 33 percent additional tariff on brooms from Mexico to allow U.S. manufacturers to increase their efficiency so that they could compete against imports. It repealed this tax two years later, noting that the industry had not taken advantage of this protection period to improve its efficiency.[42] As of 2013, the United States was still subjecting brooms to a tariff-rate quota (see Section 16.2.1).[43]

These taxes are designed to increase revenues for the importing country, protect less efficient domestic industries, and punish importers, while respecting the letter—but certainly not the intent—of WTO agreements.

16.1.7 Value-Added Tax

value-added tax
A tax collected by many countries that is very similar to a sales tax, but is based on the increase in the value of the product at each step of the manufacturing process.

In some countries, an additional tax is collected in addition to the duty, but is generally considered to have no bearing on importers—even if it adds up to a significant amount—because it is collected from domestic producers as well as from importers, and is eventually paid by only consumers: the Value-Added Tax (VAT). The idea of VAT is somewhat simple in its concept: the tax is collected on the value added by each firm involved in adding value to a good, from the first one in the production chain to the last one. The implementation of a VAT is somewhat complex, though.

It is probably best to explain the VAT concept and its implementation—as it is practiced in the European Union countries, at least—with a simplified example:

1. A farmer purchases seeds, fertilizer, pesticides, and fuel to produce corn. On each of her production-related purchases, she pays the VAT. She keeps track of the VAT she has paid in a special bookkeeping account, as a debit. She then sells the corn she has produced and collects VAT from her customer, which she records in that account as a credit. At the end of the quarter, she deducts the VAT she has paid from the VAT she has collected, and sends the difference to her government.

2. The corn is purchased by a mill that promptly transforms it into several products, including corn syrup. On all the products it sells to wholesalers and retailers, the mill collects VAT, an amount it records in a special bookkeeping account. At the end of the quarter, the mill deducts all the VAT it has paid to farmers for corn and all the VAT it has paid for its other purchases from the VAT it has collected from its customers and sends the difference to its government.

3. The corn syrup is purchased by a consumer who uses it for cooking. The consumer pays the VAT, but has no way to collect any, so it is the consumer who bears the tax's entire burden.

For imports, the concept is the same. The VAT is collected from the importer, but the importer can deduct the value of the VAT it has paid from the VAT it eventually collects from its customers; therefore, the tax is not an actual cost to the importer. However, this is somewhat incorrect: in reality, there are substantial accounting and cash-flow costs associated with this method of garnering taxes. Nevertheless, because both domestic and imported products are taxed the same way, there are no advantages garnered by either in their final costs to the consumer. The cost is quite a substantial one for the ultimate consumer, though, as the VAT rate in the European Union is approximately 20 percent.

In the E.U., the VAT is computed on the sum of the value of the imported goods and the duty levied at importation.

16.2 Non-Tariff Barriers

Some countries use high tariffs to attempt to limit the import of certain goods. However, steady pressure from the General Agreement on Tariffs and Trade, and now the World Trade Organization, has reduced considerably the duty paid by most goods in most countries. While there are still some exceptions, the trend is still toward ever-lower duty rates, with many countries having adopted tariffs that are rarely above 10 percent for most goods.

At the same time, the WTO has also been very active in attempting to decrease the number of non-tariff trade barriers that countries can place on imports. Nevertheless, several of those alternatives are still in place, which effectively limit exporters' access to certain markets. Non-tariff trade barriers are those policies and actions that have the effect of reducing the number of items imported in a specific country. Often, not surprisingly, what is perceived as a trade barrier by an international trader is presented as an innocuous requirement by the importing country's government.

16.2.1 Quotas

The primary method used by countries to limit imports is a system of quotas, which limit the quantity of goods that can enter a particular country. A quota can take either of two forms:

- **An absolute quota**, which places a yearly limit on the number of items entering a country under a specific Harmonized-System (HS) number. On occasion, the quota can be implemented using the value of the goods imported by placing a ceiling on the total value of goods imported under a specific HS number. Once the quota is reached, goods in that category can no longer be imported. Some countries, whose products are subject to quotas, have established a system of visas to monitor how much of a given quota has been filled by its exporters (see Section 16.3.7).

- **A tariff-rate quota**, which places a two-tiered tariff rate on a specific category of products. Until a specific number of goods are entered, the tariff is low, but once the quota is reached, the tariff changes to a much higher percentage. Nevertheless, the goods can still be legally imported.

quota A limit, set by the importing country's government, on the quantity of a commodity that can be imported in a given year.

Quotas are usually placed on very specific items coming from a specific country of origin. As of 2013, the United States no longer has absolute quotas, but it did until January 1, 2009. Until then, a complex system of quotas for textiles and apparel was followed by the United States and other developed countries for products originating in some developing countries, which was outlined in an international treaty called the Multi-Fiber Agreement (MFA). Those quotas restricted the number of textile items imported from a large number of developing countries. The WTO negotiated the Agreement on Textiles and Clothing to eliminate these quotas, and all developed countries' textile quotas were supposed to have been lifted by January 1, 2005. However, practical considerations made the United States and China negotiate three one-year agreements under which there was a limit on the number of certain textile items exported from China into the United States, called the "safeguard quotas."[44] This had been anticipated, should the elimination of quotas be harmful to the economies of the importing countries. However, the elimination of quotas was particularly harmful to the developing countries that were competing with China. Under the MFA quota system, many countries gained access to the large markets of Europe and the United States because Chinese firms were limited in the number of products they could sell. After the quotas were lifted, the Chinese firms, being the world's chief low-cost producers of textile apparel and having seemingly unlimited capacity, displaced these other countries' products and created economic hardship there.

The Sugar Quota

The United States has had a tariff-rate quota on sugar for many years. The total amount of raw sugar that could be imported in 2012 at the low tariff rate of U.S.$ 0.01406 per kilogram is 1,116,498 metric tonnes,[45] and any amount above that is charged U.S.$ 0.3574 per kilogram.[46] The world market price for sugar fluctuates between U.S.$ 0.25 and U.S.$ 0.60 per kilogram,[47] so the tariff can double the cost of sugar for U.S. importers.

A number of powerful groups of sugar producers in the United States are vocal supporters of this tariff-rate quota and are substantial financial backers of both political parties, so it has never been abolished, even though the WTO has ruled against it.

Under this tariff-rate quota system, each producing country is allocated a given portion of the quota; in 2012, for example, India's share of the quota is 13,063 metric tonnes, and Brazil, the world's largest producer, is allowed 236,770 tonnes.[48] These quotas are very low. Consider that a Handysize ship can hold 35,000 tonnes. Essentially, the largest producer of sugar in the world (38,600,000 metric tonnes)[49] can ship only about seven small boatloads of sugar (0.6 percent of its production) to the fourth largest market in the world, which has an annual consumption of 10,342,000 metric tonnes.[50] Brazilian sugar imports represent therefore about 1.9 percent of the total U.S. consumption. India, the second largest producer of sugar in the world at 27,430,000 tonnes, can only export about one third of a Handysize ship, representing 0.04 percent of its production and 0.13 percent of the total U.S. market. The Indian share represents less than half of what the U.S. consumes in a day.

The quota has an impact on the sugar market in the United States. Although consumers are largely unaffected by the high price of sugar because it represents a small portion of people's expenses, the overall market size is much smaller than it would be if there were no sugar quota; many industrial users of sugar have substituted corn syrup (soft drink manufacturers) or moved abroad (candy manufacturers are producing in Mexico and Canada to ship to the U.S. market) to circumvent the artificially high cost of sugar. This restriction also distorts the export market for American products: Mexico has a retaliatory 20 percent tax on soft drinks made with corn syrup, for example.[51]

However, the impact of the sugar quota is greatest on the economies of the Caribbean and Central American countries that cannot export one of their largest agricultural crops to the United States. Table 16.1 shows the

---

*The quotas for Haiti were 0 for 2010, 2011, and 2012. In 2009, Haiti had been allowed to export 7,258 tonnes

quota allocations for these countries. Note the disparities between the quotas of Haiti* and the Dominican Republic, which have about the same size population; whether it is a cause or a consequence, the gross domestic product of the Dominican Republic is roughly seven times that of Haiti.[52]

A possible move to sugar-based ethanol as a substitute for gasoline in automobile engines, which is common in Brazil, may change this situation, as the United States would need to import much larger quantities of sugar; however, as of July 2013, there were no signs that ending the quota was even being considered.

Selected Sugar Quota Quantities in metric tonnes

Country	Quota
Argentina	70,215
Barbados	11,430
Belize	17,962
Brazil	236,770
Costa Rica	24,493
Dominican Republic	218,908
El Salvador	42,455
Haiti	0
India	13,063
Jamaica	4,000
Panama	47,354

Table 16.1: Selected Sugar Quota Allocations (in tonnes)
United States Customs and Border Protection.

The United States has retained a fairly large number of tariff-rate quotas on milk, cream, dried milk, cheddar cheese, ice cream, peanuts, cocoa powder, sugar, and a substantial number of other products, that apply to all countries of origin.[53]

Quotas can also be "voluntary." Under pressure from the importing government, exporters agree to limit their exports "voluntarily" to a certain quantity. Such was the case during the early 1980s in the United States when Japanese automobile manufacturers agreed to absolute quotas for automobiles and light trucks.

Finally, quotas can come in the form of export quotas, when an exporting country limits the quantity of a certain type of good that firms can export from its territory (see Chapter 9).

16.2.2 Adherence to National Standards

Unfortunately, quotas are hardly the only non-tariff trade barriers placed by countries to restrict imports. In many instances, countries enact "safety measures" designed to ostensibly protect their populations from defective, dangerous, or unhealthy products from abroad. While most of these restrictions are justified and necessary, some of them are based on dubious data and are simply a form of undisguised protectionism for less efficient domestic producers.

Countries certainly can demand that products sold within their borders meet the standards that their governments have enacted—for example, there are many requirements regarding the quality of consumer products in developed countries. The most prominent ones are the *Deutsche Industrie Normen* (DIN) in Germany, the Japanese Industry Standards (JIS) in Japan, the *Normes Françaises* (NF) in France, and the American National Standard Institute (ANSI) in the United States. A few international standards exist as well, such as those defined by the International Organization for Standardization in its ISO set of requirements. Most of these requirements are legitimate in that they reflect national preferences and sentiment toward consumer protection, health standards, and safety. For example, the European Union requires that vehicles be equipped with rear turn signals that are distinct from the brake lights, and the United States requires that automobiles be equipped with airbags. Both are obviously worthy requirements.

The point at which these requirements become non-tariff barriers is unclear. An exporter is often unwilling to incorporate into its products an additional feature that is costly or that it deems unnecessary, and claims that the requirement is a non-tariff barrier, when it may just be an unwillingness to deal with one of the differences and difficulties of selling a product in a foreign country.[54] In a parallel fashion, such a requirement may not be a non-tariff barrier, even if it is required only of imported products and not of domestic manufacturers, if it is to protect a country from importing a disease that has not yet been observed domestically. Such was the case when non-European countries tried to protect themselves against the threat of mad-cow disease.

Nevertheless, countries' efforts to make imports adhere to national standards are often considered to be trade barriers. There have been lengthy spats over the safety of Mexican avocados in the United States,[55] of U.S. cherries in Mexico,[56] of New Zealand apples in Japan,[57] and of U.S. hormone-treated beef[58] and genetically-modified cereals[59] in the European Union. The dispute with Japan over the safety of U.S. tomatoes lasted 46 years before being resolved in favor of U.S. exporters.[60]

Banana Wars

In 1993, the European Union, in an effort to support the economies of some of its members' former colonies in the Caribbean and Africa, devised a complex system of quotas, preferential tariffs, and import licenses to favor bananas imported from these countries. Even though it is not an exporter of bananas, the United States got tangled in this dispute because two of the companies that were affected by these restrictions were Dole Foods and Chiquita Brands, two American firms exporting bananas grown in Central America to Europe.[61]

Even after three rulings against this practice by the WTO, the European Union still maintained this convoluted system of preferential treatment, and the United States eventually retaliated with higher tariffs on products from Europe. The "banana wars" escalated to a point where it involved the highest levels of government, and it took years to be resolved, despite the efforts of WTO panels to ease the tension and resolve the issue.[62]

16.2 Non-Tariff Barriers

In early 2001, Chiquita Brands took the unusual step of suing the European Union for U.S.$ 525 million, which the company claims were the lost profits the company had incurred because of the restrictions and which caused it to default on its bond payments.[63]

The spat between the United States and the European Union is now over, and European consumers end up paying slightly less for bananas today than they did when the trade barrier was in place. However, there are still conflicts between the European Union and some of the countries in which the bananas are produced; in 2012, the WTO ruled in favor of Ecuador in a dispute that alleged that the European Union's trade policies favored Caribbean and African producers of bananas.[64]

16.2.3 Other Non-tariff Barriers

Countries have enacted some very creative means to slow or restrict imports without having recourse to high tariffs, quotas, or standardization requirements. Here are several examples, which certainly do not constitute an exhaustive list:

- In the very early 1980s, France decided that it needed to protect its nascent industry in videocassette recorders (VCRs). It achieved this goal by requiring that every VCR entering the country be inspected, that a sticker be placed on every machine, and that the inspection take place in Poitiers, a landlocked small town about 250 miles from the port of Le Havre, through which most VCRs were shipped. Moreover, the inspection station was a one-man operation.[65] Countless countries have enacted similar "slow" Customs clearance processes, in order to deter imports by increasing costs to importers for additional storage, and creating potential marketing delays.

- Another tactic is to require a mind-numbing number of documents and approvals. For example, in the late 1990s, in India, "an exporter has to complete and process fifty-four documents [...]: twenty-seven pre-shipment documents, fourteen for Customs clearance, and thirteen for post-shipment realization of bills. As many as 16 approvals are needed from departments of the central government."[66] The process has been largely simplified since: as of 2013, there were eleven documents necessary to import in India, which is still twice the number of the average for countries that are members of the Organisation for Economic Co-operation and Development (OECD).[67]

- Another way to slow Customs entries is to request additional papers that are not readily available or that are close to impossible to gather. The United States requests the "sewing tickets" for some garments, an internal work document of the garment factory, as well as the time cards of the employees working there, in an attempt to determine the country of origin of textile products.[68]

- Republic of Korea has been tremendously effective at keeping foreign cars out of its domestic market. In 2012, there were 1,260,000 Korean-made automobiles sold on the U.S. market, but fewer than 10,000 U.S.-made automobiles sold in Korea, and only 130,858 foreign-made cars.[69] This was achieved, despite relatively low tariffs of 8 percent, with a systematic campaign designed to portray the purchase of a foreign car as unpatriotic. To bolster this perception, the government of the Republic of Korea has all but threatened all purchasers of foreign cars with an income tax audit.[70]

- Russia asked the U.S. exporters of chicken parts (legs and wings) to individually inspect every bird for specific diseases before they can enter the country, effectively preventing all U.S. imports of such parts.[71]

16.2.4 Pre-shipment Inspections

pre-shipment inspection The inspection, conducted by an independent company, that allows the determination that the goods conform to the description contained in the exporter's invoice.

Pre-shipment inspections (PSIs) are performed by independent companies at the point of departure of goods destined to be exported. The firm determines that the goods shipped are the ones ordered by the importer, in the correct quantity, and sufficiently well packed for an international shipment. When the independent firm has ascertained that all of these aspects conform to the invoice, it issues a Certificate of Inspection (see Chapter 9) to the importer. Inspection companies have representatives in most ports and generally can handle just about any sort of shipment; on many occasions, though, the exporter experiences delays with PSIs as the workload of inspectors can be substantial, and as the expertise needed for a specific shipment may not be available.

Pre-shipment inspections are sometimes requested by importers to ensure that exporters are shipping the correct product in the correct quantity; they are used when the importer is purchasing on a cash-in-advance basis or on a letter of credit. However, most PSIs are required by countries as part of their import process. There are several reasons for this requirement:

- The country wants an expert opinion on the classification and the value of the products that are about to enter its territory.

- The country wants to fight corruption in its own ports of entry. By having a foreign, independent firm determine the classification and value of imported goods, its own Customs authorities have lost the ability to change their classifications and valuations for a bribe. Such was the motivation when Indonesia demanded that any good shipped into Indonesia had to be pre-inspected by the Société Générale de Surveillance.[72]

- The country wants an estimate of the currency requirements it will face in the short term, and uses the value of the shipments, as determined by the PSIs, to forecast its foreign currency needs.

- The country wants to generate some revenues in addition to the tariff it charges. Most of the countries requiring PSIs have long-term contracts giving an exclusive right to a single inspection company to inspect all of the goods about to enter its territory. Although it is pure speculation, it is likely that inspection companies compensate the country for this exclusive right by transferring a portion of the revenues generated by inspections to the national treasury.

16.3 Customs Clearing Process

The Customs clearing process differs from country to country and tends to be arcane and cumbersome. In most countries, because of the complexity of the task, only certified Customs brokers or Customs agents are allowed to file the paperwork necessary to clear Customs. This section will give only a brief overview of the processes generally followed by Customs authorities worldwide and give examples based upon the U.S. system.

16.3.1 General Process

In some countries, the process starts with an application for an import license, a request for the express authorization to import a certain product. Import licenses are usually granted according to a number of criteria, most of which are based on the availability of foreign currency to pay for the import and on the availability of domestic substitutes. Generally speaking, countries with scarce foreign currency resources will attempt to limit the granting of import licenses to those companies that have generated export revenues, and to those companies purchasing goods for which no close domestic substitute is available.

For most countries, however, the process starts when an importer files an entry (*i.e.*, notifies the Customs authorities that it will import—or has imported—a particular product). There is usually an electronic or paper form (see Figure 16.2 on page 443) that has to be filed and which must accompany all the documentation necessary for the import: invoice, Certificate of Origin, Certificate of Inspection (when required), Certificate of Insurance, and other forms as required by the Customs rules of the importing country.

In most developed countries, the importer is usually responsible for classifying the goods according to the tariff schedule of the importing country, and for determining the amount of duty. In many developing countries, this task is still left to the Customs authorities, a requirement which often delays the process of clearance. In most instances, the goods are not released to the importer (cleared) until after the duty is paid or after there is evidence from the importer that it will pay, a requirement often met with a Customs bond. Generally, Customs authorities will review a percentage of the entries made by importers after the goods have been cleared and will have a few months to a couple of years to challenge them. If an entry is reviewed satisfactorily, the entry is deemed liquidated. In some countries, such as the United States, an importer dissatisfied with the final decision of Customs authorities has a brief period of time to protest a liquidated entry and request a review before it is finally settled.

16.3.2 Customs Brokers

Because of the complexity and time-consuming nature of filling out Customs entries, many countries demand that importers delegate the task of interacting with Customs to a Customs broker, a representative of the importer that has acquired the knowledge and experience required to deal effectively and efficiently with Customs. In many countries, Customs brokers are the only entities qualified to enter goods (*i.e.*, fill out the paperwork necessary to import goods). It is not the case in the United States, though, where importers can complete their own entries, as long as they have posted a Customs bond (see Section 16.3.3). Customs brokers are usually compensated on a fee basis for each entry they handle. In the United States, Customs brokers are highly qualified individuals who have to take a grueling test on issues of classification, duty computation, and quotas before being allowed to manage importers' entries.

---

entry
The process by which an importer notifies Customs that it has imported a product.

cleared
The term used to indicate that the goods were imported in the country and that the importer paid the correct amount of duty.

liquidated entry
An entry that has been successfully reviewed by Customs authorities, and for which duty has been paid.

protest
A process by which an importer can file a grievance after an entry is liquidated, so that Customs reviews classification, valuation, and country of origin.

Customs broker
A person authorized by Customs authorities to file entries.

16.3.3 Customs Bonds

In most countries, the importer has to pay the duty to Customs before the shipment can be legally released. However, this can be extremely unwieldy, especially in those cases where the shipment is an express package or is time sensitive (*e.g.*, perishable produce). Therefore, Customs authorities allow importers (or Customs brokers entering goods on their behalf) to post a surety bond, which is a guarantee that the importer or the Customs broker will eventually pay the duty due. A bond is generally a sum of money deposited with Customs, from which any unpaid duty can be withdrawn, or an insurance policy with a surety company that acts as a guarantor of the importer or the Customs broker, and which it would be required to pay if the duty were not paid on time. This process allows goods to be entered before the duty is paid. In some cases, actually, the goods are sold long before the entry is liquidated.

In the United States, the bond is not just a guarantee that the duty will be paid on time; it is also a contract that obligates the importer or the Customs broker to perform all Customs-related functions in a timely manner, such as filing entries that are complete and accurate, as well as presenting Customs with the goods after they have physically entered the country, generally for inspection purposes.

Customs bond
A sum of money collected by Customs from Customs brokers, that is held as a guarantee that duty will be paid in the correct amount.

16.3.4 Reasonable Care

Out of the U.S. Customs Modification Act of 1993 came the concepts of informed compliance and reasonable care, neither of which can be easily defined, but which have become pivotal to the efforts of the Customs Service in the United States.

The idea behind informed compliance is that, if an importer has been trained in classifying and valuing goods for import purposes, it is more likely to perform these tasks correctly. If the importer has been found to exert reasonable care in the past, the likelihood that one of its shipments is going to be inspected is minimal, thereby minimizing delays at entry and allowing the importer to organize its supply chain more predictably. It also lowers costs, as merchandise is cleared quickly and does not languish in some bonded warehouse while the importer and Customs argue about its correct classification, valuation, or country of origin.

In order for an importer to be found compliant, it must show that it exercised reasonable care in the filing of its Customs entries. In order to demonstrate reasonable care, the importer must follow a long list of obligations that the U.S. Customs Service provides.[73] The obligations center on making sure that the importer employs a Customs specialist, who will make sure that all—including the most recent—Customs regulations are followed and that it has put into place a process by which it correctly determines the valuation, classification, and country of origin of an import. Reasonable care is monitored through a system of compliance audits organized by U.S. Customs.[74]

informed compliance
A standard of behavior, enforced by U.S. Customs, that is expected of importers if they want their entries to be cleared quickly and inspections kept to a minimum.

reasonable care
A standard of behavior, enforced by U.S. Customs, that is expected of importers if they want their entries to be cleared quickly and inspections kept to a minimum.

16.3 Customs Clearing Process

Figure 16.2: Canadian Import Form for Food Products. Canadian Food Inspection Agency.

16.3.5 Required Documentation

The documentation required by any Customs authority can be extensive. Ideally speaking, there should be only three documents required in every country to make an entry:

- A form designated for entry (specific to the record-keeping requirements of the importing country)

- A Certificate of Origin to ascertain the country of origin

- A commercial invoice with enough information to determine value and classification

However, many more can be included, from an import license to a series of certificates or other documents (most of these documents were introduced and explained in Chapter 9). Many countries' requirements are available on the web; a good number of them can be accessed through the export.gov website, maintained by the U.S. Department of Commerce's International Trade Administration.[75]

The critical element of import documentation is that it is established on a per-transaction basis. Every import, however small, needs to have its own specific entry, which can lead to an inordinate amount of paperwork, under which both the importer and the Customs authorities are drowning.

16.3.6 Required Markings

Products imported into a country often require a marking—*made in [country]* or *product of [country]*—printed or affixed on the product itself or its packaging. Rules differ from country to country on the location of the marking, its size, and whether it needs to be permanently attached to the product. The determination of the country placed on the marking is also left to the country of importation. However, there are no known instances of a country on the marking being different from the country of origin for Customs duty purposes.

In the United States, markings are required for most products, although there is a list of exceptions, maintained by the U.S. Customs Office, mostly products on which it is difficult or impossible to place a marking. All markings must be legible, conspicuous, and durable. However, the United States has an additional, unusual requirement. No product imported into the United States can have a name or package such that it may mislead the public as to its country of origin. It is therefore prohibited to include words such as "American," "United States," or "U.S.A." on the package that may lead consumers into thinking that the product is of U.S. origin. Inappropriate or missing markings are subject to penalties, liquidated damages, and seizures by U.S. Customs.

Finally, there is the issue of the *made in the USA* label, which is often a marketing advantage for U.S. companies in the U.S. market. Although the Federal Trade Commission considered lowering the minimum United States content to 75 percent of a product's value, it has maintained this content at "all or virtually all" of a product for the foreseeable future, making it all but impossible to mark a product as made in the United States unless it is entirely domestically produced.[76]

16.3.7 Merchandise Visas

For those products whose importation is limited by quotas, and particularly for textile products, a bilateral monitoring system is sometimes implemented by the importing and exporting countries.

Because there is a maximum quantity of goods that can be imported into a given country in a calendar year, the government of the country of export will grant the right to export a set quantity of a specific good to the country that maintains the import quota. Such authorization is a merchandise visa. The exporting country's government can grant the export visa through a lottery, through a determination made upon prior sales, or simply sell the export visa to an exporting firm. The visa specifies the type of good (by Harmonized System number), the quantity, and the destination country to which the exporter is allowed to sell.

For products for which such a system is in place, the visa is one of the required documents that must be presented to the Customs authorities of the importing countries, and often to the Customs authorities of the exporting country as well. As quotas are slowly eliminated, so should be the visa requirements. Nevertheless, although merchandise visas were once predicted to become obsolete, they have not disappeared, and they are often required as part of the documentation package for a given import.

merchandise visa
A document, provided by the exporting country, that allows an exporter to ship goods subject to a quota in the importing country.

16.3.8 Duty Drawbacks

Several countries, including the United States, grant a substantial tax break to exporters who are using imported parts in the products they export. Such a tax break is called a duty drawback.

In the United States, the Customs Service will refund 99 percent of the duty paid by an importer in one of three cases:

- For merchandise that is rejected by the importer as non-conforming to the original purchase order

- For imported products that are re-exported unused

- For imported parts that are used—without substantial transformation—in the assembly or manufacturing of products that are eventually re-exported

duty drawback
A process by which an exporter can be reimbursed for duty that it paid on products that it imported but which products it eventually exported.

Note that this duty drawback is not available for products exported to NAFTA countries.

This drawback can represent a considerable savings in many cases. However, few U.S. firms take advantage of this duty drawback opportunity, either because they do not know about it or because they fear the paperwork requirements that accompany this program. Actually, the paperwork requirements used to be mind-boggling: for example, in order to take advantage of the "unused" drawback, Customs required importers to track individual items from their import to their leaving the country. However, the requirements have been relaxed, allowing "commercially interchangeable goods" to qualify as exports for the drawback.[77] In exchange for this flexibility, Customs has substantially stiffened penalties for illegitimate drawbacks.

Duty drawbacks can be used by some countries to bolster exports. Historically, Korea and Taiwan region supported their exporters by allowing them to engage in aggressive duty drawbacks, for example.[78] In other cases, countries have been accused to use drawbacks to engage in protectionism. Since exporters using imported goods get reimbursed for the duty that they pay upon importing them, the tariff rates can be high, and the companies do not complain. However, these high duty rates prevent other importers, who would sell the goods in the country, from being competitive.[79]

16.4 Foreign Trade Zones

Foreign Trade Zones (FTZs) are specific locations of a country that have acquired a special Customs status. Foreign Trade Zones—sometimes called Free Trade Zones—are areas of a country that, for Customs purposes, still are located "outside" of a country. Practically, that means that goods can be shipped to the FTZ without being subject to the duties, quotas, and Customs regulations of the host country. In most countries, however, including the United States, goods admitted into an FTZ must be legal in the country in which the zone is located; the exemption applies only to Customs purposes, not to other legal requirements. For example, medical devices not yet approved in the country in which the FTZ is located would not be acceptable in that FTZ, even though the devices may be perfectly legal in other countries.

Once in the FTZ, the goods can be warehoused until they are sent to their final destination, either in the host or in a foreign country. If the goods are sold in the host country, they are dutiable only at the time of that transaction. If they are sold abroad, they are dutiable only in the importing country; the country in which the FTZ is located will never collect any duty on the value of that merchandise. The country of origin used for Customs purposes remains the country from which the goods originated, and not the country in which the FTZ is located.

Foreign Trade Zones exist in one form or another in just about every country. The most common form of FTZ is a location through which cargo transits. For example, most of the ports of the world are FTZs, so that cargo can be unloaded from a ship, temporarily stored in a warehouse, and then loaded onto another vessel to its final destination. Such cargo, although physically present in the country in which the port is located, never enters the country from a Customs' Office perspective, and is therefore never assessed duty. Because shipping companies are moving toward a system of very large containerships serving very large hub ports, from which smaller, so-called feeder ships are serving smaller ports, the importance of FTZs is expected to increase. Airports, which often operate on the same concept of "hub and spoke," also often possess a few warehouses in an FTZ. Because such FTZs are available to all companies involved in international trade, the United States calls them General Purpose (Foreign Trade) Zones.

Foreign Trade Zones

Another type of FTZ is not located in a port or cargo area, but at the place of business of a corporation, such as a plant or a refinery. In most of these types of trade zones, some economic activity beyond simple warehousing is conducted, such as manufacturing, assembly, repackaging, and refining. The FTZ is created with the purpose of creating jobs in the host country by providing a lower cost structure to the businesses using them, because they do not have to pay duty on the goods that they are processing and eventually

16.4 Foreign Trade Zones

re-exporting.

Another way a business can save money by obtaining FTZ status is when the host country has an "inverted" tariff structure (*i.e.*, the tariffs charged on parts are higher than the tariffs charged on the final product). Such FTZ locations are called "subzones" in the United States, affiliated for legal purposes with a General Purpose Foreign Trade Zone, because these locations are available to only one specific company and not to others.

An interesting issue arises when a substantial transformation takes place in an FTZ and the goods change from one Harmonized System (HS) classification to another. Even though the rules of origin call for the goods to be "made" in the country in which this change of HS number took place—the country in which the FTZ is located, in this case—negotiations between Customs and the company determine the country of origin that will be used for duty purposes, be it the country of origin of the parts used, or that of the main component, or yet some other alternative. In any case, it is never the country in which the change in HS took place.

Foreign Trade Zones can be quite advantageous to hold goods in inventory until they are sold, improving the cash flow of their owners, to wait for a numerical quota to open, or for an inspection by the host country's government. However, in view of the progress made in the last few years by the WTO to lead countries toward lower tariffs and increased trade, FTZs created for other purposes than cargo transfers may have a limited future because their advantages are dwindling.

Review and Discussion Questions

1. What is the concept of a Harmonized System number? How is it used? What are the advantages of such a system?

2. Explain the concept of valuation from the perspective of Customs. Why is it particularly important to have a detailed commercial invoice for valuation?

3. Explain the concept of classification from the perspective of Customs. Why is it particularly important to have a detailed commercial invoice for classification?

4. Explain the concept of country of origin. How is it currently determined? Why is it such a difficult concept? Why is it important?

5. What are non-tariff barriers? Why are they used? Give a few examples.

6. What types of quotas are there? How does the United States enforce the quotas it imposes? What is a merchandise visa?

Notes

[1] "Membership," World Customs Organization, http://www.wcoomd.org/en/about-us/wco-members/membership.aspx, retrieved March 11, 2013.

[2] "General Rules of Interpretation," *Harmonized Tariff Schedule of the United States (2013) (rev.1)*, United States International Trade Commission, Washington, District of Columbia.

[3] "Requirements for Electronic Ruling Requests," June 22, 2009, United States Customs and Border Protection, http://www.cbp.gov/xp/cgov/trade/legal/rulings/eRulingRequirements.xml, retrieved July 5, 2013.

[4] Lucentini, Jack, "Customs, Importers Urge ITC to Review Tariff Classifications," *Journal of Commerce*, May 1, 2000, p. 3.

[5] Neville Peterson Williams (attorneys), "Cat Antlers and 'Neckties In Bottles'," *Journal of Commerce*, January 14, 1998, p. 11C.

[6] Green, Paula, "A Costly Halloween Question: Are Costumes Toys or Clothing?", *Journal of Commerce*, March 26, 1998, p. 1A.

[7] Rushford, Greg, "When Is a Duck Not Like a Bedspread?", *Asian Wall Street Journal*, February 24, 1997, p. 12.

[8] Ungar, Ed, "Closing a Literal Loophole," *U.S. News & World Report*, April 27, 1998, p. 32.

[9] Cowan, Richard, "Weyerhauser Seeks Tax to End Canada Lumber Fight," *Reuters* press release, November 20, 2002, http://ca.news.yahoo.com/021120/5/qdat.html, accessed December 12, 2002.

[10] King, Neil Jr., "Is Wolverine Human? A Judge Answers No; Fans Howl in Protest," *The Wall Street Journal*, January 20, 2003, p. A1.

[11] "Technical Information on Customs Valuation," World Trade Organization, http://www.wto.org/english/tratop_e/cusval_e/cusval_info_e.htm, retrieved July 5, 2013.

[12] *Ibid.*

[13] "Understanding the Agreements," World Trade Organization, http://www.wto.org/english/thewto_e/whatis_e/tif_e/agrm9_e.htm#origin, retrieved July 5, 2013.

[14] "WTO Agreement on Rules of Origin," Trade Compliance Center, http://tcc.export.gov/Trade_Agreements/Exporters_Guides/List_All_Guides/exp_005553.asp, retrieved July 5, 2013.

[15] Bangsberg, P. T., "Textile Dispute Impedes Hong Kong Export Growth," *Journal of Commerce*, February 3, 1997, p. 5A.

[16] Green, Paula L., "Customs Puts 63 More Firms on Violation List," *Journal of Commerce*, November 12, 1998, p. 3A.

[17] Roth, Martin S., and Jean B. Romeo, "Matching Product Category and Country Image Perceptions: A Framework for Managing Country-of-Origin Effects," *Journal of International Business Studies*, third quarter 1992, pp. 477-97.

[18] Neville Peterson Williams (attorneys), "Meeting of the Trade Minds: Discussing the Country-of-Origin Marking Travesty," *Journal of Commerce*, July 30, 1997, p. 13C.

[19] Weiser, Steven S., and Arthur W. Bodek, "Which Came First, the Chicks Hatched in England or the South African Ostrich Eggs?", *Journal of Commerce*, August 19, 1998, p. 11C.

[20] Jehl, Douglas, "Whose Lingerie Is It? A New Mid-East Secret," *The New York Times*, December 25, 1996, p. 6.

[21] Tagliabue, John, "Italian Silk Makers Upset by New U.S. Trade Law," *The New York Times*, April 10, 1997.

[22] Lawrence, Richard, "U.S., EU Smooth Over Differences on Country-of-Origin Regulations," *Journal of Commerce*, April 16, 1998, p. 4A.

[23] Levy, Clifford, "The Olive Oil Seems Fine. Whether It's Italian Is the Issue," *The New York Times*, May 7, 2004.

[24] "Rules of Origin (Preference Criteria)," North American Free Trade Agreement, U.S. Customs and Border Protection, http://www.cbp.gov/xp/cgov/trade/trade_programs/international_agreements/free_trade/nafta/rules_of_origin/, accessed July 5, 2013.

[25] "General Aspects of Preferential Origin," Taxation and Customs Union, http://ec.europa.eu/taxation_customs/customs/customs_duties/rules_origin/preferential/index_en.htm, retrieved July 5, 2013.

[26] Gillis, Chris, "Origin Compliance Challenges Shippers," *American Shipper*, March 2004, pp. 36Ű37.

[27] General Note 3: Rates of Duty, "Harmonized Tariff Schedule Online Reference Tool," 2013, United States International Trade Commission, http://hts.usitc.gov, retrieved July 5, 2013.

[28] "Generalized System of Preferences (GSP)," Office of the United States Trade Representative, http://www.ustr.gov/trade-topics/trade-development/preference-programs/generalized-system-preference-gsp, retrieved July 5, 2013.

[29] Jones, Vivian, "Generalized System of Preferences: Background and Renewal Debate," January 9, 2013, Congressional Research Service, www.fas.org/sgp/crs/misc/RL33663.pdf, retrieved July 5, 2013.

[30] "Harmonized Tariff Schedule Online Reference Tool," 2013, United States International Trade Commission, http://hts.usitc.gov, retrieved July 5, 2013.

[31] Barbaro, Michael, "Clothing Makers Allege Sex Discrimination in U.S. Tariffs," *The New York Times*, April 29, 2007.

[32] Kelly, Claire, "Court of Appeals for the Federal Circuit Announces Equal Protection Exception for Customs Cases: Totes-Isotoner v. United States," American Society of International Law, http://www.asil.org/insights100517.cfm#_ednref2, retrieved July 5, 2013.

[33] Donahue, Bill, "Ann Taylor Latest To Sue Over Gender-Based Tariffs," *Law360*, http://www.law360.com/articles/440379/ann-taylor-latest-to-sue-over-gender-based-tariffs, retrieved July 5, 2013.

[34] *Ibid*.

[35] *Country Commercial Guide: Switzerland*, Fiscal Year 2012, U.S. & Foreign Commercial Service and U.S. Department of State, April 5, 2012, http://buyusainfo.net/docs/x_9156644.pdf, retrieved July 5, 2013.

[36] Kulish, Eric, "Dumped On," *American Shipper*, July 2004, pp. 7-16.

[37] *2004 Annual Report*, The Timken Company, Canton, Ohio.

[38] Meller, Paul, and Elizabeth Becker, "U.S. Loses Trade Cases and Faces Penalties," *The New York Times*, September 1, 2004.

[39] Phillips, Michael M., "U.S. Plans Punitive Tariffs in Dispute with EU," *The Wall Street Journal*, December 22, 1998, p. A2.

[40] Helmer, John, "Russia Imposes Tax on Border Traffic," *The Journal of Commerce*, January 27, 1997, p. 3A.

[41] "Chronological list of disputes cases," World Trade Organization, http://www.wto.org/english/tratop_e/dispu_e/dispu_status_e.htm, retrieved July 5, 2013.

[42] Lucentini, Jack, "Clinton, in Pro-Trade Move, Ends Tariffs on Brooms," *The Journal of Commerce*, December 8, 1998, p. 3A.

[43] Chapter 96, "Harmonized Tariff Schedule Online Reference Tool," 2013, United States International Trade Commission, http://hts.usitc.gov, retrieved July 5, 2013.

[44] *Office of International Trade Textile and Quota Newsletter*, January 2012, http://www.cbp.gov/linkhandler/cgov/trade/trade_outreach/trade_newsletter/textile_jan.ctt/textile_jan.pdf, retrieved July 5, 2013.

[45] Sterk, Ron, "U.S.D.A. Sets 2012-13 Sugar Import Quotas," *Food Business News*, September 10, 2012.

[46] Chapter 17, "Harmonized Tariff Schedule Online Reference Tool," 2013, United States International Trade Commission, http://hts.usitc.gov, retrieved July 5, 2013.

[47] "Sugar Monthly Price—US cents per Pound," Index Mundi, http://www.indexmundi.com/commodities/?commodity=sugar&months=60, retrieved July 5, 2013.

[48] "Historical Tariff-Rate Quota/Tariff Preference Level Fill Rate," U.S. Customs and Border Protection, http://www.cbp.gov/xp/cgov/trade/trade_programs/textiles_and_quotas, retrieved July 5, 2013.

[49] "Sugar: World Markets and Trade," May 2013, Foreign Agricultural Service, United States Department of Agriculture, www.fas.usda.gov/psdonline/circulars/sugar.pdf, retrieved July 5, 2013.

[50] *Ibid.*

[51] Malkin, Elisabeth, "In Mexico, Sugar vs. Corn Syrup," *The New York Times*, June 9, 2004.

[52] Dominican Republic, "The World Fact Book," and Haiti, "The World Fact Book," Central Intelligence Agency, https://www.cia.gov/library/publications/the-world-factbook, accessed July 5, 2013.

[53] "Quota Book Transmittals (QBTs)," U.S. Customs and Border Protection, http://www.cbp.gov/xp/cgov/trade/trade_programs/textiles_and_quotas/qbts/, retrieved July 5, 2013.

[54] Thornton, Emily, "The Japan That Says No to Cold Pills," *Business Week*, May 19, 1997, p. 34.

[55] "U.S.-Mexico Avocado Trade Dispute," American University in Washington, http://www1.american.edu/ted/avocado.htm, retrieved July 5, 2013.

[56] Riley, Kate, "Finally! Mexico ends its tariffs on Washington's apples and cherries and pears and...," *The Seattle Times*, July 6, 2011.

[57] "WTO disputes with New Zealand a third party complainant," New Zealand Ministry of Foreign Affairs and Trade, April 7, 2011, http://www.mfat.govt.nz/Treaties-and-International-Law/02-Trade-law-and-free-trade-agreements/0-Japan-Apples.php, retrieved July 5, 2013.

[58] "Win-win ending to the 'hormone beef trade war'," *European Parliament News*, March 14, 2011, http://www.europarl.europa.eu/news/en/pressroom/content/20120314IPR40752/html/Win-win-ending-to-the-hormone-beef-trade-war, retrieved July 5, 2013.

[59] Harmon, Amy, and Andrew Pollack, "Battle Brewing Over Labeling of Genetically Modified Food," *The New York Times*, May 24, 2012.

[60] Linn, Gene, "U.S. Renews Attack on Asian Barriers to Food Exports," *The Journal of Commerce*, April 23, 1998, p. 1A.

[61] Weinstein, Michael M., "Banana Spat Could Have Serious Consequences for World Trade," *The New York Times*, December 29, 1998.

[62] Zaroscostas, John, "EU Officials Reject Plan to Ease Banana Gridlock," *Journal of Commerce*, January 27, 1999, p. 3A.

[63] DePalma, Anthony, "Chiquita Sues Europeans, Citing Banana-Quota Losses," *The New York Times*, January 26, 2001.

[64] "European Communities—Regime for the Importation, Sale and Distribution of Bananas," November 8, 2012, World Trade Organization, http://www.wto.org/english/tratop_e/dispu_e/cases_e/ds27_e.htm, retrieved July 5, 2013.

[65] "The Second Battle of Poitiers," *Time*, December 6, 1982, p. 31.

[66] Rao, N. Vasuki, "India to Introduce EDI to Cut Paperwork," *Journal of Commerce*, November 24, 1998, p. 3A.

[67] Business Planet: Mapping the Business Environment, The World Bank Group, http://rru.worldbank.org.

[68] "Customs Law Advisory—Court Decision Details The Costs of Failure to Maintain Records To Support Import Declaration," Steptoe and Johnson, LLP, January 30, 2007, http://www.steptoe.com/publications-4183.html, retrieved July 5, 2013.

[69] "130,858 Imported Cars were Newly Registered in 2012," Korea Automobile Importers and Distributors Association, January 7, 2013, http://www.kaida.co.kr/brand/BrandMain.jsp?pageId=2&articleId=45892, retrieved July 5, 2013.

[70] "What are these Korean non-tariff barriers to U.S. cars and trucks?", Korea-U.S. FTA, July 2, 2010, http://benmuse.typepad.com/koreaus_fta/2010/07/what-are-these-korean-nontariff-barriers-to-us-auto-imports.html, retrieved July 5, 2013.

[71] Banerjee, Neela, and Helene Cooper, "Are Russians Playing a Game of Chicken with ... Chickens?", *The Wall Street Journal*, March 18, 1996, p. B1.

[72] Borsuk, Richard, "Changing of the Port Guards: Some Importers Fear a Return to Corruption," *Asian Wall Street Journal*, April 7, 1997, p. 14.

[73] "What Every Member of the Trade Community Should Know About: Reasonable Care," February 2004, U.S. Customs and Border Protection, http://www.cbp.gov/linkhandler/cgov/trade/legal/informed_compliance_pubs/icp021.ctt/icp021.pdf, retrieved July 6, 2013.

[74] "Customs Compliance and Reasonable Care under the Mod Act," Samuel Shapiro and Company, Inc., http://www.shapiro.com/html/Compliance1.html, retrieved July 6, 2013.

[75] http://export.gov/logistics, retrieved July 6, 2013.

[76] "Complying with the Made in USA Standard," Bureau of Consumer Protection, Business Center, http://business.ftc.gov/documents/bus03-complying-made-usa-standard, retrieved July 6, 2013.

[77] MacCausland, Shawn, "CBP Eases Process for Claiming Drawback on Unused Merchandise," Sandler, Travis & Rosenberg Trade Report, http://www.strtrade.com/publications-cbp-unused-merchandise-draw-back-040913.html, retrieved July 6, 2013.

[78] "Export Competitiveness and Duty Drawback," The World Bank, http://go.worldbank.org/KV8U1ULIT0, retrieved July 5, 2013.

[79] Cadot, Olivier, Jaime de Melo, and Marcelo Olarreaga, "Can duty-drawbacks have a protectionist bias? Evidence from MERCOSUR," January 31, 2010, The World Bank, http://go.worldbank.org/70G3A9ZRB0, retrieved July 6, 2013.

Chapter 17

Developing a Competitive Advantage

17.1 Communication Challenges 454

17.2 International English 455

17.3 Special English 457

17.4 Metric System 458

17.5 Cultural Sensitivity 461

17.6 Specific Advice 462

The preceding chapters outlined many of the challenges that an international logistics manager faces in an international environment. They covered the infrastructure of international business, the management of financial and transportation risks, and the choices related to international transportation and packaging, all of which are eminently more complex than for domestic transactions.

However, a good export manager should not see these challenges as obstacles, but as opportunities to offer a higher level of service than his or her competitors. This can be done relatively simply by following a number of elementary points. The recommendations that follow may not be sufficient to clinch the sale; however, they will certainly help in all circumstances.

Consider that an importer, in most situations, is getting several quotes from several exporters located in different countries. Although the alternative bids are likely to be evaluated on a large number of criteria (price, support, after-sale service, delivery terms, and so on), one of the most important issues will be the ease with which the purchase transaction will take place. From the importer's perspective, the easiest alternative is to purchase from a supplier who communicates clearly, who is flexible in his approach, who offers terms of sale that are convenient to the buyer, who is careful in handling paperwork and transportation, and who packages the goods carefully. When all else is the same, the well-prepared exporter will earn the sale by being better prepared on those logistical details.

The good management of international logistics can be a competitive advantage.

17.1 Communication Challenges

One of the most challenging aspects of international business is effective communication. Conducting business with people in foreign countries is often hampered by language barriers. It can be quite difficult to conduct business when two people from different languages and cultures are communicating. An additional challenge for the international logistics manager is that most communications with foreign counterparts are conducted in an impersonal fashion, by e-mail, fax, and letters. This detached type of contact does not allow for the subtleties of in-person communication, such as tone of voice or gestures, which often help make communications more intelligible. There is also no opportunity to ask for immediate clarification, as there is in verbal communication, and the possibility of errors or misunderstandings is greatly increased.

The U.S. Department of State classifies languages by the degree of difficulty that they present for a native English speaker intent on learning that language. Table 17.1[1] outlines these categories and languages. The greater the differences are between two persons' languages, the greater the likelihood is that communication will be difficult. Sentences can often be interpreted differently, and both parties will then be left to wonder what the other person meant by a certain word, phrase, or sentence.

Classification of Languages in Terms of Difficulty To Learn for a Native English Speaker	
Languages closest to English, Easiest to Learn	
Roman alphabet	Spanish, French, Italian
Similar grammar	Dutch, German, Norwegian
Similar syntax	Swedish, Romanian
Languages Difficulty to Learn	
Roman alphabet	Turkish, Indonesian, Icelandic
Different grammar	Czech, Hungarian, Polish
Different syntax	Vietnamese, Finnish
Languages Very Difficult to Learn	
Different alphabet	Hebrew, Russian, Greek
Different grammar	Hindi, Thai
Very different syntax	
Languages Extremely Difficult to Learn	
Complex alphabet, multiple alphabets, or no alphabet	Chinese Arabic Korean
Very different grammar	Japanese
Very different syntax	

Table 17.1: Classification of Languages, by Difficulty
Effective Language Learning and U.S. Department of State.

To the international logistician, the diversity of languages and associated possible misunderstandings means that extreme care should be extended to communication, to ensure that the correct meaning is conveyed every time.

Conveniently for the native speaker of English, most international communication takes place in that language. English has become everybody's second language, not only because it is the easiest language to learn,* but also because it is the language of the largest trading partners of most countries. However, the advantage of being able to communicate in one's own language means that there are significant responsibilities attached to it.

17.2 International English

International logistics professionals engage mostly in written communications with their counterparts abroad (by e-mail, fax, or other written documents), and therefore it is important that they communicate clearly in writing. A specific style of writing for native English speakers has developed to increase the probability that non-native speakers of English can clearly understand what is written. This technique, dubbed International English by Edmond Weiss, was outlined in his outstanding book *The Elements of International English Style* in 2005.[2]

Writing in International English means following a fairly large number of rules (Weiss lists 57 of them), but the most important one is that the native English speaker should strive to make the meaning of the communication absolutely clear to the non-native speaker: "Business and technical documents intended for those who read English as their second language must be unusually simple, unambiguous, and literal. Ideally, they should be edited for ease of translation."[3] The most important rules are:

international English
A technique of written communication that attempts to remove all ambiguities, so that a person with limited knowledge of English can understand it.

- Always assume that the person for whom English is a second language is relying on a dictionary for some words. That means that the word definition used should preferably be the first one in the dictionary and should always be unambiguous. For example: "The company's sales took off 25 percent last year" should be replaced with "The company's sales increased 25 percent last year," for several reasons. First, "to take" is probably one of the longest entries in the English dictionary, and the meaning of "to take off" is listed toward the end of that entry. Another reason is that one of the first meanings listed of "to take off" is "to remove (one's clothes);" therefore there is a strong possibility that the sentence will be understood as "sales [removed] decreased 25 percent." A convenience sample of foreign students in the author's classes reinforced this point; about 30 percent of them thought it meant a decrease. By using a precise and accurate verb, "to increase," no confusion is possible. This recommendation is often contrary to the common caution to write in "simple words" that is often advocated by English teachers everywhere. In practicality, more complex words tend to be more precise and have the smallest number of alternative meanings, and therefore are far better for International English communication.

---

*Contrary to a commonly held belief in the United States and Britain, English actually is one of the easiest languages to learn because of its relatively simple grammar, its lack of gender forms, and its smaller number of tenses.

- Always proofread carefully and avoid all grammatical and spelling errors. There is a strong possibility of confusion in a sentence that reads, "The customer purchases products from company A and it's marketing services form company B." The reader is left to determine whether there are two typos (*it's* rather than *its* and *form* rather than *from*) or just one (*form*). Is it that the customer purchases products from company A and marketing services from company B, or is it that it is purchasing products from company A and providing marketing services to (for) company B? Actually, a non-native speaker would probably not understand that there are possible typos in that sentence and not grasp its meaning at all.

  Other common misspellings result from the confusion between *there*, *they're*, and *their*; between *accept* and *except*; between *too*, *two* and *to*; and between *effect* and *affect*. Then there is also the frequently found "should of done" instead of "should have done," which is only understandable to a native speaker who "hears" English rather than reads it. For example, it is very likely that a foreign reader will not comprehend the sentence "Our company would like to except your company's proposal," as she will not understand that the word "except" was used instead of "accept." Actually, it is more likely that she will understand the opposite of what was meant, and that the company rejected the proposal.

  Another issue for native English speakers is the correct usage of the final *s* in forming the plural and possessive. It is important to make sure that documents are proofread so that *shipments* does not appear as *shipment's*, an error that can create confusion. Is the document referring to all shipments or just one?

- Always make sure that quantitative information will be understood without question. A date of 12/11/13 can be understood three different ways: A U.S. reader will understand it as December 11, 2013; a French, British or German reader will understand it as 12 November 2013; and a Chinese reader will understand it as 13 November 2012. It is best to follow the practice of spelling all dates fully: "11 December 2013" is unambiguous.

  The number 10^9 is 1 billion to a North American reader, but 1,000 million (or 1 milliard) to a British or German reader, for whom a billion is 10^{12}; meanwhile, 10^9 is 100 crore (or 10,000 lakhs) to an Indian, Pakistani, or Nepalese. Writing the number (1,000,000,000) in its entirety leaves no doubt and is always the best strategy.

  It is common in some countries to abbreviate 35,000 to 35k, and 23,000,000 to 23M, but certainly not in all. Therefore the preference is to spell out the entire number rather than cause a possible doubt in the reader's mind.

- Always use simple and short sentences. As much as possible, the sentences should contain only one main idea. If there are possible writing shortcuts, they should be avoided—for example, "The company requests the report be sent early in the month" should be changed to "The company requests that the report should be sent between the first and the fifth day of the month." When in doubt, punctuation should be added to enhance clarification, even if it seems too heavily punctuated to a native speaker.

- Never use idioms that are sports or military related, as they are rarely, if ever, understood properly. Writing that a salesperson "struck out" on a deal or that she "hit a home run" will confuse a foreigner, who, in looking it up in the dictionary will read that she "ran around the bases with one hit."[4] A correct sentence conveying the same meaning would say that she was "unsuccessful" or "successful beyond our expectations."

  Military terminology should also be avoided. Terms such as "plan of attack" or "price war" tend to be difficult to translate or offensive to some cultures.[5]

  If there is any doubt that foreign sport terminology is incomprehensible to the uninitiated, a quick visit to a British newspaper, such as *The Guardian*,[6] or an Indian newspaper, such as *The Telegraph*,[7] and a glance at the cricket page would quickly dispel it.

The concept behind International English is that communication should be easy to understand and devoid of cultural references. One of the most effective ways to determine whether a particular message is written clearly enough to be understood by a foreign reader is to translate it using machine-translation software into another language (preferably one that is not a European language) and translate it back into English. It will rarely, if ever, be the same as the original text; however, if its original meaning is still understandable, then the text was written in an English that can be properly understood by a non-native speaker.

17.3 Special English

For communications conducted orally, the challenge is much greater, as there is less time to refine the sentences used and to make sure that the meaning is clear. It is important to realize that one of the greatest difficulties experienced by a non-native speaker—of any language—is to talk on the telephone. There are no visual cues that help communication and, on occasion, there are technical difficulties that hamper good communication.

In order to communicate clearly in English with foreigners, it is useful to become familiar with Special English, a reduced-vocabulary English developed by the Voice of America, the U.S. government-sponsored news organization that broadcasts worldwide. While the Voice of America is prohibited from broadcasting in the United States,[8] it is possible to hear its broadcast on the Internet.[9] Here are its main characteristics:

special English
A technique of oral communication that uses a limited vocabulary and short sentences, so that a person with limited knowledge of English can understand it.

- Sentences should be short and contain only one idea. It is more effective to use two sentences ("Sentences should be short. Sentences should contain only one idea.") than to confuse the listener, who is trying to understand a particular word or sentence structure and cannot remember how the sentence started. It takes a little practice, but it is certainly easy for a native speaker to learn to speak in such a way.

- The vocabulary should be limited to correct and accurate terms. All sorts of sports-related imagery exists in American English, but it should be avoided; stating that a contract negotiation is still "in the first inning" (it is in the very first stages, with only one of the two parties having made its points) or that the companies competing for a particular sale are "not on a level-playing field" (one of the competitors has an unfair advantage over the other) is unlikely to ever be understood correctly by a non-native speaker of English. The same is true of terms such as "stand up to" or "roll over," which should be replaced with their precise equivalents: "confront" or "reinvest." Even expressions that are clearly understood in one English-speaking country can be difficult for others: "carrying coals to Newcastle" makes as little sense to U.S. English speakers as "selling refrigerators to Eskimos" makes to Australians.

- The speed at which the sentences are spoken should be slower. The broadcasts of the Voice of America aim for two-thirds of the speed of normal speech. From the author's personal experience, people from the southern part of the United States are much more easily understood than people from the north because they tend to speak at a slower pace. The U.S. southern accent is much less of an issue for foreigners, who tend to visualize the words as they are spoken.

- Finally, if a foreigner asks a native speaker to repeat a sentence, the native speaker should not repeat the sentence louder, as if the person had difficulty hearing. The issue is generally about a word that the listener did not understand or a sentence that was too complicated. It is best to just repeat the sentence using slightly different vocabulary or repeat the sentence and offer an alternative word. For example, "Our company would like to sleep on that proposal for a few days" (a sentence that violates the principles listed above, and is likely to be misunderstood) can be repeated as "Our company would like to sleep on that proposal, think about it, for a few days." In this manner, the non-native speaker better understands the sentence and gains a new bit of vocabulary.

17.4 Metric System

metric system
A decimal system of measurements, part of the International System of Units, that is widely adopted worldwide.

Communication is also better served by using what is familiar. Unfortunately, U.S. exporters and importers do not use the system of measures—the metric system—that every other country in the world uses (except for Liberia and Myanmar, which do not use the metric system either) but instead uses a system which even its everyday users find difficult to understand. Foreigners, thus, tend to be entirely baffled by the U.S. system of measurement.

For example, within the so-called English system of measures, there are three types of tons: (1) the short ton, which is a measure of weight and weighs 2,000 pounds; (2) the long ton, also a measure of weight at 2,240 pounds; and (3) the gross (registered) or net ton, which is a measure of volume and equal to 100 cubic feet. And there is often no indication of which ton is the correct one. Only tradition and context dictate which "ton" is the one that is intended.

Measurement can get much more complicated. There are five types of ounces: (1) an *avoirdupois* weight unit of 437.5 grains; (2) an apothecary or Troy weight unit of 480 grains; (3) a U.S. fluid ounce, which is a measure of volume worth six teaspoons; (4) its "equivalent" regulatory fluid ounce, which is defined as 30 milliliters or 1.5 percent more than a U.S. fluid ounce; and (5) an imperial fluid ounce, which is 4 percent smaller than the U.S. unit. There is generally no indication of which unit is the correct one in a document or regulation.[10] As if this were not enough, there are traditional units in some industries that use the same terminology very differently.

17.4 Metric System

For example, leather is measured in the United States in ounces, which, in this case, is a measure not of weight nor of volume, but of thickness: "Two-ounce leather such as calf or goat skin is about 1/32 inches thick, while eight-ounce leather is a full 1/8 inches."[11]

Another peculiarity of the English measurement system is that a measurement may not refer to the actual dimensions of the product, but to a nominal measurement whose origins may be only loosely linked to its actual dimensions. If a measurement is given as $\frac{1}{2}$ inch, there are countless instances in which the measurement is actually **not** 0.5 inches:

- A 1/2-in copper pipe has an external diameter of 0.75 inches, and an internal diameter that depends on the thickness of the pipe's wall, but none of them is equal to 0.5 inches (they are between 0.528 and 0.569 inches).

- A 1/2-in electrical conduit pipe made of polyvinyl chloride (PVC) has an inside diameter of 0.622 inches, and an external diameter of 0.84 inches. If it is made of galvanized metal, its inside diameter is 0.634 inches and outside diameter is 0.84 inches.

- A 1/2-in piece of plywood is generally only 15/32 inches thick, but can be as thin as 7/16 inches thick.

The problem extends to other measurements as well:

- A piece of lumber to which every American refers as a 2-by-4 stud [2 × 4] measures actually 1.5 × 3.5 inches. A 2 × 6 piece of lumber is 1.5 × 5.5 inches, but a 2 × 8 is 1.5 × 7.25 inches.

A few more peculiarities of the English measurement system make it difficult for non-Americans. U.S. measurements are often given as a fraction, rather than a decimal; for example a measurement will be given as $2^{\frac{5}{16}}$ inches rather than 2.3125 in, a preference which is disconcerting to people who are used to a metric system that is entirely decimal.

This mathematical notation can also be confusing as it is an unconventional way to display a quantity without an operator (whether ×, +, ˆ, −, or ÷). What is meant by $2^{\frac{5}{16}}$ (sometimes noted as $2\frac{5}{16}$), is determined by context.

In American usage, in the absence of the operator, the quantity $2^{\frac{5}{16}}$ can be read three different ways:

- $2 + \dfrac{5}{16}$, what is generally meant, but it can mean

- $2 \times \dfrac{5}{16}$ or possibly

- $2 \char`\^ \frac{5}{16}$, that is, 2 to the power of $\frac{5}{16}$

as it would normally be in mathematical expressions.

Because of the issues presented by communications made in English measurements, it is to the advantage of everyone involved in a transaction to use the metric system, which has a very well defined set of measures, all of which are clearly and accurately established. A kilogram is a measure of mass, a liter a measure of volume, and a meter a measure of distance. There are convenient ways to cross over from one unit set to the next: one liter is exactly equal to a cube of side 0.1 meter (10^{-3} cubic meters), and a kilogram is equal to the mass of water contained in a liter. There are conventions for the names of multiples (kilo, hecto, deka) and for the names of fractions (deci, centi, and milli), all of which are decimal. More importantly, there are no ambiguous usages.

While this utilization of the metric system may represent a challenge for a U.S. exporter or importer, its customers or suppliers will understand much better what it intends to communicate, and this effort will result in a greater probability of making a sale.

Converting to the metric system, though, is more than just multiplying by the correct coefficient. Selling a product in 3.785-liter bottles (equivalent to one U.S. gallon bottle) does not satisfy the admonition to use the metric system; while it is a convenient conversion of a common English unit, it is an unusual unit of volume for a person used to the metric system, for whom products are generally sold in one- or two-liter bottles. A correct conversion would therefore use round units of measurement rather than direct translations of round units in the English system into awkward decimal quantities in the metric system.

Calculating a Shipment's Weight and Volume

There are substantial differences between the effort extended by a shipper using the metric system and that of a shipper using the English system. Consider two juice manufacturers, one American, the other European, who need to decide whether an identical shipment of juice boxes can fit in a 40-foot container. Will the shipment weigh less than the maximum allowable weight? Will it physically fit inside the box? The American will use the so-called traditional English system, and the European will use the metric system. Both shipments are made of 5,000 cartons of 24 juice boxes of the same identical size.

- **The American shipper**

The American shipper must first determine the weight of this shipment of juice boxes. Each juice box contains 7 fluid ounces of apple juice. Ignoring the fact that apple juice has a slightly higher density than water, and having found that 1 fluid ounce weighs 1.04 avoirdupois ounce, he determines that each juice box weighs 7.28 ounces. The total weight of the shipment is therefore $5,000 \times 24 \times 7.28 = 873,600$ ounces. Because 1 pound is 16 ounces, he then divides that result by 16 to obtain the total shipment's weight of 54,600 pounds. Will that shipment fit in a container whose maximum capacity is 26.29 long tons? He needs to divide 54,600 pounds by 2,240 and ends up with 24.375 long tons. Even accounting for the additional weight of packaging and dunnage, it is well within the container's weight limit.

Each juice box measures $1\frac{5}{8}$ inches by $2\frac{1}{2}$ inches by $3\frac{1}{2}$ inches. Will this shipment fit in a regular 40-foot container whose inside measurements are 39 feet 6 inches long by 7 feet $8\frac{1}{8}$ inches wide by 7 feet $5\frac{3}{4}$ inches high? The shipper must first determine the volume of each juice box: $1.625 \times 2.5 \times 3.5 = 14$ cubic inches. Then, he determines the volume of the entire shipment: $5,000 \times 24 \times 14 = 1,680,000$ cubic inches. Finally he needs to determine the volume of the container and, for that, needs to calculate how many inches there are in each dimension: 39 feet 6 inches is $(39 \times 12) + 6$ inches or 474 inches in length, 7 feet $8\frac{1}{8}$ inches is $(7 \times 12) + 8.125$ inches or 92.125 inches in width, and 7 feet $5\frac{3}{4}$ inches is $(7 \times 12) + 5.75$ inches or 89.75 inches in height. The entire volume of the container is therefore $474 \times 89.75 \times 92.125 = 3,919,136$ cubic inches. The shipment of 1,680,000 cubic inches fits without problem, even accounting for the space taken by packaging and dunnage. Converting those dimensions to feet and calculating in cubic feet would not have simplified the task at all.

- **The European shipper**
Using a similar shipment, the European shipper can make the same calculations much faster in the metric system. The capacity of each juice box is 205 milliliters and therefore it weighs 205 grams, if the slightly higher density of juice is ignored. The total shipment weighs $5,000 \times 24 \times 205$ grams $= 24,600,000$ grams or 24.6 tonnes. Because the capacity of the container is 26.72 tonnes, there is no issue, even after packaging and dunnage are added. The dimensions of each juice box are $4.1 \times 6.3 \times 8.9$ centimeters. Each box therefore has a volume of 230 cubic centimeters or 230 milliliters. (This is more than the volume of the juice itself, which is 205 cubic centimeters, and that is due to the fact that the juice boxes tend to have sides that are slightly concave. This was also the case for the American juice boxes but was unnoticeable because of the units used.) The entire shipment is therefore 27,600,000 cubic centimeters or 27.6 cubic meters. The container is the same, with inside dimensions of 1,204 centimeters long by 234 centimeters wide by 228 centimeters high. Its total volume is $1,204 \times 234 \times 228 = 64,235,808$ cubic centimeters or 64.23 cubic meters, and therefore the shipment fits without difficulty, even after the packaging and dunnage are added.

Unless he knew it by heart, the American shipper needed a dictionary to find out that a fluid ounce weighs 1.04 ounces and that a long ton is 2,240 pounds. He may also have glanced at a decimal equivalency table to know that $\frac{1}{8} = 0.125$. He certainly needed a piece of paper to keep it all straight, as well as a calculator. The European shipper only needed a calculator.

17.5 Cultural Sensitivity

Although communicating information clearly is fundamental to become a better international logistician, it is also very valuable to become savvy about others' cultures. Unfortunately, if there is one aspect of international business about which it is difficult to generalize, it is culture. There is little about culture that can be pinpointed in a few sentences, and when such an attempt is made, exceptions abound. In the long run, the best that an international logistician can do is to study intercultural communication. In the meantime, a few of these pointers can help.

One aspect of communication that is shaped by culture is the way people address each other in person, in the mail, or over the telephone. In some cultures, the forms of address are quite formal (France), and in others (Australia) quite informal. In some cultures, people are very sensitive to titles (Germany), in others much less so (Canada). U.S. culture is among those that care the least about titles and formalities, although there are a few notable exceptions to that rule. In all cases, because it is difficult to offend someone by being too formal, an astute international logistics manager will therefore always err on the side of formality, and communicate as politely and formally as possible until there is evidence that it is appropriate to adopt a less formal tone.

Another area in which it is easy to make quick progress is in understanding the work culture of a country. First, the international logistician should consider the separation between work and private life. In some countries, there is a considerable divide between work and family, and the two never or rarely intersect (Japan). In others, the two are closely tied to one another (Indonesia). When in doubt, it is generally better to consider that personal life and work life are separate, unless there is evidence on the part of the foreign interlocutor that it is appropriate to mention family and private life in business communications.

Another area in which there are culturally determined differences is the speed at which people operate in the workplace. In some countries, it is expected of business persons to answer an inquiry very quickly, in order to show that the inquiry is important and that it commands their full attention (Germany). A delay implies a lack of interest. In others, it is impolite to answer too quickly, as a response should be given careful thought (Saudi Arabia). There is no specific ideal way to handle these discrepancies, but the advice for international logisticians is, again, to learn the appropriate response time from what their foreign counterparts do and mirror that behavior.

Finally, culture influences the way people spend their workday; the time at which they arrive at work, leave work in the evening, and eat during the day. Culture also influences the amount of time that they spend at each meal and the days of the week that they work. Finally, it influences the different holidays that are celebrated. Countries have different holidays, and different customs during identical holidays. Sometimes it is appropriate for an exporter or importer to send a card or a greeting, in others it is not. In those cases, the CultureGrams[12] mentioned in Chapter 1 are most useful. In any case, for the international logistician, a delayed response to a request on a certain day may simply be due to a holiday rather than a lack of interest. Considering that India, due to its multiplicity of religions, has a total of 43 official holidays, it is more likely than not that there is some celebration during a given week.

17.6 Specific Advice

In addition to the general advice presented so far, the international logistician has the opportunity to gain a competitive advantage by following a number of strategies in specific areas. Some of these strategies were presented in earlier chapters, but they bear repeating.

17.6.1 Terms of Payment

Although the choice of the term of sale is dependent on the level of experience of both the exporter and the importer and on the level of confidence that the exporter has in the ability of the importer to make the payment, there are some alternatives

17.6 Specific Advice

that are definitely preferable and will increase an exporter's probability to clinch the sale.

An importer, in most situations, is getting several possible quotes from several exporters located in different countries. Alternative bids are evaluated on a large number of criteria (price, specific capabilities, after-sale service, delivery terms, and so on), and on the ease with which the purchase transaction will take place. From the importer's perspective, the easiest alternative is to purchase on an open-account basis. It is likely that at least one of the potential suppliers will offer such terms, and that others will ask for a letter of credit or a documentary collection. Therefore, the supplier offering an open-account transaction has an advantage over the others. If that supplier has purchased credit insurance, that decision does not affect its probability of getting paid.

Therefore, an exporter intent on increasing its sales should choose to display that it is confident in the ability of the importer to pay for the goods by using an open account. If it is unsure about the ability of the importer to pay, it should consider purchasing a credit insurance policy.

17.6.2 Currency of Payment

In an international transaction, the choice of the currency exposes the exporter (or the importer) to the risk of currency exchange rate fluctuation. Rather than consider this risk to be a drawback in an international sale, a good exporter should consider it an opportunity and take advantage of the several alternatives it has to reduce its risk of currency fluctuation.

Because of the intense competition that an exporter faces in international markets, it is very likely that a significant percentage of the companies competing for the importer's business will offer quotes in the importer's currency. Because it is easier for the importer to handle a purchase in its own currency, it would place an exporter at a strategic disadvantage not to quote in that currency.

An exporter intent on increasing its sales abroad should therefore offer (all of its) quotes in the importer's currency and discuss with its banker the most appropriate hedging strategy for that particular transaction.

17.6.3 Incoterms® Rule Choice

In some cases, a strategic advantage can be gained by an exporter willing to facilitate the sale of its products by assisting a novice importer in the handling of a shipment. In others, a price advantage may be obtained by an experienced importer willing to perform all or most of the tasks involved in the shipment.

Generally speaking, an exporter does not like to determine which Incoterms® rule to use on a case-by-case basis. It adopts a policy to include in international quotes those services that it feels competent providing. It is difficult for an exporter to adapt its Incoterms® strategy to accommodate the requirements of an importer, as it may require the exporter to be responsible for tasks that it has decided it would rather not perform. However, should the importer want to perform more tasks than what the exporter prefers, it is certainly possible for the exporter to do less than what it expected, and use a different Incoterms® rule on that transaction, one for which it is responsible for less.

An exporter intent on increasing its sales should therefore offer to provide the importer with the most customer-friendly Incoterms® rule quotes (either DAP or

DDP) and, if necessary, use the services of a competent freight forwarder. Should the importer want to shoulder more responsibilities, it is always possible for the exporter to reduce its involvement and quote FCA or even EXW. The best type of quote would be one in which the exporter lists different prices for different Incoterms® rules, leaving the importer with the decision to choose which is best for its specific case.

For example, an exporter could submit a quote that reads:

FCA · 2500 Industrial Parkway, Cleveland, OH 44114, USA _____ $10,000

FCA · Terminal 5, Cincinnati Airport, Covington, KY 41048, USA _____ $11,000

CIP · CDG Cargo, route des badaux, 95700 Roissy-en-France, France _____ $15,500

DAP · 114 rue de Prat, 63100 Clermont-Ferrand, France _____ $16,500

DDP · 114 rue de Prat, 63100 Clermont-Ferrand, France _____ $17,800

and leave the customer to decide which of the Incoterms® rule it would like to choose. The *pro forma* invoice would then be created after that decision has been reached.

17.6.4 Document Preparation

Accurate and timely document preparation and delivery are an essential part of international logistics and of the smooth transfer of goods from an exporter to an importer.

Any failure to provide complete documents in a timely manner is likely to delay a shipment, generate additional costs by requiring last-minute mailings of critical documents, or create difficulties for one or more of the parties involved in the transaction. Because the responsibility of proper document preparation falls mostly on the exporter, regardless of the Incoterms® rule used in a transaction, an exporter can turn its ability to do a good and thorough job in this aspect of international logistics into a marketing advantage.

An exporter intent on increasing its sales should therefore be thorough and meticulous in the way it prepares the documents that it provides to the importer. This should be reflected in the first contact, the *pro forma* invoice, and be communicated to the importer by emphasizing the experience of the company at providing accurate and thorough documents.

17.6.5 Packaging

Good handling of the packaging requirements by the exporter will also help considerably in the smooth transfer of goods from the exporter to the importer.

The most important way of looking at packaging is to prepare for the worst. The exporter should truly imagine the worst-case scenario and the roughest possible journey in packaging the goods that it ships at export. It is only under this premise that it will adequately serve the needs of the importer to receive goods in sellable and usable conditions.

Although good packaging procedures are expensive, the benefits are substantial. First, they allow the goods to arrive in perfect shape to their destination and be

17.6 Specific Advice

immediately sellable or usable by the importer. Good packaging also reduces the costs of repackaging or the costs of damaged goods. In addition, because poor packaging can always be used by insurance companies to decline a claim, it pays to have a track record of stellar packaging.

However, the greatest benefits from such a good packaging policy are the goodwill that it generates between the importer and the exporter, and the marketing benefits that can be derived from it. Because the importer is obviously not interested in having to challenge invoices or having to ask for allowances for goods that were damaged in transit, it welcomes shipments that arrive packaged carefully.

Careful packaging, meticulous document preparation, and considerate choices in terms of payment and Incoterms® rule selection will enhance the relationship between exporter and importer through goodwill and trust. Learning and understanding these skills will help an international logistician gain a substantial competitive advantage.

Review and Discussion Questions

1. What are the advantages of learning to use International English and Special English in communicating with non-native speakers of English?

2. What are the advantages of using the metric system in international commerce?

3. What are the trade-offs between utilizing a standardized policy and remaining flexible for an exporter? You can choose either terms of payment or Incoterms® rules to illustrate your points.

4. In your opinion, why is it important for an exporter to sell in the importer country's currency?

5. What are the advantages of having an "environmentally friendly" packaging policy for an exporter?

Notes

[1] Adapted from "Language Difficulty Ranking," Effective Language Learning, http://www.effectivelanguagelearning.com/language-guide/language-difficulty, retrieved July 2, 2013.

[2] Weiss, Edmond H., *The Elements of International English Style: A Guide to Writing Correspondence, Reports, Technical Documents, Internet Pages for a Global Audience*, 2005, Armonk, NY.

[3] *Ibid*.

[4] *New College German Dictionary: German-English, English-German*, Duncan, SC: Langenscheidt, 1973.

[5] Beamer, Linda, and Iris Varner, *Intercultural Communication in the Global Workplace*, 2001, McGraw-Hill-Irwin, New York, New York.

[6] http://www.guardian.co.uk

[7] http://www.telegraphindia.com

[8] Chmela, Holli, "A Language to Air News of America to the World," *The New York Times*, July 31, 2006.

[9] "Special English News," Voice of America, http://www.voanews.com/specialenglish.

[10] "Nutrition Labeling of Food," *Code of Federal Regulations*, Title 21, Volume 2, Section 101.9, Food and Drug Administration, 21 CFR 101.9, April 1, 2004, U.S. Government Printing Office, http://edocket.access.gpo.gov/cfr_2004/aprqtr/21cfr101.9.htm.

[11] "Leather and Leatherworking Tips," *Legio XX Online Handbook*, May 6, 2003, http://www.larp.com/legioxx/leather.html.

[12] CultureGrams, http://culturegram.stores.yahoo.net/incul.html.

Index

10+2 rule, 413
24-hour rule, 413

absolute advantage, 16
advanced shipping notification, 305
agent, 94, 96
    vs. distributor, 99, 124, 126
air mail service, 313
air waybill, 266
aircraft
    combi, 318
    freighter, 320
    passenger, 317
    quick change, 320
    security, 330
    special, 323
    types, 316
aircraft lease, 266, 315
    ACMI, 315
    damp, 315
    dry, 315
    wet, 315
Aircraft, Crew, Maintenance and Insurance (ACMI) lease, 315
airfreight
    charter, 314
    express, 313
    forwarder, 316
    mail, 313
    scheduled, 314
    tariffs, 327
airport
    hours of operation, 68
    infrastructure, 66
    runway, 66
    warehousing, 68
Alice Tully Theater, 3
anti-bribery convention, 114
Antonov, 323
arbitration, 131, 136
Authorized Economic Operator (AEO), 414

aval, 195

bag, 380
Baltic Exchange, 297
bank
    infrastructure, 83
Bank for International Settlements, 232
bank guarantee, 199
bank institutions, 231
banker's acceptance, 195
barge, 361
Beluga, 323
Big Mac Index, 222
bill of exchange, 193
bill of lading, 261
Bolero, 271
Bosporus, 63
box, 377
box ship, 285
breach of contract, 123
breakbulk cargo
    bag, 380
    box, 377
    crate, 377
    drum, 381
    flexible intermediate bulk container, 381
    general, 376
breakbulk ship, 289
Bretton-Woods Conference, 6

C-TPAT, 331
cabotage, 300
Canada-U.S. bridges, 76
Capesize ship, 282
car manufacturers, 13
car production, 14
carriage, 141
Carriage and Insurance Paid to (CIP), 151
Carriage Paid To (CPT), 150
carriers' liability limits

    general, 301
    Hague Rules, 301
    Hague-Visby Rules, 301
    Hamburg Rules, 301
    Rotterdam Rules, 302
cash in advance, 178
Caterpillar, 45
cell phones, 79
certificate of analysis, 257
certificate of certification, 257
certificate of free sale, 260
certificate of inspection, 253
certificate of insurance, 261
certificate of manufacture, 253
certificate of origin, 253
Certified Cargo Screening Program, 330
charter airfreight, 314
charter party, 266
chemical carrier, 291
Chep Lak Kok Airport, 67
cherries, 327
CISG, 121, 172
classification, 421, 422
Cluster Theory, 22
co-modal, 347
Colombia, 326
combination ship, 290
Commerce Control List, 247
commercial risk, 176
comparative advantage, 17
competition drivers, 13
consular invoice, 240
Container Security Initiative (CSI), 412
containers
    aircraft, 357
    dry, 348
    dry bulk, 349
    extended length, 350
    flat rack, 350
    hanger, 352
    high cube, 351
    historical development, 32, 348
    liquid bulk, 349
    open top, 350
    reefer, 351
    refrigerated, 351
    sizes, 348
    types, 348
    unit load device, 357, 385
containership, 284

contract
    acceptance, 123
    agent, 126
    arbitration, 131
    breach, 123
    choice of forum, 130
    choice of law, 130
    commission, 132
    corporate accounts, 128
    creation, 123
    distributor, 126
    force majeure, 127
    good faith, 127
    intellectual property, 132
    language, 127
    mediation, 131
    misc. clauses, 133
    offer, 122
    sales, 121
    scope of appointment, 128
    term of appointment, 129
    termination, 134
    territory, 128
contract manufacturing, 103
Convention on Contracts for the International Sale of Goods, 121, 172
Corinth Canal, 64
Cost and Freight (CFR), 161
cost drivers, 12
Cost, Insurance and Freight (CIF), 162
counterfeit goods, 113
country data sources, 23
country of origin, 421, 426
country risk, 175
cradle to cradle, 46
crate, 377
credit insurance, 179
crude carrier, 291
cultural sensitivity, 461
Curitiba, Brazil, 46
currency
    bloc, 218
    convertible, 206
    exporter's, 207
    floating, 217
    hard, 207
    importer's, 207
    pegged, 218
    third country's, 207
Customs bond, 442

INDEX

Customs broker, 441
Customs process, 441
Customs Security Programme (CSP), 415
Customs-Trade Partnership Against Terrorism (C-TPAT), 331, 409

damp lease, 315
dangerous goods, 268
deadweight tonnage, 278
deemed export, 249
Delivered At Place(DAP), 154
Delivered At Terminal (DAT), 152
Delivered Duty Paid (DDP), 155
Denied Persons List, 248
DHL, 313
diamonds, 390
dimensional weight, 327
Distribution Resources Planning, 34
distributor, 98
    vs. agent, 99, 124, 126
documentary collection
    acceptance, 195
    bill of exchange, 193
    definition, 192
    drafts, 193
    instruction letter, 192, 194
    presenting bank, 193
    remitting bank, 192
    URC 522, 195
documents
    air waybill, 266
    aircraft lease, 266
    bill of lading, 261
    certificate of analysis, 257
    certificate of certification, 257
    certificate of inspection, 253
    certificate of insurance, 261
    certificate of manufacture, 253
    certificate of origin, 253
    certification of free sale, 260
    charter party, 266
    end-use certificate, 250
    export documents, 242
    export license, 244
    import documents, 250
    import license, 260
    intermodal bill of lading, 266
    invoice, 238, 240
    manifest, 269
    ocean bill of lading, 261
    packing list, 267
    phyto-sanitary certificate, 257
    requirements, 237
    Shipper's Export Declaration, 242
    shipper's letter of instruction, 267
    transportation documents, 261
    uniform bill of lading, 263
dollar(s)
    constant, 4
    current, 4
double stack, 345
drafts
    date, 194
    definition, 193
    sight, 193
    time, 194
Dreamliner, 323
DRP, 34
drum, 381
dry lease, 315
dry-bulk ship, 294
dumping, 432
duty, 421
duty drawback, 445
duty rate, 429

EDI, 270
electronic data interchange, 270
end-use certificate, 250
Entity List, 248
error
    type I, 407
    type II, 407
euro, 7, 208
Ex-Im Bank, 233
ex-works(EXW), 146
exchange rate
    definition, 210
    forecasting, 224
    forward, 213
    futures, 214
    options, 215
    risk, 206
    spot, 213
exchange rate quote
    direct, 211
    indirect, 211
export
    active, 96
    indirect, 92

strategy coordination, 101
export controls
    general, 244
    United States, 246
export license, 244
export management corporation, 94
export quotas, 250
export tax, 250
export trading company, 93
exposure, 177, 227
express freight service, 313

Factor Endowment Theory, 18
factoring, 179
FedEx, 313, 327
Fisher effect, 222
flag, 298
    convenience, 298
    open registry, 298
flexible intermediate bulk container, 381
FOB point, 159
forefaiting, 196
Foreign Corrupt Practices Act, 115
foreign exchange
    hedge, 228
foreign sales corporation, 102
foreign trade zone, 446
Foreign Trade Zones, 114
forward-market hedge, 228
franchising, 105
Free Alongside Ship (FAS), 156
Free and Secure Trade (FAST), 363, 412
Free Carrier (FCA), 148
Free On Board (FOB), 158, 165
freight corridor, 342
freight forwarder, 359
freight tonne kilometer, 309
freighter aircraft, 320
FTZs, 114

GATT, 6
General Agreement of Tariffs and Trade, 6
General Rules of Interpretation, 422
general-merchandise ship, 289
geo fencing, 416
good faith, 127
goods, counterfeit, 113
gray market, 111
gross registered tonnage, 279

gross tonnage, 279

Hague Rules, 301
Hague-Visby Rules, 301
Hamburg Rules, 301
handysize ship, 282
Harmonized System, 422
hazardous cargo, 391
Hecksher-Ohlin, 18
hedge
    forward market, 228
    money market, 229
    options market, 230
Hong Kong Airport, 67

Ideal X, 33
IMF, 6
import license, 260
Importer Security Filing, 413
imports, parallel, 111
Incoterms
    2010 vs. 2000, 155
    by commodity, 167
    carrier's premises, 148
    CFR, 161
    choice, 143
    CIF, 162
    CIP, 151
    confusion with domestic terms, 165
    confusion with older Incoterms, 166
    CPT, 150
    DAP, 154
    DAT, 152
    DDP, 155
    exporter's premises, 148
    EXW, 146
    FAS, 156
    FCA, 148
    FOB, 158
    history, 142
    marketing tool, 167
    summary, 163
    transfer of responsibility, 143
informed compliance, 442
infrastructure
    airport, 66
    banking, 83
    cell phones, 79
    communication, 77
    courts, 84

definition, 51
electricity, 81
intellectual property, 85
Internet, 80
landlines, 78
leap frogging, 79
logistics services, 84
mail, 77
pipeline, 83
port, 52
rail, 69
roads, 72
telecommunications, 78
transportation, 52
utilities, 80
warehousing, 76
water and sewer, 82
instruction letter, 192
insurance certificate, 261
intellectual property, 85, 104, 132
intercultural communication, 23, 454
Interest Rate Parity, 223
intermodal, 347
intermodal bill of lading, 266
International Air Transport Association (IATA), 328
International Chamber of Commerce, 142, 404
International Civil Aviation Organization (ICAO), 328
international English, 455
International Fisher Effect, 223
international logistics
    definition, 39
    economic importance, 43
    elements, 41
    reverse, 44
International Maritime Organization, 402
International Monetary Fund, 6, 232
International Plant Protection Convention, 382
International Product Life Cycle, 20
International Ship and Port Facility Security, 402
international supply chain management
    definition, 39
international trade, 1
    growth, 1
Internet, 80
invoice

commercial, 238
consular, 240
pro forma, 240

JIT, 34
joint venture, 107
Just-in-Time, 34

Kai Tak Airport, 67
Kraft Foods, 110

land bridge, 71, 354
landlines, 79
largest exporting countries, 10
largest importing countries, 11
Lauder, Estée, 45
law
    choice of, 130
    contract, 125
    labor, 125
leap frogging, 79
letter of credit
    advising bank, 185
    amendment, 188
    back-to-back, 191
    confirming bank, 185
    correspondent bank, 186
    definition, 180
    discrepancy, 188
    draft, 190
    irrevocable, 188
    issuance, 181
    issuing bank, 181
    payment, 184
    shipment, 182
    stand-by, 191, 199
    transferable, 191
    UCP 600, 186
    URR 725, 188
Lex Mercatoria, 120
liability conventions
    air, 328
    ocean, 301
    rail, 357
    road, 357
licensing, 104
Lincoln Center, 3
liner ship, 278
liquefied natural gas, 296
load lines, 280

logistics
    and supply chain management, 38
    definition, 37
    development, 27
    economic importance, 42
    evolution, 38
    history, 27
    military, 28
    reverse, 44
Logistics Cluster Theory, 22
longshoreman, 29

mail, 77
main carriage, 141
Manufacturing Resources Planning, 33
maobi tree, 3
maquiladoras, 114
maritime security, 305
Maritime Transportation Security Act, 411
market drivers, 14
market entry strategy, 91
Materials Requirements Planning, 33
McDonald's restaurants, 106
McLean, Malcom, 32
mediation, 131, 137
merchandise visa, 445
methods of payment
    alternatives, 174
    bank guarantee, 199
    cash in advance, 178
    credit insurance, 179
    documentary collection, 192
    factoring, 179
    forfaiting, 196
    letter of credit, 180
    open account, 178
    purchasing cards, 197
    TradeCard, 198
metric system, 458
Millau bridge, 75
money-market hedge, 229
Mriya, 323
MRP, 33

net tonnage, 279
Nicaragua, 64
non-tariff barriers, 435
NVOCC-non-vessel-operating common carrier, 303

ocean bill of lading, 261

on-carriage, 141
onboard courier, 318
one-hundred-percent inspection, 400
open account, 178
open-sky agreement, 328
options
    call, 216
    put, 216
options-market hedge, 230
Oresund Fixed Link, 75
outsourcing, 12
ouvrages d'art, 74

packaging
    bag, 380
    box, 377
    breakbulk cargo, 376
    container stuffing, 375
    corrugated box, 373
    crate, 377
    drum, 381
    dunnage, 374
    flexible intermediate bulk container, 381
    full container load, 370
    functions, 368
    legal issues, 394
    less than container load, 375
    marketing tool, 395
    markings, 383
    mishandling detectors, 378
    non-unitized cargo, 374
    ocean, 370
    pallets, 371
    primary, 367
    retail issues, 393
    security, 389
    size, 394
    unitized cargo, 371
    wood requirements, 382
packing list, 267
pallets, 371
Panama Canal, 61, 63, 356
Panamax ship, 55, 281
parallel imports, 111
passenger aircraft, 317
personal computers, China, 388
pet shop, 104
photographs, 15
phyto-sanitary certificate, 257

piggy-backing, 95, 340
pipeline, 360
Plimsoll Mark, 280
port
    air draft, 54
    bridge clearance, 54
    capacity, 60
    cranes, 55
    depth, 54
    draft, 54
    infrastructure, 52
    land connections, 59
    warehousing, 58
    work rules, 57
Port Revel, 294
Porter, Michael, 22
post-Panamax ship, 55, 281
pre-carriage, 141
pre-shipment inspections, 254, 440
precious cargo, 390
principal, 96
pro forma invoice, 189, 240
product carrier, 291
project cargo, 359
purchasing cards, 197
Purchasing Power Parity, 220

quick-change aircraft, 320
quota, sugar, 436
quotas, 435

railroad
    double stack, 345
    freight, 341
    freiht corridor, 342
    gauge, 69
    infrastructure, 69
    land bridge, 71
    multimodal, 70
    passenger vs. merchandise, 69
    single stack, 345
reasonable care, 442
recycling, 46
refrigerated goods, 392
reshoring, 13
revenue tonne kilometer, 309
Ricardo, David, 17
risk retention, 227
road
    bridges, 74
    congestion, 72
    infrastructure, 72
    ouvrages d'art, 74
    quality, 72
    street signage, 74
road train, 340
roll-on/roll-off ship, 288
Rotterdam Rules, 302, 357
royalty, 104
Ruslan, 323

SAFE-Security and Accountability for Every Port, 411
SAFE-Security and Facilitation in a Global Environment, 404
Saint Lawrence Seaway, 63
sales contract, 121
scheduled airfreight service, 314
SCM, 35
security
    air transport, 330
    interdiction, 407
    ocean transportation, 305
    surface transportation, 363
    United States, 406
Security and Accountability for Every Port (SAFE), 411
Security and Facilitation in a Global Environment (SAFE), 404
SED, 242
semi-truck, 338
Shanghai Port, 55
Sheffi, Yossi, 22
ship
    box ship, 285
    breakbulk, 289
    Capesize, 282
    chemical carrier, 291
    combination, 290
    containership, 284
    crude carrier, 291
    dry bulk, 294
    flag, 298
    general merchandise, 289
    handysize, 282
    liner, 278
    liquefied natural gas, 296
    Panamax, 55, 281
    post Panamax, 55, 281
    product carrier, 291

roll-on/roll-off, 288
security, 305
Suez-Max, 282
tramp, 278
ultra large crude carrier, 283, 292
very large crude carrier, 282, 292
ship's rail, 159
Shipper's Export Declaration, 242
shipper's letter of instruction, 267
single stack, 345
Smith, Adam, 16
Society for Worldwide Interbank Financial Telecommunication (SWIFT), 233, 271
sogo shosha, 93
special English, 457
stevedore, 29
street signage, 74
subsidiary, 109
    marketing, 100
Suez Canal, 63
Suez-Max ship, 282
sugar quota, 436
Supply Chain Management, 35
supply chain management
    and logistics, 38
    definition, 38
SWIFT, 233, 271

tariff, 429
tariff rate, 429
technology drivers, 15
telecommunications, 78
telephone, 79
termination, 134
    convenience, 135
    just cause, 135
terms of trade, 142
Theory of Absolute Advantage, 16
Theory of Comparative Advantage, 17
tonnage
    deadweight, 278
    gross, 279
    gross registered, 279
    net, 279
top 15 cargo airports, 310
Total Security Management, 415
trade acceptance, 195
trade, international, 1
TradeCard, 198, 271

tramp ship, 278
Transportation Security Administration, 330, 407
Transportation Workers' Identification Credential (TWIC), 412
Treaty of Rome, 7
truck
    overloaded, 340
    piggy back, 340
    road train, 340
    security, 363
    semi, 338
trucking
    Europe, 338
    United States, 338
Type I error, 407
Type II error, 407

ultra large crude carrier, 283, 292
uniform bill of lading, 263
unit load device, 357
Unverified List, 248
UPS, 313

Valentine's Day, 326
valuation, 421, 425
value-added tax, 434
Vernon, Raymond, 20
very large crude carrier, 282, 292
Vienna Convention, 121
Virgin Atlantic, 329
volume weight, 327

water and sewer, 82
wet lease, 315
wood requirements, packaging, 382
World Bank, 233
World Customs Organization, 404
world trade, 4
World Trade Organization, 6
WTO, 6

Yangshan Port, 55